AMERICAN WOMEN WRITERS

AMERICAN WOMEN WRITERS

Bibliographical Essays

Edited by Maurice Duke,
Jackson R. Bryer, and
M. Thomas Inge

GREENWOOD PRESS
WESTPORT, CONNECTICUT
LONDON, ENGLAND

Library of Congress Cataloging in Publication Data

Main entry under title:

American women writers.

Includes index.
1. American literature—Women authors—History and criticism—Bibliography. I. Duke, Maurice. II. Bryer, Jackson R. III. Inge, M. Thomas.
Z1229.W8A44 [PS147] 016.81'09'9287 82-6156
ISBN 0-313-22116-2 (lib. bdg.) AACR2

Library of Congress Catalog Card Number: 82-6156
ISBN: 0-313-22116-2

First published in 1983

Greenwood Press
A division of Congressional Information Service, Inc.
88 Post Road West
Westport, Connecticut 06881

Printed in the United States of America

10 9 8 7 6 5 4 3 2 1

Contents

Preface

The plan for this book grew from a two-fold change that has taken place in the criticism of American literature since the 1950s. One of those changes centers on the ways that critical writings have been collected and organized. The other centers on a revaluation of American literature that actively began in the late 1960s, following several decades of passive fermentation.

When Floyd Stovall published his now-famous *Eight American Authors* in 1956, he ushered in a new trend in the bibliographical study of authors of the United States. For the first time on record, there was a systematic attempt to present to the scholarly world the full response that the country's major writers of the nineteenth century had evoked. Following Stovall's study came other similar ones, such as Jackson R. Bryer's *Fifteen Modern American Authors* and his subsequent *Sixteen Modern American Authors*, Robert A. Rees and Earl N. Harbert's *Fifteen American Authors Before 1900*, and our own *Black American Writers* (2 volumes). The present book, then, is in keeping with the trend established by Stovall and continued to the present. As was the case with the works cited above, the current volume attempts to present to the scholar and advanced student of American literature an authoritative guide to the work that has been published on some of the country's most important writers.

The social changes of the late 1960s and early 1970s ushered in a new way of looking at American literature. Prior to that time the writers singled out for extensive critical attention—with few notable exceptions—were male, the myriad minority and female writers rarely being the subject of serious scholarly inquiry. The situation has now changed. The present collection attempts to add in a systematic way to the continuing body of criticism about the country's women writers.

The coverage in the current volume is naturally selective. In the first place, a number of America's women writers have already been the subjects of bibliographical essays similar to the ones included here. Thus, to duplicate the work of other researchers would be wasted effort. In addition, given the opportunity, no two scholars would arrive at parallel lists of whom to include and exclude in a book such as this. We have, however, attempted to reflect the major contributions that women writers have made to American literature both historically and technically. Therefore we have tried to present their literary longevity by starting our coverage at as early a time as possible—with Anne Bradstreet. We have sought to reflect the innovations made by women writers by including the works of such experimentalists as Anaïs Nin and Djuna Barnes, as well as the unique contributions of Gertrude Stein, who stands alone in the literature of our country. Each essay is current through the fall of 1981.

In citing periodical essays, we have used the abbreviations for journals currently used in *PMLA*. When periodicals for which *PMLA* does not cite an abbreviation appear, we have created a workable abbreviation. A complete list of these abbreviations is included. Each citation of a periodical reference includes the name of the periodical and the date. In citing the places that books were published, we have included locations, unless the publisher is based in New York City; therefore, when no location is mentioned, the reader can assume the place of publication to be New York. Locations of university presses are determined by the name of the city in question, followed by the name of the press and the state with which it is affiliated (for example: Charlottesville: University Press of Virginia).

Finally, we have made no attempt to have as contributors to the book only female scholars. We did attempt to solicit the best people to do the individual chapters, and we believe that we were successful. The reader will notice, however, that the greater number of contributors to *American Women Writers* are themselves female. It happened that these particular scholars were the best qualified to do the present job.

Maurice Duke
Jackson R. Bryer
M. Thomas Inge

Abbreviations

A&D	*Arts and Decoration*
AI	*American Imago: A Psychoanalytic Journal for Culture, Science, and the Arts*
AJP	*American Journal of Psychology*
AL	*American Literature: A Journal of Literary History, Criticism and Bibliography*
ALR	*American Literary Realism, 1870-1910*
AMer	*American Mercury*
AmLS	*American Literary Scholarship: An Annual*
AmR	*American Review*
AmS	*American Spectator*
AN&Q	*American Notes and Queries*
AntigR	*Antigonish Review*
AppalJ	*Appalachian Journal*
APR	*The American Poetry Review*
AQ	*American Quarterly*
ArQ	*Arizona Quarterly*
AtM	*Atlantic Monthly*
BA	*Books Abroad*
BALF	*Black American Literature Forum*
BB	*Bulletin of Bibliography*
BC	*The Book Collector*
B Forum	*Black Forum*
BI	*Books at Iowa*
BlackR	*Black Review*
BlackSch	*Black Scholar*

BlackW	*Black World*
BNYPL	*Bulletin of the New York Public Library*
BSUF	*Ball State University Forum*
BUJ	*Boston University Journal*
BuR	*Bucknell Review: A Scholarly Journal of Letters, Arts, and Science*
BW	*Book Week*
C&L	*Christianity and Literature*
CC	*Christian Century*
CE	*College English*
CEA	*CEA Critic: An Official Journal of the College English Association*
CEJ	*California English Journal*
CennR	*Centennial Review*
ChC	*Chinese Culture: A Quarterly Review*
Cit	*Cithora*
CLAJ	*College Language Association Journal*
CLQ	*Colby Library Quarterly*
CLS	*Comparative Literature Studies*
CollL	*College Literature*
ConL	*Contemporary Literature*
ColQ	*Colorado Quarterly*
CP	*Concerning Poetry* (Bellingham, Wash.)
CR	*The Critical Review* (Canberra, Australia)
CRB	*Cahiers de la Compagnie Madeleine Renaud-Jean Louis Barrault*
CRevAS	*Canadian Review of American Studies*
Crit	*Critique: Studies in Modern Fiction*
CritI	*Critical Inquiry*
Criticism	*Criticism: A Quarterly for Literature and Arts*
CritQ	*Critical Quarterly*
CW	*Catholic World*
DAI	*Dissertation Abstracts International*
DR	*Dalhousie Review*
EA	*Etudes Anglaises: Grande-Bretagne, Etats-Unis*
EAL	*Early American Literature*
Edda	*Nordisk Tidsskrift for Literaturforskning*
EGN	*Ellen Glasgow Newsletter* (Ashland, Va.)
EIC	*Essays in Criticism: A Quarterly Journal of Literary Criticism* (Oxford, England)
EIHC	*Essex Institute Historical Collection*

EJ	*The English Journal*
ELitT	*Essays in Literature and Thought*
ELWIU	*Essays in Literature* (Macomb, Ill.)
EngR	*English Record*
ESC	*English Studies in Canada*
ESQ	*ESQ: A Journal of the American Renaissance*
ESRS	*Emporia State Research Studies*
EST	*English Studies Today*
ETHSP	*East Tennessee Historical Society's Publications*
EUQ	*Emory University Quarterly*
EWN	*Eudora Welty Newsletter*
FemS	*Feminist Studies*
FHA	*Fitzgerald/Hemingway Annual*
FiN	*Filmmakers Newsletter*
FHQ	*Florida Historical Quarterly*
FOB	*Flannery O'Connor Bulletin*
ForumH	*Forum* (Houston, Texas)
Frontiers	*Frontiers: A Journal of Women Studies*
GaR	*The Georgia Review*
GyS	*Gypsy Scholar: A Graduate Forum for Literary Criticism*
HB	*Harper's Bazaar*
HC	*The Hollins Critic*
HM	*Harper's Monthly*
HQ	*Hopkins Quarterly*
HudR	*Hudson Review*
IFR	*International Fiction Review*
IJWS	*International Journal of Women's Studies*
IowaR	*The Iowa Review*
JA	*Jarbüch für Amerikastudien*
JoA	*Journal of Aesthetics*
JAF	*Journal of American Folklore*
JAmS	*Journal of American Studies*
JCMVASA	*Journal of the Central Mississippi Valley American Studies Association*
JMH	*Journal of Mississippi History*
JML	*Journal of Modern Literature*
JNT	*Journal of Narrative Technique*
JORA	*Journal of the Otto Rank Association*

KanMag	*Kansas Magazine*
KanQ	*Kansas Quarterly*
KCN	*Kate Chopin Newsletter*
KR	*The Kenyon Review*
KRev	*The Kentucky Review*
LaH	*Louisiana History*
L&U	*The Lion and the Unicorn*
Lang&S	*Language and Style: An International Journal*
L&P	*Literature and Psychology* (Teaneck, N.J.)
LaS	*Louisiana Studies*
LFQ	*Literature/Film Quarterly*
LGJ	*Lost Generation Journal*
LJ	*Library Journal*
LNL	*Linguistics in Literature*
LR	*Les Lettres Romanes*
MarkhamR	*Markham Review*
MArt	*Mundus Artium: A Journal of International Literature and the Arts*
MagA	*Magazine of Art*
MASJ	*Midcontinent American Studies Journal*
MD	*Modern Drama*
MDAC	*Mystery and Detection Annual*
MFS	*Modern Fiction Studies*
MHRev	*Malahat Review: An International Quarterly of Life and Letters*
MissQ	*Mississippi Quarterly: The Journal of Southern Culture*
MinnR	*Minnesota Review*
MLN	*Modern Language Notes*
MMN	*Marianne Moore Newsletter*
ModA	*Modern Age: A Quarterly Review*
MoHSB	*Missouri Historical Society Bulletin*
MPS	*Modern Poetry Studies*
MQ	*Midwest Quarterly*
MQR	*Michigan Quarterly Review*
MR	*Massachusetts Review: A Quarterly of Literature, the Arts and Public Affairs* (Amherst, Mass.)
Ms.	*Ms. Magazine*
MSE	*Massachusetts Studies in English*
MWN	*Mary Wollstonecraft Newsletter*
MWR	*Midwest Review*
NALF	*Negro American Literature Forum*
NAR	*North American Review*

NBR	*New Boston Review*
NC	*Nineteenth Century*
NCF	*Nineteenth-Century Fiction*
NCFS	*Nineteenth-Century French Studies*
NCol	*The New Colophon*
NConL	*Notes on Contemporary Literature*
ND	*Negro Digest*
NEQ	*The New England Quarterly: A Historical Review of New England Life and Letters*
NewI	*The New Iconography*
NewM	*New Masses*
NewR	*New Republic*
NHB	*Negro History Bulletin*
NLauR	*New Laurel Revue*
NLd	*New Leader*
NMAL	*Notes on Modern American Literature*
NMQ	*New Mexico Quarterly*
NMW	*Notes on Mississippi Writers*
NOR	*New Orleans Review*
Novel	*Novel: A Forum on Fiction* (Providence, R.I.)
NR	*The Nassau Review: The Journal of Nassau Community College Devoted to Arts, Letters, and Science*
NSN	*New Statesman and Nation*
NY	*New Yorker*
NYHT	*New York Herald Tribune*
NYHTBR	*New York Herald Tribune Book Review*
NYHTBW	*New York Herald Tribune Book World*
NYRB	*New York Review of Books*
NYT	*New York Times*
NYTBR	*New York Times Book Review*
OUR	*Ohio University Review*
PAPA	*Publications of the Arkansas Philological Association*
PArJ	*Performing Arts Journal*
PBSA	*Papers of the Bibliographical Society of America*
PeM	*Pembroke Magazine*
PLL	*Papers on Language and Literature: A Journal for Scholars and Critics of Language and Literature*
PMHS	*Proceedings of the Massachusetts Historical Society*
PMLA	*Publications of the Modern Language Association of America*
PMPA	*Publications of the Missouri Philological Association*
PQ	*Philological Quarterly* (Iowa City, Ia.)

PR	*Partisan Review*
PrS	*Prairie Schooner*
PW	*Publishers Weekly*
QR	*Quarterly Review*
RALS	*Resources for American Literary Study*
RANAM	*Recherches Anglaises et Américaines*
RB	*Redbook*
RevP	*Revue de Paris*
RevR	*Review of Reviews*
RFI	*Regionalism and the Female Imagination*
RLLR	*Revue de Louisiane/Louisiana Review*
RLV	*Revue des Langues Vivantes*
RS	*Research Studies* (Pullman, Wash.)
SA	*Studi Americani*
SAB	*South Atlantic Bulletin*
SAF	*Studies in American Fiction*
S&C	*Studies and Critiques*
SAQ	*South Atlantic Quarterly*
SatR	*Saturday Review*
SatRL	*Saturday Review of Literature*
SB	*Studies in Bibliography: Papers of the Bibliographical Society of the University of Virginia*
SBL	*Studies in Black Literature*
SCB	*South Central Bulletin*
SCN	*Seventeenth Century News*
SCR	*South Carolina Review*
SDR	*South Dakota Review*
SEP	*Saturday Evening Post*
SFQ	*Southern Folklore Quarterly*
SHR	*Southern Humanities Review*
Signs	*Signs: Journal of Women in Culture and Society*
SLJ	*Southern Literary Journal*
SLM	*Southern Literary Messenger*
SNNTS	*Studies in the Novel*
SoQ	*The Southern Quarterly: A Journal of the Arts in the South* (Hattiesburg, Miss.)
SoR	*The Southern Review* (Baton Rouge, La.)
SoRA	*Southern Review: Literary and Interdisciplinary Essays*
SoS	*Syn og Segn: Norsk Tidsskrift*
SoSt	*Southern Studies: An Interdisciplinary Journal of the South*

SSC Review	*Shippensburg State College Review*
SR	*Sewanee Review*
StTC	*Studies in Twentieth Century Literature*
SSF	*Studies in Short Fiction* (Newberry, S.C.)
SwAL	*Southwestern American Literature*
SWR	*Southwest Review*
TamR	*Tamarack Review*
Tb	*The Tablet*
TCL	*Twentieth Century Literature: A Scholarly and Critical Journal*
TFSB	*Tennessee Folklore Society Bulletin*
THQ	*Tennessee Historical Quarterly*
TLS	(London) *Times Literary Supplement*
TR	*Transatlantic Review*
TriQ	*TriQuarterly* (Evanston, Ill.)
TSE	*Tulane Studies in English*
TSL	*Tennessee Studies in Literature*
TSLL	*Texas Studies in Literature and Language: A Journal of the Humanities*
TUSAS	Twayne's United States Authors Series
UcR	*Uclan Review*
UKCR	*University of Kansas City Review*
UMPAW	University of Minnesota Pamphlets on American Writers
UMPWS	*University of Michigan Papers in Women's Studies*
UR	*University Review* (Kansas City, Mo.)
USP	*Under the Sign: Anaïs Nin and Her Circle*
UTQ	*University of Toronto Quarterly*
UWB	*University of Wichita Bulletin*
UWR	*University of Windsor Review* (Windsor, Ontario)
VQR	*Virginia Quarterly Review*
W&L	*Women & Literature*
WCR	*West Coast Review*
WiC	*Widening Circle*
WHR	*Western Humanities Review*
WLB	*Wilson Bulletin for Libraries*
WMQ	*William and Mary Quarterly*
WR	*World Review*
WS	*Women's Studies: An Interdisciplinary Journal*
WSCL	*Wisconsin Studies in Contemporary Literature*

WVUPP	*West Virginia University Philological Papers*
WWR	*Walt Whitman Review*
XUS	*Xavier University Studies*
YR	*The Yale Review: A National Quarterly*
Y/T	*Yale Theatre*
YULG	*Yale University Library Gazette*

AMERICAN WOMEN
WRITERS

1 ANN STANFORD

Three Puritan Women: Anne Bradstreet, Mary Rowlandson, and Sarah Kemble Knight

ANNE BRADSTREET

BIBLIOGRAPHY

The most recent bibliography on Anne Bradstreet is that by William J. Scheick and JoElla Doggett in *Seventeenth-Century American Poetry: A Reference Guide* (Boston: G. K. Hall, 1977). It lists secondary criticism from 1884, including a few substantial comments on the author in essays on other subjects. All entries have annotations describing contents and noting the inclusion of biographical or bibliographical material. This listing is virtually complete to spring 1975, as far as the poetry is concerned, though it, of course, omits essays on the prose as well as several minor essays or references to the poet.

Some of the omitted essays published through 1968 may be found in "Anne Bradstreet, An Annotated Checklist" (*BB*, April-June 1970) by Ann Stanford. A selected list of criticism since 1930 appears in Stanford's *Anne Bradstreet: The Worldly Puritan* (Burt Franklin, 1974), but much important scholarship on Bradstreet has appeared since this book and the Scheick and Doggett bibliography appeared.

Josephine K. Piercy's *Anne Bradstreet* (Twayne, 1965) came out before the current upsurge in early American studies, though it lists several overviews of American poetry that might be useful in a study of the history of the poet's reputation.

EDITIONS

The first edition of Anne Bradstreet's poems, *The Tenth Muse Lately sprung up in America*, originally published in 1650 by Stephen Bowtell in

London, was reprinted in 1965 (Gainesville, Fla.: Scholars' Facsimiles & Reprints). In 1678 the Boston printer John Foster brought out a second edition under the title *Several Poems*. It contained all the poems of *The Tenth Muse* plus others gathered from manuscripts in the hands of friends and relatives. Modern editions are based on this volume, which, according to the title page, was "Corrected by the Author," although she had died six years before its publication. According to Jeannine Hensley, John Rogers, Bradstreet's nephew-in-law, probably served as editor ("The Editor of Anne Bradstreet's *Several Poems*," *AL*, January 1964).

In 1867 John Harvard Ellis added to the contents of *Several Poems* the entries in a manuscript book containing prose and additional poems by the author, as well as a long introduction combining biography and suggestions regarding sources for many of the passages in the poems. Ellis's edition, *The Works of Anne Bradstreet in Prose and Verse* (Charlestown, Mass.: Abram E. Cutter), preserves the spelling of the original, and his footnotes show many of the variations from the text of *The Tenth Muse*. It was reprinted by Peter Smith (1932; Gloucester, Mass., 1962) and has long been a standard text for scholars who prefer the earlier spelling.

An excellent text with modern spelling and punctuation is that edited by Jeannine Hensley, *The Works of Anne Bradstreet* (Cambridge, Mass.: Belknap Press of Harvard University Press, 1967). Hensley's copy text is the edition of *Several Poems* owned by the Massachusetts Historical Society as corrected by an errata leaf in the Prince Collection in the Boston Public Library. Like Ellis, Hensley has added the contents of the manuscript book. An appendix gives a location file for copies of the two seventeenth-century editions and the press variants within each of them.

In 1969 Robert Hutchinson edited a paperback selection of the poems and some of the prose arranged by genre and followed the text of the Ellis edition with the corrections made by the errata leaf used by Hensley (*Poems of Anne Bradstreet*, Dover). It has since gone out of print but is a good text for those having access to a copy.

Joseph R. McElrath, Jr., warns that all editions of the poet's work based on Ellis's edition should be suspect and that even the facsimile version of *The Tenth Muse* has been "editorially doctored by an unknown hand" and only the small amount of prose and poetry still preserved in the author's hand in the Andover manuscript (which will be discussed shortly) can show clear evidence of the author's intention ("The Text of Anne Bradstreet: Biographical and Critical Consequences," *SCN*, Summer-Fall 1976).

In order to present a text that comes as close to the author's own version as possible, McElrath and Allan P. Robb have brought out a new edition, *The Complete Works of Anne Bradstreet* (Boston: Twayne, 1981). For this, the editors have chosen the versions of poems closest in time to the original writing. Their work makes use of four copy texts, including *The Tenth*

Muse. However, because Bradstreet saw neither of her volumes through the press, we are still left in doubt about her intentions, except in the cases of the few poems in the Andover manuscript book.

MANUSCRIPTS AND LETTERS

The only manuscript written in Bradstreet's hand consists of a letter addressed to her son Simon and seventy-seven prose aphorisms titled "Meditations Divine and Moral" together with the poem beginning "As weary pilgrim, now at rest." These are written in a small notebook, six-by-three-and-three-quarters inches in size, now in the possession of the Stephens Memorial Library in North Andover, Massachusetts.

A second manuscript in the same notebook is in the handwriting of her son Simon, prefaced by his note: "A true copy of a book left by my hon'd & dear mother to her children & found among some papers after her Death." The manuscript contains a letter to her children, as well as meditations and diary entries in poetry and prose.

The Houghton Library at Harvard has a manuscript copy of the notebook, which was owned by Simon's sister, Sarah Hubbard. A comparison of this copy with the Andover manuscripts shows a few variations from the originals.

BIOGRAPHY

Anne Bradstreet "The Tenth Muse" by Elizabeth Wade White (Oxford University Press, 1971) remains the best and only full-scale biography. White covers what is known of the author and places the events of her life against a well-developed background of family descent, the intellectual milieu of the age, especially with regard to women, and the circumstances of the Bradstreet family life in the New World.

The course of Bradstreet's literary career as demonstrated in her poems is outlined in Ann Stanford's *Anne Bradstreet: The Worldly Puritan* (Burt Franklin, 1974). Josephine Piercy, in *Anne Bradstreet* (Twayne, 1965), gives an overview of Bradstreet's life in connection with her commentary on the poems; and the introductions to the *Works* edited by Ellis (1867) and Hensley (1967) and the *Poems* (1969) edited by Henderson, all cited above, contain biographical material, as does Stanford's essay "Anne Bradstreet" in *Major Writers of Early American Literature*, edited by Everett Emerson (Madison: University of Wisconsin Press, 1972). A brief biography with comments on the more important groups of poems is Cheryl Walker's "Anne Bradstreet" in *American Writers: A Collection of Literary Biographies*, edited by Leonard Unger, Supplement I, Part 1 (Charles Scribner's, 1979).

Because the author saw neither of the two seventeenth-century editions before publication, Joseph R. McElrath, Jr., in "The Text of Anne Bradstreet: Biographical and Critical Consequences'' (*SCN*, Summer-Fall 1976), warns against making assertions about the poet's biography or state of mind on the basis of differences between the two editions.

CRITICISM

Growth of Bradstreet's Reputation

Early criticism and comments on the work focused on the merits—or demerits—of her poetry. In her own time and shortly thereafter, her poetry was lavishly praised, never more so than in John Norton's ''Funeral Elogy,'' which appeared in the 1678 edition of her *Several Poems*. Cotton Mather's tribute in *Magnalia Christi Americana* (London, T. Parkhurst, 1702) was almost as excessive. In England her work was praised by Bathsua Makin in *An Essay to Revive the Antient Education of Gentlewomen in Religion, Manners, Arts & Tongues* (London, 1673). Her *Several Poems* was the only book of poetry in Edward Taylor's library; and in 1755 the governor of Connecticut used lines from one of her elegies in lamenting the death of his son (JoElla Doggett, ''Another Eighteenth-Century Instance of Anne Bradstreet's Continuing Appeal,'' *EIHC*, April 1975).

During the nineteenth century Bradstreet's reputation plummeted; Moses Coit Tyler, in *A History of American Literature* (G. P. Putnam's, 1879; Ithaca: Cornell University Press, 1949), found in her work an occasional "ingot of genuine poetry'' but noted that her prose was more attractive; and even John Harvard Ellis, the editor of her *Works*, was condescending about her poetry, while admitting that in ''Contemplations'' she revealed ''true poetic feeling.''

The revival of Bradstreet's poetic reputation began with Charles William Pearson, whose essay ''Early American Poetry'' (*Literary and Biographical Essays*, Boston: Sherman, French, 1908) praised her as a genuine poet and predicted that she would be ''remembered and honored more.'' Conrad Aiken, in editing *American Poetry 1671-1928* (Modern Library, 1929), included more of her work than that of Lowell, Longfellow, or Bryant. Possibly the greatest impetus to the revaluation of the poetry came with Samuel Eliot Morison's praise in ''Mistress Anne Bradstreet'' (*Builders of the Bay Colony*, Boston: Houghton Mifflin, 1930; rev. ed., 1964). George Frisbie Whicher's brief book *Alas All's Vanity, or A Leaf from the first American Edition of "Several Poems" by Anne Bradstreet* (Spiral Press, 1942) contained an essay praising the poet.

Elizabeth Wade White's ''The Tenth Muse—A Tercentenary Appraisal of Anne Bradstreet'' (*WMQ*, July 1951) was the first essay in a scholarly journal on the author; it placed the poet in the progression of women writers of the Renaissance and the seventeenth century. Her conclusion was that ''certainly no Englishwoman writing before Anne Bradstreet created a body of verse which has been remembered with so much respect . . . historically she deserves the earliest place among the women poets of England.''

White in part bases this assessment on the seriousness of Bradstreet as one who chose for her occupation the writing of poetry.

A more recent essay by Jennifer R. Waller, "'My Hand a Needle Better Fits:' Anne Bradstreet and Women Poets in the Renaissance" (*DR*, Autumn 1974), covers many of the same writers and comes to much the same conclusion.

A more extensive overview of Bradstreet's place in the sequence of earlier writers occurs in "Anne Bradstreet in the Tradition of English Women Writers," a dissertation by Jimmie Carol Still Durr (University of Mississippi, 1978). Durr finds that Bradstreet combined "the traditional feminine role with the still revolutionary one of woman as a writer." She concludes that Bradstreet adds to English literature a "feminine view of the human dilemma" not seen before, and that her emigration was important in her development.

Nina M. Scott, in "The Tenth Muse" (*Américas*, February 1978), compares Bradstreet to another American colonial, Sor Juana Inés de la Cruz, describing similarities in their use of the feminine point of view in their inner crises and in their struggles against opposition to themselves as writers. Also searching for similarities, Emily Stipes Watts, in *The Poetry of American Women from 1632 to 1945* (Austin: University of Texas Press, 1977), says that Bradstreet expressed in poetry the "communal" sense of being a woman and was probably the first in either England or America to write from a woman's point of view about children, childbirth, love for a spouse, and family life.

Since 1950, however, the high place of Anne Bradstreet in early American letters has been assured, and most of the scholarship has concentrated on individual poems, on tracing her sources in various authors or literary practices of her time, and on her life and work as a woman.

"CONTEMPLATIONS"

Many commentators have noted the tension in Bradstreet's work resulting from her tendency to cling to this world while being aware of the next. Several writers deal with the way she handles this tension in "Contemplations."

Robert D. Richardson, Jr., in "The Puritan Poetry of Anne Bradstreet" (*TSLL*, Autumn 1967), denies the idea of a rebellion against puritanism but contends that the tension in her poems comes from "the Puritan ideal of living in the world without being of it." Although he finds no otherworldliness in the early poems, in "Contemplations" he sees the poet reaching a balance between this world and the next in the "green world" of nature after "the speculative trying of a faith" by her circlings throughout the poem.

Alvin H. Rosenfeld, in "Anne Bradstreet's 'Contemplations': Patterns of Form and Meaning" (*NEQ*, March 1970), discovers the organization of the poem in "certain patterns of imagery and ideas." First is the seasonal metaphor, which takes the poet through autumn and winter toward an eternal spring and summer. In such imagery, Rosenfeld claims, the poet anticipates the Romantics. But he finds also that the clash between the Puritan religious conscience and the free imagination continues to rein in the full expression of "Wordsworthian joy." In the last stanza, however, the poet transcends time by both a religious and an aesthetic promise.

William J. Irvin, in a closely argued essay ("Allegory and Typology 'Imbrace and Greet': Anne Bradstreet's 'Contemplations,'" *EAL*, Spring 1975), explains that what has appeared to be a rebellion against Puritan tenets on the one hand and an attitude toward nature that points toward the coming age of romanticism on the other is actually neither of these. The poem is unified by the cyclical view of nature and the linear view of history derived from allegory and typology. The poet works her way through a series of allegories in which she views mankind as part of nature, and finding such comparisons unsatisfactory, turns to history, which "'makes things gone perpetually to last.'" But the poet continues to stress the "duality of fear and joy," the fear being "an essential part of the joy" in the total emotional structure of the poem. The poem ends in the final conversion experience, in which the soul is able to move beyond nature.

In a more literal way, Anne Hildebrand ("Anne Bradstreet's Quaternions and 'Contemplations,'" *EAL*, Fall 1973) argues that the "shadows as well as the lights of this world indicate the presence of God." The essay shows that the structure of "Contemplations" follows the order of the elements—fire, earth, water, air—in the passages concerned with the sun, the ancestors of mankind, the stream, and the bird. As in the quaternions, Bradstreet takes up each of these in turn showing their shortcomings. They serve as a prelude to her religious discovery that "secure good lies outside a world whose elements contain as much evil, or vanity, as good." This essay is excellent in showing the consistency in Bradstreet's thought patterns over a period of time.

In "Anne Bradstreet as a Meditative Writer" (*CEJ*, Winter 1966), Ann Stanford places "Contemplations" in the meditative and emblematic traditions. The poem is a series of short meditative pieces with a composition of place and an argument, followed by a resolution, or at least a series of unanswerable questions, resolved only in the final stanza of the poem, which serves as a colloquy.

The question of whether Bradstreet might properly be called a "pre-Romantic" often arises as a secondary consideration in connection with "Contemplations." Ellen Moers, in "The American muse" (*Harvard Magazine*, January-February 1979), adds to other arguments for "Romantic sensibility" Bradstreet's access to a wild and open landscape capable of drawing forth ecstasy and wonder, as well as an "immense ego" in judging and absorbing nature.

OTHER POEMS AND PROSE

The quaternions, which Hildebrand saw as the basis of "Contemplations," are considered also by Jane Donahue Eberwein in "The 'Unrefined Ore' of Anne Bradstreet's Quaternions" (*EAL*, Spring 1974). Eberwein suggests that the knowledge contained and classified in the quaternions, together with the rhetoric and logic used in the style of debate, enlivened such poems as the letters to her husband, the elegies, and "Contemplations" and enabled Bradstreet to resolve the tensions and problems revealed in the personal poems.

The poet's tensions are noted also in "Anne Bradstreet: Dogmatist and Rebel" (*NEQ*, September 1966) by Ann Stanford. She describes the pattern of questioning and submission followed by the poet in her first coming to New England, in her decision to write despite community criticism, in the letter to her children, and in the final elegies.

Kenneth A. Requa, in "Anne Bradstreet's Poetic Voices" (*EAL*, Spring 1974), draws a distinction between Bradstreet's public voice, as displayed in the elegy on Sir Philip Sidney, and the private voice of the personal poems. Her public poems, he says, are imitative in contrast to the originality of the private ones. Bradstreet felt uneasy in her role as public poet; hence, she felt a need to apologize within the poems themselves. Apology was unnecessary in the private poems, where she could abandon the popular classical references and rely on imagery drawn from her own experience. In the private poetry she also uses a greater variety of verse forms. Requa discusses control and imagery in such poems as "To Her Father with Some Verses" and "In Reference to Her Children" and the stanzas of thanksgiving. Commenting as he does on so many aspects of the poet's work, Requa's is an important essay on the less-discussed poems.

Another attempt to pull together resemblances among the poems is made by Rosemary M. Laughlin in "Anne Bradstreet: Poet in Search of Form" (*AL*, March 1970). She finds that various of the better poems are unified by the use of single conceits or images or by the use of dramatic argument.

Emily Stipes Watts looks at Bradstreet's search in even broader terms. In "The posy Unity: Anne Bradstreet's Search for Order" (*Puritan Influences in American Literature*, ed. Emory Elliott, Urbana: University of Illinois Press, 1979), she says that the poet from first to last seeks a cosmological order that will include man, nature, and God in one circle. Watts finds the quest both lifelong and melancholy. She cites the breakdown of the analogies in the second two quaternions as a failure of the poet to find an intellectual unity in the world. Bradstreet could find no redemptive pattern in history, as shown in the "Four Monarchies"; and in "Contemplations" the poet discovered not unity but a split between man and nature, to be transcended only by a despair of the world and a trust in the hereafter. With Roy Harvey Pearce in *The Continuity of American Poetry* (Princeton: Princeton University Press, 1961), Watts views the personal and domestic poems as lacking in imagination. The love poems, Watts says, "are uncomplicated and direct and say very little about the nature" of the Bradstreets' love.

Rosamund Rosenmeier ("'Divine Translation': A Contribution to the Study of Anne Bradstreet's Method in the Marriage Poems," *EAL*, Fall 1977) sees the marriage poems as representative of Bradstreet's method throughout her poetic career: "Her lifelong subject seems to have been the problem of comprehending the relationship between opposites." In these poems the use of biblical types helps her resolve the "oppositions she was struggling with" in such poems as "The Vanity of All Worldly Things" and "The Flesh and Spirit." She diffuses references in the marriage poems so that the figure of Christ as the Sun of Righteousness is put to personal use. Her husband is imaged as the sun, and his return "has many of the same effects on the poet as the dawning of the sun, the coming of the spring, or the renewal of her sense of Christ's promises." The poems' complexity results from her use of "types" by which real relationships may prefigure the invisible union to come. Rosenmeier also discusses "Upon the Burning of Our House" as a prefiguration.

Robert D. Arner's "The Structure of Anne Bradstreet's Tenth Muse," in *Discoveries & Considerations: Essays on Early American Literature & Aesthetics*, edited by Calvin Israel (Albany: State University of New York Press, 1976), argues that *The Tenth Muse* is more impressive considered as a unit than as isolated individual poems. In tracing the thematic and imagistic connections, Arner finds that the book has a complexity heretofore unnoticed and that it is more valuable as literary history and as poetry than has been suspected. In the course of his argument, Arner treats "The Four Monarchies" and gives special attention to relating its parts, discovering that in it Bradstreet moves away from her unquestioning attitude toward male supremacy. Arner's is the most comprehensive look at this long poem yet provided.

"The Prologue," which Bradstreet's editor placed at the beginning of *The Tenth Muse*, may have been originally an introduction to "The Four Monarchies." Jane Donahue Eberwein, in a close reading of the poem ("'No Rhet'ric We Expect': Argumentation in Bradstreet's 'The Prologue,'" *EAL*, Spring 1981), contends that the poet's lines disclaiming she will write about wars, captains, and kings are ironic. Throughout "The Prologue" Bradstreet argues by claiming incapacity and demonstrating command. By making concessions Bradstreet pushes her opponents' arguments to absurdity, contriving "to sound meek and vulnerable, even in the act of choosing among crowns."

Daniel B. Shea, Jr.'s "Puritan Spiritual Narratives," in his *Spiritual Autobiography in Early America* (Princeton: Princeton University Press, 1968), offers one of the few commentaries on Bradstreet's letter titled "To My Dear Children." He says that it differs from other Puritans' spiritual autobiographies in that it does not describe "the emergence of grace in its various signs and stages—and instead appears to substitute a kind of rudimentary apologetics." Actually, he comments, her argument is that parents cannot persuade their children to grace. The poet attempts to prepare her children for a stoical and loving resignation to Providence. In doing this, she represents her life in its afflictions, giving small scope to its joys.

According to Robert C. Wess's "Religious Tension in the Poetry of Anne Bradstreet" (*Christianity and Religion*, Winter 1976), such poems as "The Vanity of All Worldly Things" and "As Weary Pilgrim" reveal a sincere and simple faith in Bradstreet's religious beliefs in contrast to the doubts expressed in "To My Dear Children" and the poems on illness and recovery in the Andover manuscript. He traces the pattern of these poems "from anguish to supplication to consolation." Wess finds two kinds of tension in the poems: that between religious doubt and faith and that between material things and spiritual values, especially as expressed in "The Flesh and the Spirit" and "Upon the Burning of Our House." Such tensions, he contends, help show the Puritans as real human beings, confronted by a spiritual combat still present between an individual Christian's "public creed and private natural impulses."

Such tensions reach their apex in the late elegies on Bradstreet's grandchildren. A number of writers have commented, sometimes briefly, on these. Randall R. Mawer, however, devotes an entire essay to the question of resistance versus resignation in the elegies, seeing in the elegy on Elizabeth a "rebellion that is almost triumph" ("'Farewel Dear Babe': Bradstreet's Elegy for Elizabeth," *EAL*, Spring 1980). Mawer begins with what he considers the perennial question of Puritan New Englanders, "what are the uses of adversity?" He asserts that Bradstreet asks this question throughout her writing and that in "Farewel Dear Babe" she tells of her failure to achieve the resignation she purports to describe. Mawer gives a close reading, including a discussion of the techniques, meter, diction, and stanzaic repetition that contribute to the effectiveness of the poem.

Few writers on Bradstreet have considered the wit in many of the poems, aside from noting that it tends to be metaphysical, including paradoxes, puns, and plays on words, as well as satire. A brief beginning, placing Bradstreet in the stream of American humor as practiced by women, is made by Jacqueline Hornstein ("Comic Vision in the Literature of New England Women before 1800," *RFI*, Fall 1977 and Winter 1977-1978). Hornstein finds gentle humor in the extended bird metaphor of "In Reference to Her Children" and in the "mocking parody of her own creative talents in 'To Her Book.'" In both poems, she says, Bradstreet uses wit and humor to express her ideas about motherhood and creativity in a fallen world.

Sources and Influences

A number of essays have focused on influences on the poet by other writers or by ideas current in her time. A most important influence was the work of Guillaume DuBartas as translated by Joshua Sylvester. Though the influence of DuBartas in the early poems, particularly the quaternions, is obvious, Kenneth A. Requa ("Anne Bradstreet's Use of DuBartas in 'Contemplations,'" *EIHC*, January 1974) indicates that Bradstreet extensively borrowed ideas and point of view from DuBartas even in that late poem.

Helen McMahon, in "Anne Bradstreet, Jean Bertault, and Dr. Crooke" (*EAL*, Fall 1968), notes indebtedness to those two authors, and Dorothea Kehler points out indebtedness to Edmund Spenser for several images in "Contemplations" ("Anne Bradstreet and Spenser," *AN&Q*, May 1970).

In *Anne Bradstreet*, Piercy's chapter, "The Apprentice," suggests a relationship between the quarrels of "The Four Elements" and the bickerings within the young colony, as well as the possibility that "The Four Ages" may contain portraits of actual persons. In "Anne Bradstreet's Portrait of Sir Philip Sidney" (*EAL*, Winter 1966-67), Stanford finds such a character in the depiction of "Youth."

Piercy also relates Bradstreet to the emblematic genre in her chapter 5, "The Prose Writer," where she discusses "Meditations Divine and Moral" as emblems. In addition, this chapter contains an excellent examination of the prose style of Bradstreet. It is perhaps the only essay that has undertaken the task.

An essay in *Studi Americani 14*, edited by Augustino Lombardo (Rome: Edizioni Di Storia e Letteratura, 1968) titled "Anne Bradstreet, il Petrarchismo e il 'Plain Style,'" by Alessandra Contenti, points out Bradstreet's ability to use borrowed passages and techniques in new ways and cites her use of DuBartas and Quarles. Through Quarles's *Sions Sonets* she receives and responds to the influence of Petrarchan love poems with their antitheses and puns.

Feminist Criticism

Given Anne Bradstreet's position at the fountainhead of American poetry and her accomplishments despite the attitudes of a patriarchal society, interest has grown in her as an articulate woman and sometime advocate of the feminist position.

Wendy Martin, in "Anne Bradstreet's Poetry: A Study of Subversive Piety," *Shakespeare's Sisters: Feminist Essays on Women Poets*, edited by Sandra M. Gilbert and Susan Gubar (Bloomington and London: Indiana University Press, 1979), outlines the scope of Bradstreet's private rebellion. Bradstreet, she says, observed Puritan restrictions on the feminine role in her domestic life but expresses her feminism in her poetry. In such work as the quaternions she advocated "unity based on cooperation, not order based on dominance."

In "Anne Hutchinson and Anne Bradstreet: Literature and Experience, Faith and Works in Massachusetts Bay Colony" (*International Journal of Women's Studies*, September-October 1978), Anne King compares the lives and the nature of the work of the two women. She finds both heroic; both present the problem of the "individual voice unconnected with an orthodox organization" as well as the problem of the woman's role. They resolved their dilemmas in opposite ways—Hutchinson by scorn of tradition and approval, Bradstreet by making small compromises.

In "Images of Women in Early American Literature," *What Manner of Woman: Essays on English and American Life and Literature*, edited by Marlene Springer (New York University Press, 1977), Ann Stanford describes Bradstreet as setting forth the place of the Puritan matron in her elegy on her mother and as fitting into a typical Puritan family configuration.

Karl Keller, in his *The Only Kangaroo Among the Beauty: Emily Dickinson and America* (Baltimore: The Johns Hopkins University Press, 1979), cautions against seeing too much feminism in Bradstreet's poetry. He reminds us that Puritan theology gave importance to women as being responsible for their own souls; that responsibility included duties within the society; and that women, though subservient to their husbands in secular affairs, were equal in the "spiritual scale." Woman had a world within, and she, like every individual, had to discover her own abilities and worth. For Bradstreet the discovery involved her challenges to God, in which God won because she let him win, but nevertheless she was a partner in the struggle because God had made a covenant with mankind, and she was participating in bringing about God's will. Keller's well-considered argument arises out of his comparison of Bradstreet and Emily Dickinson as two whose womanhood in a background of puritanism enlivened their poetry.

FURTHER STUDY

Although the volume of Bradstreet scholarship has increased in recent years, much remains to be done. Additions to the biography and to the background of Bradstreet's domestic life may be made by further study of the activities of those around her and of the configurations of her social milieu. One author, for example, has suggested that the Bradstreets moved to Andover to be nearer the frontier where Simon was interested in the fur trade. Did Anne Bradstreet accompany her husband to Boston or did she visit her father's family or her sisters or was she left forever in Andover once she arrived? Helen Stuart Campbell provided some historical background material in her *Anne Bradstreet and Her Time* (Boston: D. Lothrop, 1891), but she used it without references, so that the reader is not sure where fiction begins. The kind of background she gives would be welcome if it could be documented.

Literary scholars have tended to concentrate on the personal poems. More work might be done on the earlier, public poems and the prose. A recent dissertation, Lewis Morse Baldwin II's "Moses and Mannerism: An Aesthetic for the Poetry of Colonial New England" (Syracuse University, 1973), suggests the importance of the metaphysical in Puritan aesthetics.

The study of the use of iconography by Puritans, too, is just beginning, and further study of Bradstreet in connection with the emblem books may prove fruitful.

MARY ROWLANDSON

BIBLIOGRAPHY

The historian Douglas Edward Leach, in the entry "Mary Rowlandson," *Notable American Women 1607-1950: A Biographical Dictionary*, edited by Edward T. James (Cambridge, Mass.: Belknap Press of Harvard University Press, 1971), has assembled references on the biography of this author.

EDITIONS

The first edition of the Rowlandson narrative was printed by Samuel Green, Jr., at Boston in 1682 under the title *The Soveraignty & Goodness of God, Together, with the Faithfulness of His Promises Displayed; Being a Narrative of the Captivity and Restauration of Mrs. Mary Rowlandson.* The second edition, "Corrected and amended," was printed at Cambridge, again in 1682, by Samuel Green, Sr. In the same year a London edition was set from the first edition. A rare copy of the Cambridge second edition in the Prince Collection of the Boston Public Library is the source for the best modern editions.

A list of later editions may be found in the version edited by Frederick Lewis Weis (Boston: Houghton Mifflin, 1930), but the eighteenth-century texts contain emendations that make them unreliable.

The 1682 Cambridge text is reprinted in Charles H. Lincoln's edition of *Narratives of the Indian Wars, 1675-1699* (Charles Scribner's, 1913). This edition, still available in many libraries, has been reproduced in a more recent collection, *Held Captive by Indians: Selected Narratives 1642-1836*, edited by Richard VanDerBeets (Knoxville: University of Tennessee Press, 1973). A text of the second edition with modern spelling may also be found in *So Dreadfull a Judgment: Puritan Responses to King Philip's War, 1676-1677*, edited by Richard Slotkin and James K. Folsom (Middletown, Conn.: Wesleyan University Press, 1978).

Robert Kent Diebold's doctoral dissertation ("A Critical Edition of Mrs. Mary Rowlandson's Captivity Narrative," Yale University Press, 1972) reports the finding of four leaves from the lost first edition that had been used as lining papers in a contemporary book. His examination of the two exposed leaves indicates that the London edition of 1682 "is probably the most reliable of the extant complete early editions."

MANUSCRIPTS AND LETTERS

There are no extant manuscripts or letters written by Mary Rowlandson.

BIOGRAPHY

There is no full-length biography of Mary Rowlandson. A good brief biography is the one cited above by Douglas Edward Leach in *Notable American Women 1607-1950.*

CRITICISM

Moses Coit Tyler found the diction of Mary Rowlandson to be "the pure, idiomatic, and sinewy English of a cultivated American matron." Yet, despite the many merits of her narrative, it has received more attention as history and as representative of Puritan thought than as a literary work.

Two essays trace Rowlandson's movements during her captivity. The first, Henry S. Nourse's "Mrs. Mary Rowlandson's Removes," *Proceedings of the American Antiquarian Society October 1897-October 1898*, N.S. 12 (Worcester, Mass.: American Antiquarian Society, 1899), maps out the places she stayed. The second, Douglas Edward Leach's "The 'Whens' of Mary Rowlandson's Captivity" (*NEQ*, September 1961), determines the dates and times of the removes by reference not only to Rowlandson, but to the known dates of other events she mentions.

Richard VanDerBeets, in his excellent essay, "The Indian Captivity Narrative as Ritual" (*AL*, January 1972), describes the common events and changes that occur among subjects of Indian captivities and that move the captives toward an acceptance and imitation of the ways of their captors. Ann Stanford's "Mary Rowlandson's Journey to Redemption" (*Ariel*, July 1976) describes Mary Rowlandson's gradual adjustment to captivity. She notes that Rowlandson's story is both a literal and allegorical journey representing the progress of the individual toward redemption and that both the saving of New England and of Rowlandson herself came only after there seemed no help but in the Lord.

This latter point is stressed by Paola Cabibbo in "Mary Rowlandson, Prigioniera degli Indiani," *Studi Americani 13*, edited by Augustino Lombardo (Rome: Edizioni Di Storia e Letteratura, 1967). Cabibbo points out the symmetrical form of the narrative as consisting of a prologue—the attack on Lancaster—the twenty removes, approximately half of them away from Lancaster and the others returning, and the moral conclusion. She sees the narrative as an answer to Urian Oakes's call for "Remembrancers" of the Lord's dealings: every occurrence of the journey, however small, becomes evidence of divine mercy or displeasure. The work is a fine piece of literature with good character sketches of the Indians. It moves from the opening scene with a rhythmic speed, filled with images of movement that hurry the story along. Rowlandson's use of dialogue is lively, including the readings from the Bible that show correspondences between the events of the captivity and those of the sacred word. The Bible is both real and a symbol, helping to furnish a symbolic narrative of a Christian passing through the wilderness as well as the story of a single captive. This is an excellent commentary on Rowlandson's narrative, suggestive of avenues for further exploration. It would be good to have it available in English translation.

Several essays analyze Rowlandson's story as a model for the long-lived genre of captivity narratives. David L. Minter, in "By Dens of Lions: Notes on Stylization in Early Puritan Captivity Narratives" (*AL*, November 1973), sees the early narratives as familiar stories of providential delivery placed in a new setting. Behind them lay a view that God's design ruled even "'the most unruly'" and a welcoming of affliction as beneficial. Both the protagonist and her captors are actors in a divine drama. In the Puritan view, Minter continues, all life is a prison from which the only delivery is death; release from captivity becomes a prefiguring of such release and salvation; yet even this suffering does not guarantee election, and the Rowlandson narrative moves through a rhythmic repetition of near despair and hope revived. The act of writing out the experience continues this rhythm. Rowlandson can act on several levels at once because her personal experience so embodies the social code; thus she becomes a figure of "heroic proportion" and gives meaning to "individual adventure."

Richard Slotkin and James K. Folsom go into even more detail in their anthology *So Dreadfull a Judgment: Puritan Responses to King Philip's War, 1676-1677* (Middletown, Conn.: Wesleyan University Press, 1978). According to them the captivity narrative was an archetype of a "mythology in which the colonial experience was symbolized by the peril of a white Christian woman in the Indian-haunted wilderness." Rowlandson's account marks the change in the settlers' view of the Indians, who became savages rather than convertible heathens. Though Rowlandson states this view, she becomes increasingly aware of the Indians as individuals. Her story is a psychological as well as historical document involving both the conversion experience and the trauma of emigration.

Here and in his own *Regeneration through Violence: The Mythology of the American Frontier, 1600-1860* (Middletown, Conn.: Wesleyan University Press, 1973), Slotkin connects Rowlandson's narrative to other American literary documents and to the myths of "self-transcendence." His comments are rich and complex and constitute essential reading on this author.

The question of style is addressed by David Downing in "'Streams of Scripture Comfort': Mary Rowlandson's Typological Use of the Bible" (*EAL*, Winter 1980-1981). Downing finds a change from the vigorous homely diction of her narrative to a more exalted language when she comments upon day-to-day events. In such passages she uses biblical quotations and echoes. This alternation runs through the narrative to the conclusion, where the biblical references pile up in her meditation on her release in terms close to those of a conversion experience. Downing notes the large number of passages assuring salvation and remarks on the prevalence of Old Testament passages.

FURTHER STUDY

Rowlandson's story has been among the most highly praised of the captivity narratives. Roy Harvey Pearce ("The Significances of the Captivity Narrative," *AL*, March 1947) calls Rowlandson's "the best known (and deservedly so) of the narratives." He finds in it "vivid immediacy and religious intensity" and an "aesthetic quality which derives from the freshness and concreteness of detail with which the narrator explores her experience." In his biographical sketch Leach speaks of her "vivid episodic narration" in a "vigorous, earthy style." Yet except for the studies cited and for scattered references in accounts of the captivity genre, there have been few critical writings on this important document.

Mrs. Rowlandson's account is much more lively and attractive to modern readers than many other pieces of our early literature. Rowlandson's journey grows out of tragedy, yet she includes scenes of sharply observed mundane details ironically shadowed by the impending doom of the Indian characters, as well as the loss of her daughter and other colonists and the bloody waste of such a war. Her prose is fresh and readable, while laden with biblical and symbolic imagery. The piece is long enough for extensive study of its style, imagery, symbolism, and form.

SARAH KEMBLE KNIGHT

BIBLIOGRAPHY

William J. Scheick and JoElla Doggett's *Seventeenth-Century American Poetry: A Reference Guide* (Boston: G. K. Hall, 1977) lists only four items on this author between 1879 and 1964. Because their bibliography covers only poetry, they have omitted introductions to recent editions and a few scattered or later essays. Further references to the family of Madam Knight, her journey, and the history of the *Journal* will be found under "Sarah Kemble Knight" by Malcolm Freiberg in *Notable American Women 1607-1950: A Biographical Dictionary*, edited by Edward T. James (Cambridge, Mass.: Belknap Press of Harvard University Press, 1971).

EDITIONS

The Journals of Madam Knight, and Rev. Mr. Buckingham were first published together in a volume edited by Theodore Dwight, Jr. (Wilder and Campbell, 1825). Though the *Journal* was reprinted several times during the nineteenth century, the best and most available editions are *The Journal of Madam Knight With an Introductory Note by George Parker Winship*

(Boston: Small, Maynard, 1920; New York, Peter Smith, 1935) and *The Journal of Madam Knight Including an introductory note by Malcolm Freiberg and wood engravings by Michael McCurdy* (Boston: David R. Godine, 1972).

An account of the nineteenth-century editions will be found in "The Editing and Publication of 'The Journal of Madam Knight'" (*PBSA*, First Quarter 1964) by Alan Margolies.

BIOGRAPHY

There is no full-length biography of this author. The best account of her life will be found in Malcolm Freiberg's brief introductory note to the Godine Press edition of the *Journal*. Before Freiberg's investigation the standard biography of the author was that by Anson Titus, "Madam Sarah Knight: Her Diary and Her Times 1666-1726" (*Boston Society Publications*, Vol. 9, Boston, 1912). Freiberg disagrees with Titus with regard to the identity of the author's husband and disputes other points on the basis of negative evidence for Titus' statements. However, Titus gives some material omitted by Freiberg, and his account is still worthy of consideration.

Erastus Worthington's "Madam Knight's Journal" (*Dedham Historical Register*, Vol. 1, Dedham, Mass.: Dedham Historical Society, 1890) describes the terrain Knight crossed and the history of the two taverns she visited on her first afternoon's journey—that kept by Joshua Fisher and the Billings Tavern, both now torn down. He suggests that on her return journey she stayed at a house on Centre Street in Roxbury, which was once owned by someone named Draper and was still standing in 1890.

MANUSCRIPTS AND LETTERS

The original manuscript of the *Journal* has disappeared, as has the copy made of it by Theodore Dwight, Jr., which served as the copy text for the 1825 edition. No other prose or poetry by this author has yet been discovered.

A manuscript collection pertaining to the life of Madam Knight was gathered by William R. Deane for a projected life of the author; it contains a single copy of her autograph. The collection is held by the New England Historic Genealogical Society in Boston.

Alan Margolies (cited above) gives a history of the manuscript and corrects errors made in the introductions to various editions of the *Journal*.

CRITICISM

Although Moses Coit Tyler found the *Journal* "an amusing little book" that in contrast to other diaries of the time was "refreshingly carnal, external, and healthy," few scholars have written about it in this century.

Two essays have attempted to place Knight in various genres of travel literature. Robert O. Stephens, in "The Odyssey of Sarah Kemble Knight" (*CLAJ*, March 1964), suggests that she wrote with Homer's *Odyssey* in mind, treating her own journey in mock heroic fashion. Thus, as a Bostonian, she represents the Greek among barbarians, taking the various practices of hospitality as a measure of civilization. Her stop at Mr. Devil's house represents an underworld journey, and she is enchanted by Cynthia, the moon goddess. At New Haven she witnesses the epic games of the locals. In thus mingling the Homeric and Puritan world views, Knight indicates the mythic rather than wholly realistic nature of her narrative.

Peter Thorpe places her journal in the picaresque tradition ("Sarah Kemble Knight and the Picaresque Tradition," *CLAJ*, December 1966) on the basis of a number of characteristics, among them: the element of travelling, with numerous episodes; the use of the first person narrator; the function of comment on morals and manners of those encountered; the use of comedy; and the seriousness of the close. Thorpe's comments in support of each of these points are well-taken.

In "Images of Women in Early American Literature" (*What Manner of Woman: Essays on English and American Life and Literature*, ed. Marlene Springer, New York University Press, 1977), Ann Stanford discusses the changes in the attitude toward religion between the early and later years of the seventeenth century, as illustrated by Bradstreet and Knight, and suggests that Knight represents a figure of the enlightenment and a forerunner of the romanticism of such Gothic writers as Washington Irving.

Knight's keen sense of humor is noted by Hollis L. Cate, who compares one of her passages with one from Mark Twain and finds a number of parallels ("Two American Bumpkins," *RS*, March 1973).

Jacqueline Hornstein ("Comic Vision in the Literature of New England Women before 1800," *RFI*, Fall 1977/Winter 1977-1978) also comments on humor in Knight's *Journal*. The travelogue, she says, "contains the whole spectrum of comic modes . . . from satiric tableaus of backwoods settlers and anecdotes about local Connecticut manners to self-parody to humorous light-hearted poems to scatological material and finally to witty turns on Biblical references." Hornstein gives a few examples of Knight's general comic method and concludes that the comic moments in the *Journal* are balanced by darker sections representative of worldly evil; hence she feels that Knight, like other Puritans, wrote of her experiences "in the service of her religion."

FURTHER STUDY

The starting point for further study of this author might be the manuscript collection made by William R. Deane. Even if it should not furnish enough material for a full-length biography, it might add to the few published facts we now have on the life of this author and on her time.

Madam Knight's reading opens another avenue for research. She appears familiar with some of the romances that were then available in pamphlet form, as well as with some of the better-known poets and prose writers of her time and the immediately preceding period. Besides the suggestion made in Hollis L. Cate's essay that her humor resembled that of Mark Twain, it precedes that of other American humorists as well; some of these resemblances might be the focus of further study.

Her career as a wife, mother, landlady, and woman of business should interest scholars looking into activities of women in the pre-Revolutionary era.

Local Colorists: Sarah Orne Jewett, Mary E. Wilkins Freeman, and Mary N. Murfree

The critical reputations of Sarah Orne Jewett, Mary E. Wilkins Freeman, and Mary N. Murfree have been inextricably entwined with the fate of the local color movement they have been taken to represent. At the height of the local color movement in the late nineteenth century, all three enjoyed widespread acclaim, both popular and critical. With the passage of time, however, the local color tag has become something of a hindrance to the full appreciation of their work. The term itself has acquired a slightly pejorative tone so that it is not uncommon to hear, for example, that Jewett rose above "mere local color" in *The Country of the Pointed Firs*. To some extent, of course, labels such as "local colorist" are unavoidable in literary history and criticism. Like most clichés, there is more than a little truth in applying that term to the works of these three women. However, the history of criticism of their writings is illustrative of the tendency for influential early labels and attitudes to shape and direct the research and criticism done for many years afterward. It is hard enough to effect change in critical attitudes toward major writers. It is doubly hard when one is dealing with writers not deemed to be of the first rank. Greater appreciation of the importance of minor writers has, in recent years, directed more attention to them. Jewett, Freeman, and Murfree have also benefited some from the general increase in interest in women writers. Out of this new wave may come at last the means for them to escape the local color pigeonhole or at least a better understanding of the importance of local colorists.

Of the three, criticism of Sarah Orne Jewett has been most fully developed. This fact is attributable in part to her having written *The Country of the Pointed Firs*, which is generally acknowledged to be a minor masterpiece, if that is not a contradiction in terms. Even the adulation heaped on the *Pointed Firs*, however, illustrates a problem plaguing criticism of these writers: a tendency to focus on a few outstanding works with only passing attention to the rest of the writer's output. Yet a writer's most important work can be understood best in the context of the total output of a career. Along with the shedding or reassessment of the local color stereotype, a reconsideration of these writers should bring about a closer inspection of their total production. Indeed the latter is probably a necessary condition for the former.

SARAH ORNE JEWETT

BIBLIOGRAPHY

The first full-scale bibliography of Jewett was Clara Carter Weber and Carl J. Weber's *A Bibliography of the Published Writings of Sarah Orne Jewett* (Waterville, Me.: Colby College Press, 1949). The Webers' book might be termed a "comprehensive bibliography," for it is both a primary bibliography of Jewett's writings and a secondary bibliography of writings about her. Its treatment of Jewett's books is not really descriptive, however, and for accurate descriptions of first editions, the reader should consult the Jewett entry in volume five of Jacob Blanck's *Bibliography of American Literature* (New Haven: Yale University Press, 1969). Blanck's treatment of Jewett's books is enhanced by his use of the records of her publisher, Houghton Mifflin. As a bibliography of Jewett's writings, therefore, the Webers' volume is most useful now principally for its listings of her periodical contributions, of the many reprintings of her stories in other books, and of foreign translations. Two articles in *CLQ* supplement the Webers's listing of Jewett's writings: John Eldridge Frost's "Sarah Orne Jewett Bibliography: 1949-1963" (June 1964) and Richard Cary's "Some Bibliographic Ghosts of Sarah Orne Jewett" (September 1968). See also two notes by David Bonnell Green in "Sarah Orne Jewett's 'A Dark Night'" (*PBSA*, October-December 1959) and in "The Sarah Orne Jewett Canon: Additions and a Correction" (*PBSA*, April-June 1961).

The Webers' annotated listing of critical comment on Jewett has been superseded by Gwen L. Nagel and James Nagel's *Sarah Orne Jewett: A Reference Guide* (Boston: G. K. Hall, 1978). This volume is an indispensable guide to Jewett criticism and scholarship. Covering the years from 1873 to 1976, the book provides annotated listings of contemporary reviews of Jewett's books as well as all significant later scholarship and additional references to Jewett. The book also has a valuable introduction, which surveys the course of Jewett criticism over the years.

The Nagels' landmark work replaces several other listings of secondary comment published after the Webers' bibliography. These include the articles by Frost and Cary cited above and Clayton L. Eichelberger's "Sarah Orne Jewett (1849-1909): A Critical Bibliography of Secondary

Comment'' (*ALR*, Fall 1969). Richard Cary has also provided a concise but now somewhat dated survey of Jewett scholarship in "Sarah Orne Jewett (1849-1909)'' (*ALR*, Fall 1967). All of these listings are still of some value, but they lack the comprehensiveness of the Nagels' volume. Although a full descriptive bibliography of Jewett would be welcome, it must be said that Jewett has, on the whole, been well served by her bibliographers.

EDITIONS

There is no satisfactory collected edition of Jewett's writings, although all of the books for adults published during her lifetime are in print today, mostly as facsimiles issued by reprint publishers. *Stories and Tales*, an early edition (1910) from Houghton Mifflin, consists of seven volumes reprinted from the original plates.

Undoubtedly the most influential edition has been *The Best Short Stories of Sarah Orne Jewett* (Boston: Houghton Mifflin, 1925) selected and with an introduction by Willa Cather. This edition has *The Country of the Pointed Firs* as well as eleven short stories. The text of the *Pointed Firs* in this edition includes "A Dunnet Shepherdess,'' "The Queen's Twin,'' and "William's Wedding,'' the three related stories added to the book after Jewett's death. Originally published in two volumes, Cather's collection was issued in 1954 as an Anchor paperback, *The Country of the Pointed Firs and Other Stories* (Garden City, N.Y.: Doubleday). The problem with the text in this edition is that it is better to read the *Pointed Firs* in twenty-one chapters as it was first published in 1896. This text has been made available by David Bonnell Green in *The World of Dunnet Landing: A Sarah Orne Jewett Collection* (Lincoln: University of Nebraska Press, 1962). To the original text Green has appended the three stories that had been included in the book after Jewett's death and a fourth story related to Dunnet Landing, "The Foreigner.'' The second part of *The World of Dunnet Landing* contains five critical essays on Jewett and *The Country of the Pointed Firs*. A recent edition, which also prints the *Pointed Firs* in its original form, is *Short Fiction of Sarah Orne Jewett and Mary Wilkins Freeman* (Signet Classics, New American Library, 1978). This edition also includes the four related stories and reprints five other Jewett short stories. It has an introduction by Barbara H. Solomon.

Jewett's first book has been issued along with several stories and sketches in *Deephaven and Other Stories*, edited with an introduction by Richard Cary (New Haven: College and University Press, 1966). Cary has also edited an important volume, now unfortunately out of print, *The Uncollected Short Stories of Sarah Orne Jewett* (Waterville, Me.: Colby College Press, 1971). This book contains forty-four stories that Jewett never collected in the various volumes published during her lifetime. The stories that Cary omits from the volume are "keyed in substance, style, and spirit to children's comprehension.'' Jewett's last book, *The Tory Lover*, which many consider to be her weakest, was reissued in 1975 by the Old Berwick Historical Society with an introduction by Marie Donahue.

MANUSCRIPTS AND LETTERS

Two years after Jewett's death, her intimate friend, Annie Fields, saw through the press *Letters of Sarah Orne Jewett* (Boston: Houghton Mifflin, 1911), the first collection of Jewett's letters. Fields employed a heavy editorial hand with the texts of the letters, however, and the result was a volume that is ultimately unsatisfactory by modern scholarly standards. Unfortunately the originals of some of the letters Fields had access to have disappeared, so that her edition is still of value, although it must be used with caution.

Colby College has done a great deal to further Jewett scholarship, and the publication of the Jewett letters at Colby is one of the most significant accomplishments. Richard Cary has edited *Sarah Orne Jewett Letters* (Waterville, Me.: Colby College Press, 1967), which contains 142 letters. This edition is a revised and expanded version of Cary's 1956 edition of *Sarah Orne Jewett Letters.* That 1956 edition, in turn, had expanded upon Carl J. Weber's *Letters of Sarah Orne Jewett Now in the Colby College Library*, published by the Colby College Press in 1947.

Many other Jewett letters have been published in scattered articles, and these can be located by using the index entry to "Letters" in the Nagels' Jewett reference guide. The most important miscellaneous collections that have been printed are: C. Carroll Hollis's "Letters of Sarah Orne Jewett to Anna Laurens Dawes" (*CLQ*, September 1968); Richard Cary's "'Yours Always Lovingly': Sarah Orne Jewett to John Greenleaf Whittier" (*EIHC*, October 1971); and Richard Cary's "Jewett to Dresel: 33 Letters" (*CLQ*, March 1975).

John Eldridge Frost has published a checklist of Jewett's letters, both published and unpublished, in "The Letters of Sarah Orne Jewett" (*CLQ*, September 1959). The most important collections of letters and manuscripts are at the Houghton Library, Harvard University; the Society for the Preservation of New England Antiquities (SPNEA), Boston; and the Colby College Library. The Houghton collection includes extensive correspondence, manuscripts, diaries, and scrapbooks. The SPNEA collection has 974 letters from Jewett to her sister, Mary Rice Jewett. The listing of Jewett manuscripts in the second edition of *American Literary Manuscripts* (Athens: University of Georgia Press, 1977) is more up to date than Frost's 1959 article, although it does not describe a library's holdings in the same detail that Frost does.

While many Jewett letters have been published, there is still a need for a comprehensive edition. The many extant Jewett manuscripts would seem to offer rich resources for textual study that has also not yet been undertaken.

BIOGRAPHY

Sarah Orne Jewett has been the subject of two book-length biographies. It has certainly been a boon to her critical reputation that the first of these, *Sarah Orne Jewett* (Boston: Houghton Mifflin, 1929), was by F. O. Matthiessen. Gracefully written, it can, however, scarcely be called definitive. It does not draw extensively on manuscript sources, for example, and it is short on both facts and documentation. Its style is impressionistic and caused one reviewer to compare it to a Jewett story in the way it recreates "the atmosphere in which its heroine moved." Matthiessen suggests that Jewett's style was her great strength, and he declares Jewett and Emily Dickinson to be the two best women writers America has produced. Because of the quality of the book itself and because of Matthiessen's later stature as a critic, this book, his first, will remain an important contribution to Jewett studies.

The second biography is John Eldridge Frost's *Sarah Orne Jewett* (Kittery Point, Me.: The Gundalow Club, 1960). Originally a dissertation at New York University, it was published in an edition of only three hundred copies. It complements Matthiessen's book well in the sense that it is scrupulously researched and documented, if not as gracefully written. Frost's book is largely biographical, and his criticism of Jewett's writings is laudatory. Although a fuller critical biography of Jewett is necessary, Frost's life is a solid piece of work which deserves to be reprinted so that it can be more widely available.

Two brief accounts of Jewett's life are Warner Berthoff's sketch in *Notable American Women* and the first chapter of Richard Cary's TUSAS volume, *Sarah Orne Jewett* (1962). In addition to these general accounts, there are a few articles that elaborate more specific aspects of her life. Richard Cary's "Sarah Orne Jewett and the Rich Tradition" (*CLQ*, November 1957) touches on the influence of her family background on her writing. Cary's "Miss Jewett and Madame Blanc" (*CLQ*, September 1967) discusses the relationship between Jewett and Marie Thérèse Blanc, the French writer and critic who translated several of Jewett's stories. In another article, "The Other Face of Jewett's Coin" (*ALR*, Fall 1969), Cary discusses what can be learned about Jewett by a reading of the letters sent to her. Susan Allen Toth's "Sarah Orne Jewett and Friends: A Community of Interest" (*SSF*, Summer 1972) discusses the relationships between Jewett and three other New England writers, Rose Terry Cooke, Mary E. Wilkins Freeman, and Alice Brown.

CRITICISM

There are two useful overviews of Jewett criticism. Richard Cary's introduction to *Appreciation of Sarah Orne Jewett: 29 Interpretive Essays* (Waterville, Me.: Colby College Press, 1973) reviews in general terms the reception Jewett has received over the decades. He does not, for the most part, discuss individual works but rather suggests the way in which Jewett's reputation has slowly developed. The essay was first published as "The Rise, Decline, and Rise of Sarah Orne Jewett" (*CLQ*, December 1972). The introduction to *Sarah Orne Jewett: A Reference Guide* by Gwen L. Nagel and James Nagel examines more specifically some of the paths in which Jewett criticism has fallen. Their opening comment is that a review of Jewett scholarship over the years "reveals a progressive sophistication of insight within a relatively narrow range." In fact, they have found that most of the principal areas of criticism of Jewett, with the exception of pastoralism and literary impressionism, were established soon after *Deephaven*, her first book, was published in 1877. Their introduction traces these lines of inquiry and gives a general evaluation of Jewett scholarship. It has generally offered a balanced view of her strengths and weaknesses, but there has been too much "undocumented work, showing less than rigorous research, which proffers judgments problematic in their critical formulations."

The two most important books of Jewett criticism are Richard Cary's Twayne's United States Authors Series (TUSAS) volume and *Appreciation of Sarah Orne Jewett*. The latter volume reprints many of the most important critical articles on Jewett beginning with Marie Thérèse Blanc's 1885 essay in *Revue des Deux Mondes*, "Le Roman de la Femme-Médecin." Most of the critical essays on Jewett discussed in this essay that were published before 1973 are reprinted in *Appreciation of Sarah Orne Jewett*.

Cary's TUSAS volume for many years was the only comprehensive critical survey of her entire oeuvre. It is a conscious attempt "to redress the balance" of critical work on Jewett, which has concentrated on *The Country of the Pointed Firs* and one or two short stories to the exclusion of the rest of her work. The book is truly comprehensive. After a lengthy analysis of Jewett's style, characters, and themes, Cary systematically examines her sketches, sketch stories, short stories, and novels. He even gives a passing look at her writing for children and her historical work, *The Story of the Normans*. Cary's critical assessments are judicious. He concludes, "It is not too much to claim that Sarah Orne Jewett is without peer among her contemporaries in the reliable description of her chosen time, place, and personalities." He places her work somewhere between romanticism and realism, but rejects the local color label because there is more to her fiction than the rendering of local scenes, characters, and customs. For an informed, albeit necessarily sometimes brief, reading of nearly all of Jewett's fiction, Cary's volume is invaluable. It is an essential tool for Jewett studies.

Equally handy is Josephine Donovan's brief survey of Jewett's writings, *Sarah Orne Jewett* (New York: Ungar, 1980). Donovan examines Jewett's stories and novels roughly in chronological order and discusses her development of such themes as the conflict between country and city, individualism and communal concerns, and the role of women in society. She also includes a discussion of Jewett's critical theories and of her literary influence. Donovan's approach tends to be encyclopedic, but that is part of the book's value, for she comments on nearly every Jewett tale and fits each one into the context of her evolving literary career.

Before Cary's volume there were many general interpretive pieces on Jewett, though certainly none as comprehensive as his book. These pieces represent a kind of intermediate stage between the reviews which greeted her books on publication and the academic writings on Jewett that began to appear with some consistency in the 1950s. Mixing biography and criticism, these essays tend to follow well-worn paths and to repeat commonplace phrases such as a praise for the delicacy of her art. Although not without some insight, they are not rigorously analytical.

One of the earliest comprehensive pieces on Jewett was Charles Miner Thompson's "The Art of Miss Jewett" (*AtM*, October 1904). He detects three motives in her work: to interpret the rural folk to the city resident, to chronicle the speech and customs of the country people, and to interpret the town to the country. He sees her naturally "aristocratic point of view" preventing her from clearing up the misunderstandings between town and country. In *A History of American Literature Since 1870* (Century, 1915), Fred Lewis Pattee sees this same kind of patrician aloofness in Jewett's work. He argues that, brilliant as her work is in technique, it lacks "the final touch of art" because it is "*too* literary." Edward M. Chapman praises Jewett's "intimacy with her material" in "The New England of Sarah Orne Jewett" (*YR*, October 1913), though this intimacy was not translated into stark realism. Chapman emphasizes Jewett's use of New England weather and the changing seasons in her work. Willa Cather's introduction to *The Best Short Stories of Sarah Orne Jewett* has probably been the most influential early assessment. Cather asserts that Jewett's best works have a beauty in their simplicity. Here also Cather makes the claim that *The Country of the Pointed Firs* is worthy of joining *The Scarlet Letter* and *Huckleberry Finn* as the three most enduring works of American literature.

The traditional literary history approach has been to treat Jewett and the other New England local colorists as recorders of decline and then to differentiate between their approaches to this general subject. Thus in *Acres of Flint: Writers of Rural New England, 1870-1900* (Washington: Scarecrow Press, 1951), Perry D. Westbrook sees Jewett's work as a celebration of preindustrial America. In *Harvests of Change: American Literature 1865-1914* (Englewood Cliffs, N.J.: Prentice-Hall, 1967), Jay Martin also focuses on Jewett's world as one which time has passed by. He notes her persistent desire to escape into an idealized childhood of the past. The triumph of the *Pointed Firs*, however, is the ambivalent attitude toward this idealized world.

A good brief introduction to Jewett is Margaret Farrand Thorp's essay, *Sarah Orne Jewett*, in the University of Minnesota Pamphlets on American Writers Series (Minneapolis: University of Minnesota Press, 1966). It is a mix of biography and criticism, but it does not venture any new interpretations.

Of the specialized studies of Jewett's work, the bulk of attention has been given, of course, to *The Country of the Pointed Firs*. When it was published in 1896, reviewers recognized it as a kind of capstone to Jewett's writing career. Alice Brown wrote that "perhaps no such beautiful work has ever been done in America" (*Book Buyer*, October 1897). Willa Cather's praise of it in her 1925 introduction cited above echoes Brown's judgment. Clearly *The Country of the Pointed Firs* has been responsible for preventing Jewett's reputation from slipping as much over the years as has that of other local colorists. Discussion of the book has revolved around questions of its form and unity. More recently it has become the focal point for discussion of the pastoral mode in Jewett's writings.

One of the most important articles on the book is Warner Berthoff's "The Art of Jewett's *Pointed Firs*" (*NEQ*, March 1959). Berthoff calls the book "a masterpiece of the local-color school" and feels that this "is not at all to talk it down," for regional fiction can offer a powerful critique of the new social order emerging in the nineteenth century. In *The Country of the Pointed Firs* Jewett has conveyed the fatalistic "sense of American life as requiring, as being *founded* upon, the pitiless extinction of the past, the violent extirpation of amenity and beauty and of every temporary establishment of that truly civil order which is the earliest of American dreams." Berthoff sees unity in the cumulative power of the events of the book to reveal this sociological and historical insight.

The question of the unity of *The Country of the Pointed Firs* has been a vexing one, for it seems to be less than a well-wrought novel, and yet it is clearly more than just a series of related sketches. In "The Unity of *The Country of the Pointed Firs*" (*TCL*, July 1959), Hyatt H. Waggoner suggests that apart from a unity of tone or setting, the book possesses a central unifying vision that is essentially humanistic and religious. Jewett has been able "to transmute felt reality into symbol," to portray Dunnet Landing as a place where "the permanent human situation may be discovered and the abiding human values discerned."

Taking issue with Berthoff's essentially sociological interpretation of the book, Francis Fike argues in "An Interpretation of *Pointed Firs*" (*NEQ*, December 1961) that instead of portraying human life as determined by "the great natural contingencies" of economic life, Jewett has discerned "the timeless and universal capacity of human nature to endure creatively and resourcefully in the face of great natural and social odds.'' Fike's interpretation emphasizes the three additional Dunnet Landing sketches added to the book after Jewett's death. The problem of what to do with these additional pieces has been taken up by David Bonnell Green in ''The World of Dunnet Landing'' (*NEQ*, December 1961; reprinted in *The World of Dunnet Landing: A Sarah Orne Jewett Collection*). He argues that ''The Queen's Twin,'' ''A Dunnet Shepherdess,'' ''William's Wedding,'' and ''The Foreigner'' should be included in discussions of the *Pointed Firs* because they are authentic enlargements of Jewett's fictional world.

The question of whether *The Country of the Pointed Firs* should be considered a novel at all is answered in the affirmative by Paul D. Voelker in ''*The Country of the Pointed Firs*: A Novel by Sarah Orne Jewett'' (*CLQ*, December 1970). Although it has been granted that the book has a certain unity, structure, and theme, he suggests that it has not been considered a novel because of its lack of ''growth and development of character.'' Voelker goes on to argue that the narrator undergoes a subtle development over the course of the book, which transforms her from an outsider to an intimate of the Dunnet Landing community.

One attempt to get the *Pointed Firs* out of the local color slot is Robin Magowan's ''Pastoral and the Art of Landscape in *The Country of the Pointed Firs*'' (*NEQ*, June 1963). Magowan suggests that the book differs from *Deephaven* principally in Jewett's adoption of the pastoral form, which he describes as presenting ''a summer vision of life.'' ''At its most intense, pastoral expresses man's dream of a perfectly ordered, self-contained, civil existence.'' Jewett's style is pictorial and compared to the impressionism of Winslow Homer. She has a ''mastery of perspective'' for placing objects in the context of their background so that they carry the maximum symbolic suggestion. The pastoral analysis also figures in Magowan's ''The Outer Island Sequence in *Pointed Firs*'' (*CLQ*, June 1964), in which the outer islands represent differing quests for ideals. Barton L. St. Armand dissents from Magowan's comparison of Jewett to Homer and suggests in ''Jewett and Marin: The Inner Vision'' (*CLQ*, December 1972) that she is better compared with ''a more modern impressionist, John Marin.'' Marin and Jewett share the same ''angle of vision, the perspective, the framing of the perceiving consciousness.'' Their art is human-centered while Homer's is more naturalistic.

In ''*The Country of the Pointed Firs:* A Pastoral of Innocence'' (*CLQ*, December 1970), David Stouck suggests that the narrator's quest for a return to childhood innocence at Dunnet Landing gives the book its pastoral quality. The book's achievement lies in the ''emotional ambiguity'' it evokes in the reader, who is always ''aware of the impossibility of regaining such innocence'' yet constantly feels drawn to the world the book presents.

Michael W. Vella's ''Sarah Orne Jewett: A Reading of *The Country of the Pointed Firs*" (*ESQ*, Fourth Quarter 1973) locates the sources for the book in the Emersonian perception of nature as symbolic and in the emphasis on verisimilitude of the realists. The unity of the book centers in the narrator's coming to understand life at Dunnet Landing by a sharpening of what Emerson called the "corresponding faculty," which is the ability to see transcendent reality in natural phenomena. Out of this growing perception, the narrator realizes her oneness with humanity.

In another analysis of the form of the book, Priscilla Leder in "The Gifts of Peace: Sarah Orne Jewett's Vision of Romance" (*GyS*, Winter 1977) considers the *Pointed Firs* in terms of Richard Chase's theory that the American novel has traditionally tended toward the romance. She sees Jewett's incorporation of romantic elements in the book as providing a unifying pattern. The romantic elements "are presented in relation to the community and are an integral and perhaps indispensable part of its functioning." Whereas in novels by men the romantic elements are often destructive forces, here Jewett uses them to enhance the idea of protective security in the community of Dunnet Landing. The sense of community is obviously a central theme in *The Country of the Pointed Firs*, and it figures prominently in Paul John Eakin's article, "Sarah Orne Jewett and the Meaning of Country Life" (*AL*, January 1967). Eakin discusses the book in the context of Jewett's earlier work. He finds a celebration of the social order of the community and a persistent "quest for permanence in her scenes of country life."

As Richard Cary notes in his TUSAS volume, little critical attention has been devoted to Jewett's work apart from the *Pointed Firs*. Slowly this seems to be changing. Her first book, *Deephaven*, has generally been looked at as an early attempt to write the kind of book Jewett later wrote successfully in the *Pointed Firs*. In his introduction to *Deephaven and Other Stories*, Cary describes it as standing "in relation to the rest of her work as the embryo to the adult organism." Robert L. Horn, however, has tried to examine the book on its own merits in "The Power of Jewett's *Deephaven*" (*CLQ*, December 1972). His conclusion is that once the reader gets by "the cloying narrative frame and the obvious technical unevenness" in the book he finds a startling picture: "some of the most devastating portrayals of isolation, frustration, self-delusion, human dry-rot, and, at times, indomitability in all of Jewett's fiction."

Even more neglected than *Deephaven* has been *A Marsh Island*, which Randall R. Mawer, in "Setting as Symbol in Jewett's *A Marsh Island*" (*CLQ*, June 1976), sees as a successful blending of story and local color setting. Jewett's historical novel, *The Tory Lover*, has not really had its dismal critical reputation enhanced, however. In "*The Tory Lover*, *Oliver Wiswell*, and *Richard Carvel*" (*CLQ*, December 1970), Helen V. Parsons finds Jewett's novel particularly unconvincing when compared to two more successful historical novels. Jewett's book is deficient in plotting and in its treatment of violence and love.

Among Jewett's short stories, "A White Heron" has long been recognized as perhaps the finest. There have been four recent articles devoted to it. Theodore R. Hovet examines the different worlds of Sylvia and the male hunter in "America's 'Lonely Country Child': The Theme of Separation in Sarah Orne Jewett's 'A White Heron'" (*CLQ*, September 1978). He sees in this contrast a "social enactment of the psychological drama of separation, the separation from bodily union with a nurturing environment which each individual must undergo in the process of maturation." It is a conflict between a child whose life is dependent on nature and the aggressive forces of the modern world. In "'Once Upon a Time': Sarah Orne Jewett's 'A White Heron' as a Fairy Tale" (*SSF*, Winter 1978), Hovet explores Jewett's use of the fairy tale form to present the conflict between modern and provincial America. Richard Brenzo's "Free Heron or Dead Sparrow: Sylvia's Choice in Sarah Orne Jewett's 'A White Heron'" (*CLQ*, March 1978) is a study of Jewett's use of symbols in the story to give it universal meaning. A more specialized study of the story's symbolism is James Ellis's "The World of Dreams: Sexual Symbolism in 'A White Heron'" (*NR*, 1977).

Apart from studies of specific works by Jewett, there are a number of useful articles on particular themes in her writing and on aspects of her craftsmanship. Richard Cary has written two articles based on Jewett letters that touch on her attitudes toward writing. In "Jewett on Writing Short Stories" (*CLQ*, June 1964), he prints a series of letters to Celia Thaxter's son John, who was struggling to write fiction. Jewett urges him to strive for verisimilitude and scolds him for heavy plotting. In "Jewett's Literary Canons" (*CLQ*, June 1965), he prints an 1885 letter in which she advocates a simple realism that promotes the "common ideal."

A longer study of Jewett, which focuses on her attitudes toward writing, is A. M. Buchan's *"Our Dear Sarah": An Essay on Sarah Orne Jewett* (Washington University Studies No. 24, St Louis: Washington University Press, 1953). Buchan contrasts Jewett's theory of writing with the realistic approach represented by Howells. For Jewett writing was a personal experience in which the writer draws not so much on the world about him as on "the transfigured memory of the past." Thus the artist renders reality "only from a vantage point distinctively his own." Buchan argues that these were values which Jewett shared with Willa Cather and that they represent a uniquely feminine approach to writing.

The literary relationship between Jewett and Cather that Buchan comments on has been the subject of other studies. Eleanor M. Smith in "The Literary Relationship of Sarah Orne Jewett and Willa Sibert Cather" (*NEQ*, December 1956) notes many similarities in style and approach between the two. Cather had a broader range, however, and her writing is more realistic than Jewett's. Given the differences between the times in which these women wrote, however, Smith finds it remarkable that there are as many similarities as there are. On the other hand, James Woodress argues in "Sarah Orne Jewett and Willa Cather: Anti-Realists" (*EST*, Fifth

Series, 1973) that Jewett influenced Cather to abandon a Jamesean approach to writing in favor of a Wordsworthian one, thereby turning Cather into a twentieth-century romantic. Richard Cary's "The Sculptor and the Spinster: Jewett's 'Influence' on Cather" (*CLQ*, September 1973) focuses on a comparison of Cather's "The Sculptor's Funeral" with Jewett's "Miss Tempy's Watchers."

Jean Boggio-Sola, in "The Poetic Realism of Sarah Orne Jewett" (*CLQ*, June 1965), likens her art to painting and says that her realism is of a higher order than social realism. "Her power of suggestion, heightened by her easy flowing style, rests in great part on a complete identification with her material at large, and more particularly with nature in a manner that recalls Thoreau." This emphasis on Jewett's treatment of setting recurs in Robert D. Rhode's "Sarah Orne Jewett and 'The Palpable Present Intimate'" (*CLQ*, September 1968). Rhode argues that "through her personification of nature" she gave her stories "a quality of personality that compensated for her lack of suspenseful drama."

In "To Calm and Uplift 'Against the Dark': Sarah Orne Jewett's Lyric Narratives" (*CLQ*, December 1975), Bert Bender argues that the traditional reading of Jewett as a local colorist has prevented an appreciation of the lyric depth of her stories.

Catherine Barnes Stevenson has discussed some of the conflicting forces at work in Jewett in "The Double Consciousness of the Narrator in Sarah Orne Jewett's Fiction" (*CLQ*, March 1975). Her narrators are often torn between their nostalgic impulses and a recognition of the necessity and inevitablity of change. Stevenson sees the sea in *The Country of the Pointed Firs* as a symbol of the forces that simultaneously sustain and threaten the security of Dunnet Landing.

Two articles touch on the contradictory themes of childhood and old age. In "The Child in Sarah Orne Jewett" (*CLQ*, September 1967), Eugene Hillhouse Pool engages in some risky biographical criticism. He finds Jewett's life "an uneasy middle road between childhood and adulthood" and sees the tension of this dilemma transferred to some of her characters. Susan Allen Toth's "The Value of Age in the Fiction of Sarah Orne Jewett" (*SSF*, Summer 1971) examines Jewett's positive and sympathetic portrayal of her older characters. In contrast to Mary E. Wilkins Freeman's older characters, there is a contentment and harmonious relationship between Jewett's characters and the community.

Jewett's historical consciousness has long been acknowledged. It forms the basis of Ferman Bishop's "The Sense of the Past in Sarah Orne Jewett" (*UWB*, February 1959). Bishop traces the historicist element through Jewett's books. Given this bent of mind in Jewett, Bishop does not see *The Tory Lover* as being inconsistent with the rest of her work. Time present and time past do converge in Jewett's fiction, and Mary C. Kraus has analyzed her concept and use of time in "Sarah Orne Jewett and Temporal

Continuity'' (*CLQ*, September 1979). Jewett viewed time as a continuum in which the past and the present are interdependent. She ''consistently tended toward, and sought to evoke, a state of permanence in which distinctions between past and present dissolve and are subsumed by certain humanistic and religious values in light of which such distinctions are irrelevant.'' Kraus's analysis covers a wide range of Jewett's writings and convincingly demonstrates the links between her use of the past and her vision of an ''orderly, harmonious world.''

Although critics have commonly observed that Jewett's fictional world is largely inhabited by women, there has not been very much feminist-oriented interpretation of her work. Barbara H. Solomon, in her introduction to *Short Fiction of Sarah Orne Jewett and Mary Wilkins Freeman*, says that *The Country of the Pointed Firs* has been neglected because ''it is so thoroughly a women's book about the world of women—old women at that.'' Yet her contention that the book has been neglected is clearly debatable. In ''The Literature of Impoverishment: The Women Local Colorists in America 1865-1914'' (*WS*, No. 1, 1972), Ann Douglas Wood says that Jewett and Freeman were the first American women writers good enough to merit a lasting reputation. She contrasts the lives of the local colorists with the earlier writers of sentimental fiction and sees the local color writers as portraying the demise of the world of the sentimental women writers of the previous generation. Carolyn Forrey briefly discusses *A Country Doctor* as a study of the new woman in ''The New Woman Revisited'' (*WS*, No. 1, 1974).

The most thorough ''women's'' reading of Jewett is Josephine Donovan's recent article, ''A Woman's Vision of Transcendence: A New Interpretation of the Works of Sarah Orne Jewett'' (*MR*, Summer 1980). Donovan sees Jewett's elegiac tone as stemming from the theme of alienation, particularly the alienation felt by women. To cope with women's efforts to transcend their condition, she argues that Jewett posits ''a kind of women's religion . . . a kind of matriarchal Christianity'' in which the sense of community ''is sustained by women and their ethos of hospitality.''

The nature of the intense friendships between women in the nineteenth century is an intriguing, albeit somewhat elusive, topic treated in two recent articles. In ''Pure and Passionate: Female Friendship in Sarah Orne Jewett's 'Martha's Lady''' (*SSF*, Winter 1980), Glenda Hobbs interprets ''Martha's Lady'' as Jewett's depiction of an idealized, passionate, sensuous—but not physical—love between two women. Jewett herself had such friendships with many women. Her closest alliance was with Annie Fields, and that relationship is the focus of Josephine Donovan's ''The Unpublished Love Poems of Sarah Orne Jewett'' (*Frontiers*, Fall 1979). These verses, ostensibly written to Fields and other women friends, have been ignored by scholars content to portray Jewett as a ''passionless 'spinster.''' Although Donovan necessarily equivocates on the question of the precise nature of the Jewett-Fields relationship, it is clear that past editors and scholars, including Fields herself, have chosen to mask or ignore elements in Jewett's character reflected in this poetry.

MARY E. WILKINS FREEMAN

BIBLIOGRAPHY

No full-scale descriptive bibliography exists for Freeman, but there is the excellent bibliography of books and contributions to books in volume three of Jacob Blanck's *Bibliography of American Literature* (*BAL*) (New Haven: Yale University Press, 1959). The *BAL* listing has been supplemented by three notes in *PBSA:* Jacob Blanck's "*BAL* Addenda" on *The Portion of Labor* (April-June 1961); Roger B. O'Connor's "*BAL* Addenda" on *"Doc" Gordon* (April-June 1967); and Philip B. Eppard's "*BAL* Addenda: Cooke, Frederic, Freeman, and Fuller" (April-June 1980).

Freeman was a prolific contributor of stories, sketches, and verse to periodicals and newspapers. Philip B. Eppard has been compiling a checklist of all of her periodical contributions, and it is nearly ready for publication. Until it is published, the most complete listing is the bibliography of Edward Foster's biography, *Mary E. Wilkins Freeman* (Hendricks House, 1956). Foster does not, however, give the periodical publication for stories Freeman later collected in book form; nor does he record any of her voluminous writings for children's magazines. Foster's list has been supplemented by George Monteiro's "Addenda to Foster's *Freeman*" (*PBSA*, July-September 1975).

For secondary works on Freeman, the most useful surveys so far are the bibliography of Perry D. Westbrook's TUSAS volume, *Mary Wilkins Freeman* (1967) and his bibliographical essay on Freeman scholarship (*ALR*, Summer 1969). Although Westbrook's bibliographies are now somewhat out of date, his work marks the beginning of new interest in Freeman. Therefore his surveys of criticism are useful summaries of the Freeman criticism on which the work of the last fifteen years has been building.

Brent L. Kendrick has given a detailed analysis of doctoral dissertations on Freeman (*ALR*, Summer 1975). He notes twelve unpublished dissertations in whole or in part devoted to Freeman, but he laments the quality of much of the work done. Significantly, eight of these twelve dissertations were completed between 1969 and 1975. Kendrick is at work on a comprehensive bibliography of secondary comment on Freeman, which will include a survey of contemporary reviews of her books. Access to a selected listing of such reviews can now be had by using Clayton L. Eichelberger's *A Guide to Critical Reviews of United States Fiction, 1870-1910* (2 vols.; Metuchen, N.J.: Scarecrow Press, 1971-1974).

EDITIONS

Mary E. Wilkins Freeman was a Harper author, and that firm kept some of her work in print until the late 1940s. After several years of publishers' neglect, Freeman's books began to be reissued again in the 1960s, principally by the reprint houses. Consequently, most of her short story collections and some of her novels are available today. Although prices for these editions tend to be high, the increasing scarcity of some of Freeman's titles in the original editions on the used-book market make these reprints useful. They are, however, chiefly facsimiles with no critical or biographical commentary. More useful to the student are editions readily available with interpretive introductions. The Signet Classic edition, *Short Fiction of Sarah Orne Jewett and Mary Wilkins Freeman* (New American Library, 1978), has an introduction by Barbara H. Solomon. It reprints fourteen Freeman stories, including four from collections later than *A Humble Romance* and *A New England Nun*. In view of the comparative neglect that Freeman's later stories have suffered, it is worth noting that her last book for Harper's, *The Best Stories of Mary E. Wilkins* (1927), contains twenty-five stories, only nine of which are from *A Humble Romance* and *A New England Nun*. This edition has been reprinted by the Scholarly Press. Perry D. Westbrook's edition of *Pembroke* (New Haven: College and University Press, 1971) makes available what many consider to be Freeman's best novel. Arkham House, the fantasy publisher, has issued Freeman's *Collected Ghost Stories* (Sauk City, Wisconsin, 1974) with an introduction by Edward Wagenknecht. This collection includes the six stories from *The Wind in the Rose-Bush and Other Stories* as well as five other Freeman stories with a supernatural element. The Feminist Press selection of Freeman stories, *The Revolt of Mother and Other Stories* (Old Westbury, N.Y., 1974), reprints eight stories from *A Humble Romance* and *A New England Nun* with an afterword by Michele Clark. It has recently gone out of print.

In short, a good percentage of Freeman's output is available today in some form or another. There is, however, a shortage of editions suitable for classroom use. None of her writings have been subjected to modern textual editing. Nor has the vast amount of her uncollected writings been resurrected for the modern reader. A uniform edition of her best work would be welcome.

MANUSCRIPTS AND LETTERS

There is no single outstanding collection of Freeman's papers, and undoubtedly scholarship has been hampered by the lack of such a collection. Furthermore, the letters that have survived have been little used by researchers. The most important collections of Freeman letters are at Columbia University, the University of Virginia, the New York Public

Library, and the American Academy of Arts and Letters. Columbia has much of her correspondence with Harper's. Her letters to Mary Louise Booth, editor of *Harper's Bazaar*, are at Virginia; and letters to Hayden Carruth, editor of *Woman's Home Companion*, are at the New York Public Library. The American Academy of Arts and Letters has her correspondence with the Academy. Scattered letters and manuscripts can be located through the second edition of *American Literary Manuscripts* (Athens: University of Georgia Press, 1977).

A landmark in Freeman scholarship is the completion of Brent L. Kendrick's 1981 dissertation at the University of South Carolina, "The Infant Sphinx: The Collected Letters of Mary E. Wilkins Freeman" (*DAI*, June 1982). Kendrick has assembled just over five hundred of Freeman's letters, including those in private hands as well as those at institutions. Fully annotated, it presents the most complete picture available of Freeman's career as a professional author. The fact that Kendrick's extensive searches turned up only five hundred letters suggests the relatively low survival rate for Freeman manuscript material, for surely that figure must represent only a fraction of her total correspondence over a long career. It should be noted that Kendrick was unable to locate any of the manuscript letters and stories cited in Edward Foster's biography, although his edition includes the texts of those unlocated letters as quoted in Foster.

BIOGRAPHY

Edward Foster's *Mary E. Wilkins Freeman* is the only book-length biography of Freeman. It began in the 1930s as a doctoral dissertation at Harvard under F. O. Matthiessen. At that time Foster was able to interview many friends and relatives of Freeman, and the material gleaned from these interviews gives the book much of its strength. The book mixes analysis of some of Freeman's fiction with biography, and Foster argues that Freeman's "personality informs her stories more than has been assumed by earlier critics." Harry R. Warfel noted in his review of the biography (*AL*, March 1957), "The artistry of Mrs. Freeman and the sources of her art interest Mr. Foster a good deal more than some of the biographical cruxes of her life story."

For shorter summaries of Freeman's life, there is Foster's sketch in *Notable American Women*. There is also a short biographical chapter in Abigail Ann Hamblen's *The New England Art of Mary E. Wilkins Freeman* (Amherst, Mass.: Green Knight Press, 1966). There are also biographical elements in Westbrook's TUSAS volume. The availability of Freeman's complete correspondence in Brent Kendrick's edition will fill in some of the biographical gaps in Foster. Nevertheless, Foster, while clearly not the definitive biography that is needed, is indispensable and will remain so because of the unique source material he assembled.

CRITICISM

There is a brief history of Freeman's literary reputation in chapter ten of Westbrook's TUSAS volume. When her stories and books were first being published, Mary E. Wilkins, as she was then known, was inevitably compared to Sarah Orne Jewett. In a review of *A Humble Romance and Other Stories* (*HM*, September 1887), William Dean Howells makes the comparison but says, "The fun is opener and less demure, the literature is less refined, the poetry is a little cruder [in Wilkins's stories]." He detects an occasional sentimental or romantic note but praises the stories' "directness and simplicity" as being "like the best modern work everywhere." In "New England in the Short Story" (*AtM*, June 1891), Horace E. Scudder says of *A New England Nun and Other Stories*, "The compression of these stories is remarkable, and almost unique in our literature." He notes "a common character" to the stories, "an undertone of hardship, of loss, or repressed life, of sacrifice, of the idolatry of duty." Scudder concludes that Freeman's "pungent" humor was sometimes the only feature preventing some stories "from oppressing the reader unduly." By contrast he finds Jewett's humor "more pervasive, more genial, more kindly and winning." Thus quite early Freeman was established as a recorder of the darker side of New England life, a characteristic made evident in her style as well as in her subject matter. This has been the standard approach to her writings ever since.

This interpretation of Freeman's work is evident in the first important analysis of her writing, Charles Miner Thompson's "Miss Wilkins: An Idealist in Masquerade" (*AtM*, May 1899). Thompson focuses on Freeman's attention to examples of distorted will among the descendants of the Puritans and suggests that while her portrait is realistic, it is an incomplete representation of New England life. He devotes some attention to Freeman's novels and finds that they resemble short-story incidents strung together; that her style is not well adapted to the novel form. He also notes significantly, "Although she is ranked in the popular judgment as a realist, there is in her work the purest vein of romance and ideality, and even a certain touch of mysticism and allegory, which allies her, however distantly to the literary family of Hawthorne." Thompson's essay, along with its discussion of Freeman as the portrayer of the Puritan will in stages of degeneration, therefore touches on two other familiar themes of Freeman criticism: the relative inferiority of her novels to her stories and the conflict between realism and romanticism in her work.

Paul Elmer More pursues the Hawthorne connection and the interpretation of Freeman as an analyst of the latter-day Puritan will in an essay, "Hawthorne: Looking Before and After" in *The Shelburne Essays, Second Series* (Putnam's, 1905). More identifies three stages of New England consciousness represented by the dogmatic faith of Cotton Mather, the lonely idealism of Hawthorne, and the mere "nervous impotence" of Freeman's characters. The struggles of will and conscience have played themselves out leaving only a barrenness of feeling in Freeman's New Englanders.

Of the early generation of Freeman critics, Fred Lewis Pattee was the most significant. He discusses her extensively in *A History of American Literature Since 1870* (Century, 1915) and in *The Development of the American Short Story* (Harper, 1923). Pattee's views are best summed up in an essay "On the Terminal Moraine of New England Puritanism" printed in *Sidelights on American Literature* (Century, 1922). He also notes her kinship with Hawthorne rather than the realists. In fact he argues that she equals Hawthorne "in her command of pathos and of emotional intensity" and surpasses "him in her command of gripping situation and her powers of compelling characterization."

F. O. Matthiessen, who speaks somewhat slightingly of Freeman in his biography of Sarah Orne Jewett, is more respectful in an essay on "New England Stories" in John Macy, ed., *American Writers on American Literature* (Liveright, 1931). He praises the directness of her tales and calls her "unsurpassed among all American writers in her ability to give the breathless intensity of a moment." Van Wyck Brooks devotes some attention to Freeman as a recorder of New England decline in *New England: Indian Summer* (Dutton, 1940). He says that her best work equals Jewett's and that it is even more eminent because of the depth of feeling that informs her art.

Modern scholarly attention to Freeman begins with Perry D. Westbrook's *Acres of Flint: Writers of Rural New England 1870-1900* (Washington: Scarecrow Press, 1951). Westbrook places Freeman in the context of other New England writers of her time, but his comments generally follow the path of criticism laid out half a century before. In *The New England Art of Mary E. Wilkins Freeman*, Abigail Ann Hamblen provides a brief survey of Freeman's writings, arguing that she was faithfully reproducing the life and mind of New England in her time.

Westbrook's TUSAS volume on Freeman provides an overview of her entire writing career, with the exception of her writings for children and her poetry for adults. The bulk of Westbrook's analysis rests on his assertion that Freeman "is the supreme analyst of the Puritan will in its noble strength, in its aberrations, and in its decadence into mere whim and stubborness." When Freeman departs from this theme, her writing loses much of its power. Westbrook does cover Freeman's later books, although his work is heavily weighted towards her earlier writings. Of the books published after her marriage in 1902, only *Six Trees*, *By the Light of the Soul*, and *The Shoulders of Atlas* receive any kind of extended treatment. A sympathetic appreciation of Freeman, which also places her in the tradition of New Englanders who grappled with the problem of conscience, appears in

Austin Warren's *The New England Conscience* (Ann Arbor: University of Michigan Press, 1966).

Larzer Ziff, in *The American 1890s: Life and Times of a Lost Generation* (Viking, 1966), gives a few brief, but incisive pages to Freeman. He notes themes of rebellion and sexual sublimation in her fiction. Of the comparison to Jewett he says, "Although not so fully realized—episodes too often substituting for the art of the story—Mary Wilkins Freeman's work aims at a range of impressions well beyond Miss Jewett's ken." For the modern reader, however, he finds in Freeman "an artificiality from which Miss Jewett is almost entirely free." He also notes a salient biographical fact that must be kept in mind in comparing the total outputs of Freeman and Jewett: "Another thing Sarah Jewett had during her career that Mary Freeman had not was an estate of some $75,000 invested in United States Steel, the Pennsylvania Railroad, Calumet and Hecla, and other corporations." Freeman retained throughout her life a fear of poverty. Although she made good money with her writing, she never lost sight of the fact that economic necessity was one of the forces behind her writing career.

The first piece of scholarship to go beyond the traditional line of interpretation of Freeman was David H. Hirsch's "Subdued Meaning in 'A New England Nun'" (*SSF*, Winter 1965). In a close reading of one of Freeman's best stories, Hirsch dissects how Freeman's subtle use of detail reflects the inner conflicts in her heroine that make the story "almost a case study of an obsessive neurosis."

Another signal attempt at reinterpretation of Freeman is Susan Allen Toth's "Defiant Light: A Positive View of Mary Wilkins Freeman" (*NEQ*, March 1973). Toth argues that the emphasis on Freeman as a recorder of New England decay "has obscured the real dramatic conflict at the heart of Freeman's best short stories." Toth discusses the conflicts between individuals and the community and says that Freeman's characters display "integrity, strength, and initiative" that offset their barren environments. John W. Crowley echoes some of Toth's argument in "Freeman's Yankee Tragedy: 'Amanda and Love'" (*MarkhamR*, Spring 1976). Crowley dissents from the view expressed in Jay Martin's *Harvests of Change: American Literature 1865-1914* (Englewood Cliffs, N.J.: Prentice-Hall, 1967). Martin sees Freeman's characters as pathetic survivors lacking the capacity for heroic action.

Alice Glarden Brand's "Mary Wilkins Freeman: Misanthropy as Propaganda" (*NEQ*, March 1977) also argues that Freeman's work has been underestimated. She sees her as a "civilized critic of destructive human behaviors," behaviors fostered by a rural parochialism and the heavy hand of tradition. There are elements of a feminist critique in Brand's article, for she devotes a good deal of attention to the sexual conflicts in Freeman's fiction. Her wider view of Freeman's critique of the social order keeps the article from being only a feminist reading. Not so fortunate is Michele Clark's afterword to the Feminist Press collection, *The Revolt of Mother and Other Stories*, which finds meaning in Freeman's stories because they show women relating to other women. Barbara H. Solomon concentrates on Freeman's treatment of her female characters in her introduction to *Short Fiction of Sarah Orne Jewett and Mary Wilkins Freeman*, but her analysis is restricted to brief readings of the stories included in the collection. One of Freeman's female characters is closely analyzed by Sarah W. Sherman in "The Great Goddess in New England: Mary Wilkins Freeman's 'Christmas Jenny'" (*SSF*, Spring 1980). Sherman sees in this neglected short story a picture of an "archaic woman" who exhibits characteristics of an ancient matriarchal age.

One of Freeman's most famous stories, "The Revolt of 'Mother,'" has been the subject of two recent articles. Marilyn Davis DeEulis briefly discusses the story's spatial imagery in "'Her Box of a House' Spatial Restriction as Psychic Signpost in Mary Wilkins Freeman's 'The Revolt of "Mother" (*MarkhamR*, Spring 1979). Joseph R. McElrath, Jr., analyzes the structure of the story in terms of the requirements of magazine fiction. In "The Artistry of Mary E. Wilkins Freeman's 'The Revolt'" (*SSF*, Summer 1980), he sees the story as a series of crisis/climax situations designed to maintain the reader's interest. He argues that Freeman deftly brings off a surprise ending which, with its "reassuring testimony to the admixture of good and evil in human nature...is vintage Howellsian realism at its enduring best."

Two other articles on Freeman are worth noting. In "Mary Wilkins Freeman's Parable of Wasted Life" (*AL*, January 1971), Susan Allen Toth examines the story "The Three Old Sisters and the Old Beau" and finds echoes of Hawthorne's "The Wedding Knell" in its "theme and imagery." She sees it as a critique of the decline in New England society. In "Character Types in the Fiction of Mary Wilkins Freeman" (*CLQ*, December 1971), James H. Quina, Jr., delineates four different character types: those in the control group, who seek to maintain the status quo; the ascetics, who withdraw from life; the rebels, who take a stand against the status quo; and the mediators, who attempt to "moderate the tension created between the second and third character types." He finds that in this fourth type Freeman "conveys her deepest insight into human compassion."

MARY N. MURFREE

BIBLIOGRAPHY

Mary N. Murfree, famous during her lifetime as Charles Egbert Craddock, has not been accorded the honor of a full-scale bibliography devoted solely to her. Nevertheless, her books and contributions to books are treated superbly in the sixth volume of Jacob Blanck's *Bibliography of American Literature* (New Haven: Yale University Press, 1973). A short listing of her books and periodical contributions appears in the bibliography of Edd Winfield Parks's biography, *Charles Egbert Craddock (Mary Noailles Murfree)* (Chapel Hill: University of North Carolina Press, 1941). Fuller bibliographical information on Murfree's periodical publications may be found in Reese M. Carleton's "Mary Noailles Murfree (1850-1922): An Annotated Bibliography" (*ALR*, Autumn 1974). The bulk of Carleton's piece is an annotated listing of secondary comment on Murfree from 1881 to 1973. Its coverage of reviews is invaluable for any study of Murfree's critical reception, and its listing of later scholarship and comment is an essential tool in evaluating her later critical reputation. An earlier survey of scholarship on Murfree is by Richard Cary, "Mary Noailles Murfree (1850-1922)" (*ALR*, Fall 1967). Cary has also provided a selective annotated listing of writings on Murfree in the bibliography of his TUSAS volume, *Mary N. Murfree* (1967).

EDITIONS

Mary N. Murfree published twenty-five books in her lifetime. In 1967 Richard Cary noted, "Not a single title of the original editions is currently in print, nor are any reprints available." The reprint industry has rectified this situation somewhat so that approximately a third of her books are in print today. The only noteworthy edition, however, is the University of Tennessee Press edition of *In the Tennessee Mountains* (Knoxville, 1970) with an introduction by Nathalia Wright. No textual edition has been done even for Murfree's most famous book, however, and there is no really suitable edition of her writings, apart from Wright's, for classroom use.

Two pieces of fiction by Murfree have been published posthumously in periodical form. "The Erskine Honeymoon," her last novel, was published serially in the *Nashville Banner* (29 December 1930-31 March 31) but has never been published in book form. William B. Dillingham has edited an unpublished short story "When Old Baldy Spoke" (*EUQ*, Summer 1962).

MANUSCRIPTS AND LETTERS

Reese M. Carleton's annotated bibliography of Murfree in *ALR*, cited above, includes a listing of her manuscripts and letters. Notable holdings include: the manuscript of *The Prophet of the Great Smoky Mountains* and an incomplete manuscript of *In the Clouds* at the Houghton Library, Harvard University; four chapters of *His Vanished Star* at the University of North Carolina; and the manuscript of Murfree's incomplete and unpublished novel *Allegheny Winds and Waters* at the Emory University Library. Emory also has some manuscripts of unpublished stories and an unpublished essay. The Tennessee State Library and Archives in Nashville has part of the manuscript of *His Vanished Star*, some typewritten manuscripts, and some publishing contracts.

Among letters, perhaps the most significant collection is her correspondence with Houghton Mifflin at Harvard's Houghton Library. There is also a small collection of letters to the editors of the *Century* at the New York Public Library. In addition Emory has one box of letters to, from, and about Murfree.

Although Edd Winfield Parks used some of her correspondence with editors and publishers in his biography, there has been no edition of her letters. One letter to James R. Osgood & Company has been published, with a facsimile, in R. Baird Shuman's "Mary Murfree's Battle" (*TSL*, 1961).

BIOGRAPHY

The only book-length biography of Mary N. Murfree is Edd Winfield Parks's, *Charles Egbert Craddock (Mary Noailles Murfree)*. Originally Parks's doctoral dissertation at Vanderbilt University in 1932, it gives an excellent overview of Murfree's career. It draws heavily on unpublished letters and is especially strong in its treatment of Murfree's relations with editors and publishers and of her writing habits. The rest of the Murfree family figures prominently in the biography, and the whole story is set in the swiftly changing historical circumstances of the South in the second half of the nineteenth century. Parks discusses Murfree's books in the context of her career, but there is little sustained critical analysis. The biography incorporates material Parks published earlier in "Craddock's First Pseudonym" (*ETHSP*, 1934). Parks also wrote the sketch of Murfree for *Notable American Women*. Another brief survey of Murfree's life can be found in the first chapter of Richard Cary's TUSAS volume.

Two master of arts theses from George Peabody College in 1928 contribute to a biographical study of Murfree. Mary Sue Mooney's "An Intimate Study of Mary Noailles Murfree, Charles Egbert Craddock" draws on interviews with Murfree's sister for some of its biographical information. More valuable is Mooney's reproduction of newspaper and magazine reviews of Murfree's books. Eleanor B. Spence's "Collected Reminiscences of Mary N. Murfree" contains assorted anecdotes about the writer's life.

The first significant biographical account of Murfree was in William Malone Baskervill's *Southern Writers: Biographical and Critical Studies* (Nashville: M. B. Church, 1897). Another volume with personal reminiscences of Murfree is John M. Stahl's *Growing with the West: The Story of a Busy, Quiet Life* (London & New York: Longmans, Green, 1930). An interesting contemporary glimpse of Murfree can be found in Doris Lainer's "Mary Noailles Murfree: An Interview" (*THQ*, Fall 1972), which reprints an 1885 interview with a man who had recently encountered Murfree at

Montvale Springs, Tennessee. Dennis Loyd's "Tennessee's Mystery Woman Novelist" (*THQ*, Fall 1970) is wholly derivative from other secondary sources.

CRITICISM

Mary N. Murfree's career had a pattern similar to that of many other American writers. Her first book, *In the Tennessee Mountains*, was a critical and popular success, and she was to spend the rest of her life trying to live up to the achievement of that book. Today she is remembered chiefly for the stories that make up that volume and to a lesser extent for her novel *The Prophet of the Great Smoky Mountains*. It is interesting to note, in fact, that Houghton Mifflin kept that novel in print until the 1950s, so that it was the last of Murfree's books to go out of print from the original edition. More than either Jewett or Freeman, Murfree was a novelist. Only six of her twenty-five books were short story collections. Thus she provides an interesting case study of the adaptability of local color material to the novel.

As with Jewett and Freeman, Murfree's strengths and weaknesses were recognized early in her career. In a review of *The Prophet of the Great Smoky Mountains* (*HM*, January 1886), William Dean Howells compliments her fresh and faithful presentation of a strange world. He dismisses her lapses into romanticism as comparatively insignificant but closes on a somewhat ominous note: "The art of the book is, for the most part, very good; there is little comment; the people speak for themselves. If we are perhaps called too often to look at the landscape, the landscape is certainly always worth looking at, and the book, where it escapes from tradition, both satisfies and piques. After one has finished it, one wants to know what Miss Murfree's next book will be like." Here one can see the main lines of Murfree criticism already drawn. Her strength is in her realistic portrayal of life in the Tennessee mountains. Her weaknesses are her lapses into sentimentality, her tendency to overdo descriptions of the landscape, and her failure to move beyond the territory staked out in her first books without losing her power. Unlike the criticism of Jewett and Freeman, there has not been a really concerted effort to get Murfree out of the local color pigeonhole.

Early assessments of Murfree's work stressed her understanding of the lives of her mountain characters. Henry C. Vedder's chapter on her in *American Writers of Today* (Boston: Silver, Burdett, 1894) approves the cultivation of mind that Murfree brings to her studies of character, and he praises her descriptive powers. William Malone Baskervill points out the moral lessons to be learned from the struggles of her characters, and he acknowledges her tendency to overdo descriptions. In *Social Historians* (Boston: R. G. Badger, 1911) Harry Aubrey Toulmin, Jr., asserts that her achievement is in recording hitherto unstudied phases of the social history of the South. A critique of the more strictly literary aspects of her work by Fred Lewis Pattee in *A History of American Literature Since 1870* (Century, 1915) is harsh. Pattee points out that Murfree was familiar with her material only as a visitor to the mountains and that her work has more the quality of impressionistic painting than of realism. He indicts her characterizations, and while admiring her style, laments her tendency to lapse into floridness. Her impressionistic techniques could create at best a scattered effect. Pattee's judgment in *The Development of the American Short Story* (Harper, 1923) is even harsher. He finds much of her style artificial and even concludes that the seed of her ultimate failure lay in the thinness of her material.

It took a long time for critical analysis of Murfree to advance beyond this state. Edd Winfield Parks's biography does not delve into criticism for the most part, and when it does it tends to be apologetic. He even suggests that Murfree's reputation would be much higher had she died in 1885 after publishing her first four books. Alexander Cowie gives a sympathetic few pages to Murfree in *The Rise of the American Novel* (American Book Co., 1948). He finds her work's validity in its fresh experience, a familiar critical line. Cowie also notes her tendency to emphasize setting but does not explore this potentially interesting area very far. He concludes, however, that she could not write effectively outside of the narrow range of material offered by the Tennessee mountains.

It is against this critical background that the first assessment of Murfree's total output, Richard Cary's TUSAS volume, was published in 1967. Cary has arranged the book topically, so that he considers Murfree's fiction dealing with the mountains, the Civil War, the frontier, Mississippi, and her juvenilia. His conclusion is that Murfree "stands among the most eminent of American local colorists." He sees her best work in *In the Tennessee Mountains, The Prophet of the Great Smoky Mountains, In the "Stranger People's" Country, Where the Battle Was Fought*, and in various snippets from her other writings, including her Mississippi stories with their glimpses of plantation life. Indeed, Cary suggests that Murfree could have pursued better a distinguished career as a novelist of manners and a chronicler of high society than as a portrayer of the life of the southern mountaineer. This conviction no doubt stems from his feeling that Murfree too often stands outside or above her mountain characters. She was, in fact, not really one of them.

There are a few noteworthy shorter studies of Murfree, though they do not for the most part break any new ground. Archer Taylor, in "Proverbs and Proverbial Phrases in the Writings of Mary N. Murfree" (*TFSB*, March 1958), finds little variety or novelty in her use of local sayings. Merrill Maguire Skaggs's *The Folk of Southern Fiction* (Athens: University of Georgia Press, 1972) discusses Murfree's mountaineers in the context of a wider southern literary tradition. Mary Nilles, in "Craddock's Girls: A Look at Some Unliberated Women" (*MarkhamR*, October 1972), concludes, not too surprisingly, that Murfree's women "were the antithesis of 'modern' or 'liberated' women." A more interesting, though brief, feminist analysis appears in Ann Douglas Wood's "The Literature of Impoverishment: The Women Local Colorists in America 1865-1914" (*WS*, No. 1, 1972). Wood sees the situation of Cynthia Ware in "Drifting Down Lost Creek" as a prime example of the dilemma of women that concerned most of the female local color writers.

Nathalia Wright's introduction to the reissue of *In the Tennessee Mountains* sympathetically surveys the stories with special attention to the types of characters, the dialect, and the use of setting. Wright's edition elicited a very favorable essay-review by Harry R. Warfel, "Local Color and Literary Artistry: Mary Noailles Murfree's *In the Tennessee Mountains*" (*SLJ*, Fall 1970). Warfel argues that "Murfree was more concerned to manipulate artistic literary techniques than to photograph the places and people." Her work is idealistic and romantic, qualities inherent in all local color writing. Her aloofness to her material is also part of the local color approach. But in the end Warfel concludes that local color was not her chief end. "It is as a romantic artist who, while seeming to be local in subject matter and dialect, transcended the immediate into the universal that Miss Murfree is memorable." Warfel's provocative article achieves the feat of making artistic virtues out of characteristics that previous critics had deemed to be defects in Murfree's work.

A more restricted study of one aspect of Murfree's first book is Allison Ensor's "The Geography of Mary Noailles Murfree's *In the Tennessee Mountains*" (*MissQ*, Spring 1978). Ensor discusses Murfree's failure to use real place names in her stories but finds that one notable exception is "Drifting Down Lost Creek." Specific references in this story may stem from a hitherto unmentioned visit Murfree made to Sparta, Tennessee. An earlier note on Murfree's geography is Nathalia Wright's "A Note on the Setting of Mary Noailles Murfree's 'The "Harnt" That Walks Chilhowee'" (*MLN*, April 1947).

In "Mary Noailles Murfree: A Reappraisal" (*AppalJ*, Spring 1979), Durwood Dunn explores the extent to which Murfree's picture of Tennessee mountain life corresponds to nineteenth-century reality. He finds her descriptions of the physical environment of the mountains generally accurate but argues that her picture of a static, homogeneous mountaineer life is distorted. Unfortunately, Dunn says, Murfree's stereotypes have been so powerful that they have hindered a true understanding of the varied culture of the region.

The only comprehensive study of Murfree's work since Cary's TUSAS volume is a dissertation by Reese Monroe Carleton, "Conflict in Direction: Realistic, Romantic, and Romanticistic Elements in the Fiction of Mary N. Murfree" (University of Wisconsin, Madison, 1976). The fact that Murfree never developed a single approach to her writing was responsible for the unevenness of her output, Carleton suggests. The pressure of writing serialized novels tended to push her toward the romanticistic, that is, dramatic action with a sentimental plot.

CONCLUSION

This chapter began with an observation that the critical attitudes toward Sarah Orne Jewett, Mary E. Wilkins Freeman, and Mary N. Murfree had been in large part determined by their association with the local color movement and that that association had tended to preclude much serious analysis of their work. The problem of using the category "local color" or "regionalism" is that it is difficult to define these terms to everyone's satisfaction. In order to get a full appreciation of these writers, we must be ready to read their works "on their own carefully developed and detailed terms," to use Susan Allen Toth's comments on Freeman's stories. The local color or regional factor will probably figure in such readings, but it will not determine or restrict the area of investigation. For Jewett this broader approach is fairly well advanced, although it needs to be applied more generally to works other than *The Country of the Pointed Firs*. For Freeman this approach has begun, but unlike Jewett, she has lacked that one important longer work that attracts critics. For Murfree very little criticism has been done to advance her reputation beyond that established during her lifetime.

The importance of having the essential tools of scholarship for each of these writers should not be underestimated in any evaluation of the critical work done on them. Certainly Jewett scholarship would not be nearly so far advanced were it not for the efforts of Colby College in issuing a bibliography, an edition of letters, and an edition of her uncollected stories. Without the biographical, editorial, and critical work of Richard Cary and without the forum of the *Colby Library Quarterly*, Sarah Orne Jewett studies would probably not be in a much better state than Freeman scholarship. Yet even with all the work that has been done on Jewett, there is still a need for an updated descriptive bibliography, a more comprehensive edition of letters, a new critical biography, and better editions of her works. For Freeman the needs are nearly the same, with the exception that an edition of her letters has now been completed. Mary N. Murfree stands in need of these same scholarly tools.

The point is that good scholarship tends to beget better scholarship and criticism. With the necessary tools available, the serious reconsideration of these writers can be advanced beyond the lines indicated here. The "relatively narrow range" which Gwen L. Nagel and James Nagel found that Jewett scholarship fell into is a phrase that even more accurately describes the criticism of Freeman and Murfree. Despite the avalanche of research and criticism published in recent years, much of the work of Sarah Orne Jewett, Mary E. Wilkins Freeman, and Mary N. Murfree is comparatively unexplored territory.

3 TONETTE BOND INGE

Kate Chopin

Kate O'Flaherty Chopin did not begin seriously writing fiction until she was a thirty-nine-year-old widowed mother of six children. In her one decade or so of literary creativity, she published two collections of short stories that gained her national recognition as a local colorist and a novel that, though generally recognized as possessing artistic merit, was denounced for its immoral theme. After the public failure of *The Awakening*, Kate Chopin wrote very little, and when she died she was all but forgotten.

Until the 1960s Chopin gained mention in literary histories and biographies mainly as a writer of local color stories in which the Creoles and Cajuns of Cane River County, Louisiana, are sensitively and frequently boldly characterized. *The Awakening* was generally ignored until the 1960s, when a few critics recognized the novel's merits and urged its reappraisal. The appearance in 1969 of Per Seyersted's *Critical Biography* and the *Complete Works* initiated an outburst of critical interest in Chopin. Critics of the 1970s continued Seyersted's investigation of Chopin as a pioneering realist and extended the critical appraisal and examination to include all aspects of her works and practically every critical preoccupation. Especial Chopin's works became the province of feminist approaches to life and literature and the interaction between them.

BIBLIOGRAPHY

The scholar or student will find numerous bibliographical aids to Kate Chopin's works and to critical studies of her works. Jacob Blanck lists the primary works and their reprints in the *Bibliography of American Literature*, Vol. 2 (New Haven: Yale University Press, 1957). Generally available is Lyle H. Wright's *American Fiction, 1876-1900* (San Marino, Calif.:

Huntington Library, 1966), which lists Chopin's works, their contents, and locations of first editions.

Chapter 9 of Per Seyersted's *Kate Chopin: A Critical Biography* (Baton Rouge: Louisiana State University Press, 1969) contains a bibliographic essay focusing on the trends in the critical response to Chopin's works up to 1968. Seyersted lists secondary materials on Chopin for Louis D. Rubin's *A Bibliographical Guide to the Study of Southern Literature* (Baton Rouge: Louisiana State University Press, 1969) with prefatory remarks about the general critical neglect of Chopin's "urge to apply a French realism to the description of emancipated women." Still useful is Per Seyersted's annotated essay "Kate Chopin (1851-1904)" (*ALR*, Spring 1970) listing primary and secondary materials and indicating areas for further study. Rubin's *Bibliographical Guide* is updated through 1975 by *Southern Literature, 1968-1975: A Checklist of Scholarship* (Boston: G. K. Hall, 1978), edited by Jerry T. Williams, which annotates thirty-eight books and articles on Chopin. In "Kate Chopin and Her Critics: An Annotated Checklist" (*MoHSB*, July 1970), Richard H. Potter annotates theses, dissertations, book reviews, and articles and books treating Chopin's life and works. This attempt at a complete bibliography is supplemented, updated, and extended by Thomas Bonner, Jr.'s, "Kate Chopin: An Annotated Bibliography" (*BB*, July-September 1975). Bonner lists editions, reprints, and collections and carefully annotates theses and dissertations, bibliographies, reviews of Seyersted's *The Complete Works of Kate Chopin* (1969), and criticism published since 1970. Lists of reviews of Chopin's novels and short story collections are contained in volumes one and two of Clayton L. Eichelberger's *A Guide to Critical Reviews of United States Fiction, 1870-1910* (Metuchen, N.J.: Scarecrow Press, 1971 and 1974, respectively). *The Kate Chopin Newsletter* (KCN)—renamed in Spring 1977 *Regionalism and the Female Imagination* and now defunct—though generally inaccessible, is a useful bibliographic source for secondary materials up through its discontinuation with the winter 1976-1977 issue.

Elizabeth S. Muhlenfeld ("Kate Chopin," *ALR*, Summer 1975) reviews the nine dissertations on Chopin written through early 1975 and concludes that, except for Bernard J. Koloski's "Kate Chopin and the Search for a Code of Behavior" (University of Arizona, 1972), the surge of interest in Chopin since 1970 has failed "to inspire any fresh, reasoned critical appraisals."

In 1976 G. K. Hall published Marlene Springer's *Edith Wharton and Kate Chopin: A Reference Guide*, which includes annotations for scholarly items, criticism, reviews, and miscellaneous commentary published between 1890 and 1973. It mentions two items for 1975 yet ignores *The Kate Chopin Newsletter*, which was begun in the Spring of 1975. In reviewing the bibliography, Anne Rowe praises Springer's history of the critical reception of

Chopin's work and, in spite of a number of small errors, considers it a "useful, accessible tool for scholars" (*RALS*, Spring 1978).

An index to the growth in Kate Chopin criticism is provided by Lewis Leary, who, in *Articles on American Literature, 1900-1950* (Durham, N.C.: Duke University Press, 1954), lists one Chopin entry; then in *Articles, 1950-1967* (Durham, N.C.: Duke University Press, 1970), three. Most recently, in *Articles, 1968-1975* (Durham, N.C.: Duke University Press, 1979 in the preparation of which he was assisted by John Auchard), he cites sixty-four entries in over three pages of text.

Daniel S. Rankin's chronological listing of primary Chopin works in *Kate Chopin and Her Creole Stories* (Philadelphia: University of Pennsylvania Press, 1932) and Per Seyersted's appendix in *The Complete Works of Kate Chopin*, Vol. 2 (Baton Rouge: Louisiana State University Press, 1969) still have some value; however, *A Kate Chopin Miscellany*, published in late 1979 by Northwestern State University Press (Natchitoches, La.), edited by Per Seyersted and Emily Toth, supersedes all earlier listings with a complete bibliography of primary works, including as well Chopin's statements, extant letters, inscriptions, pieces of music, translations, and a complete annotated bibliography of secondary criticism, including dissertations.

EDITIONS

In Per Seyersted's two-volume *The Complete Works of Kate Chopin* (Baton Rouge: Louisiana State University Press, 1969), ten stories, one essay, ten poems, and a juvenile fable appear for the first time. John Espey, in his review essay of Seyersted's *Complete Works* and Chopin biography finds the term "complete" inappropriate since the *Complete Works* "include none of [Chopin's] translations, nor any part of the 1894 diary . . . nor three unfinished stories, nor 'In Spring,' her one poem to receive wide circulation" (*NCF*, September 1970). Espey quarrels further with Seyersted's ordering of the stories by date of composition, for such an organization prevents the reconstruction of the sequence of stories in Chopin's two published collections and ignores the stories planned for collection under the title "A Vocation and a Voice."

In *A Kate Chopin Miscellany* (Natchitoches, La.: Northwestern State University Press, 1979), Per Seyersted and Emily Toth publish all extant writings of Kate Chopin not included in *Complete Works*. These include the three stories Chopin left unfinished, the fragment of a tale she destroyed, twenty-five mainly occasional poems, and two diaries. Thus the two collections together constitute a complete and scholarly compilation of Kate Chopin's writings.

Though in 1953 the French Americanist Cyrille Arnavon had published a translation of *The Awakening* (titled *Edna*), Kenneth Eble's 1964 Capricorn reprint of *The Awakening* was the first reissue of Chopin's work since the last reprint of *Bayou Folk* in 1911. In his introductory essay (essentially the same essay Eble published in the *Western Humanities Review*, Summer 1956), Eble called *The Awakening* "a first-rate novel," anticipating in many respects the modern novel and deserving to be restored.

In the Rinehart Edition of *The Awakening and Other Stories by Kate Chopin* (Holt, Rinehart, and Winston, 1970), Lewis Leary annotates twenty stories, arranged in the order of their first publication, and the novel. Leary's selections from Kate Chopin's writings are impeccably chosen to represent her various skills. Margaret Culley, in "Kate Chopin and Recent Obscenities" (*KCN*, Fall 1975), however, indicts this edition and the 1972 Avon paperpack edition for their careless treatment of the text itself. Culley praises Kenneth Eble's handling of the text in his facsimile edition (Capricorn, 1964) and Per Seyersted's in the 1969 *Complete Works* and in the 1974 Feminist Press reprint where, in all three cases, the text is left "almost as it first appeared." Both the 1964 Capricorn and the 1974 Feminist Press editions are out of print, mirroring the recent settling of interest in Kate Chopin. For the highly accessible Norton Critical Edition, *Kate Chopin: The Awakening, An Authoritative Text, Contexts, Criticism* (1976), Margaret Culley used the text of the novel's first edition with one minor addition. A few hardcover editions of Chopin's works remain in print. In 1972 Mss. Information Corporation (Edison, N.J.) published expensive reprints of both the 1894 edition of *Bayou Folk* and the 1897 edition of *A Night in Acadie*. In less accessible editions, Gordon Press Publishers (Green Station, N.Y.) brought out in 1974 *Bayou Folk, A Night in Acadie*, and *The Awakening*.

MANUSCRIPTS AND LETTERS

In 1931 Daniel S. Rankin, Kate Chopin's first biographer, salvaged Kate Chopin's manuscripts from a St. Louis, Missouri, attic. Almost all her manuscripts, memorabilia, letters, and materials are on file with the Missouri Historical Society. Anyone interested in a catalogue of these materials and of the letters and manuscripts known to exist elsewhere should consult Per Seyersted's "Kate Chopin (1851-1904)" (*ALR*, Spring 1970).

With the late 1979 publication of the carefully annotated *A Kate Chopin Miscellany*, all extant Kate Chopin manuscripts, letters, inscriptions, statements, and translations have been published, including the important 1894 notebook entitled "Impressions." The *Miscellany* also publishes Chopin's only musical composition and five pages of family photographs. In the exhaustive bibliography of primary materials, the editors indicate a work's composition date, its first published appearance, and its inclusion in collections. The *Miscellany* also presents all known letters written to Chopin.

BIOGRAPHY

Two important early biographical sketches of Kate Chopin written by her literary friends are "Mrs. Kate Chopin," attributed by Per Seyersted to Sue V. Moore (*St. Louis Life*, 9 June 1894) and "Kate Chopin," by William Schuyler (*Writer*, August 1894). These two appreciative essays and Alexander Nicholas DeMenil's biographical sketch and critical evaluation "A Century of Missouri Literature" (*MoHR*, October 1920) are reprinted in *A Kate Chopin Miscellany*. DeMenil's remarks in the 1904 version of the essay *The Literature of the Louisiana Territory* (St. Louis: St. Louis News, 1904) reflect the prejudices of the male literary establishment: "she has . . . no serious purposes, no lesson to teach in life. . . . She is simply a bright, unaffected, unpresuming and womanly woman."

Other first-hand primary biographical information is contained in the notes from a 1949 interview the Missouri Historical Society conducted with Felix Chopin, Kate Chopin's son. These notes are also published in the *Miscellany*.

For his 1932 biography *Kate Chopin and Her Creole Stories* (Philadelphia: University of Pennsylvania Press), Daniel S. Rankin had access to Kate Chopin's manuscripts and journals and interviewed the writer's relatives and acquaintances. Though many of Rankin's critical statements may be outmoded and limited, some of his biographical insights have proved permanently useful. Rankin believed that the themes of Chopin's novels and tales owed their origins to "the story telling days of impressionable youth": Kate Chopin's imagination, "as a very young girl, through the zeal and the story-telling propensity of her great-grandmother, had been saturated with a keen interest in woman's nature, and its mysterious vagaries." He recognized that she read voluminously and that she had "a contemporary mind" energetically resisting direct literary influence.

Per Seyersted's 1969 study, *Kate Chopin: A Critical Biography* (Baton Rouge: Louisiana State University Press), which Octagon Books has reprinted and which Louisiana State University Press has made available in a paperback edition, is the standard biography. Much of the foundation of Seyersted's biography is built upon the interviews and unnamed sources of Rankin's work, though Seyersted also had access to a previously unknown diary from 1894 and a manuscript from 1896. Reviewing the book, Lewis Leary argues in "Kate Chopin, Liberationist?" (*SLJ*, Fall 1970) that Seyersted "allows a reader to place too much emphasis on Mrs. Chopin as a crusader for the rights of women," but that he is more on target when he views her as a link between George Sand and Simone de Beauvoir. Seyersted's biography has been judged "solemn and effusive" by Jean Stafford in "Sensuous Woman" (*NYRB*, 23 September 1971), where she nevertheless found it competent in execution and illuminating in its biographical details.

More extensive evaluative commentary is to be found in the dissertation critique of Seyersted's work by David Aaron and Sigmund Skard (*Edda*, Hefte 6, 1971). For Aaron the biography's strength lies in Seyersted's convincing delineation of the stages in Chopin's development as a literary artist. Aaron's most weighty charge against Seyersted is that he does not go far enough in "thickening the obstacles Kate Chopin had to overcome," which included her "private struggle with the critical priesthood." Sigmund Skard concludes that though Seyersted's portrait of Chopin is not altogether new, it improves substantially upon Rankin's in that it interprets the biographical documents in the light of Chopin's total literary output.

Four articles in *The Kate Chopin Newsletter* should be consulted for biographical corrections. Using doctors' bills and an order and bill for a casket, in "The Misdated Death of Oscar Chopin" (Fall 1975) Emily Toth establishes Oscar Chopin's death as occurring in December 1882 rather than January 1883, as stated in Rankin and Seyersted. An unsigned note, "The Practical Side of Oscar Chopin's Death" (Winter 1975-1976), reports that according to recently uncovered documents, Oscar Chopin died on 17 December 1882, though his coffin was ordered on 10 December. In "Kate Chopin Remembered" (Winter 1975-1976), Emily Toth records family anecdotes and firsthand reminiscences gleaned from conversations with Chopin's descendants and includes a genealogy. Most significantly, in "Kate Chopin's Family: Fallacies and Facts, Including Kate's 'True Birthdate,'" (Winter 1976-1977), Mary Helen Wilson uses census records to establish Kate Chopin's birth date as 12 July 1850, not 8 February 1851, as usually reported.

In "Colorful Characters from Kate's Past" (*KCN*, Spring 1976), the scholar will also find useful Elizabeth Shown Mills's discussion of the enterprising and unconventional female ancestors whose stories might have been passed on to the young Kate by her great-grandmother Victoire Verdon Charleville.

CRITICISM

Students of trends and issues in Kate Chopin criticism have two helpful aids accessible to them. Margaret Culley's *Kate Chopin, The Awakening: An Authoritative Text, Contexts, Criticism* (W. W. Norton, 1976) reprints excerpts from largely inaccessible contemporary reviews documenting the critical controversy the novel engendered. Excerpts from contemporary scholarship and journalism as well as an editorial essay detailing the legal and social position of women during the 1890s provide a useful framework for the moral and social issues raised in the novel. The criticism excerpted in the Norton edition ranges from Percival Pollard's satirical discussion in *Their Day in Court* (Neale, 1909) to two previously unpublished essays prepared expressly for the edition. Other excerpted essays show the trends in Chopin criticism from her rediscovery in the late 1950s to the early 1970s.

A Kate Chopin Miscellany publishes the 1894 biographical-critical sketches by Sue V. Moore (*St. Louis Life*, 9 June 1894) and William Schuyler (*Writer*, August 1894) as well as later critical statements and essays and, of most value perhaps, a competent translation of Cyrille Arnavon's introduction to *Edna*, the 1953 French translation of *The Awakening*, which served to spur the revival of American scholarly interest in Chopin during the 1960s.

CRITICISM OF CHOPIN'S WORKS THROUGH THE 1960S

Perhaps following the lead of William Schuyler in his early sketch of Chopin (*Writer*, August 1894), her early critics tended to ascribe the highly sensuous qualities of her storytelling not to art but to the influences of her French ancestry. Most of the reviewers who were courageous enough to attend to *The Awakening* (1899) admired its style but were repulsed by its theme. An excellent sampling of these early reviews is reprinted in Culley's Norton edition of *The Awakening*. Even the most positive of the earlier reviewers, C. L. Deyo, though conceding the novel's "flawless art," considered its theme of female sexuality "positively unseemly" in "The Newest Books" (*St. Louis Post-Dispatch*, 20 May 1899).

The critical views of another of Chopin's critic friends, Alexander Nicholas DeMenil, exemplify the prejudices of the literary establishment that Chopin battled throughout her brief writing career. In "Kate Chopin" (*The Literature of the Louisiana Territory*, St. Louis: *St. Louis News* 1904), DeMenil praises her facility in handling the Creole dialect, admires her "femininely subtle" insight, and, not surprisingly, compliments her complete lack of literary pretensions. In the 1920s, Fred Lewis Pattee, like DeMenil, cannot view Chopin as a conscious literary artist. Calling Chopin's stories "primitively original" in *Century Readings in the American Short Story* (Century, 1927), Pattee, in *The Development of the American Short Story* (Harper, 1923), had previously emphasized their uncultivated spontaneity: "Without models, without study or short-story art, without revision, and usually at a sitting, she produced what often are masterpieces before which one can only wonder and conjecture."

In "Kate Chopin (*Library of Southern Literature*, Vol. 2, Atlanta: Martin and Hoyt, 1907), Leonidas Rutledge Whipple praises Chopin's short stories for their "delicate sensuous realism" and recognizes her novels as "studies of complex feminine natures" and thus anticipates the direction later critics will take in assessing Chopin's fictional achievements. However, he says that her "lasting fame" will depend on her two collections of Creole short stories, for, though *The Awakening* shows "art of the finest kind," it "fails of greatness because its themes and its persons are not usual."

In the early decades of this century, literary historians most commonly viewed Chopin's stories as "delicate studies of Creole life . . . not inferior to those of Cable," to cite a representative comment by Edward J. H. O'Brien in *The Advance of the American Short Story* (Dodd, Mead, 1923). With the passing of time, increasing recognition was given to Chopin's characterization—"her people are not names but three dimensional and quick with life" —says Joseph J. Reilly in "Stories by Kate Chopin" (*Commonweal*, 26 March 1937). At the same time others, such as Lizzie C. McVoy in "Kate Chopin" (*Louisiana in the Short Story*, Baton Rouge: Louisiana State University Press, 1940), recognized her "keen knowledge of dramatic values." See also Shields McIlwaine's *The Southern Poor-White from Lubberland to Tobacco Road* (Norman: University of Oklahoma Press, 1939). In 1942 Joseph J. Reilly in *Of Books and Men* (Julian Messner) acknowledges Maupassant's influence on Chopin, and praises "Athénaïse" and "Désirée's Baby" for their economy in creating atmosphere and their fully realized characters. Reilly further shows that a reversal has occurred in the critical approach to her stories: "Mrs. Chopin knew before setting pen to paper exactly whither she was bound," for her conclusions are inherent either "in the situation or in the psychology of the chief character." By the 1950s such literary historians as Clarence Gohdes considered Chopin a better "fabricator of *contes*" than Cable. "Désirée's Baby" is to be admired for its Maupassantian "crispness of structure," and *The Awakening*, as a delineation of "a philandering woman . . . deserves a worthy place in the history of sterner realism in nineteenth-century America" asserts Gohdes in "Exploitation of the Provinces" (*The Literature of the American People: An Historical and Critical Survey*, ed. Arthur Hobson Quinn, Appleton-Century-Crofts, 1951).

Cyrille Arnavon, in his introductory essay to the 1953 French translation of *The Awakening*, was the first critic to take a psychoanalytic approach to the novel's heroine and its author. Arnavon, who describes Chopin as "in many ways a Victorian *grande dame*" who wrote "chiefly to amuse herself," finds the primary weakness of this "American *Madame Bovary*" in its "unlikely . . . rather too schematic" dénouement, which spoils the novel's psychological realism. The suicide is attributable to a regressive fixation and denial of sexuality in Edna and "through her, in her creator" (reprinted in *A Kate Chopin Miscellany*).

In "*The Awakening* by Kate Chopin," Robert Cantwell, reflecting the shift in critical esteem from the stories to the novel, ranks the novel "among the world's masterpieces of short fiction" but considers her stories "fragmentary" and only partially imagined: "they more often seem translations of experiences from the sophisticated world into the backwoods than evocations of that backwoods life itself" (*GaR*, Winter 1956).

In the 1960s critics began to investigate Kate Chopin's relationship with literary tradition. For Edmund Wilson, her works do not connect with an inherited tradition: rather, in her recurring treatment of the theme of marital infidelity, Kate Chopin anticipates D. H. Lawrence (*Patriotic Gore: Studies in the Literature of the American Civil War*, Oxford University

Press, 1962). In "An Important St. Louis Writer Reconsidered," Per Seyersted treats Kate Chopin as a "forgotten early American realist" (*MoHSB*, January 1963). While Warner Berthoff, in *The Ferment of Realism: American Literature 1884-1919* (The Free Press, 1965), views *The Awakening* as "a New Orleans version of the familiar transcendentalist fable of the soul's emergence, or 'lapse,' into life" as well as a "period-piece of post-Darwinian ethics." Larzer Ziff's *The American 1890s: Life and Times of a Lost Generation* (Viking, 1966) finds the characters' situations in Chopin's local color stories "conventionalized" and in some cases even exploited for quaintness. However, *The Awakening* "was the most important piece of fiction about the sexual life of a woman written to date in America, and the first fully to face the fact that marriage ... was but an episode in her continuous growth." As a realist, Chopin shows Edna Pontellier inextricably caught between her illusions and the conditions society imposes upon women.

In "Kate Chopin's Other Novel" (*SLJ*, August 1966), the single treatment of *At Fault* before the 1970s, Lewis Leary points out the weaknesses in plot and narrative consistency but considers the novel's chief fault its thin characterization: "motivation, when present, seems superimposed rather than an inevitable precursor of action." Its chief influences seem to be Dickens and the American local colorists rather than Flaubert or Mme. de Staël. Yet, concludes Leary, there is "much good in it, for an artist can be seen at work, learning her trade."

Two essays published near decade's end approach Chopin's fiction from a feminist vantage. In an essay of enduring value, "The Southern Woman in the Fiction of Kate Chopin" (*LaH*, Spring 1966), Marie Fletcher examines Kate Chopin's treatment of her Southern heroines and concludes that in spite of Chopin's realistic treatment of human situations, her heroines "follow the same ideals of faithfulness, loyalty, and chastity honored by the ladies of wealth and social prominence in the sentimental and historical fiction of pre-war days." More ephemerally, Joan Zlotnick, in "A Woman's Will: Kate Chopin on Selfhood, Wifehood, and Motherhood" (*MarkhamR*, October 1968), finds that unlike D. H. Lawrence's heroines, Chopin's Edna can reconcile the demands of the body and soul only in death, a formula devised by Chopin to question society's ordination of marriage and motherhood as integral to woman's happiness.

George Arms, in "Kate Chopin's *The Awakening* in the Perspective of her Literary Career," is the first critic to give just recognition to the complexity of Kate Chopin's ironic method. *The Awakening* is worked out through a pattern of complex and even blurred oppositions demonstrating with "philosophical pragmatism" an unwillingness "to extract a final truth." In the short stories, though, "it is hard to see a regular progression toward the complex sense of opposition that she realized in *The Awakening*" (*Essays in American Literature in Honor of J. B. Hubbell*, edited by Clarence Gohdes, Durham, N.C.: Duke University Press, 1967).

Another early discussion of the modernity of *The Awakening* occurs in Richard P. Adams's "Southern Literature in the 1890's" (*MissQ*, Fall 1968), in which he sees Chopin's novel as evidence of "the existence of a genuine proto-modern tradition in Southern literature" and as anticipating Faulkner's *Absalom, Absalom!* in its use of contrasting cultures.

In the first book-length critical study, Per Seyersted closes out the decade of Kate Chopin's critical rediscovery with a sensitive reading of Chopin's life and works in *Kate Chopin: A Critical Biography* (Baton Rouge: Louisiana State University Press, 1969). Seyersted wants to show that Chopin's vision transcended the particulars of her locale to achieve a universal view of the human struggle: "What Kate Chopin wanted was nothing less than to describe post-Darwinian man with the openness of modern French writers." Her particular achievement was the development of what Seyersted calls a "female realism . . . a more powerful realism than that introduced by Mme. de Staël or George Sand" with which "to describe woman, to give a true picture of the fundamentals of her existence." In applying a "unique pessimistic realism" to woman's unchanging condition, Kate Chopin "broke new ground in American literature." Per Seyersted's essay introducing *The Complete Works of Kate Chopin* (Baton Rouge: Louisiana State University Press, 1969) remains a valuable analysis of the nature and worth of Kate Chopin's literary achievement. Seyersted is the first critic to draw attention to the seriousness and scope of Chopin's literary ambitions. He further shows that her significance lies in her artistry and in the bold treatment of her primary theme: "the immutable impulses of love and sex" in the psychology of the individual. For Seyersted, Kate Chopin's unsentimental and amoral view of woman as "a toy in the hands of nature's procreational imperative" allies her more closely with Theodore Dreiser than with any other American writer of her day.

CRITICISM IN THE 1970S: GENERAL TREATMENTS OF CHOPIN'S WORKS

In the general treatments of Chopin's works in the 1970s, critics concerned themselves principally with her artistry and narrative methods, with the psychology of her characters, with her philosophy, and with the feminist social and literary issues raised by her fictional characters and their situations.

In "Love in Louisiana—Kate Chopin: A Forgotten Southern Novelist" (*TLS*, 9 October 1970), an anonymous reviewer of Seyersted's *Kate Chopin: A Critical Biography* states that Chopin shares with Hawthorne a "deep awareness of the truths of the human heart" and emulates Balzac and anticipates Faulkner in the creation of recurring characters solidly placed in a fully imagined locale.

Daniel Aaron amplifies Seyersted's biography with an acute discussion of the personal and cultural limitations which Chopin "circumvented" in her best work in "Per Seyersted: Kate Chopin. A Critical Biography" (*Edda*,

1971). Aaron also contributes a valuable discussion of Chopin's realism: Unafraid to suggest the perverse or the grotesque, preferring the absurd and wayward over the quaint, Chopin is best viewed as a precursor of such later writers as Katharine Anne Porter, Eudora Welty, Carson McCullers, and Flannery O'Connor. Sigmund Skard, in the same critique, acknowledges Chopin's debts to European naturalism.

In his introduction to *"The Storm" and Other Stories by Kate Chopin: With The Awakening* (Old Westbury, N.Y.: Feminist Press, 1974), Per Seyersted provides an excellent and thorough commentary on Chopin's critical fortunes and her artistic achievement. Clement Eaton treats Chopin as an artistic rebel against the literary traditions of a patriarchal and sentimental South in "Breaking a Path for the Liberation of Women in the South" (*GaR*, Summer 1974).

Beginning in the 1930s, social historians and literary critics have shown interest in Chopin's portrayals of blacks and Creoles, generally concluding that though her Creoles are individualized, her blacks are essentially stereotypes (see M. Clifford Harrison, *Social Types in Southern Prose Fiction*, Ann Arbor, Mich.: Edwards, 1932; and Sterling Brown, *The Negro in American Fiction*, Washington, D.C.: Associates in Negro Folk Education, 1937). By the 1970s, however, Merrill Skaggs finds that Chopin "never really challenges the Creole stereotype" first elaborated by G. W. Cable; thus, her stories appear both "dated and contrived." In *The Folk of Southern Fiction* (Athens: University of Georgia Press, 1972), Skaggs points out, on the other hand, that *The Awakening*—"the best novel to be published by a self-consciously southern writer before the twentieth-century"—has timeless and universal qualities because it exposes neither the New Woman nor the Creoles but "any society in which the rights of one individual are automatically less than those of another."

In a lackluster treatment, "Negroes in the Fiction of Kate Chopin" (*LaH*, Winter 1971), Richard H. Potter plods through Chopin's fiction to show that in it the author departs from the traditional stereotypes to make her portraits of blacks realistic and humanistic. The essay reminds us that in *At Fault*, Chopin treats racial subjects that were taboo in her day fifty years before Faulkner and Harper Lee gave them currency.

Patricia Hopkins Lattin's "Kate Chopin's Repeating Characters" (*MissQ*, Winter 1979-1980), is probably the most penetrating treatment of Chopin's characterization to appear in recent years. Lattin shows how Chopin's fictional themes, like Faulkner's after her, increase in scope and richness when the recurring characters are analyzed within their extended contexts.

The most significant general treatment of Chopin's artistry in the 1970s is Robert D. Arner's monograph-length study "Kate Chopin" (*LaS*, Spring 1975). Arner presents a close analysis of Chopin's narrative techniques to show that "her artistic development kept pace with her expanding vision . . . of the human mind." Her primary technique of achieving "psychological verisimilitude" is through the use of natural symbols to establish a correspondence between inner and outer worlds. In *The Awakening* Chopin "paints a landscape of the mind and spirit" which indicates that at her best she "should be ranked with Poe, Hawthorne, Melville and other writers whose images are symbols of an inner world." The stories to have been collected under the title *A Vocation and a Voice*, which Arner considers Chopin's best work next to *The Awakening*, explore "with penetrating insight the underside of human consciousness." In an introduction to Arner's study, Lewis Simpson contends that Kate Chopin shares with Shakespeare and with Faulkner the vision of man alienated from a past authoritative religious tradition: "In her fiction, notably in *The Awakening*, Kate Chopin offers a dramatization of the psychic expense of the destruction of the moral order—the process of self-damnation through self-salvation."

The 1970s produced a mélange of useful essays on feminist issues, some narrowly focused on Chopin's works and some projecting Chopin's fiction into broader feminist contexts. In her study of Kate Chopin and other nineteenth-century women writers, "The Independent Woman and 'Free' Love" (*MR*, Autumn 1975), Emily Toth concludes that though the traditional approaches to the independent woman are present in Chopin's work, "they are sometimes transformed and usually with a new view of the sexual relation." Sharon O'Brien's "Sentiment, Local Color, and the New Woman Writer: Kate Chopin and Willa Cather" (*KCN*, Winter 1976-1977) shows that Kate Chopin figured prominently in the late nineteenth-century "shift from the sentimental vision of the woman writer as moralist to the later view of the woman as artist." Patricia Hopkins Lattin provides a convenient summary of Chopin's fictional treatment of childbirth and motherhood in "Childbirth and Motherhood in Kate Chopin's Fiction" (*RFI*, Spring 1978). Noting that earlier women writers like Glasgow, Wharton, Chopin, and Cather challenged their societies' assumptions about the price of passion, Susan R. Horton laments that "contemporary women novelists begin and end by taking as a given exactly what they ought to be questioning" in "Desire and Depression in Women's Fiction: The Problematics and the Economics of Desire" (*MFS*, Summer 1978).

Criticism in the 1970s: Individual Works other than *The Awakening*

In a careful and thorough analysis, "Landscape Symbolism in Kate Chopin's *At Fault*" (*LaS*, Fall 1970), Robert D. Arner locates the structural coherence of *At Fault* (1890) in the theme of "the past and its pressures on the present," to place it in the mainstream of Southern fiction, and shows that Chopin anticipates Faulkner in her uses of the landscape symbolism inherent in the pastoral and Gothic modes employed in Southern writing. Bernard J. Koloski argues that unlike Edna Pontellier in *The Awakening*, the heroine of *At Fault* achieves fulfillment through the uniting of inner and outer realities made possible by her "willingness to adjust to a changing community and a changing morality." Chopin realizes this theme through "a well conceived succession of contrasts," states Koloski in "The Structure of Kate Chopin's *At Fault*" (*SAF*, Spring 1975). Focusing on theme and setting rather than on character, Donald A. Ringe, in "Cane River World: Kate Chopin's *At Fault* and Related Stories" (*SAF*, Autumn 1975), centers the novel's dynamics in the "intrusion of modern industry into the agricultural world of the plantation." William Warnken examines the fire-light-darkness image pattern to conclude that this cycle of images provided Chopin with "a relevant controlling force" for her venture into the fiction of social consciousness in "Fire, Light, and Darkness in Kate Chopin's *At Fault*" (*KCN*, Fall 1975). Thomas Bonner, Jr., provides a helpful summary of the narrative devices used in *At Fault* and an analysis of its structural strengths and weaknesses in "Kate Chopin's *At Fault* and *The Awakening*" (*MarkhamR*, Fall 1977).

James E. Rocks provides a useful though loosely focused discussion of Chopin's thematic and narrative irony, principally in the short stories in "Kate Chopin's Ironic Vision" (*RLLR*, Winter 1972). Rocks states that in her use of the technique of the epiphany, Chopin anticipates Joyce. Bert Bender's "Kate Chopin's Lyric Short Stories" (*SSF*, Summer 1974) calls Chopin's stories "fictional songs of the self" and argues that they are unconventional in tone as well as theme. In "St. Louis and the Fiction of Kate Chopin" (*MoHSB*, October 1975), Emily Toth examines *At Fault* and the stories set in St. Louis to show that Chopin, "as a questioner of established modern values," used her native city as the specific symbol representing "restrictions on female potential and mobility."

Two essays focus on the fruitful connection between Chopin's life and art. Thomas Bonner, Jr., in "Kate Chopin's European Consciousness" (*ALR*, Summer 1975), discusses the thematic contributions of setting in "Wiser Than a God," "A Point at Issue," and "Lilacs." Bonner asserts that the fictional themes of "self-knowledge and eroticism" for which these three stories functioned as "laboratory experiments," have their origins in Chopin's own awakening to freedom experienced during her wedding journey through Europe. Bernice Larson Webb, in "The Circular Structure of Kate Chopin's Life and Writing" (*NLauR*, Fall 1976), analyzes in three stories—"Charlie," "Athénaïse," and "Nég Créol"—the function of the journey of quest and discovery, a pattern reflected in Chopin's life.

Viewing Kate Chopin mainly as a "pioneering realist," Robert D. Arner published in the early 1970s three essays of continuing value that examine the craft of Chopin's stories. In "Kate Chopin's Realism: 'At the 'Cadian Ball' and 'The Storm' " (*MarkhamR*, February 1970), Arner uses "At the 'Cadian Ball" as a yardstick to measure Chopin's development "away from slickness and local color sentimentality" toward the "genuine realism" realized in "The Storm," a story notable for its unconventionality and artistic integrity. "Characterization and the Colloquial Style in Kate Chopin's 'Vagabonds'" examines Chopin's use of language to develop the theme of the alter ego (*MarkhamR*, May 1971). In "Pride and Prejudice: Kate Chopin's 'Désirée's Baby'" (*MissQ*, Spring 1972), Arner successfully rehabilitates the critical reputation of "Désirée's Baby" in a thorough revelation of its artistic integrity. Even more provocative, though, is Arner's contention that the story, which combines "racial themes and a transmuted seduction theme," is a hybrid mix of the *Uncle Tom's Cabin* and the *Clarissa* traditions.

Peggy Skaggs examines the theme of male possessiveness, appearing in stories spanning Chopin's entire writing career, to demonstrate Chopin's developing maturity in both perception and technique in "'The Man-Instinct of Possession': A Persistent Theme in Kate Chopin's Stories" (*LaS*, Fall 1975). Anne Rowe sees "Beyond the Bayou," in its use of "symbolic setting, complex psychological portraiture, and the freedom versus confinement theme," as an important harbinger of the "treatment of physical and psychological freedom in *The Awakening*" in "A Note on Kate Chopin's 'Beyond the Bayou'" (*KCN*, Fall 1975). In the same issue Emily Toth's "The Cult of Domesticity and 'A Sentimental Soul'" provides a useful analysis of "A Sentimental Soul" showing that "Kate Chopin uses the trappings of American sentimental fiction as a way of pursuing new questions more characteristic of a French view," and Pamela Gaudé presents a somewhat scanty analysis of the influence of two Maupassant stories upon "The Storm" in "Kate Chopin's 'The Storm': A Study of Maupassant's Influence." In an essay generally devoid of fresh insight, "Kate Chopin's *Bayou Folk* Revisited" (*NLauR*, Fall 1977), Thomas Bonner, Jr., surveys the artistry of the tales collected in *Bayou Folk*.

In another of her excellent readings of Chopin, this time of "Désirée's Baby," Cynthia G. Wolff demonstrates, in "Kate Chopin and the Fiction of Limits: 'Désirée's Baby'" (*SLJ*, Spring 1978), the technical means by which Chopin creates "the fiction of limits": what Chopin consistently treats in her fiction is the "ominous and insistent presence of the margin" defining the precariousness of the human condition. In "Kate Chopin and the Pull of Faith: A Note on 'Lilacs'" (*SoS*, Spring 1979), Elmo Howell uses "Lilacs" to demonstrate that counter to most critics' claims, Chopin was no amoralist. Rather, her fictional aim is to dramatize the conflict between body and soul, an indication that Chopin "never let go her hold on traditional values." In those stories in which she insists on a moral, as in "A Vocation and a Voice" and "Two Portraits," "her stories turn into allegory." In "The Boy's Quest in Kate Chopin's 'A Vocation and a Voice'" (*AL*, May 1979), a fine essay reminding us that modern critics continue to do Chopin an injustice when they try to make her "a spokeswoman for only the female half of the human family," Peggy Skaggs examines the masculine point of view in "A Vocation and a Voice" to argue that Chopin was concerned not with sexual identity but with human identity.

In an essay admirable for its freshness and thoroughness, "Kate Chopin's Sources for 'Mrs. Mobry's Reason'" (*AL*, January 1980), Susan Wolstenholme provides a penetrating analysis of the strengths and weaknesses of "Mrs. Mobry's Reason" in light of its sources in Ibsen and Wagner.

CRITICISM IN THE 1970S: *THE AWAKENING*

A survey of the criticism of *The Awakening* since its publication in 1899 shows that until the late 1950s the novel was either ignored, ridiculed, or misunderstood by most critics and literary historians. Percival Pollard, in *Their Day in Court* (Neale, 1909), finds that the novel's theme—the sexual awakening of a twenty-eight-year-old wife and mother of two children—stretches the reader's credulity. Daniel S. Rankin, Chopin's first biographer, in *Kate Chopin and Her Creole Stories* (Philadelphia: University of Pennsylvania Press, 1932), finds the novel is an "analytical study of the character of a selfish, capricious woman" that grew out of a fin de siècle imagination. Arthur Hobson Quinn's *American Fiction: An Historical and Critical Survey* (Appleton-Century, 1936) places the novel among studies of "morbid psychology." In *The Confident Years: 1885-1915* (E. P. Dutton, 1952), Van Wyck Brooks calls the novel "one small perfect book" but misunderstands its theme. Not until Kenneth Eble's 1956 essay, "A Forgotten Novel: Kate Chopin's *The Awakening*" (*WHR*, Summer), prompted by the French Americanist Cyrille Arnavon's interest in the novel, does an American scholar strive to discern the exact nature of the novel's achievement. Eble considers *The Awakening* "a first-rate novel . . . advanced in theme and technique over the novels of its day, and . . . anticipat[ing] in many respects the modern novel." Eble praises the novel's portraiture, its structure, its symbolic imagery, and identifies Edna's conflict as "the struggle with *eros* itself." Stanley Kauffmann, in "The Really Lost Generation" (*NewR*, 3 December 1966), regards *The Awakening* as "an excellent and prodigiously courageous study of marital infidelity [that] deserves a place in the line of major American fiction." Though flawed by some of the mannerisms of its day, its "insistence on emotional truth [and] the confrontation of the resultant consequences without plot contrivance or escape" identify it as an "anachronistic, lonely, existentialist voice out of the mid-twentieth century."

In the 1970s the critics opened a full examination into the artistry of Chopin's novel, devoting particular attention to the novel's narrative technique.

John R. May, in "Local Color in *The Awakening*" (*SoR*, Autumn 1970), argues that the Creole setting is symbolically integral to Edna's psychological conflict. In the introductory essay to the 1970 Rinehart edition of *The*

Awakening and Other Stories by Kate Chopin, Lewis Leary provides a still highly useful examination of the novel's imagery to show its organic wholeness and conscious artistry. In "Kate Chopin's *The Awakening:* Ambiguity as Art" (*JAmS*, August 1971), Kenneth M. Rosen attributes the ambiguities of the novel's ending to the ambiguities of the myth it presents: Edna Pontellier enacts the mythic role of unawakened woman "in a world which denies the very nature of the woman herself."

Ruth Sullivan and Stewart Smith's "Narrative Stance in Kate Chopin's *The Awakening*" (*SAF*, Spring 1973) argues that a dual narrative stance that is not objective but omniscient and judicial shapes the novel's theme. The partisan narrative view, which "speaks for a romantic vision of life's possibilities," becomes unreliable when it equates Edna's sexual awakening with existential insight. For the alternate stance, which "speaks for a realistic understanding and acceptance of human limits," shows that Edna does not "know what she is doing, where she is going, or what she wants." The theme of the novel granted by this double posture is that only the exceptionally strong survive the tumult of rebirth. However, for Jane P. Tompkins, in "*The Awakening*: An Evaluation" (*FemS*, Spring-Summer 1976), this narrative technique of alternative views of reality—and the concomitant alternation of lyric and satiric moods—leaves unexplored the epistemological problem of synthesis. The meaning and value of Edna's suicidal choice remain "unclear because Chopin has withheld her own view of it."

With George M. Spangler's essay, "Kate Chopin's *The Awakening:* A Partial Dissent" (*Novel*, Spring 1970), the issue of the novel's conclusion moves to the critical foreground. Spangler finds much to praise in Chopin's skillful characterization and in the novel's "cultural dimension." However, the novel's conclusion, "a painful failure of vision," is contrived to provide "the pathos and poetic justice prized by the sentimental and moralistic readers of her day." Also focusing on the novel's conclusion, Peggy Skaggs, in "Three Tragic Figures in Kate Chopin's *The Awakening*" (*LaS*, Winter 1974), argues that although all three female figures in the novel are tragically unable to achieve "a fully realized human identity," Edna Pontellier experiences tragic failure because only she is unwilling to compromise with her social milieu.

Cynthia G. Wolff, in "Thanatos and Eros: Kate Chopin's *The Awakening*" (*AQ*, October 1973), challenges those readings of the novel's conclusion that emphasize Edna as a victim of societal pressures. Wolff sees Edna's portrait as a psychological study of a regressive personality. In "The New Woman Revisited" (*WS*, No. 1, 1974), Carolyn Forrey explains Edna's suicide as indicative of Chopin's inability, in a society that had no place for the New Woman, to imagine a satisfactory new role for her awakened heroine. Joyce Ruddell Ladenson's "Paths to Suicide: Rebellion Against Victorian Womanhood in Kate Chopin's *The Awakening*" (*Intellect*, July 1975) interprets Edna's suicide as "a final act of self-assertion" and rejection of her cultural conditioning.

Several critics approach the novel's literary and social issues from a broad feminist perspective. Jules Chametzky, for instance, examines Chopin's treatment in *The Awakening* of woman's biological and cultural entrapment but concludes that finally Chopin was "at a loss as to how to break through to newer and more humane conventions." Chametzky contends, in "Our Decentralized Literature: A Consideration of Regional, Ethnic, Racial and Sexual Factors" (*JA*, 1972), that *The Awakening* along with the works of such other so-called regionalists as Cable, Chesnutt, and Cahan was poorly received because it challenged "the dominant class's notion of a culturally homogeneous nation." Annette Kolodny traces to *The Awakening* the beginnings in women's writings of such inversions as suicide and death imagined as comforting and attractive in "Some Notes on Defining a 'Feminist Literary Criticism'" (*CritI*, Autumn 1975). In *The Female Imagination* (Alfred A. Knopf, 1975), Patricia M. Spacks contributes to Kate Chopin criticism a brilliant discussion of the moral philosophy and feminist psychology in *The Awakening*: "*The Awakening* depicts a world of emotional needs and social commandments in which morality must be discovered, not assumed," and Spacks points out that Edna's first moral responsibility is to "separate reality from fantasy." Unwilling to confront the struggle between actuality and dream, Edna "drowns in her own romanticism." Spacks concludes that for Chopin and her British predecessors writing the fiction of revolt against patriarchal injustice, "nineteenth-century women . . . share a dream of dependency. Gratified, it may give them the opportunity of control, or it may lead to the recognition that it involves some fundamental denial of the self."

Barbara Bellow Watson, in "On Power and the Literary Text" (*Signs*, Autumn 1975), turns to Chopin's novel to illustrate a realistic treatment of women's experience of power. Edna Pontellier exercises a kind of negative power that, though incapable of winning battles, can judge and refuse. In "Kate Chopin's *The Awakening* as Feminist Criticism" (*LaS*, Fall 1976), Emily Toth asserts that Chopin transformed the abstract insights of the feminist social critics inherent in her culture into concrete fiction. Irene Dash's "The Literature of Birth and Abortion" (*RFI*, Spring 1977) examines selections from the writings of Anne Bradstreet, Kate Chopin, Anne Sexton, and Gwendolyn Brooks to show that in women's writings the female artist is forced to choose between absolutes: "life or death, children or their rejection." Judith Fryer, in "Edna Pontellier: The New Woman as Woman," in her *The Faces of Eve: Women in the Nineteenth-Century American Novel* (Oxford University Press, 1976), contrasts Edna with her European cousins Emma Bovary and Anna Karenina and with her American sisters to illustrate the difference between male and female perceptions of women. Fryer views Edna's awakening as a Whitmanian song of herself, her suicide a rebirth.

Recently critical attention has been profitably directed toward placing the novel in its intellectual and literary milieux. In a bold essay closely examining the novel's imagery, "Romantic Imagery in Kate Chopin's *The Awakening*" (*AL*, January 1972), Donald A. Ringe concludes that Chopin's theme and characterization in *The Awakening* were shaped by the philosophy and psychology of nineteenth-century transcendentalism.

Otis B. Wheeler's "The Five Awakenings of Edna Pontellier" (*SoR*, January 1975) takes an opposing view. According to Wheeler, *The Awakening* examines and then rejects as inauthentic the Victorian myths of self-consecrating love and Church-consecrated love. In Edna's realizing that she will always be imprisoned by both the biological and the social orders, Chopin dismisses the transcendental myth of the "unlimited outward expansion of the self." Sharon O'Brien, in "The Limits of Passion: Willa Cather's Review of *The Awakening*" (*W&L*, Fall 1975), discusses the only contemporary evaluation of Chopin's novel by a major critic but notes that Cather's assessment is prejudiced by her deep-seated distrust of human passion.

Desiring to place *The Awakening* in "a clearer relationship with its time," Carol B. Gartner, in "Three Ednas" (*KCN*, Winter 1975-1976), examines two earlier Ednas—in Edward L. Wheeler's *Old Avalanche* and in Dinah Maria Mulock's *The Woman's Kingdom*—to show how Chopin's heroine departs from a pattern established in the dime novels of her day.

In the second half of the 1970s, criticism of the novel becomes self-conscious and concerned to treat the sexual issues raised in the novel in specific psychological or sociological terms or within a specific literary context or tradition.

Following Per Seyersted's suggestions that Kate Chopin may have wished to retain her original title of the novel as its subtitle, Margaret Culley's "Edna Pontellier: 'A Solitary Soul,'" in *Kate Chopin, The Awakening: An Authoritative Text, Contexts, Criticism*, edited by Margaret Culley (W. W. Norton, 1976), analyzes Chopin's treatment of solitude, a theme she was attracted to in Maupassant. Edna awakes to the painful realization that she is alone in a society that defines women through role relationships with men. For Paula S. Berggren, in "'A Lost Soul': Work Without Hope in *The Awakening*" (*RFI*, Spring 1977), Edna, though avoiding the self-abnegation required by her cultural role, is "fatally undefined, a lost soul with no purpose in life," whereas Adèle Ratignolle is the novel's "most awakened being, totally in harmony with her physical being and totally responsive to her vocation. . . ."

In an essay not devoid of feminist impatience, Priscilla Allen charges today's male critics, who generally overstate and isolate Edna's sexuality, with misreading the novel: "Edna is not accepted as representative of the human spirit simply because she is female," states Allen's article, "Old Critics and New: The Treatment of Chopin's *The Awakening*," in *The Authority of Experience*, edited by Arlyn Diamond and Lee R. Edwards (Amherst: University of Massachusetts Press, 1977). Though James H.

Justus does not agree with Allen that sexual politics is the central issue in the novel—"The focus of *The Awakening* is upon one woman's dilemma."—he sees universal significance in Edna's dilemma in his "The Unawakening of Edna Pontellier" (*SLJ*, Spring 1978). Justus interprets *The Awakening* as a challenge to one of the enduring pieties of twentieth-century American literature: "that self-knowledge is the threshold to psychic health, the instrument by which the trapped sensibility may be free." Edna occupies a middle ground between such characters as Crane's Maggie, Norris's McTeague, and Dreiser's Carrie and Clyde who passively accept their fates without benefit of self-knowledge and those like London's Wolf Larsen and Martin Eden, Dreiser's Hurstwood, Norris's Presley, and Wharton's Lily Bart who, though they gain self-knowledge, find that it "exacerbates their feeling of helplessness and ineffectuality." Chopin grants Edna enough insight to begin her search for a satisfying alternative to her societal roles, "but that alternative cannot be conceived in terms of maturity but only in the regressive reenactment of the egoism of childhood."

In "Beyond Sex: The Dark Romanticism of Kate Chopin's *The Awakening*" (*BSUF*, Winter 1978), Ottavio M. Casale places the novel among the mythic treatments of the fall from innocence of Hawthorne and Melville. Chopin's sea is akin not to Whitman's but to Melville's and to Hawthorne's forest, environs reflecting psychological states.

Nancy Walker, in "Feminist or Naturalist: The Social Context of Kate Chopin's *The Awakening*" (*SoQ*, Winter 1979), insists that Edna's awakening is "a realization of her sensual nature, not of her equality or freedom as an individual." Chopin uses the conventions of literary naturalism to explore Edna's sexual awakening within a setting of two colliding cultures. Walker further argues that Edna "is controlled by her own emotions, not by men or society."

An article stylistically laborious but useful to undergraduates thinking about gender stereotypes in literature, Anne-Lise Paulsen's "The Masculine Dilemma in Kate Chopin's *The Awakening*" (*SoS*, Winter 1979) examines the novel's male and female types and concludes that Chopin presents "the conflict between the traditional 'masculine' and 'feminine' principles."

A more supple discussion in the same journal, Elizabeth Fox-Genovese's "Kate Chopin's Awakening" (*SoS*, Fall 1979), applies the tools of psychoanalytic criticism to Chopin to explain the contradictions in the novel's structure and dynamic. In uniting a "serious critique of bourgeois patriarchalism" with a "case history of an aberrant individual," Chopin may have been "killing off a part of herself—a residual adolescent dependency—even as she played with criticizing a society that had, by and large, treated her well."

The criticism focusing on the fertile connection between Chopin's *The Awakening* and the fiction of other writers has produced fairly useful insights.

In "Kate Chopin and Walt Whitman" (*WWR*, December 1970), Lewis Leary finds that Chopin uses quotations and echoes from Whitman's "Out of the Cradle Endlessly Rocking" and "Song of Myself" to extend the range of thematic nuances in *The Awakening*. Gregory L. Candela establishes imagistic connections between Whitman's and Chopin's mockingbirds in "Walt Whitman and Kate Chopin: A Further Connection" (*WWR*, December 1978). John Espey briefly argues that Chopin's characteristic tone suggests the Goncourts as significant French influences upon Chopin's novel in an untitled review (*NCF*, September 1970), and Bernard J. Koloski notes the atmospheric contributions of the Swinburne lines from "The Cameo" in "The Swinburne Lines in *The Awakening*" (*AL*, January 1974).

In a limpid treatment of the links between Chopin's novel and Ibsen's *A Doll's House*, William Warnken establishes the similarities of theme, imagery, and dramatic method to conclude that "Chopin was in some ways influenced by Ibsen" in "Kate Chopin and Henrik Ibsen: A Study of *The Awakening* and *A Doll's House*" (*MSE*, Autumn 1974-Winter 1975).

Though ungracefully written, Pamela Gaudé's "A Comparative Study of Kate Chopin's *The Awakening* and Guy de Maupassant's *Une Vie*" (*RLLR*, Winter 1975) provides some worthwhile insights into Chopin's novel. In an interesting but rather opaque argument, in "The French Influence in Kate Chopin's *The Awakening*" (*NCFS*, Spring 1976), Eliane Jasenas reads *The Awakening* as a narrative self-consciously liberating itself from the influences of French culture, specifically the pessimism of Maupassant, Flaubert, and Baudelaire.

In developing a feminist criticism, Emily Toth uses Chopin's *The Awakening* and Dreiser's *Sister Carrie* to define the masculine model of novelistic time—which is public, purposeful, causal, linear, and materialistic—and the feminine model—which is private, lyrical, cyclical, and epiphanic in "Timely and Timeless: The Treatment of Time in *The Awakening* and *Sister Carrie*" (*SoS*, Fall 1977).

Charles W. Mayer's article, "Isabel Archer, Edna Pontellier, and the Romantic Self" (*RS*, June 1979), is a well-considered and revealing discussion of the similarities and differences to be found in the characterizations of Henry James's heroine and Chopin's. Like James, Chopin defines her character within terms that challenge the tenets of a native American individualism, the Emersonian belief in the inviolate self. Both characters achieve illumination "in the form of a violent shock revealing that their vaunted freedom is an illusion." But while "James and the older realists hold romantic characters up to critical view in order to show how the knowledge of reality might lead them into consciousness and choice," Chopin denies Edna the "freedom of choice arrived at through self-awareness." Hence, *The Awakening* remains "a picture of a romantic mind in the grip of an inexorable force."

Three scholars have undertaken profitable studies in the relationship between Chopin's novel and the fiction of women writers who followed

Chopin. Gladys W. Milliner, in "The Tragic Imperative: *The Awakening* and *The Bell Jar*" (*MWN*, December 1973), sees both Edna Pontellier and Esther Greenwood as caught in the biological trap and both Chopin and Plath as exemplars of women awakened to the nightmare of unrealizable potential. In "Chopin and Atwood: Woman Drowning, Woman Surfacing" (*KCN*, Winter 1975-1976), Cathy N. Davidson convincingly demonstrates that Margaret Atwood's 1972 novel *Surfacing* effectively revises Chopin's *The Awakening*: "The two novels, taken together, suggest that 'awakening' is always relative and never an easy task." Robert McIlvaine argues rather persuasively that Margaret Deland's 1906 novel *The Awakening of Helena Richie* "was intended to be an answer to and a criticism of Kate Chopin's notorious novel" in "Two Awakenings: Edna Pontellier and Helena Richie" (*RFI*, Winter 1979).

Chopin Studies at the Beginning of the 1980s and Future Needs in Chopin Criticism

Publishers continue to show interest in making Chopin's stories accessible to a wider audience. In 1979 The Women's Press (London) published a collection of Kate Chopin's stories under the title *Portraits: Short Stories Selected and Introduced by Helen Taylor*. This anthology contains twenty-nine stories from Chopin's three collections and a brief bibliography. In her introduction Taylor shows that Chopin consciously used the short story form because it suited her particular artistic purposes. However, Taylor's principal concern is to place Chopin in the context of the peculiarly American literary traditions which she inherited, especially those associated with the local colorists. For Taylor these nineteenth-century women local colorists are the ancestors of such twentieth-century women writers as Cather, Welty, McCullers, and O'Connor. Cynthia G. Wolff has included seven Chopin stories in the anthology *Classic American Women Writers* (Harper & Row, 1980), which includes a Chopin chronology and a highly selective bibliography. In her introduction, Wolff identifies the central dilemma in Chopin's fiction as the maintenance of emotional stability amid the precarious conditions of marriage and motherhood. Wolff places *The Awakening* as "one of the three or four great novels of the American nineteenth century."

Scholarly interest in Chopin, after the eruption in the mid-seventies, remains active into the eighties. Joyce C. Dyer has examined Chopin's treatment of her male characters in the stories "Azélie," "At Chênière Caminada," and "A Vocation and a Voice" to show that Chopin's "point of view was not strictly feminine." Dyer notes that "both males and females . . . have no choice but to discover their passion, in spite of risks, confusion, and guilt" in "Kate Chopin's Sleeping Bruties" (*MarkhamR*, Fall-Winter 1980-1981). But *The Awakening* continues to elicit the most scholarly attention.

In a chapter entitled "Spiritual Liberation, Social Defeat: Kate Chopin," in *Diving Deep and Surfacing: Women Writers on Spiritual Quest* (Boston: Beacon Press, 1980), Carol P. Christ explores the thesis that in *The Awakening* "Edna's suicide reflects spiritual triumph but social defeat." For Christ, Chopin's novel is weakened by the fact that "Chopin could not envision any person who could give Edna support in her quest nor imagine any alternative for Edna other than spiritual or physical death." Jerome Klinkowitz includes a sometimes perfunctory chapter on *The Awakening* in *The Practice of Fiction in American Writers from Hawthorne to the Present* (Ames: Iowa State University Press, 1980). Chopin's novel is "simply... an advance in American literature, and the areas of its achievement are clearly ones pioneered by naturalism." Klinkowitz sees in Chopin's writing the reflection in miniature of the "larger movement in American literature from romanticism and local color to realism and naturalism." Klinkowitz summarizes, Chopin's "theme is a romantic imaginative awakening; the catalyst for it is drawn from the materials of local color; and her method of following the action is naturalistic." In an unusually thoughtful and well-written essay, "*The Awakening:* A Political Romance" (*AL*, March 1980), Lawrence Thornton makes some useful contrasts between Chopin's Edna Pontellier and Flaubert's Emma Bovary. Though Edna and Emma "are both narcissists, Edna becomes aware of political crises related to her position within Creole society that sharply distinguish her from Emma, who responds to French provincial society only as a mirror of her romantic fantasies...." Joseph L. Candela, Jr., takes up *The Awakening* under the subheading "Individualism and Society" in a valuable article entitled "The Domestic Orientation of American Novels, 1893-1918" (*ALR*, Spring 1980). Candela's concern is to place Chopin's novel and the questions it raises within the context of the feminist revolution of the Progressive Era. In his useful examination of Chopin's brand of feminism, Candela concludes that "the most profound aspect of her novel lies in the realization that feminism is a part of a larger problem, involving the tension between individualism and responsibility. Her conclusion demonstrates the sterility of unfettered individualism, equating it to selfishness...."

Chopin scholars have announced considerable work in progress. Thomas Bonner, Jr., has contracted with Garland to prepare a manuscript tentatively entitled "Kate Chopin: A Dictionary of Characters and Places in Her Fiction." A potentially useful reference for students, it will contain commentary, plot summaries, and a glossary of localisms. A book-length critical work on Chopin has been announced by Robert Arner (G. K. Hall, publisher). Dorothy Weil is under contract to Harper & Row for a new biography of Chopin, and Thomas Bonner, Jr., is planning an edition of Chopin's translations of Maupassant. In her forthcoming book *Female Wits*, Emily Toth will devote a chapter to Chopin's contributions to American women's humor.

Topics needing further attention include comparisons of Chopin's works and works of such writers as Ellen Glasgow, Colette, D. H. Lawrence, and Simone de Beauvoir. Book-length works could profitably be written on the place of Chopin's work in Southern literature and on Chopin's connections with American realism and naturalism. Critics need to continue to reevaluate accepted critical positions on Chopin and to continue the examination of her craft and her ironic voice. Much of Chopin criticism has been ground in the mill of academe's publish-or-perish ethos. Nonetheless, critics of the 1970s succeeded in securing a place for Chopin's works in American literature. Their business in the eighties should be a deliberate and comprehensive evaluation of her achievement.

4 JAMES W. TUTTLETON

Edith Wharton

BIBLIOGRAPHY

While we await Jacob Blanck's slow but steady progress toward the letter W, we may take note of the following bibliographical aids to the study of Edith Wharton's work: Lawson McClung Melish's *A Bibliography of the Collected Writings of Edith Wharton* (Brick Row Book Shop, 1927) lists first editions by publication dates, ending with Mrs. Wharton's *Here and Beyond* (1926). Both this title and "American First Editions . . . Edith Wharton," by Merle Johnson and Frederick M. Hopkins, (*PW*, March 10, 1923), Number 24 of a series of bibliographic checklists of American authors, are superseded by Merle D. Johnson's *American First Editions*, 4th edition, revised and enlarged by Jacob Blanck (R. R. Bowker, 1942).

Lavinia Riker Davis's *A Bibliography of the Writings of Edith Wharton* (Portland, Me.: Southworth Press, 1933), published in 325 copies, is divided into five sections: (1) full collations of the first American editions; (2) uncollected essays, poems, and stories in magazines; (3) articles, reviews, and appreciations of Mrs. Wharton appearing in American and European magazines; (4) contributions to books, including prefaces, translations, and so forth, and (5) comment on Edith Wharton's work appearing in essays and books by others. This last section is valuable for a partial list of early reviews. Aside from being relatively inaccessible, this bibliography is incomplete since it was published before Mrs. Wharton's death. In "A Bibliography of the Writings of Edith Wharton by Lavinia Davis" (*PW*, June 17, 1933), D. A. Randall points out that Davis is actually less valuable on first editions than the Melish bibliography. Davis ignores the existence of multiple states, binding variations, author-signed editions, and the like.

This essay originally appeared in slightly different form in *Resources for American Literary Study*. It is reprinted here with the permission of the editors.

Both Melish and Davis, however, are inadequate on English editions. Randall characterizes the Davis bibliography as falling into the "worth while if you want it, but by no means necessary" category. Randall feels that Davis's work "proves again that most bibliographers of modern authors could well afford to be less hasty in publishing careless and incomplete work." All of these were superseded by Vito J. Brenni's *Edith Wharton: A Bibliography* (Morgantown: West Virginia University Library, 1966), some ninety pages of bibliographical information.

Selected but valuable checklists of Edith Wharton criticism are published in Davis's *A Bibliography*. . . ; in Louis Auchincloss's Minnesota pamphlet *Edith Wharton* (Minneapolis: University of Minnesota Press, 1961); in Irving Howe's compilation *Edith Wharton: A Collection of Critical Essays* (Englewood Cliffs, N.J.: Prentice-Hall, 1962); in Blake Nevius's *Edith Wharton: A Study of Her Fiction* (Berkeley: University of California Press, 1953); and in Geoffrey Walton's *Edith Wharton: A Critical Interpretation* (Rutherford, N.J.: Fairleigh Dickinson University Press, 1970). Less readily accessible but extremely valuable (through 1961) is Patricia R. Plante's dissertation "The Critical Reception of Edith Wharton's Fiction in America and England with an Annotated Enumerative Bibliography of Wharton Criticism from 1900 to 1961" (Boston University, 1962).

James W. Tuttleton's "Edith Wharton: An Essay in Bibliography" (*RALS*, Autumn 1973) offers an overview of Wharton criticism organized identically with and incorporated in this chapter. It should be noted, however, that new biographical information about Mrs. Wharton's private diary for 1908, mentioned in the *RALS* article, permits the following correction: the anonymous lover mentioned in the diary was Morton Fullerton, not Walter Berry, as was thought for many years.

All of these checklists of Wharton criticism have now been superseded by Marlene Springer's *Edith Wharton and Kate Chopin: A Reference Guide* (Boston: G. K. Hall, 1976), which lists and briefly annotates each item of published criticism in chronological order up to 1975.

EDITIONS

Charles Scribner's Sons—Mrs. Wharton's publisher until 1916—is largely responsible for the Wharton titles now in print. Scribner's began to reissue her works in the hardback "Centennial Edition" in 1962, the centenary of Mrs. Wharton's birth. These unedited reissues, which include all of the major novels, are a welcome basis for the continuing critical examination of her work. They are not scholarly editions, however, and do not merit the faith we have in texts meticulously prepared for the Center for Scholarly Editions.

In addition to the major novels and her autobiography, *A Backward Glance*, the Scribner reissues include a two-volume collection entitled *The Collected Short Stories of Edith Wharton* (1968), edited and introduced by

R. W. B. Lewis. The question of choice and taste aside, the value of this collection is twofold: it makes available samplings from *The Greater Inclination, Crucial Instances, The Descent of Man*, and other collections; and it brings together for the first time a number of uncollected stories that Mrs. Wharton either suppressed or ignored in compiling her own collections of stories. Wayne Andrews's edition of *The Best Short Stories of Edith Wharton* (Scribners, 1958), with an introduction revealing sensational biographical details, is not a part of the Centennial Edition but may be mentioned here as a tasteful selection of Mrs. Wharton's short story art. Also available in the Scribner Centennial Edition is *The Edith Wharton Reader* (1965), which presents 700 pages of Mrs. Wharton's best fiction, poetry, and critical prose, impeccably chosen by the editor, Louis Auchincloss.

In addition to these Scribner reissues, a number of Mrs. Wharton's works, mostly those out of copyright, have been issued in hardback by reprint houses. *Crucial Instances, The Greater Inclination, The Touchstone*, and *The Valley of Decision* have been recently reprinted by the AMS Press. *Summer* has been reprinted by the Scholarly Press. Octagon Books has reprinted *The Writing of Fiction*, and the Gregg Press has reprinted *Sanctuary*.

Scribner's has also reissued the following titles in the "Scribner Library" paperback series: *The House of Mirth, Roman Fever and Other Stories, Summer, The Reef, Old New York, The Custom of the Country, The Age of Innocence, Ethan Frome*, and *The Edith Wharton Reader*, edited by Louis Auchincloss. *Edith Wharton's Ethan Frome: The Story with Sources and Commentary*, edited by Blake Nevius, was published in 1968 by Scribner's as part of its Scribner Research Anthologies paperback series.

The novels published after 1916, when Edith Wharton broke with Charles Scribner and moved over to Appleton, are generally unavailable in paperback, doubtless owing to copyright problems, the absence of an appropriate Appleton paperback line, and the lesser quality of the later fiction. Nevertheless, some other publishers have issued paperbacks of some of her novels. *Hudson River Bracketed*, with an "Afterword" by Louis Auchincloss, is available in a New American Library Signet edition; *The Age of Innocence* is available in a Houghton Mifflin Riverside edition, a Modern Library edition, and a New American Library edition; and *The House of Mirth* is also available in the New York University Press, New American Library, and Rinehart paperback editions.

Most of the manuscript fragments and authorial *disjecta membra* at Yale and elsewhere have not yet been published. But one new title has been brought into print, Mrs. Wharton's juvenile attempt at a novel. It has been edited by Viola Hopkins Winner under the title *Fast and Loose, A Novelette by David Olivieri* (Charlottesville: University Press of Virginia, 1977). This 130-page splurge of sentimentality was inexplicably reprinted by *Redbook* (April 1978).

MANUSCRIPTS AND LETTERS

There is no census of Edith Wharton manuscripts and letters. The largest collection of her papers was deposited in the Yale University Library in 1938 after her death. It consists of some 50,000 items, including manuscripts, letters, diaries, journals, and notebooks. Other important collections are owned by William Royall Tyler at Dumbarton Oaks in Washington; by Louis Auchincloss in New York; by Harvard's Houghton Library and Villa I Tatti research center in Settignano, Italy; by the Firestone Library at Princeton; and by the libraries at Amherst College, the University of California (Berkeley), The Wisconsin State Historical Society, and The New York Public Library. R. W. B. Lewis reports that Mary Pitlick is preparing an edition of Wharton's letters.

BIOGRAPHY

The best brief biographical essay, by one who knew her, is Leon Edel's "Edith Wharton" in the *Dictionary of American Biography* (Charles Scribner's, 1958), Volume 23. It should be read in conjunction with her autobiography, *A Backward Glance* (Charles Scribner's, 1934), a memoir marked by intriguing evasions and omissions. On the title page, Mrs. Wharton quoted Chateaubriand's *"Je veux remonter le penchant de mes belles années."* But by limiting herself to her *"belles années,"* she unfortunately presented an extremely distorted portrait of herself. Personal and intimate details are passed over in silence. She did not even mention her mother's death in 1901, her divorce from Edward Wharton, nor that bittersweet relationship with Walter Berry. Mrs. Wharton was unusually reserved. The most passionate affair of her life, with Morton Fullerton in 1908, is discreetly omitted. She threw practically no light on her beginnings as a writer, and the one chapter devoted to the "secret garden" of her writing career was so selective in detail as to be positively misleading. Louis Auchincloss has expressed admiration for the reticence of Mrs. Wharton's autobiography, in contrast to the tell-all memoirs of women like Caitlin Thomas and Diana Barrymore. However that may be, there is no question that the reticence of this autobiography and the thirty-year ban imposed on the examination of her private papers stifled rather than encouraged critical and biographical interest in Mrs. Wharton and her work for many years.

As autobiography, *A Backward Glance* was unsatisfactory even to Mrs. Wharton. Not long before her death, she undertook to enlarge the record of her life in an essay originally entitled "A Further Glance" but posthumously published in *Harper's Magazine* (March 1938) as "A Little Girl's New York." Based on what she called the "mountains of wreckage" that now divide "my contemporaries from the era of the New Deal," she lovingly recreated the brownstone era of the 1870s and 1880s, all the while recognizing that Old New York was never a very significant social milieu.

The reticence that marks *A Backward Glance* also characterizes Percy Lubbock's *Portrait of Edith Wharton* (D. Appleton-Century, 1947), the first long study of the woman after her death. As discreet as a Victorian family biography, Lubbock's portrait subordinated the facts of her life to what he felt was the quality of her experience in Paris and Hyères, where she maintained her palatial residences. Lubbock knew little about Mrs. Wharton's childhood and young womanhood in America and, though he solicited "recollections" from her friends, he made little effort to find out about her past, expecting later biographers to fill in his gaps. Even though it is "a good literary achievement based on her life," by one who knew her, Bernard Berenson, a close friend of Mrs. Wharton, wrote to Henry Coster the year that it appeared that Lubbock's biography, however enjoyable, was "oh! so skin-deep! Foreseeing it would be, I got out of contributing any pages toward it."

One of the obvious points to be made about Lubbock's biography is that he did not like Mrs. Wharton. Frankly, a number of people did not care for her. And of those who have written about her life, Lubbock has been most candid about sketching in the traits that alienated her contemporaries—her worldliness, her impatience, her restlessness, her snobbishness, her boredom with dull people, her asperity, the malice of her wit. It would be vain in the company of those who knew Edith Wharton, Lubbock wrote, "to pretend that she was always sweetly and mercifully kind; we shall too often catch one another's eye over our memories of her at moments when she was nothing of the sort." Lubbock observed that she was "capable at times of marked—and often apparently quite uncalled-for—asperity. She was one of the few people I have ever known who did what severe ladies used to do so readily in novels: she 'drew herself up' . . . and wasn't at all disturbed by the embarrassment or confusion she created."

Lubbock, a friend of Henry James, could never quite forgive Edith her treatment of the Master, her masculine aggressiveness, her irritation over Lubbock's marriage, her tendency to dominate or disrupt conversation, her inevitable rows in public—with hotel keepers, tradesmen, taxi drivers, and the like. Although short on fact, one of the values of Lubbock's biography is that it throws into prominent relief the friendship of Mrs. Wharton and Walter Berry. Curiously, Lubbock ascribes the feebleness of her later fiction to his malign influence. None of her friends, according to Lubbock, "thought she was the better for the surrender of her fine free spirit to the control of a man . . . of a dry and narrow and supercilious temper." A lawyer of modest international reputation, Berry met Mrs. Wharton about the time of her marriage, and their friendship was unusually close until his death in 1927. During their long friendship, she submitted much of her writing to his eye and followed his critical judgment to a degree that Lubbock called disastrous. Dogmatic, egotistical, and snobbish, Berry inflicted "hurts in her growth," according to Lubbock, that "were lasting." Most of the deficiencies of her work, of her attitude toward life, and of her treatment of those around her, in fact, Lubbock attributed to this man. However that may be, Mrs. Wharton loved Berry, praised him in *A Backward Glance* for his critical discernment and assistance and, at her death, was buried next to him in the Cimetière des Gouards at Versailles. Even so, as Edmund Wilson points out in "Edith Wharton: A Memoir by an English Friend" (*Classics and Commercials*, Farrar, Straus, 1950), there are as yet no facts to deny Lubbock's reading of the Wharton-Berry relationship.

Mrs. Wharton's capacity for passionate love was first revealed in the introduction to Wayne Andrews's edition of *The Best Short Stories of Edith Wharton* (Charles Scribner's, 1958), which published part of Mrs. Wharton's private diary for 1908. The effect of this publication, however, was to mislead readers into thinking that Berry was the object of her love. In fact her lover was Morton Fullerton, a ne'er-do-well journalist with whom Mrs. Wharton had a brief but intense liaison. For a while it appeared that Andrews might delve deeper—his introduction was subtitled "Fragment of a Biography in Progress"—but the fragment was never completed.

A number of other writers have touched on the life of "that handsome, disagreeable little Pussy Jones, always scribbling," in less sensational ways. And anyone wishing to examine the biographical record would do well to consult the following books and essays. Janet Flanner's "Dearest Edith" (*NY*, 2 March 1929; rptd. in *An American in Paris: Profile of an Interlude Between Two Wars*, Simon and Schuster, 1940) is a suggestive, snide, and witty profile. Miss Flanner provides intriguing glimpses of the woman, equates her work with her life, and denies that the writer understood the social change which had wiped out the Four Hundred: "She spent her life formally proving that the wages of sin were social death and lived to see the grandchildren of her characters comfortably and popularly relaxing into open scandals." Flanner ignored the stringent satirical novels of the 1920s, emphasizing the historian.

Robert Sencourt's "Edith Wharton" (*Cornhill Magazine*, June 1938) and Logan Pearsall Smith's *Unforgotten Years* (Boston: Little, Brown, 1939) throw a more favorable light on her life, particularly her friendships in the later years when she and Smith cruised the Mediterranean. Smith's "Slices of Cake" (*NSN*, 5 June 1943) also yields some charming anecdotes about James, Mrs. Wharton, and Santayana in London. Caresse Crosby, a relative of Walter Berry who tried to displace Mrs. Wharton as his hostess, provided an acerbic account of the Berry affair in *The Passionate Years* (Dial, 1953). And Nicky Mariano's *Forty Years with Berenson* (Alfred A. Knopf, 1966) likewise emphasizes Mrs. Wharton's disagreeableness to those who knew her only slightly; but to "BB" and Nicky herself Mrs. Wharton eventually became an intimate and warm friend. Such intimacy is also suggested in Margaret Terry (Mrs. Winthrop) Chanler's "Winters in Paris"

(*AM*, October 1936; rptd. in *Autumn in the Valley*, Boston: Little, Brown, 1936). A child of Edith's New York, Mrs. Chanler emphasized their friendship with Theodore Roosevelt: "It was said of Edith Wharton and Theodore Roosevelt that they were both self-made men; she was pleased with the saying and repeated it to me." Mrs. Chanler noted the difficulty "for one brought up in worldly security, with the mental and spiritual inertia it so often engenders, to put himself through the discipline of attaining professional mastery in any field." Both of them, Mrs. Chanler observed, "grew up in the complacent atmosphere of New York's *haute bourgeoisie* in the later nineteenth century, and both won name and fame through their own efforts. . . ."

A considerable amount of solid biographical information and intelligent inference is also available in Millicent Bell's *Edith Wharton and Henry James: The Story of Their Friendship* (George Braziller, 1965). The record of this friendship is also enriched by the story as told from James's side, in Leon Edel's *Henry James: The Master, 1901-1916* (Philadelphia: J. B. Lippincott, 1972). More speculative, from the biographical viewpoint, is R. B. Dooley's "A Footnote to Edith Wharton" (*AL*, March 1954), which sees the novels as romans à clef, with one-to-one correspondences between Edith's acquaintances and her characters. A reliable and well-informed retrospective by one who knew her well is William R. Tyler's "Personal Memories of Edith Wharton" (*PMHS*, 1973).

Olivia Coolidge's *Edith Wharton: 1862-1937* (Charles Scribner's, 1964) is an engagingly written juvenile biography for girls and does not attempt to go beyond what is already known to the scholar about Mrs. Wharton as woman and writer. Grace Kellogg's *The Two Lives of Edith Wharton: The Woman and Her Work* (D. Appleton-Century, 1965) uncovers a few hitherto unpublicized facts about the novelist, but Miss Kellogg has an undisciplined imagination and is given to flights of fancy so extravagant that any student of the novelist who accepts her conclusions does so at his own risk. No scholar can concur with the biographer who concludes, on *no* evidence whatsoever, that the source of *Ethan Frome* must have been a familiar folk tale of Brittany, the Basque country, or some Alpine village, simply because New England winters are "too cheerful" to be described as Mrs. Wharton describes them in the work. On the other hand, a visually delightful book, but one sound in its critical overview of the woman, is Louis Auchincloss's pictorial biography, *Edith Wharton: A Woman in Her Time* (Viking Press, 1971), which contains more than one hundred photographs of Edith Wharton and her world.

Prior to the appearance of R. W. B. Lewis' *Edith Wharton: A Biography* (Harper & Row, 1975), Millicent Bell offered the supposition in *Edith Wharton and Henry James* that "the closed Yale collection will contain fewer revelations than most scholars have supposed." And E. K. Brown noted in "Edith Wharton" (*EA*, January-March, 1938) that "it is to her work that she would wish attention to be devoted, to her life and character only in so far as knowledge of them proved indispensable to illuminate her work."

But Lewis's biography, the definitive treatment of the novelist's life, did produce some surprises. A Pulitzer Prize winner, this massive work of nearly 600 pages, predicated in part on Erik Erikson's identity theory, covers (perhaps too briefly) the childhood of the writer in New York and Europe and, more comprehensively, the life of the social set in which Mrs. Wharton and her husband moved, her friendships, her development as a writer, her expatriation to Paris, and the years of maturity and decline. While the biography does not significantly alter our image of the woman and writer, Lewis's work does settle the nagging question of Edith Jones's paternity (she *was* her father's daughter). It also identifies Morton Fullerton, the American journalist in Paris, as the man with whom Mrs. Wharton had the torrid, if brief, love affair in 1908. And it prints for the first time the stunning fragment of fiction "Beatrice Palmato." This work outdoes Henry Miller for incestuous eroticism, if not for pornography. That the grande dame of American letters, sometimes written off as stiffly starched and hyperconservative, could have written so intensely erotic a story—and saved it for her future readers—indicates that Edith Wharton was not all whalebone and snobbish propriety. Lewis's biography tells her life with sensitivity and tact; it is not likely to be superseded in the near future.

CRITICISM

This section moves from early estimates to later, from general overviews to focused studies of issues, genres, books, and techniques—occasionally violating chronology to link essays and studies that overlap or treat comparable problems. Doctoral dissertations and newspaper reviews are omitted unless special attention seems warranted. For a list of dissertations the reader may consult Edward A. Sklepowich's "Edith Wharton" (*ALR*, Autumn 1975).

Before 1920

During the early years of Mrs. Wharton's career, she was the frequent subject of generally appreciative articles surveying broadly the whole, or a significant part, of her work. Taken together, these early essays raise most of the significant critical issues that still preoccupy her readers. Anna McClure Sholl's "The Work of Edith Wharton" (*Gunton's Magazine*, November 1903), for example, praised Mrs. Wharton's style, which, though she thought it artificial, is effectively illustrated in *The Greater Inclination* and *Crucial Instances*. Sholl spoke of Edith's "lambent masculine humor" in "The Pelican," which she called "one of the best short stories ever written." For Sholl, it is "for her beauty of style—artificial it may be, yet really beautiful—that Mrs. Wharton will always be read."

The publication of *The House of Mirth* (1905), a best seller, provoked a number of new critical studies. Louise Collier Willcox's "Edith Wharton" (*Outlook*, 25 November 1905) was apparently based on an interview, for, in analyzing the stories up through 1905, it cites a number of literary influences including James and de Maupassant; but "it is to Goethe above all other literary influences that Mrs. Wharton feels indebted." Erskine Steele's "Fiction and Social Ethics" (*SAQ*, July 1906) cited an important letter from Mrs. Wharton indicating her intention: to show the disastrous consequences to the individual who has no tradition of endearing values or center of early pieties. Charles Waldstein used *The House of Mirth* as the basis for a long essay on the classical and modern definition of tragedy and society in "Social Ideals" (*NAR*, June 1906).

Others were less complimentary. Henry Dwight Sedgwick, in "The Novels of Mrs. Wharton" (*AM*, August 1906), remarked on Mrs. Wharton's "cleverness" but not originality, arguing that her fiction was based on literature, not life, on artifice rather than on feeling. Sedgwick laid great stress on her feminine point of view in characterization, plot choice, and mentality. Her much remarked culture, evident in *The Valley of Decision*, Sedgwick described as "got up" from books. He felt that *The House of Mirth* lacked inevitability and failed to advance her talent, for, though it lacked poetry, it was nevertheless unobservant of "the regulations of realism and determinism." These views he expanded in *The New American Type and Other Essays* (Boston: Houghton Mifflin, 1908), where he condemned her lack of "originality, poetic feeling, humor, insight, romance, energy, or power." None of her characters had any reality for Sedgwick, and her works relied too much on chance, failing to observe "the primary tenets of realism." Sedgwick thought her next novel, *The Fruit of the Tree*, superior to *The House of Mirth* because of its more "serious purpose," and in a gesture at faint praise, he concluded, "who that is writing to-day can dispute with Mrs. Wharton the title to the term of brilliancy?"

To jump somewhat ahead, John Curtis Underwood's *Literature and Insurgency: Ten Studies in Racial Evolution* (Mitchell Kennerley, 1914) picked up Sedgwick's adjective in observing that "brilliancy is a patrician quality, of the superficial, by the superficial, for the superficial. It is intrinsically alien to the genius of the Anglo-Saxon world, in particular to that of its male half; and the great mass of the world in general has some reason for looking at it with suspicion." In this radical attack on the Genteel establishment, and on Mrs. Wharton as an "academician" in her art, Underwood condemned *The House of Mirth* as "one of the most insidiously immoral novels ever written." Still, he had to admit that Mrs. Wharton was "our most distinguished woman in American literature." This kind of attack on the patrician class she wrote about is also characteristic of the criticism of Robert Herrick, whose "Two Studies in Luxury" (*The Critic*, October-November 1906) condemned our "singularly unreal and aristocratic literature." Somewhat later, in "Mrs. Wharton's World" (*NewR*, 13 February 1915), Herrick went on to argue that Mrs. Wharton was too technically proficient, that she wrote "perhaps too consciously well." Herrick thought her even hampered by too close a knowledge of her social materials. For Herrick, Mrs. Wharton contributed little toward "painting in our national canvas" and was not, in fact, a "social historian." Herrick felt that her best work was about psychological problems not endemic to high society—stories about imaginary people she could not have known, like Ethan and Mattie, Justine and Amherst. In contemplating these criticisms, it is perhaps well to remember that Mrs. Wharton denied the claim that the novelist must deal only with the common experience, and she resented the view that the "social and educated being is an unreality unworthy of his attention, and that only the man with the dinner-pail is human, and hence available for his purpose" ("The Great American Novel," *YR*, July 1927).

If Henry D. Sedgwick emphasized Mrs. Wharton's feminine point of view, H. G. Dwight carried the theme one step further in "Edith Wharton" (*Putnam's Magazine*, February 1908). With some anxiety but more self-directed, male-deprecating humor, Dwight noted the emergence of women in America as a major aesthetic force and the problem of comparing them with men: "With Mrs. Wharton it is no longer a question of sex and comparisons." Dwight felt that the workmanship and significance of her thirteen books "set them entirely apart from the mass of contemporary writing." Dwight praised the high standard she maintained from book to book, and concluded that "she, almost alone among American writers, is not afraid to face the fact that the sorrow of the world often outweighs its joy, that good is most strangely intershot with evil, and that there are questions which it is worth asking how far soever they may lead." Who else, in the age of *Freckles* and *A Girl of the Limberlost*, was exploring such forbidden themes as euthanasia, as Mrs. Wharton did in *The Fruit of the Tree*?

Under the magazine pen name of "Calvin Winter," Frederick Taber Cooper's "Edith Wharton" (*Bookman*, May 1911) praised Mrs. Wharton's "rare mental subtlety and unusual breadth of culture," describing her as "a worldly-wise person with rather wide cosmopolitan sympathies yet with a rigid social caste." A few months later, after the appearance of *Ethan Frome*, Cooper condemned her, in "The Bigger Issues in Some Recent Books" (*Bookman*, November 1911), "for the utter remorselessness" of the *nouvelle*, observing that art for "art's sake is the one justification of a piece of work as perfect in technique as it is relentless in substance." Cooper expanded these views in *Some American Story Tellers* (Henry Holt, 1911), criticizing Mrs. Wharton's "relentless pursuit of a motive down to its ultimate analysis, her deliberate stripping off of the very last veils of pretense, showing us the sordidness and cowardice of human souls in all their nudity."

Edwin Björkman, in *Voices of To-Morrow* (Mitchell Kennerley, 1913), criticized *Ethan Frome* as being too one-sided, ignoring the social problems of rural poverty. James Huneker, in "Three Disagreeable Girls" (*Forum*, November 1914), linked Undine Spragg with Hedda Gabler and George Moore's Mildred Lawson as unpleasant types but not New Women. W. H. Boynton, in "Mrs. Wharton's Manner" (*Nation*, October 13, 1913), described her manner as suave, sophisticated, and feminine but full of latent restlessness. In captivating a magazine audience of women readers, in *The House of Mirth* and *The Custom of the Country*, Boynton argued, she gave fictional equivalents of the chit-chat of society columns like *Town-Talk*.

Henry James's *Notes on Novelists* (London: J. M. Dent, 1914) is rather more complimentary; in fact she is the only American noticed in his chapter on "The New Novel." Focusing on *The Custom of the Country*, with its concentrated distillation of novelistic elements and almost "scientific" satire, James praised the way her "masculine conclusion" tends "so to crown the feminine observation." Percy Lubbock's "The Novels of Edith Wharton" (*QR*, January 1915) surveyed all of the major novels before World War I and concluded that her books reflect "an imagination far more easily stimulated to work than induced to ruminate." Lubbock believed that the defect of the group was "their curious lack of anything that could be disengaged as a philosophy of life, a characteristic synthesis of belief." Lubbock also felt that Mrs. Wharton's fastidiousness cost her "the fullest possible intimacy with the stuff of character—especially of social character as opposed to individual."

During the war, William Lyon Phelps, in *The Advance of the English Novel* (Dodd, Mead, 1916), dissented from the common view that Edith Wharton was, if not "our foremost novelist," at least "at the head of all living American women who write books." He granted only *Ethan Frome* the title of "masterpiece," condemning *The Fruit of the Tree* as immoral on the ground that Justine is a murderer, not in the act of committing euthanasia but in referring to the wild horse: "the moment she mentions that dangerous beast, she is guilty of murder." Later, in *Twentieth Century American Novels* (Chicago: American Library Assn., 1927), Phelps dropped his dissent against her preeminence, observing that "By common consent, Edith Wharton stands at the head of American contemporary writers of fiction, and her career is synonymous with the century." "Professor Billy's" inconsistency, however, was often matched by his eccentricity: he once praised an unknown Edith Minter above Edith Wharton.

Meanwhile, Lawrence Gilman argued unsuccessfully, in "The Book of the Month: Mrs. Wharton Reverts to Shaw" (*NAR*, August 1917), that *Summer* owed its power to the Shavian theory of "the natural attraction of the sexes for one another." Gilman's theory that Charity Royall's affair illustrates the operation of the Life Force fulfilling its demand for motherhood is interesting but not demonstrated by this *nouvelle*.

Francis Hackett's "Mrs. Wharton's Art" (*NewR*, 10 February 1917; rptd. in *Horizons*, B. W. Heubsch, 1918) criticized the narrowness of Mrs. Wharton's character types, particularly in *Xingu and Other Stories*, observing that "these are not the kind of people with whom you share cracker-jack in a day coach. These are not the lads and lasses who put the skids under William H. Taft in 1912, abandoned themselves to 'Onward Christian Soldiers' at Chicago, and helped Mr. [Theodore] Roosevelt to be a traitor to his class." Nevertheless, Hackett liked her short fiction, singling out "Bunner Sisters" and "The Long Run," concluding that "Mrs. Wharton comes very near affording complete gratification with this volume of short stories." And while Régis Michaud's *Mystiques et réalistes anglo-saxons d'Emerson à Bernard Shaw* (Paris: A. Colin, 1918) was linking Mrs. Wharton with the realists, Helen Thomas and Wilson Follett were arguing, in *Some Modern Novelists* (Henry Holt, 1919), that her innovations broke down the barriers between genres and celebrating her "poised perfection of phrase."

EDITH WHARTON IN THE TWENTIES

By the 1920s, then, Mrs. Wharton was clearly a figure to reckon with, although appreciation was clearly divided by the critics' attitudes toward her style, subjects, and tone. In the year of *The Age of Innocence*, Charles Trueblood's "Edith Wharton" (*Dial*, January 1920) led off the decade by emphasizing, like Sedgwick, her "cleverness" and lack of originality. In judging her satire to be as noteworthy as her creative talent, Trueblood emphasized her detachment. Mrs. Wharton, Trueblood felt, failed to give us the "epic of America," and he denied her a place among the New Women: "The art of fiction would seem by now almost a traditional field for the assertion of feminine emancipation"; but according to Trueblood, Mrs. Wharton did not play that theme: "The emancipation of her sex is a note she does not sound, doubtless because she believes in equality." If she is to be called a New Woman, Trueblood concluded, she is doing "a relatively new thing for a New Woman to do: namely, defending some of the oldest things in civilization."

Carl Van Doren's "Contemporary American Authors: Edith Wharton" (*Nation*, 12 January 1921), which was subsumed into his *Contemporary American Novelists, 1900-1920* (Macmillan, 1922), contrasted her Four Hundred to O. Henry's Four Million as "ethnological exhibits." He found her a powerful analyst of social authority in *The House of Mirth*, of the tragedy of circumstance in *Ethan Frome* and *Summer*, and of the pathos of poverty in "Bunner Sisters." In defining her "natural instinctive habitat" as "a true tower of irony," Van Doren noted that she lacked James's "exuberance and richness of texture" but had "more intelligence than he."

This was more praise than V. L. Parrington was willing to give her in "Our Literary Aristocrat" in the *Pacific Review* (June 1921). Dismissing *The Age of Innocence* for ideological reasons made explicit in his *Main Currents*, he observed that "there is more hope for our literature in the honest crudities of the younger naturalists, than in her classic irony; they at least are trying to understand America as it is."

Katherine Fullerton Gerould, a novelist always paired with Mrs. Wharton as a disciple of James, observed of Mrs. Wharton's aristocrats, "let us hope that she never will abandon them." Mrs. Gerould's *Edith Wharton: A Critical Study* (D. Appleton, 1922) was an appreciative eleven-page publicity pamphlet distributed by Mrs. Wharton's publisher. In the same year, Henry Seidel Canby's *Definitions* (Harcourt, Brace, 1922) devoted a chapter to *The Age of Innocence*, noting that "a little canvas is enough for a great picture if the painting is good." Canby felt that if Mrs. Wharton was narrow, it was because her vision was beautifully focused. He concluded that the novel is "a fruit of our soil" and has "a reality that epics lack."

If Björkman had called Mrs. Wharton one of the "voices of tomorrow" in 1913, Percy Boynton saw her as an old-fashioned throwback to the age of Howells and James. In "American Authors Today: Edith Wharton" (*EJ*, January 1923; rptd. in *Some Contemporary Americans* (Chicago: University of Chicago Press, 1924), and enlarged in *Literature and American Life* (Boston: Ginn, 1936), Boynton sneered at her characters, observing, "God made them, therefore let them pass for men and women." In condemning the New York society her novels portray, Boynton observed of her personae that "spiritually they have the kind of phosphorescence that is caused in some organic matter by decay."

In *American Night's Entertainment* (D. Appleton, 1923; rptd. in *Authors of the Day*, Doran, 1924), and in *Cargoes for Crusoes* (D. Appleton, 1924), Grant Overton praised *The Age of Innocence* as "the novel of character at its finest" and quarreled with nitpickers who found factual inaccuracies in it. His judgment is called into question, however, by his ranking *Old New York* as superior to *The Age of Innocence*, calling these *nouvelles* "the finest things Mrs. Wharton has ever done with the exception of *Ethan Frome*." Later, in *The Women Who Make Our Novels* (Dodd, Mead, 1928), Grant Overton surveyed the novels and short stories, overpraising *The Mother's Recompense* but concluding that "No one of our time can write more beautifully." An interesting observation of Overton's suggests that there may be a regional bias, as well as an ideological one, involved in some of the critics' judgments of Mrs. Wharton. Speaking of Percy Boynton's *Some Contemporary Americans*, Overton argued, "Naturally a Chicagoan despises the effete society of Mrs. Wharton's pages." If so, the rather severe criticism of Herrick, Boynton, and Robert Morss Lovett should perhaps be seen in the light of Chicago's failure to become the literary capital Hamlin Garland and others hoped it would be.

Lovett's *Edith Wharton* (Robert M. McBride, 1925), a monograph in the "Modern American Writers" series, emphasized, from a liberal viewpoint, her treatment of the themes of culture, class, and morality. In noting her coldness, her defensive critical views, her snobbish personality, and the lucidity of her style, Lovett called her "profoundly ignorant of the relations of class with class, which is the vital issue of social morality today." In *The Main Stream* (Charles Scribner's, 1927), Stuart P. Sherman roundly contradicted Lovett's view of her knowledge of social relations and praised *The Mother's Recompense* for "the perfection of the design with its dainty intricacies all so perfectly subordinated to its unity of effect, and the neatness and completeness of the workmanship."

If Joseph Collins's *Taking the Literary Pulse* (Doran, 1924) argued that "one of Mrs. Wharton's greatest distinctions is that she is not sentimental," Osburt Burdett's "Edith Wharton" (*London Mercury*, November 1925; rptd. in *Contemporary American Authors*, edited by J. C. Squire, Henry Holt, 1928), called her characters "a projection less of intuition than of thought," but he praised her technical mastery as comparable to George Eliot's: "She has her craft, at least, at her finger's ends. In her novels we see the European tradition of the art of prose narrative essaying to master the contrast of life in the States." Other appreciative essays were written by Wilbur Cross in "Edith Wharton" (*Bookman*, August 1926), "Great Novelist of the American Scene" (*WR*, May 1929), and *Edith Wharton* (D. Appleton, 1926), a publisher's publicity pamphlet based on the *Bookman* essay. Meanwhile, Régis Michaud returned to her in *The American Novel To-Day* (Boston: Little, Brown, 1928), applying the psychoanalytic method, to excess, in the examination of her fiction.

At the close of the decade one of the most penetrating studies of the writer was published by Catherine Gilbertson in "Mrs. Wharton" (*Century*, August 1929). Disputing Lovett's claim that Mrs. Wharton was a throwback to the Victorians, Gilbertson praised her for the qualities of reasonableness, clarity, orderliness, the aristocratic tone and temper, dignity, poise founded on intelligence and sympathy, and the courage to be loyal to her vision of wisdom and beauty—the "enveloping virtues of the work she has produced." Gilbertson linked Mrs. Wharton's conception of culture and art to Arnold and Pater, preferring it to "the younger generation, intent upon its own antics," which is "looking the other way," and to "a generation not so young" which prefers "to drown in noisy naturalism the well-modulated voice of her better taste and greater wisdom." Gilbertson defended Mrs. Wharton from Carl Van Doren's charge that she was spectatorial and unpartisan, identifying her viewpoint as the "complete honesty that refuses to dogmatize, to tie itself up with causes and movements." Gilbertson also scored the militant feminists of the 1920s for misunderstanding *The Reef*, for failing to see that Mrs. Wharton's refusal to be propagandistic, her detached intelligence, made the novel still worth reading in 1929, even though the double standard in sexual mores was passing away. For Gilbertson, Mrs. Wharton's audience did not die out in 1914; the novelist still had a great deal to say to the generation of the 1920s and 1930s.

EDITH WHARTON IN THE THIRTIES

Blake Nevius begins his book on Mrs. Wharton by noting that "to a generation of writers nurtured on social realism, . . . she had nothing to teach except by way of negative example." The proletarian passion, for better or worse, also infused the criticism of the decade, reinforcing the twenties' attack on the genteel tradition, its customs and moral conventions. Granville Hicks, for example, argued in *The Great Tradition* (Macmillan, 1935) that Mrs. Wharton surrendered the obligation to criticize contemporary America and turned instead to historical romances like *The Age of Innocence* (revealing thereby that he had not read *Twilight Sleep, The Glimpses of the Moon, The Children*—works of the 1920s which, however weak, do satirize postwar manners). Ludwig Lewisohn's *Expression in America* (Harper & Bros., 1932) dismissed Mrs. Wharton rather smugly, wondering "that at so late an age a woman as intelligent as Edith Wharton could have taken seriously the conventions of a small and unimportant social group." Even Henry Seidel Canby, who had praised her "fine art of narrative" as "a fruit of our soil" in *Definitions* (Harcourt, Brace, 1922), changed his tune in the 1930s, dismissing her because "Mrs. Wharton did not have America to write about. She had only the soiled egret feathers and false decorations" (*SatRL*, 21 August 1937). When Canby came to write on her work in the *Literary History of the United States* (Macmillan, 1948) he tempered his view, observing merely that Glasgow, Gale, and other "regional" novelists of manners "saw America in a national perspective as Edith could not."

Pelham Edgar returns the focus from geography to aesthetics in "Edith Wharton" in *The Art of the Novel* (Macmillan, 1933), as does Frances T. Russell in "Edith Wharton's Use of Imagery" (*EJ*, June 1932), a perceptive early study of the ways images convey her themes. Less complimentary is Frances T. Russell's "Melodramatic Mrs. Wharton" (*SR*, October-December 1932), which identifies a penchant in Mrs. Wharton for the sentimental, soft, and melodramatic. Equally critical is Harry Hartwick's overview of the novels in *The Foreground of American Fiction* (American Book Co., 1934), which subsumes the works under two themes: the decline of the old aristocracy and the inevitability of punishment for social transgressors, no matter how unfair the punishment may be. Hartwick argues, rather unsuccessfully, that Mrs. Wharton's problems are problems "of a class rather than those of mankind, problems that would never arise outside of a drawing-room." Russell Blankenship's *American Literature as an Expression of the National Mind* (Henry Holt, 1936) characterizes Mrs.

Wharton as a first-rate disciple of James and a satirist in the Lewis mode. In claiming her as "one of the finest novelists now writing in English," he notes only one major defect in her work—"her reticent objectivity sometimes leads her into a chilliness of temper." But in an age of proletarian passion, Blankenship finds the change of tone "refreshing."

E. K. Brown's *Edith Wharton: Etude Critique* (Paris: E. Droz, 1935), the second full-length study of the novelist (Lovett's was the first), is a revision of Brown's Sorbonne dissertation and is written in French. Brown was a perceptive critic, always pleasurable to read; his analysis of the novels and stories is informed and sensitive. Occasionally, however, he was dazzled by works which are no longer highly valued. *The Children*, for example, he thought one of her best; recent critics have given it short shrift. He did not think very highly of *The House of Mirth*; it may well be her best. An index of the difference between Lovett and Brown is that Lovett saw Mrs. Wharton's world view as essentially comic, whereas Brown saw her view of life as ironic. A fine overview of her work in English is also available in E. K. Brown's "Edith Wharton" (*EA*, January-March 1938).

Arthur Hobson Quinn's *American Fiction: An Historical and Critical Survey* (D. Appleton-Century, 1936) surveys Mrs. Wharton's work, identifying her as "our chief social satirist," noting that "with Edith Wharton the supreme artist in modern American fiction emerges"—high praise indeed in a comprehensive survey of the art of fiction. A comparable judgment is recorded in Harlan Hatcher's *Creating the Modern American Novel* (Farrar and Rinehart, 1935), which claims for her "an honored and unique place" in the development of the modern novel in America: "She is an artist." Less perceptive is Walter Fuller Taylor's *A History of American Letters* (American Book Co., 1936), which wrongly asserts a preference in Edith Wharton for "a symmetrically formed novel." In surveying her major works, he also wrongly proposes that Mrs. Wharton "adopted the highly unified point of view employed in James's *The Ambassadors*." For some reason Taylor feels that "Mrs. Wharton thus eschews the loose, biographical method so popular in the English novel, in favor of the more classical, more deliberately architectonic planning characteristic of James." This claim is flatly contradicted by *A Backward Glance*, where Mrs. Wharton condemns James's sacrifice of everything to geometrical design. Novels like *The Custom of the Country, Hudson River Bracketed, The Buccaneers,* and others are principally biographical and unroll as episodic chronical novels.

In a chapter called "The Feminine Novel," Fred Lewis Pattee's *The New American Literature, 1890-1930* (Century, 1937) grouped Mrs. Wharton with Gertrude Atherton, Kate Douglas Wiggin, Ellen Glasgow, Willa Cather, and Zona Gale, emphasizing how she applied a "Gallic" technique (under the influence of Stendhal, Balzac, Flaubert, and Turgenev) to American materials of limited scope. An easy mark for those critics who wanted the great American novel, Mrs. Wharton is dismissed by Pattee with the observation that "of the great, quivering, suffering, laboring human mass, she knows little...." Q. D. Leavis, however, was more complimentary, in "Henry James's Heiress" (*Scrutiny*, December 1938), although she argued that Mrs. Wharton's values are principally negative: "her values emerging I suppose as something other than what she exposes as worthless." Mrs. Leavis held that "this is not very nourishing, and it is on similar grounds that Flaubert, so long admired as the ideal artist of the novel, has begun to lose esteem. It seems to be the fault of the disintegrating and spiritually impoverished society she analyzes. Her value," for Mrs. Leavis, "is that she does analyze and is not content to reflect."

At the time of her death, Wilson Follett, in "What Edith Wharton Did—and Might Have Done" (*NYTBR*, 5 September 1937) was stunned by the size of her *oeuvre.* Noting that "the critical historian who would see Mrs. Wharton whole has to begin his study with four feet of books," Follett praised her consummate style, her achievement having "a quantitative solidity almost monumental and not exceeded by the more obvious brilliance of its parts...." He marveled at her variety of themes, character types, and styles, suggesting that she changed her audience with her changing themes. Follett noted that late in her life she discovered American history; he felt that if she had lived longer she might also have discovered America itself and produced living novels about the "real life" of the country. A comparable summary article, at her death, was written by C. John McCole, in "Some Notes on Edith Wharton" (*CW*, January 1938). Her weaknesses, for McCole, were these: she should have stopped writing fifteen years earlier, before her work became tenuous and tedious; she maintained a "tiresome allegiance to the thin outer shell of society, rather than to the inner core of humanity"; she gave too much emphasis to social, not enough to moral, sanctions; her use of coincidence was excessive; and she was too much given to melodrama. Her strengths he identified as her artistry in "recreating atmospheres"; her gift for scenic development; her facility for making the significant detail serve the plot; her feeling for undertones and overtones of compressed emotion; her gift for the telling phrase put to the service of irony and satire; her effective sense of humor; her command of *le mot juste*; her technical proficiency in various fictional forms; and her support of the idea of tradition in a chaotic and discontinuous age.

Edith Wharton Since 1940

Mrs. Wharton's death in 1937, as some of the previous essays suggest, called for a comprehensive overview of the woman and her work. And the overall thinness of many of the criticisms of her work during her lifetime led Edmund Wilson to observe at her death that her critics had done her "something less than justice." Although other writers had received comprehensive attention, at the time of her death only two brief book-length studies had been devoted to her work—one a partial portrait by Lovett (written when she still had fourteen books yet to publish), the other, by Brown, written in French.

Wilson sought to rectify the problem in "Justice to Edith Wharton" (*NewR*, 19 June 1938; rptd. in *The Wound and the Bow*, Oxford University Press, 1941). Wilson defended her as a woman whose failed marriage and maladjustment in the society of New York turned her into "a passionate social prophet." In thus identifying the psychic genesis of her art, Wilson described her as "a brilliant example of the writer who relieves an emotional strain by denouncing his generation."

In a like effort to do justice to the novelist, Olga Avendaño de Valdivia published a long study, in six chapters and an appendix, in the *Andean Quarterly* for the Summer 1943-1944; Summer 1944; Winter 1944; Spring 1944; and Christmas, 1944 issues. Entitled "Edith Wharton," this sensible study of nearly ninety double-columned pages is broad in scope, treating the writer's life (based on *A Backward Glance*), her theory of the novel, *nouvelle*, and short story (based on *The Writing of Fiction*), her themes and characters, her literary influences, her psychological predispositions, her international preoccupations, her sense of style, her conception of morality, and her philosophy of life. An instance of Olga de Valdivia's provocative analysis is suggested by her claim that Mrs. Wharton unconsciously reflected the New Humanism of Irving Babbitt in adhering to a belief "in the sense of decorum as a guide to moral behaviour."

The first scholarly full-length treatment of Mrs. Wharton's work after her death was Blake Nevius's *Edith Wharton: A Study of Her Fiction* (Berkeley: University of California Press, 1953). Although his study lacks biographical data and the evidence contained in her restricted papers, Nevius competently interwove what was generally known about Mrs. Wharton with illuminating criticism of her novels and stories. His study was based on the claim that there are three major reasons why Edith Wharton should have a permanent claim on our attention. First, she is "the only American novelist who has dealt successfully and at length with that feudal remainder in New York society which hardly survived the beginning of the present century." Second, Mrs. Wharton overcame her limitations by exploiting two great interlocking themes; one was "the spectacle of a large and generous nature . . . trapped by circumstances ironically of its own devising into consanguinity with a meaner nature"; the other was the related problem of trying to define "the nature and limits of individual responsibility, to determine what allowance of freedom or rebellion can be made for her trapped protagonist without at the same time threatening the structure of society." The third reason why Mrs. Wharton deserves study is that "she is, next to Henry James, our most successful novelist of manners—not an extravagant claim in view of the limited competition in what to Americans seems to be an alien and difficult genre." While Nevius is inaccurate as to the importance and prevalence of this genre, his study is a useful and instructive introduction to her fiction.

Less satisfying is Marilyn Jones Lyde's *Edith Wharton: Convention and Morality in the Work of a Novelist* (Norman: University of Oklahoma Press, 1959). This study, full of illuminating insights, is given over to an unfortunately rigid thesis about convention and morals. In Lyde's scheme, the moral issues in Mrs. Wharton's work are always analyzed into the three terms of a syllogism, of which the components are the individual, society, and a resulting action of either revolt or submission.

Millicent Bell's *Edith Wharton and Henry James: The Story of Their Friendship* (George Braziller, 1965) is the best source for details about the literary and biographical relationship between these two fascinating writers. Based on a fresh and extensive use of many unpublished letters in the Houghton Library of Harvard University, the book completes in an admirable way the picture suggested in Professor Bell's earlier article, "Edith Wharton and Henry James: The Literary Relationship" (*PMLA*, December 1959).

Geoffrey Walton's *Edith Wharton: A Critical Introduction* (Rutherford, N.J.: Fairleigh Dickinson University Press, 1970) argues that Mrs. Wharton is greatly misunderstood by the critics—"Brooks, for example, or Blake Nevius, who devoted a whole critical book to her novels" but who "shows less understanding of her than did Henry Dwight Sedgwick or R. M. Lovett writing in her lifetime." Walton sought to rectify the misunderstanding by surveying Mrs. Wharton's fiction in thematic groups—tragedy in the upper-class and middle-class society; comedy in society; satire on society; social change and moral problems; the writer in the community, and so forth. Walton, an English critic, does not pretend to know the New York City or New England worlds Mrs. Wharton wrote about, and his analysis lacks adequate reference to the literary history of Mrs. Wharton's time. Nevertheless, with "proper diffidence," Walton concludes that Edith Wharton is the equal of Jane Austen.

Gary Lindberg's *Edith Wharton and the Novel of Manners* (Charlottesville: University Press of Virginia, 1975) undertakes to "assess Edith Wharton's qualities and contributions as a novelist"; "to explore ways of analyzing the novel of manners and the meaning of society in fiction"; and "to provide careful and broad-based readings of her three most important novels"—*The House of Mirth, The Custom of the Country*, and *The Age of Innocence*. These ambitions are perhaps too grand for so exiguous a book, lacking, as it does, an adequate definition of manners, of the novel of manners, and of techniques endemic to the form. Lindberg is at his best in giving partial analyses of the three novels, but a fundamental, unresolved philosophic antipathy divides him from Mrs. Wharton's characters and their plights: he is basically unsympathetic to the effects of the power of social convention as she dramatizes it and prefers "Adamic" rebels (Hester, Huck) in conflict with the powers of social convention, characters who "as Melville puts it, . . . say NO! in thunder." In other words, Lindberg prefers romances, not novels of manners. For Mrs. Wharton, the idea of the

Adamic character was naive, since there is no self independent of what she called "the web of custom, manners, culture" which the self "has elaborately spun about itself."

The Twayne's United States Authors Series continues to expand and now includes Margaret McDowell's *Edith Wharton* (Boston: Twayne, 1976), which includes "Viewing the Custom of Her Country: Edith Wharton's Feminism" (*ConL*, Autumn 1974) and much else so as to make a fine introduction to the study of Mrs. Wharton's work. Also introductory in intent is Richard H. Lawson's *Edith Wharton* (Frederick Ungar, 1977), a 118-page contribution to the publisher's Modern Literary Monographs series.

One of the most effective recent book-length critical studies is Cynthia Griffin Wolff's *A Feast of Words: The Triumph of Edith Wharton* (Oxford University Press, 1977), which undertakes to explain how Edith Wharton, "one of the half-dozen greatest novelists that America has produced," should have written as well as she did, and indeed, why she wrote at all. Wolff's questions are elucidated by means of psychological analysis. Wolff believes that Edith "sustained neglect at what Erik Erikson has called the 'oral-respiratory-sensory stage.'" Her mother's rejection of the sensitive child becomes apparent in the pervasive imagery, throughout the novels, of coldness, claustral isolation, and starvation. As a compensation for her "oral deprivation," young Edith Jones turned to orality— words—and substituted "the act of communication for the more gratifying comforts of passive receptivity." While this puts the matter rather baldly, Wolff argues her thesis with subtlety and tact in identifying the sources of tension in Wharton's work. Perhaps the most original aspect of the book is the treatment of *The Custom of the Country*, where the obnoxious Undine Spragg is shown convincingly to be a reflection of the author's drive and psychic energy.

These book-length studies of Mrs. Wharton's work have begun the task of recovering her critical reputation—or at least of putting it in a clearer and truer historical and critical perspective. Werner Berthoff has claimed in *The Ferment of Realism* (The Free Press, 1965) that "rumors of critical neglect of Edith Wharton have been exaggerated." But, now that the biographical record is available, much remains to be done to make Mrs. Wharton's works understood and more justly appreciated. For as Irving Howe noted in 1962 in editing a collection of articles on her fiction, "the amount of first-rate criticism devoted to Mrs. Wharton's novels is small"; he was led to conclude that "justice has not yet come to Edith Wharton."

Some of that first-rate criticism is of course reprinted in Howe's *Edith Wharton: A Collection of Critical Essays* (Englewood Cliffs, N.J.: Prentice-Hall, 1962), which, of the works so far discussed, includes Wilson's "Justice to Edith Wharton," Lubbock's "The Novels of Edith Wharton," Brown's "Edith Wharton," Q. D. Leavis's "Henry James's Heiress: The Importance of Edith Wharton," Parrington's "Our Literary Aristocrat," Wilson's review of Lubbock's biography called "Edith

Wharton: A Memoir by an English Friend," and excerpts from Nevius's *Edith Wharton* which discuss *Ethan Frome* and *The Age of Innocence*. In addition to these are a number of other valuable essays. Louis Auchincloss's "Edith Wharton and Her New Yorks" (*PR*, July-August 1951; rptd. here and in Auchincloss's *Reflections of a Jacobite*, Boston: Houghton Mifflin, 1961) argues that the subject of her main study was "the assault upon an old and conservative group by the multitudes enriched, and fabulously enriched, by the business expansion of the preceding decades." At her best Auchincloss judges her as "an analyst of the paralysis that attends failure in the market place and of the coarseness that attends success," observing that "hers was not a world where romance was apt to flourish." (These views are expanded in Auchincloss's fine Minnesota pamphlet *Edith Wharton* [Minneapolis: University of Minnesota Press, 1961]; rptd. in *Seven Modern American Novelists* [Minneapolis: University of Minnesota Press, 1964], edited by William Van O'Connor).

Irving Howe's collection also includes Alfred Kazin's discussion of Mrs. Wharton, first published as "The Lady and the Tiger: Edith Wharton and Theodore Dreiser" (*VQR*, Winter 1941) and reprinted in *On Native Grounds* (Doubleday, 1942). Kazin's thesis is that Mrs. Wharton was "not so much interested in the accession of the new class as she was in the destruction of her own, in the eclipse of its finest spirits." In this, Kazin feels that she missed her true subject, "the emerging new class of brokers and industrialists, the makers and promoters of the industrial era. . . ." The upshot of her alienation was a disposition to tragedy and a commitment to art. But since Wharton never gave us a "conception of America as a unified and dynamic economy, or even as a single culture," "a great artist, even a completely devoted artist, she never became." Kazin finds Dreiser admirable by comparison, for reasons which those interested in art may find difficult to fathom. Irving Howe also reprints E. K. Brown's "Edith Wharton: The Art of the Novel," originally published in *The Art of the Novel*, edited by Pelham Edgar (Macmillan, 1933). In this essay Brown contrasts her with George Eliot, analyzes her narrative point of view, explores her friendship with Theodore Roosevelt, and defines the principles of his social criticism as "not far removed from the better principles of his social action." (Other essays in the Howe anthology will be discussed later, in connection with the specific novels to which they refer.)

Topics and Issues; Individual Works

From here on, the criticism will be grouped according to topics and issues that recur in the article- or chapter-length criticism of Mrs. Wharton's work.

On Edith Wharton as a novelist of manners, the reader may profitably consult, in addition to Lindberg's book, Christof Wegelin's "The Rise of the International Novel" (*PMLA*, June 1962), which links her to the tradition of Howells and James, and H. E. Hierth's "The Class Novel" (*CEA*,

December 1964), which explores her sense of social stratification. H. Wayne Morgan's essay "Edith Wharton: The Novelist of Manners and Morals" in *Writers in Transition* (Hill and Wang, 1963) is marred by factual errors but is sensitive to "the central theme which emerged from Mrs. Wharton's work"—"not manners, but morality—the question of ethical conduct in society amid the problems of human relations." James W. Tuttleton's "Edith Wharton: Social Historian of Old New York" in *The Novel of Manners in America* (Chapel Hill: University of North Carolina Press, 1972) relates Mrs. Wharton to the American tradition of the social novel, which is by no means a genre alien to this country, as Nevius mistakenly suggests. In exploring the way manners determine the fate of her characters, Tuttleton establishes Mrs. Wharton as the major link between the generation of Howells and James and that of Fitzgerald, Lewis, and Auchincloss, between the nineteenth- and twentieth-century American novel of manners.

Among her older critics, Sedgwick, Dwight, and Overton linked Mrs. Wharton with the issue of feminism. In addition to the book-length studies of McDowell and Wolff this fruitful approach is also reflected in Josephine L. Jessup's *The Faith of Our Feminists* (Richard R. Smith, 1950). If there is a claim to be made on the score of Mrs. Wharton's "feminism," Jessup does the job inadequately, failing to convince the reader that "for the space of twenty novels she attempts to show woman preëminent, man trailing at heel." Rather more sensible is George Snell's essay in *The Shapers of American Fiction, 1798-1947* (E. P. Dutton, 1947), which argues that Mrs. Wharton, a Jamesian, was a valuable model of the woman writer for Willa Cather, Susan Glaspell, Ellen Glasgow, and Ruth Suckow. The culmination of F. L. Pattee's many studies of women as writers and subjects of fiction seems to be Louis Auchincloss's *Pioneers and Caretakers: A Study of Nine American Women Novelists* (Minneapolis: University of Minnesota Press, 1965), which argues that our major women novelists, Mrs. Wharton among them, are "conservators" of our cultural, social, and moral traditions.

On Edith Wharton as a poet, the reader may consult Brian Hooker's "Some Springtime Verse" (*Bookman*, June 1909). Hooker found the poetry intellectual and dry, modelled on Tennyson, Stephen Phillips, Rossetti, and Browning, cumbersome in its blank verse, and troubled in its rhymes. He concluded that it was not good poetry but that the volume showed "how high in poetry a thoroughly cultivated prose artist may attain." The reader may also consult Robert Sencourt's "The Poetry of Edith Wharton" (*Bookman*, July 1931), which overpraises her verse; and Blake Nevius's "Pussie Jones's Verses: A Bibliographical Note on Edith Wharton" (*AL*, January 1952).

On Edith Wharton and her correspondence, the reader will profit from Louis Auchincloss's "Edith Wharton and Her Letters" (*Hofstra Review*, Winter 1967); Hilda Fife's "Letters from Edith Wharton to Vernon Lee" (*CLQ*, February 1953); and Frederick R. Karl's "Three Conrad Letters in the Edith Wharton Papers" (*YULG*, January 1970). As previously noted, there is as yet no edition of Mrs. Wharton's letters. Mary Pitlick is reportedly preparing one, however.

On Edith Wharton as a writer of short stories and *nouvelles*, the following essays are invaluable. Blanche C. Williams's discussion of Mrs. Wharton in *Our Short Story Writers* (Moffat, Yard, 1920) analyzes various "crucial instances" in the tales, noting the inversion so often since remarked. Pattee's *The Development of the American Short Story* (Harper and Bros., 1923) rates Mrs. Wharton very highly, observing that her short fiction "shines among the mass of writings of the period like a diamond in a tray of beads." Edward J. O'Brien's *The Advance of the American Short Story* (Dodd, Mead, 1931) lumped Mrs. Wharton with Gerould and Anne Douglas Sedgwick as a member of "The School of Henry James," noting her "arctic frigidity" and concluding that "her collected short stories form a superb *pastiche* of Henry James with little added."

Patricia R. Plante's "Edith Wharton as Short Story Writer" (*MQR*, July 1963) is especially useful for determining the critical reception of Mrs. Wharton's volumes of short stories. In view of the high praise initially given them, Plante is rightly puzzled at the decline in Mrs. Wharton's reputation as a short story writer. Although it is clear that Mrs. Wharton's tales were put in the shade by the short stories of Anderson, Hemingway, Fitzgerald, and Faulkner, Plante expresses the hope that Edith Wharton will "continue to be read by a discriminating audience because of her mastery of form and language and because of a few ideas which will always deserve universal attention."

Margaret B. McDowell's "Edith Wharton's Ghost Stories" (*Criticism*, Spring 1970) takes a less exalted stance, comparing Mrs. Wharton to James and Hawthorne. In McDowell's judgment, the ghost stories are "the work of a mature and sophisticated artist." R. W. B. Lewis's "Powers of Darkness" (*TLS*, 13 June 1975) is also acutely illuminating on the ghost tales. Joan V. Greenwood has published three studies of the short fiction: "The Implications of Marital Status in Edith Wharton's Short Stories and *Nouvelles*"; "The Importance of Milieu in Edith Wharton's Short Stories and *Nouvelles*"; and "The Nature and Results of Conflict in Edith Wharton's Short Stories and *Nouvelles*." All three appeared in *Kobe College Studies* (in the October 1958, February 1959, and June 1959 issues). Further evidence of Japanese interest in Mrs. Wharton is suggested by Ichiro Tanjimoto's ambiguously entitled "The Stream of the Views on the Short Story in America" (*Cultural Science Reports*, October 1962). Finally, R. W. B. Lewis's "Introduction" to *The Collected Short Stories of Edith Wharton* (Charles Scribner's, 1968) offers an eighteen-page discussion of some of the eighty-six tales she wrote, of which Lewis judges twenty to be "very good indeed."

On Edith Wharton's juvenilia and early career, the reader may consult "The Early Edith Wharton" (*TLS*, 20 March 1953), as well as Viola Hopkins Winner's very fine essay, "Convention and Prediction in Edith

Wharton's *Fast and Loose*" (*AL*, March 1970), which sees her now published juvenile novella as foreshadowing the subjects, themes and style of Mrs. Wharton's mature works. G. M. Loney has admirably described Mrs. Wharton's connection with the playwright Clyde Fitch in "Edith Wharton and *The House of Mirth:* The Novelist Writes for the Theater" (*MD*, Spring 1961). And Mrs. Wharton's complicated relationship with her publisher Charles Scribner and her editors William Crary Brownell and Edward Burlingame is admirably told in Millicent Bell's "Lady into Author: Edith Wharton and the House of Scribner" (*AQ*, Fall 1957). Mrs. Wharton's break with Charles Scribner over the publication of *Literature* and her shift to Appleton in 1917 reveal a hardheaded practicality from which Scribner never recovered. Edith Wharton's activities during World War I and the literary reflection of them in *The Marne*, *Fighting France* and *A Son at the Front* are intelligently discussed in Peter Buitenhuis's "Edith Wharton and the First World War" (*AQ*, Fall 1966). Buitenhuis offers her attitudes toward European civilization as a useful corrective of the more negative views of Pound and others, for whom Europe was a "botched civilization." A comparably useful overview of her treatment of the war is offered by David Clough in "Edith Wharton's War Novels: A Reappraisal" (*TCL*, January 1973), which should be read alongside Stanley Cooperman's *World War I and the American Novel* (Baltimore: The Johns Hopkins University Press, 1967).

The fruitful connection between Edith Wharton and other writers has been a rich field for Wharton criticism. Her relationship with James has of course received greatest attention—most extensively in Millicent Bell's *Edith Wharton and Henry James*, which incorporates her earlier essays, for example, "A James Gift to Edith Wharton" (*MLN*, March 1957), and in Leon Edel's *Henry James: The Master*, which gathers up some of the information in his 1966 address, "Henry James, Edith Wharton and Newport," published by the Redwood Library and Newport Atheneum. This relationship, though admirably close and mutually fulfilling, was not always satisfying for James, who was fond of calling her the "Angel of Devastation" and the "pendulum" woman. Adeline R. Tintner finds a Jamesian satire on Mrs. Wharton in "James's Mock Epic: 'The Velvet Glove,' Edith Wharton, and Other Late Tales" (*MFS*, Winter 1971-1972). Tintner also examines the writers' satiric treatment of each other in "The Metamorphoses of Edith Wharton in Henry James's *The Finer Grain*" (*TCL*, December 1975) and in "'The Hermit and the Wild Woman': Edith Wharton's 'Fictioning' of Henry James" (*JML*, September 1974).

The literary relation is also explored in James W. Tuttleton's "Henry James and Edith Wharton: Fiction As the House of Fame" (*MASJ*, Spring 1966), which explores the old argument between behaviorist and impressionist novelists over whether houses, furniture, clothes, and the like can, in fiction, "constitute" or express character. Abigail Ann Hamblen's "The

Jamesian Note in Edith Wharton's *The Children*" (*UKCR*, March 1965) and Vittoria Sanna's "I romanzi di Edith Wharton e la narrativa jamesiana" (*SA*, 1964) also explore the Master's technical influence. On this score, Q. D. Leavis's "Henry James's Heiress: The Importance of Edith Wharton," reprinted in the Howe anthology cited above, should be mentioned here, for Mrs. Leavis accurately notes, in surveying the writer's work, that "the American novel grew up with Henry James and achieved a tradition with Mrs. Wharton."

The connection between Mrs. Wharton and Sinclair Lewis has been less definitively handled. K. S. Rothwell has been most acute in "From Society to Babbittry: Lewis' Debt to Edith Wharton" (*JCMVASA*, Spring 1960). Hilton Anderson has identified "A Whartonian Woman in *Dodsworth*" in the *Sinclair Lewis Newsletter* (Spring 1969). Anderson even sees Mrs. Wharton as a character in her own novels in "Edith Wharton as a Fictional Heroine" (*SAQ*, Winter 1970). Incidentally, Mrs. Wharton is said to be fictionally satirized in Hamilton Basso's *The Greenroom* (Doubleday, 1949).

Edith Wharton's notorious meeting with F. Scott Fitzgerald is taken up in "What Really Happened at the Pavillon Colombe" (*Fitzgerald Newsletter*, Fall 1959) and Arthur Mizener gives his version of the encounter in *The Far Side of Paradise* (Boston: Houghton Mifflin, 1965) and in "Scott Fitzgerald and Edith Wharton" (*TLS*, 7 July 1966). But Andrew Turnbull defends his own version of the tale in the *TLS* for 29 September 1966. None of this biographical bickering has the central importance of Frederick J. Hoffman's excellent essay "Points of Moral Reference: A Comparative Study of Edith Wharton and F. Scott Fitzgerald," in the *English Institute Essays, 1949* (Columbia University Press, 1950). Aspects of this relationship—suggested by Gilbert Seldes's claim in "Spring Flight" (*Dial*, August 1925) that Fitzgerald learned the scenic method from James through the example of Mrs. Wharton—are also explored in Tuttleton's *The Novel of Manners in America.* Aside from James, Lewis, and Fitzgerald, the literary connections are rather thin and not easily documented, although a number of peripheral articles listed in Springer's reference guide and the annual bibliographies of *PMLA* are suggestive.

The following sections will deal with articles on individual novels, which, incidentally, are also analyzed in many of the book-length studies discussed above. In "*The House of Mirth* Revisited" (*HB*, December 1947; rptd. in the *American Scholar*, Winter 1962-1963, and in the Howe anthology), Diana Trilling argues that *The House of Mirth* is a "class" novel expressing "one of the most telling indictments of a social system based on the chance distribution of wealth, and therefore of social privilege, that has ever been put on paper." Marie Bristol's "Life Among the Ungentle Genteel: Edith Wharton's *The House of Mirth* Revisited" (*WHR*, Autumn 1962) argues that Edith Wharton was a naturalist and resents the automatic inclusion of

Mrs. Wharton among the Genteel writers, including James ("that dried-up old virgin who never did anything more strenuous than lift an oyster fork."). Less rhetorically flamboyant, and less appreciative, is V. S. Pritchett's essay in *The Living Novel and Later Appreciations* (Random House, 1964), which describes Mrs. Wharton's "republic of the spirit" as "a new kind of puritan snobbery" and *The Age of Innocence* as "a surrender to the established bourgeois standard." He notes that "we mistrust her at once when, late in life, she becomes benign."

One of the best interpretations of the novel is Irving Howe's "Introduction" to *The House of Mirth* in the Rinehart paperback edition (1962). There Howe observes that "when one reads and submits to the urgencies of a novel like *The House of Mirth*, the effect is that of being held in a steady, inexorable enclosure. Mrs. Wharton's sense of the inescapability of waste—the waste of spirit, the waste of energy, the waste of beauty—comes to seem a root condition of human life." R. W. B. Lewis's essay on *The House of Mirth* in *Trials of the Word* (New Haven: Yale University Press 1965) is a reprint of his Introduction to the New York University Press paperback edition of the novel. Its value lies in Lewis's analysis of Mrs. Wharton's manuscript revisions.

At the end of *The House of Mirth*, an "unspoken word" passes between Lily and Selden, which Mrs. Wharton does not articulate. James W. Gargano undertakes to identify it as "faith" in "*The House of Mirth:* Social Utility and Faith" (*AL*, March 1972). For Gargano, Mrs. Wharton's theme "insists that personal integrity represents an act of faith in a spiritual order beyond the disorder of the world of appearances."

Richard Poirier, however, differs on the convincingness of the ending. In *"The House of Mirth"* in *The American Novel from James Fenimore Cooper to William Faulkner*, edited by Wallace Stegner (Basic Books, 1965), a paper originally designed for oral presentation over the Voice of America, Poirier argues rather persuasively that Mrs. Wharton could not "authenticate her sentiments about compassion and kinship," so that the conclusion of the novel seems contrived. Walter Rideout is preoccupied with fictional links in "Edith Wharton's *The House of Mirth*" in *Twelve Original Essays on Great American Novels*, edited by Charles Shapiro (Detroit: Wayne State University Press, 1958). Arguing that the accidents of Mrs. Wharton's chronology prevent us from doing her total justice, Rideout objects to our dismissing her "as one of the best in a bad time, without quite realizing how good in an absolute sense that best could be." He rectifies the injustice by providing a close reading of the novel's overall structure in terms of the chapter organization of the book.

A number of the more recent articles on *The House of Mirth* have accentuated Lily Bart as a beautiful object, made so by the marital mores of the time and by the materialism of New York society. Robert McIlvaine's "Edith Wharton's American Beauty Rose" (*JAmS*, August 1973) finds the flower imagery of the novel to derive from John D. Rockefeller's 1902 speech comparing the cultivation of the American Beauty Rose to American business practices. Cynthia G. Wolff's "Lily Bart and the Beautiful Death" (*AL*, March 1974) and Judith Fetterley's "'The Temptation to Be a Beautiful Object': Double Standard and Double Bind in *The House of Mirth*" (*SAF*, Autumn 1979) both explore the cost to human fineness of the treatment by society of Lily Bart. Much the same critical orientation is expressed by Constance Rooke in "Beauty in Distress: *Daniel Deronda* and *The House of Mirth*" (*W&L*, Fall 1976).

Anne Friman has grappled with the question of free will versus determinism in *The House of Mirth* in "Determinism and Point of View in *The House of Mirth*" (*PLL*, Summer 1966). And James W. Tuttleton's "Edith Wharton: High Priestess of Reason" (*Personalist*, Summer 1966) concludes, on the basis of this novel, that Mrs. Wharton's determinism is more apparent than real.

The Age of Innocence has also drawn a great deal of attention, as the previous decade survey has suggested. Here let me group some of the more recent essays. Louis Kronenberger's "Edith Wharton's New York: Two Period Pieces" (*MQR*, Winter 1965; rptd. in *The Polished Surface: Essays in the Literature of Worldliness*, Alfred A. Knopf, 1969), is a model of graceful analysis, exploring *The House of Mirth* and *The Age of Innocence* as "unsurpassed portraits of a compact social world, an established social 'order,' at two differing stages of its existence," written in two different moods. Though the latter book contains a great deal of sharp satire, this quality is underplayed in J. A. McManis's "Edith Wharton's Hymns to Respectability" (*SoR*, October 1971). Similarly, Van Wyck Brooks in *The Confident Years* (E. P. Dutton, 1952) dismissed the "social amenity" and "financial incorruptibility" of Old New York as an inadequate basis on which to establish the values of her genteel and respectable aristocracy. Something of the same point of view is expressed in Edward Wagenknecht's *Cavalcade of the American Novel* (Henry Holt, 1952) and in Joseph Warren Beach's *The Twentieth Century Novel* (Century, 1932). Beach finds the social ideal of Old New York "represented by May Welland," whose victory over Newland seems to be sanctioned by the author herself.

Arthur Mizener confronts the conclusion of the novel more directly in his essay in *Twelve Great American Novels* (New American Library, 1967), where he observes that the "moral realism" of the epilogue expresses unequivocally Mrs. Wharton's view that "the only endurable life is one that preserves the values that have governed Newland and Ellen's lives," even though the cost to the individuals involved is the loss of spontaneous feeling. John J. Murphy finds these ironies embedded in the form of the novel, in "The Satiric Structure of Wharton's *The Age of Innocence*" (*MarkhamR*, May 1970). C. C. Doyle explores how the theme of innocence is conveyed through style and imagery in "Emblems of Innocence: Imagery

Patterns in Wharton's *The Age of Innocence*" (*XUS*, Fall 1971), an approach beautifully complemented by Viola Hopkins's excellent essay, "The Ordering Style of *The Age of Innocence*" (*AL*, November 1958), which examines the way language (syntax, diction, and imagery) actually works to convey Mrs. Wharton's themes in the novel. Nevius has observed of *The Age of Innocence* in *Edith Wharton* that "it is a triumph of style, of the perfect adaptation of means to a conception fully grasped from the outset. It would be difficult to say that she faltered or overreached herself at any point." Others may wonder, however, if the catalogue of physical changes in New York City between 1870 and 1900 is adequately integrated into her design. And Heinrich Straumann, more or less in answer to Lewisohn, Hicks, Brooks, and others, has observed in *American Literature in the Twentieth Century* (London: Hutchinson's University Library, 1951) that "for those readers to whom the cruelty of social conventions is not a reality, a good deal of Edith Wharton's art will be lost." Blanche H. Gelfant focuses on these cruelties in *The American City Novel* (Norman: University of Oklahoma Press, 1954), concluding that in Mrs. Wharton's fashionable but destructive city, "as in Dreiser's Chicago, the promise of personal self-fulfillment is illusory."

Very good readings of the novel are to be found in Louis Auchincloss's Introduction to the New American Library paperback (1962) and R. W. B. Lewis's Introduction to the Scribner paperback. Less satisfying is Lillie B. Lamar's "Edith Wharton's Foreknowledge in *The Age of Innocence*" (*TSLL*, Fall 1966), which points out a few errors in family relationships in the novel as evidenced that Mrs. Wharton's last page really was not always implicit in the first, as she once said. Lamar concludes, on the basis of this trivial evidence, that Mrs. Wharton "knew somewhat less about her own creative process than she boasts of in *A Backward Glance*." Comparably thin is Edwin Mosely's "Edith Wharton's Weak Faust" (*CE*, December 1959). Kimi Ishimoto has studied the novel in "On *The Age of Innocence*" (*ELitT*, March 1963), as has Agostino Lombardo in "L'eta dell' innocenza" (*Il Mondo*, 11 October 1960), neither of which I have seen. I find Louis O. Coxe's essay "What Edith Wharton Saw in Innocence" (*NewR*, 27 June 1955), reprinted in the Howe anthology, a most sensitive account of the buried emotions of Mrs. Wharton's Old New Yorkers.

The loss of such perceptions, as well as the disappearance of the physical setting of Old New York, is also explored in James W. Tuttleton's "Edith Wharton: The Archeological Motive" (*YR*, Summer 1972), which proposes that after World War I Mrs. Wharton undertook imaginatively to revive and recover for the modern sensibility certain modes of thought and feeling eclipsed by the roar of the modern, discontinuous universe.

The Age of Innocence does not fare well in James W. Gargano's "*The Age of Innocence*: Art or Artifice?" (*RS*, March 1970). Not surprisingly, given the title, Gargano finds it contrived and failing in style, characterization, and intent. The author concludes that "since it does not searchingly explore the problem of freedom, with which it purportedly deals, it does not earn its rather righteous and insipid resolution." In a somewhat similar vein, Brenda Niall finds the character of Newland Archer weighing in the balance in "Prufrock in Brownstone: Edith Wharton's *The Age of Innocence*" (*SoRA*, No. 3, 1971). Niall's conclusion is that the novel is far from a nostalgic look at Old New York, as Eleanor Widmer had argued in "Edith Wharton: The Nostalgia for Innocence," in *The Twenties: Fiction, Poetry, Drama*, edited by Warren French (Deland, Fla.: Everett/Edwards, 1967). Niall sees the novel instead as an attack on the human waste caused by Old New York. Cynthia Griffin Wolff's "*The Age of Innocence:* Wharton's 'Portrait of a Gentleman'" (*SoR*, July 1976), subsumed in her *Feast of Words*, likewise studies Newland Archer in the context of James's portrait of Isabel Archer; while Irving F. Jacobson offers a thematic study of the novel in "Perception, Communication, and Growth as Correlative Themes in Edith Wharton's *The Age of Innocence*" (*Agora: A Journal in the Humanities and Social Sciences*, Fall 1973).

The short novel by which Mrs. Wharton is best known—*Ethan Frome*—has also elicited a great deal of criticism, much of it controversial and vitriolic. One of the principal subjects of this criticism is Mrs. Wharton's relation to her regional materials. F. O. Matthiessen, in "New England Stories" in *American Writers on American Literature* (Liveright, 1931), observed that *Ethan Frome* "is the work of a woman whose life has been passed elsewhere." Mrs. Wharton denied this claim, arguing that she spent many summers in the environs of Lenox, where she discovered a grayness much grimmer than the rosy-colored regionalism of Jewett and Freeman. Abigail Ann Hamblen's "Edith Wharton in New England" (*NEQ*, June 1965) rejects this defense, arguing that *Ethan Frome* was just slumming. Comparing her work to Mary Wilkins's *Pembroke* suggests Mrs. Wharton's ignorance and, worse, her pity for the people of the area. Hamblen believes that Mrs. Wharton is a better writer when she deals with the society of New York.

Less argumentative and more instructive are Alan Henry Rose's "'Such Depths of Sad Initiation': Edith Wharton and New England" (*NEQ*, September 1977) and Nancy R. Leach's "New England in the Stories of Edith Wharton" (*NEQ*, March 1957), which analyzes the fragments of three manuscript novels left unfinished at Mrs. Wharton's death: *Mother Earth, The Cruise of the Fleetwing*, and *New England.* These fragments, all set in the area, "emphasize the virtues and defects of her understanding and interpretation of the region," which is closer to O'Neill's than to Jewett's. According to Mrs. Leach, New England meant for Wharton a lack of culture and economic opportunity in the depopulated villages; narrow people "going to seed"; the fake culture of the back-country college towns; and a certain character type—"proud, ignorant, superstitious, melancholy, capable of hard physical labor and infinite human suffering."

These criticisms are mild compared to others. J. D. Thomas's "Marginalia on *Ethan Frome*" (*AL*, November 1955) nitpicks the chronology of the story and deplores the narrator as ill-chosen. Thomas thought Mrs. Wharton did not know what the real life of farmers and sawmill operators was like; hence the *nouvelle*, he believes, is full of errors. Thomas continues in the same vein in "Three American Tragedies: Notes on the Responsibilities of Fiction" (*SCB*, Winter 1960), a study which includes *Kingsblood Royal* and *An American Tragedy*.

Thomas's criticism of the narrator of the story is the subject of John Crowe Ransom's study of *Ethan Frome* in "Characters and Character: A Note on Fiction" (*AmR*, January 1936), where he observes that Mrs. Wharton failed adequately to identify herself with this narrator, fearing to become too detached from her own mentality: "Clearly and sternly conscience says to the authors of fiction: Identify yourself with your characters. . . ." Bernard DeVoto, in the Introduction to the Scribner edition (1938), argued that all the characters were puppets rather than living characters. Elizabeth Shepley Sergeant's dialogue in "Idealized New England" (*NewR*, 8 May 1915) saw the book as "an example of what hate can accomplish as creative inspiration; and of the difference between observation and understanding." And James Hafley's "The Case Against *Ethan Frome*" (*Fresco*, Spring, 1961) should be mentioned as a wild diatribe against Mrs. Wharton's story, for reasons that are totally incomprehensible.

Doubtless the most interesting and controversial essay on the story is Lionel Trilling's "The Morality of Inertia" in *Great Moral Dilemmas*, edited by Robert MacIver (Institute for Religious and Social Studies, 1956; rptd. in Trilling's *A Gathering of Fugitives*, Boston: Beacon Press, 1956), which I judge to be one of the great failures of this great critic's career. Trilling feels that "it isn't a great book or even a fine book. It seemed to me a factitious book, perhaps even a cruel book." He observes that Mrs. Wharton suffered here "a limitation of heart." The basis for these judgments is that "when the characters of a story suffer, they do so at the behest of their author—the author is responsible for their suffering and must justify his cruelty by the seriousness of his moral intention." Mrs. Wharton, according to Trilling, could not "lay claim to any such justification." Trilling finds objectionable that, in Ethan's crisis, Mrs. Wharton does not have him "deal with the dilemma" (Mattie vs. Zeena) in "the high way that literature and moral philosophy prescribe, by reason and choice. Choice is incompatible with his idea of his existence; he can only elect to die." Why readers should regard Ethan's existential choice as the product of inertia few people will understand.

A much more helpful avenue to understanding this *nouvelle*, I think, is offered by David Eggenschwiler, whose "The Ordered Disorder of *Ethan Frome*" (*SNNTS*, Fall 1977) argues that this *nouvelle* has more design than at first may be apparent. Also instructive is the view of Kenneth Bernard, who argues in "Imagery and Symbolism in *Ethan Frome*" (*CE*, December 1961) that the depth of the story inheres in its imagery and symbolism rather than in her characterization. Bernard believes that "to overcome the deficiencies of their natural reticence (and perhaps her own), to retain the strength of the severe and rugged setting . . . , she resorted to a brilliant pattern of interlocking imagery and symbolism"—namely, the grayness of Starkfield, frozen emotion and infertility, the isolation of the farmhouse, the sense of entrapment, light and dark imagery, and sexual symbolism (barrenness, infertility, and emasculation). Charles Bruce's "Circularity: Theme and Structure in *Ethan Frome*" (*S&C*, 1966) and Joseph X. Brennan's "*Ethan Frome*: Structure and Metaphor" (*MFS*, Winter 1961-1962) account for the book's success in terms of its form. Brennan studies the narrator's perceptions and sensitivity as the key to the contrasts and metaphors which govern the story (the Norway spruces versus the farmhouse bedroom, light and shadow, imagery of birds vs. the cat, reds versus grays or stark whites, and so on). Brennan's conclusion establishes the propriety of judging the novel "in terms of the special character of the narrator's mind—his predilection for poetic, symbolic design and an abstract ideal of human nature—rather than in terms of psychological realism." A number of lesser articles, too numerous to list, also exist on *Ethan Frome*.

Mrs. Wharton's other novels and stories have received, understandably, less critical attention than her best three. Nevertheless, the following miscellaneous articles repay attention. On *The Fruit of the Tree*, the reader may consult H. E. Woodbridge's *"The Fruit of the Tree* and Ibsen's *Rosmersholm"* (*Nation*, 5 December 1907). On *The Valley of Decision*, John J. Murphy's "Edith Wharton's Italian Triptych: *The Valley of Decision*" (*XUS*, May 1965) and Anne Fremantle's "Edith Wharton: Values and Vulgarity" in *Fifty Years of the American Novel: A Christian Appraisal*, edited by H. C. Gardiner, S. J. (Charles Scribner's, 1952). Mrs. Fremantle is rather exercised by Mrs. Wharton's treatment of the Church in this historical romance of *settecento* Italy, dismisses her smug Protestant sensibility, and concludes that Mrs. Wharton "had no message; she had nothing, even, that she very desperately wanted to say." Van Wyck Brooks is less condemnatory in *The Dream of Arcadia: American Writers and Artists in Italy, 1760-1915* (E. P. Dutton, 1958). Studying her many Italian books and stories in the context of contemporary collectors of *objets d'art*, Brooks praises her for having brought to the front "certain unappreciated phases of Italian culture . . . which nobody seemed to know anything about, or care anything about, when she began to write." Brooks's work is also useful in correcting an error of fact in Blake Nevius's study: the model for Lewis Racie in *False Dawn* was not James Jackson Jarves, as Nevius argues, but Thomas Jefferson Bryan, who collected Italian primitives and established a Museum of Christian Art in Old New York.

On *The Reef*, Louis Auchincloss's introduction to the Scribner paperback (1965) may be read with profit, alongside Elizabeth Ammons's "Fairy-Tale Love and *The Reef*" (*AL*, January 1976) and James W. Gargano's "Edith Wharton's *The Reef*: The Genteel Woman's Quest for Knowledge" (*Novel*, Fall 1976), both dealing with Anna Leath's idealization of love and revulsion against its sexual side, as productive of Anna's Old New York education in averting one's eyes from the facts of life. Henry James's extraordinary letter to Mrs. Wharton, written on 4 December 1912 and reprinted in the Howe anthology, called *The Reef* "quite the finest thing you have done." James thought so well of the novel that he called Mrs. Wharton "a lost and recovered 'ancient' whom George Eliot might have read. Those who appreciate the Jamesian novel of geometric design, tightly controlled in the point of view, will like *The Reef.* Lubbock did, calling it "the most compellingly beautiful thing in all her works."

On *The Custom of the Country*, the reader may profitably consult Michael Millgate's "The Novelist and the Businessman: Henry James, Edith Wharton, Frank Norris" (*SA*, 1959), together with Millgate's excellent study *American Social Fiction: James to Cozzens* (Edinburgh: Oliver and Boyd, 1964), for a discussion of Mrs. Wharton's sense of society. Less complimentary is H. W. L. Chapman, who in "Books in General" (*NSN*, 20 January 1945) singled out *The Custom of the Country* as exemplifying best the work of "an extremely competent professional novelist" whose cleverness lay in creating the illusion of character out of what were in fact puppets and dolls. Adeline R. Tintner finds "A Source from *Roderick Hudson* for the Title of *The Custom of the Country*" (*NMAL*, Fall 1977), while Elizabeth Ammons continues with the frequently studied topic of "The Business of Marriage in Edith Wharton's *The Custom of the Country*" (*Criticism* Fall 1974). *The Children* is practically unnoticed, as it probably should be, except for Abigail Hamblen's "The Jamesian Note in Edith Wharton's *The Children*" (*UKCR*, March 1965).

Nancy Leach has illuminatingly discussed Edith Wharton's unpublished *kunstlerroman* entitled *Literature* in "Edith Wharton's Unpublished Novel" (*AL*, November 1953). Much of this material found its way, transformed, into *Hudson River Bracketed* and *The Gods Arrive*, which are ably discussed in Louis Auchincloss's "Afterword" to the New American Library edition for the former novel and in Alexander M. Buchan's "Edith Wharton and 'The Elusive Bright-Winged Thing'" (*NEQ*, Spring 1964). Viewing these novels in the light of her theory of literature expressed in *A Backward Glance* and *The Writing of Fiction*, Buchan concludes that her personal life and her imaginative life, "the two worlds she would fain have believed isolated from each other," were, "in not so secret ways, one and the same." The international novels of the 1920s and 1930s differ from the earlier books by including as satirical subjects the vulgarity of the modern European sensibility. John Harvey's "Contrasting Worlds: A Study in the Novels of Edith Wharton" (*EA*, Spring 1954) explores the significance of her expatriation in a most perceptive way, emphasizing the sense of her observation about Paul Bourget's *Outremer*. The altered tone of Mrs. Wharton's later studies of the international theme is sensitively analyzed in Christof Wegelin's "Edith Wharton and the Twilight of the International Novel" (*SoR*, April 1969). Occasional essays are devoted to Mrs. Wharton's lesser novels and may be found listed in Springer's reference guide and in annual *PMLA* listings.

In conclusion, let me mention a number of essays and studies that deal with technique. On Mrs. Wharton as a critic, of her own and other writing, the reader should consult her own essays: "Confessions of a Novelist" (*AM*, April 1933); "The Criticism of Fiction" (*TLS*, 14 May 1914; rptd. in *Living Age*, July 1914); "The Great American Novel" (*YR*, July 1927); "Henry James in His Letters" (*QR*, July 1926); "Permanent Values in Fiction" (*SatRL*, 7 April 1934); "The Vice of Reading" (*NAR*, October 1903); and "Visibility in Fiction" (*YR*, March 1929). To these essays, which explore her critical principles about reading and writing, must be added her books *A Backward Glance* (Charles Scribner's, 1934), especially the chapters on Henry James and her "secret garden" of writing, and *The Writing of Fiction* (Charles Scribner's, 1925), which sets forth her guiding principles as a novelist and writer of short fiction. Her unpublished novel *Literature*, discussed in the Nancy Leach article cited above, *Hudson River Bracketed*, and *The Gods Arrive* are also full of literary observation. Eric LaGuardia's "Edith Wharton on Critics and Criticism" (*MLN*, December 1958) gives a brief but valuable summary of her critical views. Finally, Mrs. Wharton's creative orientation, viewed from a feminine perspective, is also explored in Cynthia Griffin Wolff's "Edith Wharton and the 'Visionary' Imagination" (*Frontiers*, Fall 1977).

On Edith Wharton's imagery, Frances T. Russell's "Edith Wharton's Use of Imagery" (*EJ*, June 1932); C. C. Doyle's "Emblems of Innocence: Imagery Patterns in Wharton's *The Age of Innocence*" (*XUS*, Fall 1971); James W. Tuttleton's "Edith Wharton and Henry James" (*MASJ*, Spring 1966), and Kenneth Bernard's "Imagery and Symbolism in *Ethan Frome*" (*CE*, December 1961), which have already been discussed, should be consulted. On the structure of her fiction, see Charles Bruce's "Circularity: Theme and Structure in *Ethan Frome*" (*S&C*, I, 1966); J. J. Murphy's "The Satiric Structure of Wharton's *The Age of Innocence*" (*MarkhamR*, May 1970); and Joseph X. Brennan's "Ethan Frome: Structure and Metaphor" (*MFS*, Winter 1961-1962); all of these are fully discussed above. James W. Tuttleton's "Edith Wharton: Form and the Epistemology of

Artistic Creation" (*Criticism*, Fall 1968) analyzes Mrs. Wharton's formal aesthetic theory and her experimental innovations, with special reference to *Hudson River Bracketed*.

On Mrs. Wharton's characterization, a number of suggestive essays repay perusal. Edmund Wilson's analysis of her male protagonists as ineffectual dilettantes modelled on Walter Berry (in "Justice to Edith Wharton," cited fully above) has led Winifred Lynskey to argue in "The 'Heroes' of Edith Wharton" (*UTQ*, July 1954) that they are not so much based on Berry as on a sentimentalized projection of Mrs. Wharton herself. Something of the same point of view is conveyed in Marius Bewley's *Masks and Mirrors: Essays in Criticism* (Athenaeum, 1970), which, in rejecting Trilling's theory of the morality of inertia, argues on the basis of biographical evidence that her characters reflect her own preoccupations, in particular that she is "vulgarly capitalizing on her private experiences in *Ethan Frome*." This vulgarity is projected onto her *arrivistes*, according to Hilton Anderson in "Edith Wharton and the Vulgar American" (*SoQ*, October 1968). The invader is also the subject of Patricia R. Plante's "Edith Wharton and the Invading Goths" (*MASJ*, Fall 1964). Both Anderson and Plante survey the novels dealing with the assault on the inner citadel, Anderson concluding that Mrs. Wharton found vulgarians more numerous and "more interesting as literary types" than cultured Americans, and she gave them names like Looty Arlington, Indiana Frusk, and Undine Spragg. Robert L. Coard's "Names in the Fiction of Edith Wharton" (*Names*, March 1965) explores the implications of some of Mrs. Wharton's names.

A more clinical, psychoanalytic study of Mrs. Wharton's personae is offered in Dr. Henry J. Friedman's "The Masochistic Character in the Work of Edith Wharton" (*Seminars in Psychiatry*, August 1973), which is preoccupied with "the compliance of individuals with the rules of society when these rules are detrimental to their own personal happiness and well being." Dr. Friedman studies four major novels in order to show that the protagonists' suffering "had a self-induced aspect" arising out of their own "unconscious sense of guilt," which in turn results from an overdeveloped superego working in combination with "strong but unconsciously unacceptable impulses," usually anger and rage.

Mrs. Wharton's use of settings is also the subject of a number of instructive essays. As does Blanche Gelfant's *The American City Novel*, Jay Martin's essay in *Harvests of Change* (Englewood Cliffs, N.J.: Prentice Hall, 1967) emphasizes the alienation theme in the urban setting. Annette K. Baxter's "Caste and Class: Howells' Boston and Wharton's New York" (*MQ*, July 1963) studies upward social mobility in both cities, finding it easier in New York than in Boston. The essays by Louis Kronenberger, Louis Auchincloss, Joan Greenwood, and John Harvey—all fully cited and discussed above—also throw light on the importance of the settings of the stories. James W. Tuttleton's "Leisure, Wealth, and Luxury: Edith

Wharton's Old New York'' (*MQ*, July 1966), finally, explores the function of beauty and moral freedom in the opulent settings of her historical fiction.

The determinant of setting bears closely on the problem of naturalism in her fiction, and Edmund Wilson in ''Justice to Edith Wharton'' (fully cited above) remarks how the objects of her novels, the rugs, chandeliers, vases, and so on, become the agents of tragedy: the ''people of Edith Wharton are pursued by them as by spirits of doom and ultimately crushed by their accumulation.'' Wilson called her ''not only one of the great pioneers, but also the poet, of interior decoration.'' This preoccupation is also noted by Willard Thorp in *American Writing in the Twentieth Century* (Cambridge, Mass.: Harvard University Press, 1960), who describes as one of her ''greatest assets'' her ''love of detail and her accuracy in using it.'' This line of inquiry is also profitably followed by Jan Cohn in ''The House of Fiction: Domestic Architecture in Howells and Edith Wharton'' (*TSLL*, Fall 1973), and by Sarah M. McGinty in her superbly illustrated essay ''Houses and Interiors as Characters in Edith Wharton's Novels'' (*NCF*, Spring 1979).

Quite a number of critics, however, have resented the sheer accumulation of objects in Mrs. Wharton and others, notably Willa Cather, who argued in ''The Novel Démeublé'' in *Willa Cather on Writing* (Alfred A. Knopf, 1949) that ''the novel, for a long while, has been over-furnished'' and that ''we have had too much of the interior decorator since [Balzac's] day.'' Picking up this lead, Louise Bogan, in ''The Decoration of Novels'' in *Selected Criticism* (Noonday, 1955), condemns Mrs. Wharton's ''excessive'' attention to interiors in *The Buccaneers*. A rather better opinion of the novel, exploring the international settings and characterization, is Gaillard Lapsley's ''A Note on *The Buccaneers*,'' an afterword to the Appleton-Century edition (1938). Finally, in ''Aspects of Naturalism in Four Novels by Edith Wharton'' (*TCL*, January 1957), Larry Rubin moves from objects to philosophy, studying four major novels as examples of Mrs. Wharton's naturalism, which he sees as comparable to Dreiser's world view. The subtleties of her irony are such that the wide disparities in critical definitions of her world view will probably never be reconciled.

On Mrs. Wharton's style, Viola Hopkins's ''The Ordering Style of *The Age of Innocence*'' (fully cited above) is one of the best studies of the subject. Lillie B. Lamar's ''Edith Wharton and the Book of Common Prayer'' (*AN&Q*, November 1968) points to the profound influence of the rhythms of the Anglican prayerbook, which Mrs. Wharton loved, as a child, to hear read aloud. Richard Poirier's *A World Elsewhere* (Oxford University Press, 1966) finds Mrs. Wharton's work ''a precarious mixture of tones, an evidence of discrepancy between the subject of her satire, which is uniquely American and contemporary, and her dependence at certain points on English writers, especially Jane Austen and George Eliot.'' When that discrepancy became too great, as Louis Auchincloss has noted in *Reflections of a Jacobite*, Mrs. Wharton's "style [lost] its old precision and [began] to take on the slickness of a popular magazine story." Still, Helen Thomas and Wilson Follett gave high praise to her "poised perfection of phrase" in *Some Modern Novelists*, and Grant C. Knight, in *American Literature and Culture* (R. Long and R. R. Smith, 1932), claimed that "When in her best moods she is equalled by few Americans in point of style."

What should be said, finally, about Edith Wharton's achievement, as expressed in this overview of criticism? Was Mrs. Wharton, as N. Elizabeth Monroe insisted in *The Novel and Society* (Chapel Hill: University of North Carolina Press, 1941), the greatest novelist America has known? Was she the American equivalent of Jane Austen or George Eliot? Certainly Edmund Wilson was right in calling her "a passionate social prophet" and Q. D. Leavis perceptive in claiming Mrs. Wharton as "an extraordinarily acute and far-sighted social critic." But what can be said to account for the decline in her reputation in the two decades since her death? Was she the victim of a literary criticism, especially prominent since the 1930s, which has demanded a reformist vitality, a necessarily liberal if not leftist point of view? Patricia R. Plante, in "Edith Wharton: A Prophet Without Due Honor" (*MWR*, 1962), explained Mrs. Wharton's decline in reputation by contrasting her subjects with those of the more recently popular naturalists (Dreiser, Hemingway, Farrell) and by observing that her themes are too subtle for "readers faced with problems such as nuclear warfare and industrial organization. . . ." Mrs. Plante concludes that "One may also add to the above possible reasons for Mrs. Wharton's decline her cool detachment in an age when sincerity is tested by passionate partisanship; her conviction against divorce when the divorce rate in America is one of the highest in the world; her rejection of both the slice of life and stream of consciousness techniques in a day when both are still widely appreciated and defended; and finally, her emphasis upon order and form in a decade of literary experimentation and often chaos."

Recently, however, Mrs. Wharton's reputation as a writer has been on the ascendant. While her readers still struggle with the question of justice to Edith Wharton, first raised by Edmund Wilson in the 1930s and more recently by Cynthia Ozick in "Justice (Again) to Edith Wharton" (*Commentary*, October 1976), the Lewis biography has generated fresh interest in the woman, and Wolff's *A Feast of Words* has disclosed rich complexities in the fiction not previously perceived. It therefore comes as not quite a surprise when Gore Vidal remarks, in "Of Writers and Class: In Praise of Edith Wharton" (*AM*, February 1978), that "At best, there are only three or four American novelists who can be thought of as 'major' and Edith Wharton is one." He regards Wharton and James as "the two great American masters of the novel." And he observes that "now that the prejudice against the female writer is on the wane, they look to be exactly what they are: giants, equals, the tutelary and benign gods of our American literature." If such a judgment, by such a writer, does not do justice to Edith Wharton, justice will be a long time in coming to her.

It seems to me that Mrs. Wharton will continue to be read, principally for those reasons suggested by E. K. Brown in "Edith Wharton" (*EA*, January-March 1938)—namely, for "her interest in technique, an interest which makes her novels and her shorter pieces of fiction suggestive to the reader who cares, as she did, about the processes of art. It will also be because of the clarity of her social observation," and "because of the temper of her mind, which has given a special tone to her best writing. . . ." Brown believed that it was "not the tone of the highest art indeed, but a tone which is unfailingly interesting and stimulating, that 'particular fine asperity' which Henry James spoke of in summing up her intelligence."

The best of these critics have suggested, in varying ways, that in spite of her manifest limitations, Mrs. Wharton was a serious and deeply committed artist with a high respect for the professional demands of her craft, a woman praiseworthy for the generally high quality and range of her *oeuvre*, a novelist who wrote some of the most important fiction in the first quarter of the twentieth century, perhaps in our literary history.

5 JAYNE L. WALKER

Gertrude Stein

BIBLIOGRAPHY

The first three sections of Robert Wilson's *Gertrude Stein: A Bibliography* (The Phoenix Bookshop, 1974) present a comprehensive listing of Stein's published writings. Section B includes a useful guide to excerpts from her letters published in books of biography and criticism. Section D, the first survey of translations of Stein's writings, is less comprehensive than the previous ones. Although it begins to suggest the wide diffusion of her texts in foreign countries from Japan to Czechoslovakia, it does not fully record the surge of European translations that appeared in the 1970s, most notably in France. Subsequent sections of Wilson's bibliography list musical settings and recordings of Stein's texts, the published works of Alice B. Toklas, and "ephemera and miscellanea" of interest primarily to book collectors.

Wilson's volume was preceded by a number of other bibliographical projects, the first of which was Stein's own "Bibliography," a chronological listing of her published and unpublished work in *transition* (February 1929). Julian Sawyer catalogued Stein's published writings and miscellaneous items in *Gertrude Stein, A Bibliography* (Arrow, 1941) and "Gertrude Stein: A Bibliography 1941-1948" (*BB*, May-August, September-December 1948). And in 1954 George James Firmage compiled *A Check-List of the Published Writings of Gertrude Stein* (Amherst: University of Massachusetts, 1954). Prior to Wilson's book, the most comprehensive bibliography was Robert Bartlett Haas and Donald Clifford Gallup's *A Catalogue of the Published and Unpublished Writings of Gertrude Stein* (New Haven: Yale University Library, 1941). Wilson's bibliography supersedes all these previous inventories of Stein's published works. Gallup and Haas's "A Chronological List of Published and Unpublished Writings of Gertrude Stein," the final section of their 1941 volume, is an invaluable scholarly resource, although its dating of Stein's texts, especially those from her early period, is occasionally imprecise. Richard Bridgman's *Gertrude Stein in Pieces* (Oxford University Press, 1970) includes a supplemented version of this chronological inventory of Stein's literary production, adding Stein's later texts and citations of the volumes in which the shorter works were published.

Unfortunately, the only fairly comprehensive checklist of Stein criticism was compiled in 1943: Julian Sawyer's "Gertrude Stein (1874-): A Checklist Comprising Critical and Miscellaneous Writings about Her Work, Life and Personality from 1913-1942" (*BB*, January-April, May-August 1943), which Sawyer supplemented in 1948 (*BB*, January-April). To construct a reasonably comprehensive bibliography of Stein criticism, scholars must also consult all of the recent selected bibliographies—Bridgman's in *Gertrude Stein in Pieces*, Wilson's in his 1974 *Bibliography*, Edward Burns's in the Gertrude Stein issue of *TCL* (Spring 1978) and Michael J. Hoffman's, which is annotated, in his *Gertrude Stein* (Boston: Twayne, 1976)—plus the annual listings in *PMLA* and other standard sources.

Both James R. Mellow's *Charmed Circle: Gertrude Stein and Company* (Praeger, 1974) and Linda Simon's *The Biography of Alice B. Toklas* (Garden City, N.Y.: Doubleday, 1977) provide extensive listings of biographical source materials.

EDITIONS

More than two-thirds of the books Stein published during her lifetime are currently in print, nearly all of them in paperback editions. *Portraits and Prayers* is the most important volume that is still out of print.

During the years after Stein's death in 1946, a series of volumes prepared from the unpublished manuscripts she bequeathed to the Yale University Library began to appear: *Four in America*, with an introduction by Thornton Wilder (New Haven: Yale University Press, 1947); *Blood on the Dining-Room Floor* (Pawlet, Vt.: Banyan Press, 1948), with a foreword by Donald Gallup; and *Last Operas and Plays* (Rinehart, 1949), with an introduction by Carl Van Vechten. Stein's Radcliffe themes were published in Rosalind S. Miller's *Gertrude Stein: Form and Intelligibility* (Exposition Press, 1949). Under the general editorship of Carl Van Vechten, with an advisory committee of Donald Gallup, Donald Sutherland, and Thornton Wilder, Yale University Press issued the eight-volume *Yale Edition of the Unpublished Writings of Gertrude Stein* between 1951 and 1958: *Two: Gertrude Stein and Her Brother and Other Early Portraits (1908-1912)*, with a foreword by Janet Flanner (1951); *Mrs. Reynolds and Five Earlier Novelettes (1931-1942)*, with a foreword by Lloyd Frankenberg (1952); *Bee Time Vine and Other Pieces (1913-1927)*, with a preface and notes by Virgil Thomson (1953); *As Fine As Melanctha (1914-1930)*, with a foreword by

Natalie Clifford Barney (1954); *Painted Lace and Other Pieces (1914-1937)*, with an informative introduction by Daniel-Henry Kahnweiler (1955); *Stanzas in Meditation and Other Poems (1929-1933)*, with a preface by Donald Sutherland (1956); *Alphabets and Birthdays*, with an introduction by Donald Gallup (1957); and *A Novel of Thank You*, with an introduction by Carl Van Vechten (1958).

In the 1970s the volume *Fernhurst, Q.E.D., and Other Early Writings* (Liveright, 1971) made available Stein's earliest narratives; this edition restores the original text of *Q.E.D.*, which was slightly altered in the 1950 edition entitled *Things As They Are* (Pawlet, Vt.: Banyan Press). The sumptuously illustrated *Gertrude Stein on Picasso*, edited by Edward Burns (Liveright, 1970), includes the first published excerpts from the notebooks Stein wrote between 1902 and 1911, the only substantial portion of her work that remains unpublished. Leon Katz is editing these notebooks for eventual publication.

Carl Van Vechten's *Selected Writings of Gertrude Stein* (Modern Library, 1962), which is prefaced by F. W. Dupee's excellent 1962 "General Introduction," is still the best all-purpose anthology of her work, representing the major periods and genres of her literary production. Readers should note, however, that it reprints the opera libretto of *Four Saints in Three Acts*, not Stein's original text, first published in *Operas and Plays* (1932) and reprinted in *Selected Operas and Plays*, edited with an introduction by John Malcolm Brinnin (Pittsburgh: University of Pittsburgh Press, 1970). All of the texts included in Brinnin's volume were authenticated by Donald Gallup. Unfortunately, these are the only texts originally published during Stein's lifetime that have received the same scrupulous editing as those issued after her death.

A number of other anthologies of Stein's work have appeared in recent years. Robert Bartlett Haas's *A Primer for the Gradual Understanding of Gertrude Stein* (Los Angeles: Black Sparrow Press, 1971) presents a chronological selection of her writings from her Radcliffe themes to *The Mother of Us All*, chosen to illustrate her changing aesthetic and stylistic principles, which Haas discusses in his brief introductions to each section. This volume also includes Donald Sutherland's 1964 essay "Gertrude Stein and the Twentieth Century." *Gertrude Stein: Writings and Lectures 1911-1945* (London: Peter Owen, 1967), edited by Patricia Meyerowitz, presents a well-chosen selection of Stein's theoretical essays and her more difficult texts, including *Tender Buttons* and a generous sampling of the portraits. The 1971 Penguin American paperback edition is currently out of print, but the British edition is still available. *Gertrude Stein's America*, edited by Gilbert A. Harrison (Washington, D.C.: Robert B. Luce, 1965), is a collection excerpted mainly from her autobiographical works and *Brewsie and Willie*, with a few selections from uncollected magazine articles. Robert Bartlett Haas has edited a two-volume collection of pieces originally published in periodicals: *Reflections on the Atom Bomb* (Los Angeles: Black

Sparrow Press, 1973) and *How Writing is Written* (Los Angeles: Black Sparrow Press, 1974). And the 1980 volume *The Yale Gertrude Stein*, edited and with an introduction by Richard Kostelanetz (New Haven: Yale University Press), presents a selection of texts chosen from the eight-volume *Yale Edition of the Unpublished Writings of Gertrude Stein*.

MANUSCRIPTS AND LETTERS

A number of university libraries have several Stein letters in their collections; fewer have small manuscript collections. Berkeley's Bancroft Library houses a small but valuable Stein collection, notable primarily for its biographical materials related to her early life, including her first years in Paris. But the vast majority of Stein's manuscripts are assembled in the Beinecke Library at Yale. In "The Gertrude Stein Collection" (*YULG*, October 1947), Donald Gallup, until recently the curator of Yale's Collection of American Literature, reports that the Collection includes approximately 90 percent of Stein's manuscripts and 80 percent of her typescripts. The Collection also contains nearly all of the letters received by the Stein household, as well as a large number of letters written by Stein. *The Flowers of Friendship: Letters Written to Gertrude Stein*, edited by Gallup (Alfred A. Knopf, 1953), a tantalizing sampling of the former, only suggests the enormous scope and interest of this part of the Collection. In addition to the manuscripts and correspondence, Stein's bequest to Yale also included her extensive collection of photographs, newspaper clippings, and other memorabilia, as well as the contents of her personal library. The Beinecke also houses the papers of Alice B. Toklas and Leo Stein, as well as those of many of Stein's friends, including Alfred Stieglitz, Marsden Hartley, Hutchins Hapgood, and Mabel Dodge Luhan. Gallup describes the acquisition of these related collections in "Du Côté de Chez Stein" (*BC*, Summer 1970).

Until Gallup completes the edition of Stein's letters that he is currently preparing for publication, readers can sample her correspondence in a number of his essays that include extensive quotations from her letters. "Gertrude Stein and the *Atlantic*" (*YULG*, January 1954) reproduces her amusing correspondence with Ellery Sedgwick concerning publication of her work. "Always Gertrude Stein" (*SWR*, Summer 1949) contains ten of her letters to Gallup. "A Book is a Book is a Book" (*NCol*, January 1948) and "The Making of *The Making of Americans*" (1950; reprinted in *Fernhurst, Q.E.D., and Other Early Writings*) are studies of correspondence related to Stein's efforts to publish *Three Lives* and *The Making of Americans*. More recently, *Sherwood Anderson/Gertrude Stein: Correspondence and Personal Essays*, edited by Ray Lewis White (Chapel Hill: University of North Carolina Press, 1972), provides an interesting record of this literary friendship. And *Dear Sammy: Letters from Gertrude Stein and Alice B.*

Toklas (Boston: Houghton Mifflin, 1977), edited by Samuel M. Steward, contains forty-four of Stein's letters to Steward as well as a large number written to him by Toklas after Stein's death.

In addition to Gallup's forthcoming edition of Stein's letters, readers can also look forward to future publication of her correspondence with Virgil Thomson, edited by Richard France, and her extensive correspondence with Carl Van Vechten, edited by Edward Burns.

Stein scholars may regret Edward Burns's decision to publish only letters Toklas wrote after Stein's death in his *Staying on Alone: Letters of Alice B. Toklas* (Liveright, 1973). Still, what emerges from this volume is a far more vivid self-portrait than the one Toklas presents in her memoir *What Is Remembered* (Holt, Rinehart and Winston, 1963).

BIOGRAPHY

Stein's artful narratives of her own life in *The Autobiography of Alice B. Toklas* (Harcourt, Brace, 1933), *Everybody's Autobiography* (Random House, 1937) and *Wars I Have Seen* (Random House, 1945) have served as the inevitable point of departure for all subsequent biographical studies. *The Autobiography* provoked strenuous protests from Matisse, Braque, Tzara, and the Jolases, who impugned both Stein's veracity and her understanding in *Testimony Against Gertrude Stein*, a supplement to *transition* (February 1935). The autobiographical writings of Stein's brother Leo in *Appreciations: Painting, Poetry and Prose* (Crown, 1947) and *Journey into the Self*, edited by Edmund Fuller (Crown, 1950), also challenge Stein's judgment and her version of events. These writings are also useful for what they reveal about the elder brother who powerfully influenced her early life.

Other published reminiscences of Stein written by friends and acquaintances are so numerous that the twenty-three selections included in *Gertrude Stein: A Composite Portrait*, edited by Linda Simon (Avon, 1974), do not begin to exhaust this rich vein of material. Simon's collection serves as a convenient starting point for further study of the sources it excerpts. Among the most interesting of these are Virgil Thomson's discussion of his collaborations with Stein in his *Virgil Thomson* (Alfred A. Knopf, 1966), Thornton Wilder's descriptions of Stein's working methods in his "Introduction" to Stein's *Four in America*, and Bravig Imbs's lively account of the Stein salon in the mid-twenties in his *Confessions of Another Young Man* (Henkle-Yewdale, 1936). Among the memoirs not represented in Simon's collection, Mabel Dodge Luhan's *Movers and Shakers* (Harcourt, Brace, 1939) and Hutchins Hapgood's *A Victorian in the Modern World* (Harcourt, Brace, 1939) contain particularly revealing reminiscences of Stein before she became a public figure. W. G. Rogers's *When This You See Remember Me: Gertrude Stein in Person* (Rinehart, 1948) is primarily an account of the author's acquaintance with Stein in the 1930s and 1940s.

And Sir Francis Rose's pamphlet *Gertrude Stein and Painting* (London: Book Collecting and Library Monthly, 1968) provides interesting anecdotal descriptions of Stein's taste in painting. The bibliographies in James R. Mellow's *Charmed Circle: Gertrude Stein and Company* and in Linda Simon's *The Biography of Alice B. Toklas* provide more comprehensive listings of published and unpublished memoirs and biographies that present information on Stein.

Elizabeth Sprigge, Stein's first academic biographer, rarely makes use of any of these other sources to question the authority of Stein's autobiographical writings. Despite the promise of its title, Sprigge's *Gertrude Stein: Her Life and Work* (Harper, 1957) is not a critical biography in any sense of the term. Filled with extensive quotations from Stein's texts, this study provides details that supplement Stein's own account, but it does not create an independent vantage point for understanding her life and work. Still, Sprigge's original research remains useful, particularly her interviews with Stein's friends at Radcliffe and Johns Hopkins and her neighbors at Bilignin and Belley. Sprigge's earlier essay "Gertrude Stein's American Years" (*Reporter*, 11 August 1955) contains some additional material drawn from interviews.

A more ambitious study then Sprigge's, John Malcolm Brinnin's critical biography *The Third Rose: Gertrude Stein and Her World* (Boston: Little, Brown, 1959) attempts to correct what this critic terms the "myopia" of Stein's autobiographical writings by supplementing her accounts of events with those of other participants. As a biography, Brinnin's book has largely been superseded by Mellow's *Charmed Circle*, but its lively exploration of the relationship of Stein's writings to the major artistic and intellectual currents of her time is still of interest.

Mellow's is by far the most comprehensive biography that has appeared. This well-documented study draws on a wide range of sources, including an extensive array of memoirs and a sampling of Stein's voluminous unpublished correspondence, to create a richly detailed, eminently readable account of her life and her artistic and social milieu. Although it chronicles the events of her literary career, commenting briefly on her major texts, *Charmed Circle* is not a critical biography. Its wealth of detail amplifies the portrait of Stein's well-known public self without penetrating far beneath its surface.

The two critics whose studies illuminate the relationship between Stein's life and her writings are Leon Katz and Richard Bridgman. In his unpublished doctoral dissertation, "The First Making of *The Making of Americans:* A Study Based on Gertrude Stein's Notebooks and Early Versions of her Novel (1902-8)" (Columbia University, 1963) and in his "Introduction" to *Fernhurst, Q.E.D., and Other Early Writings*, Katz reveals the strong dependence of Stein's early works on autobiographical sources. The publication of Katz's long-awaited critical biography of Stein's early years, which will draw on both his study of her unpublished notebooks and extensive interviews with Toklas, promises to be a major event in Stein scholarship. The autobiographical dimension of Stein's writings is a central concern of Richard Bridgman's brilliant chronological study of her works in *Gertrude Stein in Pieces*. Three appendices to Bridgman's study are also of biographical interest: a detailed chronology of Stein's life, an index of names mentioned in *The Autobiography of Alice B. Toklas* and *Everybody's Autobiography*, and a list of Stein's grades at Radcliffe and Johns Hopkins.

In its use of quotations from Stein's texts as biographical facts, Linda Simon's *The Biography of Alice B. Toklas* lacks the critical tact of Bridgman's approach, but this biography provides a useful study of Stein's relationship with Toklas. Until the 1970s, lesbianism was the great unvoiced issue among the great majority of Stein's biographers and critics, with the notable exception of Katz. One early breach of this silence was Edmund Wilson's speculation, in a 1951 review of *Things As They Are*, reprinted in "Gertrude Stein Old and Young," in *The Shores of Light* (Farrar, Straus, and Young, 1952), that the opacity of Stein's later styles stemmed from the problem of writing about the taboo subject of "relationships among women." The most subtle, productive exploration of this issue is Catharine R. Stimpson's "The Mind, the Body, and Gertrude Stein" (*CritI*, Spring 1977), which examines Stein's changing strategies for dealing with her sexual identity in her life and her writings, within the larger historical context of the "mind/body problem" confronted by American women of Stein's generation.

In a different vein, a number of biographical studies assess Stein's friendships with writers and painters. Mark Schorer's engaging essay "Some Relationships: Gertrude Stein, Sherwood Anderson, F. Scott Fitzgerald, and Ernest Hemingway," in his *The World We Imagine* (Farrar, Straus, and Giroux, 1968), traces the growth and decline of personal intimacies and literary affinities among these four American writers. Not surprisingly, Stein's tempestuous relationship with Hemingway has stimulated more commentary than her friendship with any other writer. In "Hemingway and the Autobiographies of Gertrude Stein" (*FHA*, 1970), Lawrence D. Stewart focuses on the mutual detestation of Hemingway and Toklas, apparent in their writings and in *The Autobiography of Alice B. Toklas*. And in "Alice and Gertrude and Others" (*PrS*, Winter 1971-1972), Donald Sutherland reports Toklas's conviction, expressed during one of his last meetings with her, that by "get[ting] rid of Hemingway," she was "breaking up a triangle or an incipient affair." Stein's long and unusually placid friendship with Carl Van Vechten has also been the subject of two studies. Donald Gallup discusses their friendship, their mutual regard for each other's work, and Van Vechten's years of service to Stein's memory in "Carl Van Vechten's Gertrude Stein" (*YULG*, October 1952), a study based on their extensive correspondence in Yale's Stein Collection. And Bruce Kellner's "Baby Woojums in Iowa" (*BI*, April 1977) provides a more anecdotal account of their relationship, including a richly detailed description of their first meetings, drawn from Carl Van Vechten's unpublished journals.

Donald Gallup's "The Weaving of a Pattern: Marsden Hartley and Gertrude Stein" (*MagA*, November 1948) and Douglas Cooper's "Gertrude Stein and Juan Gris" in *Four Americans in Paris: The Collections of Gertrude Stein and Her Family* (The Museum of Modern Art, 1970) are biographical studies of Stein's friendships with these painters, based on correspondence in the Stein Collection.

Aline B. Saarinen's chapter "Americans in Paris: Gertrude, Leo, Michael, and Sarah Stein" in her book *The Proud Possessors* (Random House, 1958) has largely been superseded by the excellent individual studies of the Stein and the Cone families' activities as art collectors that are published in *Four Americans in Paris*. This indispensable volume also contains an informative illustrated catalogue of the paintings in the Museum of Modern Art's 1970 exhibition and a chronological series of photographs of Stein's atelier that records the development of her collection, with useful captions identifying the paintings.

Hugh Ford's *Published in Paris: American and British Writers, Printers, and Publishers in Paris 1920-1939* (Macmillan, 1975) presents a thoroughly researched history of Stein's relationships with publishers, agents, and printers throughout her career.

The most extensive of Stein's published interviews, Robert Bartlett Haas's "Gertrude Stein Talking: A Transatlantic Interview" (*UcR*, Summer 1962, Spring 1963, Winter 1964), is marred by unfortunate errors of transcription. A shorter version is more conveniently available in Haas's *A Primer for the Gradual Understanding of Gertrude Stein*.

The award-winning 1972 film biography *Gertrude Stein: When This You See, Remember Me*, produced and directed by Perry Miller Adato for National Educational Television, merits the attention of Stein scholars. Adato discusses the genesis of this film, with its rich array of visual materials and its interviews with Kahnweiler, Lipschitz, Thomson, and others, in "Gertrude Stein: When This You See, Remember Me" (*FiN*, March 1972). This film is available for classroom rental from McGraw-Hill Films.

Both this film and the four popularized biographies that were published in the 1970s testify to the continuing appeal of Stein's legendary life. Three of these recent biographies are written for a young adult audience: Howard Greenfeld's *Gertrude Stein: A Biography* (Crown, 1973), Ellen Wilson's *They Named Me Gertrude Stein* (Farrar, Straus, and Giroux, 1973), and W. G. Rogers's *Gertrude Stein Is Gertrude Stein Is Gertrude Stein: Her Life and Work* (Thomas Y. Crowell, 1973). Janet Hobhouse's *Everybody Who Was Anybody: A Biography of Gertrude Stein* (London: Weidenfeld and Nicolson, 1975) is well written and lavishly illustrated, but it makes no significant scholarly contribution.

CRITICISM

CRITICISM BEFORE STEIN'S DEATH

The few essays on Stein's work that appeared between 1910 and 1920 served more to promulgate the legend of her involvement with modernist painting than to elucidate her texts. In August 1912 her verbal portraits of Picasso and Matisse appeared in Alfred Stieglitz's influential magazine *Camera Work*, accompanied by an editorial that emphasized the analogy between Stein's innovative techniques and the equally unconventional methods of the painters who served as their subjects. The following year Stein became one of the journalistic sensations of the Armory Show after Mabel Dodge's essay "Speculations, or Post-Impressionism in Prose" announced, "Gertrude Stein is doing with words what Picasso is doing in paint" (*A&D*, March 1913). Carl Van Vechten's "How to Read Gertrude Stein" (*Trend*, August 1914) emphasizes Stein's friendship with Picasso and Matisse, suggesting that they may have influenced the course of her writing, and also calls attention to Stein's "intimate association with the studies of William James." Both Dodge and Van Vechten emphasize the predominance of sound over sense in Stein's writings, recommending that the reader "drift along," enjoying the "sensuous charm of her art."

In "Engineering with Words" (*Dial*, April 1923), a review of *Geography and Plays*, Kenneth Burke grants that Stein's writings proffer this immediate appeal of "significant form," but he contends that by underemphasizing the selection of subject matter, Stein created an "art by subtraction" that suggests the "insignificance of significant form." During the next few years, however, Stein's methods were eloquently defended by fellow writers, beginning with Sherwood Anderson in "The Work of Gertrude Stein," his preface to *Geography and Plays* (Boston: Four Seasons Press, 1922). Both Marianne Moore (*Dial*, February 1926) and Katherine Anne Porter (*New York Herald Tribune Books*, 16 January 1927; reprinted in *The Days Before*, Harcourt, Brace, 1952) published appreciative reviews of *The Making of Americans*. In the "Communications" section of *TR* (October and November 1924), Mina Loy directly counters Burke's argument with brilliant readings of "A Sweet Tail (Gypsies)" and other texts, demonstrating the thematic clarity that gradually emerges from what she terms their "intercepted cinema of suggestion."

Beginning in 1926 *transition* provided a congenial organ of dissemination for Stein's writings. In "K.O.R.A.A." (June 1927) the editors praise Stein and Joyce for their equally successful efforts to "restore to the act of reading its integral and proper pleasures." This essay describes much of Stein's work as "abstract," but in "A Note on the Writing of Gertrude Stein" in the Fall 1928 issue, Ralph Church objects to this common characterization, arguing that Stein's texts manifest the kind of "intrinsic" meaning that is proper to literature. In his 1930 essay "The Works of Gertrude Stein" (reprinted in *Imaginations*, New Directions, 1970),

William Carlos Williams professes more interest in the revolutionary implications of Stein's "breakaway from th[e] paralyzing vulgarity of logic" in her later writings than in the "thrilling clinical record" she created in "Melanctha." Edith Sitwell's *Aspects of Modern Poetry* (London: Duckworth, 1934) credits Stein and Joyce with the modern "rebirth of the medium." Sitwell's earlier *Poetry and Criticism* (London: Hogarth Press, 1925) emphasized Stein's "making of abstract patterns," but her later study praises both the extraordinary semantic force of Stein's rhythmic patterns and the clarity of the visual impressions she creates. In *By Way of Art* (Coward-McCann, 1928), Paul Rosenfeld discusses the "retrospective discovery" of Stein's writings by contemporary poets and novelists who share her sense of the "primacy of rhythm and the consequent conceptions of literature as pattern and language as relativity."

In 1936 in a disparaging review of *Narration* (*Criterion*, July 1936), Hugh Sykes Davies notes, "Not many years ago, Miss Stein was honorably mentioned in most lists of the leaders of modern literature, even short ones." The apogee of this trend proved to be Edmund Wilson's inclusion of a chapter on Stein in *Axel's Castle* (Charles Scribner's, 1931). In this famous study of the impact of French Symbolist aesthetics on modern literature, Stein appears in the company of Yeats, Valéry, Eliot, Proust, and Joyce, as the most extreme practitioner of the poetics of suggestion, with its concomitant withdrawal from common life: "[S]he has gone so far that she no longer even suggests." Despite his salutory warning that "one should not talk about 'nonsense' until one has decided what 'sense' consists of," Wilson has little sympathy for Stein's work after *Three Lives*, which he wholeheartedly admires.

In the 1920s, as Stein came to be regarded as a major figure in contemporary literature, her work frequently served as a lightning rod for critical assaults on the larger modernist movement. Max Eastman's derisive account of Stein as one of the leaders of what he terms the "cult of unintelligibility," in his book *The Literary Mind* (Charles Scribner's, 1931), typifies this practice. By far the most interesting studies in this vein are Laura Riding's "T. E. Hulme, the New Barbarism, and Gertrude Stein" in her *Contemporaries and Snobs* (London: Jonathan Cape, 1928) and Wyndham Lewis's in his *Time and Western Man* (London: Chatto & Windus, 1927). Riding argues that Stein is the only writer to follow the anti-Romantic, antihumanist theoretical program of Hulme, Pound, and others to its logical conclusion: a "coherent barbarism" grounded in the theory of an absolute, collective time-sense and the practice of using words, purged of history, "automatically to record pure and ultimate obviousness." A slightly different version of this discussion of Stein appears in the "Conclusion" of Riding's and Robert Graves's *A Survey of Modernist Poetry* (London: W. Heinemann, 1927). Unlike Riding, Lewis considers Stein a romantic writer, a leading exponent of the modern "time-cult"—the "school of Bergson-Einstein, Stein-Proust"—that his book attacks. Lewis compares Stein's style with Anita Loos's in *Gentlemen Prefer Blondes* to enforce his characterization of Stein as a "colossus among the practitioners of infancy," which he regards as a byproduct of this modern obsession with time.

During the decade following publication of *The Autobiography of Alice B. Toklas* (1933), critical commentary on Stein's experimental writings became less polemical, as the version of modernism she represented was displaced from the center of the literary scene. The *Autobiography* was greeted by a suggestive review by William Troy (*Nation*, 6 September 1933), who insists that the value of her work cannot be determined until her artistic intentions are more fully understood. According to Troy, Stein's "so-called naive or primitive writing . . . represents such a complex synthesis" of influences—William James, Bergson, and Whitehead and also Cézanne, Picasso, and Juan Gris—that "the most painstaking analysis is required to reveal them with any degree of clarity." During the next few years, critics began to explore her affinities with James and Whitehead but not always with the degree of subtlety that Troy prescribes.

B. F. Skinner's essay "Has Gertrude Stein a Secret?" (*AtM*, January 1934) alleges that Stein's works in the "*Tender Buttons* manner" were written "automatically and unconsciously," according to the laboratory methods described in the essays she wrote for the *Psychological Review* while she was working under the direction of William James at Harvard. In "Gertrude Stein" (*AmS*, April 1934), Sherwood Anderson attempted to defuse Skinner's charge by arguing that "good writing" is always "half automatic." And in *Everybody's Autobiography*, Stein herself took pains to deny that her writing was "automatic." In a seminal essay "Gertrude Stein, William James, and Grammar" (*AJP*, January 1941), Ronald B. Levinson counters Skinner's argument with a more subtle account of the use Stein made of her studies with James. Levinson suggests that Stein's writing was consciously shaped by "grammatical doctrines" that closely parallel William James's theories of language—particularly in the unusual prominence they both grant to the "transitive parts" of speech, especially conjunctions and prepositions. In "Gertrude Stein and the Solid World," published in *American Stuff* (Viking, 1937), Dorothy Van Ghent proposes that Stein's writings enact the metaphysics of Alfred North Whitehead by "attempt[ing] to cancel the gaps between one thing and another, between space and time, between past and present, between concept and precept."

The more neutral, more academic Stein criticism that began to appear in the 1930s continued in the few essays devoted to her work in the next decade. Harvey Eagleson's "Gertrude Stein: Method in Madness" (*SR*, April 1936) discusses the theory and practice of repetition in her early works and demonstrates that much of *Four Saints in Three Acts* becomes intelligible against the background of extrinsic knowledge about Saint Therese and Saint Ignatius. George Haines's "Forms of Imaginative Prose: 1900-1940" (*SoR*, Spring 1942) grants Stein a prominent place among modern novelists who use language primarily as "imitation of reality" rather than as "reference" to it. Haines's later study, "Gertrude Stein and Composition" (*SR*, Summer 1949), an appreciative survey of her work, demonstrates that techniques of poetic analysis illuminate her writings more effectively than those of prose criticism.

Three critical studies of Stein's work appeared in France during this period. Bernard Faÿ's generally impressionistic account of her life and literary achievement in "Gertrude Stein, poète de l'Amérique" (*RevP*, 15 November 1935) contains a number of provocative critical insights. Approaching Stein's "pure poetry" in the context of the Symbolists' pursuit of musicality, Marcel Brion praises her more rigorous construction, which he compares to a Bach fugue, in "Le Contrepoint poétique de Gertrude Stein" (*Échanges*, June 1930). And Pierre Brodin's *Les Écrivains américains du vingtième siècle* (Paris: Horizons de France, 1947) includes a chapter that sympathetically surveys Stein's life and work.

Books

The first book of Stein criticism appeared three years after her death. Rosalind S. Miller's *Gertrude Stein: Form and Intelligibility* (Exposition Press, 1949) is a modest study intended to provide the "average reader" with an introductory guide to Stein's theories of composition and to her major works. This volume is of interest to contemporary readers for its inclusion of Stein's Radcliffe themes, which Miller edited for publication.

The two books of Stein criticism published in the 1950s—Donald Sutherland's *Gertrude Stein: A Bibliography of Her Work* (New Haven: Yale University Press, 1951) and Benjamin L. Reid's *Art By Subtraction: A Dissenting Opinion of Gertrude Stein* (Norman: University of Oklahoma Press, 1958)—reenact the impassioned polemics that surrounded Stein's writings in the 1920s. One of the few indispensable books of Stein criticism, Sutherland's brilliant partisan defense of her work combines an elaborate metaphorical style with lucid, precise critical insights. Sutherland's first chapter is still the best consideration of the role of James and Münsterberg in shaping the terms of Stein's explorations of consciousness. His chronological study of her major texts emphasizes that none of her various styles is devoid of sense, but that they each constitute a profound critique of conventional forms of discourse that expresses a serious philosophical position. Sutherland contends that Stein's central achievement was to "restore the sense of immediate unprepared experience" to literature. But he is careful to insist that Stein's texts cannot be reduced to the experience or to the ideas that generated them, because her writing is, above all, a "thing existing in itself, . . . an absolute and absolutely present literary work."

While Sutherland praises Stein as the purest literary practitioner of what he takes to be the central achievement of modern art, "the isolation and extrication of immediate quality from the whole unending complex of practical relations," B. L. Reid vigorously condemns what he calls (following Kenneth Burke) Stein's "art by subtraction" as "sweepingly antimoral and anti-intellectual." Concentrating on Stein's theoretical writings, Reid demonstrates the logical coherence of her "complex and frequently impressive aesthetics," which he nonetheless deplores. Although he never acknowledges the broader implications of his attack on Stein's aesthetics, the terms of his condemnation constitute a full-scale rejection of some of the fundamental premises of Symbolist and modernist art. At the heart of Reid's polemic is a moral repugnance for any art that refuses to supply "usable truth" for the "business of living." For Reid, the most damning symptom of Stein's "fatal alienation of art from life" is what he presumes is her intention to use words as if they were "essentially empty counters," to create an absolutely private language. William Gass's "Gertrude Stein: Her Escape from Protective Language" (*Accent*, Autumn 1958) is a brilliant critique of the terms of Reid's argument.

At the end of his book, Reid declares Stein "effectively dead as a writer." But already in the 1950s, a new generation of American poets and playwrights were becoming vitally interested in her work, and in the 1960s a number of academic scholars turned their attention to Stein. Compared with Sutherland's and Reid's books, Frederick J. Hoffman's pamphlet *Gertrude Stein* for the University of Minnesota Pamphlets on American Writers Series (Minneapolis: University of Minnesota Press, 1961) is remarkable for its judicious neutrality. This generally perceptive introduction to Stein's writings focuses on her theories of composition and the development of her early work from *Three Lives* to *Tender Buttons*. While emphasizing the "objective" analysis of consciousness, derived from William James, that informs all of her writings, Hoffman also characterizes her texts beginning with *Tender Buttons* as "non-representational"—an unresolved contradiction that is remarkably common in Stein criticism. The most outstanding contribution of Hoffman's study is his brilliant analysis of "Melanctha."

Michael J. Hoffman's *The Development of Abstractionism in the Writings of Gertrude Stein* (Philadelphia: University of Pennsylvania Press, 1965) describes the local stylistic features of Stein's writings as a "progressive 'leaving-out'" of conventional elements of realistic verisimilitude and verbal communication and characterizes her development during this period as a steady progression "down the path of abstractionism to non-representationalism." Like many previous critics, Hoffman assumes, too readily, that Stein's emulation of modernist painting led her to create a mode of writing that functioned "plastically . . . exclusive of the symbolic nature of words." The limitation of this study, inherent in its methodology, is its premise that Stein's deviations from conventions necessarily entail a flight from meaning, an assumption that fails to recognize the semantic force of formal innovation.

In *Gertrude Stein and the Present* (Cambridge, Mass.: Harvard University Press, 1967), Allegra Stewart argues that Stein's writings are unified by the informing psychological experience of contemplation or "ingatheredness," characterized by "creative dissociation," which served as the source of both her linguistic practices and her theories of creativity. Few readers will unreservedly accept all the intricacies of Stewart's analyses of *Tender Buttons* as a verbal mandala, unified by a network of interconnecting etymological roots, and of *Doctor Faustus Lights the Lights* as a play of Jungian archetypes enacting a "psychic monodrama" of "self-realization or individuation." But her more general discussion of the quality of Stein's "sacramental view of human creativity," grounded in a strictly empirical experience of "presence," highlights an important dimension of Stein's writings that has not been as thoroughly studied by other critics.

A slighter book than Stewart's, Norman Weinstein's *Gertrude Stein and the Literature of the Modern Consciousness* (Frederick Ungar, 1970) explores affinities between Stein's writings and a wide range of modern hypotheses concerning the relationship between language and consciousness. The major argument of this study is the familiar contention that Stein's literary work "represents an attempt to capture [William] James' pluralistic universe through the development of an experimental syntax." Weinstein's descriptions of what he terms the "consciousness-altering" characteristics of Stein's texts are so frequently imprecise and his introduction of other intellectual and artistic contexts is so unsystematic that his potentially interesting study has little scholarly merit.

Richard Bridgman's *Gertrude Stein in Pieces*, which Bridgman modestly describes as a "preliminary inventory of Gertrude Stein's literary estate," set a new standard for Stein criticism. By charting the enormous corpus of Stein's writings and opening it to serious textual analysis, this book lays the groundwork for all subsequent studies of her literary production. The greatest strengths of Bridgman's study derive from his assumption that the way to begin reading the "unruly melange" of Stein's texts is to "familiarize oneself with its actual features." His survey of Stein's writings reveals the range of signifying practices encompassed by what most previous critics termed her "abstract" or "non-representational" style and demonstrates that even a text like *Tender Buttons* will begin to "yield its meanings as readers grow more familiar with it." Bridgman's study tends to concentrate on the autobiographical dimension of Stein's texts, frequently emphasizing psychological motivations over aesthetic concerns as the sources of her writings. The narrative of the author's inner life that emerges from Bridgman's chronological readings of her texts, which highlight (for the first time) the rich erotic strain in her writings, is an invaluable corrective to the common assumption that Stein's work was totally divorced from human, emotional concerns.

Michael J. Hoffman's *Gertrude Stein* is an introductory survey of Stein's career written for the Twayne's United States Authors Series. A less forbidding book for the beginning student of Stein's writings than Bridgman's, it is a less engaging introduction to her work than Sutherland's. Its first half recapitulates the argument of Hoffman's earlier book, tracing what he terms the "development of abstractionism" from *Q.E.D.* to *Tender Buttons*. Its second half considers, in turn, Stein's later operas and plays, novels, and theoretical and autobiographical writings, emphasizing their deviations from generic conventions and briefly summarizing their thematic content. But like Hoffman's previous study, this one tends more to discourage than to stimulate efforts to decipher her more unconventional texts.

Carolyn Copeland's *Language and Time and Gertrude Stein* (Iowa City: University of Iowa Press, 1975) claims to be a generic study of Stein's narrative techniques, focusing on her changing uses of the narrator. The absence of *The Making of Americans* (omitted because of its length) is only one indication of the lack of rigor of Copeland's approach. Her methodological framework, derived from Percy Lubbock and Wayne Booth, cannot adequately account for many of Stein's textual strategies, especially those of her middle period. Not surprisingly, the strongest sections of this book are those that deal with Stein's less unconventional texts, the early narratives and the autobiographies.

In contrast, Wendy Steiner's *Exact Resemblance to Exact Resemblance: The Literary Portraiture of Gertrude Stein* (New Haven, Conn.: Yale University Press, 1978), by far the most important book of Stein criticism since Bridgman's *Gertrude Stein in Pieces*, should serve as a model for future generic studies of Stein's narratives and plays. Steiner begins by tracing the history of the portrait, making brilliant use of semiotic theory to clarify the problem of mimesis inherent in the genre, and proceeds to use Stein's theoretical writings as a framework for analyzing the three historical phases of her portraits. Subsequent chapters explore parallels between Stein's changing techniques of portraiture and those of "analytic" and "synthetic" Cubism and assess the place of the portrait within the corpus of her writings. Steiner's generic approach, which isolates the portraits from the chronological sequence of texts within which they were produced and derives Stein's theories of portraiture almost exclusively from her later writings, has evident historical limitations, especially in dealing with the crucial change from the early portraits to those in the style of *Tender Buttons*. Still, this excellent study has many compensating virtues, not the least of which is this critic's resolute effort to decipher Stein's difficult texts.

Essays, Chapters in Books, and Dissertations

Stein and the Literary Tradition

Before Stein's death critics had already begun efforts to situate her writings within the American literary tradition—a context that increasingly supplanted her earlier identification with the major figures of international modernism. In his extraordinary 1933 review, William Troy suggests that

Stein's writings represent the culmination of the "orientation from experience toward the abstract," which he contends characterizes the American literary tradition from Hawthorne to James. Wendell Wilcox makes the same argument in "A Note on Stein and Abstraction" (*Poetry*, February 1940).

Oscar Cargill's *Intellectual America: Ideas on the March* (Macmillan, 1941) was the first of a series of studies to assess the impact of Stein's writings on subsequent American writers. Praising "Melanctha" as the "first genuinely primitivistic study in American literature," Cargill argues that *Three Lives* provided the "generic force" for Sherwood Anderson's *Winesburg, Ohio* and served as the crucial model for both Anderson's and Hemingway's "studied, conscious simplicity of style." Cargill roundly condemns the more "decadent" writings that followed *Three Lives*. Van Wyck Brooks offers a similar assessment of Stein's work in *The Confident Years: 1885-1915* (E. P. Dutton, 1952), deploring what he regards as her withdrawal into the "infantile" style and sensibility of her later writings. In *The Twenties: American Writing in the Postwar Decade* (Viking, 1955), Frederick J. Hoffman takes a broader view of the importance of Stein's writings for Hemingway and others, suggesting that her most significant contributions to the American tradition were "a sense of the immediate present and a fully documented discussion of the aesthetic strategies required to make immediacy functional within a prose text." Linda Wagner's more recent essay, "Sherwood, Stein, The Sentence, and Grape Sugar and Oranges," in *Sherwood Anderson: Dimensions of His Literary Art*, edited by David D. Anderson (East Lansing: Michigan State University Press, 1976), is a comparative study of Anderson's style and Stein's in *Three Lives*. Frank Baldanza's "Faulkner and Stein: A Study in Stylistic Intransigence" (*GaR*, Fall 1959) describes a number of similar stylistic features that characterize these writers' prose styles, which "have restored syntax to a dominating rhythmic importance that reconciles modern prose to its earlier poetic roots."

Richard Bridgman's invaluable study *The Colloquial Style in America* (Oxford University Press, 1966) assigns Stein's writings a prominent place within the stylistic tradition it traces. By highlighting the predominance of repetition of words, sounds, and certain syntactical patterns in the works of earlier American writers, most notably Henry James, as well as in those of writers who followed Stein, Bridgman forcefully demonstrates that Stein's characteristic stylistic features are a conscious synthesis of elements integral to this ongoing tradition. Stein's writings are equally central to the American literary tradition as Tony Tanner characterizes it in *The Reign of Wonder: Naïvety and Reality in American Literature* (Cambridge, England: University Press, 1965). Tanner argues that, beginning with the Transcendentalists, American writers have dedicated themselves to re-creating a naive vision concentrated exclusively on the present moment, through the immediacy of colloquial speech. While he emphasizes how closely Stein's theoretical writings accord with these interests, he concludes that, except for "Melanctha," Stein's "new way of writing was not a successful communication of her new way of seeing."

James M. Cox's "Autobiography and America" (*VQR*, Spring 1971) was the first of a series of essays that assess Stein's place within the tradition of American autobiography. Cox argues that Stein logically extended the tradition of Franklin, Thoreau, and Adams, each of whom used autobiography as an exemplary form of American history, by creating "[h]er life in words, a total present [which] would be the living fact on which to base a genuine vision of American autobiography as American history." In *Educated Lives: The Rise of Modern Autobiography in America* (Columbus: Ohio State University Press, 1976), Thomas Cooley contends that Stein's theoretical concerns led her to create "narratives of existing rather than of becoming or being educated," which have more in common with Franklin's and Thoreau's "chronicles of the timeless self" than with the autobiographical forms produced by Henry Adams and other writers of his generation. G. Thomas Couser's "Of Time and Identity: Walt Whitman and Gertrude Stein as Autobiographers" (*TSLL*, Winter 1976) develops a series of sometimes strained comparisons between Stein's autobiographical writings and Whitman's, focusing on their shared commitment to transcending the limitations of individual identity and chronological time.

Three essays consider the relationships of other texts to earlier American writers and traditions. Sharon Shaw's comparative study "Gertrude Stein and Henry James: The Difference Between Accident and Coincidence" (*PeM*, 1974) focuses on these writers' shared belief that "only through language can one hope to bring to light the endlessly subtle meanderings of consciousness." In "The Great American Novel: Final Chapter" (*AQ*, Winter 1969), George Knox argues that Stein's "antinovelistic" efforts to "essentialize American life" in *The Making of Americans* function as a "super-spoof" of the idea of the Great American Novel. And Judith P. Saunders's "Gertrude Stein's *Paris France* and the American Literary Tradition" (*SDR*, Spring 1977) argues that this text creates a fictional paradise in the tradition of the "quintessentially American myth of escape."

These studies are the exceptions to the widespread neglect of Stein's writings among scholars of American literature, most strikingly evident in the absence of her work from all but the most recent editions of the standard anthologies of American literature. Except for Bridgman's and Tanner's books, none of the major studies of the American literary tradition produced in the last twenty years have seriously considered her works. Unfortunately, Stein specialists have done little to counter this neglect. Since Stein criticism became the domain of scholars instead of fellow writers, the most common procedure has been to treat Stein's works in isolation—not only from the American literary tradition but from the international context of literary modernism as well. The bold forays of Edmund Wilson and John Malcolm Brinnin have had too few successors.

Only three recent studies have attempted to situate Stein's works within the tradition of European modernism. William Wasserstrom's lively essay "The Sursymamericubealism of Gertrude Stein" (*TCL*, February 1975) displays no profound knowledge of Stein's texts, but it is nonetheless a provocative exploration of her links to both the American tradition of Emerson, William James, and Henry Adams and the European modernism of Mallarmé, the Cubists, and the Surrealists. James Rother's "Gertrude Stein and the Translation of Experience" (*ELWIU*, Spring 1976) more systematically discusses Stein's "discipline of translating the objects of consciousness" into verbal forms as part of the European revolt against classic realism from Flaubert and Mallarmé to Beckett. Bruce F. Kawin's discussion of Stein in *Telling It Again and Again: Repetition in Literature and Film* (Ithaca, N.Y.: Cornell University Press, 1972) considers her uses of repetition in the context of those of other writers from Proust to Robbe-Grillet and features a detailed comparison between her writings and Beckett's.

Kawin was not the first critic to consider Stein's writings in relation to contemporary French narrative. Strother B. Purdy's 1970 essay "Gertrude Stein at Marienbad" (*PMLA*, October 1970) compares her theories and practice of repetition with Robbe-Grillet's in his film script *L'Année dernière à Marienbad*, arguing that Stein's theories are "ideally, and only, realizable by a film." More recently, in a brief study "Gertrude Stein: The Forerunner of Nathalie Sarraute" (*IFR*, July 1978), Ethel F. Cornwell suggests that Stein's theories of narrative anticipate those of the French New Novelists, especially Sarraute—a topic that merits more thorough investigation. Neil Schmitz's suggestive exploration of the congruence between the textual strategies of *Tender Buttons* and the central concerns of post-modernist narrative and contemporary literary theory in "Gertrude Stein as Post-Modernist: The Rhetoric of *Tender Buttons*" (*JML*, July 1974) should stimulate future research in this area.

Anna Gibbs's "Hélène Cixous and Gertrude Stein: New Directions in Feminist Criticism" (*Meanjin*, September 1979) proposes that Cixous's writings—both her narratives and her studies of "écriture féminine"—suggest a new mode of feminist criticism that illuminates Stein's textual strategies. And in "Gertrude Stein's 'Composition as Explanation'" (*TCL*, Spring 1978), Bruce Bassoff traces affinities between the theories Stein develops in this essay and those of Benjamin, Derrida, and especially Lévi-Strauss.

Despite the resurgence of interest in Stein's writings among contemporary American artists, there have been few studies of this phenomenon. Both Julian Beck, director of the Living Theatre and author of "Storming the Barricades," in Kenneth H. Brown's *The Brig* (Hill and Wang, 1965) and Lawrence Kornfeld, who directed six of Stein's plays between 1957 and

1974 and authored "How the Curtain Did Come, Conflict and Change: The Theatre of Gertrude Stein" (*PArJ*, Spring 1976), eloquently testify to Stein's importance for the contemporary American theater. But the only scholarly efforts to assess the nature of this impact have been Marie-Claire Pasquier's brief essay in French, "Le Théâtre comme paysage: Gertrude Stein et le théâtre américain d'aujourd'hui" (*CRB*, First trimester 1977), which focuses on Robert Wilson, Richard Foreman, and Meredith Monk, and Kate Davy's more detailed study, "Richard Foreman's Ontological-Hysteric Theatre: The Influence of Gertrude Stein" (*TCL*, Spring 1978). The only study of Stein's writings as a model for contemporary American poets has been Jayne L. Walker's "Exercises in Disorder: Duncan's Imitations of Gertrude Stein," in *Robert Duncan: Scales of the Marvelous*, edited by Robert J. Bertholf and Ian W. Reid (New Directions, 1979).

Stein and Painting

Comparisons between Stein's writings and Cubist painting have pervaded Stein criticism since its beginning. Until recently discussions of this relationship have generally been based on the erroneous premise that Cubism is an "abstract," "nonrepresentational" art. As early as 1955, in the "Introduction" to Stein's *Painted Lace*, Daniel-Henry Kahnweiler, the art dealer for the Cubists, insisted that Stein's work, like that of the Cubists, is a "realistic art" which "exists by itself, while *signifying* something else." But Kahnweiler's brilliant discussion went unread, while John Malcolm Brinnin's contention, in *The Third Rose*, that Stein modeled her work on nonrepresentational painting (his erroneous characterization of Cubism) influenced many subsequent approaches to Stein's writings.

Samuel H. McMillan's doctoral dissertation "Gertrude Stein, the Cubists, and the Futurists" (University of Texas, 1964) is a disappointing ahistorical study based on outmoded textbook generalizations about Cubism. L. T. Fitz's comparative study "Gertrude Stein and Picasso: The Language of Surfaces" (*AL*, May 1973), based solely on Stein's *Picasso* (1938), reaches the familiar conclusions that Stein shared with Picasso a commitment to flat surfaces and to language as a purely plastic entity. Marilyn Gaddis Rose's "Gertrude Stein and Cubist Narrative" (*MFS*, Winter 1976-1977), another ahistorical study, finds what this critic takes to be Cubist techniques of abstraction, juxtaposition, and rearrangement in *Three Lives, Lucy Church Amiably*, and *Ida*. And Earl Fendelman discusses Stein's thematic and structural uses of Cubist aesthetics in *The Autobiography of Alice B. Toklas* in his essay "Gertrude Stein Among the Cubists" (*JML*, November 1972). None of these studies exhibits more than the most superficial understanding of the techniques, aesthetics, or historical development of Cubism.

Two little-known essays should serve as points of departure for all future studies of Stein's writings in the context of modernist painting. Leon Katz's "Matisse, Picasso and Gertrude Stein," published in *Four Americans in Paris*, is an invaluable historical study of Stein's personal and artistic involvement with Cézanne, Matisse, and Picasso, based primarily on evidence from Stein's unpublished notebooks. The essay by Leon Katz and Edward Burns, "'They Walk in the Light': Gertrude Stein and Pablo Picasso," published in *Gertrude Stein on Picasso*, is a slightly different version of the material on Picasso that appears in Katz's "Matisse, Picasso and Gertrude Stein." David Antin's brilliant interview, "Some Questions About Modernism" (*Occident*, Spring 1974), contains only brief comments on Stein, whom he regards as the only writer who understood "how profoundly Cubism opened up the possibilities of *representation*," but his brilliant discussion of the central issues of modernism from the perspective of art history provides an invaluable context for approaching the study of Stein's relationship to painting.

Three recent studies of this problem are grounded in an understanding that Cubist painting retained a representational element. Jayne L. Walker's doctoral dissertation, "Gertrude Stein and Her Objects: From 'Melanctha' to *Tender Buttons*" (University of California, Berkeley, 1975), based in part on Stein's unpublished notebooks, demonstrates that the changes in Stein's writings from 1905 to 1912 closely parallel developments in Picasso's paintings during the same period. Wendy Steiner's chapter "Literary Cubism" in *Exact Resemblance to Exact Resemblance* (New Haven: Yale University Press, 1978) is a detailed study of similarities between the techniques of Stein's first two phases of portraiture and those of "analytic" and "synthetic" Cubist portraits. And Marjorie Perloff's wide-ranging discussion of the significance of Stein's various styles in "Poetry as Word-System: The Art of Gertrude Stein" (*APR*, September-October 1979) includes an excellent reading of "Susie Asado" as a portrait manifesting Cubist strategies of "instability, indeterminacy, and acoherence."

Considerations of Stein's writings in the context of painting have always centered on Picasso's Cubism. The only major exception is Henry M. Sayre's "Imagining the Mind: Juan Gris and Gertrude Stein" (*SHR*, Spring 1977), which focuses on the problematic links between signs and images in Stein's 1926 volume *A Book Concluding With As A Wife Has A Cow: A Love Story*, illustrated by Gris. Although many critics have acknowledged Stein's indebtedness to Cézanne, no one has published a detailed study of this important issue.

Other Intellectual Contexts

After the pioneering studies of Levinson and Sutherland, most of Stein's critics have acknowledged her affinities with Jamesian psychology and philosophy. Frederick J. Hoffman's *Gertrude Stein* and Robert Bartlett Haas's "Another Garland for Gertrude Stein" in *What Are Masterpieces* (Pitman, 1970) are two of the most forceful arguments for the influence of Jamesian pragmatism on her writings. The only critic to challenge the primacy of James's influence has been Leon Katz, whose important essay "Weininger and *The Making of Americans*" (*TCL*, Spring 1978) convincingly documents Stein's rejection of Jamesian pragmatism in favor of the Kantian idealism of Otto Weininger's *Sex and Character* while she was writing *The Making of Americans*.

Textual Analyses

The high percentage of textual studies that have focused on the early period of Stein's writings suggests that scholars have generally been more interested in the radical changes in her style from the earliest texts to *Tender Buttons* than in the issues posed by her later works. Haldeen Braddy's essay "The Primitive in Gertrude Stein's 'Melanctha'" (*NMQ*, Autumn 1950) was the first systematic study of the style of this text. Although Braddy's pseudo-anthropological premises lead him to questionable conclusions about its characters and themes, his discussion of its "primitive" style is still valid. Richard Bridgman's "Melanctha" (*AL*, November 1961), a more detailed study of its style, emphasizes the extent to which this text is a "full-scale reworking" of *Things As They Are*, Stein's earlier lesbian novel. In "Continuity of Romantic Irony: Stein's Homage to Laforgue in *Three Lives*" (*CLS*, June 1975), Carl Wood discusses ways in which thematic repetition unifies the stories in *Three Lives* and heightens their Laforguean irony.

The Making of Americans is the crucial text for understanding the changes in Stein's style between *Three Lives* and *Tender Buttons*. Although several excellent specialized studies of this work have appeared, too few critics have given it the attention it deserves. The genesis of this text is the major subject of Leon Katz's invaluable unpublished doctoral dissertation, "The First Making of *The Making of Americans*," (Diss., Columbia University, 1963) which should be the starting point for all serious studies of the early period of Stein's work. Katz's study focuses on the development of Stein's project from 1902 to 1908, emphasizing the changes in her theoretical premises and working methods that preceded the final version of the text. But this wide-ranging study, which contains a wealth of biographical details, also includes illuminating discussions of *Q.E.D.* and *Three Lives* and new information concerning the intellectual and artistic contexts that helped to shape Stein's early writings. Building on Katz's work, Clive Bush proffers a complex, difficult exploration of the epistemology of the text, which he regards as a satire of Aristotelian (and Jamesian) certainties, in "Toward the Outside: The Quest for Discontinuity in Gertrude Stein's *The Making of Americans; Being a History of a Family's Progress*" (*TCL*, Spring 1978). Kenneth Frieling's "The Becoming of Gertrude Stein's *The Making of Americans*" in *The Twenties: Fiction, Poetry, Drama*, edited by Warren French (Deland, Fla.: Everett/Edwards, 1975), offers a simpler account of the work's changing textual strategies, arguing that both the "outside phenomena" and the theories of reality with which it began gradually cede to the "abstract" rhythms of authorial consciousness. Linda Jeanne McMeniman's doctoral dissertation, "Design and Experiment in *The*

Making of Americans by Gertrude Stein'' (University of Pennsylvania, 1976), a valuable detailed analysis of the text, demonstrates that oppositions and paradoxical unifications underlie the novel's structure, style, and thematic development. Its fourth chapter, a brilliant stylistic analysis employing the methodology of transformational grammar, is by far the most sophisticated discussion of the significance of Stein's deviant syntactical structures that has yet appeared.

Until fairly recently *Tender Buttons* was generally presumed to be illegible, but since Bridgman's pioneering study, a number of critics have taken up the challenge of attempting to read this text. While David D. Cooper's "Gertrude Stein's 'Magnificent Asparagus': Horizontal Vision and Unmeaning in 'Tender Buttons' " (*MFS*, Autumn 1974) describes the text as a "horizontal visionary work" informed by the "recognition of chaos and necessary *un-meaningfulness*," others have explored the meanings produced by its unconventional verbal structures. Two paraphrases of individual sections of the text have appeared in *The Explicator:* Jonathan C. George's "Stein's 'A Box' " (February 1973) and Ruth H. Brady's "Stein's 'A Long Dress' " (February 1976). Joel Porte's "Gertrude Stein and the Rhythms of Life" (*NBR*, June 1975) argues that the meaning of this text and others of the same period is grounded in the physical functions and rhythms of the body. And Wayne A. Howitt's doctoral dissertation, "Reading as a Creative Effort: A Study Utilizing Gertrude Stein's *Tender Buttons*" (State University of New York, Buffalo, 1975) uses this work as a case study for observing the psychology of reader response. More interesting than these studies are two essays that directly confront the question of how meaning is produced in this text. After an intelligent consideration of this problem in "Spreading the Difference: One Way to Read Gertrude Stein's *Tender Buttons*" (*TCL*, Spring 1978), Pamela Hadas offers a reductive interpretation of the work as an oblique memoir, a continuation of the study of differences between Stein and her brother Leo that she began in *Two*. The brilliant reading that Neil Schmitz presents in "Gertrude Stein as Post-Modernist: The Rhetoric of *Tender Buttons*" should stimulate future efforts to elucidate what he terms the "core of its linguistic pact."

In the mid-1970s three studies appeared that use Roman Jakobson's model of the metaphoric and metonymic polarities of discourse to elucidate the radical change in Stein's style from *The Making of Americans* to *Tender Buttons:* David Lodge's "Gertrude Stein" in his book *The Modes of Modern Writing* (Ithaca, N.Y.: Cornell University Press, 1977; an earlier version of his study of Stein appeared in "Metaphor and Metonymy in Modern Fiction," *CritQ*, Spring 1975); Randa K. Dubnick's "Two Types of Obscurity in the Writings of Gertrude Stein" (*ESRS*, Winter 1976); and Jayne L. Walker's doctoral dissertation, "Gertrude Stein and Her Objects: From 'Melanctha' to *Tender Buttons*." Walker's detailed readings of the early portraits of artists, the crucial transitional text *Two*, and *Tender Buttons* elucidate the theoretical concerns that motivated the gradual shifts in Stein's textual strategies from *The Making of Americans* to *Tender Buttons*.

Next to the works of her early period, Stein's autobiographies have commanded the greatest interest among recent critics—stimulated, perhaps, by a new surge of interest in this genre in the 1970s. In addition to the studies discussed above, which assess their place in the tradition of American autobiography, a number of studies, beginning with Bridgman's, have analyzed the literary techniques of these texts, which were long regarded merely as naive historical memoirs. Although several critics have noted that *Everybody's Autobiography* accords more closely with Stein's theories of narrative than does *The Autobiography of Alice B. Toklas*, not surprisingly it is Stein's creation of the point of view and voice of Alice B. Toklas that has attracted the most extensive critical commentary. In "Remarks As Literature: *The Autobiography of Alice B. Toklas* by Gertrude Stein" (*MQR*, Fall 1978), Lawrence Raab concludes, more readily than most critics, that Stein's strategy of re-creating her past "within the 'actual moment' of the speaking voice of Alice B. Toklas" fulfills her theoretical commitment to present-tense composition. Lynn Z. Bloom delineates what she terms the "egotistical, interpretative, and objective functions" of the "ventriloquistic persona" of the *Autobiography*, in "Gertrude Is Alice Is Everybody: Innovation and Point of View in Gertrude Stein's Autobiographies" (*TCL*, Spring 1978). Bloom contends that this innovative strategy is unrepeatable, but in "The Mock-Autobiography of Alice B. Toklas" (*AN&Q*, September 1977), Timothy Dow suggests that the mock-autobiography, inaugurated by Stein, has emerged as an important subgenre of contemporary narrative.

A number of recent studies have emphasized the extent to which Stein's *Autobiography* subverts the conventional mimetic expectations of the genre. In "Visual Rhetoric in *The Autobiography of Alice B. Toklas*" (*CritI*, June 1975), an analysis of the illustrations included in the original text, Paul K. Alkon suggests that the gradual displacement of photographs of reality by photographs of paintings and, finally, by a manuscript page "mirrors a final transformation . . . of both Gertrude and Alice into works of art." James E. Breslin's "Gertrude Stein and the Problems of Autobiography" (*GaR*, Winter 1979) links the ambivalent status of the text—both "historical memoir" and "fictional construct"—to its contradictory presentation of both the character and the theories of Gertrude Stein in his argument that Stein's struggle with the conventions of autobiography led her to create a "book with an elusive center and a discontinuous design." In a provocative, wide-ranging essay, "Portrait, Patriarchy, Mythos: The Revenge of Gertrude Stein" (*Salmagundi*, Winter 1978), Neil Schmitz argues that the *Autobiography* turns on an act of revenge, flaunting the absence of the writer's "disembodied I" from the "bogus materiality" of Alice's portrait of Gertrude Stein and from Picasso's famous portrait of her as well. In "The Autobiography as Generic 'Continuous Present': *Paris France* and *Wars I Have Seen*'' (*ESC*, Summer 1978), the only study of Stein's autobiographical writings that considers these later texts, Shirley Swartz contends that their stronger thematic organization indicates a new strategy, a shift of focus from "what the human mind experiences" to "what the human mind knows."

In contrast to the autobiographies, Stein's operas and plays have received little systematic critical attention, except in Bridgman's chronological study of Stein's literary production and chapters devoted to this genre in books by Sutherland and Hoffman (1976). Two early studies explicate the religious imagery and themes of *Four Saints in Three Acts*: Julian Sawyer's "A Key to *Four Saints in Three Acts*" (*NewI*, Fall 1947) and Harvey R. Garvin's "Sound and Sense in *Four Saints in Three Acts*" (*BuR*, December 1954). These essays, which are concerned solely with wresting paraphrasable meaning from this text, are the only detailed analyses of individual plays that have appeared, except for Allegra Stewart's Jungian interpretation of *Doctor Faustus Lights the Lights* in *Gertrude Stein and the Present*. John McCaffrey's "'Any of Mine Without Music to Help Them': The Operas and Plays of Gertrude Stein" (*Y/T*, Summer 1973) is primarily concerned with musical settings of Stein's texts. Elizabeth Fifer's "Put Language in the Waist: Stein's Critique of Women in *Geography and Plays*" (*UMPWS*, 1975) examines Stein's "feminist critique" of traditional female roles and heterosexual romantic love and marriage in a series of plays about women. Especially in light of the interest Stein's plays have aroused among contemporary playwrights and directors, a systematic study of this genre of her writings would be an important contribution to Stein scholarship.

Except for sections in books by Bridgman, Hoffman (1976), Sutherland, and Copeland, the only study that treats any of Stein's later narratives is Cynthia Secor's "*Ida*, A Great American Novel" (*TCL*, Spring 1978), which interprets the novel as a dream-like portrait of the "human mind" of an ordinary woman of her period in search of marriage. Again, a systematic generic study of Stein's narratives is needed. More detailed analyses of individual texts, especially *Ida* and *Mrs. Reynolds*, would also be useful.

Critics have studied Stein's work in various subgenres. Virginia J. Tufte's "Gertrude Stein's Prothalamium: A Unique Poem in a Classical Mode" (*YULG*, July 1968) reprints Stein's privately-issued 1939 poem "Prothalamium for Bobolink and His Louisa" and discusses its use of conventional motifs. Lawrence D. Stewart's "Gertrude Stein and the Vital Dead" (*MDAC*, 1972) explores the terms of Stein's involvement with detective fiction, especially in the decade of the 1930s. Laura Hoffeld's essay "Gertrude Stein's Unmentionables" (*L&U*, Spring 1978) is a thematic analysis of the children's book *The World is Round*. And "Is Flesh Advisable? The Interior Theater of Gertrude Stein" (*Signs*, Spring 1979), Elizabeth Fifer's study of Stein's erotic writings, elucidates the "disguised autobiography" encoded in their imagery.

Several volumes of Stein's works are prefaced by useful critical studies of the texts they contain. Thornton Wilder's introductions to *The Geographical History of America* (Random House, 1936; reprinted in Random House/Vintage, 1973) and to *Four in America*, Donald Sutherland's "Preface: The Turning Point" in *Stanzas in Meditation* (New Haven: Yale University Press, 1956), and William Gass's wide-ranging introduction to the 1973 edition of *The Geographical History of America* are particularly valuable. An expanded version of Gass's essay entitled "Gertrude Stein and the Geography of the Sentence," which includes a brilliant discussion of *Tender Buttons*, appears in his book *The World Within the Word* (Alfred A. Knopf, 1978).

Except for *TCL*'s special issue on Stein and the less scholarly special issues of *WiC* (Fall 1973) and *LGJ* (Winter 1974), the only collection of essays on Stein that has appeared is the Italian volume of critical studies *Gertrude Stein: l'esperimento dello scrivere*, edited by Biancamaria Tedeschini Lalli (Naples: Liguori, 1976). This collection and the work of two other Italian critics, Fernanda Pivano's "Gertrude Stein: pioniera di un secolo," in her *La balena bianca e altri miti* (Milan: Arnoldo Mondadori, 1961) and Barbara Lanati's chapters on Stein in her *L'avanguardia americana: tre esperimenti: Faulkner, Stein, W. C. Williams* (Turin: Einaudi, 1977) are the only significant foreign studies of Stein that have appeared since her death, except for the essays by Brodin and Pasquier discussed above. However, Jacques Roubaud's "Gertrude Stein, Gertrude Stein et Gertrude Stein" in *Critique: Revue Générale des Publications Françaises et Etrangères* (Paris, France) (December 1978), the most interesting of the spate of reviews that greeted recent translations of her work in France, and Viviane Forrester's brief discussion of Stein's writings in her *Tel Quel* essay "Féminin pluriel" (Winter 1977) indicate that French literary scholars are becoming aware of the significance of Stein's texts.

The vast majority of Stein's texts have barely begun to be read. The sheer bulk of her literary corpus could make explications of individual texts a growth industry in English departments for years to come. But subsequent research should produce more subtle analyses of the significance of Stein's various textual strategies and more systematic studies of the periods and genres of her writings. Serious feminist criticism of Stein's work has barely begun. More generally, the burgeoning interest in literary theories and methodologies should stimulate new approaches to Stein's texts and provide more refined instruments for analyzing both their individual operations and their relationships to painting and psychology. Historically grounded studies of the artistic and intellectual sources that helped to shape her writings are also needed. Serious reconsiderations of her work in the context of literary modernism, both Anglo-American and international, are long overdue. And it is time for more, and more detailed, studies of contemporary American and continental writers' affinities with Stein.

6 BARBARA J. GRIFFIN

Two Experimental Writers: Djuna Barnes and Anaïs Nin

The early careers of Djuna Barnes and Anaïs Nin have much in common. Both lived in or near New York City for a time and later in Paris where they were associated with the colony of expatriate writers that flourished there until the outbreak of World War II. In addition, both wrote in a manner which so departed from the established conventions for novels, short stories, and plays that readers have continued to find their work difficult and sometimes baffling.

In 1939-1940 both writers returned from Paris to New York, and from this point on the paths of their careers diverge. By 1940 when she left Paris, Barnes had already published six volumes of fiction and received a great deal of critical acclaim for *Nightwood*, which had been published in both British and American editions (London: Faber and Faber, 1936; New York: Harcourt Brace, 1937). Her readership was not large, but her works were being issued by influential publishers such as Harcourt Brace, Faber and Faber, and Horace Liveright. Barnes had become a well known and colorful member of the expatriate circle of writers that dispersed at the end of the 1930s, but when she returned to New York in 1940 her public life ended. She became, as she described herself in a rare interview in 1971, "a recluse, a form of Trappist" (*NYTBR*, 24 May 1971). After 1938 the only new work she published was *The Antiphon*, a verse play first published in 1958 (New York: Farrar, Straus and Cudahy; London: Faber and Faber), and five poems, the most recent of these in the *New Yorker* ("Quarry," 27 December 1969 and "Walking-mort," 15 May 1971). A discussion of all five of these poems can be found in the last chapter of Louis Kannenstine's *The Art of Djuna Barnes: Duality and Damnation* (New York University Press, 1977). Because she withdrew from any kind of public life and published so little in the last four decades, Barnes's work is probably less widely known today than in 1940.

Anaïs Nin's career has followed a very different course. In 1939 when she returned to the United States, Nin had published only three volumes: *D. H. Lawrence: An Unprofessional Study* (Paris: E. W. Titus, 1932), *The House of Incest* (Paris: Siana Editions, 1936), and *The Winter of Artifice* (Paris: Obelisk Press, 1939). Both volumes of fiction were published in limited editions by small independent presses either established by Nin and Henry Miller or with which they were closely associated. In the first years following her return to the United States, Nin's work was rejected by commercial publishers, so that she again found it necessary to establish her own press and publish it herself. Nin desired a wider readership and critical appreciation of her work, but neither of these things came about until 1966 when she began publishing the volumes of her *Diary*. With the publication of the first *Diary* volume and increasingly in the next decade, Nin became a public figure in whom there was great interest. She toured colleges and universities throughout the United States, giving lectures and readings, and answering questions, and seems to have delighted in the fame and recognition that finally came to her. As a result Nin's work is better known today than ever before, and there is much critical interest in her.

DJUNA BARNES

Djuna Barnes's decision to become a recluse in 1940 and her scorn of interviews, autobiography, and memoirs mean that study of Barnes's career as a writer mainly was undertaken without her assistance. We can't help but regret this, because of the light she might have shed on her own career and work and on the lives and careers of writers with whom she was associated in the 1920s and 1930s. But this may also mean that we avoid the problem encountered with some of the criticism of Anaïs Nin published during the 1960s and 1970s—that it was done by people who knew Nin personally and admired her a great deal. Critical assessments of Barnes's work are, in almost all cases, rendered free of the bias that close personal association with her might produce.

BIBLIOGRAPHY

There are two Barnes bibliographies. The first, done by Robert Hipkiss in 1968 and published in *Twentieth Century Literature* (October 1968), is mentioned here only because it should be avoided. As Douglas Messerli points out in the introduction to his 1975 bibliography *Djuna Barnes: A Bibliography* (David Lewis), the Hipkiss bibliography is incomplete and contains errors. Messerli's bibliography attempts to provide as complete a list as possible of works by and about Barnes. He also lists her contributions to books, and as many of her contributions to newspapers and magazines as can be identified, though he notes that because of her early and prolific career as a journalist, during which period many of her writings were unsigned, this list is almost certainly not complete.

Messerli's list of works about Barnes is long because, he explains, "So little is known about Barnes that I thought it necessary to include every book or article that ever mentioned her." He recognizes that not all of these make a "contribution to Barnes study," and his brief annotations of each entry help indicate which items are worth looking at. Messerli also includes a short list of writings about Barnes not in English, which includes reviews of the 1961 Stockholm production of the Dag Hammerskjöld translation of *The Antiphon*. In both the English and non-English sections of his bibliography of secondary materials, Messerli has grouped reviews of particular volumes together, so that it is possible to see quickly the kind of reception a volume received. The only limitation of Messerli's bibliography is its lack of a full index. His introduction provides a useful summary of Barnes's career and critical history.

EDITIONS

At the present time three volumes of Barnes's work are in print: *Nightwood* (New Directions), *Ryder* (St. Martin's), and *Selected Works* (Farrar, Straus, and Giroux). *Selected Works*, first published in 1962, contains *Spillway* (a collection of nine stories), *The Antiphon*, and *Nightwood*. According to Messerli, most of the stories have been "considerably revised for this edition," and the version of *The Antiphon* published here is Barnes's "preferred edition." In addition, *Selected Works* reprints T. S. Eliot's 1937 introduction to *Nightwood* and a 1949 note in which Eliot says he is leaving his original preface to the novel unchanged. As recently as 1972, *Ladies Almanack*, first published in Paris in 1928, was published in a facsimile edition by Harper and Row. Barnes's first published volume *The Book of Repulsive Women* (1915) was reissued by the Alicat Bookshop Press (New York) in 1948 and has not been reissued. According to Messerli, Barnes suppressed this edition. The contents of the early volume of stories *A Book* (Boni & Liveright, 1923) reappeared in the volume *A Night Among the Horses* (Horace Liveright, 1929), along with three additional stories. The *Spillway* collection of stories in the *Selected Works* contains several stories from *A Night Among the Horses* revised. Therefore, though neither *A Book* nor *A Night Among the Horses* has been reissued in its original form, some of the stories from these volumes are still in print. Much of the small body of Barnes's published work (aside from her journalistic writings) is thus available in current or fairly recent editions.

Some of Barnes's work has been translated and published outside the United States. *Nightwood*, for example, has been published in French, German, Dutch, Danish, Italian, and Spanish. One of the most interesting instances of this is the translation of her play *The Antiphon* completed in 1960 by Dag Hammarskjöld in conjunction with Karl Ragnar Gierow, who was then director of the Swedish Royal Dramatic Theater. According to Hammarskjöld's biographer, Brian Urquhart (*Hammarskjöld*, Alfred A.

Knopf, 1972), Hammarskjöld first wrote to Barnes about his difficulty in grasping the play's meaning, but he came to feel, after talking with Barnes and working with the play, that it was not obscure. Henry Raymont, writing in the *New York Times Book Review* (24 May 1971) of his interview with Barnes, refers to "a commission for 40 new poems from the Suhrkamp Verlag of Frankfurt." In a 1975 essay James Baird remarks that "presumably new poems are shortly to be published" in Germany and cites the 1971 interview article as the basis for his statement. At present, however, I can find no indication that a volume of new poems has appeared in German or in English.

MANUSCRIPTS AND LETTERS

A large collection of Djuna Barnes's papers was deposited with the McKeldin Library, University of Maryland, College Park, in 1970. This collection contains extensive correspondence, typescripts, page proofs, and such miscellaneous materials as newspaper clippings, notebooks, drawings, and playbills. Some of the correspondence and certain of the other materials are restricted, that is, "not open for use at the present time." All of the materials, however, have been cataloged, and it is possible to obtain an inventory of the collection as well as an indication of those items which are restricted by writing to McKeldin Library.

BIOGRAPHY

There is no book-length biography of Barnes and no prospect for one at the present time. Henry Raymont, who interviewed her in 1971, described the one-room apartment in which she lived after 1940 as cluttered with the "accumulation of more than 30 years of correspondence, manuscripts, paintings and books" (*NYTBR*, 24 May 1971). But when asked if she might publish something in the nature of memoirs or autobiography, Barnes reacted with horror: "How can you ask me such a question? Lillian Hellman's and all those people's memoirs are so disgusting . . . why should I want to add to it?" It seems unlikely, therefore, that Barnes chose a biographer or cooperated with anyone attempting to do a biography.

For biographical information about Barnes we can turn to three kinds of sources. The first of these is literary history, often in the form of memoirs. Because she was such a colorful and active participant in the Parisian expatriate community during the 1920s and 1930s, almost any account of the group contains references to her. Typical of this kind of source are Sylvia Beach's *Shakespeare and Company* (Harcourt Brace, 1956), Hugh Ford's *Published in Paris: American and British Writers, Printers, and Publishers in Paris, 1920-1939* (Macmillan, 1975), and Burton Rascoe's *A Bookman's Daybook* (Horace Liveright, 1929). Such sources offer important glimpses of Barnes's relationships with and responses to other literary figures of this period. Rascoe, for example, in an entry for 14 July 1922, gives an account of an evening spent with Barnes and Edmund Wilson in the course of which Barnes made her frequently quoted remark about Joyce's *Ulysses*: "I shall never write another line. . . . Who has the nerve to after that?" A similar source for a later period is Willa Muir's *Belonging: A Memoir* (London: Hogarth Press, 1968), in which she describes Barnes's relationship with T. S. Eliot. A second place to seek biographical information about Barnes is in such standard biographical reference works as *Contemporary Authors: A Bio-bibliographical Guide to Current Authors and Their Works* and the *Dictionary of Literary Biography* (both published in Detroit, by the Gale Research Company). *The Dictionary of Literary Biography* has just issued a volume called *American Writers in Paris 1920-1939*, edited by Karen Lane Rood (Doubleday, 1980). Its five-page entry on Barnes by Louis Kannenstine deals primarily with the content and nature of her various works but provides some information about her early life. Finally we can look at the two book-length critical studies that have been done of Barnes: *Djuna Barnes* by James Scott (Boston: Twayne, 1976), and *The Art of Djuna Barnes: Duality and Damnation* by Louis Kannenstine (New York University Press, 1977). Kannestine deals in some detail with Barnes's early career as a writer (though not with her personal life). Scott discusses the influences of Barnes's parents; her paternal grandmother, Zadel Barnes; and early family life on her work.

CRITICISM

A useful place to begin an examination of Barnes criticism is with essays that both survey and try to interpret Barnes's critical history. One of the best of these is Douglas Messerli's introduction to his 1975 *Djuna Barnes: A Bibliography*. In it he notes the decidedly positive response in 1936 and 1937 to the English and American editions of *Nightwood*. But he also recognizes that in 1936 and 1975 Barnes "has yet to be universally appreciated," and that "even in the universities, few have ever heard of Djuna Barnes or know anything of her rich career." As reasons for this he cites the "complexity and elusiveness of her work," and the fact that she "refused to mythologize herself through memoirs or reminiscences," so that "few of her readers know anything of her personal life." Critics themselves are in part responsible for her lack of recognition, he believes. Both *Nightwood* and *The Antiphon* "simply demanded a greater perception than many critics possessed," and recently the tendencies of critics to "concentrate almost entirely upon *Nightwood*," and to "work not toward an evaluation and interpretation of Barnes as much as they do toward broader literary theories of their own" have worked against wider understanding and appreciation of Barnes's work.

Erika Duncan in another 1976 essay, "Djuna Barnes and *Nightwood*" (*B Forum*, No. 4), also raises the question of what has "deterred a more widespread appreciation" of Barnes, but she offers a somewhat different answer. She believes it is because both readers and critics are unwilling to accept "the validity of pain as an experience." As a result, reviewers, while praising her style, bemoan the bitterness, decadence, and perversion of her vision and "even those critics who have recognized the literary importance of *Nightwood* have concentrated more on its structure and its language than its content."

Duncan's view that both critics and readers have resisted Barnes's work in order to repudiate the view of life it offers seems borne out by at least one early review. Floyd Dell, writing in *The Nation* on 2 January 1924, says of the stories in *A Book*, "Each of her stories seems to be leading impressively up to an inevitable end; but the inevitable never happens." This has the effect, he says, of reducing fiction to "just such a meaningless chaos of accident as life itself appears to sensitive and troubled minds." This, he argues, is opposed to one of the very purposes of art, which is to impose order: "we are accustomed, in fiction, to find life's chaos thought out and arranged in some fairly orderly and intelligible pattern: that, indeed, is supposed to be one of the purposes of art."

Barnes's work clearly does not arrange life's chaos in any kind of orderly pattern, and yet from the beginning responses to it have been remarkably positive. Even Dell finds much to praise in these stories, and Kenneth Burke, in a 1924 review of *A Book* (*The Dial*, May), says its pages "have a force, an ingenuity," and that in it "the will to tragedy is maintained with a sureness which is very rarely met with in contemporary writing."

Barnes's 1928 novel *Ryder* also evoked generally favorable responses. Ernest Bates begins his review in the *Saturday Review of Literature* (17 November 1928) by saying, "No one need be entirely unhappy this fall with such a book as 'Ryder' newly come into this world." Even a reviewer who finds this novel too derivative—"in the Joyce-out-of-Rabelais manner"—describes Barnes as "richly and authentically gifted" (*NewR*, 24 October 1928).

It is for *Nightwood*, however, in 1936 and 1937, that Barnes first received widespread critical recognition. Peter Quennell, writing in response to the British edition of it in 1936, describes it as "a very remarkable production," "strangely original," and "extremely moral" (*NSN*, 17 October 1936). Graham Greene comments that "a sick spiritual condition may have gone [in] to this book, but it is rare in contemporary fiction to be able to trace any spiritual experience whatever, and the accent, I think is sometimes that of a major poet" (*Tb*, 14 November 1936).

The American edition of *Nightwood*, published in 1937, included an introduction by T. S. Eliot in which he praised the novel for the "great achievement" of its style, the "brilliance" of its wit and characterization, and "a quality of horror and doom very nearly related to that of Elizabethan tragedy." American reviewers felt it necessary to comment both on the novel and upon Eliot's assessment of it. Though Alfred Kazin, writing in the *New York Times Book Review* (7 March 1937), takes issue with Eliot's view of *Nightwood* and gives the novel itself a very qualified review, Mark Van Doren says that Eliot "has praised Miss Barnes for what I consider the best of reasons; . . . the merits he discovers in *Nightwood* are clearly there" (*SoR*, Summer 1937). In similar fashion, Clifton Fadiman, in the *New Yorker* (13 March 1937), calls *Nightwood* "this extraordinary novel" and praises Eliot's "brilliant introduction." Even reviewers who dislike the book and who claim to be baffled by Eliot's admiration for it, almost without exception praise "the force and distinction of Miss Barnes's writing" (*NewR*, 31 March 1937). Reviewers who have the highest praise for *Nightwood* are those who admire both the power of Barnes's language in the novel and the novel's dark vision. This is true of Rose Feld, writing in the *New York Herald Tribune* (7 March 1937): "for a philosophy and a wisdom convoluted and complicated with a knowledge of good and evil, for language that has deep-flowing rhythm and Saxon hardihood, for the maintenance of a mood that is strange and dark, Djuna Barnes achieves distinction."

In the four decades since the publication of *Nightwood*, these first reviews of it have been succeeded by more extended attempts to study the novel's vision and technique and to relate these to trends in modern literature. Joseph Frank devotes the long middle section of his three-part essay, "Spatial Form in Modern Literature" (*SR*, Spring, Summer, Autumn 1945), to a detailed exposition of *Nightwood*, in which he argues that we cannot approach the novel "expecting to find a coherent temporal pattern," for it "lacks a narrative structure in the ordinary sense." Its chapters, he says, are "knit together, not by the progress of any action—either physical action, or as in a stream-of-consciousness novel, the act of thinking," but by "a pattern arising from the spatial interweaving of images and phrases independently of any time sequence." He further believes that in *Nightwood* "the evolution of spatial form in the novel [is carried] forward to a point where it is practically indistinguishable from modern poetry." Frank's essay has been frequently reprinted, and in a 1957 article, "The Literary Image and the Reader: A Consideration of the Theory of Spatial Form" (*JA*, September 1957), Walter Sutton sets out to "test his [Frank's] idea of spatial form . . . by reference to the actual reading of the . . . novel." Sutton's conclusion is that he must reject Frank's view that *Nightwood* has a pattern or structure independent of time-sequence. Rather, he says the "chief burden" of the novel is its "oppressive time-consciousness of a particular place and time in history—the cosmopolitan world of displaced Europeans and expatriated Americans in the post-World-War-I years."

Frank's and Sutton's essays are typical of those that try to place *Nightwood* in relation to the theory and practice of modern fiction. This continues to be a concern in critical writing about Barnes. For example, the

1976 essay by Michael Vella, "Djuna Barnes Gains Despite Critics' Poll" (*LGJ*, Winter 1976) argues that "Barnes absorbed so much" from the Surrealist movement centered in Paris in the 1920s and 1930s that "*Nightwood* is one of the most thoroughly surrealistic of American novels." But increasingly in the 1960s and 1970s there appear essays that focus more exclusively on the novel itself. Ulrich Weisstein's essay "Beast, Doll, and Woman: Djuna Barnes's Human Bestiary" (*Renascence*, Fall 1962), Kenneth Burke's "Version, Con-, Per-, and In-" (*SoR*, April 1966), and Edward Gunn's "Myth and Style in Djuna Barnes's *Nightwood*" (*MFS*, Winter 1973-1974) are essays of this type. In 1976 and 1978 two essays appeared on the style of *Nightwood*, Elizabeth Pohoda's "Style's Hoax: A Reading of Djuna Barnes' *Nightwood*" (*TCL*, May 1976) and Carolyn Allen's "'Dressing the Unknowable in the Garments of the Known': The Style of Djuna Barnes' *Nightwood*" in *Women's Language and Style: Studies in Contemporary Literature #1* (Akron, Ohio: University of Akron, 1978).

Nightwood continues to be the central focus of Barnes criticism, but a few critics have broadened their study of Barnes to examine her other work. A relatively early example of this is an essay by Alan Williamson, "The Divided Image: The Quest for Identity in the Works of Djuna Barnes" (*Crit*, Spring 1964). Suzanne Ferguson examines Barnes's short stories in a 1969 essay "Djuna Barnes's Short Stories: An Estrangement of the Heart" (*SoR*, Winter 1969). One of the most important of these general essays is by Louis Kannenstine and appears in the 1972 *Festschrift for Djuna Barnes on Her 80th Birthday* (Kent, Ohio, Kent State Libraries). The festschrift itself is a disappointing collection of brief tributes in poetry and prose, but Kannenstine's essay is a thoughtful overview of Barnes's work and how it has been received. In it he argues that "the collective work of Djuna Barnes has been a consistent whole, both in terms of its formal integrity and the philosophical point of view it suggests," but that this has not been recognized.

Barnes's 1958 verse play *The Antiphon* has been another focus of Barnes criticism, though it has received neither the attention nor the praise that has been accorded *Nightwood.* Dudley Fitts, writing in the *New York Times Book Review* (20 April 1958), gives it a mixed review: "It is scarcely a play: one cannot imagine it on any stage . . . but it is dramatic poetry of a curious and sometimes high order." Reviewers generally echo Fitts's view, admiring the play's language but regarding it as "unplayable" drama. Two helpful assessments of *The Antiphon* are those by Marie Ponsot, "'Careful Sorrow and Observed Compline'" (*Poetry*, October 1959), and Donna Gerstenberger, "Three Verse Playwrights and the American Fifties" in *Modern American Drama: Essays in Criticism*, edited by William Taylor (Deland, Fla.: Everett/Edwards, 1968).

Until quite recently there was no published book-length study of Barnes, but in 1976 and 1977 two such studies apeared. James B. Scott's *Djuna*

Barnes (Boston: Twayne, 1976) is a Twayne's United States Authors Series book and is addressed, Scott says in his preface, "to readers who for the main part have yet to read the works herein discussed." It begins with a chapter on Barnes's "Early Life" and devotes subsequent chapters to her stories, one-act plays, to *Ryder, Ladies Almanack, Nightwood*, and *The Antiphon*. Scott's view of Barnes is that she is a naturalist and not an existentialist, because "the naturalist believes . . . in the capability of logic and reason to understand life, even though he or his characters may be powerless to alter its hard realities." The existentialist, Scott says, sees life as "irrational" and "beyond understanding," while the purpose of the naturalist is to help us understand life, to show us "*how* and *why* life is tragic and painful." This thesis about Barnes is not one with which we may immediately agree, and the same is true of his concluding statement about *The Antiphon*, that it is "dramatically unified and sound" and "works" in performance.

Louis Kannenstine's *The Art of Djuna Barnes: Duality and Damnation* (New York University Press, 1977) attempts to "give Djuna Barnes her due, first by establishing the literary context within which her work belongs, and second by recognizing its formal achievement and thematic consistency, qualities not readily apparent upon a piecemeal examination." His view of Barnes is significantly at odds with that of Scott, for Kannenstine believes that "a root theme in Miss Barnes's work involves mystery, or, more precisely, the human condition of nonunderstanding, of ontological bewilderment following from the historical loss of the patterns of existence available in the old faiths." Barnes sees civilized man, Kannenstine says, as cut off from "the primitive element within himself," and also from a "state of holy grace." He lives, then, in an "intermediate existence" which is "wholly enigmatic." Kannenstine believes that Barnes's "middle vision" is most fully expressed in *Nightwood* and that "that immaculate novel is indeed a masterpiece." Like Scott, Kannestine devotes chapters to Barnes's early career, to the short stories, *Ryder*, *Ladies Almanack*, *Nightwood*, and *The Antiphon*. He also includes, however, two chapters on Barnes's poetry. In a chapter entitled "The Early Poems," he examines the poems which appear in *The Book of Repulsive Women* (1923), and in the last chapter, "Postscript," he looks at the five poems which have been published since 1938.

THE FUTURE OF BARNES CRITICISM

There is still a very limited amount of critical work being done on Barnes, though, after so many years, the publication of two book-length studies of her work may indicate that this situation is changing. The books themselves, Kannenstine's in particular, may revive interest in her work. The problem is, in part, that Barnes virtually stopped publishing in 1958 with the appearance of *The Antiphon*. The few short poems that have appeared since then have not been enough to spark new interest in her or to provide us with additional insights about her work. If, in the next few years, we gain access to materials that suggest new ways to think about her work, then we can expect a renewal of critical interest in her.

ANAÏS NIN

Anaïs Nin's first book, *D. H. Lawrence: An Unprofessional Study,* was published in 1932 when she was twenty-nine years old. When she died in 1977, she had been writing for over forty years, producing short stories, novels, a few works of criticism, and the many volumes of her diary. Until 1966, when publication of the edited *Diary* began, she was not widely known or admired as a writer. Oliver Evans, who published the first book-length study of her work in 1968, notes that for years it was customary to think of Nin as "an artist whose literary virtue was its own—and almost its only—reward," and as one whose "integrity stubbornly resists the commercial compromise." Nin's integrity was rewarded during the last decade of her life when the publication of six volumes of the *Diary* brought her a large and enthusiastic audience of readers and caused critics and scholars to begin serious study of her work.

BIBLIOGRAPHY

Benjamin Franklin V is the primary bibliographer of works by Anaïs Nin. In his 1973 book, *Anaïs Nin: A Bibliography* (Kent, Ohio: Kent State University Press), he attempts to provide a "complete record of Miss Nin's appearances in print in English, exclusive of Canadian editions of her books." At the beginning of this volume he solicits notice of omissions or errors and expresses doubt about the completeness of two sections, "Contributions to Books" and "Contributions to Periodicals," but his work seems, in fact, to have been remarkably thorough. His listing includes, in addition to her books, pamphlets, and the contributions mentioned above, published interviews, recordings of Nin reading her own work, her editorial affiliations and letters written to her and subsequently published. This last list of letters, he acknowledges, is a somewhat "unorthodox" inclusion. But it does alert us to the important volume of letters from Henry Miller, *Letters to Anaïs Nin*, edited by Gunther Stuhlmann (New York: G. P. Putnam's Sons, and London: Peter Owen, 1965), and also to Miller's "Letter to Anaïs Nin Regarding One of Her Books," which was published in Miller's *Sunday After the War* (Norfolk, Conn.: New Directions, 1944) as "More About Anaïs Nin." These letters contain useful commentary on her work and are not noted in Rose Marie Cutting's *Anaïs Nin: A Reference Guide* (Boston: G. K. Hall, 1978), which lists "Writings About Anaïs Nin, 1937-1977."

Perhaps the greatest value of Franklin's book is its clarification of the publishing history and shifting contents of particular volumes and titles of Nin's work. In "Anaïs Nin: A Bibliographical Essay" in *A Casebook on Anaïs Nin*, edited by Robert Zaller (New York and Scarsborough, Ontario: New American Library; London: New English Library, 1974), an essay written just prior to the publication of *Anaïs Nin: A Bibliography*, Franklin remarks that Nin's "publishing history is . . . so complex that it has . . . prevented interested scholars from turning their much needed critical insights toward her literary creations." Franklin demonstrates that complexity in this essay by discussing "Titles with Changing Contents," "Compositions with Changing Titles," and "Titles Referring to More Than One Work." In *Anaïs Nin: A Bibliography* he presents in detail the publishing history of individual volumes and titles.

Franklin's 1973 book is supplemented in part by his own subsequent work. During 1973, while still an editor of the journal, *Under the Sign of Pisces: Anaïs Nin and Her Circle* (published at Ohio State University in Columbus, Ohio), Franklin regularly reported on new Nin publications. Richard Centing, an editor of *Under the Sign of Pisces* since it began in 1970 and its sole editor since the last issue of the 1973 volume, has continued to report to the journal's readers on new publications of Nin's work. Elsewhere, as in an essay appearing in the special Nin issue of *Mosaic* (Winter 1978), Franklin again examines and clarifies the details of a chapter of Nin's publishing history.

"A Checklist of the Writings of Anaïs Nin, 1973-1976," compiled by Reesa Marcinczyk and published in the Winter 1977 issue of *Under the Sign of Pisces*, further updates Franklin's 1973 list. Marcinczyk attempts, as does Franklin, to be complete and arranges her bibliography in much the same way as his. Marcinczyk's list contains many more items than those reported on in *Under the Sign of Pisces* between 1973 and 1977.

Since Marcinczyk's checklist there has been no systematic attempt to add to the bibliography of Nin's work. During 1976 Nin's health was failing and, aside from volume six of the *Diary* (*The Diary of Anaïs Nin, 1955-1966*), little previously unpublished work appeared. Since her death in January of 1977, several volumes of early work have been published for the first time. These include an early volume of the *Diary, Linotte: The Early Diary of Anaïs Nin 1914-1920* (Harcourt Brace Jovanovich, 1978), two volumes of erotica, *Delta of Venus* (Harcourt Brace Jovanovich, 1977), and *Little Birds* (Harcourt Brace Jovanovich, 1979), and some early stories, *Waste of Timelessness and Other Early Stories* (Weston, Conn.: Magic Circle Press, 1977). An additional volume of the *Diary* for the years 1966-1974 was published in 1980 by Harcourt Brace Jovanovich.

With Nin's reputation as an important writer now established and interest in her work running high, it is no longer difficult to keep track of new publications of Nin's own work. But staying in touch with articles and books being published about Nin is quite a different story. Richard Centing points out that Nin scholarship has become "a thriving academic industry" (*USP*, Fall 1979). In addition, Nin's life and work have stimulated published responses which are not, strictly speaking, scholarly or critical. For example, *Celebration with Anaïs Nin*, edited by Valerie Harms (Riverside, Conn.: Magic Circle Press, 1973), is an account of a "weekend dialogue among thirty diverse strangers . . . Anaïs Nin, and some important persons from her life and work." There is a real need, therefore, for bibliographical sources that will keep us informed of what is being published about Nin and that will help us sort through and evaluate these publications. Rose Marie Cutting's *Anaïs Nin: A Reference Guide* (Boston: G. K. Hall, 1978) does the first of these things for the period 1937-1977, by providing an annotated bibliography of writings about Nin published during those years. Richard Centing notes that this is "certainly the most complete list of secondary sources on Nin now in existence" (*USP*, Fall 1979). In addition, Cutting's chronological arrangement makes it easy to survey the history of interest in Nin and responses to her work. Cutting's annotations seem to be careful attempts to indicate the nature of the works she lists ("a review," "a descriptive bibliography," and so on) and to summarize their contents (in the case of books, she does this at surprising length, chapter by chapter) without making any judgment of their value. For this reason, her *Guide* fails to help us identify the most important work being published about Nin at the present time.

Under the Sign of Pisces, itself an outlet for Nin criticism, reviews book-length studies of Nin's work as they appear and has, since the journal's inception, made note of articles on Nin that have appeared elsewhere. The Spring 1980 issue of *Under the Sign of Pisces* published "A First Supplement to Rose Marie Cutting's *Anaïs Nin: A Reference Guide* (Boston: G. K. Hall, 1978)." This was compiled by *USP*'s editor, Richard Centing, and includes writings about Nin published since Cutting's 1977 cutoff date, as well as earlier items not listed by Cutting. These supplements are continuing to appear in *USP*. The Winter 1981 issue includes a "A Fourth Supplement" to Cutting's *Reference Guide*. Centing's annotations are especially helpful in directing us to the most interesting of the items he lists.

EDITIONS

Nin's long years of struggling to have her works published and of publishing many of them herself came to an end in 1961 when Alan Swallow agreed to become her United States publisher (see the *Diary, 1955-1966*, for the exchange of letters between Nin and Swallow regarding this). With *Seduction of the Minotaur* in that year, Swallow began publishing her new work and at the same time reissuing previous work. Swallow died in 1966, but the Swallow Press has kept in print the volumes of her fiction and also *D. H. Lawrence: An Unprofessional Study*. In addition, it has published

The Anaïs Nin Reader, edited by Philip Jason (1973), and *A Woman Speaks: The Lectures, Seminars and Interviews of Anaïs Nin*, edited by Evelyn J. Hinz (1975).

In 1964 Nin began to consider seriously publication of the diary and to discuss this possibility with Gunther Stuhlmann and Alan Swallow. They were, she reports in the *Diary, 1955-1966*, "encouraging," but Swallow "felt it might be too big a burden for him." Several large publishers considered and decided against publishing the diary before Harcourt Brace agreed to do so. The first volume of the edited *Diary* was issued in 1966 and eight volumes of it are now in print. Volumes One through Six, covering the years from 1931 through 1966, appeared between 1966 and 1976. *Linotte: The Early Diary of Anaïs Nin, 1914-1920* was published in 1978. It is actually the seventh volume of the *Diary* to be published, but is not referred to as Volume Seven because it covers a period much prior to that of the first six volumes. *The Diary of Anaïs Nin, 1966-1974*, published in 1980, is the eighth volume of the *Diary* to be published, but is called Volume Seven because it picks up where Volume Six ended in 1966. In addition, Harcourt Brace Jovanovich has published *A Photographic Supplement to the Diary of Anaïs Nin* (1974), a collection of essays, interviews and lectures called *In Favor of the Sensitive Man and Other Essays* (1976); and the two volumes of erotica written in the 1940s, *Delta of Venus* (1977), and *Little Birds* (1979). Two volumes of Nin's work have been published by other American presses. *The Novel of the Future*, in which Nin takes up again some of the critical issues raised in her two pamphlets of 1946 and 1947, *Realism and Reality* and *On Writing*, was published in 1978 by Macmillan. *Waste of Timelessness and Other Early Stories* was published by the Magic Circle Press (Weston, Conn.) in 1977. This volume is made up of stories that Nin says, in a preface, she was "persuaded" would be of interest, though she describes them as "immature" and "never intended . . . to be published." In 1979 another volume of Nin's work, *Portrait in Three Dimensions*, was published by Renata Druks (Malibu, Calif.: Concentric Circle Press) in a limited edition of one thousand copies. It consists of comments by Nin on both the personality and art of her friend, Renata Druks, whom she met in 1953. According to Richard Centing (see *USP*, Winter 1980), Nin's brief introduction to this volume had not been published previously, though the rest of it consists of exerpts from *Collages, The Novel of the Future* and Volume Five of the *Diary*. Centing says the volume was completed in 1967, but not published at that time because the color plates of Druks's paintings would have made it too expensive.

Most of Nin's published work is also available from English publishers, primarily Peter Owen, and much of it is now available or becoming available in translation in French, Spanish, and even Japanese. The availability of almost all of Nin's work in the United States and elsewhere indicates the present high level of interest in her.

MANUSCRIPTS AND LETTERS

There are two large collections of Nin manuscript materials of which anyone studying Nin should be aware. One of these is among the Special Collections of the Northwestern University Library. It was purchased from Nin in 1952, and a checklist of its contents done by Nancy Zee was published in *Under the Sign of Pisces* in the Spring 1972 issue. In 1976, Valerie Harms published a detailed discussion of some early and unpublished novels and stories that are a part of this collection. This essay appears in *Stars in My Sky: Maria Montessori, Anaïs Nin, Frances Steloff* (Riverside, Conn.: Magic Circle Press). In 1977 the Magic Circle Press, with which Valerie Harms is associated, published sixteen short stories from this manuscript collection in the volume *Waste of Timelessness and Other Early Stories*. Finally, in the special Nin issue of *Mosaic* edited by Evelyn Hinz (Winter 1978), Marie Clare Van der Elst published an article called "The Manuscripts of Anaïs Nin at Northwestern." Elst notes that this collection contains "practically all the manuscripts of Anaïs Nin's fiction—published as well as unpublished—together with two drafts of what was to become *D. H. Lawrence: An Unprofessional Study*." Elst's article, along with the checklist by Zee and the work done by Harms, gives a very detailed account of the contents of this collection.

By contrast, there is less specific knowledge of and less ready access to the other large collection of Nin manuscripts, which is among the Special Collections of the University of California, Los Angeles Library. In the Fall 1976 issue of *Under the Sign of Pisces*, Richard Centing published the following note: "I have been informed that the manuscript of Anaïs Nin's *Diary* has been sold to the University of California, Los Angeles. If any of my readers could write a story on the sale . . . I would be glad to publish it." As late as the Winter 1981 issue of *USP*, no reader had come forward with the details of this sale. In response to my inquiry, I was told: "UCLA has acquired the literary papers of Anaïs Nin. These papers were purchased with particular restrictions regarding use. Any unpublished material is sealed until after publication. Of the 149 diaries which comprise the bulk of the collection, the first 6 which have been published are available for use." The phrase "the literary papers" is slightly misleading here, since, in fact, a very significant part of Nin's literary papers are in the Northwestern collection. But these two collections together give us a large body of valuable and potentially revealing manuscript material. Hopefully the material at UCLA will eventually become as available for study as that at Northwestern, since it should allow us to study the editing of the diaries by both Nin and Stuhlmann.

Other Nin materials are scattered in libraries throughout the United States. These consist largely of letters to and from Nin and occasionally of typescripts or proofs of published works. Two additional libraries hold collections of some size and significance. These are at Southern Illinois

University in Carbondale, Illinois, and the University of Kansas at Lawrence, Kansas. The Southern Illinois collection consists of seventy-one letters from Nin to Lawrence Durrell, whom she met in 1937, and twenty-two other letters from Nin to various individuals. This library also has some Nin materials in its Caresse Crosby collection, but that collection was described as unprocessed in response to my inquiry in October 1979.

The University of Kansas materials are in the *Two Cities* Archives collection in the Department of Special Collections at the Kenneth Spencer Research Library. *Two Cities* was a bilingual magazine conceived by Jean Fanchette, a young medical student whom Nin met in Paris in the winter of 1958-1959. The first issue of *Two Cities* appeared on 15 April 1959, with Nin as its New York editor and Fanchette listed as "Directeur." (See the table of contents page of this issue reproduced in the Nin issue of *Mosaic* [Winter 1978].) Only nine issues of the journal were published, but Nin's relationship with Fanchette was an important and typical one. In its early stages Nin was warmly and enthusiastically appreciative of Fanchette's understanding of her work. The first issue of *Two Cities* contained an essay on Nin by Fanchette, "Pour une preface." In the 1955-1966 volume of the *Diary*, Nin calls this article "nearly perfect, so near the target in insight," and says of Fanchette, "I count him my best friend in France." Soon, however, she began to find both the work of editing the journal and Fanchette's repeated demands for money burdensome and upsetting. At the same time, she also saw this relationship as resembling the many relationships in which she had given a great deal of herself and her resources and then come to feel used or betrayed. Her discussions of the relationship with Dr. Inge Bognar (with whom she was undergoing analysis at the time) constituted an attempt to break this pattern.

The University of Kansas *Two Cities* Archives collection is described by Manuscripts Librarian Ann Hyde as consisting of "proofs, accepted and rejected manuscripts, . . . correspondence with contributors to the literary magazine" and "about 88 letters from Nin to the editor Jean Fanchette." Given the intensity of Nin's early relationship with Fanchette and her awareness that the relationship was evolving in a familiar way, it seems probable that these materials offer glimpses of an important episode in Nin's life.

BIOGRAPHY

With the publication of the *Diary* beginning in 1966, Anaïs Nin became a figure in whom there was widespread and intense public interest. In their recent critical study of her work, *Anaïs Nin: An Introduction* (Athens: Ohio University Press, 1979), Benjamin Franklin V and Duane Schneider note that "the great popularity that Nin earned through the *Diary* . . . made her a celebrity." From 1966 until the last year or so of her life, when she had become too ill, Nin traveled frequently throughout the United States, lecturing at colleges and universities, reading from her work, talking with groups of students and readers, and answering questions. Evelyn Hinz, in the introduction to the volume she has edited, *A Woman Speaks: The Lectures, Seminars and Interviews of Anaïs Nin* (Chicago: Swallow Press, 1975), says that Nin came to feel that readers wanted to see her in person in order to relieve their fear "that possibly the woman with whose struggles one had identified . . . was not real but a fictional creation, . . . [that] this apparently painstaking record of an individual's search for viable truths might be discovered to be partially or totally a masterful fabrication."

Those who heard Nin speak and perhaps met her as she traveled about the country were struck by her warmth and seeming openness and by the way "she gave herself to everyone" (see "Report on 'Celebration: A Weekend with Anaïs Nin,'" in *USP*, Fall 1972). The public idea of Nin that emerges from 1966 on is that of a person eager to make herself and her experiences available to others, both through her writing and through warm personal encounters with individuals and groups. Yet despite this, there is, at present, no biography of Nin, and precise biographical information about her is not readily available. Franklin and Schneider provide a biographical footnote near the beginning of their study of Nin that is both brief and cautiously worded:

> Anaïs Nin was born in Neuilly, France, on 21 February 1903. Anaïs, her mother (Rose Culmell), and two brothers (Thorvald and Joaquin) were deserted by her father (Joaquin, the musician) in about 1912. The four of them moved to New York City where young Anaïs enrolled in P.S. No. 9. She did not complete her formal schooling, and in her teenage years she was a model and a dancer. She was married at about the age of eighteen and returned to Paris, presumably with her husband, in the 1920's.

The paradox is that we know so much about Nin, from the *Diary* and from her fiction, lectures, and interviews, and, at the same time, so little. We know, for example, nothing about her marriage, except when it took place, that Ian Hugo is still alive, and that they collaborated on the illustrating and filming of some of her work. Hugo is mentioned in the *Diary* only as an illustrator. Critics commenting on the *Diary* note repeatedly how much is omitted from this account of her life and how much those omissions affect the character of the account:

> The edited versions of the diary nearly all appear to be concealing more than they reveal. There is nothing, for example, about Nin's long marriage. We are left to guess who exactly were and were not Nin's lovers. There is very little about her daily domestic life or the source of the money on which she lives. ("Anaïs Nin" by Laurie Stone in *The Village Voice*, 26 July 1976).

Lynn Sukenick remarks that "in certain respects the diaries are as elusive as the father they are written to—the absence of Nin's husband in these pages, for instance, necessarily leaves a fissure which would make all other relationships undergo a geological shift" ("The 'Diaries' of Anaïs Nin," *Shenandoah*, Spring 1976). In trying to characterize Nin's relation to the reader of the *Diary*, Sukenick says, "she creates an atmosphere of intimacy at the same time that she refrains from a policy of open disclosure." Nin seems to have related in much the same way to those who came to know her personally. What she did not tell of herself in the pages of the *Diary* was not necessarily revealed outside of them. During her lifetime the impression one received of Nin outside the pages of her work seems to have been as carefully shaped and controlled as the persona created in the *Diary*.

Perhaps the most important biographical document that comes out of the period prior to Nin's death is the film "Anaïs Nin Observed: A Film Portrait of a Woman as Artist" done by Robert Snyder in 1973. A notice in the Winter 1973 issue of *Under the Sign of Pisces* announces that this film has "been shown recently at UCLA, the College of Marin, and Dartmouth, and has met with a most enthusiastic response." In 1976 the Swallow Press published *Anaïs Nin Observed: From a Film Portrait of a Woman as Artist*. This is a book of photographs and text that Snyder describes as "derived" from the film. In the acknowledgments to this volume, Snyder expresses his special gratitude to Rupert Pole, who assisted him in making both the film and the book. He notes that Pole's "devotion to Anaïs and his knowledge of her work and the vast archives of extant pictures, mss., and texts eased the burden on Anaïs and made my job smoother."

Despite the interest this film and the book based on it have for us, they are both products of the period during which Nin or someone close to her, such as Rupert Pole, effectively controlled our knowledge and view of her. In 1975, however, two years prior to her death, Nin appointed Evelyn Hinz as her official biographer and provided her with a statement to that effect. This statement, addressed "To Whom it May Concern," stipulates that Hinz will have access to "the original diaries . . . and other pertinent materials." The Fall 1977 issue of *Under the Sign of Pisces* prints Nin's statement and Hinz' own soliciting information for the biography. We can expect, then, in the future, to know considerably more about Nin's life and experiences than we do now. It will be interesting to see how this information will affect critical discussion of her work, particularly of the *Diary*.

CRITICISM

Rose Marie Cutting's bibliography of "Writings about Anaïs Nin, 1937-1977" in *Anaïs Nin: A Reference Guide* lists no book-length studies prior to 1968 and only about 100 shorter writings for the period of nearly thirty years before 1966, when the first volume of the *Diary* appeared. In 1966 alone, however, thirty-five articles were published, and in 1967 another twenty-eight appeared in response to the second volume of the *Diary*. In 1968, though no new volume of the *Diary* was published, twenty more articles appeared and in 1969, when yet another diary volume was issued, there were thirty-five articles. In the years since 1969 the quantity of writings about Nin has continued to increase, and there are now five book-length critical studies of her work. Because both the quantity and focus of Nin criticism shifted so dramatically in 1966 when publication of the *Diary* began, Nin's critical history consists of at least two chapters, the first a fairly brief one and the second longer and more complex.

1937-1966

Henry Miller initiated the public discussion of Nin as a writer in his essay "Un Être Etoilique," which appeared in *The Criterion* in October 1937. At that time, Nin's only published books were *D. H. Lawrence: An Unprofessional Study* (1932) and *The House of Incest* (1936). Miller's essay does not comment on either of these, but instead on the unpublished diary, which he describes as "a monument of confession which when given to the world will take its place beside the revelations of St. Augustine, Petronius, Abelard, Rousseau, Proust and others." Miller's statement was frequently reprinted in the nearly thirty years between 1937 and the publication of the first volume of the diary in 1966. During these years curiosity about and interest in the diary grew, and portions of it were read in manuscript by Nin's friends and literary associates. Critics and readers in general, however, had no access to the diary, and therefore published criticism of Nin's work before 1966 focuses on the fiction.

Here again Miller gives us one of the earliest responses in a "Letter to Anaïs Nin, regarding one of her books." This was not published until 1944 in Miller's *Sunday After the War* (Norfolk, Conn.: New Directions), but the letter is dated 1933 and was apparently written after Miller had read a version of *The House of Incest.* His comments are appreciative and insightful and include detailed analyses of passages, but they are also of interest to us because in them he notes many of those qualities of Nin's work that critics have noted ever since. He comments, for example, on the uniqueness of her style ("I do not recall anyone to whom you bear the slightest resemblance"), on the difficulty of what she is attempting ("what you are trying to put into words defies language"), and on the modernness of her language and her use of material from dreams or the unconscious ("it is the language of modernity, . . . of nerves, repressions, larval thoughts and processes, the images not entirely divorced from their dream content"). He notes that the novel contains passages that "hover on the borders of hallucination," and that she sometimes withholds too many clues from the reader—"there are too many holes between your utterances." He is struck most of all by her powers of insight, especially as they are applied to women—"you have said such tremendous things, such revelatory things, that you appear to me like a sorceress."

The third volume of Nin's *Diary* (1939-1944) records her difficulty in finding an audience for her work in the United States. At the end of that volume, however, she prints the whole of a brief but appreciative essay by Edmund Wilson that appeared in the *New Yorker* on 1 April 1944. Wilson's positive review of *Under a Glass Bell*, which she had printed herself, was her first recognition by the American literary establishment. In it Wilson notes some of the same qualities that Miller had commented on: that these are "half stories, half dreams," that some "passages . . . suffer a little from an hallucinatory vein of writing which the Surrealists have overdone," and that the stories take place in a world of "feminine perception." Finally, Wilson says "Miss Nin is a very good artist." We can judge the impact of this review by a passage in the opening entry of the fourth volume of the *Diary* (dated April 1944): "we . . . have to work on a second printing of *Under a Glass Bell*. The first edition of three hundred copies was sold quickly. A publisher who met me at a party said: 'How did you get so well known with three hundred copies of a book?' "

Nin's reputation was not made, however, by this review and the subsequent sales of *Under a Glass Bell*. Many, if not most, critics remained hostile to her work. Diana Trilling, in a review of *This Hunger* in *The Nation* on 16 January 1946, says Nin's "method" is that of "clinical history," and her stories "more like case histories." In noting Nin's use of the material of psychoanalysis in her fiction, Trilling is remarking on a facet of Nin's writing that will be both admired and criticized in the next several decades of response to her work. The objection to this implicit in Trilling's comment that Nin's stories are "more like case histories than . . . short fiction" is that Nin's writings are not finally works of art. This objection to Nin's use of psychoanalytical material is not as frequently expressed as we might expect. But admirers and defenders of her work have continued to refute it. Harriet Zinnes, in a 1963 article, "Anaïs Nin's Works Reissued" (*BA*, Summer 1963), argues that "it is far more accurate to characterize Miss Nin's work as 'poetic' . . . than psychoanalytic." Zinnes acknowledges that one does find at times in the novels "the pointed psychoanalytic revelation of a character's action," but she goes on to say that "the unfolding of the action derives from a primary poetic conception which is conveyed by the act of language, by the symbolism, by the texture and rhythm of words, the color and movement of lines."

Trilling is also annoyed because Nin leaves out so much that we are ordinarily told about characters in a work of fiction. She notes that this "abstraction of her characters from the context of their real lives . . . gives a certain surrealist quality to her stories," but says that "her approach is not properly described as surrealist, since . . . Nin is primarily concerned to lay out a case."

A review of *Under a Glass Bell* by Elizabeth Hardwick in the *Partisan Review* (June 1948) further illustrates the irritated and impatient response that Nin's fiction often received in the 1940s and 1950s. Hardwick remarks that Nin's "attraction to the inexpressible is fatal," that Nin "shuns the real world" and writes instead about the "psychological underworld," that "she likes abstractions" and has "a pathological appetite for mystification."

During these early years, many critics seemed not to understand what Nin was attempting in her fiction. For this reason, William Burford in an essay, "The Art of Anaïs Nin" (published in *Anaïs Nin: On Writing*, by Alicat Press, 1947, along with Nin's essay "On Writing"), states that critics "should view new writing by new standards." The "patterns of Jane Austen," he argues, "represent the spirit of the eighteenth century, . . . but in the twentieth century . . . we must have a fresh order." Nin, he says, has the "ability to create an order which seems to us more valid in our contemporary world than the order of Jane Austen." The "realism" of writers like Steinbeck and Hemingway is, Burford claims, a "dead end."

Burford makes reference in this essay to Nin's own essay "Realism and Reality" of which 750 copies were published in 1946 (also by the Alicat Press). This essay was not widely read in 1946, but in Nin's book *The Novel of the Future*, published in 1968 by Macmillan, she looks back to that essay and places it in the context of a dialogue in which she was then engaged with "publishers . . . critics, . . . close friends and people whose opinions I respected" about the nature of her work. Specifically, she says, she received "sharp" and "probing" questions about the fact that she "left out so much of the realistic trappings and concentrated only on those having a direct relation to the emotional drama." These questions led her to begin "what seemed at first a purely defensive interpretation of abstraction, of deleting the unessential, the upholstery, the commonplace, and the obvious." Finally, she says, she found it necessary "to formulate a theory." The "main theme" of that theory was "that one could only find reality by discarding realism." She notes that this theory was not new even at that time in France, but that in America in the 1940s "Surrealism was an unpopular term," and "no one" seemed inclined "to follow the direction indicated by D. H. Lawrence, James Joyce, Djuna Barnes, or André Breton." She realizes, therefore, that in 1946 she was "speaking of psychological reality to an audience conditioned to representational social realism."

Nin's statements here typify her attempt throughout her career to clarify her intentions as a writer and to persuade readers and critics of the value and desirability of those intentions. They also reflect her continuing belief that those who do not understand or respond well to her work have not yet grasped those intentions and are responding out of outmoded expectations.

During the 1950s critical responses to Nin's work were more temperate and generally more favorable. Maxwell Geismar, for example, in his review of *A Spy in the House of Love* (*The Nation*, 24 July 1954), calls it "the best of her series of novels published in this country." He also praises it for its "psychological realism," and says of Nin that she is "one of the few women writers in our literary tradition to affirm the centrality of the biological impulses for her own sex," and that, furthermore, "she is prepared to describe these emotions from the feminine point of view with the same ruthless honesty that marked a D. H. Lawrence or a Dreiser."

Nin was delighted by one assessment of her work that was published during this period, the essay by Jean Fanchette published in *Two Cities: La Revue Bilingue de Paris* on 15 April 1959. (See the discussion of Fanchette above.) Fanchette notes that Nin is known in France through her preface to Henry Miller's *Tropic of Cancer*, since her own work has not yet been translated into French, but he views her as a writer of great importance and originality and ranks her with Virginia Woolf.

Fanchette's essay was not widely read and has never been reprinted, but it is significant as an early and very positive response to Nin's work from outside the United States and her immediate circle of friends and literary associates. Nin seems to have felt at this time that the critical tide so long running against her was now turning: "Jean Fanchette is translating *Spy* into French. For twenty years I have been vilified and excluded, and for the first time this summer felt appreciated" (*Diary 1955-1966*).

In Fall 1962 an article on Nin's fiction, "Anaïs Nin and the Discovery of Inner Space," appeared in the *Prairie Schooner*. It is still a helpful analysis of her fiction, but in 1962 it was unusual in several ways. Its author, Oliver Evans, was a university professor writing an extended essay on Nin's work in a scholarly journal. Though he alludes near the end of the essay to "the publication by Alan Swallow last fall of Miss Nin's collected works," his purpose is not to review a recent Nin publication, but rather to examine closely and at some length the career of a writer whom he treats as a major literary figure. He notes that the audience for Nin's work, "though discriminating, has never been a large one." But he praises her "integrity" and her "obstinacy" in "ignoring the advice" of the "Saturday Reviewers of Literature" and continuing to write "in her own very special way." Prior to Evans's essay, critics of Nin's work had been, with only a few exceptions, reviewers writing for magazines like the *Saturday Review*. This continued to be true for a while longer, but gradually in the 1960s and increasingly in the 1970s, Nin's work began to receive the serious attention of academic critics writing for scholarly journals.

Harriet Zinnes's essay "Anaïs Nin's Works Reissued" (*BA*, Summer 1963) is written in response to the Swallow publication of her work, but like Evans's essay, it is an assessment of the whole of her work thus far. Zinnes's essay is an appreciative but balanced examination of some of the influences on Nin's work—her "close sympathy with Lawrence," for example; her aims as a writer as expressed in the 1947 pamphlet "On Writing"; Nin's characteristic theme, "What is the self?"; and the success and "occasional failures" of her technique. Like Evans, Zinnes treats Nin as an important writer. Her fiction, Zinnes says, has the "stamp of genius."

Another significant piece of criticism that comes out of this period in the 1960s before the publication of Nin's *Diary* is the chapter on Nin in Pierre

Brodin's *Présence contemporaines: écrivains américans d'aujourd'hui* (Paris: Nouvelles Editions Debresse, 1964). Like Evans and Zinnes, Brodin treats Nin as a major writer. He recognizes that she has written in a manner contrary to most of the contemporary trends in American literature, but he predicts that "Le jour n'est pas loin où elle sera, à juste titre, considérée comme un des écrivains les plus importants de son temps."

In 1964 Nin's *Collages* was published by the Swallow Press. Responses to it were mixed but more favorable than not. Nin was coming to be seen at this time as a fiction writer of much artistry whose works are difficult and unusual and who will always be read and admired by a small and select audience. *Collages* is Nin's last work of fiction, and with the publication of the first volume of the *Diary* in 1966, Nin's whole situation with respect to readers and critics changed.

Publication of the *Diary* came about through an arrangement between the Swallow Press and Harcourt Brace and World. Alan Swallow, who had been publishing Nin's fiction in the United States since 1961, is reported by Nin to have felt that the diary "might be too big . . . for him." Whatever Swallow meant by this, his premonition was correct. Benjamin Franklin V and Duane Schneider, in *Anaïs Nin: An Introduction* (Athens: Ohio University Press, 1979), refer to "the huge success of the first volume," and Bettina Knapp, in her *Anaïs Nin* (Frederick Ungar, 1978), says that "reviews, public appearances, television programs and celebrations" followed the publication of the *Diary*'s first volume.

Suddenly Nin's readership was a large and enthusiastic one, and she was being asked to give interviews, do readings and go on lecture tours. As discussion of the *Diary* by reviewers and critics began, and as subsequent volumes of the diary were published, more and more critical study of Nin's work was undertaken. During the period from 1966 to 1979, hundreds of articles and five book-length critical studies of Nin were written. Interestingly, though Nin wrote no new fiction after the publication of *Collages* in 1964, much critical attention was directed during this period to the fiction as well as the *Diary*. Novels and short stories several decades old (*The House of Incest*, *Under a Glass Bell*, for example) received intense critical scrutiny. There was much interest in her unpublished fiction, and she was finally persuaded to publish a volume of early stories, *Waste of Timelessness and Other Early Stories* (Weston, Conn.: Magic Circle Press, 1977). Gradually all that Nin did became of interest to her growing numbers of admirers (many of them young and many of them women). College students packed lecture halls to hear her speak, read, and answer questions. She was hailed by some leaders of the women's movement as a woman who had achieved liberation, and a great many readers wrote to her about their own experiences and their responses to the *Diary*.

During this period a whole new set of critical issues and problems arose. Not the least of these was the emergence of a cult-like attitude toward Nin, which threatened to bias critical assessment of her work as much as the early hostility towards her had done. This was, in part, the result of her strikingly attractive manner and appearance and the warmth and interest she seemed to direct at those who came to hear and meet her. With the passage of time, this devotion to Nin the person, as opposed to Nin the writer, will undoubtedly diminish.

1966-1979, THE DIARY

Critical discussion of the *Diary* during these years returns again and again to many of the same issues. One of these has to do with just what the *Diary* is—journal, memoir, autobiography, novel? Is it "true" and therefore valuable as social and literary history? Or is it fiction? Is it a shaped and conscious work of art? If so, is it, perhaps, a new kind of work for which we have, presently, no category? Leon Edel, in a 7 May 1966 review (*SatR*), treats it simply as a journal, "a document rather than an act of creation." He notes the purposes these "voluminous notebooks of the self" seemed to have served for Nin personally and sees the value of the *Diary*'s first volume as consisting of the "portraits" it offers of such people as Otto Rank, and of the "early Depression years in Paris after most American expatriates had fled."

As early as these first reviews, however, Karl Shapiro (*BW*, 1 May 1966) says that the *Diary* has "the full dimensions of the novel (character, 'plot,' exposition, dialogue, causal action, and . . . in addition the quality of perception, the precision of imagery, the intricate organization, and the exquisite feminine sensibility . . . of the poet." Shapiro concludes by saying it is finally "unclassifiable as a book at all," but he clearly views it as a conscious and created work of art. Few reviewers and critics in 1966 or since have treated the *Diary* as Edel did. Nearly all have seen it as the work of a conscious literary artist, and most apply to it concepts and terminology borrowed from novel criticism. Jean Garrigue, in her *New York Times* review (24 April 1966), speaks of the "principal characters" of this first volume. Marguerite Young, writing in 1967 (see *Voyages: A National Literary Magazine*, Autumn) says "the diary is replete with fictive elements." Daniel Stern, in an essay called "Princess of the Underground," appearing on 4 March 1968 in *The Nation*, says that Nin "is so much the novelist that the 'others' in her *Diary* are as real as the 'I'." The people in the *Diary* have, he says, "the density of fully imagined characters." In a later essay in *The Nation* (29 November 1971), Stern says that in the *Diary* Nin is "creating a novel in the form of a continuous diary."

Treating the *Diary* as a kind of novel raises other questions. One of these is the question of just who or what Nin herself is in this new kind of novel. Duane Schneider dealt with this question as early as 1970 in an essay called "The Art of Anaïs Nin" (*SoR*, Spring 1970), in which he argues that in the *Diary* Nin is defining "a single, primary, multifaceted character, Anaïs

Nin," who is "the artist's conception of herself." He develops this argument further in a later essay, "Anaïs Nin in the *Diary:* The Creation and Development of a Persona" (*Mosaic*, Winter 1978), in which he says that the "central consciousness" in the *Diary* is "that of a persona" whom we must be careful not to confuse with Nin the "real person." Schneider goes on to say that the *Diary* is, in fact, a "new art form—the journal-novel."

Generally, critics have accepted the view that the *Diary* is a new kind of work that combines qualities of the diary and the novel, but this raises the question of how we should view the contents of the *Diary*—as truth or fiction? Critics who address this question seem, at times, to be speaking a kind of double-talk. Wayne McEvilly, for example, in a 1971 essay called "The Bread of Tradition: Reflections on the Diary of Anaïs Nin" (*PrS*, Summer 1971), says that "Nin's diaries are fiction even if true." But he also says, as do a number of critics that "the matter of... truth" is "inessential." Paul Kuntz, in an essay, "Art as Public Dream," published in *A Casebook on Anaïs Nin*, edited by Robert Zaller (New American Library, 1974), says simply that "the standards of factual truth are inappropriate to works of art," and Tristine Rainer, in an essay, "Anaïs Nin's Diary I: The Birth of the Young Woman as an Artist," also published in the *Casebook*, argues that "Nin's journals... transcend the artificial Western categories of fact and fiction, life and art, in order to discover the power of truth combined with the poetry of fiction."

The issue of the "truth" of the *Diary* will perhaps never be put quite to rest. Rather, statements like those above about the irrelevancy of this issue seem to have resulted in a refocusing of discussion on a closely related issue —that of the omissions from and editing of the *Diary*. Since the volumes of the *Diary* first began appearing, readers and critics have been troubled by the fact that so much has been left out of what seems at first an intimate and full account of Nin's experiences. In her public appearances Nin received frequent questions from readers about these omissions and her response was consistently that they occurred out of respect for those who did not wish—as she did—to share their lives. "I have a right to share my life, but I do not have the right to impose that on people who do not wish to," affirms Nin in *A Woman Speaks*, edited by Evelyn Hinz (Chicago: Swallow Press, 1975). Nin also addressed this issue in "Genesis of the Diary," the fifth chapter of *The Novel of the Future* (Macmillan, 1968), in which she says, "As a diarist I drew my own boundary lines indicating that a respect for the life of a human being is more important than satisfying the curiosity of invaders, violators of human rights." She further claims in this chapter, however, that the portraits of those people who do appear in the *Diary* are "very full," and that "nothing essential to a portrait was left out of the diary."

In discussing the editing of the *Diary* here, Nin mentions the "constant coeditorship of Gunther Stuhlmann" and speaks of "my method of editing combined with Gunther Stuhlmann's objectivity." Just how Stuhlmann has functioned as an editor of the *Diary* is a subject that evokes much critical curiosity. Benjamin Franklin V and Duane Schneider, in their 1979 book *Anaïs Nin: An Introduction*, say that the *Diary* is "a product of careful editing and selection," and then go on to probe speculatively into the process by which the "private diary" was transformed into the "public diary." Their discussion is the most useful that we have on the editing of the *Diary*. Until the manuscripts of the private diary have been carefully studied, however, we can do no more than speculate.

A focus of more productive critical discussion has been the relationship between the *Diary* and Nin's fiction. Interest in this has been stimulated by the fact that many of the episodes in Nin's fiction also appear in the *Diary*. Again Nin herself has commented on this relationship in *The Novel of the Future* (see especially chapters four and six). She notes that, "At first diary and fiction conflicted. I was asked to choose, to abandon one in favor of the other. Dr. Rank as an analyst and Henry Miller as fiction writer and friend wanted me to surrender it, so I might become a novelist." But in 1968 she is able to say, "Today they no longer conflict... they ended by nurturing one another." The diary she says "was the notebook I depended on for characters and themes." Marianne Hauser, writing in the *Journal of the Otto Rank Association* in June of 1970, says that Nin's "vast diary" became the "alchemist's laboratory where her acute observations, dreams and human encounters" were "distilled into art." Nin, Hauser says, "draws from her source, the diary, and through added dimensions creates an intensified reality, i.e. fiction." One of the most useful and frequently quoted descriptions of the relationship between the *Diary* and the fiction is that by Anna Balakian in her essay, "The Poetic Reality of Anaïs Nin" in *A Casebook on Anaïs Nin*. Balakian says that "the diary and the creative work are like two communicating vessels, and the division is an imaginary one; they feed each other constantly, the diary feeds the imagination with encounter and experience, the creative process invades the diary... transforming the perceptions of the author in regard to her sensory data and emotional reactions to events."

Some of the most helpful discussions of the *Diary* that come out of the period between 1966 and 1979 are those which go beyond the issues of its genre, truth, and relation to the fiction, and examine it much as we might examine any work of literature, with attention to its primary motifs and recurring theme or themes. Marianne Hauser and Wayne McEvilly both published essays of this type in 1968 (*StTCL*, Fall 1968). In "Anaïs Nin: Myth and Reality" Hauser says the *Diary* is a "quest for the hidden self," and in "Portrait of Anaïs Nin as a Bodhisattva: Reflection on the *Diary, 1934-1939*" McEvilly perceives a three-part thematic structure in the *Diary*: "the bodhisattva theme, or the strand of compassion and giving...; the weaving theme, or the strand of belief in the possibility of transforming every event . . . into something rich and strange . . . ; and [the] music theme, or the conscious insistence on the strange fact that whatever comes to us as vitally important . . . speaks to us in the mode of music."

THE FICTION

Nin wrote no new fiction after the publication of *Collages* in 1964, and though the readership of her fiction was somewhat expanded by the publication of the *Diary*, it remained (and will probably always remain) small, relative to the large audience of the *Diary*. Critics, however, have taken great interest in Nin's fiction since publication of the *Diary* began, and much critical and scholarly discussion of the stories and novels has been published during this period. Textual study has begun (see Benjamin Franklin V's study of a section of "Houseboat" in the Winter 1978 issue of *Mosaic*). Early works of fiction, such as *The House of Incest* and *Under a Glass Bell*, have received a kind of critical attention they did not receive before the publication of the *Diary*, in both general essays (see Balakian's "The Poetic Reality of Anaïs Nin" cited above) and essays focused on single works of fiction (see, for example, "The Importance of *Under a Glass Bell*" by Kent Ekberg in *USP*, Spring 1977). Nin's "continuous novel," *Cities of the Interior*, has been a particular focus for discussion of Nin's fiction. Sharon Spencer first examined the structure and style of *Cities of the Interior* in her book, *Space, Time and Structure in the Modern Novel* (New York University Press) in 1971 and published two more essays on this work in 1974 and 1976 (see *A Casebook on Anaïs Nin*, 1974; and *USP*, Summer 1976). In her 1977 book on Nin, *Collage of Dreams* (Chicago: Swallow Press), she examines *Cities of the Interior* again in relation to Nin's other works of fiction. In 1969 Wayne McEvilly did an analysis of the last section of *Cities of the Interior, Seduction of the Minotaur*, which appeared in 1972 as an afterword to the Swallow Press edition of *Seduction of the Minotaur*. That essay has been reprinted several times (most recently in *A Casebook*, 1974), and was described by Philip Jason in "The Future of Nin Criticism" as "probably the best close examination of a single work" (*JORA*, June 1972). In addition, the several book-length studies besides Spencer's which appeared during this period all give close attention to Nin's fiction. Interestingly, all the critical scrutiny that Nin's fiction has recently received has not produced a consensus as to which of Nin's works of fiction are the best or most successful. Benjamin Franklin V and Duane Schneider, for example, view *The House of Incest* as her "best and most challenging volume of prose fiction" (*Anaïs Nin: An Introduction*), while Ekberg calls *Under a Glass Bell* a turning point in Nin's career and says that it is the book in which she seems to have conquered "emotional and artistic problems," and "reached a new plateau of self-knowledge and understanding" (*USP*, Spring 1977).

Anaïs Nin as Artist in the Diary and the Fiction

A primary way in which Nin has been approached as an artist is through the sources of her work. There is disagreement among critics as to which of these are the most important and which constitute real influences on her work. Generally, however, there is agreement that among the figures, works, and movements with which Nin came in contact in ways that were significant to her early development as an artist are the following: D. H. Lawrence, Henry Miller, Antonin Artaud, André Breton, surrealism, Theater of the Absurd, psychoanalysis, René Allendy, the Symbolist Movement, Proust's *A la recherche du temps perdu*, Otto Rank and through him the work of Carl Jung. The *Journal of the Otto Rank Association* frequently publishes essays on Nin. In the December 1972 issue it published two essays on Nin written by Rank himself in 1935, a "Preface" to the early diary, and another to *The House of Incest*. The Summer 1977 issue of this journal was a special tribute issue to Nin and contains a particularly useful analysis by Sharon Spencer of the ways in which Rank encouraged and discouraged Nin's development as an artist. Spencer notes that, "In every way but one—his quite understandable feeling that the Diary was harmful to her productivity as a formal writer—Rank affirmed Nin's aspirations for herself as woman and as artist." Anna Balakian in her essay, "The Poetic Reality of Anaïs Nin" (*A Casebook on Anaïs Nin*, 1974), discusses the influence on Nin's early work of her symbolist "heritage" and of her contacts with Artaud, Breton, and surrealism. Orville Clark, in an essay called "Anaïs Nin: Studies in the New Erotology" (*A Casebook on Anaïs Nin*, 1974), sees a close affinity between Nin and D. H. Lawrence. In addition to the many essays like these, which examine sources of Nin's work, each of the book-length studies that have appeared since 1968 has dealt with these early influences.

In this same period (1966-1979), much discussion of Nin as an artist has focused on whether or not Nin is a "female artist" and what that means. In a 1971 review of *A Spy in the House of Love*, the *Times Literary Supplement* hailed that novel as "an impassioned cry for Women's Lib" and Nin herself as an "intensely feminine writer" who champions "the emancipation of women's psyche" (*TLS*, 29 January 1971). Nin never characterized herself in quite this way, and when asked to comment on the issue of women's liberation often qualified her remarks by saying that she believed that liberation was something that must happen not to "one segment of people" but to "all of us" (*A Woman Speaks*). A more pertinent question is that of the extent to which Nin's vision and style are "feminine" and whether or not these are strengths or weaknesses in her work. Ellen Killoh, in "The Woman Writer and the Element of Destruction" (*CE*, October 1972), and Sharon Spencer, in "'Femininity' and the Woman Writer: Doris Lessing's *The Golden Notebook* and the *Diary of* Anaïs Nin" (*WS*, No. 3,

1973), both deal with the conflict that Nin and women artists in general must face between what Killoh calls the "mutually exclusive categories" of woman and artist. Both critics see Nin's *Diary* as an account of her long struggle to "become a creator" (Spencer) and to reconcile the roles of woman and artist. Killoh believes Nin finally failed in this, but Spencer believes Nin's and Lessing's work are "daring and powerful portraits of woman as artist."

Wallace Fowlie, in a 1973 essay (*NYTBR*, 9 September 1973), notes the "leading characteristic of Miss Nin's art that has often been rehearsed in print by such eminent writers as Edmund Wilson, Lawrence Durrell, and William Carlos Williams, namely, the feminine quality of her writing." In particular, he says, Nin's work evidences its feminine character in its "deep subjectivism . . . , the lucidity about herself she manifests in moments of crisis or distress, and her concern with personal relationships." Wayne McEvilly, in his essay on *Seduction of the Minotaur* (*A Casebook on Anaïs Nin*, 1974), also notes that Nin's femininity as a writer has "been universally acknowledged," but he goes on to ask what this means and to claim that "not every woman who writes has this feminine touch," and that it is a power of "insight" or "clairvoyance" that Nin possesses more as artist than as woman.

The fullest assessments of Nin as an artist are to be found in the five book-length studies of her that were published from 1968 through 1979. The earliest of these is Oliver Evans's *Anaïs Nin* (Carbondale: Southern Illinois University Press, 1968). In it, Evans examines the *Diary* and the fiction, but treats the *Diary* primarily as "the source of all her fiction," and as autobiography and social and literary history. The *Diary*, he says, is "one of the most accurately factual descriptions in English of Bohemian life in Paris during the early thirties, and one of the most intelligent first-hand commentaries that have appeared in this country on the growth of literary Surrealism during those exciting years." Evans's view of the *Diary* is no longer generally held, but the subsequent chapters in which he examines the themes and techniques of her novels and stories provide an analysis and overview of Nin as a fiction writer that is still useful and widely respected. Nin herself was much interested in and, at times, troubled by this first full study of her work as it was being written. The *Diary* for the years 1955-1966 records some of Nin's responses to Evans's manuscript and prints three letters from Nin to Evans that should be read for the comments Nin makes about ways in which she feels her work should and should not be approached.

The second full-length study of Nin's work is Evelyn Hinz's *The Mirror and the Garden: Realism and Reality in the Writings of Anaïs Nin* (Columbus: The Ohio State University Libraries Publication Committee, 1971; Harcourt Brace Jovanovich, 1973). In her introduction Hinz summarizes the state of things with respect to criticism of Nin's work by saying that for too long "literary scholars" have ignored Nin's work, leaving "the task of interpretation . . . largely in the hands of 'friends.'" This has remained true, she says, though Nin's audience has expanded, and Nin has been taken up by "recent liberation movements," which tended to bury "Nin, the artist . . . under the . . . woman and the rebel." In addition, attention has been diverted almost exclusively to the *Diary*, to the neglect of the rest of her work. Hinz's purpose is to consider Nin's work from a literary rather than a personal or political point of view and to focus in particular on the fiction and the criticism. The mirror and the garden of Hinz's title are symbols taken from Nin's 1947 essay "On Writing." For Nin, Hinz says, "the mirror as symbol . . . has three referents: on the metaphysical level the empirical world, on the aesthetic level realism and on the psychological level neurosis." By contrast, the garden "represents all that is positive, creative and healthy. On the metaphysical level it refers to transcendental reality; on the aesthetic level it refers to a poetic style and organic form; and on the psychological level it refers to naturalness, spontaneity, and creativity." In her use of the garden as symbol, Hinz believes that Nin reveals the clear influence of Emerson and American transcendentalism: "As a symbol of reality, Nin's garden is the equivalent of Emerson's 'nature,' and the man who is able to read this symbolic text becomes like Emerson's poet, 'the transparent eyeball.'" Three of the chapters of Hinz's book deal with particular works, *D. H. Lawrence: An Unprofessional Study, The Novel of the Future*, and the *Diary*. Hinz's view of the *Diary* is that it "provides the seminal context for her fiction and that it is important in itself as a literary creation." But these facts, she believes, should not cause us to "relegate the fiction to second place." The other chapters of this study deal with Nin's fiction in terms of its themes, structure, characters, and language. The 1971 and 1973 editions of Hinz's book are in no way outdated by the critical work that has been done on Nin since they were published, and Nin's choice of her as official biographer in 1975 suggests that Nin perceived in Hinz sympathy for and understanding of her work.

In 1975 the Swallow Press published Sharon Spencer's *Collage of Dreams: The Writings of Anaïs Nin*. In a review of this book (*USP*, Spring 1978), Kent Ekberg calls this the "least 'academic' and . . . most original work of criticism on Nin yet to appear." He also notes that it is the most comprehensive study thus far, touching on the fiction, the six volumes of the *Diary*, and even on the volume of essays (*A Woman Speaks*). Spencer's approach, Ekberg says, is "intuitive and idiosyncratic," and her book "will probably be regarded as the best general introduction to her work for many years to come." Spencer operates from several premises about Nin in this book. One is that "the central motivation in Nin's life and art is a passionate desire to transform every thing, every experience, and every person, into a meaningful and valuable... entity." Nin's central metaphor for the "process through which art transforms the ordinary into the extraordinary" is that of alchemy. In addition, Spencer claims, "collage as a concept underlies Anaïs Nin's sense of art," and can be defined as "visual alchemy." Both Nin's fiction and her *Diary* are "collage compositions." Spencer sees Nin as influenced by the collage artist Jean Varda, by the Symbolists of the late nineteenth century, by Proust, and by the Surrealists. But in discussing each of these influences, she is quite specific as to the nature and extent of its impact on Nin's theory and practice as an artist. In discussing Nin's relation to surrealism, for example, Spencer points out that Nin "praises the Surrealists for emphasizing man's need for liberty and for locating the source of this liberty in the unconscious." But she also notes that Nin "criticizes their insistence on presenting the raw contents of the unconscious, the results of automatic writing, without interpreting them."

With the exception of two chapters devoted to the *Diary*, Spencer's book is not organized around particular works, but around such themes as "The Dream"—"Nin's vision of the dream gives continuity and profundity to her meaning as woman and artist alike," and "rediscovering Woman." Her view of the *Diary* is that it "cannot be assigned to a genre," that "there is nothing else like it in our literature," and that it "is as close to a complete, comprehensive, and deep expression of a human life as any one can think of or even imagine." She believes also that the "literary work... Nin's Diary most resembles is Proust's... *A la recherche du temps perdu.*" In the *Diary*, she says, Nin "speaks with the voice of a woman," but "not only for women." For the *Diary* is, in fact, "the first autobiography of the artist in the United States."

Spencer's last chapter is called "The Narcissus Pool," and in it she defends Nin against the charge of narcissism that continues, at times, to be made against her. The answer to that charge, Spencer believes, lies in Otto Rank's study and account of the "creative personality" and the "personal evolution of the artist." When we understand these, then we will recognize that "Anaïs Nin's life work... gives us both the books that exonerate the artist from the charge of selfishness and the history of a life devoted to the actualization of all its capabilities, not the least of which is the gift of love for others."

Bettina Knapp's *Anaïs Nin* (Frederick Ungar, 1978) is the first book about Nin published after her death in January 1977, and its tone is, at times, very much that of a tribute to Nin. It seems to have been intended as an introduction to Nin's life and work for those who may be just beginning their study of her. Knapp supplies a chronology of major events in Nin's life and of the composition and publication dates of her works and organizes the book itself chronologically. This book has, however, curious omissions and imbalances. The *Diary* is dealt with briefly and only as a basis for the brief biographical sketch that makes up the whole of chapter one. Nin's book on Lawrence is studied at some length in chapter two, as is *The House of Incest* in chapter three. Knapp's discussion of surrealism and of Nin's experience of psychoanalysis with Allendy and Rank as background for *The House of Incest* is detailed and helpful and so are her chapters on *Winter of Artifice* and *The Voice* and on *Cities of the Interior*. But there is no discussion of *Under a Glass Bell* or of the last volume of fiction, *Collages*, nor does she deal with any of Nin's other critical writings, "On Writing," "Realism and Reality," and *The Novel of the Future*.

The most recent book-length study of Nin is *Anaïs Nin: An Introduction* by Benjamin Franklin V and Duane Schneider. Its publication represents the culmination of many years of Nin criticism and scholarship by its authors. Its focus is entirely upon Nin's work rather than her biography or personality and is about equally divided between the fiction and the *Diary*, with a third and shorter section devoted to criticism and nonfiction. Part One devotes a chapter to each of the volumes of fiction in order of their publication, including the five novels that were eventually published together as *Cities of the Interior* and the last volume, *Collages*. The authors view *The House of Incest* as her best volume of prose fiction and believe that it contains "the basic ideas, themes, and images that Nin develops more fully (and yet less satisfactorily) in the five volumes that make up her continuous novel." Part Two begins with a general chapter on the *Diary*, which deals with the issues of its editing and genre, and then devotes a full chapter to each of the *Diary*'s six volumes. This is the closest and most detailed analysis of the *Diary* that has been done. The authors' view of the published *Diary* is that it is "a new and created work of art rather than . . . a reproduction of Nin's private journal," and that "as a work of literature it succeeds as well as if not better than most of her fiction because it is rooted firmly in an identifiable and substantial context." In addition, they regard "the character of Nin in the *Diary* as a persona." They call the *Diary* "Nin's real continuous novel." In their chapters on the individual volumes of the *Diary*, they assess the quality of the separate volumes in terms of the degree of "unity, coherence, drama and intensity" that they possess, judging the first volume to be "the strongest."

THE FUTURE OF NIN CRITICISM

In a 1972 essay, "The Future of Nin Criticism" (*JORA*, June 1972), Philip Jason outlined areas of Nin's work and career that needed study. By 1979 few of the areas he had mentioned earlier remained entirely unexplored. A measure of her acceptance by the academic establishment is the increasing number of doctoral dissertations that are being written about her. It seems unlikely that interest in Nin will wane any time soon. The publication since her death of a second volume of erotica, as well as a volume of the early diary, and the projected publication of a diary volume, which follows chronologically the one for 1955-1966, give continuing impetus to the study of her work. The biography being written by Evelyn Hinz is a subject of great curiosity. Finally, there are the manuscripts of the private diaries in the University of California at Los Angeles library which hold, we presume, the answers to many of our questions about the editing of the *Diary*.

7 EDGAR E. MACDONALD

Ellen Glasgow

BIBLIOGRAPHY

The first extensive checklist of Ellen Glasgow's works was William H. Egly's "Bibliography of Ellen Anderson Gholson Glasgow" (*BB*, September-December 1940), which was revised and expanded by W. D. Quesenbery, Jr., in his "Ellen Glasgow: A Critical Bibliography" (*BB*, May-August and September-December 1959). These lists have, however, been superseded by later compilations.

Ellen Glasgow, A Bibliography, by William W. Kelly, and edited by Oliver Steele (Charlottesville: Bibliographical Society of Virginia, 1964) was designed to fill the need for a comprehensive critical, analytical, and enumerative bibliography. It is divided into three major sections: (1) "Writings of Ellen Glasgow and Book Reviews," containing books and reviews, collected editions, stories in periodicals, and contributions to books; (2) "Ellen Glasgow Biography and Criticism," containing biographical portraits, honors, and sketches, biographical and critical material in periodicals, and dissertations completed on Ellen Glasgow; and (3) "Manuscripts in the Ellen Glasgow Collection," containing a checklist of letters to Ellen Glasgow, chronology of letters to Ellen Glasgow, catalogue of Ellen Glasgow manuscripts, notebooks, biography, poems, miscellaneous manuscripts and letters, letters, genealogy, and fiction. The book concludes with a twenty-seven-page index. Kelly's Introduction is perceptive in its review of Ellen Glasgow's literary fortunes, and his description of the manuscripts in the Alderman Library Ellen Glasgow Collection at the University of Virginia is of solid value to the student. The collector of Glasgow, however, will be

This essay originally appeared in slightly different form in *Resources for American Literary Study*. It is reprinted here with the permission of the editors.

disappointed in Section A of Part I, "Writings of Ellen Glasgow and Book Reviews," especially in light of the editor's assertion that "the notes are sufficient to identify any copy of an Ellen Glasgow book printed to date." A random application of the descriptive criteria in this bibliography reveals many discrepancies or what appear to be variants from the norms. The editor does not list an 1899 edition of *The Descendant* nor a 1903 edition of *The Battle Ground*, and one suspects he may have overlooked other editions. In his Preface, Steele professes an attempt "to list all the impressions of Ellen Glasgow's books" but advises that "the descriptions are not fully analytical." He assures us, however, that "the notes are the result of a thorough bibliographical analysis." Given that statement, we must assume that he elected not to report the complete results of that analysis. The frequency of "copy seen rebound" and "no copy seen" can only mean that the bibliographer has not consulted "the required large number of copies for examination" that Fredson Bowers advises in *Principles of Bibliographical Description* (Princeton: Princeton University Press, 1949). Keeping in mind the admonition, once again by Bowers, that "one must recognize that the complex methods of modern printing and sale do not lend themselves readily to classification, one can still express disappointment that the enlightenment promised by the bibliographer was not forthcoming. Since publication, three "Addenda to Kelly" have appeared in the *Papers of the Bibliographical Society of America*. These three are: William L. Godshalk's "Addendum to Kelly: Ellen Glasgow's *Voice of the People* (*PBSA*, January-March 1973); George Monteiro's "Addenda to the Bibliographies of Glasgow *et al.*" (*PBSA*, April-June 1975); and Gene DeGruson's "Addenda to Kelly: Ellen Glasgow" (*PBSA*, April-June 1977). These criticisms aside, the *Bibliography* is attractive as a book, it contains a large amount of information necessary for a detailed study of Glasgow, and even the disappointed collector will find it useful if used with discretion.

Frederick P. W. McDowell supplied an Ellen Glasgow checklist of limited value in *A Bibliographical Guide to the Study of Southern Literature*, edited by Louis D. Rubin, Jr. (Baton Rouge: Louisiana State University Press, 1969). This was doubtless owing to editorial restrictions. Edgar E. MacDonald reassessed much of the criticism listed in Kelly and supplemented it in "Ellen Glasgow: An Essay in Bibliography" (*RALS*, Autumn 1972). This essay was reprinted in slightly amended form in *Ellen Glasgow: Centennial Essays*, edited by M. Thomas Inge (Charlottesville: University Press of Virginia, 1976), and it is incorporated in the present essay. Jan Zlotnik Schmidt continued to update Glasgow scholarship in "Ellen Glasgow: An Annotated Checklist, 1973-Present" (*EGN*, October 1978).

Ellen Glasgow is included in *First Printings of American Authors: Contributions Toward Descriptive Checklists*, Vol. 2 (Detroit: Gale, 1978), and twenty-five title pages of her works are reproduced, purporting to be those of first editions. Richard Layman cites Kelly's *Bibliography* as his sole reference, but the title page of *The Voice of the People* shown here does not include the publisher's device in the center of the page that his reference indicates.

EDITIONS

Except for *A Certain Measure* and *The Woman Within*, first editions of Ellen Glasgow's works are described in Merle D. Johnson's *American First Editions*, fourth edition revised and enlarged by Jacob Blanck (Mark Press, 1942). First and later editions are also listed in the Kelly *Bibliography* and *First Printings of American Authors*, but there the reservations detailed in the previous section should be noted. The *Old Dominion Edition of the Works of Ellen Glasgow* (Garden City, N.Y.: Doubleday, 1923-1933) and *The Virginia Edition of the Works of Ellen Glasgow* (Charles Scribner's, 1938) were neither complete, the first containing eight novels and excluding eight as well as the stories and poems, and the latter including twelve novels and excluding six earlier novels as well as the stories and poems. *The Virginia Edition* was reproduced in Kyoto, Japan, in 1974, in recognition of the Glasgow centennial.

Certain Glasgow titles remain in print; in addition, certain of her writings have appeared in print for the first time during the last decade. In the former category are *The Descendant*, *The Voice of the People*, *Barren Ground*, *The Romantic Comedians*, *The Sheltered Life*, *Vein of Iron*, *The Freeman and Other Poems*, and *A Certain Measure*. *Voice, Barren Ground, The Sheltered Life*, and *Vein of Iron* are available in paperback. New Glasgow publications embrace a variety of matter; letters will be considered below.

A previously unpublished short story by Ellen Glasgow, "The Professional Instinct," has been edited by William W. Kelly (*WHR*, Autumn 1962). It is a parable of a woman who willingly sacrifices all her attainments and security for an egotistical male unworthy of her sacrifice. Richard K. Meeker later included it in his collection of Ellen Glasgow stories and sees it as a reflection of Glasgow's relationship with Henry Anderson; this reader rather sees it as Glasgow and almost any male.

Ellen Glasgow appears in charming guise in "'Literary Realism or Nominalism' by Ellen Glasgow: An Unpublished Essay," edited by Luther Y. Gore (*AL*, March 1962). Light in tone and deft in phrase, the essay is presented as an imaginary conversation, a dialogue discussing writers and writing, treating less ponderously the realism-romantic debate that Cabell and others jousted in during the 1920s:

> We have no literary criticism, merely reviews of fashions; we are primarily concerned with neither philosophy nor method, but with the tasteful display of either fancy

dress or homespun. Our one permanent interest is in externals. The first demand we make of our novelists is that they shall follow what the authors of "fashion notes" in the daily press describe as "the prevailing style."

In *The Collected Stories of Ellen Glasgow* (Baton Rouge: Louisiana State University Press, 1963), Richard K. Meeker brought together the eleven short stories published during her life and the one published posthumously. In a graceful introduction he situates them in her development as a writer, categorizes them neatly, and comments on their relationship with the novels. He rather convinces us that although she held the genre in small esteem, she displayed considerable talent in their composition, and that they should not be neglected in a total assessment. These stories were issued in paperback in 1966.

In 1966 Luther Y. Gore's doctoral dissertation, the editing and annotating of Ellen Glasgow's last work, *Beyond Defeat*, was published (Charlottesville: University Press of Virginia). *Beyond Defeat* was the work of a dying woman well beyond her literary prime, and this inconsequential epilogue could have no interest for a general reader and indeed would misrepresent Glasgow in a cruel way. For those scholars interested in her work as a totality, there are the manuscripts of *Beyond Defeat* at the University of Virginia, there is Gore's dissertation, there is an analysis of this work in Joan Foster Santas's *Ellen Glasgow's American Dream* (considered below), and there is the extended treatment given to this material in the Kelly *Bibliography*. In Section B, Part III, of the latter, over fifty pages are given to the three drafts of *Beyond Defeat* with all the significant changes that Ellen Glasgow made in each. In his Introduction Gore states that "the decision not to publish *Beyond Defeat* was probably well taken on Ellen Glasgow's part," yet he makes no direct case for his publishing the work. His commentaries on her methods of composition are cogent, but none of his observations justified the appearance of this work in print.

Glasgow scholars deplore the fact that at the present writing several of her major novels are not in print. The irony of her peripheral work being made available instead of an early masterpiece, *Virginia*, would not have been lost on Miss Glasgow.

MANUSCRIPTS AND LETTERS

The Kelly *Bibliography* gives a detailed listing of manuscripts in the Ellen Glasgow Papers at the University of Virginia but ignores holdings in other libraries. *American Literary Manuscripts* (2d edition, Athens: University of Georgia Press, 1977) lists a number of libraries with Glasgow material, in particular Harvard, the New York Public Library, the University of North Carolina, Princeton, and Yale. Harvard, as the repository of the papers of Walter Hines Page and Howard Mumford Jones, holds letters that span the half century of Ellen Glasgow's career. The University of Virginia, as the holder of the papers of a number of Glasgow correspondents, has the largest collection of Glasgow letters. Owing to James Branch Cabell's system of filing letters from correspondents in presentation copies of their works, the James Branch Cabell Library at Virginia Commonwealth University has acquired a number of notes, postcards, and letters from Ellen Glasgow along with his library.

Letters of Ellen Glasgow (Harcourt, Brace & World, 1958) is a genteel selection edited by Blair Rouse, who is neither amazed with their profundity of thought nor impressed with their generosity of observation. Included in this volume are letters indicating that Glasgow held her person and her work in proper esteem, bowing to neither popular opinion nor critical indifference. Supplementing these letters, others have since been published.

James B. Colvert edited "Agent and Author: Ellen Glasgow's Letters to Paul Revere Reynolds" (*SB*, 1961). These letters underline her concern for a "discriminating audience," her desire to be published in England, her predilection for the novel over the short story, and her small regard for serialization.

Ellen Glasgow also appears in charming form in *Five Letters from Ellen Glasgow Concerning Censorship* (Richmond, Va.: Friends of the Richmond Public Library, 1962). This elegant pamphlet has an Introductory Note by Louis D. Rubin, Jr., and the letters present Glasgow assessing *Elmer Gantry* negatively as literature but defending its right to appear on library shelves, expressing distaste for Charles Wertenbaker's *Boojum*, but overall affirming her conviction "that there should be no moral censorship of literature."

In "Ellen Glasgow's Letters to the Saxtons" (*AL*, May 1963), Douglas Day presents and comments on five letters to Eugene F. and Martha Saxton in which, among other details of minor interest, Miss Glasgow touches on her duties as a judge in the Harper Prize Novel Competition in 1933: "I wish somebody would write a novel on the idea that there is as much life in sitting still with one's own soul as there is in speeding to nowhere.... Do you know anybody brave enough to write such a book?" One will occasionally come across a letter of Ellen Glasgow's published in the letters of another writer, such as Gertrude Stein or Upton Sinclair. She corresponded with a large number of people, usually expressing herself strongly on whatever topic that engaged her at the moment. Some sixteen letters have appeared in *The Ellen Glasgow Newsletter*, annotated by Jan Zlotnick Schmidt. Three letters to Seymour Frank were published by Guy R. Woodall, in "Letters by Ellen Glasgow and Others on the First Editions of Three of Her Novels" (*TSL*, 1976). In light of the wealth of Glasgow letters at the University of Virginia alone, a new selection would be welcome in published form, one that would give a more rounded portrait of the writer with less concern for a genteel image.

BIOGRAPHY

The *New York Times Index* and the Kelly bibliography record the numerous interviews given by Ellen Glasgow and the impressions of her contemporaries. Her many letters also give us insight into the personality of the woman, but the truly objective portraits did not appear until after her death.

When her autobiography, *The Woman Within* (Harcourt Brace, 1954), appeared posthumously, it provoked a wide spectrum of reactions. Her literary executors had waited for the death of Henry Anderson before revealing Ellen Glasgow's unflattering and inaccurate account of their engagement. The book was hailed as "Ellen Glasgow's 'Honest' Autobiography," although James Branch Cabell wrote that he distrusted "the entire book throughout as a factual record." Ellen Glasgow may have intended the work to be a truthful recounting of her life as she experienced it, but she was accustomed to writing novels. As for many writers, her emotional life and her career were the same. Seeing people and events through a "filter," she gives accounts that are not always in accord with the facts as recorded in letters and the observations of others. In the major studies of Ellen Glasgow, Monique Parent early cast a dubious eye on certain details as given in *The Woman Within*; other Glasgow scholars continue to accept it as factual biography. Ellen Glasgow's translation of incidents into intense feeling will have to be delicately balanced by anyone attempting to evaluate the woman or her work.

In "Speaks with Candor of a Great Lady," a chapter in *As I Remember It* (Robert McBride, 1955), James Branch Cabell makes the well-substantiated claim that he knew Ellen Glasgow for the last twenty years of her life better than anyone else. In particular, he recounts his role in her designation as a "social historian" and his revisions of *In This Our Life*. His portrait of her late years is deftly sketched, blending irony and admiration in his account of their relationship.

In 1962 two studies of Glasgow appeared: Blair Rouse's *Ellen Glasgow* (Twayne) and Monique Parent's monumental, 574-page *Ellen Glasgow: Romancière* (Paris: A. G. Nizet). The former will be considered below, but owing to the exhaustive biographical research that went in the latter, it is reviewed here. Monique Parent, a Parisienne by birth and education, undertook her research on Ellen Glasgow for the French *doctorat d'état*. She made many trips to Virginia, where she interviewed those who had known, seen, or, in some cases, heard of Ellen Glasgow, in particular Glasgow's sister Rebe Tutwiler, her long-time companion Anne Virginia Bennett, her life-long friend Roberta Wellford, her literary executrix Irita Van Doren, and, of course, James Branch Cabell. Parent made many friends in Virginia, and she was accorded an insight into the mores and personality of its people, which she interpreted with finesse; she had an instinctive feeling for the environment that formed the woman and writer that Ellen Glasgow became.

Parent divided her work into the classic three parts of French literary analysis, "The Environment," "The Woman," and "The Work." The first part is a comprehensive view of the South and its history, which she felt necessary for her French readers but which also has value for American students studying Ellen Glasgow in depth. Her second part, "The Woman," is of greater value, for she first gives us a deftly realized exterior portrait, such as others have only approached, and then goes on to penetrate the masks for a character analysis that is intimately revealing yet still generous. The third part, dealing with the novels, is sound but does not surpass the critical evaluations of McDowell or Rouse. While her three-fold approach inevitably leads to some overlapping, a general fault with many French theses, the resulting depth of Parent's work compensates for minor flaws. This work was received with its highest accolade by the faculty of the Sorbonne in 1960 and was published in 1962. William W. Kelly, in his *Ellen Glasgow: A Bibliography*, sees it as "probably the most exhaustive and comprehensive discussion of Miss Glasgow's life and career yet published." McDowell's reaction to this work in *A Bibliographical Guide to the Study of Southern Literature* is critical: "The complex of social, ethical, philosophical, and religious values out of which Ellen Glasgow wrote requires sharper definition than they have received from Monique Parent." But it is peculiarly in these areas that she excels. For depth, breadth, balance, and psychological insight, hers is the best portrait of Ellen Glasgow to date.

The latest biography to appear is *Ellen Glasgow and the Woman Within* (Baton Rouge: Louisiana State University Press, 1972), by E. Stanly Godbold, Jr. In it Godbold makes a noble attempt to reveal Ellen Glasgow as a personage, and doubtless his truthfulness concerning many aspects of her life will come as a surprise to those who have been nourished on the public image she cultivated and projected during her lifetime. While it may be "the first full biography" of Ellen Glasgow, as the dust wrapper asserts, it is far from being the "definitive account of her life" that is further proclaimed. Her early formative years are not covered in depth, and indeed J. R. Raper gives a more detailed analysis of these years in his *Without Shelter* (see below). Godbold is the first to rely heavily on the notes that Marjorie Kinnan Rawlings made for her projected biography, but he seems unaware that some of Mrs. Rawlings's sources were less than candid, and some may have actually withheld information of vital interest for a biographer. Faced with equivocal "evidence," Mrs. Rawlings herself relinquished the objective of an intimate biography of Ellen Glasgow. Although Godbold relies on the Rawlings Papers extensively, he ignores, at least in any acknowledgment, the serious biographical research done by Monique Parent in her *Ellen Glasgow: Romancière*. In his personal interviews with Richmond "friends of Miss Glasgow," in several notable instances he accepts and quotes information supplied by a person who had no social or literary contact with Ellen Glasgow whatsoever. In treating Ellen Glasgow's affair with "Gerald B.," Godbold wavers between well-founded caution—"How much of her imagination went into the writing of the chapter is impossible to say"—and incautious assertion—"Gerald died in 1905." As Godbold moves toward Ellen Glasgow's later years with their copious documentation and fresher memories, his portrait takes on veracity. Chapter 11, "Historical Revelations," seems rather an insertion, perhaps lifted from an earlier paper, but it sums up with cogency her role as a social historian. Like other assessments of Ellen Glasgow as a writer, *Ellen Glasgow and the Woman Within* leaves the reader vaguely uncomfortable about her place in American letters. A reading of the novels in an attempt to analyze the writer's psyche may be valid, but only if the work under scrutiny is also assessed as having vitality apart from the force that created it. As for the woman, Godbold gives us Ellen Glasgow the eccentric, very true in many respects but certainly not the final delineation.

Brief biographical sketches and notes continue to appear. C. Hugh Holman supplied her entry for the *Dictionary of American Biography*, Supplement Three, (Charles Scribner's, 1973). Julius R. Raper assesses the influence of Walter McCormack on Glasgow in "The Man Ellen Glasgow Could Respect" (*EGN*, March 1975); he adds insights into her early personality in "European Initiation of Ellen Glasgow" (*EGN*, October 1976); and he deftly summarizes her career in *Southern Writers: A Biographical Dictionary*, edited by Robert Bain, Joseph M. Flora, Louis D. Rubin, Jr., (Baton Rouge: Louisiana State University Press, 1979). Edgar E. MacDonald touched on her birth date and the identity of "Gerald B" in "Biographical Notes on Ellen Glasgow" (*RALS*, Autumn 1973; rptd. in *Centennial Essays*, Charlottesville: University Press of Virginia, 1976). MacDonald also gives peripheral views of Glasgow in her criticism of the work of a close friend, "Emma Gray Trigg" (*EGN*, October 1975), and in her close relationship with her niece, "Lellie: Ellen Glasgow and Josephine Clark" (*EGN*, March 1976).

CRITICISM

Critical Reception during Her Life

The best of the contemporary assessments of Glasgow's works have been assimilated in the full-length studies that are listed below in "Books," none of which actually appeared in her lifetime. All these materials have been admirably annotated by McDowell and Rouse, and the reader is referred to the following section for a discussion of these works. Rouse's résumé in Chapter 10 of his *Ellen Glasgow* is a model of concise critical reporting.

For the most part, Ellen Glasgow's novels enjoyed a favorable critical reception during her literary career. She early announced her serious intent as an artist, and her shortcomings as a writer, even her lapses into dullness, were generally overlooked out of respect for her ethical ideals. She cultivated critics who reviewed favorably and indeed directed their attention to those aspects of her work that she wished underlined for the less observant. This is not to imply that the criticism of James Southall Wilson, Howard Mumford Jones, James Branch Cabell, and others classified as admiring friends is not worth the scholar's attention today; however, these acolytes all wrote with the realization that the surfacely Olympian, interiorly intense woman of whom they wrote would pass judgment on their work. Carl Van Doren, Stuart Pratt Sherman, Carl Van Vechten, Henry Seidel Canby, and J. Donald Adams were also among the illustrious who commented on her work in terms highly acceptable to the author. But Ellen Glasgow was an astute scholar as well as an instructor; her friendly reviewers helped her to define her aims, and her abilities grew as her own perceptions of art and life expanded. She wrote that she had read almost every treatise on writing that was available, and her library, as catalogued by her nephew, Carrington Cabell Tutwiler, Jr., *Ellen Glasgow's Library* (Charlottesville: University Press of Virginia, 1969), a descriptive pamphlet of thirty-one pages, and *A Catalogue of the Library of Ellen Glasgow* (Charlottesville: University Press of Virginia, 1969), a book of 287 pages, attests to her wide reading of the major Western novelists.

Having read the criticism of others during a lifetime, she absorbed, assimilated, recollected, and in time became her own best spokeswoman for the work she had intended to write. *A Certain Measure*, her last work to appear in her lifetime, is Ellen Glasgow at her best. Wise, witty, sometimes factual, she discourses with ease on literature in general and her works in particular. Growing out of earlier prefaces to her novels, prefaces in which critical opinion had helped her to codify her thoughts concerning literary techniques (in a formula suggested by Cabell), this work considers both objectively and subjectively her novels in terms of objectives and fulfillment, always generously. As Cabell observed, these essays read well, and there is evidence that some of the urbanity is his. Edgar E. MacDonald, in "The Glasgow-Cabell Entente" (*AL*, March 1969), and E. Stanly Godbold, Jr., in *Ellen Glasgow and the Woman Within*, see his hand in their composition; Cabell intended a heavy irony in his review of *A Certain Measure* when he wrote pointedly: "It is, in brief, all Ellen Glasgow." But the true irony is that it remains a book about Ellen Glasgow by Ellen Glasgow. Despite her neuroses and biases, she was a perceptive critic, and herein she carefully chose her best efforts to amplify in comment. *A Certain Measure* remains an interesting, even valuable commentary on her work.

William W. Kelly's doctoral dissertation, "Struggle for Recognition: A Study of the Literary Reputation of Ellen Glasgow" (Duke University, 1957), has proved of value for scholars interested in the contemporary criticism of her work. In the review of critical articles in periodicals below, the emphasis will be, for the most part, on the more objective criticism following the death of Ellen Glasgow in 1945.

BOOKS

Frederick P. W. McDowell's *Ellen Glasgow and the Ironic Art of Fiction* (Madison: University of Wisconsin Press, 1960) was the first book-length study of Glasgow to appear. Chapter I, "The Artist and Her Time," is adequate in recounting the basic facts of Glasgow's career; it conveys however, no intimacy of feeling for the writer or her environment. The bulk of McDowell's book is devoted to an analysis of the Glasgow opus, her theory and practice, and his presentation is accurate and solid. His bibliography sums up in an exemplary manner the major Glasgow criticism to that time. In *Ellen Glasgow* Blair Rouse terms his work an "excellent" critical study; C. Hugh Holman sees it as "not too perceptive or critically discerning a treatment" in *Three Modes of Southern Fiction*, to be discussed later.

Two years later, two new studies of Glasgow were published: Monique Parent's *Ellen Glasgow: Romancière* and Blair Rouse's *Ellen Glasgow* in Twayne's U.S. Authors Series (Twayne, 1962). Rouse had earlier edited the *Letters of Ellen Glasgow* (Harcourt, Brace, 1958); he had an interest in Glasgow of long standing, having been accorded a personal interview with her in 1941. While the compact format of the Twayne Series doubtless imposed restrictions on him, his is a more than adequate overview and is in some respects superior to other titles in that series. As the same time it is somewhat pedestrian in observation, and his championship of Glasgow understandably has him citing her more favorable critics. Wholly commendable is his bibliography, wherein he gives concise evaluations of previous Glasgow scholarship. This work, available in paper as well as hardcover, is of special value in the classroom, giving the student the essential details for a rounded understanding of the social critic and novelist.

Louis Auchincloss's *Ellen Glasgow* (Minneapolis: University of Minnesota Press, 1964), No. 33 in the University of Minnesota Pamphlets on American Writers, brings us the insight of a critic who is himself a novelist. Into a brief forty pages he instills a remarkably clear and balanced assessment of Ellen Glasgow, written in an urbane style that pleases as it informs. This study was incorporated into Auchincloss's *Pioneers and Caretakers* (Minneapolis: University of Minnesota Press, 1965). Like the Rouse work, this pamphlet too is a handy aid for the classroom student.

Joan Foster Santas's *Ellen Glasgow's American Dream* (Charlottesville: University Press of Virginia, 1965) is a dissertation perpetrated in print. A rehash of every pronouncement Glasgow ever made about writing, as well as a rewarming of almost every observation made about her by others, its breezy prolixity successfully buries Santas's "thesis." This type of work is the antithesis of Parent's painstaking research.

In *Without Shelter: The Early Career of Ellen Glasgow* (Baton Rouge: Louisiana State University Press, 1971), also an outgrowth of a dissertation, J. R. Raper analyzes Ellen Glasgow's early fiction with the object of illustrating the Darwinian influences. In addition he takes issue with Joan Santas, Blair Rouse, and Barbara Giles's "Character and Fate: The Novels of Ellen Glasgow" (*Mainstream*, September 1956) on points of interpretation and attempts to expand in more specific detail certain biographical episodes that bear on Ellen Glasgow's work. While this aspect of his study is not perfectly realized, it moves in the direction of greatest need in Glasgow studies, which is for a psychological understanding of the woman who turned weakness into strength in her struggle for comprehension and self-realization. Raper's critical analyses of the novels are wholly admirable; his bibliography is a catch-all of miscellanea.

Marion K. Richards's thesis, *Ellen Glasgow's Development as a Novelist* (The Hague: Mouton, 1971), appeared in print some years after it was written. Richards's approach is to examine the novels through *Barren Ground* in the light of the revelations in *A Certain Measure* and *The Woman Within.* This approach might have had some validity when she wrote it, but now this work is simply an out-of-date thesis. Also, her bibliography is the most anemic of all those in the studies reviewed above, since it was not updated after completion as a dissertation. Although she has read the novels perceptively, her easy acceptance of critic Glasgow commenting on the writer appears naive. References to Mary Johnston as Mrs. Johnston shock the reader. Summing up all Glasgow's earlier work (in terms of betrayal theme, setting, symbolism, style, and structure) as reflected in *Barren Ground* is a tidy thesis device, but it cannot be justified as an extramural contribution to Glasgow scholarship. The studies that precede excel *Ellen Glasgow's Development as a Novelist* too comprehensively for anyone to find this limited work of any significant value.

Ellen Glasgow: Centennial Essays, edited by M. Thomas Inge (Charlottesville: University Press of Virginia, 1976), was an outgrowth of observances of the writer's centennial at Mary Baldwin College and at the Richmond Public Library. In "Ellen Glasgow as Feminist," Monique Parent Frazee establishes the writer's credentials, giving us Glasgow's 1914 definition of feminism. Then she develops the thesis that Glasgow's interests lay less in the political and economic areas than in the philosophical. Frazee finds the writer's goals in accord with those of today's feminists but underlines that her style in attaining these goals was in marked contrast to that of the vocal sisters of the movement today. Howard Mumford Jones, a personal friend and long-time critic of the author, contributed two essays. In "The Earliest Novels" he compares her apprentice work in *The Descendant* and *Phases of an Inferior Planet* favorably with Hemingway's *The Torrents of Spring* and Fitzgerald's *This Side of Paradise.* While Glasgow's early works were flawed, they gave evidence of the work that was to follow in matters of style, technique, and theme; all that she needed was the experience that would inform her later works. This article also appeared in *A Festschrift for Marguerite Roberts*, edited by F. Elaine Penninger (Richmond: University of Richmond, 1976). In "Northern Exposure: Southern Style," Jones, after reviewing literary history in the United States, advises a modern reader not to categorize Glasgow in narrow definitions but to view her widely as a novelist of "the human condition," one who sought "the fusion of experience with universals"; she is "the novelist of sweetness and austerity." In "The Prewar Novels," Frederick P. W. McDowell touches on the strengths of Ellen Glasgow's fiction before *Barren Ground* but treats *The Deliverance, The Miller of Old Church*, and *Virginia* as "more consistent aesthetic successes." Always a perceptive critic, McDowell determines that in *The Deliverance* she "convincingly embedded some of the mythic aspects of . . . Southern civilization"; *The Miller* "is one of the most compendious of Miss Glasgow's books; its scope is broad, and the modes of experience which it encompasses, from the tragic to the comic, make it distinctive"; "The vigor and asperity of Miss Glasgow's ironic vision in *Virginia* give it a strength which the later elegiac novel *The Sheltered Life* does not always attain." In "Ellen Glasgow's Civilized Men" Blair Rouse analyzes the terms "civilized" and "civilization" and the attributes she accords "a small number of her characters, all men." Rouse considers some five male characters who qualify as civilized; of the females, he sees only Roy Timberlake in *In This Our Life* as approaching the ideal. Edgar E. MacDonald's "Glasgow, Cabell, and Richmond," Dorothy Scura's "Glasgow and the Southern Renaissance," C. Hugh Holman's "The Comedies of Manners," and Edgar E. MacDonald's "An Essay in Bibliography," all having been previously published, are commented on below.

Elizabeth Gallup Myer undertakes the defense of Ellen Glasgow as a neglected feminist in *The Social Situation of Women in the Novels of Ellen Glasgow* (Hicksville, N.Y.: Exposition Press, 1978). A small book of some eighty pages, and introductory in nature, the author's intent is earnest, her appreciation of Glasgow is sincere, and her presentation is amiable, but the total effect is little more than that of a book-club talk. Five of its six "chapters" are very brief. Chapter V, "Categories," is "the heart of Miss Myer's essay." It is divided into Social Situation (twenty pages), Economical (six-and-a-half pages) Political (one page), Religious (three pages), and Educational (three pages). This little treatise must have been written some time in the past, for the latest critical work cited in the text is dated 1958. Even in a "Supplemental Bibliography" the names of such Glasgow scholars as Parent, Holman, and Raper are conspicuously absent. Further, the author appears unaware of the criticism devoted to Glasgow in scholarly periodicals. Myer's weak tea might be served to children, but it's an insipid infusion for anyone who has already met Glasgow.

Another thesis given publication is Barbro Ekman's *The End of a Legend: Ellen Glasgow's History of Southern Women* (Uppsala: Studia Anglistica Upsaliensia, 1979). Ekman categorizes the female characters of the novels, sees them as victims of the Southern Code of Chivalry, traces their evolution, and summarizes their plights. All Glasgow critics seem to have equal value for Ekman, and she scrambles early and later critics in a context that makes them appear to be contemporaries. She is also given to overstatement: "Glasgow spent the first sixteen years of her career portraying, for the most part, the Southern Belles." In a review, Monique Parent Frazee, who sat on Barbro Ekman's doctoral jury, objects to the absence of any reference to Glasgow's black females, to an overemphasis on the role of local tradition at the expense of universalities, and to the limited scope of the work "as a study of social history rather than as a contribution to literary criticism" (*EGN*, October 1979). Ekman makes many valid observations, but there is little in her work of original interest. Presented in her native Swedish, this thesis might have served as a useful introduction to the work of Ellen Glasgow for Swedish students; as a contribution in English to international understanding of the Glasgow opus, *The End of a Legend* is of peripheral value.

The best scholar can convince us that our reading of a work has been deficient in understanding and make us thank him or her. Julius Rowan Raper brilliantly essays the role of the enlightener, and his *From the Sunken Garden: The Fiction of Ellen Glasgow, 1916-1945* (Baton Rouge: Louisiana State University Press, 1980) gives Glasgow students an entirely new perspective from which to view that writer. In "A Personal Note" he tells us that he turned from the biographical, critical approach employed earlier in *Without Shelter* to "the invisible core that seems to drive Glasgow's characters," recognizing that in mid-career she had developed—or stumbled on—"a technique combining devices as literary as the foil and the double with a process as psychological as projection," thus allowing her "to create characters arguably more complex than the "tripartite figures of the Freudians." With this focus Raper surveys Glasgow's work starting with *Life and Gabriella* (1916) and continuing through the posthumous *Beyond Defeat* (1945). Raper's psychological analysis skilfully avoids impressionistic effusions and adds an entirely new critical dimension to the Glasgow canon. The success of any artist must be measured against what that artist attempted, the flawed masterpiece having a greater revelatory value for us than the perfection of the bibelot. In the growth of her mind, in her dedication "to endow 'every tree' with 'a name of its own and a special identity,'" in her lifelong attempt to transform human experience into words that would hold the ephemeral moment for attentive analysis, in the desire to *know*, Ellen Glasgow is a phenomenon in American letters. Like an Emily Dickinson or a Virginia Woolf, she used all of herself, and *From the Sunken Garden* makes us realize the value her distillation holds for us. It is a "magic by which we see ourselves in a mirror of words that at some point cease to be words and become people—people who are, at first, someone else walking around inside our head—and, finally, only ourselves." If Raper has grown from his study of Glasgow, we grow from our study of Raper.

Chapters and Commentaries in Books

As an avowed and accepted interpreter of a time and place, Ellen Glasgow continues to enjoy consideration in the general surveys of American social thought and the American novel. Remarkably enough, she has elicited rather kind appraisals from the more acidulous critics, such as Kazin and Geismar, and has been cavalierly derided by the usually kinder omnipotents.

Alfred Kazin, a social critic scornful of the 1920s, castigated the sophisticates of the "James Branch Cabell School" in *On Native Grounds* (Reynal & Hitchock, 1942; rev. ed., Garden City, N.Y.: Doubleday, 1956; rptd. in *Literature in America*, edited by Philip Rahv, New York: Meridian Books, 1957). On the other hand, he wrote glowingly of Ellen Glasgow, comparing her *Sheltered Life* with Chekhov's *Cherry Orchard*:

> When she discovered about 1913, the year she published *Virginia*, that the comedy of manners was her work, she made it serve what the very best comedies of manners have always served: as an index to the qualities of a civilization, and as a subtle guide to its covert tragedy. From one point of view, of course, her talent was only the highest expression of the society she lampooned; but her attacks on Southern complacency were never complacent in themselves. She belonged to a tradition and lived out her career in it; and her understanding seemed all the more moving because she was so deeply and immovably a participant in a world she scorned.

In a briefer but equally kind consideration, Henry Steele Commager in *The American Mind* (New Haven, Conn.: Yale University Press, 1950) underlined Glasgow's growing disenchantement with the New South and its material values as well as the irony of her finding strength in a past she had rejected.

In *The Faith of Our Feminists: A Study in the Novels of Edith Wharton, Ellen Glasgow, Willa Cather* (Richard R. Smith, 1950), Josephine Lurie Jessup gives us a perfectly innocuous if pedestrian review of the Glasgow opus. She advises us that Ellen Glasgow's "mission was to magnify woman." She admits, rather charmingly, that *Virginia* contradicts her thesis.

Frederick J. Hoffman, in *The Modern Novel in America, 1900-1950* (Chicago: Henry Regnery, 1951; rev. ed., Henry Regnery, 1956), elected to treat only Glasgow's later novels. He admired her social comedies, her subtle uses of viewpoint, but found her irony at times intrusive—characters became puppets for her commentaries. On the other hand, Dorinda in *Barren Ground* was too much the "model of heroic womanhood." *Vein of Iron* was impregnated with "too much contrived pathos." Thus the reader is prevented from viewing the characters of the comedies seriously and on the other hand is told that he cannot view the characters of the fortitude novels seriously enough.

Majl Ewing, in "The Civilized Uses of Irony: Ellen Glasgow," in *English Studies in Honor of James Southall Wilson*, edited by Fredson T. Bowers (Charlottesville: University Press of Virginia, 1951), sees Ellen Glasgow's gift for irony springing from her awareness of the absurdities attendant on male-female sexual relationships and detects this gift as early as *The Wheel of Life* (1906). In this work Ellen Glasgow "has discovered the life force—biological attraction—which henceforth makes so much of the comedy and tragedy of her novels. Her gift flowered in the three comedies of the city. Ewing speculates, as have others, on the possible influence of Cabell on its first major appearance in *The Romantic Comedians*.

N. Elizabeth Monroe contributed "Ellen Glasgow: Ironist of Manners" to *Fifty Years of the American Novel: A Christian Appraisal*, edited by Harold C. Gardiner (Charles Scribner's, 1951), a revision of her article first published in *America* (April 1951). She touches on the neglect accorded Ellen Glasgow at that date but concludes: "A writer with so much to say and so conscious of the means to saying it need not worry about neglect." While generally laudatory in tone, Monroe reproaches Ellen Glasgow for presenting "too many frustrated people, too many despairing moods, too many gallant poses." Recalling the subtitle of this survey, she adds that "religion is always treated skeptically and ironically, as though the novelist herself saw religion only as part of an outworn code." Monroe had earlier written a long critical appraisal, "Contemplation of Manners in Ellen Glasgow," in *The Novel and Society: A Critical Study of the Modern Novel* (Chapel Hill: University of North Carolina Press, 1941), which Ellen Glasgow is said to have found imperceptive. Perhaps Glasgow did not care for such assertions as: "She has never turned her art inward on the processes of her own thought and feeling." On the whole, though, it was a needed review of Glasgow's total work at the time, and much of what Monroe had to say remains valid today.

Van Wyck Brooks saw Ellen Glasgow as more than a regionalist in *The Confident Years: 1885-1915* (E.P. Dutton, 1952): "In her reaffirmation of reality and life against what used to be called the dead hand of tradition, Ellen Glasgow was a part of the world movement of her time—just as her Virginia scene was, in fact, a wider scene, the all-American scene of two generations." Brooks also presented brief critical and personal sketches in *Our Literary Heritage: A Pictorial History of the Writer in America* (E.P.

Dutton, 1956) and *From the Shadow of the Mountain: My Post-Meridian Years* (E.P. Dutton, 1961).

Edward Wagenknecht devotes a generous chapter, "Ellen Glasgow: Triumph and Despair," to the writer in his *Cavalcade of the American Novel* (Holt, Rinehart and Winston, 1952). Ever a kind reviewer, it is his usual warm appreciation, taking the pronouncements of the author under consideration at face value. Blair Rouse sees Wagenknecht's critique as a "somewhat inaccurate account of her career," but other than its acceptance of Glasgow as a reliable critic of Glasgow the writer, a course many scholars readily follow, it is a relatively accurate and comprehensive overview of her work. Wagenknecht sees her characters as "better Stoics than Christians," although they, like their creator, never quite abandon a mystic vision of a final unity.

Maxwell Geismar also devotes a generous chapter to Glasgow in *Rebels and Ancestors: The American Novel, 1890-1915* (Cambridge, Mass.: Houghton Mifflin, 1953), underscoring the fact that her best work appeared after she was fifty: "In this late blooming Indian summer she broke through the double armor of culture and temperament." Geismar generally writes approvingly of Glasgow, but along with other sociologically attuned critics, he expresses dismay that her "Colonels" and "darkies" speak the clichés of stereotypes, implying that in these instances she ceases to be the realist. As an interesting and privileged critic, Geismar indulges in mild audacities that gently titillate the professorial drudge; he compares *The Wheel of Life* (1906) with *The Great Gatsby*. He makes that early work sound better than most readers seem to remember it; but then we are reassured when he adds that "the moralistic tone of the conclusion is probably the main reason why *The Wheel of Life* has been an unduly neglected work." And then he sees *The Miller of Old Church*, which some of us seem to remember as having some charm, as an inferior work. What one would be tempted to term plot rehashes in another critic's commentary become with Geismar a matter of debate so that in the end he gives us a probing, enlightening analysis. He underlines more clearly than any previous Glasgow critic how the growth of moral discernment in her characters paralleled her personal emotional dilemmas and their resolution, a growth marked by the mixed tone of her work, "both elegiac and ironic." In finally escaping "from the constrictive sexuality at the center of her own emotions . . . she was able, in her last period of work, to break through the armor of the southern legend itself."

In contrast to these on-the-whole favorable commentaries, John Edward Hardy in "Ellen Glasgow," in *Southern Renascence*, edited by Louis D. Rubin, Jr., and Robert D. Jacobs (Baltimore: Johns Hopkins University Press, 1953), is negative, condescending, and gloriously unprophetic. The essay has some interest as a classic example of the critic being superior to the artist and to other critics in lauding a minor work over other novels, in this instance *The Miller of Old Church*. He states that "Ellen Glasgow . . . is in no way essentially a realist. She is . . . essentially a sentimentalist." He does "not advocate a Glasgow critical revival," advice prodigiously ignored in the intervening twenty-seven years by a large number of perceptive critics, including one of his editors.

The South in American Literature, 1607-1900 (Durham, N.C.: Duke University Press, 1954), by Jay B. Hubbell, gives us a brief review of the Glasgow opus. Hubbell traces her development as a novelist and suggests a heterogeneous collection of influences—James, Howells, Cable, and Cabell. In his "Ellen Glasgow: Artist and Social Historian," in *South and Southwest: Literary Essays and Reminiscences* (Durham, N.C.: Duke University Press, 1965), Hubbell is discursive and charmingly anecdotal, recounting his long acquaintance with Glasgow's work and his personal association with the woman. He sees her as a pioneer, more representative of a place than Faulkner. He defends her claim to having conceived a "history of Virginian manners" quite early, as opposed to Cabell's revelation that it was his conception rather late in her career. Hubbell states, "I do not think Cabell's memory on these points accurate. . . . Ellen Glasgow was quite aware of what she was doing." Another personal reminiscence is given us by Isaac F. Marcosson in *Before I Forget* (Dodd, Mead, 1959). Associated with Walter Hines Page in the Doubleday, Page Company, Marcosson sketches a long (since 1900), admiring, literary friendship with Ellen Glasgow, revealing the totally committed devotion a contemporary could feel for the writer and the woman.

In "Ellen Glasgow and the Southern Literary Tradition," in *Virginia in History and Tradition*, edited by R. C. Simonini, Jr. (Farmville, Va.: Institute of Southern Culture, 1958), C. Hugh Holman comments on those writers who, judged by an older Southern literary tradition, were excluded from the classification of Southern writer, notably Poe, Glasgow, Wolfe, and Faulkner. In an easy, broadly allusive style, he convinces the reader that, rather than being outside, these writers are most representative of a tradition of Southern literary art. Glasgow shares with them

> a sense of evil, pessimism about man's potential, tragic sense of life, a deep-rooted sense of the interplay of past and present, a peculiar sensitivity of time as a complex element in narrative art, a sense of place as a dramatic dimension, and a thoroughgoing belief in the intrinsic value of art as an end in itself, with an attendant Aristotelian concern with forms and techniques.

In *Three Modes of Southern Fiction* (Athens: University of Georgia Press, 1966), Holman gives a further analysis of Ellen Glasgow's work in relation to that of Faulkner and Wolfe. His broad scholarly background brings clarity to diversity, especially in his opening and closing chapters wherein he melds history and geography in defining the complex nuances of "southern." In the chapter devoted specifically to Glasgow, "The Novelist of Manners as Social Critic," Holman observes that the novel of manners in the tradition of Jane Austen presents the testing of "men and women by accepted standards of conduct in a sharply arrested moment in history." Ellen Glasgow's comedies of manners differ in that "her characters are tested not by their conformity to a meaningful code but by their futile rebellions against a dead one." Ellen Glasgow's attitude toward her culture was ultimately ambivalent: "Not to love it was, for Miss Glasgow at least, impossible; and yet to fail to subject it to ironic analysis would be to succumb to its worst failings." The clarity and urbanity of Holman's style raises the scholarly essay to an art form. This essay was later included in Holman's *The Roots of Southern Writing* (Athens: University of Georgia Press, 1972). Holman's later contributions to Glasgow scholarship contained in *The Immoderate Past: The Southern Writer and History* (Athens: University of Georgia Press, 1977) and *Windows on the World: Essays in American Social Fiction* (Knoxville: University of Tennessee Press, 1979) are considered in the following section as they appeared first in periodicals.

Louis D. Rubin, Jr., observed Miss Glasgow with his left eye, slightly jaundiced, while beaming with his right upon James Branch Cabell in *No Place on Earth* (Austin: University of Texas Press, 1959). Rubin makes no claim to having exhaustively reread all the works of either author, but he has read selectively in depth and gives us insights not found elsewhere. His approach to Miss Glasgow, however, seems rather severe and results in the type of commentary where Gideon Vetch of *One Man in His Time* (1922), a minor novel in the Glasgow canon, is compared with Willie Stark in *All the King's Men*, Warren's masterpiece. Although Rubin challenges, with reason, Ellen Glasgow's claims to literary prescience in projecting her social history, he accepts Cabell's claims to olympian forethought in planning an epic cycle, although the latter was from the beginning of his career suspected of being a falsifier of a large order. On the positive side, Rubin's analysis points up the common problem of many Glasgow heroines of marrying beneath them or of not marrying at all. He admires her awareness of the implications in the confrontations of members of the First Families of Virginia with people of lower status; consequently he prefers her comedies to her novels of "high seriousness." His final word for Ellen Glasgow is "transitional."

Three years after *No Place on Earth* appeared, Rubin covered the same material in an address given before the Friends of the Richmond Public Library, published by that group in 1966 under the title *Richmond as a Literary Capital.* His thesis is the same: that Glasgow's and Cabell's Richmond was a strange translation of the Richmond of mundane experience. Here he again favors the comedies; however, in a more mellow mood he stresses the idea that there were *two* Ellen Glasgows, related to be sure. This assessment judges her "a very heroic woman, not only for what she did, but for what she tried to do." The ideas he expostulates in the above are presented again in "Two in Richmond," first in *South: Modern Southern Literature in Its Cultural Setting*, (Garden City, N.Y.: Doubleday, 1961) and later in his *The Curious Death of the Novel* (Baton Rouge: Louisiana State University Press, 1967). Rubin briefly discusses point of view in *Barren Ground* in his *The Teller of The Tale* (Seattle: University of Washington Press, 1967). He contributed the "Introduction" to *Ellen Glasgow: Centennial Essays*, edited by M. Thomas Inge, (Charlottesville: University Press of Virginia, 1976) in which he gracefully commented on her status in southern letters.

Willard Thorp in *American Writing in the Twentieth Century* (Cambridge, Mass.: Harvard University Press, 1960), like Rubin, favors the comedies and regrets that Glasgow discovered her "vein of high comedy" late in life, owing, perhaps, to her early adherence to the "realism preached by W. D. Howells and his disciples." H. Wayne Morgan terms his essays in *Writers in Transition* (Hill & Wang, 1963) "old-fashioned appreciations," and his "Ellen Glasgow: The Qualities of Endurance" does not belie that genial classification nor does it exclude reasonable balance. As his chapter title indicates, he writes of Glasgow's efforts to define human fortitude; in her work we feel the stresses inherent in the "shift from agrarian to industrial America." John R. Welsh's essay, "Egdon Heath Revisited: Ellen Glasgow's *Barren Ground*," in *Reality and Myth* (Nashville, Tenn.: Vanderbilt University Press, 1964), develops the expected comparison of *The Return of the Native* with *Barren Ground*, in particular the analogies of characters (especially rustics), symbol (heather-broomsedge), theme (environment versus human will), and circumstance (sexual attraction versus common sense). Both novels are tributes to the human spirit of survival in adverse environments ("the world").

Warner Berthoff, in his brief and gloomy assessment of Ellen Glasgow in *The Ferment of Realism* (Free Press, 1965), informs us that "the buried vein of authenticity in Ellen Glasgow's work is almost entirely subjective and emotional." Then he flatly states that "as social history and social criticism her novels are well-bred fantasy." Howard Mumford Jones, in *Jeffersonianism and the American Novel* (Teachers College Press, 1966), sees three ladies in particular, Wharton, Cather, and Glasgow, bridging the gap between the writers of "the golden age" of the later nineteenth century and their successors who abandoned the premises of the "natural aristocracy."

Robert E. Spiller refreshingly treats Ellen Glasgow as a novelist rather than as a historian in his *The Cycle of American Literature* (Macmillan, 1955, rptd. 1967), seeing her efforts as a writer bent on achieving "something like Hawthorne's truth to the human heart." In her slow but determined advancement in ability, he sees her succeeding where others have failed: "With a flexible style, capable of almost tragic intensity or comic irony at will, she was able to interpret, out of her own understanding of herself, the shift in values which had so completely altered the society of which she was a part."

A segment of a doctoral dissertation, "The Decline of the Southern Gentlemen Ideal: Indian Summer," by Kenneth M. England (Vanderbilt University, 1957), was published by Georgia State College as one of its *School of Arts and Sciences Research Papers* (April 1967). In this segment, England exhaustively analyzes the character of Asa Timberlake of *In This Our Life*. Asa's code is based on an idealized concept of a beautiful self-sacrificing mother who is symbolic of Mother South. While Asa is in the pattern of the Southern gentleman, his noble actions seem peculiarly lacking in conviction; but we are assured "he possesses character and maintains it, and that is in itself a triumph even though he represents ideals that no longer prevail."

William Leigh Godshalk contributed a preface and copious notes for a new edition of *The Voice of the People* (New Haven, Conn.: College and University Press, 1972). He reviews the sociology for which the work has been abundantly praised but goes on to suggest that its merits in this area have overshadowed its artistic values. He credits Glasgow for her skillful development of the theme of isolation and a style which has "historical density." In characterization, he sees the novel's heroine as "the central figure, standing between the opposed forces of Nick and Dudley, polar characters contrasting in their actions, their physical and mental attributes, and their political ideals." Godshalk especially admires the symbolism of the novel, and as for the constantly shifting point of view, he sees it as a device to achieve ironic effect. "Though the overall impression is dark and autumnal, the artistry is impeccable, and *The Voice of the People* is a much better novel than many critics have been willing to admit."

In Chapter 7, "'The Diminished Grandeur of Washington Street': Ellen Glasgow's *The Sheltered Life*," of *Shifting World: Social Change and Nostalgia in the American Novel* (Lewisburg, Pa.: Bucknell University Press, 1976), David C. Stineback traces the theme of multiple deceptions in the novel and concludes, "The society of lower Washington Street, Queenborough, Virginia, has turned on itself and committed suicide." James S. Wamsley and Anne M. Cooper, in *Idols, Victims, Pioneers: Virginia's Women from 1607* (Richmond: Virginia State Chamber of Commerce, 1976), give a superficial summary of Glasgow's life and career. As late as 1977 Richard Gray asserts that "little of great critical merit has been written on Glasgow despite her obvious importance." In his "The New South and the Old Problems: Ellen Glasgow" (*The Literature of Memory*, Baltimore: Johns Hopkins University Press, 1977), Gray discusses Ellen Glasgow's vision of a new agrarian society based on the plain man of character and her perceptive alteration of this vision through the years. He makes a strong defense of *In This Our Life*, "a complete volte-face," seeing its indictment of the industrialized South as a proof of Glasgow's strength of character.

"The situation was steeped in irony, like something from one of her own comic novels. Ellen Glasgow, the self-appointed advocate of the plain man, had ended her creative life with a novel that celebrated the virtues of the old patrimony." Her personal dilemma, however, paralleled that of the new society.

Seven American Women Writers of the Twentieth Century: An Introduction (Minneapolis: University of Minnesota Press, 1977) includes Louis Auchincloss's suave and understanding *Ellen Glasgow* from the Minnesota Pamphlet Series. As editor, Maureen Howard contributes an hilarious preface in which she comments on four of Glasgow's works: "*The Romantic Comedians* holds up nicely"; of *Barren Ground*, "The Price of Dorinda's Success Is Awful"; Jenny Blair, at the end of *The Sheltered Life*, "can be saved from George's shallow and corrupting romantic ideas"; in *The Woman Within*, Glasgow "is given to defensive overevaluations of her work and then spilling the beans of self-doubt much like Norman Mailer."

Serafina Kent Bathwick contributes an interesting chapter to *The Modern American Novel and the Movies*, edited by Gerald Peary and Roger Shatzkin, (Frederick Ungar, 1978) with her essay on *In This Our Life*, "Independent Woman, Doomed Sister." Bathwick discusses the novel in depth indicating how its emphasis on inner monologue posed problems for the film adapter, Howard Koch. His four film scripts, moving progressively from meditation to action, reversed Glasgow's sister symbolism, and Roy, the philosophical iconoclast, is shown as the conventional stay-at-home good woman. John Huston, the director, further emphasized the reversal showing Stanley (Bette Davis) in constant motion and Roy (Olivia de Havilland) in studied repose. The film resulted in melodrama rather than a philosophical statement on the changing social order. Bathwick's scholarly analysis tells us much about the techniques of filmmaking in the early 1940s and even more about the problems of translating literature into film.

As his chapter title indicates, "Ellen Glasgow and William Faulkner: Vestigial Calvinism and Naturalism Combined," Perry D. Westbrook in *Free Will and Determinism in American Literature* (Cranbury, N.J.: Associated University Presses, 1979) scrutinizes *Barren Ground* and *Vein of Iron* as works that illustrate his thesis. He acknowledges that Glasgow creates her own special vocabulary but judges that the results are the same. "Pragmatically, Dreiser's chemisms and instincts, Miss Glasgow's vein of iron, and Calvin's grace of God are identical, and none dispels the inscrutability of ultimate cause." He is also inclined to associate Glasgow's fleeting transcendental ecstasies with religious exaltation. Yet Westbrook gives due credit to all the philosophical influences found in her work. He finds *Barren Ground* "remarkable for its synthesis of Calvinist predestination, scientific determinism, and a transcendentalism that was derived from Plotinus, the religions of the East, and German philosophy. These three strands—so important both singly and in combination in the life of the

American mind and soul—are brought together in *Barren Ground* with a plausibility seldom equaled in American literature."

"Ellen Glasgow in Richmond" is included as one of the thirty chapters in *No Castles on Main Street: American Authors and Their Homes* by Stephanie Kraft (Rand McNally, 1979), which purports to give glimpses of the environment where authors lived and worked. The chapter devoted to Glasgow's 1841 Greek Revival residence has the feel of a tourist visit. Ellen Glasgow's associations with houses has been touched on in greater depth in the *Ellen Glasgow Newsletter*, and they are mentioned here for their relevance. Dorothy Scura gives an intimate view of the house and its evolution in "One West Main" (October 1974); and in "A Lost Memorial to Ellen Glasgow" (March 1980), Scura details the efforts of Arthur Glasgow and Henry Anderson to keep the house as the writer had left it. In "Fertile Ground" (March 1978), Antoinette W. Roades traces the history of Jerdone Castle, the house and farm beloved by Ellen Glasgow in her childhood and which figures in her work. In "Ellen Glasgow and Rockbridge County" (October 1978), Roger Hunt Carroll writes of the Glasgow estates in that county, in particular "Green Forest" (*glas-gow* in Gaelic); he also recounts her visits there in her research for *Vein of Iron*.

Recent Articles in Periodicals

The current diversity of interest in Ellen Glasgow is especially apparent in the variety of periodicals, in particular the smaller ones, that are presenting articles on every aspect of her work. She has been accorded handsome recognition in the Communist publication *Mainstream* (Barbara Giles, "Character and Fate: The Novels of Ellen Glasgow," September 1956), as well as in the Catholic weekly *America* (Nellie Elizabeth Monroe, "Ellen Glasgow: Ironist of Manners," April 1951).

The controversy surrounding the inception of Glasgow's social history has elicited a continuing discussion in periodicals as well as in books. The first article treating the subject in depth, reviewing the evidence from early to late, is Daniel W. Patterson's "Ellen Glasgow's Plan for a Social History of Virginia" (*MFS*, Winter 1959-1960). This reasonable presentation of Cabell versus Glasgow as the "planner" provoked a rather ill-tempered rereading of the evidence by Oliver J. Steele in "Ellen Glasgow, Social History, and the 'Virginia Edition'" (*MFS*, Summer 1961). Steele is the author of several articles on plate damage and impressions of Glasgow novels and the editor of the Kelly bibliography; he also presented a memoir from a Glasgow notebook, "Gertrude Stein and Ellen Glasgow: Memoir of a Meeting" (*AL*, March 1961). Edgar E. MacDonald in "The Glasgow-Cabell Entente" (*AL*, March 1969) cites letters and notes that support Cabell's claims to first seeing the Glasgow opus as a planned history. The formula for prefaces that resulted in *A Certain Measure* was his, he supplied the title for that work, and his hand is evident elsewhere. The continuing discussion is due in part to the phrasing of Ellen Glasgow's intentions in her early letters; whatever her early intent may have been, a body of work that constitutes a social history resulted.

Frederick P. W. McDowell, author of the first book-length study of Glasgow, earlier gave us an overview of her work in "Ellen Glasgow and the Art of the Novel" (*PQ*, July 1951), an analysis of her literary techniques as enunciated in *A Certain Measure*, and their application to her novels. In "'The Old Pagan Scorn of Everlasting Mercy'—Ellen Glasgow's *The Deliverance*" (*TCL*, January 1959), McDowell points up the vitality of her earlier novels. He analyzes the symbolic values of the characters in that novel and, more specifically, Christopher Blake's revenge motivation and its consequences. McDowell sees *The Deliverance* as "more significant as a psychological than as a sociological study," the character of Guy Carraway serving as "Miss Glasgow's disinterested Jamesean spectator." He concludes that the matured sense of form that unites social scene and characters, the larger motivating forces as well as the emotional, and "her realization of the close relationship between the tragic and the comic in human affairs all indicate the stature of this novel." In "Theme and Artistry in Ellen Glasgow's *The Sheltered Life*" (*TSLL*, Winter 1960), McDowell, in a masterly analysis, a definitive exposition, presents the case that *The Sheltered Life* is not only Glasgow's best novel but one of the artistic achievements of her time.

Allen W. Becker's studies for his dissertation, "Ellen Glasgow: Her Novels and Their Place in the Development of Southern Fiction" (Johns Hopkins University, 1956), resulted in three articles in scholarly publications. In "Ellen Glasgow's Social History" (*TeSE*, 1957), he discusses six of her earlier novels as a chronological series intended to document the impact of the New South upon the Old. In *Voice, Battle, Deliverance, Romance, Virginia*, and *Life and Gabriella*, Glasgow employed a technique of allowing a character to epitomize a segment of Southern society, but the results are marred by sentiment, auctorial intrusion, and distortion of the character for the sake of her thesis. These novels are the esquisses for the more successful treatment of the same material in *Barren Ground, The Sheltered Life*, and *Vein of Iron*. Becker contributed the central section, "The Period 1865-1925," of a three-part article, "Agrarianism as a Theme in Southern Literature" (*GaR*, Summer 1957). Here he situates Glasgow between Thomas Nelson Page and James Branch Cabell, terming *Barren Ground* "the most openly agrarian work of the period under consideration." Dorinda Oakley attempts "to recapture her soul by marrying it to the land." Glasgow, however, became disillusioned with the industrialization she welcomed in her earlier novels. The agrarian South, which her first hero left in *The Descendant*, is symbolically returned to by her last hero in *Beyond Defeat*. In "Ellen Glasgow and the Southern Literary Tradition" (*MFS*, Winter 1959), Becker asserts that she "brought to Southern letters the first conscious literary realism," her most radical innovation lying in her rejection of the aristocratic basis of society. Yet Glasgow did not totally abandon the romantic love story, the noble Southern woman, nor the rhetorical style of earlier writers. Her later novels, "in their new outlook on industrialism, in their regionalism, and in their use of the family as a symbol, display the central concerns and viewpoints in the fiction of the Southern revival." Some scholars might take exception to Becker's assertion that interest in Glasgow's novels "lies in their 'history,' for none are literary successes."

Newton Baird, in "Leadership in Ideal Proportions: Ellen Glasgow's *The Voice of the People*" (*Talisman*, Winter-Spring 1956-1957), treats that novel to a detailed analysis, in particular the character of Nicholas Burr, the honest country boy, morally and politically victorious over a decadent aristocracy. Sentimentality is the one weakness "of a quite brilliant author," one who "was able to construct in this novel an intricate triangular relationship of courage, integrity, and betrayal. Within the triangle is the dominant theme of the author's entire body of work: the destructive or uncivilized element in human nature as opposed to moral intelligence." Robert Holland, in "Miss Glasgow's 'Prufrock'" (*AQ*, Winter 1957), postulates that in her chronicles of Virginia, Ellen Glasgow viewed World War I as "the ridge which separates, in a general way, the struggles of order from the death of order: beyond this ridge loom confusion and loss of will." Bracketing the contemporary wasteland are *The Sheltered Life* and *In This Our Life*, with *They Stooped to Folly* lying between them, in point of time treated. Holland makes an extended comparison of Virginius Curle Littlepage of the latter novel with Eliot's "Prufrock." Glasgow's "modern" hero is impotent because "will and desire are at secret odds, so that desire is constantly thwarted by will. Reflecting the fragmented state of modern consciousness, the personal spirit of Mr. Littlepage is torn between two worlds and two cultural claims." Holland's final paragraph, a scholium "in which the words *success* and *failure* have the same pair of referents," will benumb all but the resolute logician.

Joan Curlee's "Ellen Glasgow's South" (*BSUF*, Winter 1961-1962) is a brief overall review of Glasgow's work with the emphasis on her interpretation of the South, Old and New. Curlee relies heavily on *A Certain Measure* and cites older critical opinions. R. H. Dillard, in "The Writer's Best Solace: Textual Revisions in Ellen Glasgow's *The Past*" (*SB*, 1966), assures us that Glasgow was the conscientious reviser she claimed to be. "The Past," the work Dillard considered, is her short story, not to be confused with "The Deep Past," the central section of *The Sheltered Life*. William F. Heald sees a number of Ellen Glasgow's "vividly realized minor characters" as grotesques. His "Ellen Glasgow and the Grotesque" (*MissQ*, Winter 1965-1966) thus associates her with a host of latter-day

European and Southern writers. This focusing on the incongruities of characters grows out of an author's "realization that man is both sublime and ridiculous, that man's life is both laughable and terrifying." Too bad, concludes Heald, that Ellen Glasgow's feeling for *bienséance* made her shrink from presenting "the violent and the extreme" in her larger portraits. K. A. Heineman, in "Ellen Glasgow: The Death of the Chivalrous Tradition" (*ForumH*, Fall 1967), postulates that Glasgow's upholding of the rights of women and the dignity of the common man helped to break the spell of the chivalrous tradition. Robert Hudspeth reexamines the contrasting points of view, youth and age, as a thematic device in "Point of View in Ellen Glasgow's *The Sheltered Life*" (*Thoth*, Spring 1963). Edgar E. MacDonald's "Glasgow and James: On the Techniques of the Novel" (*Stylus*, Randolph-Macon College, Fall 1965) redefines Glasgow's "romantic-realistic" position in relation to other writers and places her close to Henry James in literary philosophy. Nancy Minter McCollum skims over several analogous points in "Glasgow's and Cabell's Comedies of Virginia" (*GaR*, Summer 1964). Both authors wrote "of the prolonged worship of the chivalric tradition during the late nineteenth century and early twentieth century in Virginia," Glasgow sprinkling salt, Cabell sugar. They shared an "inherited sense of delicacy." While Glasgow's optimism is restricted, Cabell's gaiety is only the surface of his pessimism. Styles differ greatly, Cabell's "mannered, high-flown, irreverent, flamboyant, iconoclastic," Glasgow's "logical, restrained, catholic. Yet the end result for both is poetic prose of a pure and controlled nature." J. J. Murphy's theme in "Marriage and Desire in Ellen Glasgow's *They Stooped to Folly*" (*Decant*, Texas Christian University, Fall 1965) is that in this work Glasgow embraced the Victorian concept of mutual responsibility in marriage. Victorian?

Blair Rouse, the most dedicated of all Glasgow scholars, has devoted some thirty-five years to championing her work and defending her honor against critical onslaughts. His earlier commentaries are incorporated in his *Ellen Glasgow*, reviewed above, but more recent articles attest to his continuing zeal. In "Ellen Glasgow: The Novelist in America" (*The Cabellian*, Autumn 1971), he takes us on a leisurely consideration of the role of the professional novelist in America from Cooper to Faulkner and treats more particularly Glasgow's search for "an intelligent recognition from critics and readers whom she could respect." The true artist is one who treats "experience" as "an illumination of life," and this was ever Glasgow's goal. In "Ellen Glasgow: Manners and Art" (*The Cabellian*, Spring 1972), Rouse reviews the most serious critical objections to her work, acknowledging that her faults as a novelist—oversimplification, a reliance on Victorian serial techniques, a stubborn adherence to intuition for characterization—do indeed exist. Then he asks: "What, on the other hand, were her achievements?'' The answer: ''In her nineteen novels Ellen Glasgow created complex patterns which enable one to understand more clearly the meaning of life during the past century.'' Rouse proceeds to develop the positive characteristics inherent in her work and concludes that, ''Ellen Glasgow, like other American and European novelists of our time, faced the problem of writing fiction that would be serious and intelligent as well as affirmative in statement yet would be neither oversimplified nor ambiguous.'' Ironically, as her champion points out perceptively, she occasionally ''found her answer in the affirmation of a tragic character—in tragic meanings.'' More recently he has given us an affectionate memoir in ''I Remember Miss Ellen'' (*EGN*, March 1977) based on his visit with her ''on a mild December day—December 19, 1941.'' He records his impressions, her comments on her works, and includes four letters that she wrote him.

As a devotee of Darwin, Ellen Glasgow has attracted the attention of Marxist critics from time to time. In ''Work and Love, or How the Fittest Survive: A Study of Ellen Glasgow's 'Life and Gabriella' '' (*Language and Literature*, November 1973), Marianne Kristiansen presents a textbook reading of that novel with little depth of research. ''Bourgeois'' and ''bourgeoisie'' are recurring terms. ''The petty bourgeoisie is primarily characterized by its subjective adherence to an anachronistic ideology, which no longer coheres with its material situation, e.g. its notion of the female as an ornament.'' While the author's English is passably comprehensible, it is heavily an economics textbook, further weighted with *underlined* words. The article abounds with charts purporting to trace developments. One little chart contrasting the attributes of ''lady'' and ''businesswoman'' carries the explanation: ''Groups 1-3 are defined on the basis of material, objective criteria, whereas group 4 stands for the genteel lady-norms of the petty bourgeoisie. The conflict between the two female roles is dissolved by way of the contrast EXTERNAL versus INTERNAL.'' One gathers, rather dejectedly, that Marianne Kristiansen sees Gabriella's ''life-force'' as a masculine rejection of traditional female virtues.

Clement Eaton, in ''Breaking a Path for the Liberation of Women in the South'' (*GaR*, Summer 1974), gives Glasgow her due in the process, analyzes *Virginia*, and concludes that ''she was too great an artist to use her novels, with the single exception of *The Builders*, as propaganda instruments, even for women's rights.''

The Fall 1974 issue of the *Mississippi Quarterly* contains a special section entitled ''Richmond, Virginia, and Southern Writing,'' introduced by M. Thomas Inge. Maurice Duke's ''Cabell's and Glasgow's Richmond: The Intellectual Background of the City'' focuses on its cultural life, the four sections of the essay treating the History, the Reading, the Theater, the Writing. In his conclusion, Duke gives an overview of the impact of the city on Ellen Glasgow and James Branch Cabell. In ''Glasgow, Cabell, and

Richmond,'' Edgar MacDonald defines Richmond's class structure, commenting on its relative stability, its strictures, and its personality, going on to suggest how many of its attitudes entered the work of its two best-known writers of fiction. The city served exclusively as background for seven of Glasgow's novels and partially for five. Unlike Cabell, whose youthful sensibilities were wounded by gossip, Glasgow looked on Richmond's restrictive mores with amused detachment and in time questioned whether in her youth ideas had been ''any more free in Oxford or Bloomsbury than in Richmond.'' This essay was later included in *Ellen Glasgow: Centennial Essays*. Dorothy Scura, in ''Glasgow and the Southern Renaissance: The Conference at Charlottesville,'' treats at length the ''Southern Writers Conference,'' which took place at the University of Virginia on 23-24 October 1931, and gives sketches of the thirty authors who attended. She discusses Ellen Glasgow's opening speech and assesses the results of the meeting, rating it a social success but a failure ''as a forum for exchanging constructive ideas.'' It was, however, a milestone, ''a recognition, as well as a celebration, of the development in Southern writing now known as the Southern Literary Renaissance.'' This essay too was later included in *Ellen Glasgow: Centennial Essays*.

The late distinguished American scholar C. Hugh Holman continued to offer insights to the Glasgow oeuvre. In ''April in Queenborough: Ellen Glasgow's Comedies of Manners'' (*SR*, Spring 1974), he touches on the catharsis she realized from writing *Barren Ground* and her arrival at a new understanding of the art of fiction. In *The Romantic Comedians, They Stopped to Folly*, and *The Sheltered Life*, the writer is everywhere present but ''she has learned most of the lessons of point of view and author-effacement.'' Holman then details how Glasgow was able ''to re-create her world like a true Maker, and in its gravest moments to flood it with the silvery laughter of Meredithian comedy.'' Ironic detachment and knowing affection made these three novels ''succeed admirably in that difficult and rare genre, the American comedy of manners.'' This essay was included in *Ellen Glasgow: Centennial Essays* and in *Windows on the World: Essays on American Social Fiction* (Knoxville: University of Tennessee Press, 1979). In *The Immoderate Past: The Southern Writer and History* (Athens: University of Georgia Press, 1977), Holman comments on the use of time as a major dimension in the fiction of Southern novelists, whereas time has been displaced by space in the mainstream of the American novel. In support of this thesis he incorporates his ''Ellen Glasgow and History: *The Battle Ground*,'' earlier published in *Prospects* (1976). In this essay Holman observes that while *The Battle Ground* ''contains the most strictly historical elements'' of all her works, it ''is in a sense a microcosm of the whole pattern of Ellen Glasgow's social history of Virginia.'' As ''an objective symbol for an inner struggle,'' this work ''established the central social action that motivates her fictional history of the Commonwealth." Continuing with his thesis on time in *The Immoderate Past* he touches on "The Deep Past," the central section of *The Sheltered Life* wherein Glasgow "has departed from her standard realistic method, which is employed with great skill though the bulk of the novel, and has moved into a kind of poetic recollection that moves freely in time, both borrowing sequential freedom from certain aspects of the stream of consciousness tradition and borrowing poetic expression from Virginia Woolf." In "*Barren Ground* and the Shape of History" (*SAQ*, Spring 1978), Holman goes beyond the psychological and moral considerations of that novel to expound on its historical dimension. Obsessed with time, Glasgow's view is basically Hegelian, in that it sees "History as Process, the movement of large forces through sequences that lead to large cause-and-effect relationships." Her characters become "the equivalents of Faulkner's 'avatars'. . . ." Thus *Barren Ground*, "the most personal, private, and individual of Ellen Glasgow's novels, is, on one level, a microcosm of southern history." This essay too is incorporated in *Windows on the World*.

Oliver Steele in his "Ellen Glasgow's *Virginia:* Preliminary Notes" (*SB*, 1974) gives us a fascinating insight into the writer's creative thought. He describes the source material and advises us that the notes "consist of two chapter by chapter outlines of the novel, . . ." giving evidence that she did not have quite the clarity of purpose she claimed in *A Certain Measure*. A significant change is in the use of Cyrus Treadwell, from arch-villain to simply an exponent of unfeeling materialism, "from a melodramatic to a realistic level." The author also changed the character of Margaret Oldcastle, the "other woman," underlining Glasgow's decision "to make Virginia's tragedy a matter of her own character, rather than of external circumstance." These early drafts "record the stages by which, for the writer, the hypothetical and abstract became concrete and actual." Steele appends thirteen pages of notes, calling attention to the fact that Glasgow wrote no less than nine separate versions of the opening scene of the novel.

In a perceptive reading of the Glasgow canon, "Ellen Glasgow: The Great Tradition and the New Morality" (*CLQ*, June 1975), N. E. Dunn sets forth Miss Ellen's juxtaposition of the code of "beautiful behavior" versus the "new morality." "Although Glasgow saw some values in both the old and the new codes, her very uncertainty about which code to subscribe to revealed that she was much more aware of what was wrong with them than what was right." Glasgow's oeuvre, while analyzing the exterior masks of society, probes into the psyche of man, in particular the author's own. "Conflict between the old and the new codes is not merely a matter of conflict between the generations in her work. In the novels Miss Glasgow's own inner conflict is often expressed in terms of conflict within a single character's consciousness." Despite a minor reservation or two—"the red-headed [?] lady from Richmond," the assertion that Asa Timberlake sided with the family against the Negro youth, Parry Clay—Dunn's analysis of the philosophical Glasgow ranks with the best scholarship devoted to any author. It summarizes Glasgow's life-long search for "something to live by," and it underlines the final irony of successful failure.

In "History in *Barren Ground* and *Vein of Iron*: Theory, Structure, and Symbol" (*SLJ*, Fall 1975), Judy Smith Murr sees the structure of the two novels as illustrating Glasgow's translation "of the movement of personal history into a structural and thematic aesthetic," which encompasses "many levels of history in the novels: universal, social, familial, and individual. . . ." The patterns are similar on each level, and Murr illustrates her thesis primarily by considering the emotional outlooks of Dorinda and Ada, "Glasgow's iron-veined individuals [who] assert a theory of history which places primacy on the individual."

Katherine C. Turner, in "To the Heart of Oakley and Woodruff" (*SHR*, Fall 1976), juxtaposes Glasgow's Dorinda Oakley of *Barren Ground* and John Fowles's Sarah Woodruff of *The French Lieutenant's Woman*. "Twins of a sort in their brainchild birth," they give us, "partially through the articulations of their authors," insights into "the curious art of composition." Both authors owe a debt to Hardy, but both respect the independent natures of their heroines. "Dorinda Oakley and Sarah Woodruff are linked by more than the wood in their names and by their cutting across the grain of life."

The Winter 1977-1978 issue of the *Mississippi Quarterly* presented a special section devoted to Glasgow entitled "The Apprenticeship of Ellen Glasgow," edited by M. Thomas Inge. The lead article, contributed by Julius Rowan Raper, "Ambivalence Toward Authority: A Look at Glasgow's Library, 1890-1908," assesses the writer's reading during her formative years and points out that in addition to her predilection for the Darwinists, she also favored the early writers of "wisdom" literature such as Epictetus, Marcus Aurelius, and Plato. To these she added the Buddhists and the sacred texts of the East. Raper assures us that indeed "Glasgow did not exaggerate the extent and nature of her early intellectual rebellion, that she did read, and mark very perceptively, all the authors the autobiography mentions. . . ." Dorothy McInnis Scura, in "The Southern Lady in the Early Novels of Ellen Glasgow," outlines "the number, variety, and complexity of Ellen Glasgow's women characters in her early novels" but goes on to underline that "it was not until her tenth novel that Glasgow chose a fragile female gentlewoman for her protagonist." In *Virginia* she was prepared to treat in definitive terms "the full-length, three-dimensional portrait . . . of the external conformist as well as reveal for the first time the doubting iconoclast within." In her study of the first ten Glasgow novels, "Toward a Perfect Place: Setting in the Early Novels of Ellen Glasgow," Dorothy Kish's thesis is that "a pulsating sense of place, whether the massive tobacco fields of *The Deliverance* or the charming gardens of the

Richmond novels, harmonizes with the other elements of the stories." A feeling for natural beauty mingled with artistic vision taught her to extend a "character's mood into the setting." Her artistic integration of character and setting flowered in *Virginia*, from an "intense sweetness" in the April promise, through "the splendour of the Indian summer," to the bleakness of the winter that symbolizes Virginia's failed marriage. "As she settles into a life of stoicism, an ensemble of subdued images—falling leaves, fading sunlight, shaded sick-rooms—signifies the end of her bright days." In "A Finger on the Pulse of Life: Ellen Glasgow's Search for a Style," Edgar MacDonald sees her early career as a movement from ideas per se to a quest for a proper vehicle for the expression of the ideas in artistic images. She studied the French and English determinists, but found her inspiration in Tolstoy. She learned the value of the objective observer, the commenting chorus, and gradually let her characters develop from within their own psyches. "Imagery, a striking feature of her style from the beginning, she refines into a subtle art, especially in her use of light and shadow; at the same time her symbolism moves from the theatrical to the poetically suggestive, an evocation of a time, place, mood, an inherent part of the fabric she wove as a mature artist." In the same issue of the *Mississippi Quarterly*, Ladell Payne offers "Ellen Glasgow's *Vein of Iron*: Vanity, Irony, Idiocy" in which he gives a close reading of this novel, revealing his interest in Faulkner studies in expounding on its theme of endurance and fortitude. Glasgow, Payne observes, had the "ability to see the vanity, the irony, and the idiocy of man's life and still affirm some value to endurance. . . ." We can even achieve brief illusions of happiness. The human spirit triumphs irrationally. "Moreover, there is nothing to affirm *but* life, existence in all its idiocy. This is both the irony and the glory of being human."

J. R. Raper's in-depth studies of Glasgow's life and work have grown into the definitive statements concerning the writer. "Glasgow's Psychology of Deceptions and *The Sheltered Life*" (*SLJ*, Fall 1975) presents an incisive analysis of the novel in which General Archbald is seen as "a dramatized point of view to be judged against the real events of the book." From this perspective we become aware "that the tragedy of Eva and George and Jenny is very much like an Ibsen play enacted before the eyes of the General and that it is the interposition of his complex sensibility between the play and the reader which makes this novel capable of probing shadowy corners of the mind." Judging this work as Glasgow's finest achievement, Raper convinces us that "*The Sheltered Life* is the most intense study Glasgow ever made of the themes she handled best throughout her career, those associated with evasive idealism." Raper's essay, "Invisible Things: The Short Stories of Ellen Glasgow" (*SLJ*, Spring 1977), presents the thesis that these stories appeared at a low period of novel-making in Glasgow's career and that they represent experiments in characterization. In her studies of psychoanalysis, in particular the theories of Jung, from whom she mastered "the technique for revealing a character's unconscious side by projecting it upon other characters." Raper outlines her experiments with male-female relationships in "The Professional Instinct," "Thinking Makes It So," "The Difference," "The Artless Age," and "Romance and Sally Byrd." In the so-called ghost stories—"The Shadowy Third," "Dare's Gift," "The Past," "Whispering Leaves," and "Jorden's End"—Raper points out that in actuality they are less ghostly than psychological: "The Narrator dreams his or her way to the core of his psyche, identifies what is still vital there, rescues it, and allows the dead past to be finally dead." In these studies, "With this insight and these stories, Ellen Glasgow transcended the flat realism based on external details that had generally been her metier before 1916...." Raper again utilizes his psychological projection theory in "The Landscape of Revenge: *Barren Ground*" (*SHR*, Winter 1979). After a discussion of point-of-view in the novel, he suggests that "the narrator gives us enough information unavailable to Dorinda to suggest that Dorinda's psyche develops through four phases." To understand the complex forces working within her, "we must turn from dream and myth symbols to the way Dorinda sees other people through masks that her mind has created of previously unrecognized contents of her own psyche." In her multiple references to nature, "Glasgow uses the landscape as an alternate screen upon which to project" Dorinda's inner being. "But the landscape has an existence of its own.... This independence makes it at times a choral presence commenting upon the action. Its commentary may be trusted more completely than Dorinda's—perhaps even more than the narrator's." Raper further situates this novel in the mainstream of southern writing, seeing its agrarianism not as an anachronistic escape but "as another manifestation of a hunger" expressed in the southern imagination, like that of the "denizens of Faulkner's hamlet when they lust after the wild energy of Flem's Texas ponies." These three essays have been incorporated into Raper's very fine study, *From the Sunken Garden: the Fiction of Ellen Glasgow, 1916-1945* (Baton Rouge: Louisiana State University Press, 1980).

The *Mississippi Quarterly* again accorded a special section to essays on Glasgow in its Fall 1979 issue. "*Barren Ground:* Ellen Glasgow's Critical Arrival" is introduced by Dorothy McInnis Scura, who deftly touches on background details in commenting on the differing perspectives of four scholars new to Glasgow studies. Linda Wagner, in "*Barren Ground's* Vein of Iron: Dorinda Oakley and Some Concepts of the Heroine in 1925," compares Glasgow's creation with four other contemporary fictional women, including Fitzgerald's Daisy Buchanan and Hemingway's Lady Brett Ashley: "For today's readers, especially those interested in women characters and their choices, Glasgow's *Barren Ground* may well be the strongest of these mid-1920s novels, precisely because it does attempt to avoid the formula." Like other critics, Wagner sees the resolution of

Dorinda's conflicts as reflecting Glasgow's purging of her own and an acceptance of the ambivalence of experience. In "Pastoral Transformations in *Barren Ground*," Tonette L. Bond postulates that Dorinda's story "is the record of her redemption through the reordering of her physical and mental environments to accord with the pastoral ideal. . . ." In her own quest for meaning, Glasgow reconsidered the power of humanized nature in reconciling the mind to life in a fallen world. "By endowing her heroine with the 'subjective vision' and the 'creative impulse' to 'remould' her fallen world, Glasgow can use the story of Dorinda's self-redemption through pastoral vision as a means of prophesying a new South built upon the permanent values of the mind made universal in art." In "Hardy and Ellen Glasgow: *Barren Ground*," James W. Tuttleton sees Glasgow's heroine as a "composite of many Hardean figures" but goes on to point out the novel's parallels with *The Return of the Native*. "Nevertheless, in *Barren Ground* Ellen Glasgow achieved a magisterial vision of human will and fortitude, a work complex in the forms of its indebtedness to the mind and art of Thomas Hardy, but a work transcendently her own." Judith B. Wittenberg, in "The Critical Fortunes of *Barren Ground*," observes that "the trends in Glasgow criticism have been far from orderly." While "Southern reviewers naturally focused on the regionalism of the novel," the Northern reviewers, for the most part, "emphasized the book's American qualities. . . ." Upon Glasgow's death in 1945 critical assessments began to diverge. The 1960s "saw the healing of at least one critical schism; the either-or approach to Glasgow and Faulkner was made obsolete" by Holman's *Three Modes of Southern Fiction*. Alfred Kazin had suggested in the early 1940s that Glasgow was "a martyr to American criticism," and Wittenberg illustrates convincingly that "*Barren Ground* has suffered . . . from changing critical fashions."

The title of Wayne Lesser's essay, "The Problematics of Regionalism and the Dilemma of Glasgow's *Barren Ground*" (*SLJ*, Spring 1979), alerts the reader that here is an analysis of the novel that goes deeper than most. Lesser carefully defines his terms and proposes "a reading of *Barren Ground* which comes to terms with the difficulties created by its narrative heterodoxy," regarding it "as paradigmatic; for the relationship between specificity and universality which informs the text is representative of the fictional dynamics which characterize those novels we identify as works of 'serious' regional literature." He then examines the specificity aspect in tracing Dorinda's contemplation of the self. "Paradox" is the key word in a pattern of withdrawal and engagement. In Dorinda's "success in preserving the creative self while directing its energy toward the practical experience of living," she "manages to meet the strange demands of this paradoxical situation by reversing the spirit of each process: by changing the process of withdrawal from one of denial to celebration, and by changing the process of engagement from one of embracement to selective confrontation." In the next section Lesser considers the universality aspect. Here, he avers, Glasgow has utilized a technique which "repeatedly rejects the usual significance of literary and social forms and yet elicits meaning from such denials by a selective commemoration of them." In allying the reader's dilemma with that of Dorinda's, he sees the test as having "two distinct conceptual areas: the representational-specific; the evaluative-universal." In creating a novel based on conflicting modes of discourse, Glasgow prefigured in this work that "more complexly realized later in the novels of Faulkner, Warren, Tate, and Welty."

In "Sexual Reversals in Thomas Hardy and Ellen Glasgow" (*SHR*, Winter 1979), Velma Bourgeois Richmond sees Ellen Glasgow's final novel, *In This Our Life*, as "perhaps the most eloquent tribute of her indebtedness to Hardy's life-long influence, in particular to *Jude the Obscure*." Richmond compares the roles of Jude and Asa in their respective novels, showing how the assumption of the female role leads to Jude's destruction and to Asa's survival. Each novel has a pair of females representing spirit and flesh. Asa tells Roy (spirit) at the end: "In seeking there is not ever an end, nor is there an end in seeking and not finding." According to Richmond, "This belief in continuity, in new possibilities regardless of rational arguments against hopefulness, distinguishes Ellen Glasgow's vision: "instinct, not reason, decides a man's life in the end.'" Asa's "abnegation of narrowly restrictive sexual roles," representative of "the diffused mental and emotional outlook of a whole community," illustrates that "for all her pursuit of intellect, of rational philosophy, [Glasgow] rests her final case on her intuitions, however unfashionable." Richmond illustrates how a brief essay treating one novel can effectively summarize the evolution of an author's philosophical growth.

Graduate Studies

Interest in Ellen Glasgow on the graduate level continues, reflecting an increased emphasis on Southern literature in American literary studies and the growing dominance of the feminists. Even more, the titles of recent dissertations suggest that in a world of fluctuating values, the questing student has turned instinctively to a writer whose career encompassed a life-long search for sustaining values. The Kelly *Bibliography* lists sixteen dissertations; in his bibliographical essay in *Centennial Essays* MacDonald lists forty; Schmidt adds six in her checklist in the October 1978 *Ellen Glasgow Newsletter*; and Barbra Ekman's recent dissertation is reviewed in this essay under Books.

SUMMARY OBSERVATIONS

Recent criticism has accorded Glasgow a more objective analysis than much of the earlier commentary, and perhaps the social historian and the novelist have been adequately defined. The complexity of the woman, a willful artistic ego in conflict with her environment, has been dealt with, but she has yet to be revealed in a full portrait. At one extreme in the studies, she is the smiling stoic; at the other, she is the over-emotional neurotic. Her role as social historian has both enhanced and obscured. While she wrote truthfully of her time and place in Virginia, her theme was rather of the human heart circumscribed by existential concepts. The slowness of the feminists in taking up Glasgow as an early champion, a cause for mild wonder, may be attributed to the fact that she was too much the artist to make her novels into tracts and perhaps to the suspicion that the freedom of the spirit she sought went beyond the narrow definitions of political feminism. As a novelist, she built her books in an isolation that appears the norm for literary genius in America. Her novels illustrate the inevitable defeat of the romantic in a material world as well as the inevitable seduction of the realist by romantic ideals. Life itself would seem to flaw her works, in that as an art form it consistently eludes the order the artist would impose on it. In addition, to quote R. C. Wood, "The formalist critics who dominate the serious journals today cannot get past her inconsistencies of tone, her pages of sentiment, her structural mistakes." Such judgments are applicable to almost any writer by those who wish to make them. Perhaps as J. R. Raper earlier suggested, when American criticism gives over its preoccupation with the fiction of sensation and returns to an appreciation of novels of vision, Ellen Glasgow's gifts as a novelist will rise in esteem. The most recent criticism, that of Raper, Bond, and Lesser, indicates a new awareness of this aspect of her work. Raper and C. Hugh Holman, the former of whom still treds the hallowed halls of Pulpit Hill, point the way to enlightenment. Holman, with his historical approach, saw even her earlier works as novels of manners, and Raper with his psychological approach, deeming even her "failures" as worthy of study, presents criticism that establishes Glasgow more securely as an American writer of serious merit. No less was her goal, she determined early in her career, and even those scholars who are depressed by her elegiac stoicism evince admiration for her intellectual growth, her persevering dedication, and her life-long quest for values. Roy Timberlake in her last novel cries out, "I want something to hold by!" Her father gathers her into his arms assuring her, "You will find it my child." Ellen Glasgow knew the ending was sentimental, but it also incorporated an ironic paradox: "Asa's [Healer's] refusal to surrender [hope] seemed to me to be one of those rare defeats that are victories," restoring "paradoxically, the demolished convention of the happy end." Indeed, the "happy end" can be thought of as an act of pure creation.

8 JOAN GIVNER, JANE DeMOUY AND RUTH M. ALVAREZ

Katherine Anne Porter

Katherine Anne Porter's art has over the years proved peculiarly elusive of definition. As early as 1944 Edmund Wilson admitted that he was unable "to take hold of her work in any of the obvious ways." In 1970 the anonymous *TLS* reviewer of a substantial volume of criticism of her stories concluded that the most suitable approach "largely fails to uncover the real sources of artistic power which gave them their overwhelming impact."

As these remarks suggest, the criticism of Porter's work that has proliferated for five decades has led neither to a shifting of the critical base nor to a definition of her place in modern literature.

One of the factors hampering serious criticism has been the intrusion into the work of the writer's own life and personality. This occurred partly because she drew heavily on autobiographical material for her fiction and partly because her high profile on the university lecture circuit tempted critics to fall under the spell of her charismatic presence. Accordingly, something of a cult developed around her. Robert Penn Warren has well described the effect of such a cult in his introduction to Edward Schwartz's "Katherine Anne Porter: A Critical Bibliography" (*BNYPL*, May 1953):

> The very intensity with which Miss Porter's work has laid hold on the imagination of her admirers has, however, almost done her reputation a disservice. Appreciation and devoted understanding invite their peculiar liabilities, for the appreciator and the understander are tempted, sometimes, to think of themselves as the initiated, to see themselves as acquainted uniquely with a mystery, to feel themselves members of a cult privileged to tend a special flame.

Joan Givner has contributed the first part of this chapter, pages 201-13.

His remark is borne out by the criticism. In the early years critics tended to adopt the stance of defenders of a gallant lady, vying with each other in the fulsomeness and ingenuity of their praises. After the appearance of *Ship of Fools* in 1962 they split into two camps—one of attackers, the other of embattled partisans. Neither the early adulation nor the later conflict lead to any significant elucidation of her art.

A further effect of Porter's high personal visibility has been to generate false biographical assumptions. Critics have rarely taken stock of the extent to which Porter shaped her autobiographical statements, suppressing certain incidents from the record if they seemed inappropriate and heightening or inventing others that she deemed acceptable. One of the common views is that Porter wrote out of a tradition of society and culture that had its roots planted firmly in the Old South. This premise is untrue. Porter found herself as a young woman and nourished herself as an artist by means of a fragmented cultural tradition that was largely fantasy and that, in its primary state, she could have known, if at all, only at second hand.

At last, however, fifty years after the appearance of her first volume of short stories, her letters and manuscripts are being made accessible to scholars, her biography is nearing completion, and the way is being prepared for a definitive study.

BIBLIOGRAPHY

The first comprehensive bibliography, "Katherine Anne Porter: A Critical Bibliography" by Edward Schwartz (*BNYPL*, May 1953), remained for years the chief research aid for students.

Sixteen years later, this pamphlet was superseded by *A Bibliography of the Works of Katherine Anne Porter and A Bibliography of the Criticism of the Works of Katherine Anne Porter* (Metuchen, N.J.: Scarecrow Press, 1969) by Louise Waldrip and Shirley Ann Bauer. The first part of this book is comprised of a University of Texas doctoral dissertation. "A Bibliography of Katherine Anne Porter" (1967) by Louise Waldrip. The dissertation lists essays, book reviews, poems, stories, novels, translations, symposiums, introductions, and afterwords to works of other authors, and foreign editions of her own works from 1917 through 1964. In the book Waldrip omits the dissertation's introduction, adds some new items in the Contribution to Periodicals section, and adds eighty-one additional items to the Contribution to Books section. Bauer's part of the book consists of a listing of criticism. Useful as this volume is as a research tool, it is somewhat unsatisfactory because the two halves are clumsily yoked together. The organization of the first half is in clear chronological sequence within each section. The organization of the second half is partly chronological and partly alphabetical. In the Book Reviews section, for example, the books reviewed are listed chronologically and the reviews themselves, alphabetically by author. Unaccountably, Porter's first volume of short stories, *Flowering Judas* (1930), is unlisted. The important early reviews of that book are listed along with the later reviews of the expanded edition, *Flowering Judas and Other Stories*, which appeared in 1935. In spite of its untidiness, the book contains valuable information, including new items that Porter made available to the compilers from her own collection of clippings.

The most useful list to date of Porter criticism appeared in 1976 as the first part of *Katherine Anne Porter and Carson McCullers: A Reference Guide* (Boston: G. K. Hall) by Robert F. Kiernan. Kiernan lists in chronological order, with abstracts of each work, the criticism of Porter from 1924 to 1974. The beginning date is somewhat deceptive since the 1924 reference is the biographical note in *The Best Short Stories of 1923*, edited by Edward J. O'Brien. While its inclusion quite accurately records that the promise of her story "María Concepcíon" was marked by its selection for the *Best Stories* volume, criticism of Porter's work essentially began in 1930.

The compilers of the above bibliographies are aware of the incompleteness of their work. Waldrip and Bauer explain it by saying that "records of many of Miss Porter's early writings, especially those in local newspapers, have been impossible to find." Writings in newspapers, on the contrary, are always preserved and able to be traced. Moreover, the task of finding newspaper articles about and by Porter is made easier by her tendency from an early age to appear in the newspapers wherever she was. The omission of these early items from the record is regrettable, not because they are numerically great, but because they are highly revealing of the author at an early formative period of her life.

Although in later years Porter rejected her work in journalism and considered a reference to her early career as a "newspaper woman" to be actionable libel, she did, in fact, work for several years as a journalist. She began this work in 1917 through her friendship with the editor of the *Fort Worth Critic*, Garfield Crawford, and his wife, Kitty. With their help she wrote theatrical reviews for the paper, and the experience thus gained helped her soon afterwards to secure a job with a more prestigious newspaper, the *Rocky Mountain News*, in Denver, Colorado. For a few months in 1919 she acted as drama editor of this paper and wrote weekly editorials as well as many dramatic reviews. These have been listed in Kathryn Adams Sexton's M.A. thesis, "Katherine Anne Porter's Years in Denver" (University of Colorado, 1961). The significance of these reviews in explained by Joan Givner in "Katherine Anne Porter's Journalism" (*SWR*, Autumn 1979).

In the fall of 1919 Porter left Denver and went to New York, where she found a job in the publicity department of a motion picture studio. It was not unusual for studio publicists to write articles for fan magazines, and Porter did such work in order to supplement her salary. One of her signed articles appeared in *The Motion Picture Magazine* in the fall of 1920. It seems likely that other articles were placed in similar magazines, but the task of tracing them is hampered by the fact that articles in fan magazines have not been indexed by authors.

In late 1920 Porter abandoned her publicity work for a job with the *Magazine of Mexico*, a new promotional journal backed by a group of American bankers. While she was gathering material in Mexico, she became embroiled in the political situation there and, having to flee the country at short notice, she went once again to her friends, the Crawfords, in Fort Worth. Besides his work on the local newspaper, now renamed the *Fort Worth Record*, Garfield Crawford was editing and publishing another new magazine, *The Oil Journal*. He hired Porter for this new venture, and she interviewed people and wrote articles on them. At the same time she was writing stories, and at the end of six months she decided to return to New York, give up journalism forever, and concentrate on her own fiction. Henceforth she made it a point to advise young writers to avoid journalism at all costs, to get any kind of a job, even "hashing" in a restaurant in preference. She told interviewer Barbara Thompson in 1962 (*Paris Review*, Winter-Spring 1963; rptd. in *Katherine Anne Porter: A Critical Symposium,* edited by Lodwick Hartley and George Core, Athens: University of Georgia Press, 1970) that she had been a journalist for a year once and that it did her no good. In fact, she had done it for just over four years, and it had contributed more than she realized to her art.

Another body of writing which has been overlooked, along with the journalism, is Porter's juvenilia. She told Barbara Thompson:

> I published my first story in 1923. That was "María Concepcíon," the first story I ever finished. I rewrote "María Concepcíon" fifteen or sixteen times. That was a real battle, and I was thirty-three years old. I think it is the most curious lack of judgment to publish before you are ready.

This statement not withstanding, Porter had published four stories before "María Concepcíon." One of these, "Hadji A Tale of the Turkish Coffee House," is listed in the bibliography by Edward Schwartz. Three others appeared in the children's magazine *Everyland*. These may have been suppressed because, as children's stories, she thought they did not merit serious attention. Or they may have been excluded on the grounds that they were retellings of already existing stories. However, they show a thematic link with her later stories and provide an important key to the development of her art.

That Porter aspired to write poetry at an early age is shown by the appearance of one poem in an obscure Texas trade journal in 1912. It seems likely that careful research in Texas and elsewhere will yield many examples of her early uncollected writing.

EDITIONS

In 1930, at the insistence of a group of Porter's friends—among them Matthew Josephson, Allen Tate, Caroline Gordon, Yvor Winters, and Edmund Wilson—Harcourt, Brace was persuaded to bring out a collection of her fiction. The somewhat reluctant publisher selected six from Porter's previously published stories and issued *Flowering Judas* in a limited edition of six hundred copies. The volume contained "María Concepcíon" (*Century*, December 1922), "Magic" (*transition*, Summer 1928), "Rope" (*The Second American Caravan*, 1928), "He" (*New Masses*, October 1927), "The Jilting of Granny Weatherall" (*transition*, February 1929) and "Flowering Judas" (*Hound and Horn*, Spring 1930).

The critical reception was so enthusiastic that in 1935 an expanded edition, *Flowering Judas and Other Stories*, was published by Harcourt, Brace. This added to the original six the following stories—"Theft" (*The Gyroscope*, November 1929), "That Tree" (*VQR*, July 1934), "The Cracked Looking Glass" (*Scribner's Magazine*, May 1932) and a revised version of "Hacienda" (*VQR*, October 1932).

Yet another edition of the same stories appeared in 1940 in the Modern Library. For this Porter wrote an introduction which contained the often-quoted manifesto describing her stories as "fragments of a larger plan" designed to help her understand "the logic of this terrible and majestic failure of the life of man in the Western World." This introduction was written at the time of the fall of France and reflected her disillusionment at the end of a decade of personal and cosmic disasters. Although she said of the past decade that "we none of us flourished in those times" she had, in fact, written during this time most of her best short stories.

Two years before the appearance of the last edition of *Flowering Judas and Other Stories*, the volume *Pale Horse, Pale Rider* (Harcourt, Brace, 1939) was published. This book contained three short novels, "Old Mortality" (*SoR*, Spring 1938), "Noon Wine" (*Signatures*, Spring 1937) and the title story (*SoR*, Winter 1938). Harcourt, Brace was eager to publish more of Porter's work and especially *Promised Land*, which had been started as a fourth short novel but had grown to the dimensions of a full-length novel.

In 1942 *The Itching Parrot*, by José Joaquin Fernandez de Lizárdi, translated and with an introduction by Katherine Anne Porter, was published by Doubleday, Doran.

After some years of unfulfilled contracts, Harcourt, Brace realized that neither the novel nor a large output of new stories was forthcoming. In 1944, therefore, they published her last small collection, *The Leaning Tower and Other Stories*. It contained "The Source" (*Accent*, Spring 1941), "The Witness" and "The Last Leaf" (published as "Two Plantation

Portraits," *VQR*, January 1935), "The Circus" (*SoR*, July 1935), "The Old Order" (*SoR*, Winter 1936), "The Grave" (*VQR*, April 1935), "The Downward Path to Wisdom" (*HB*, December 1939), "A Day's Work" (*Nation*, 10 February 1940), and the title story (*SoR*, Autumn 1941).

In 1949 the Modern Library added *Pale Horse, Pale Rider* to its titles. Their doing so afforded little pleasure to Porter, who was chagrined by their decision to drop *Flowering Judas and Other Stories*.

Since 1936, when she had become part of the literary circle surrounding the *Southern Review* at Louisiana State University, Porter had written a number of critical articles. In 1952 these were collected in a volume, *The Days Before* (Harcourt, Brace) named for the title of her biographical essay on Henry James.

Harcourt, Brace continued to hope for the novel but, although it continued to appear in her list of "works in progress" with changing titles, its appearance was continually delayed by health problems, financial difficulties, and (although she did not admit this as a major factor) by compelling artistic problems. Eventually she changed publishers, managed to find financial support that freed her from the necessity of earning a living by lecturing, and *Ship of Fools* was published by Atlantic Monthly Press in 1962.

Three years later Harcourt, Brace published *The Short Stories of Katherine Anne Porter*. For this she wrote an introduction and added four previously uncollected stories—"The Martyr" (*Century*, July 1923), "Virgin Violeta" (*Century*, December 1924), "Holiday" (*Atlantic Monthly*, December 1960) and "The Fig Tree" (*Harper's Magazine*, June 1960).

In 1980 Delacorte Press published *The Collected Essays and Occasional Writings of Katherine Anne Porter*. This volume contained in addition to the essays from *The Days Before*, many essays and reviews that had been published subsequently and a selection of her early published poetry.

In 1977 Atlantic Little Brown published Porter's last work. It was *The Never-Ending Wrong*, an essay describing her experiences during the Sacco-Vanzetti trial in 1927.

Paperback editions of the short story collections, of *The Collected Essays and Occasional Writings* and of *The Collected Short Stories of Katherine Anne Porter* have been published and her works have been translated into many languages.

Of particular interest to collectors are the special limited editions of Porter's works that have been produced. In 1933 Harrison of Paris produced *Katherine Anne Porter's French Song Book*, a collection of seventeen of her favorite French songs, translated by Porter. The edition, designed by Monroe Wheeler, consisted of 15 copies of handmade paper and 595 other copies, all signed by the author. This volume has been described by Toby Widdicombe as "a masterpiece of design, harmonizing poetry, prose, and musical notation in an aesthetic whole" ("Monroe Wheeler," *Dictionary of*

Literary Biography, Vol. 4, *Americans in Paris, 1920-1939* [Detroit: Gale, 1980]).The next year Harrison of Paris produced a first edition of *Hacienda*, again designed by Monroe Wheeler, and limited to 895 copies. In 1937 Schuman's of Detroit published a first edition of *Noon Wine* in a limited edition of 250 numbered copies. In 1955 Harcourt, Brace published Porter's essay *A Defence of Circe* in a limited edition of 1,700 copies, intended for the friends of the author and the publishers as New Year's Greetings. In 1958 *Mademoiselle* published *A Christmas Story* as Christmas cards to the magazine's staff and friends. A staff member estimated the number of copies at between 2,500 and 3,000. The same story, with drawings by Ben Shahn, was republished in 1967 by the Delacorte Press.

MANUSCRIPTS AND LETTERS

In 1966 Porter named the University of Maryland, College Park, the recipient of her sizable literary archive. In order to house this gift, the University established in the McKeldin Library a suite of rooms, consisting of two offices and a larger room, which it designated as the Katherine Anne Porter Room. Here Porter placed many of her manuscripts and papers, much of her life-time's correspondence, 2,000 volumes of her personal library, 200 phonograph records, photographs of herself and her friends, and other assorted personal memorabilia, such as her spinet and the refectory table on which she worked. To these items the University over the years added its own purchases of Porter manuscripts and books. This archive constitutes the most important resource for Porter scholars.

The collection of manuscripts comprises, besides those of finished works, several unpublished stories, drafts of unfinished stories, and notes for stories that were planned and never begun.

Of the personal correspondence, the compiler of one catalogue wrote that it was freshest during the period 1931-1937 and that it was characterized by repetitiveness. She noted that the same phrases and attitudes were repeated, almost verbatim, at twenty-year intervals. In spite of the repetitiveness, many of the letters are crucial to an understanding of Porter's life and work. Among them are a series dating from 1934, which she wrote to Glenway Wescott and Monroe Wheeler. This group constitutes a detailed record of her financial, personal, and literary difficulties and especially of her long struggle to finish *Ship of Fools*. This correspondence has been described by Joan Givner in "Porter's Subsidiary Art" (*SWR*, Summer 1974). Another important set of letters was written to her husband, Eugene Pressly, while she was in Germany in 1931, in the situation that provided the basis of her story, "The Leaning Tower." These letters have been described by Joan Givner in "'Her Great Art, Her Sober Craft': Katherine Anne Porter's Creative Process" (*SWR*, Summer 1977).

Porter's library books have a value far beyond the usual record of a writer's lifetime of reading, for it was her habit to read with pencil in hand and to sprinkle the margins of her books liberally with spontaneous comments. Her marginalia, therefore, provide her uninhibited reactions to all that she read. In books by her friends she has recorded objections that loyalty prevented her from voicing elsewhere. "Robert Giroux, why did you allow this?" she wrote of certain words in the work of Flannery O'Connor. Her notes in her large collection of books on religious subjects—saints' lives and histories of the early Church—testify to her deeply ambivalent feelings on the subject. Her comments and corrections in critical works on her own fiction not only record her anger but also inadvertently provide literary and biographical insights.

The McKeldin Library also contains copies of letters from the collections in other libraries, sometimes because Porter herself kept copies of her letters and sometimes because other libraries have duplicated their holdings and placed copies in The Katherine Anne Porter Room. These copies include the correspondence with Eudora Welty, that with Genevieve Taggard from the New York Public Library, and that with Malcolm Cowley from the Newberry Library.

Other libraries have smaller collections of Porter material that is not duplicated. After the McKeldin Library, the Beinecke Rare Book Library of Yale University is the largest repository of Porter material. It contains her correspondence with George Platt Lynes, with Robert Penn Warren and, most importantly, the correspondence with her close friend and confidante, the novelist Josephine Herbst.

Some of the libraries with very small Porter holdings have very interesting items. When Porter was in the last stages of her work on *Ship of Fools*, she wrote (15 June 1961) the following note to herself:

> SOF came out of this voyage and these notes, now destroyed unless Caroline Gordon has kept her copy of it. . . . I did not copy my original notes, but wrote her a long account in letter form, working in some of the episodes from my notes, putting in others I did not keep copies for myself. I should like so much to think that they still exist, I should like to have seen them for use in the novel. . . . But all of this is over now, I need not think of this again.

The letter referred to, lost for years, reappeared (with a few pages missing) among the papers which Caroline Gordon placed in the library of Princeton University. It is a long letter of twenty pages, described by Porter herself as a log of the journey, and its relevance to the final version of the novel is described by Joan Givner in "The Genesis of *Ship of Fools*" (*SLJ*, Fall 1977).

The Harry Ransom Center of the University of Texas in Austin recently acquired three versions in typescript of the story "Holiday." Porter wrote the versions in 1924, was not satisfied with any of them, set them aside, and forgot about them. When she found them again decades later, she saw at once which was the right version, made some changes, and the story was published in *Atlantic Monthly*. The HRC also contains a Harrison Press edition of *Hacienda* in which Porter wrote a "key" indicating the actual names of the people on whom the characters of the story are based.

In spite of the eager acquisition of Porter material by the large research libraries, there still remain in private collections some items of unique value. The papers of Matthew Josephson in the possession of Eric Josephson of Sherman, Connecticut (destined eventually for the Beinecke Rare Book Library of Yale University), contain a series of letters written by Porter in 1930. These clarify the nature of her relationship with Josephson and his part, denied by Porter and disputed by her friends, in launching her career as a writer. The letters show that he was instrumental in the publication of her first book of stories, for which he wrote the "blurb" on the dust jacket.

Porter's childhood friend still owns the letters that Porter wrote in 1914 when she went to Chicago to try to break into the movies. Since Porter had given various accounts of her purpose in going to Chicago, the letters, although few in number, are important to the biographical record.

The immediate members of Porter's family still own many papers and rare volumes. Among these is a first edition of *Pale Horse, Pale Rider*, Porter's gift copy to her sister. In the margin the sister identified by name family members on whom the characters of the stories were based.

BIOGRAPHY

In 1955 after completing the bibliography of her work, Edward Schwartz asked Porter about the possibility of doing her biography. She told him in a private letter:

> I think your bibliography is a fine piece of work, and I am happy that it has been done. But I think the blood pressure of your interest is not really high enough for a biography. First place you haven't got a notion of what you are asking for. Bushels of papers and letters, filing cabinets or note books and unfinished mss. The marginal notes on my books alone was undertaken, and given up in despair by a young friend. And think of the chronology! and the places I have lived or visited and the *reasons* for my being there. Friendships, love affairs, marriages . . . ideas of a life time, varying and changing and coming round again. And the genesis of stories, and how related to my experience . . . this and a lot more is what you undertake in an honest biography.

There are even greater difficulties than those she listed. Because of her lifelong habit of covering her traces and suppressing whole areas of her experience, only a systematic search through civic documents, church records, and old newspapers can bring to light her early experiences. Even that task, however, is less hazardous than the work of disentangling fact from fiction in the more visible parts of her life, for in the accounts given in autobiographical notes, essays, and interviews she resembles her own description of Mexico, "this sphinx of countries which for every fragment of authentic history yields two riddles."

Her adjustments to the biographical record were variously motivated and took a variety of forms. She suppressed her given name, "Callie," and substituted one of her own choosing. Until she reached seventy she subtracted four years from her age. She circulated an erroneous genealogy that linked her first to Daniel Boone and, when that was proven false, to his brother Jonathan and to a number of other prominent American statesmen. (Some of the genealogical errors were not wilful since the record she used was drawn up by an amateur genealogist who made mistakes.) She suppressed an early humdrum marriage to a travelling salesman and substituted instead a romantic story of elopement from a New Orleans convent to marry a rich man, older than herself, who shut her up. This last substitution, an episode from the life of one of her aunts, illustrates Porter's tendency to annex to her own record events from the lives of others if they seemed interesting and appropriate. Her most persistent fabrication was the description of her childhood home as a sprawling mansion, equipped with a well-stocked library, which housed, besides the immediate family, numerous visitors and servants.

To even her closest friends, she spoke of dining on the plantation in a room with panelling that had been copied from the original panelling brought from England, and she displayed as family heirlooms items she had purchased in antique shops. Some of her friends developed a hearty skepticism about the stories of her life. Josephine Herbst (to whom she wrote about the panelling) said bluntly that she would not believe a word Porter said. Others loyally maintained that her tendency to romanticize her own life was of little consequence because in her art she practiced the greatest truth an artist is capable of, a truth sometimes larger than living actually permitted. Many friends, like Glenway Wescott, learned not to expect straight biographical facts from her but to accept that the "story material" was somehow more characteristic.

While a full-length biography of Porter is still to appear, a number of biographical summaries have been included in the critical studies of her works. Not surprisingly, they contain a mixture of facts and errors. George Hendrick, in his *Katherine Anne Porter* (Twayne, 1965), did valuable and imaginative research in Texas, interviewing elderly witnesses while they were still alive and communicative. The important information he thus discovered provides a basis for any biographical study of Porter. The inaccurate parts of his work are those in which he relies on Porter's own words in her published interviews. John Edward Hardy begins his study *Katherine Anne Porter* (Frederick Ungar, 1973) with "A Biographical Essay." He proceeds with caution and, being fully cognizant of the pitfalls of earlier writers on the subject, perpetuates few of the persistent errors about Porter's early life. He does not, however, realize the extent of the unreliability of her own biographical accounts. He points out, for instance, the errors of date and detail in an account of her family Christmas that she wrote for *McCall's* magazine in December 1971. But the entire description is of the family Christmas of a childhood friend of Porter's and not of her own. Robert Penn Warren's Introduction to *Katherine Anne Porter: A Collection of Critical Essays* (Englewood Cliffs, N.J.: Prentice-Hall, 1979) is a tissue of misleading information. He perpetuates such errors as the false genealogical details, the descriptions of the early family life, the education in a convent school, the elopement from the convent, the brevity of the first marriage, and the fact that her sense of vocation as an artist was from the beginning the line intact of her life.

Some of the fictions surrounding Porter's life are of little consequence. Such details, for example, as her true name, her correct age, and the authentic version of her family tree, have little bearing on her fiction. There are some biographical facts, on the other hand, that are crucial to the elucidation of her art. Among these, the simplication of the record so that her growth as a writer runs through her life as the one unbroken thread, from the time she wrote her first "Nobbel" at the age of six to the triumphant completion of *Ship of Fools* when she was seventy-two, is the most misleading.

From the beginning Porter had a multiplicity of talents. For this reason a number of careers were open to her and she attempted several. Many threads were woven into her life, and teaching, no less than acting, might be considered the chief, unbroken one. As soon as she left school she supported herself by teaching, and the advertisement for the little school she opened appeared in the newspaper of a small Texas town when she was fifteen. During her first marriage she taught Elocution and Dramatic Art, again placing an advertisement in the local paper to attract students. In 1916 she founded a small school for tubercular children in Dallas. In 1920 when she went to Mexico, she earned extra money by teaching dancing. In later years, when she was established as a writer, she taught and lectured on her art. She supported herself by "trooping the universities" as a visiting lecturer and had longer appointments at Stanford, at the University of Michigan, and at Washington and Lee University in Virginia.

In her early days it seems that she wished most of all to succeed as an actress. One of her earliest memories was of being taken out and beaten for telling a visiting clerical gentleman that she wished to be an actress. Residents of Kyle recall that Callie was always organizing the other children in dramatic performances that were staged in the Porter's front yard. Porter's closest childhood friend remembers that she spent hours trying to help Callie decide whether she wanted to be an actress or a nun. In 1914 when her first marriage ended, Porter went to Chicago to try to break into the motion picture companies there. When she left a few months later, she returned to Texas and supported herself by giving performances of songs and poems in the country towns of Texas and Louisiana. She was an active member of the Little Theatre in Denver in 1919 and again in Forth Worth in 1921.

To ignore the teaching, acting, and journalism is to ignore important elements in her career and in her development as an artist. It is in the journalism, for example, that the theme which informs all her fiction is first expressed, and it seems reasonable to conclude that the theme evolved from the journalism. Her dramatic skills made possible the memorable performances she gave for years on lecture platforms, and more importantly, they prepared the way for the dramatic qualities present in her best fiction.

Another area of confusion that has affected the evaluation of Porter's work has been her geographical and class identification. Critics who have compared "Old Mortality" and "Noon Wine" have assumed that the aristocratic world of the first story was Porter's own. Accordingly, they have praised her for the imaginative leap by which she managed to portray so vividly the plain people of "Noon Wine."

Thus, Winfred S. Emmons, in *Katherine Anne Porter: The Regional Stories* (Austin, Tex.: Steck-Vaughn, 1967), writes:

> When Miss Porter deals with such people (the Plain People) in her stories, she endows them with a certain dignity; but in the society of her childhood they were viewed with condescension by the 'good families,' just as they would be today.... Miss Porter is a snob, in a very pleasant way; it is the way she was raised.

> Given the social sense that Miss Porter had, it is noteworthy that she was able to transcend it and write two stories of the plain people in which the *noblesse oblige* is transmuted into sympathy and understanding.

Mark Schorer, in his afterword to the paperback edition of *Pale Horse, Pale Rider* (Signet, 1962), writes:

> But let us observe first what is observed before we come to contemplate that truth—Miss Porter's remarkable skill in moving into a kind of life that was not hers and into a point of view that was completely alien to her own, to Miranda's.

In fact, it was the world of "Noon Wine" that was Porter's familiar world and the atmosphere of "Old Mortality" which was achieved through a feat of the imagination. Vida Vliet, in an unpublished doctoral dissertation, "The Shape of Meaning: A Study of the Development of Katherine Anne Porter's Fictional Form" (Pennsylvania State University, 1968), did extensive research in Texas into the Porter family background. She concludes that the world of the Texas dirt farmer is truer than any other to the actual surroundings of Porter's childhood. The vivid qualities of description that critics have noted in "Noon Wine" derive from Porter's first-hand knowledge of the characters and the setting. She based her characters on members of her own family, keeping their names for the most part unchanged, and she took the setting from the farm on which she spent several weeks as a guest when she was fourteen. Some of the sources of the world of "Old Mortality" have been indicated by Joan Givner in "The Plantation of This Isle: Katherine Anne Porter's Bermuda Base" (*SWR*, Autumn 1978).

If Porter made misleading statements about her life in Texas, she made equally misleading ones about her association with Mexico. She claimed that it was never a foreign country for her because she had visited Mexico City as a child, had always known the Mexican communities in the small Texas towns of her childhood, and had grown up in San Antonio when it was full of Mexican exiles. In fact, when she wrote her essay "Why I Write About Mexico" for *Century Magazine* in 1923, explaining that Mexico was her familiar country, she had lived there for only two limited periods of time, for six months in 1921 and for less than that in 1922. Her assertion obscures a fact of some importance in tracing her mastery of her art. Before she went to Mexico she had been trying to write fiction and had acquired most of the skills that would characterize her mature work. The one element she lacked was a body of material about which to write. Mexico was a most unfamiliar and stimulating place for her and provided (as the voyage on the SS *Vera* from Veracruz to Bremerhaven was later to do for the novel) exactly what she needed: the proper stuff of fiction.

CRITICISM

Just as the absence of hard biographical facts have made Porter a personal enigma, so her work has proved something of a critical puzzle. Since the publication of *Flowering Judas* in 1930, reviewers and critics have found in her stories undeniable quality, but her method has been difficult to decipher and her subject hard to define. On the other hand, her work has offered something to just about everybody: whatever the critical viewpoint, it has been applied to Katherine Anne Porter.

Traditionalists have written about her realism, New Critics about her irony and style, mythicists her capacity to create legends out of personal history and fictions out of memory. Regionalists want to focus on her stories about the South or Southwest, while others, emphasizing her international settings and her pessimism, call her a Modernist. In the last five years, structuralists and feminists have begun to take their turns. Her themes are myriad. She is influenced by Joyce, say some; there are ties to Hawthorne and James; she is influenced by no one, say others.

What has emerged from this plethora is a continuing desire among critics to synthesize, to make all-inclusive statements about Porter's work. Several have attempted it, but so far no one has succeeded. Among those who have tried, there tend to be two approaches: there are those who offer unequivocal praise, and there are those among whom one detects a fretful impatience with Porter and her indefinable reputation. They wish she would produce more, presumably so they could classify her. Some see her concerns as universal, while others find her literature essentially negative.

When *Ship of Fools* was published in 1962, some twenty years after Porter had published her last fiction, it was not surprising that many tried to assess her career on the basis of her novel, and that many found her wanting. However, she won the National Book Award and the Pulitzer Prize for Fiction in 1966, and the controversy surrounding *Ship of Fools*, combined with the prizes, motivated more critical attention than she had had before.

Her death in September 1980, after a career spanning fifty years, should generate a new wave of criticism. Although the definitive work on her remains to be done, there is nevertheless valuable comment on Porter, some of it from the best critical minds of the period. Critical reaction to Porter has necessarily followed the course of her publications, with reviews often generating scholarly analysis. There are few full-length books; because of the lack of synthesis, the most penetrating comment exists in a few seminal essays and in interpretations of individual stories.

Thus, the most valuable book on Porter is a collection of essays. Lodwick Hartley and George Core, themselves distinguished commentators on Porter's art, put together in *Katherine Anne Porter: A Critical Symposium* (Athens: University of Georgia Press, 1969) a compendium of essays that at once reflects the high level of Porter criticism and the complex faces she presented to the reading public. The collection is admirably balanced. Barbara Thompson's *Paris Review* interview and Glenway Wescott's "Katherine Anne Porter Personally" reflect the woman speaking about herself; there are five essays—ranging from 1942 to 1966—on her method and/or achievement. Several others are standard readings of some of her best stories, such as Ray B. West's "Symbol and Theme in 'Flowering Judas.'"

Of the most written about stories, only "Noon Wine" is missing from the group, perhaps because in 1969 there was no obviously outstanding essay on that story. There are two essays on Porter's critical theory, and three on *Ship of Fools*. A selective but useful bibliography is included. In compiling this collection, Hartley and Core have managed to provide excellent scholarship from both established critics like Robert Penn Warren and Cleanth Brooks and younger, unknown critics. Opinions diverge; not all are favorable; yet one leaves these discrete essays with a far better sense of what Porter's work is all about than after reading any number of overviews of her fiction. One wishes only that this collection was available in paperback and more accessible to students.

A second collection of essays, Robert Penn Warren's *Katherine Anne Porter*, for the Twentieth Century Views Series (Englewood Cliffs, N.J.: Prentice-Hall, 1979; hereafter referred to as Warren) *is* available in paper and provides easy access to six of the essays already collected in Hartley and Core. In addition, he includes Porter's own classic essay "Noon Wine: The Sources," which says as much as anyone else can about the intuitive nature of her creative processes. Warren has written a felicitous introduction, which is unfortunately full of biographical inaccuracies. On the whole, the book is too heavily weighted to praise of *Ship of Fools*. There is only the famously negative *Commentary* review for balance; consequently, neither the range of controversy over the novel nor the reappraisal of it is reflected in this book.

1930-1950: Reviews and Early Critical Pieces

Every new author might wish for the critical reception Porter first received. As critics have repeatedly pointed out, whatever apprenticeship she had was served so quietly that when the first edition of *Flowering Judas* was published in 1930, readers wondered over the appearance of such unlooked for, mature art. Distinguished reviewers like Allan Tate, writing for *The Nation* (1 October 1930) did not hesitate to call her "a new star," whose style was simultaneously rich and spare; Ivor Winters (*Hound and Horn*, January-March 1931) called "Flowering Judas," "The Jilting of Granny Weatherall," and "Theft" "major fictions," better than the work of most contemporary American writers. Llewelyn Jones in *American Writers on American Literature*, edited by John Macy (Horace Liveright, 1931) called her the new Willa Cather.

Superlatives continued when the second edition of *Flowering Judas* (1935) appeared with additional stories like "The Cracked Looking-Glass" and "Hacienda." She was regarded by an increasing number of reviewers as the "best" and "finest" short story writer in America and was cited for her fine characterization, the complexity and depth of her stories, and the eminence of her style.

Her reputation thus established by a single volume of stories, Porter began to get notice from the respected Southern and Southwestern quarterlies. As early as 1938, Howard Baker discussed Porter's "greatness" in "The Contemporary Short Story," (*SoR*, Winter), and Glenway Wescott, in an essay appropriately titled "Praise" (*SoR*, Summer 1939), found in "Noon Wine" epic qualities that reminded him of Milton.

In 1939 reviewers of *Pale Horse, Pale Rider* repeatedly praised Porter as a stylist and reiterated the popular assessment: she was one of the best fiction writers in America. Nevertheless, the fact that reviewers could not agree on which of the three stories was best reflected the general inability to assess just what it was Porter was doing.

Clifton Fadiman (*NY*, 1 April 1939) called all three stories works of art, but liked the title story best. Paul Crume did a good job of identifying specific qualities of her art (*SoR*, January 1940): "Her approach is a curious blend of impressionism with the hardness and exactness of imagery characteristic of a writer who reports," but who "gains her effects subtly and slowly," achieving "an eloquence almost lost from the American literature of our time." In the first serious assessment of her work, Lodwick Hartley reviewed all of her stories (*SR*, April-June 1940), stating the crux of the Porter paradox: any of her work illustrates that she is one of America's most talented writers, but her stories are hard to classify. Hartley concluded that she mistrusts the short story form; one wonders why he didn't assume she was experimenting.

Margaret Marshall, writing in *The Nation* (13 April 1940), pointed out that Porter's material was intuitively absorbed and therefore unstrained. She prophetically asserted that Porter would never write "a novel of American life" because she was better at creating the individual thumbprint than at generalization. Charles Allen (*ArQ*, Summer 1946) linked Porter's powerful themes to the depth of characterization she achieved by observing man under pressure and in his cultural situation.

Just as she was fortunate in her early reviews, Porter was lucky enough to attract the attention of Robert Penn Warren, who has written both incisively and broadly about her achievement. A lifelong commentator on Porter, his "Katherine Anne Porter (Irony with a Center)" (*KR*, Winter 1942; rptd. in *Contrasts*, Harcourt, 1951; in *Selected Essays*, Random House, 1958; and in slightly revised form in Hartley and Core) is the single most important essay on her work and the standard by which others must be judged. It is a classic in its own right. He views her stylistic techniques as part of a complicated, integrated process that highlights first of all meaning in scene, which in turn illustrates the theme of the story, which is frequently ironic. Thus Porter deals in irony not for its own sake, but creates ironical structures, which force readers to confront human experiences in a new light.

Porter's solid reputation, despite the small volume of her work, was reflected in the widespread comment that greeted *The Leaning Tower* in 1944. Edmund Wilson (*NY*, 30 September 1944; rptd. in *Classics and Commercials*, Farrar, Straus, 1950, and in Warren) wrote his famous appreciation, repeating the usual terms of serious comment on Porter: "She is an absolutely first-rate artist" who creates a "self-developing organism" in her prose, but she is "baffling because one cannot take hold of her work in any of the obvious ways." Foreshadowing an approach that others will take, Wilson divides in an effort to conquer: there are stories about family life, stories about foreign countries and human values, and stories about women.

In other *Leaning Tower* reviews, Porter was again praised for her style and characterization, compared to Katherine Mansfield, applauded for "The Leaning Tower," "The Downward Path to Wisdom," and "The Grave." Some reviewers did take exception to the slightness of *The Old Order* stories. Howard Mumford Jones (*SatRL*, 30 September 1944); Marguerite Young (*KR*, Winter 1945); Theodore Spencer (*SR*, Spring 1945); F. O. Mathiessen (*Accent*, Winter 1945; rptd. in *The Responsibility of the Critic*, Oxford University Press, 1952); and Diana Trilling (*Nation*, 23 September 1944) were representative. In the spring of 1947, another important article appeared in *Accent*: Ray B. West, Jr.'s, "Symbol and Theme in 'Flowering Judas,'" discussed in this survey with other criticism of "Flowering Judas." It was the first of several penetrating essays on individual Porter stories. Thus "stylist," "realist," and "symbolist" were the terms in which Porter was discussed in this period.

1950-1962: Reputation and Elusive Assessment

During the 1950s Porter published only nonfiction (*The Days Before*, Harcourt, Brace, 1952, and "Noon Wine: The Sources," *YR*, September 1956). Readers waited for the novel announced some ten years before. It seemed a natural time for academic critics to synthesize Porter's themes and methods. Ray B. West, Jr., broke new ground in "Katherine Anne Porter and 'Historic Memory'" (*Hopkins Review*, Fall 1952; rptd. in *Southern Renascence: The Literature of the Modern South*, edited by Louis D. Rubin Jr., and Robert D. Jacobs, Baltimore: Johns Hopkins University Press, 1953; and in *South: Modern Southern Literature in Its Cultural Setting*, edited by Louis D. Rubin, Jr., and Robert D. Jacobs, Garden City, N.Y.: Doubleday, 1961; and expanded in *Katherine Anne Porter*, Minneapolis: University of Minnesota Press, 1963). He pointed out the autobiographical resonance between Porter and her characters, the significance of her Southern roots, and her tendency to create and utilize myth, rightly seeing this connection as the reason for the small quantity and high quality of her work. Because her memory is "historic," however, her past acquires the dimensions of legend or myth, a characteristic she acquired in the Southern culture in which she was raised. In Miranda, Porter finds personal definition by examining her past. West convinces us that Porter universalizes her own past, whether legendary or actual, into common human experience.

In 1957 Harry J. Mooney, Jr., published the first full-length pamphlet attempting an overview of Porter's work, *The Fiction and Criticism of Katherine Anne Porter* (Pittsburgh: University of Pittsburgh Press, rptd. in 1962 with an additional chapter on *Ship of Fools*). Mooney reasonably points out that there has been too much attention to Porter's style and not enough to content, which he proposes to remedy. He groups her stories under several thematic concepts; Porter writes out of "the psychology of human relations," each story dealing with a "mystery in man's behavior." Most often these are failures of love, or hope, or fortitude. She also deals with the disparity between the world of youth and innocence typified by the Old Order and the hard world of maturity and disillusion. While these points are sensible enough, Mooney's brevity and reliance on description rather than analysis limits the value of his monograph.

Other critics examined the negative aspects of Porter's themes. Charles A. Allen, in "Katherine Anne Porter: Psychology as Art" (*SWR*, Summer 1956), says Porter's characters are betrayed because they are frustrated by the absence of both physical and social needs. S. H. Poss (*TCL*, April-July 1958) notes that "The Circus," "Old Mortality," "Pale Horse, Pale Rider," and "The Grave" form a *Bildungsroman* wherein Miranda discovers that her hope for an ideal state is not realizable. Marjorie Ryan points out that Porter stories, though not derived from Joyce, share with *Dubliners* the theme of "moral paralysis" (*AL*, January 1960).

Echoing Ray West, Edward G. Schwartz's "Fictions of Memory" (*SWR*, Summer 1960; rptd. in Hartley and Core) asserts that Porter's reality is defined "through individual consciousness." Past and present are measured, as is the future, by memory. He finds "nearly all" of Porter's fiction related in theme and treatment to the Miranda stories, wherein the "childhood dream of changelessness is found false." Internal awareness is what provides order in the midst of twentieth-century chaos. Examining five central stories, Schwartz persuades us, like Warren, that Porter's art is not only an end in itself, but achieves a moral statement as well.

George Greene (*Thought*, Autumn 1961) and Shirley E. Johnson (*WVUPP*, December 1961) explore the dissatisfaction and disillusionment with love in Porter's stories.

The attempt to sum up Porter's achievement and identify her subject reached a high point in James William Johnson's "Another Look at Katherine Anne Porter" (*VQR*, Autumn 1960; rptd. in Hartley and Core). He intelligently identifies the critical paradox that is Porter and finds the explanation for it in her being a woman, a Southerner, both critic and fiction writer, an "admixture of abilities" that confuse discussions of her canon. Thus she is examined from narrow perspectives, as a stylist, for instance, or in terms of thematic syntheses that do not exist.

Johnson is right to insist on Porter's multiplicity of experience, but in examining her "fictional philosophy" — a task he feels made possible because she has not published a story in fifteen years—he reexamines themes already determined: the relationship of the past to the present in the mind; cultural displacement; the self-delusion in unhappy marriage; the death of love and the survival of human integrity; and man's slavery to his human nature, to suffering and to disappointment. Johnson sees these themes carried forward by Porter's complex and adroit use of symbols and "limpid prose style" into a "consistent and complete" fictional point of view. Ultimately he finds her work thoroughly realistic, tragic, incisive, and compassionate, but too limited in scope and volume. Johnson's own work is intelligent and resourceful in bringing Porter's work down to basic issues, although one is still left with a sense of the discreteness of her canon rather than its unity.

1962-1980: Criticism and Controversy

Certainly, if there was a desire to sum up Porter's contribution prior to 1962, it was only exacerbated by the long-awaited publication of *Ship of Fools*. Not only was the novel much anticipated—a fact scathingly satirized by Peter DeVries (*NY*, 16 June 1962)—but it was widely regarded as the magnum opus of a First Lady of fiction. Upon publication, it more than doubled the fictional output of Porter's whole career. Reviewers and critics leaped to assess it.

Ship of Fools was practically guaranteed popular success when it was selected by the Book-of-the-Month Club; and Porter's reputation apparently guaranteed it critical success—at least initially. The first positive response ranged from excited adultation to polite applause, and the book quickly topped the best seller list. Typical of the former was Mark Schorer's review for the *New York Times Book Review* (1 April 1962; rptd. in Warren): "Call it, for convenience, the *Middlemarch* of a later day. And be grateful."

Such effusiveness was echoed in Charles Poore's review (*NY Times*, 3 April 1962), who called it "miraculously brilliant," and "a cathedral for the damned." Sybille Bedford (*Spectator*, 16 November 1962) believed it The Great American Novel. Louis Auchincloss (*NYHT Books*, 1 April 1962), Howard Moss (*NY*, 28 April 1962), and Warren Beck (*Chicago Sunday Tribune*, 1 April 1962) all found it a masterpiece. *Harper's* Paul Pickrel (April 1962) and the *Atlantic Monthly* (Glenway Wescott, April 1962) approved. Porter was praised for her range of characterization, her intelligence and humor, and her harsh but unflinching view of human folly.

Not everyone was appreciative. John K. Hutchens (*NYHT*, 2 April 1962) found *Ship of Fools* lacking in comparison to Porter's stories; it offered no revelations, he felt, and was weak in dramatic irony and flabby in style. Stanley Hyman (*NLd*, 2 April 1962) felt that ultimately the book failed to move its reader. Stanley Kauffmann (*NewR*, 2 April 1962) felt that so much was expected of the book that it could not fail to disappoint. Kauffmann found the style labored, the characters static, and profundity lacking.

Wayne C. Booth (*YR*, Summer 1962) was shamefaced to admit his disappointment in a work too large and fragmented to be successful; Brom Weber (*MinnR*, Fall 1962) sounded two common criticisms when he complained that the characters were stereotyped and the book long-winded. But the most scathingly articulate attack was Theodore Solotaroff's *Commentary* article (October 1962; rptd. in *The Red Hot Vacuum*, Atheneum, 1970; and in Warren). It is as excessive in its condemnation as

Schorer's is in its praise. Solotaroff is unable to contain his righteous anger over sheepish reviewers who have failed to criticize the lack of plot and action, the grotesque characterization, and the downright misanthropy and revulsion for human sexuality demonstrated by the author. He also charged anti-Semitism, saying Porter's treatment of Lowenthal was "only one example of Miss Porter's compulsive tendency to simplify and close her characters and issues, to look down upon life from the perspective of towering arrogance, contempt, and disgust." Solotaroff's vituperative comment became a rallying cry for others who felt disaffected with Porter, and the critical assessment of the book soured.

The lines drawn in the *Ship of Fools* controversy were these: Was the lack of structure in the book conscious or simply the ineptness of a short-story writer attempting a novel? Were Porter's characters simply stereotypes, grotesques, or caricatures? Or were they unflinchingly realistic—or perhaps satiric—looks at human frailty? Was the unrelenting portrayal of collusion and downright evil in the course of the voyage evidence of a religious viewpoint, that is, belief in Original Sin and human responsibility, or a political statement of cold-hearted misanthropy? Was the novel epic in scope or merely long-winded? Was it tedious and flat in style or a richly embroidered portrayal of things and people?

Only a handful of essays attempt to treat the book seriously, and the best are those that refuse the kind of either/or oppositions which defined discussion of *Ship of Fools* for a decade. Most notable among them is M. M. Liberman's "Responsibility of the Novelist: The Critical Reception of *Ship of Fools*" (*Criticism*, Fall 1966), in which he argues that Porter is a classicist both philosophically and technically. She believes in Original Sin—a position Solotaroff would have her deny—and she has written not a novel, as Booth and others have presumed, but a modern apologue. He extended his remarks in "The Short Story as Chapter in *Ship of Fools*" (*Criticism*, Winter 1968) by discussing—partly in response to Paul Miller (*University Review*, Winter 1965)—the value of understanding Porter's use of short-story technique in scene after scene of her apologue. A synthesis of these two articles constitutes the first essay in Liberman's *Katherine Anne Porter's Fiction* (Detroit: Wayne State University Press, 1971) and in that form is reprinted in Hartley and Core and in Warren.

Robert B. Heilman's elegantly written "*Ship of Fools:* Notes on Style" (*Four Quarters*, November 1962; rptd. in Hartley and Core) is not an apology for the book, but uses it to explicate Porter's classic, traditionalist techniques, a style so subtle that it seems to emanate from the things and people being described. A very balanced view is Lodwick Hartley's "Dark Voyagers: A Study of Katherine Anne Porter's *Ship of Fools*" (*University Review*, Winter 1963; rptd. in Hartley and Core). He explains that Porter, in spite of her tragic insights into individual people, has eschewed tragedy in

Ship of Fools. Instead of majesty, we see the terror of human failure and focus on nightmare and the "Dark chaos of life itself," where a universal order may not be possible.

In one of the sanest discussions of both *Ship of Fools* and of Porter's real talents and limitations, "Katherine Anne Porter: The Larger Plan" (*KR*, Autumn 1963), Daniel Curley uses Porter's stories for an intelligent comparison with the novel when he asserts the significance of the Miranda persona in the most successful Porter work. Porter's use of the personal point of view in a character who searches for order in a chaotic world is infinitely more effective than a "frontal attack on the universal." Curley offers concrete reasons for considering *Ship of Fools* a bad book.

As major work from an important writer, *Ship of Fools* will probably continue to be discussed, and newer critics, like Jon Spence in "Looking Glass Reflections: Satirical Elements in *Ship of Fools*" (*SR*, Spring 1974), can bring both objectivity and insight to some of the old issues. His well-written essay illustrates Porter's integration of animal imagery and episodic structure to achieve Swiftian satire, a purpose neither misanthropic nor pessimistic.

In *The Art of Southern Fiction* (Carbondale: Southern Illinois University Press, 1967), Frederick Hoffman spoke for the more balanced critics when he called *Ship of Fools* "a flawed book . . . but also . . . a remarkable achievement," and one is reminded that *Moby-Dick* in its own time was thought massive and dull by many critics. It remains to be seen if another generation will give *Ship of Fools* a better assessment; but for the moment, the consensus is that Porter should have heeded her own advice to Eudora Welty and stuck to writing short stories.

Whatever the response, there is no doubt that with the publication of *Ship of Fools* (1962) and her *Collected Stories* (1965), Porter capped her career. She achieved fame and fortune for the novel and recognition for the stories, which won both the National Book Award and the Pulitzer Prize for Fiction. All this combined to make this decade the high tide of Porter criticism.

Five of the nine books on Porter were published during this time, and Mooney's study was updated to include discussion of *Ship of Fools* (1962). Waldrip and Bauer's bibliography appeared; *Four Quarters* (November 1962) issued a special Porter number, which like the Hartley and Core collection, is a compendium of excellent essays. Notable in addition to Robert B. Heilman's already mentioned essay on style is Joseph Wiesenfarth's seminal reading of a little-discussed story: "Illusion and Allusion: Reflections in 'The Cracked Looking-Glass.'" These are reprinted in "Katherine Anne Porter: Feeling, Form, and Truth," Hartley and Core. John V. Hagopian, in a brief effort at assessment, discusses Porter's combination of technical mastery and intense feeling to produce a unique variety of stories about self-discovery.

Without adding anything to an understanding of Porter's work, Louis Auchincloss offers a general summary in a chapter devoted to Porter in *Pioneers and Caretakers: A Study of Nine American Women Novelists* (Minneapolis: University of Minnesota Press, 1965); Denis Donoghue's "Reconsidering Katherine Anne Porter" (*NYRB*, 11 November 1965) also covers old ground in discussing the significance of her characters, who turn the past "into myths, and myths into mythologies."

In one of the most acerbic attempts at assessment, John W. Aldridge, in "Art and Passion in Katherine Anne Porter" (*Time to Murder and Create: The Contemporary Novel in Crisis*, David McKay, 1966; rptd. in Hartley and Core; and in *The Devil in the Fire* (Harper's Magazine Press, 1972), expresses his irritation with the fact that Porter is "widely recognized as a creative artist of almost awesome fastidiousness, whose very paucity of production has come to be regarded as the mark of a talent so fine it can scarcely bring itself to function." Striking chords that will be reiterated by others, he finds her best work in the short novel and in her native Southwestern and Southern settings. Unlike Hagopian, he thinks art and passion have failed to combine in her writing.

The Stories

During the early 1960s especially, there was brisk discussion of individual stories, particularly "The Jilting of Granny Weatherall," "Flowering Judas," "Noon Wine," and "The Grave." In response to the *Collected Stories* a trio of classics appeared in the *Yale Review* (Winter 1966) from three Olympians: Eudora Welty, Robert Penn Warren, and Cleanth Brooks. In an essay that eventually gave its title to her own fine collection of criticism, "The Eye of the Story" (rptd. in Hartley and Core), Eudora Welty, whose career was launched with Porter's help, explains and emphasizes the interior quality of Porter's stories and what is gained by her focusing less on what the visual eye can see than on the eye of eternity. She writes stories of the spirit, and her time is eternity.

Reviewing the *Collected Stories*, Warren gives a retrospective view of Porter's art: she writes radically modern stories that nevertheless reflect a belief in evil, ethical responsibility, and the sanctity of the individual soul. If her characters are stoic, they are, like Granny Weatherall, tough enough to survive and take joy in their strength. Brooks's contribution is the standard reading of "The Grave." In a brief essay that illustrates how much can be felicitously said in little space, he demonstrates how a typical rite of initiation—Miranda's discovery of the meaning of sex and her destiny as a woman—are raised to a social and "even a philosophical" plane (rptd. in Hartley and Core).

Reviews of the *Collected Stories* tended to praise, with Anthony Burgess (*Spectator*, 31 January 1964) and Granville Hicks (*SatR*, 25 September 1965) asserting that Porter would be remembered for her stories rather than for *Ship of Fools.* Joseph Featherstone thought so too (*New Rep*, 4 September 1965; rptd. in *The Critic as Artist*, edited by Gilbert A. Harrison, Horace Liveright, 1972) and agreed with Aldridge that her best stories were the initiation tales set in her native Texas and the South. Howard Moss (*NYTBR*, 12 September 1965) reiterated her aesthetic value and her gift for characterization and style. George Core (*GaR*, Fall 1966) praised her for never imitating herself or stooping to "mere journalism" as well as for being faithful to "her ideal of a fully organic style"; his discussion of "Holiday" in this review was extended and included in Hartley and Core.

Writing of Porter in 1965, C. Hugh Holman (*AmLS*, 1965) addressed her as a writer of secondary importance who was receiving critical attention because of the "prestige of *Ship of Fools*"; but by 1967 Warren French (*AmLS*, 1967) was calling her one of the seminal writers of the 1930s, and she has continued to be regarded as important, with attention focusing on individual stories.

It is certainly an indication of their primary significance in Porter's canon that "Flowering Judas" and "Noon Wine" have continually received the most interpretation. "The Grave," "Theft," "The Jilting of Granny Weatherall," and "Pale Horse, Pale Rider" have also been seriously examined. While good work has been done on other stories, including James Hafley on "María Concepcíon" and Joseph Wiesenfarth on "The Cracked Looking-Glass" (*Four Quarters*, November 1962), Lodwick Hartley on "The Downward Path to Wisdom" (*SSF*, Fall 1969), John Edward Hardy on "Holiday" (*SLJ*, Spring 1975), and Thomas F. Walsh on "Old Mortality" (*CollL*, Winter 1979), there has been no ongoing discussion of these. They all bear further comment, as do stories like "Virgin Violeta." Feminists have begun to discuss the "Old Order" stories as a group, but the best of them, like "The Circus" and "The Fig Tree," deserve separate examination. The future of Porter criticism, like her reputation, will probably depend a great deal on her stories.

"Flowering Judas"

By far the most significant essay, and the one that defined the terms of discussion of "Flowering Judas" is Ray B. West, Jr.'s, "Katherine Anne Porter: Symbol and Theme in 'Flowering Judas'" (*Accent*, Spring 1947; rptd. in Hartley and Core; in *Critiques and Essays on Modern Fiction: 1920-1951*, edited by John W. Aldridge, Ronald Press, 1952; in *American Literature: Readings and Critiques*, edited by Robert W. Stallman and Arthur Waldhorn, G. P. Putnam's, 1961; and in revised form in *The Art of Modern Fiction*, edited by Ray B. West, Jr., and R. W. Stallman, Rinehart, 1949). This classic study identified three areas of symbolism in the story: religious symbols related to Christian belief; secular symbols tied to Marxist ideology; and love symbols, suggesting erotic, secular, and divine love. Interaction among these fields of symbolism makes clear that religion and Marxism are sterile without love and that love is impossible unless tied to belief. West set in motion an ongoing argument about the betrayal theme when he identified Eugenio as Christ and Laura as his Judas.

Adjunct to the betrayal theme are discussions of Laura's ambivalence and her concommitant inability to act. Sr. Mary Bride, O.P. (*SSF*, Fall 1963) feels that in failing to choose between good and evil, Laura substitutes conformity for commitment. In rejecting love, she rejects life. Sam Bluefarb (*CLAJ*, March 1964) points out that the pattern of initiation is typically one of loss of innocence, temporary paralysis, and finally action. Laura, however, is locked into paralysis. Dorothy Redden (*SSF*, Winter 1969), unlike some commentators, feels that Porter does not condemn Laura, but supports the dualism Laura lives by because it is her survival. In a brief note (*NMAL*, Winter 1977), Mary Rohrberger argues that Eugenio is both Judas and Christ, and that Laura is the one betrayed. She refuses to follow this Christ in order to be true to herself. Other essays discuss the poetic techniques of language (Beverly Gross, *Style*, Spring 1968) and imagery (David Madden, *SSF*, Spring 1970) that convey theme. The best of these is Leon Gottfried's discussion of "Dantesque and Theological Symbolism" (*PMLA*, January 1969).

"Noon Wine"

Discussions of "Noon Wine" have perhaps to some extent been overshadowed by Porter's own classic essay on the story, "Noon Wine: The Sources"; no one essay stands clearly above the others, but the story has nevertheless evoked solid criticism. One of the best is Thomas Wynn's (*AL*, May 1975). In what could be a fruitful approach to other Porter stories, he examines the language of "Noon Wine" as one would examine the language of a poem, and in finding the language characteristic of the story, opens up the "logic" of Mr. Thompson's gradual estrangement from place, family, and self, and thus the necessity of his suicide. Thomas F. Walsh has done good work on the story, first in "The 'Noon Wine' Devils" (*GaR*, Spring 1968) and more importantly in "Deep Similarities in 'Noon Wine'" (*Mosaic*, Fall 1975), in which he demonstrates that Helton and Hatch are doubles for the hapless Mr. Thompson. Not only does this significantly illuminate Thompson's character, but it shows how character necessitates his tragic end. In a beautifully written essay (*Descant*, Texas Christian University, Fall 1977), Edward Groff explains the enormous complexity underlying an apparently simple story and thereby illuminates why the story is so compelling. He explicates the story as ancient tragedy, while demonstrating that Porter has used "thoroughly contemporary, peculiarly American, and hauntingly timeless material" to do so. This essay deserves broad reading. Two other discussions of "Noon Wine" as tragedy deserve mention. They are J. Oates Smith (*Renascence*, Spring 1965) and Marvin Pierce, (*OUR*, 1961). Roy R. Male (*Criticism*, Fall 1961) ties the story to other American classics that use the "mysterious stranger" theme.

"The Grave"

Cleanth Brooks's (*YR*, Winter 1966) is the most significant essay on "The Grave," but Daniel Curley (*MFS*, Winter 1963) has also written importantly about it. He sees the story as a paradigm of the "personal fable" that informs all of Porter's work, asserting that the "mind of the writer is the grave of the past." In his art, the writer's past is resurrected. *Studies in Short Fiction* for several years provided a forum for debate over two essential issues in the story: the nature and use of its symbolism, and whether the story asserts resurrection or Miranda's tendency to bury unhappy experience. (See *SSF*, Sr. M. Joselyn, O.S.B., Spring 1964; Vereen M. Bell, Fall 1965; Dale Kramer, Summer 1965; William Prater, Spring 1969). Constance Rooke and Bruce Wallis argue (*SSF*, Summer 1978) that the Adam and Eve myth informs the story: Miranda falls into knowledge as a child; twenty years later, the adult Miranda experiences new life and knowledge in the epiphany in the marketplace.

"The Jilting of Granny Weatherall"

The criticism attending Granny Weatherall does not do justice to the complex power of that story, but Joseph Wiesenfarth's discussion (*Crit*, Spring 1969) of patterns of order and disorder in Granny's life and death is worth reading. Laurence A. Becker (*EJ*, December 1966) explicates the verbal patterns of the story to illustrate the double jilting; Daniel R. Barnes and Madeline T. Barnes (*Renascence*, Spring 1969) misunderstand the significance of Hapsy in asserting that she is an illegitimate baby fathered by the jilter.

"Pale Horse, Pale Rider"

Mark Schorer's afterword to the New American Library edition (New York, 1962; rptd. in *The World We Imagine*, Farrar, Straus and Giroux, 1968) discusses the inseparability of past, present, and future in this short novel, but Sarah Youngblood's essay (*MFS*, Winter 1969; rptd. in Hartley and Core) is the more substantive reading. Like Ray B. West, Jr., on "Flowering Judas" she finds three movements in the story that are of increasing psychological significance, and she demonstrates convincingly how Miranda's death-wish and her influenza resonate with the war themes of the story. Philip R. Yanella (*SSF*, Fall 1969) reads the story in terms of Miranda's dislocation from the Old Order, and her lack of preparation for dealing with the modern world. Jane Flanders (*RFI*, Fall 1978), examining the dreams of "Pale Horse, Pale Rider," finds that the war perverts the American virtue of self-reliance into selfishness.

"Theft"

Once again, Joseph Wisenfarth (*Cithara*, May 1971) produces the most substantive discussion of a story by applying to "Theft" the concept of order and disorder he has seen in other Porter stories. This theme seems less central here, however, and the essay is more valuable for its discussion of epiphany and imagery. Joan Givner (*SSF*, Summer 1969) finds its theme related to *Ship of Fools*: it is about the failure to oppose evil, which allows evil-doers to triumph. Leonard Prager (*Perspective*, Winter 1960) states the essential theme: the protagonist has lost selfhood because of her failure in human feeling and commitment. William Bysshe Stein's (*Perspective*, Winter 1960) view of the protagonist as a woman who is unhappy because she has substituted her career for marriage and motherhood is clearly outdated. Two more recent comments in *CEA Critic* also can be skipped. Charles W. Smith (January 1976) believes the verb tense in the first sentence is not grammatically accurate. Carol Stern Simpson (May 1977) replies and explains Porter's use of the past tense. Such a catalogue illustrates that the work done on Granny Weatherall and "Theft" at least, is disappointing. In-depth readings remain to be done on these stories and others.

FULL-LENGTH BOOKS

Worthwhile criticism of Porter's major stories also appears in several of the full-length publications that appeared in this peak period of criticism, although readers should pick and choose among them. The first of these was Ray B. West, Jr.'s, *Katherine Anne Porter* (UMPAW, No. 28, Minneapolis: University of Minnesota Press, 1963). It includes a revised version of his "historic memory" essay, as well as valuable insights on individual stories. Unfortunately, it is marred by biographical errors on which he bases some assumptions. Winfred S. Emmons's aforementioned *Katherine Anne Porter: The Regional Stories* (Southwest Writers Series, Austin, Tex.: Steck-Vaughn, 1967) is sorely limited by confining itself to less than half the stories Porter wrote, and by defining "region" quite literally—as a place only.

Both more interesting and valuable as an introduction to Porter is George Hendrick's effort for the Twayne Series: *Katherine Anne Porter* (1964). Hendrick corrects some of the biographical errors in West's monograph and establishes Porter's correct year of birth, 1890; he further illuminates the sparse details of Porter's official "life" by drawing on the unpublished theses of Stallings and Sexton. Although his analyses tend to highlight basic issues in a story, they are too brief to be substantive, and the groupings of stories he creates ("The Irish," "Germans," "Southern, Southwestern and Autobiographic") fail to illuminate them in any significant way. However, his attention to literary allusions in the stories is a worthwhile addition to Porter comment, and the book contains a useful, if limited, chronology and bibliography.

By far the most ambitious of the attempts at a cohesive view of Porter's work is William Nance's *Katherine Anne Porter and the Art of Rejection* (Chapel Hill: University of North Carolina Press, 1964). Basically, Nance's study asserts that Porter's work should be divided into those stories about the "isolated autobiographical heroine most often named Miranda" and "stories employing characters inferior to Miranda and separated from her by ironic criticism." The "rejection" he finds in all of Miranda's actions are the "repeated escapes" from oppressive unions: family, marriage, and other close associations with human beings. While he attempts to be thoroughgoing in his analysis and makes many valid observations, he is the victim of his own thesis. Sometimes it is too shallow an issue: Miranda does feel oppressed in many instances, but the interesting question is, Why? And sometimes he forces the issue, as when he tortuously tries to prove that "Pale Horse, Pale Rider" is *not* a love story.

Nance's interpretation of Porter as negativistic stirs strong reaction among readers of his work, the most famous of whom is probably Caroline Gordon (*Harper's*, November 1964). She takes him to task for letting his critical apparatus get the best of him, insisting that he overanalyzes, misreads, and abuses Porter's art, which actually constitutes a *Comédie Humaine*. This scuffle is interesting because it is a microcosm of the *Ship of Fools* controversy—whether Porter should be seen as a grizzled old misanthrope, frigid and even venomous, or as an unblinking, honest reporter of a very real and human frailty.

Published in 1971, M. G. Krishnamurthi's *Katherine Anne Porter: A Study* (Mysore, India: Rao and Raghaven), is a thoroughly researched reprise of her canon. The author asserts no thesis, preferring to group the stories, yet again, under thematic headings such as rejection of family and the reality of the past. It adds nothing new.

After the denigration of *Ship of Fools* set in, M. M. Liberman established himself as a major apologist for that book by explaining in "The Responsibility of the Novelist" that it should not be judged by the standards of a novel because she had written a "kind of modern apologue, a work organized as a fictional example of the truth of a formulable statement or a series of such statements." In those terms, its wide cast of characters, its caricature, and its fragmentary qualities and unity based on theme rather than coherence of action are entirely appropriate. Liberman attracted respectful attention for this comment from both other scholars, and from Porter herself. These remarks and a later essay discussing the short story as chapter in *Ship of Fools* constitute the lead essay and major virtue of his *Katherine Anne Porter's Fiction* (Detroit: Wayne State University Press, 1971). This small collection of discrete essays discusses the verbal and rhetorical elements in several major stories, but other scholars had expected a major explication of Porter's canon. Warren French (*AmLS*, 1971) called Liberman's small book "a major disappointment."

The best of the full-length studies is John Edward Hardy's *Katherine Anne Porter* (Modern Literature Monographs, Frederick Ungar, 1973). While it fails, like its predecessors, as an overview—Hardy, like everyone else, examines the stories under four thematic headings—it is solid, sane, and perceptive both in offering biographical detail and readings of individual stories. One could do a lot worse than to begin with Hardy. In spite of these several worthy efforts, Warren French could write in 1973 that "Katherine Anne Porter still really awaits discovery." Nothing produced since alters that statement.

Feminism

Another characteristic of Porter criticism in the 1970s is the beginning of feminist criticism on Porter's work. As early as 1944 Edmund Wilson noted that Porter's most interesting works were her stories about women; Cleanth Brooks has asserted that her stories and essays reveal "a wide streak of the feminist." Warren, Nance, and Hardy all note that Porter heroines search for identity and independence. However, it was not until the mid-1970s that anyone took a feminist approach to Porter's work.

The best of these essays are Jane Flanders's "Katherine Anne Porter and the Ordeal of Southern Womanhood" (*SLJ*, Fall 1976), and Judith Fetterley's "The Struggle for Authenticity: Growing Up Female in *The Old Order*" (*KCN*, Fall 1976). Using the "stories of the Old South," Flanders asserts that Miranda learns to reject experience and human ties because she has seen the rebellion of her grandmother, her Aunt Amy, and her cousin Eva against Southern society, a male-dominated community frustrating to the real nature and personalities of women. However, all three are unworthy role models who project no positive image for her to imitate. Her discussion of the grandmother and Amy are particularly good.

Fetterley concerns herself with similar questions, although she confines herself to *The Old Order* stories, which she sees as "carefully ordered to reveal the drama of Miranda's growing up and to define its central concerns: the struggle for authenticity of experience, clarity of vision, and straightness of narration." Thus the *Bildungsroman* theme is given an extra dimension.

Rosemary Hennessy (*ColQ*, Winter 1977) also sees *The Old Order*, in conjunction with "Old Mortality" and "Pale Horse, Pale Rider," as a female *Bildungsroman* wherein forfeiting romantic love becomes the price of self-knowledge. Barbara Harrell Carson concurs in this in *The Authority of Experience: Essays in Feminist Criticism*, edited by Arlyn Diamond and Lee R. Edwards (Amherst: University of Massachusetts Press, 1977). She believes that Porter's women all seek "valid selfhood"; Miranda achieves this in her new artistic life, only at the sacrifice of Adam. In a purely descriptive essay, Margaret Bolsterli (*BuR*, Spring 1978) says the characters of Porter, Welty, and McCullers define the status of women in society before the raised consciousness of the 1960s and 1970s. Charlotte Goodman (*CQ-Connecticut Quarterly*, March 1979) compares the attitudes of Granny Weatherall and Tillie Olsen's Eva ("Tell Me a Riddle") with those of Mann's Aschenbach and Tolstoi's Ivan Ilych. While the men finally accept death as the outcome of lives in which they have made their own choices, these two women feel they are the victims of decisions made by the men in their lives and die feeling unfulfilled.

By the end of the 1970s most of the "distinguished" comment on Porter had been rendered, and treatment of her work has been taken over by scholars lesser known than the Tates, the Warrens, and the Brookses. Of her more recent critics, only Alfred Kazin (*Bright Book of Life*, Boston: Little, Brown, 1973) has a well-known reputation. Yet comment has continued at a steady pace, and it has been solid, if not outstanding. One exception is the fine work of Thomas F. Walsh, who has made several valuable contributions to Porter scholarship.

Porter's last publication, *The Never-Ending Wrong* (1977), generated little notice, much of it insubstantial, although Eudora Welty (*NYTBR*, 21 August 1977) pointed out that its theme is one that recurs in Porter's fiction. Hank Lopez's *Conversations with Katherine Anne Porter* (Boston: Little, Brown, 1981) is the first book generated by her death in September 1980. Its gossipy quality will, unfortunately, snare the unwary reader, but its slick reporting and careless scholarship ought to render it a curiousity piece at best. Certainly it cannot be depended on for biographical accuracy. In addition to this general history, there are three special topics that characterize Porter criticism.

NONFICTION

Attention to Porter's nonfiction has come primarily in reviews of her essays, *The Days Before* (1952) and *The Collected Essays* (1969). Praising most her articles on literature, commentators find her essays interesting as a self-portrait and as an expression of both her critical and personal values. Little, however, has been done to study her literature in terms of these issues.

Two comments on the essays are particularly valuable. A fine synthesis of Porter's aesthetic theory is Lodwick Hartley's "The Lady and the Temple" (*CE*, April 1953; rptd. in Hartley and Core). He sees her nonfiction not only as an index of her critical theory, but also of her limitations. Porter makes of art a temple in the classical Greek mode, seeking in the artist objectivity, nobility, and sensitivity. She says she wishes to understand the failure of life in the Western world, but for all its beauty, her own work fails to "illuminate [that] supreme tragedy."

Edward Schwartz, in another fine synthesis of Porter's philosophy of "dissent" (*WHR*, Spring 1954; rptd. in Hartley and Core; and in Warren), points out her distaste for institutionalized belief. She prefers skepticism in thought and realism in literature; art became the means by which she sought moral definition in lieu of formal religion. Likewise, she sought meaning and order in her fiction.

Joan Givner has studied Porter's letters (*SWR*, Summer 1974) and her journalism (*SWR*, Autumn 1979). Jane Flanders (*Frontiers*, Summer 1979) illustrates that Porter's nonfiction of the 1920s reveals a feminist philosophy. Walter Sullivan (*SLJ*, Fall 1970; rptd. in *Death by Melancholy: Essays on Modern Southern Literature*, Baton Rouge: Louisiana State University Press, 1972) finds the essays egotistical and Porter's judgment "narrow"; he uses them to justify his overall estimate that her art is limited.

Regionalism

While Porter declined to think of herself as a "Southern" or "Southwestern" writer, her origins in Indian Creek, Texas, and her ties to a family of genteel southern traditions, as well as stories like "Noon Wine," "Old Mortality," and *The Old Order* meant inevitably that some commentators would use regionalism as an approach to her work, as did Rebecca Smith (*SatR*, 16 May 1942). The limitations of putting Porter in the category of regional writer are evidenced amply in Winfred Emmons's aforementioned pamphlet, *Katherine Anne Porter: The Regional Stories* (Austin, Tex.: Steck-Vaughn, 1967). Little is gained by discussing stories simply on the basis of a common setting, and much is lost by eliminating a whole corpus of material that has little to do with region.

On the other hand, the question of Porter's "Southerness" throws much more light on her technique and achievement if one does not limit the concept to setting alone. Ray B. West, Jr., for instance, demonstrates that Porter's "historic memory" derives from Southern cultural attitudes and habits of mind. Likewise, Robert B. Heilman (*Hopkins Review*, Fall 1952) in an essay that discusses Porter only cursorily, defines the "Southern temper" as an identifiable attitude and taste in writers like Faulkner, Welty, Wolfe, and Warren. Cleanth Brooks places Miranda's state of hopefulness and ignorance within the context of the "Southern temper" in *The Shaping Joy: Studies in the Writer's Craft* (Harcourt Brace Jovanovich, 1971).

Frederick Hoffman, too, universalizes the idea of "Southerness" in *The Art of Southern Fiction: A Study of Some Modern Novelists* (Carbondale: Illinois Southern University Press, 1967) by illustrating that Porter depends neither on region nor history, but instead transforms "all life into art." He discusses the Miranda stories in this context and asserts that *Ship of Fools* is a book that goes beyond tradition to confront the character of the present.

John M. Bradbury, in *Renaissance in the South: A Critical History of the Literature, 1920-1960*, (Chapel Hill: University of North Carolina Press, 1963), and Elmo Howell (*SCR*, December 1971) define "Southerness" more narrowly to the detriment of their insight into Porter. More recently,

Edwin W. Gaston, Jr.'s, discussion of Southern myths that Miranda discards in the Old Order stories (*SwAL*, 1973) is too brief to be significant, and Jan Nordby Gretlund's discussion of Porter's personal and critical response to Faulkner (*NMW*, Winter 1980) based on her perusal of marginalia in the Faulkner books Porter owned, is interesting, but asserts little about Porter other than her admiration for Faulkner and their common attachment to the South.

MEXICO

Porter called Mexico her second country; although it would seem an obvious area of inquiry, little work has been done until recently on Porter and Mexico. Anyone interested in the subject should begin with Hank Lopez's interview with Porter, "A Country and Some People I Love," (*Harper's*, September 1965; rptd. in Warren), bearing in mind that Porter was not always reliable in talking about her past experience. William Nance (*SWR*, Spring 1970) sees Mexico as a kindred spirit of Porter's, where it was possible for her to be alone but not lonely and to dissent. Drewey Wayne Gunn (*American and British Writers in Mexico, 1556-1973,* Austin: University of Texas Press, 1974) agrees that she loved Mexico, in spite of the fact that her Mexican stories demonstrate her disappointment with the revolution.

Colin Partridge (*SSF*, Fall 1970), in a good overview of her Mexican material, argues that Porter's Mexican experience helped shape her life and art, and like Givner, believes that Porter's nonfiction as well as her fiction illuminates her movement from journalist to short-story writer and her continuing interest in political history. Thomas F. Walsh's new work on Mexico, is interesting. He uses Porter's unpublished "The Children of Xochitl" ("Identifying a Sketch by Katherine Anne Porter," *JML*, September 1979) to illustrate Porter's early expression of her yearning for perfect happiness. In "Xochitl: Katherine Anne Porter's Changing Goddess" (*AL*, May 1980), Walsh links this early work to "Hacienda," where Porter confronts the loss of that possibility.

In many respects, Porter commentary remains in its infancy. Joan Givner's definitive biography is not yet published; Porter's letters have not been collected and edited, and as yet, no definitive critical assessment has been achieved. Presumably the completion of these tasks will generate new comment. It seems certain that as a master of the short story her reputation will hold; it remains to be seen if she will be as fortunate in the new wave of scholars who attend her work as she was in the first.

9 PEGGY W. PRENSHAW

Eudora Welty

BIBLIOGRAPHY

The most extensive checklist of published works by Eudora Welty has been compiled by Noel Polk (*MissQ*, Spring 1973). This listing forms part of a "complete descriptive bibliography," which, according to Polk in 1981, is nearly ready for publication. The 1973 checklist covers Welty's separate publications, the prose fiction and nonfiction appearing in books and periodicals, other miscellaneous prose pieces, poetry, photographs, and interviews.

In the first issue of the *Eudora Welty Newsletter* (Winter 1977), editor W. U. McDonald, Jr., announced plans to provide a continuing list of Welty's published works and supplied a first installment for the period 1974-1976, which supplements the Polk bibliography. Subsequent issues of *EWN*, published twice annually by the University of Toledo, have furnished Welty scholars an invaluable source of information about the author's current publications and, occasionally, about earlier writings not listed by Polk.

McDonald has made an especially useful bibliographic study of *The Eye of the Story* (*EWN*, Summer 1978), in which he identifies earlier published versions of the contents of the collection and points out variations.

Important early checklists of Welty's fiction and essays were compiled by Katherine Hinds Smythe (*BB*, January-April 1956) and of the book reviews by McKelva Cole (*BB*, January-April 1963).

W. U. McDonald, Jr., has led the way in providing helpful finding lists of Eudora Welty's manuscripts (*BB*, September-December 1963 and July-September 1974; *EWN*, Winter 1978). As with published works by Welty, the *Eudora Welty Newsletter* furnishes current information about Welty's disposition of manuscripts and about the holdings in various manuscript collections. Other bibliographical sources for the manuscript holdings are

Alain Blayac on the University of Texas at Austin collection in a special issue of the French journal *Delta* (November 1977), and Ronald Tomlin (*EWN*, April 1979) and Joan Givner (*Descant*, Texas Christian University, Fall 1978) on the major collection held by the Mississippi State Department of Archives and History.

In addition to his 1973 listing of Welty's works published outside the United States, Noel Polk has compiled an additional checklist of translations and foreign language editions (*EWN*, Summer 1977). In the same issue W. U. McDonald, Jr., gives a preliminary list of Welty publications in British periodicals, and in the Winter 1979 issue provides a supplement. Clearly, additional work is needed toward a complete accounting of Welty's work in translation and in foreign language editions. At present Polk and McDonald, through *EWN*, are providing a useful clearinghouse for Welty scholars and collectors who can offer information about foreign publications.

Comprehensive bibliographies of critical commentary have been available to Welty scholars since 1960, when Seymour Gross compiled a thirty-two page checklist for the *Secretary's News Sheet* (April) of the Bibliographical Society of Virginia. Polk's bibliography for the *Mississippi Quarterly* special issue on Welty (Fall 1973) included a selective but extensive checklist of secondary materials.

In 1976 Victor Thompson published *Eudora Welty: A Reference Guide* (Boston: G. K. Hall), the most extensive listing to date of critical commentary on Welty. The Thompson guide, beginning with the year 1936 and extending through 1974 and partially into 1975, includes a great variety of materials—not only critical essays and monographs, but a wide assortment of reviews, textbook explications, interviews, newspaper items, bibliographies, and some of Welty's own critical writings, though not the book reviews. Regrettably, the guide has problems of typographical errors, particularly in the index, occasional double entries, and a puzzling "no entry" for some numbered items, but it is useful to the Welty scholar in locating many items, especially those in newspapers not elsewhere identified. Through his inclusion of a wide sampling of reviews, Thompson effectively demonstrates the steady rise in popular attention to Welty's writing. Further, his chronological listing of scholarly commentary indicates the growth of Welty's literary prominence. More than a third of the book is taken up with materials published from 1970 to 1975. Thompson's introduction and annotations, which describe but rarely evaluate the critical materials, provide useful information about the publication history and acceptance of individual works.

Polk has compiled updated supplements to his 1973 checklist in *EWN* (Summer issues, 1977, 1978, 1979). Further supplements to both Polk and Thompson are provided by Martha van Noppen (*EWN*, Summer 1978) and by Ronald Tomlin in a regular feature of *EWN*, "Clipping File," a listing of newspaper and magazine pieces that come chiefly from Mississippi and Southeastern sources.

Theses and dissertations on Welty's work are most easily located in O. B. Emerson and Marion C. Michael, compilers of *Southern Literary Culture: A Bibliography of Masters' and Doctors' Theses* (Tuscaloosa: University of Alabama Press, 1979); Jack D. Wages and William D. Andrews, compilers of "Southern Literary Culture: 1969-1975" (*MissQ*, Winter 1978-1979); and O. B. Emerson's guide to "buried" Welty theses in the *SLC* listings (*EWN*, Summer 1979).

Some students may welcome the aid of selective bibliographies offered by established Welty scholars. The most useful of these are by Ruth Vande Kieft, *American Novelists Since World War Two*, edited by Jeffrey Helterman (*Dictionary of Literary Biography:* Vol. 2; Detroit: Gale, 1978); and Michael Kreyling, *Eudora Welty's Achievement of Order* (Baton Rouge: Louisiana State University Press, 1980).

EDITIONS

Scholars can generally be grateful for the present accessibility of Eudora Welty's major works. The nine volumes of fiction, the recent volume of collected stories, the book of photographs, and the collection of essays are all currently available in either hardcover or paperback editions, or both.

A Curtain of Green (Garden City, N.Y.: Doubleday Doran, 1941) is available from Harcourt Brace Jovanovich in hardcover and in the Harvest paperback series. The collection of stories also appears with *The Wide Net and Other Stories* as the Modern Library volume, *Selected Stories of Eudora Welty* (1954), and as the first part of *The Collected Stories of Eudora Welty* (1980). All available editions, as Noel Polk notes of the Modern Library text in *EWN* (Winter 1979), follow the 1947 Harcourt, Brace edition rather than the original 1941 edition.

The Robber Bridegroom (Garden City, N.Y.: Doubleday Doran, 1942) is presently available from Harcourt, Brace in hardcover (1970) and paperback (Harvest, 1978). Also available is the Atheneum (1963) paperback edition.

Currently available in hardcover and paperback editions from Harcourt Brace Jovanovich are the following titles, all of which were initially published by Harcourt, Brace: *The Wide Net and Other Stories* (1943), *Delta Wedding* (1946), *The Golden Apples* (1949), and *The Ponder Heart* (1954). At present *The Bride of the Innisfallen and Other Stories* (Harcourt, Brace, 1955) is offered separately only in paper. *Thirteen Stories*, selected from the four volumes of stories and introduced by Ruth Vande Kieft (1965), is currently available in the Harvest series. In 1980 Harcourt Brace

Jovanovich issued *The Collected Stories of Eudora Welty*, a hardcover edition that includes *A Curtain of Green and Other Stories, The Wide Net and Other Stories, The Golden Apples, The Bride of the Innisfallen and Other Stories*, and the two previously uncollected stories, "Where Is the Voice Coming From?" and "The Demonstrators."

Random House offers the following titles both in hardcover and in the Vintage paperback series: *Losing Battles* (1970), *The Optimist's Daughter* (1972), and *The Eye of the Story* (1978). *One Time, One Place: Mississippi in the Depression, A Snapshot Album* (1971) is available from Random House only in hardcover. Welty's book for children, *The Shoe Bird* (Harcourt, Brace & World, 1964), is unfortunately no longer in print.

A number of special limited editions of Welty's short stories and essays have been issued from time to time, as, for example, *Music from Spain* (Greenville, Miss.: Levee Press, 1948) and *Short Stories* (Harcourt, Brace, 1950). Listings of these separate publications, which in the same or different versions are available in the collections listed above, are included in Polk's 1973 bibliography and in the regular feature, "Works by Welty," in the *Eudora Welty Newsletter.* In 1980 the Franklin Library, Franklin Center, Pennsylvania, issued special editions of *The Optimist's Daughter*, which includes a seven-page preface by Welty; *The Collected Stories of Eudora Welty*; and *Moon Lake and Other Stories*, which includes the thirteen stories selected by Vande Kieft for the Harvest paperback. Other recent limited editons include *Eudora Welty: Twenty Photographs* (Winston-Salem, N.C.: Palaemon Press, 1980); *Acrobats in a Park* (Northridge, Calif.: Lord John Press, 1980), an uncollected short story previously published in *South Carolina Review* (November 1978) and, in a different earlier version, in *Delta* (November 1977); and *Bye-Bye Brevoort: A Skit* (Jackson, Miss.: Palaemon Press for New Stage Theatre, 1980). Two recordings of Welty reading her stories have been issued by Caedmon: the 1952 recording of "Why I Live at the P.O.," "A Worn Path," and "A Memory," and the 1979 recording of "Powerhouse" and "Petrified Man."

The publication of *The Eye of the Story* made many of Welty's essays, sketches, and reviews easily available for the first time. One must still search, however, for some of the book reviews and early pieces, such as the essay on Jose De Creeft (*Magazine of Art*, February 1944), and for the ongoing current publications, such as "Looking Back at the First Story" (*GaR*, Winter 1979) and the ten-page "Afterword" to a recent reprinting of E. P. O'Donnell's 1941 novel, *The Great Big Doorstep* (Carbondale: Southern Illinois University Press, 1979).

Overall, the availability of trustworthy editions of the major writings serves the Welty scholar very well indeed. The only ominous note is recent reports of a declining stock of titles in hardcover, with the implication that some additional titles may soon be available only in paperback editions. For this reason the publication of *The Collected Stories of Eudora Welty* is especially welcome.

MANUSCRIPTS AND LETTERS

The principal despository for Eudora Welty's manuscripts is the Mississippi Department of Archives and History in Jackson. The second largest collection is the Humanities Research Center of the University of Texas at Austin. The checklists and bibliographical articles of McDonald, Tomlin, and Blayac, listed above, provide handy guides to the locations of the manuscripts.

The large Mississippi collection includes typescripts of *A Curtain of Green*; "Stories by Eudora Welty" (sixteen of the stories in *A Curtain of Green*, omitting "A Worn Path" and including "Acrobats in a Park"); *The Robber Bridegroom*; "Delta Cousins," an unpublished story that formed an early version of *Delta Wedding*; *The Golden Apples*; *The Ponder Heart*; versions of the seven stories composing *The Bride of the Innisfallen*; *The Shoe Bird*; *Losing Battles*; *One Time, One Place*; *The Fairy Tale of the Natchez Trace*; the early uncollected stories, "The Doll," "Magic," and "Retreat"; the sketch, "Bye-Bye Brevport"; the 1960s stories, "Where Is the Voice Coming From?" and "The Demonstrators"; "Earliest Tries at Stories '30s," which includes five unpublished stories and two published essays, "Jane Austen" and "Must the Novelist Crusade?"

Typescripts of other unpublished writings of Welty in the Mississippi collection include a dramatization of *The Robber Bridegroom*; a ballet libretto for "The Shoe Bird"; a revue written with Hildegard Dolson, "What Year Is This?" and a speech on William Faulkner delivered at a literary festival in Oxford, Mississippi, in 1966. The Mississippi Archives also has corrected printer's proof of *The Eye of the Story*, as well as galley and page proofs of many of the works, the extensive collection of photographs that Welty took of Mississippi scenes in the course of her work with the Works Progress Administration (WPA) in the 1930s, and, a recent acquisition, the typescript of a speech delivered in Jackson at the 1980 inaugural ceremonies of Governor William Winter. In 1981 the Mississippi Archives acquired papers that are among Welty's earliest compositions. A short story, designated as chapter one of an untitled longer work, and 5,000 words of notes, written in 1925 when Welty was a high school student, will be available to scholars beginning January 1986.

In the Texas collection are typescripts of *The Robber Bridegroom, The Wide Net and Other Stories, The Golden Apples, The Bride of the Innisfallen and Other Stories, The Optimist's Daughter* (xerox copy of the printer's typescript of the Random House version), and two short pieces on William Faulkner, published on the occasions of his winning the Gold

Medal for Fiction and, for the Associated Press, of his death. Corrected and revised galley and page proofs of *The Ponder Heart* are also held in the Texas collection.

The Baker Library of Dartmouth College holds the typescript of *The Robber Bridegroom* that, according to McDonald, is apparently the one used for the first edition. The University of Virginia has a carbon typescript of "How I Write" (*VQR*, Spring 1955). Other miscellaneous short typescripts are located in the Ford Foundation, New York (a grant application), the National Institute of Arts and Letters (an acceptance of the Howells Medal for Fiction), Bryn Mawr (on "Bryn Mawr's Young Writers"), and the New York Public Library Theatre Collection, Lincoln Center (a description of the visit of Jerome Chodorov and Joseph A. Fields to Mississippi in preparation for the stage production of *The Ponder Heart*; published in *EWN*, April 1979).

Eudora Welty's uncollected letters are to be found scattered among twenty-five or more libraries, which are partially located for the Welty scholar in *American Literary Manuscripts*, although not identified, and in the McDonald checklists already mentioned. Undoubtedly there are countless business and personal letters that have not been identified or located.

Many of the letters in libraries concern details of the publication of stories, as, for example, those at Yale, written to Cleanth Brooks about stories published in the *Southern Review*. Other letters are notes of thanks and appreciation, responses to invitations, business correspondence with or in behalf of such agencies as the National Institute of Arts and Letters. One major collection of letters, written in 1943-1956 to A. Lehman Engel, is in the Millsaps-Wilson Library in Jackson. Among the letters in the Mississippi Archives, one to Joseph A. Fields and Jerome Chodorov is particularly interesting for its lengthy commentary on an early draft of their dramatized version of *The Ponder Heart*. The most notable collection of personal letters is that in the Humanities Research Center of the University of Texas at Austin, written to Elizabeth Bowen during the period in which Welty was working on the stories that comprise *The Bride of the Innisfallen*.

Through the years of her career, Eudora Welty has travelled widely and maintained a large circle of friends and business and personal acquaintances with whom she has corresponded. One day many of these letters may be available in library collections to scholars, but at present most of the Welty correspondence is held privately.

BIOGRAPHY

No biography has been written. There are some short biographical summaries in several books and monographs, most notably the "Chronology" and first chapter of Ruth Vande Kieft's *Eudora Welty* (Twayne, 1962), but the sources of the most extensive information about Welty's life are the author's own writings, especially the personal essays, and the numerous interviews dating from 1941.

On several occasions Welty has firmly stated her determination to protect her private life from public, albeit scholarly, examination. In a lengthy interview for the *Paris Review* (Fall 1972), she told Linda Kuehl that she would feel "shy, and discouraged" at the thought of a biography. She went on to explain that one's private life "should be kept private." She concluded: "My own I don't think would particularly interest anybody, for that matter. But I'd guard it; I feel strongly about that. They'd have a hard time trying to find something about me. I think I'd better burn everything up. It's best to burn letters, but at least I've never kept diaries or journals."

Welty reiterated her point that the only biography that matters is the life that she transmutes into her work in an interview with Reynolds Price for the *New York Times Book Review* (7 May 1978). "I agreed with W. H. Auden," she said, "who in his will directed that everyone destroy his correspondence. I thought that was right, and I was mad when people didn't do it and went on and printed things anyway—that's accepted as the thing to do, with just a shrug. I don't think it's morally right to do such a thing."

Despite her understandable preference for maintaining her privateness, Welty has been generous indeed with her time and personal experience in conversations and correspondence with writers, critics, teachers, and students. She has a well-known reputation for graciously receiving interviewers and patiently answering all sorts of questions during the course of her travels to campuses across this country and abroad. She has given a number of filmed interviews, which are extremely interesting not only for her candid responses but for their presentation of her speech and manner of conducting herself. Frank Haines filmed an interview with Welty for the Mississippi Authority for Educational Television ("An Interview with Eudora Welty," 26 October 1971). In a telecast that has been transcribed (*MissQ*, Spring 1973), William F. Buckley, Jr., interviewed Welty and Walker Percy on "Firing Line" (Southern Educational Communications Association, December 1972). Two recent 16mm films are those by Richard R. Moore, *Eudora Welty, The Writer in America Series* (Sausalito, Calif., 1975), and *Four Women Artists* (Memphis, Tenn.: Center for Southern Folklore, 1977). In 1979 Dick Cavett conducted an hour-long interview with Welty for his program on the Public Broadcasting System.

Urgently needed now is a comprehensive checklist of the published and filmed interviews, including the newspaper pieces that report appearances and interviews of Welty in connection with her lectures and public readings. These interviews, together with the author's own autobiographical essays and the accounts of friends who have written of her and her work from time to time, form the chief source of biographical material.

Of Welty's childhood in Jackson, the most detailed information is to be found in her essays, "The Little Store" and "A Sweet Devouring." Nash K. Burger has written an affectionate account of school days he shared with Welty in "Eudora Welty's Jackson" (*Shenandoah*, Spring 1969). In Jane Reid Petty's interview of Welty, "The Town and the Writer" (*Jackson Magazine*, September 1977), there are details about the author's parents, her activities as a child, and about a number of Jackson landmarks that will immediately call to mind details in her fiction. In "Two Jackson Excursions," Peggy Prenshaw (*EWN*, Winter 1978) comments on Welty's use in "A Memory" and "A Visit of Charity" of several Jackson landmarks familiar in her youth. Ruth Vande Kieft furnishes useful information about the Welty family history in *Eudora Welty*. In a light-hearted comment, Welty once remarked that her "father's being from Ohio, a Yankee" was about the only source of suffering she remembers as a child (*WLB*, February 1942).

Welty's college years, spent at Mississippi State College for Women, the University of Wisconsin, and Columbia University School of Business, are discussed by the author in several interviews, notably Jean Todd Freeman, *Conversations with Writers II* (Detroit: Gale, 1978). A very good source for information about Welty in the 1930s, the period when she worked for the W.P.A. in Mississippi as Junior Publicity Agent, is an interview conducted by William Ferris in *Images of the South* (Southern Folklore Reports, No. 1, Memphis, Tenn.: Center for Southern Folklore, 1977). Of course, the single best record of these years is to be found in Welty's *One Time, One Place*, with its introductory essay about her travels across Mississippi during the 1930s and its collection of snapshots selected from the numerous photographs she made during the period. Patti Carr Black has assembled a striking exhibition of Welty's photographs, in which she matches selected pictures with passages from the fiction. Black's exhibition catalog, *Welty*, was published by the Mississippi State Department of Archives and History (1977), which houses the entire collection of photographs.

Frequently in interviews Welty has talked of her start in publishing and of those who were particularly helpful and encouraging. Other good sources for this period are her agent, Diarmuid Russell, in "First Work" (*Shenandoah*, Spring 1969), and Welty's good friend, the former director of the Mississippi Department of Archives and History, Charlotte Capers, in "The Narrow Escape of 'The Petrified Man': Early Eudora Welty Stories" (*JMH*, February 1979).

Finally, Katherine Anne Porter's introduction to *A Curtain of Green* has probably served as the most widely read biographical piece on Welty. Porter gives the main outline of Welty's life up to 1941, describes their meeting and her interest in Welty's work, and vividly evokes a sense of the activity and texture of Welty's life at that time—love of music, early reading, a loving family, and a normal social life. Porter quotes Welty's description of herself as "underfoot locally," and notes that "normal social life in a medium sized Southern town can become a pretty absorbing occupation." Welty herself has written something of this social life in her introduction to *The Jackson Cookbook*, "The Flavor of Jackson" (*Eye of the Story*).

Welty has written of the difficult years of the 1960s, the decade of the civil rights movement, in "Must the Novelist Crusade?" and has talked of those years in such interviews as that with Buckley on "Firing Line," and, more recently, with Tom Royals and John Little, "A Conversation with Eudora Welty" (*Bloodroot*, Spring 1979). The 1960s was also the period in which she was at work on *Losing Battles* and *The Optimist's Daughter*, and she discusses the composition of these books in the long interview conducted by Charles T. Bunting, "'The Interior World': An Interview with Eudora Welty" (*SoR*, October 1972). Other recent newspaper interviews that are detailed and worth consulting for biographical material are Henry Mitchell, "Eudora Welty: Rose-Garden Realist, Storyteller of the South" (*Washington Post*, 13 August 1972), and Don Lee Keith, "Eudora Welty: 'I Worry Over My Stories'" (*New Orleans Times-Picayune*, 16 September 1973). An engaging, very personal account of the years from about 1946 to 1966 is Charlotte Capers's "Eudora Welty: A Friend's View" in *Eudora Welty: A Form of Thanks*, edited by Louis Dollarhide and Ann J. Abadie (Jackson: University Press of Mississippi, 1979).

CRITICISM

General Estimates

In 1944 Robert Penn Warren published in the *Kenyon Review* one of the earliest and certainly one of the most influential studies of Welty's fiction. In "The Love and the Separateness of Miss Welty," reprinted in his *Selected Essays* (Random House, 1958), Warren defends Welty against reviewers who objected to her poetic technique in *The Wide Net*. In so doing he introduces several approaches to theme and technique that have become by now well established in Welty criticism: her portrayal of contrasting poles of experience, for example, love and separateness, her concern with the mysteries of the inner life and with the mythic, ritualistic qualities inherent in ordinary experience, and her experimentation with many kinds of stories, particularly with a lyrical method—the method of modern poetry—whereby the vivid and actual become expressive symbols. Because of Warren's prestige and the astuteness of his analysis, the essay set the direction for much of the Welty criticism that followed.

In the opening article of the November 1952 issue of *College English*, Granville Hicks wrote an appreciative essay that doubtless reached many teachers who were increasingly finding Welty stories in their text anthologies. Like Warren, he finds Welty's "persistent theme" to be the mystery of personality, and he regards her technique as well suited to its expression.

In his correction of reviewers who claimed Welty's important subjects were squalor and violence, Hicks is chiefly interesting now as a reminder of how obsessively some earlier critics discussed Southern writers in terms of the "gothic" and "grotesque."

Another article that saw wide circulation was Robert Daniel's "The World of Eudora Welty" in *Southern Renascence* edited by Louis D. Rubin, Jr., and Robert D. Jacobs (Baltimore: Johns Hopkins University Press, 1953), revised slightly and reprinted in Rubin and Jacobs's *South* (Garden City, N.Y.: Doubleday, 1961). Daniel's analysis consists chiefly in categorizing Welty's settings and assigning the short stories to one of four categories. Like Hicks and many others, Daniel takes up in some detail the matter of Welty's relationship to Faulkner. As is so often the case, it is a gratuitous line of commentary—and one that he drops in the 1961 revision.

Ruth M. Vande Kieft published the first full-length study of Welty in 1962 as one of the Twayne United States Authors Series (*Eudora Welty*). Since its publication it has stood as the most comprehensive and authoritative study of Welty's fiction. A revised edition that will incorporate the work published since 1962 is being prepared by Vande Kieft and should soon be available. The updating will correct the study's only serious shortcoming, for it is an exceptional work that offers perceptive, subtle readings of most of Welty's fiction. But even with its strengths, which are many, the study illustrates the problem inherent in "covering" a writer whose canon includes a great many first-rate short stories, in addition to novels and literary essays. In the case of Welty, furthermore, with stories that are particularly rich in texture and expressive imagery, the burden of coverage is acute, especially when the critic faces tight space limitations. But Vande Kieft makes her words count, and she remains the critic to be read first. On Weltian themes, Vande Kieft emphasizes the "mysteries" of the inner life (revising an article that appeared in the Spring 1961 *Georgia Review*); the dualities of experience, thus amplifying and developing Warren's "love and separateness" analysis; and the special vision of comedy and fantasy that typifies much of Welty's fiction. Vande Kieft is also very helpful in pointing up stylistic and structural techniques of *Delta Wedding, The Golden Apples*, and *The Bride of the Innisfallen*. In her conclusion she discusses Welty's relation to the South, to other Southern writers, and to the tradition of recent Western literature.

In 1965 Alfred Appel, Jr., published *A Season of Dreams*, the first book in the Louisiana State University Press's Southern Literary Series. It offered a chance for breadth and detail unavailable in the Twayne format; but, regrettably, it missed its chance. Appel drew so heavily on Vande Kieft and others as to make the book virtually unusable. A quick comparison of his and Vande Kieft's commentaries on "Livvie" and "The Purple Hat," for instance, will show the difficulty. The book marked an unfortunate turn in Welty criticism.

In the fifteen year period between the publication of *The Bride of the Innisfallen* (1955) and *Losing Battles* (1970), a number of general essays on Welty appeared in books on contemporary fiction. One of the best of these is Alun Jones's "The World of Love" in *The Creative Present*, edited by Nona Balakian and Charles Simmons (Garden City, N.Y.: Doubleday, 1963). Jones adds to the critical understanding of Welty's lyrical imagination and offers particularly astute insights into the complex manipulation of narrators in *The Golden Apples* and into the comic invention of *The Ponder Heart*. As if anticipating *Losing Battles*, which appeared the same year as his essay, Richard Rupp further develops the Jones analysis of Welty's "world of love" by tracing the author's celebratory attention to family and community in "Eudora Welty: A Continual Feast" in his *Celebration in Postwar American Fiction* (Miami, Fla.: University of Miami Press, 1970). Rupp also points readers in a productive direction for understanding *The Golden Apples* by showing that the central subject of the book is less about old myths newly embodied than about the myth-making process itself.

Three different critics in essays in the mid 1960s linked Welty with Carson McCullers, but in two of these the links seem mainly to shorten the table of contents, since few parallels between the writers are drawn. Marvin Felheim in *Contemporary American Novelists*, edited by Harry T. Moore (Carbondale: Southern Illinois University Press, 1964) and Frederick J. Hoffman in *The Art of Southern Fiction* (Carbondale: Southern Illinois University Press, 1967) give brief commentaries that cover old ground. By far the most important of the three essays is Chester Eisinger's in *Fiction of the Forties* (Chicago: University of Chicago Press, 1963). Eisinger identifies Welty as a writer of the "new fiction," discussing her in a chapter that includes Truman Capote, McCullers, Paul Bowles, and Jean Stafford. He calls her, in fact, the "pioneer" in the new fiction and attributes her clear break with the modes of the 1930s to her dedication to "the power and mystery of the imagination." In this context he suggests a kinship between Welty's aesthetics and Coleridge's theory of the imagination, and he goes on to place Welty in the modernist literary tradition. Her relation to this tradition is the subject of more extended treatment in his 1979 essay, discussed below. Eisinger is particularly good in his analysis of the formal techniques that give shape to Welty's fiction, showing that they serve and derive directly from the author's predilection for subtlety and indirection.

Four other essays of the mid-1960s analyze the full range of Welty's achievement, but they each follow a rather single line of commentary. In fact, Kurt Opitz, in "Eudora Welty: The Order of a Captive Soul" (*Crit*, Winter 1964-1965), writes a singular essay that, with the exception of some reviews, stands as the sole negative criticism amid the affirmative, appreciative essays of the past forty years. Understandably, the essay has evoked numerous rebuttals. Opitz claims that Welty holds the "pseudoromantic premise" that events are fated and beyond human control, a view that "sets certain conditions for the interpretation of the text." In his far-fetched accusation of Welty as a literary determinist, he stands alone. Whatever Welty's literary failures, they are not didacticism and message-mongering.

Although he concentrates on *The Golden Apples*, Louis D. Rubin, Jr., in *The Faraway Country* (Seattle: University of Washington Press, 1963), surveys Welty's fictional "Mississippi," somewhat rigidly distinguishing it from Faulkner's "Mississippi." In discussing *Delta Wedding* and *The Golden Apples*, he makes a strong case for the social quality of Welty's fiction. In *Violence in Recent Southern Fiction* (Durham, N.C.: Duke University Press, 1965), Louise Y. Gossett finds violence pervasive in Welty's fiction, but the effect is complex, she says, for often "squalid actuality may take on a glimmer of magic." She persuasively shows that the role of violence in Welty's fiction differs sharply from that in, say, Robert Penn Warren's, for in Welty the effect is not so much a harmful consequence as a condition for revelation, whereby a character's view of himself is changed and heightened.

John Edward Hardy begins his essay on "The Achievement of Eudora Welty" (*SHR*, Summer 1968) with Simone de Beauvoir's statement of the limitations women artists face, discouraged as women have been from any questioning of their experience. He then measures the statement against Welty's achievement, asserting that "there is no other fictionist whose writing is so thoroughly and unmistakably feminine." But Hardy's real subject is not the female imagination, rather Welty's themes of the individual's confrontation with solitude, absurdity, violence, and racism. Noting her unsentimental but sympathetic portrayals, he proposes that the distinctive perspective derives from her being a woman. His separate-but-equal premise includes the possibility that "the division of the sexes, even among artists, unlike the division of the races, is necessary and permanent in the human condition."

Five short monographs published between 1968 and 1976 are variously useful to Welty readers. J. A. Bryant, Jr., in a 1968 pamphlet for the Minnesota Series on American Writers, revised in *Seven American Women Writers of the Twentieth Century* (Minneapolis: University of Minnesota Press, 1977), gives a helpful general introduction to the early fiction with brief comments on *The Optimist's Daughter* and *Losing Battles* added in the 1977 revision. He briefly discusses Welty's critical writings. Neil Isaacs's *Eudora Welty*, in the Steck-Vaughn Southern Writers Series (Austin, Tex., 1969), will appeal to readers interested in the mythological framework of Welty's fiction. He concentrates on Welty's employment of archetypes, specifically the central myth of renewal that incorporates the summer king, winter king, and goddess figure. In one section he also gives a useful analysis of Welty's experimentation with various narrators, her "performance stories." Unlike the Bryant pamphlet, this essay is not introductory, as its format might suggest. Isaacs frankly eschews the familiar thematic and regional approaches to Welty's fiction in favor of an analysis of mythic patterns.

Two longer monographs focus exclusively on the short fiction: Marie-Antoinette Manz-Kunz's *Eudora Welty: Aspects of Reality in her Short Fiction*, in Swiss Studies in English (Bern: Francke Verlag, 1971) and Zelma Turner Howard's *The Rhetoric of Eudora Welty's Short Stories* (Jackson: University Press of Mississippi, 1973). Manz-Kunz is most suggestive in a chapter that discusses Welty's technique of evoking reality as an "experience of rhythm." She is least successful on the sociology of *The Golden Apples*. Howard employs Wayne Booth's categories and terminology from *The Rhetoric of Fiction* to describe Welty's literary techniques. Both works bear the familiar marks of graduate theses.

In 1976 Michael Kreyling prepared an introductory pamphlet on Welty for the Mississippi Library Commission's series on Mississippi writers. The essay was not widely distributed, but fortunately Kreyling has included his most original insights in his 1980 full-length study discussed below.

This same period saw two special journal issues devoted to Welty, *Shenandoah* (Spring 1969) and *Mississippi Quarterly* (Fall 1973). *Shenandoah* carries some important essays on individual works by Robert B. Heilman, Ashley Brown, and Reynolds Price, and general estimates in five appreciative tributes by Malcolm Cowley, Martha Graham, Walker Percy, Allen Tate, and Robert Penn Warren. In a short article on "The Art of Eudora Welty," Joyce Carol Oates admiringly traces Welty's subtle transformations of the ordinary and natural into artful stories that "mean very nearly everything."

Ruth M. Vande Kieft's "The Vision of Eudora Welty" in the *Mississippi Quarterly* issue offers a clear, invaluable discussion of one of the most discussed topics in Welty criticism: the author's embodiment of a distinctive vision of the world, a world of oppositions and dualities in the language and structure of the fiction. Thomas Landess's "The Function of Taste in the Fiction of Eudora Welty," another general essay, treats the author's kinship to Jane Austen and Henry James and her subtle methods of locating and validating a refined sensibility within a compassionate view of human frailty.

An article that might profitably be read in conjunction with Vande Kieft's "Vision" is Lucinda H. MacKethan's "To See Things in Their Time: The Act of Focus in Eudora Welty's Fiction" (*AL*, May 1978; rptd. in *The Dream of Arcady*, Baton Rouge: Louisiana State University Press, 1980). Beginning with comments on place and time, but ultimately discussing angles of vision, MacKethan analyzes four categories of characters who variously embody the "seeing" in time and the "being" of place.

At the end of the 1970s three collections of essays appeared, adding significantly to the body of Welty criticism. Four of the ten essays collected by John F. Desmond in *A Still Moment: Essays on the Art of Eudora Welty*

(Metuchen, N.J.: Scarecrow Press, 1978) treat general topics. John A. Allen, in an article that appeared originally in *Virginia Quarterly Review* (Autumn 1975), is exceptionally good on the nature of heroism in Welty's fiction. Other general studies are those of Jerry Harris, who seeks to establish a category that describes Welty's philosophical mind; James Neault, who writes on time—Welty's control of the arrested, "still" moment; and Albert J. Griffith on Welty's literary theory, who finds that her concept of mysteriousness explains much about her themes and use of language.

The seven papers in *Eudora Welty: A Form of Thanks*, edited by Louis Dollarhide and Ann J. Abadie (Jackson: University Press of Mississippi, 1979) were originally presented in 1977 at a symposium honoring Miss Welty at the University of Mississippi. Although all treat special rather than general topics, Cleanth Brooks on language, Peggy W. Prenshaw on women's roles, and William Jay Smith on the "poetic vision," they draw broadly from the fiction for their remarks. Reynolds Price offers a brief, but warm, tribute in "A Form of Thanks."

By far the largest collection is Peggy Whitman Prenshaw's *Eudora Welty: Critical Essays* (Jackson: University Press of Mississippi, 1979), which has twenty-five previously unpublished essays, the first nine of which are designated general studies. Many of these, however, take up special topics and are included below. Among the most valuable of the general treatments are those of Chester Eisinger, who extends his earlier assessment of Welty's work as an important translation between modernist and traditionalist literature, and John A. Allen, who discusses Welty's embodiment of mysteriousness in a host of characters ranging throughout the fiction. J. A. Bryant, Jr., looking at many examples of Welty's use of narrators, should be read in conjunction with Eisinger. Bryant perceptively shows the relation of the narrators to Welty's resolution of the modernist disjunction between the self and the world.

Finally, the most recent general estimate of Welty's art is the important full-length study by Michael Kreyling, *Eudora Welty's Achievement of Order* (Baton Rouge: Louisiana State University Press, 1980). Kreyling's strengths are his fresh, engaging prose, and his development of several new approaches to reading Welty's fiction, notably an attention to tracing connections and progressions that reveal an evolving artistry and to showing patterns that link the fiction with central motifs not only in American culture but in the "general consciousness." Kreyling, warning that analytical or argumentative criticism will not suit Welty's fiction, heeds his own advice and offers sensitive readings that are admittedly personal. In this, he implies that the decoding of the text is the critical act—one reader's reading of the work—and so he urges readers to attend the fiction, bringing with them a capacity for pleasure and passion, rather than turn toward the criticism. (This comes in Kreyling's afterword.)

With Vande Kieft, Kreyling's work provides the most profitable starting point for study of Welty's fiction. In the 2 March 1980 *New York Times Book Review*, Robert Penn Warren reviews Dollarhide and Abadie, Prenshaw, and Kreyling.

SPECIAL TOPICS

Many critics have directed their attention to Welty's identity as a Southern writer and her depiction of the South, particularly in relation to her theories about place in fiction. Both Vande Kieft and Kreyling take up the topic ably and in detail. In *The Folk of Southern Fiction* (Athens: University of Georgia Press, 1972), Merrill Skaggs traces the uses to which Welty puts nineteenth-century Southern local color, as she draws on familiar, even stereotypical, Southern characters and motifs. Charles E. Davis, in "The South in Eudora Welty's Fiction: A Changing World" (*SAF*, Autumn 1975), argues that Welty's South is central, not peripheral to her fiction, and that the changing South is a basic theme of her work. One of the most valuable discussions of Welty's development and portrayal of the region is Albert Devlin's "Eudora Welty's Mississippi" in the Prenshaw collection. Going far beyond the hollow issue of whether or not Welty is a "regionalist," a subject that has generated much print, Devlin also looks beyond the "lyrical Welty" to consider the body of her work that reflects a "cohesive view of historical reality." Many essays on individual works give insights into the Southern theme, two examples being John E. Hardy's "*Delta Wedding* as Region and Symbol" (*SR*, Summer 1952) and Peggy W. Prenshaw's "Cultural Patterns in Eudora Welty's *Delta Wedding* and 'The Demonstrators'" (*NMW*, Fall 1970). One also finds among the biographical and the appreciative essays, such as Robert Drake's "Eudora Welty's Country—and My Own" (*ModA*, Fall 1979), some information about Welty's South. Offering some further use are Elmo Howell's two essays, "Eudora Welty and the Use of Place in Southern Fiction" (*ArQ*, Autumn 1972), "Eudora Welty and the City of Man" (*GaR*, Winter 1979), and Bessie Chronaki's "Eudora Welty's Theory of Place and Human Relationships" (*SAB*, May 1978).

Understandably, style—and specifically the poetic or lyrical technique—is a chief topic of Welty criticism. Again, one should consult the major general studies. Particularly worthwhile articles are Ruth Vande Kieft's "The Vision of Eudora Welty" (*MissQ*, Fall 1973) and John F. Fleischauer's "The Focus of Mystery: Eudora Welty's Prose Style" (*SLJ*, Spring 1973). Because pursuit of this topic is necessarily grounded in concrete illustration, some of the best treatments of the topic deal with single works. Among these, one should consult Daniel Curley's "Eudora Welty and the Quondam Obstruction" (*SSF*, Spring 1968) and Robert Detweiler's "Eudora Welty's Blazing Butterfly: The Dynamics of Response" (*Lang&S*, Winter

1973). Already mentioned but noteworthy on this topic are Smith in Dollarhide and Abadie, and Allen's and Bryant's essays in Prenshaw.

Another aspect of technique that has attracted critical comment is Welty's handling of dialogue and colloquial language. An early study, still useful, is Robert Holland's "Dialogue as a Reflection of Place in *The Ponder Heart*" (*AL*, November 1963). In "Colloquialism as a Style in the First-Person-Narrator Fiction of Eudora Welty" (*MissQ*, Fall 1973), Nell Ann Pickett analyzes one of Welty's most distinctive techniques—the use of first-person narrators and, through language, the implicit control of the reader's response to them. Cleanth Brooks's recent essay in Dollarhide and Abadie, showing how Welty understands, respects, and uses the oral tradition of the Southern folk culture, is another valuable treatment of this topic.

In 1947 Eunice Glenn published an illuminating analysis of fantasy in Welty's fiction, a topic that has come to occupy many critics. Glenn's essay, in *A Southern Vanguard*, edited by Allen Tate (Prentice-Hall), offers a comprehensive study of fantasy as aspects of both form and the author's world view. Heinrich Straumann extends Glenn's analysis slightly in his commentary on Welty in *American Literature in the Twentieth Century* (Harper Torchbooks, 1965). Vande Kieft devotes a chapter to the uses of fantasy, giving a helpful treatment of the "variety of contexts and methods in and through which illusion, fantasy, and the dream world are presented." Individual studies of *The Robber Bridegroom* and of some of the short stories (for example, "Powerhouse," "Old Mr. Marblehall," "Asphodel," and "The Purple Hat") frequently concentrate on Welty's methods of combining the fantastic with the realistic.

Welty's richly complex and subtle uses of myth, often closely allied with fantasy, have generated some of the most thoughtful critical studies that have been done. Among the general studies, Isaacs's is particularly good and should be consulted, as should Vande Kieft. Thomas L. McHaney, in "Eudora Welty and the Multitudinous Golden Apples" (*MissQ*, Fall 1973), offers a learned, comprehensive study of myth in *The Golden Apples*. Early treatments of myth aimed chiefly at identifying mythological allusions in the fiction, as, for example, Harry C. Morris's "Eudora Welty's Use of Mythology" (*Shenandoah*, Spring 1955) and William M. Jones's "Name and Symbol in the Prose of Eudora Welty" (*SFQ*, December 1958). Several essays in Prenshaw add substantially to an understanding of the various roles and patterns in which Welty employs myth. John A. Allen writes about a number of characters, "demigods," whose essentially mysterious lives suggest "the other way to live" and thereby furnish the central thematic tensions in the fiction. Robert L. Phillips, Jr., does not so much turn up new ground as develop a framework for categorizing the different uses of myth and fantasy in the fiction. Demmin and Curley, discussing the "male godhead" and the "female mysteries," extend McHaney's important work on *The Golden Apples*, as does Daniele Pitavy-Souques, who writes an extremely suggestive analysis of Welty's structural use of the Perseus myth. Finally, there are a number of excellent treatments of myth that one should consult in the studies of individual works, particularly *The Robber Bridegroom, The Golden Apples, Losing Battles*, and several of the short stories. Among the many explications of stories, some of the most suggestive or comprehensive studies of myth are William M. Jones's "Eudora Welty's Use of Myth in 'Death of a Traveling Salesman'" (*JAF*, January-March 1960), Neil D. Isaacs's "Life out of Death: Ancient Myth and Ritual in Welty's 'A Worn Path'" (*NMW*, Spring 1976), Andrea Goudie's "Eudora Welty's Circe: A Goddess Who Strove with Men" (*SSF*, Fall 1976), and Peggy W. Prenshaw's "Persephone in Eudora Welty's 'Livvie'" (*SSF*, Spring 1980).

The topic of Welty's humor and comedy has not received the attention that it deserves. Some useful work has been done, however, and one should start with Vande Kieft's chapter on comedy and Seymour L. Gross's "Eudora Welty's Comic Imagination," in *The Comic Imagination*, edited by Louis D. Rubin, Jr. (New Brunswick, N.J.: Rutgers University Press, 1973). Gross's general essay examines Welty's joyful "hospitality to the diversity and energy and magical surprises of the human carnival," with comments mostly on *The Robber Bridegroom* and *The Ponder Heart*. It does not take up the kind of satiric comedy Welty employs in "Petrified Man." Charles E. Davis in Desmond discusses the tradition of old Southwestern humor in *The Robber Bridegroom*, and Merrill Skaggs is noteworthy for her account of the more general tradition of Southern humor as it infuses *The Ponder Heart* and other works. One should also see Kreyling's informative chapter on *The Ponder Heart*. Seymour Gross and Mary Anne Ferguson in Prenshaw, writing on *Losing Battles*, should be read for their illuminating comments about the comedic patterns in the novel. Also, other studies of *The Robber Bridegroom, The Ponder Heart*, and *Losing Battles* often include material on humor.

Welty's treatment of women's roles, often discussed in the context of her portrayal of marriage and the family, has drawn increased recent attention. John A. Allen's essay, reprinted in Desmond, should be read for its discussion of male and female heroes and its analysis of the conception of heroic action embodied in the fiction. He includes many of the works in his commentary, showing that the capacity for feeling and a sure sense of reality are, for Welty, the requisites of the heroic. Hardy's "Marrying Down in Eudora Welty's Novels" in Prenshaw is a richly suggestive critique of marriage and its consequences for the partners, especially the women. He shows that, at its best, marriage is a laudable compromise with the world, with the expected gains and losses that come with compromise. But in his discussion of *Losing Battles*, Hardy finds another view, which is kept submerged in the novel, "that marriage is somehow a betrayal of one's deepest identity, not only personal identity but one's essential *human* identity." In several ways extending or giving illustration to many of Hardy's observations are Jane Hinton's "The Role of the Family in *Delta Wedding, Losing Battles* and *The Optimist's Daughter*" and Elizabeth Kerr's "The World of Eudora Welty's Women" in Prenshaw. Margaret Bolsterli in "Woman's Vision: The Worlds of Women in *Delta Wedding*, *Losing Battles* and *The Optimist's Daughter*" in Prenshaw posits the coexistence of women's and men's cultures in the society portrayed by Welty, and she discusses the situation and texture of experience that shape the women's culture. A more detailed discussion of the women's culture is Peggy W. Prenshaw's "Woman's World, Man's Place: The Fiction of Eudora Welty" in Dollarhide. Prenshaw relates the roles of women to matriarchal patterns, to the desire for family membership and renewal, and to female archetypes that express the ambition for individual consciousness and heroic action. Demmin and Curley's essay in Prenshaw also gives some helpful insights into the male-female archetypal patterns in the fiction. A still useful early study of women is Mary Catherine Buswell's "The Love Relationships of Women in the Fiction of Eudora Welty" (*WVUPP*, December 1961). Buswell discusses several types of women characters—the old maid, the young unmarried girl, the married woman—in what is mainly a character study, not a critique of the female imagination or the female psychology of the characters.

Other useful critical studies cover a wide range of special topics. These include three essays on Welty's portrayal of black characters and, to some extent, her handling of racial themes. See John Edward Hardy's "Eudora Welty's Negroes" in *Images of the Negro in American Literature*, edited by Seymour L. Gross and John Edward Hardy (Chicago: University of Chicago Press, 1966) and John R. Cooley's "Blacks and Primitives in Eudora Welty's Fiction" (*BSUF*, Summer 1973). W. U. McDonald, Jr., in "Eudora Welty's Revisions of 'Pageant of Birds'" (*NMW*, Spring 1977), shows changes Welty made for the 1974 reprinting of the essay, first published in the *New Republic* in 1943. He concludes that the changes "evince a heightening of linguistic sensitivity in describing the Negro participants and delineating the narrator's response." On a different topic, Mary Catherine Buswell identifies the mountain characters in the fiction, drawing comparisons with several sociological studies of the Appalachian mountaineer in "The Mountain Figure in the Fiction of Eudora Welty" (*WVUPP*, July 1972). Anne M. Masserand, analyzing several of the short stories, finds the traveller a persistent figure and the home-versus-journey opposition a reiterated theme in "Eudora Welty's Travellers: The Journey Theme in Her Short Stories" (*SLJ*, Spring 1971). Finally, there are a number of studies devoted to explications of psychological patterns, most often focusing on individual works covered below. One general study, which unfortunately uses the fiction as so much case study material, is Raymond Tarbox's "Eudora Welty's Fiction: The Salvation Theme" (*AI*, Spring 1972).

Individual Works

A Curtain of Green

Only a few studies treat the entire collection of stories, but explications of individual stories abound in periodical and textbook essays. Katherine Anne Porter's 1941 introduction, reprinted in succeeding editions and thus widely read, pointedly recognizes the "extraordinary range of mood, pace, tone, and variety of material." She discusses the stories in three groupings, and states a preference for the lyrical story, "where external act and the internal voiceless life of the human imagination meet and mingle." (It is interesting that in Welty's next collection, *The Wide Net*, this kind of story predominates.) Porter's discussion of the satiric comedy of "Petrified Man" is apt, but in identifying Sister of "Why I Live at the P.O." as a "terrifying case of dementia praecox," Porter has given rise to a stream of comments and rebuttals that apparently has no end.

Among the most discerning of the reviewers is Louise Bogan (*The Nation*, 6 December 1941), who compares Welty's method and material to those of Gogol. Frederick Brantley, in "*A Curtain of Green:* Themes and Attitudes" (*American Prefaces*, Spring 1942), gives an astute analysis of themes, discussing "isolation" and other topics in ways that lay groundwork for the more comprehensive Warren essay coming two years later. In a much later essay, Robert J. Griffin, in "Eudora Welty's *A Curtain of Green*," in *The Forties: Fiction, Poetry, Drama*, edited by Warren French (Deland, Fla.: Everett/Edwards, 1969), concentrates on the poetic style, specifically on symbol and theme, and in effect compiles a summary of many points well established in the criticism. Still later, Barbara Fialkowski in "Psychic Distances in *A Curtain of Green:* Artistic Successes and Personal Failures," in the Desmond collection, compares the theme of human isolation in the stories to the artist's necessary separation from life. She reaches the questionable conclusion that Welty acquiesces to the condition of isolation as she capitalizes on the artist's distance—"one feels a shrug of the artist's shoulders as she pulls away from her sorry cast of characters." As far as it goes, Gary Carson's discussion of the artist in "A Memory" and "Powerhouse" is useful, but it is a topic requiring broader development than he gives it in "Versions of the Artist in *A Curtain of Green*: The Unifying Imagination in Eudora Welty's Early Fiction" (*SSF*, Fall 1978). (On the artist figure in *The Wide Net*, see Curley and Warner below.)

Significant studies of *A Curtain of Green* already mentioned are those of Devlin in Prenshaw, who writes about the deep social and historical understandings manifest in the stories, and Vande Kieft, who gives brief but illuminating comments on each of the stories. Kreyling looks at a few representative works to write of characters, often grotesques, whose stories are "discovered" by author and reader through the process of technique.

In addition to the explications of stories discussed above in the section on myth, there are many other worthwhile readings of single stories. For their insights into Welty's fiction in general, some of the most suggestive or provocative of the periodical essays are Lodwick Hartley's "Proserpina and the Old Ladies" (*MFS*, Spring 1957); Robert B. Heilman's "Salesmen's Deaths: Documentary and Myth" (*Shenandoah*, Spring 1969); Robert Detweiler's "Eudora Welty's Blazing Butterfly: The Dynamics of Response" (*Lang&S*, Winter 1973); and Charles E. May's "*Le Roy Mehaigné* in Welty's 'Keela, The Outcast Indian Maiden'" (*MFS*, Winter 1972-1973). Of the many psychological approaches to the stories, two interesting ones are Charles E. May, answering Porter on "dementia praecox" with R. D. Laing's work, in "Why Sister Lives at the P.O." (*SHR*, Summer 1978), and St. George Tucker Arnold, Jr., drawing on Erich Neumann's *The Origins and History of Consciousness*, in "The Raincloud and the Garden: Psychic Regression as Tragedy in Welty's 'A Curtain of Green'" (*SAB*, January 1979).

Though not explications, three other informative articles by W. U. McDonald, Jr., are "Revision of 'A Piece of News'" (*SSF*, Spring 1970); "Welty's Social Consciousness: Revisions of 'The Whistle'" (*MFS*, Summer 1970); and "Eudora Welty, Reviser: Some Notes on 'Flowers for Marjorie'" (*Delta*, November 1977). An illuminating background piece for reading "Powerhouse" is Whitney Balliett's "Jazz: Fats" (*NY*, 10 April 1978).

The Robber Bridegroom

Welty's 1944 "Some Notes on River Country," collected in *The Eye of the Story*, is a good starting point. Reviewers Alfred Kazin's "An Enchanted World in America," (*NYHTB*, 25 October 1942), and Marianne Hauser's "Miss Welty's Fairy Tale," (*NYTBR*, 1 November 1942) concentrate on the fairy-tale elements, with Kazin going more deeply into Welty's use of native American material. On mythic materials that give shape to the novel's structure as a romance, consult Ashley Brown's "Eudora Welty and the Mythos of Summer" (*Shenandoah*, Spring 1969) and Neil Isaacs's general study. Bryant's pamphlet gives an estimable general reading of the novel; and adding further details on the various literary and historical sources, as well as on themes, is Charles C. Clark's "*The Robber Bridegroom*: Realism and Fantasy on the Natchez Trace" (*MissQ*, Fall 1973). Gordon E. Slethaug, in "Initiation in Eudora Welty's *The Robber Bridegroom*" (*SHR*, Winter 1973), makes the commonsensical observation that Clement and Rosamond Musgrove move from a simple to complex understanding of experience—discovering that all things are double—and thereby achieve a mature view of reality. He argues persuasively that the ballad "Young Andrew" and certain of the Grimms tales furnish shaping patterns for the story's plot and the characters' initiations. Making many of the same points is another article published in 1973, Carol P. Smith's "The Journey Motif in Eudora Welty's *The Robber Bridegroom*" (*SSC Review*, Shippensburg [Pa.] State College) which discusses initiations as journeys or quests undertaken by the characters.

In "Eudora Welty's *The Robber Bridegroom* and Old Southwest Humor: A Doubleness of Vision," in the Desmond collection, Charles E. Davis examines old Southwest humor mainly to say that Welty, like the humorists, "establishes a distance between herself and her story." He devotes most of his essay to illustrating the "essential doubleness of all things," which he, like many others before him, finds the crucial theme of the novel—one that links characters, situations, history, and myth. Warren French in "'All Things are Double': Eudora Welty as a Civilized Writer," in Prenshaw, significantly extends the discussion of the "doubleness" theme by analyzing a particular set of doubles or opposites in the novel—the marketplace and the forest—which links the novel with a long tradition of American fiction. Michael Kreyling, too, should be read for his discussion of the American theme and the novel's strategy of juxtaposing pastoral and history in developing the theme. In "Clement and the Indians: Pastoral and History in *The Robber Bridegroom*," in Dollarhide and Abadie, Kreyling focuses on Clement as the character who comes to understand the conditions and costs of pioneering and, from the example of the Indians, the inevitability of change. Kreyling revises the essay for the chapter in his book, briefly developing the material on the pastoral dream with comparisons to Hawthorne and others and expanding the discussion of the characters Jamie Lockhart and Salome.

The Wide Net and Other Stories

Most essays on the collection as a whole have aimed to show a unity of the stories, with Kreyling maintaining that the connectedness is so sure as to be a foreshadowing of *The Golden Apples*. In 1943 the reviews paid little attention to unity and focused instead on the dreamlike style of the stories. Diana Trilling's review (*The Nation*, 2 October 1943), for instance, found Welty's prose self-conscious, a "ballet of words," an accusation that has given subsequent critics a seemingly endless chance for rebuttal and a convenient departure point for analyzing and defending the style. In addition to Warren's essay on "The Love and the Separateness in Miss Welty," which concerns themes and techniques, one of the best stylistic studies is Daniel Curley's "Eudora Welty and the Quondam Obstruction" (*SSF*, Spring 1968). The essay gives a clear, well-illustrated account of how Welty's prose style expresses her themes. Taking Joel Mayes of "First Love" as an artist figure comparable in some ways to the Audubon discussed by Curley, John

M. Warner, in "Eudora Welty: The Artist in 'First Love'" (*NMW*, Fall 1976), makes some useful points about the story as revelatory of Welty's conception of the artist.

The historical backgrounds of the stories and Welty's special uses of them have been given wide study. One of the best of the historical studies is Albert J. Devlin's "Eudora Welty's Historicism: Method and Vision" (*MissQ*, Spring 1977). Concentrating on "A Still Moment" and "First Love," Devlin elucidates Welty's complex process of selecting and transforming historical matter into fiction. A worthwhile source study that identifies literary and historical sources, as well as some special uses Welty makes of them, is Victor H. Thompson's "The Natchez Trace in Eudora Welty's 'A Still Moment'" (*SLJ*, Fall 1973). Related but briefer studies are Thompson's "Aaron Burr in Eudora Welty's 'First Love'" (*NMW*, Winter 1976), Devlin's "From Horse to Heron: A Source for Eudora Welty" (*NMW*, Winter 1977), and Peggy W. Prenshaw's "Coates' *The Outlaw Years* and Welty's 'A Still Moment'" (*NMAL* Spring 1978). Unlike the critics who view Welty's historicism through her treatment of sources, F. Garvin Davenport, Jr., in "Renewal and Historical Consciousness in *The Wide Net*," in Prenshaw, emphasizes the psychological growth of characters, wherein they "awaken" to their separate identities and consequently find renewed ways of ordering experience. He maintains the stories are linked by their reiteration of this pattern, which is the process by which a "historical consciousness" is achieved. In his book Kreyling makes a strong but finally only half-convincing case for the collection's unity, arguing for a single theme, a common setting, and the connections implied by certain "echoing words."

Interpretations of mythic material and symbolic patterns in the individual stories are numerous. In addition to the general studies and the explications cited in the section on myth, see Robert J. Kloss's "The Symbolic Structure of Eudora Welty's 'Livvie'" (*NMW*, Winter 1975) for a discussion of the sexual symbolism.

Delta Wedding

Most of the reviews of the novel were favorable, though again Diana Trilling, in "Fiction in Review" (*The Nation*, 11 May 1946), led the opposition with her condemnation of the "poeticism" of the book and her frank distaste for the Southern culture that was its subject. In "A Fine Novel of the Deep South" (*NYTBR*, 11 April 1946), Charles Poore admired Welty's unique perception of the South and her richly detailed portrayal of it. John Crowe Ransom's "Delta Fiction" reviewed the novel for the *Kenyon Review* (Summer 1946), calling it a "comedy of love," but concentrating on Welty's treatment of the Southern material and, further, on the future of the tradition the novel depicted. Vande Kieft has taken Ransom's "comedy of love" phrase as her main approach in a helpful discussion of Welty's management of the large cast of characters and various thematic lines.

One of the most significant and influential studies of *Delta Wedding*, one that anyone interested in the novel should read, is John Edward Hardy's "*Delta Wedding* as Region and Symbol" (*SR*, July-September 1952; rptd. in his *Man in the Modern Novel*, Seattle: University of Washington Press, 1964). Hardy gives a close reading of the details of place and people, regional details that ultimately function as symbols. As he convincingly shows, "the order of the novel is a poetic order—of recurrent themes, symbols, and motifs of symbolic metaphor. And it must be close-read, as a poem." Elmo Howell, in "Eudora Welty's Comedy of Manners" (*SAQ*, Autumn 1970), discusses *Delta Wedding* as a novel of manners set in the provinces, but he scarcely goes beyond Hardy except to provide a Fairchild family tree for the reader's convenience. In "Cultural Patterns in Eudora Welty's *Delta Wedding* and 'The Demonstrators'" (*NMW*, Fall 1970), Peggy Prenshaw discusses Welty's portrayal and interpretation of the complex social structure of the modern South.

In an interesting but rambling commentary, Richard J. Gray discusses Welty's conception of experience as a continual conflict between order and spontaneity, specifically as the conflict is given form in the characters of *Delta Wedding*, in "Eudora Welty: A Dance to the Music of Order" (*CRevAS*, Spring 1976; rptd. in his *The Literature of Memory*, Baltimore: Johns Hopkins University Press, 1977). In Prenshaw, M. E. Bradford's "Fairchild as Composite Protagonist in *Delta Wedding*" is brief, but it offers a suggestive examination of the Fairchild family as the objective representation of communal life, Southern life, which is threatened by an insistent private sensibility. Beginning with an early version of the novel, the unpublished short story, "The Delta Cousins," Michael Kreyling makes an important study of the development of the lyrical structure of the novel, thus broadening the earlier insights of Hardy. He concludes from his analysis of Welty's revisions and expansions that the novel is "a record of a writer's discovery of her distance and in that distance the relationship between herself and experience; in short, it records the discovery of a style."

In another discerning study in Prenshaw that includes comments on *Delta Wedding*, John Edward Hardy, mentioned above, discusses the thematic significance of the marriages in the novel, particularly the pattern of "marrying down," represented by George-Robbie and Dabney-Troy. Also helpful on the female characters in the novel are the essays by Prenshaw in Dollarhide and Abadie, and by Hinton, Kerr, and Bolsterli in Prenshaw. In an article entitled "Emasculating Women in *Delta Wedding*," Florence Phyfer Krause acknowledges the novel as a comedy, but she seems entirely to miss its spirit in arguing that Welty condemns and ironically exposes "the evil inherent in tenacious, pleading, emasculating, power-loving aristocratic women" (*PMPA*, 1976). Carol A. Moore analyzes a crucial chapter in the novel, showing its relation to the work's central themes, in "Aunt Studney's Sack" (*SoR*, July 1980).

The Golden Apples

Reviews were generally favorable, with attention paid chiefly to the structure of the book (the interrelated stories) and, as in the past, to Welty's unique prose style. The book's technical and thematic complexity, as well as its artistic excellence, have drawn much critical comment in subsequent essays. These tend to concentrate on the mythic material in the book, the question of the unity of the stories, and on general thematic and structural analyses.

On mythic motifs and figures in the book, one should consult Vande Kieft, who devotes the longest chapter in her study to *The Golden Apples*. McHaney, mentioned above in the section on myth, is outstanding on the Greek and Celtic mythological references, as well as on themes and imagery in general. He also gives a useful survey of the criticism up to 1973. Early criticism on Welty's use of myth tended to be overly specific, even ingenious in identifying parallels and allusions, as for example, in H. C. Morris's "Zeus and the Golden Apples" (*Perspective*, Autumn 1952). For an interesting examination of Welty's use of ancient motifs of male power and female mysteries to "create her own myth of human wholeness," see Demmin and Curley in Prenshaw. Pitavy-Souques in Prenshaw is also interested to explore ways that mythic material contributes to the book's unity. In a structuralist analysis of the Perseus myth, she shows that both the content and the organization of the myth shape the book's structure and theme.

All of the essays devoted to uses of myth are, of course, to some extent concerned with the question of unity and interrelationships. But some critics have taken different routes to the subject of the book's "wholeness." Michael Kreyling gives a sensitive, sequential reading of the stories to show "how things emerge," that is, to show how Welty evokes the natural, physical world through which a mythological network emerges and is interpreted. In some ways anticipating Kreyling's approach, though with less breadth and development, William M. Jones, in "The Plot as Search" (*SSF*, Fall 1967), finds the central unity of the book to be the author's and the reader's sharing of a "search for plot" that unites "the mundane and the mythical." Other studies of unity, offering some limited use, are Wendell V. Harris's terse essay, "The Thematic Unity of Welty's *The Golden Apples*" (*TSLL*, Spring 1964), and Franklin D. Carson's "Recurring Methaphors: An Aspect of Unity in *The Golden Apples*" (*NConL*, September 1975).

Among the most illuminating criticism of *The Golden Apples* have been thematic and structural studies devoted to the book's "doubleness," its embodiment of various kinds of dualities. Vande Kieft concentrates on the juxtaposition of two sets of characters, the wanderers and their foils, who, though seemingly passive, have their power too. J. A. Bryant, Jr., in "Seeing Double in *The Golden Apples*" (*SR*, Spring 1974), considers the distinctive Weltian vision in the book, whereby the everyday world is portrayed in its "richness and undeniable immediacy," and the visionary world is valued and validated as "a kind of miracle that can redeem life from the dullness that traditionalism and common sense have often reduced it to." Merrill Skaggs's "Morgana's Apples and Pears," in Prenshaw, similarly identifies this duality, symbolized by the controlling metaphors of "fancy pears" and "golden apples," in an analysis that usefully extends Bryant's. Douglas Messerli, in "Metronome and Music: The Encounter between History and Myth in *The Golden Apples*," in Desmond, discusses the opposition of the local and timebound to the universal and timeless by following the now familiar critical formulation of history versus myth.

Louis D. Rubin, Jr., in *The Faraway Country* (Seattle: University of Washington Press, 1963), discusses Welty's depiction of the Southern community, its susceptibility to time and change, and the capacity of art to fuse both community and change. It is an informative introductory essay, though Rubin's beginning identification of the "two Mississippis" of Faulkner and Welty poses overly neat boundaries. In *A Requiem for the Renascence* (Athens: University of Georgia Press, 1976), Walter Sullivan is also concerned with the book's portrayal of community. Following a line of analysis that Bradford takes up later, writing of *Delta Wedding* in Prenshaw, Sullivan examines the strengths of the community in its dealing with those who threaten or deviate from its values. Two articles that make useful points about *The Golden Apples* are Carol S. Manning's "Male Initiation, Welty Style" (*RFI*, Fall 1978), on the patterns of initiation of the male characters, with emphasis on "Moon Lake," and Robert S. Pawlowski's "The Process of Observation: *Winesburg, Ohio* and *The Golden Apples*" (*UR*, Summer 1971), which compares the methods and artistic aims of Anderson and Welty. Finally, offering insights into the links between structure and theme are two articles in the special issue of *Delta* (November 1977). Daniele Pitavy, in "'Shower of Gold' Ou Les Ambiguités De La Narration," discusses the story as something of a key to the book, employing as it does a dramatized narration that embodies the thematic ambiguities central to the book's subject. Neil Corcoran analyzes several of Welty's methods of evoking mystery in "The Face That Was in the Poem: Art and 'Human Truth' in 'June Recital.'"

The Ponder Heart

The novel was more widely reviewed than any of Welty's earlier books, with most reviewers expressing admiration for the comic invention, but some uncertainty about what to make of its subject. Later critical studies, mostly on the colloquial language and the ambiguity attached to the first person narration, have been few. Vande Kieft discusses the novel only in scattered comments throughout her book. An important early essay by Robert B. Holland, "Dialogue as a Reflection of Place in *The Ponder*

Heart" (*AL*, November 1963), concerns Welty's use of dialogue as a "vocalization of the design of the culture." Holland takes an approach few other critics have followed, and one that deserves further exploration for *The Ponder Heart* and other works as well. Other critical essays, dealing with different aspects of language and, especially, with the humor of the novel, are covered above in special sections.

The dramatization of the novel has given rise to a line of criticism that focuses on the relation of the first person narrator to the novel's essential nature. Welty herself has written an interesting piece about the playwrights, "Chodorov and Fields in Mississippi" (*EWN*, April 1979). Robert Y. Drake, Jr., in "The Reasons of the Heart" (*GaR*, Winter 1957), argues that the play fails to catch the crucial theme of the story, the paradoxical nature of experience. Lacking narrator Edna Earle's perspective, he maintains, the play needs balance and the Weltian spirit of "acceptance of the totality of experience, the good along with the bad." Brenda G. Cornell takes Drake's emphasis on paradox a step further in "Ambiguous Necessity: A Study of *The Ponder Heart*" in Prenshaw. Contrasting the novel with the play, Cornell convincingly argues that the overall effect and artistic excellence of the book depend upon the ambiguity consonant with Edna Earle's first person narration. Michael Kreyling elaborates the argument of Drake and Cornell in a helpful discussion of the opposites and conflicts in the novel, particularly the tensions in the pairing of the Dionysiac and Appollonian ways of Uncle Daniel and Edna Earle. The source of the comedy in *The Ponder Heart*, Kreyling observes, is the "vital balance between laughter and outrage," with Edna Earle providing a "comic version of the struggle between the sexes and between the champions of life and of order." Finally, Rachel V. Weiner, in "Eudora Welty's *The Ponder Heart:* The Judgment of Art" (*SoSt*, Fall 1980), provides a useful study of the artistry of Welty's narration and the clarity and richness of Edna Earle's tale as history of the South.

The Bride of the Innisfallen and Other Stories

Reviewers of the collection seemed generally to show a respect for the art and a discomfort with the style. Walter Elder, for example, in "That Region" (*KR*, Autumn 1955), speaks of characters whose "trivial essence" shimmers, and who are "sustained and destroyed by delicacies, by moments." Louis D. Rubin, Jr., in "Two Ladies of the South" (*SR*, Autumn 1955), finds the stories to be about time and about a character's discovery of himself. Though his commentary chiefly concerns "Kin," Rubin suggests an interpretational approach to the whole collection that Kreyling later develops and extends. Rubin writes: "The search for the meaning of the moment of time provides the structure of the story. . . . Each is a development toward inactivity, to the reality of self freed of the distractions of elapsing events."

In a suggestive commentary Vande Kieft finds that, despite the apparent departure from earlier work, *The Bride of the Innisfallen* illustrates both a consistency in Welty's vision and the signs of development—"a progress from innocence to experience." (This was the latest of Welty's works at the time of Vande Kieft's writing.) Vande Kieft distinguishes the stories with locales outside the South and discusses the experimentation in technique, particularly in "The Burning," but she finds a continuity with the earlier work in the "dominant themes, feelings, and the continued shaping influence of place." Kreyling discusses the poetic technique of the collection, using the term "rhythmic" to describe the organization of the volume and the movement within each story. He is good on the title story, which he sees as the most complex of the seven stories and, in some ways, as a summation of the collection.

In an elegantly written essay that reveals an impressive understanding of Welty's view of the world and her art of expressing it in fiction, Alun R. Jones discusses three of the stories. "A Frail Travelling Coincidence: Three Later Stories of Eudora Welty" (*Shenandoah*, Spring 1969) should be consulted not only for its discussion of themes and techniques in *The Bride of the Innisfallen* but for its general insights into Welty's art. Similarly, Noel Polk's "Water, Wanderers, and Weddings: Love in Eudora Welty," in Dollarhide and Abadie, includes some illuminating comments about Welty's treatment of love throughout the fiction, but he concentrates on two stories from *Bride*, the title story and "No Place for You, My Love," both also discussed by Jones. Unlike Jones, however, he finds in "No Place" more failure than fulfillment in the characters' search for love.

In general, there have been fewer articles on the individual stories of *The Bride of the Innisfallen* than on those of other collections. The most distinguished essay is Welty's own account of the genesis and composition of "No Place for You, My Love" in "How I Write," which appears as "Writing and Analyzing a Story" in *The Eye of the Story*. Two essays on "The Burning," Elmo Howell's "Eudora Welty's Civil War Story" (*NMW*, Spring 1969) and Edward Gallafent's "The Landscape of 'The Burning'" (*Delta*, November 1977), emphasize the outward violence and destruction in the story as symbols of the interior destruction within the sisters' minds. Gallafent, more illuminating on Welty's technique of merging mind and place, finds in the character Delilah some reconciliation of the "inside and outside worlds" that are hopelessly split in the lives of the sisters. Don Harrell, in "Death in Eudora Welty's 'The Bride of the Innisfallen'" (*NConL*, September 1973), contends that the story is about the American girl's discovering the "meaning of her own mortality." Like many others he notes that Welty characteristically expresses theme through lyrical, "impressionistic" prose. In "Mythic Elements in 'Ladies in Spring'" (*NMW*, Winter 1974), Margaret Bolsterli briefly interprets details in the story that suggest ancient rainmaking and fertility rites. A much more detailed study of mythic patterns is that of Andrea Goudie in "Eudora Welty's Circe: A Goddess Who Strove with Men" (*SSF*, Fall 1976). This is a useful thematic study, developed through a close comparison of the Odysseus-Circe stories in *The Odyssey* and in Welty's "Circe."

The Shoe Bird

Written for a juvenile audience, this book has received very little attention. Neil Isaacs briefly discusses its failings and strengths, and then goes on to examine its themes of memory and love. His interpretation, written before the publication of *The Optimist's Daughter*, calls the novel immediately to mind. Reading Isaacs, one wonders whether *The Shoe Bird* might foreshadow the later work in certain ways. Two other essayists have discussed *The Shoe Bird* in their analyses of special motifs manifest in the fiction. Jeanne R. Nostrandt, in "Eudora Welty and the Children's Hour" (*MissQ*, Winter 1975-1976), traces Welty's attention to the bird pageant in the early photographs, the essay "Pageant of Birds," and in the children's book. Similarly, Albert J. Griffith's "Henny Penny, Eudora Welty, and the Aggregation of Friends," in Prenshaw, shows the device of the aggregation of friends to function structurally and thematically in *The Shoe Bird* and in "The Wide Net" and "The Wanderers."

Losing Battles

There are interesting comments by Welty herself on the plan and composition of the novel in several interviews discussed above in the biography section. The reviews of the novel, the first major fiction in fifteen years, were numerous and strongly favorable. Fellow writers Reynolds Price and Joyce Carol Oates praised the novel, Price noting the rich plenitude of its vision and concluding of Welty that "no one writing sees more," in "Frightening Gift" (*Washington Post*, 17 April 1970). In "Eudora's Web" (*Atlantic*, April 1970), Oates admires the musical quality, the "voices" of the novel, though finally she declares that "it is not a work that will appeal to everyone." James Boatwright praises the comic invention, finding the novel overall a "major work of the imagination and a gift to cause general rejoicing" (*NYTBR*, 12 April 1970). Some reviewers used the occasion of the novel's publication to write helpful retrospective analyses and evaluations of Welty's career. Among the most illuminating of these are John W. Aldridge and Louis D. Rubin, Jr. In "Eudora Welty: Metamorphosis of a Southern Lady Writer" (*SR*, 11 April 1970; rptd. in Aldridge's *The Devil in the Fire*, Harper and Row, 1972) Aldridge sees the novel as evidence that Welty "has radically enlarged the range of her interests" and, in his view, grown from a "Southern lady writer" with "narrow" scope into a major writer of the first rank. Rubin acclaims the "high art" of the novel and of Welty's fiction generally, concluding that she is "one of the three or four most important writers to come out of twentieth-century America" (*HC*, June 1970). He acknowledges that the method of the novel—"its density of surface"—may pose a difficulty for some readers: "Everything is out on the surface, but the art is the surface, and every inch of the surface must be inspected." To illustrate Welty's literary achievement (and obviously to attract readers unfamiliar with Welty's earlier works), Rubin devotes the second half of his essay to *Delta Wedding* and *The Golden Apples* ("the masterpiece of all the books"). Louise Y. Gossett, in "Eudora Welty's New Novel: The Comedy of Loss" (*SLJ*, Fall 1970), also discusses the novel in the context of the earlier works. She notes, for example, that in pairing the Renfro-Beecham family and Miss Julia, Welty uses a familiar motif of "the pairing of alternatives." Gossett's is a well-developed review-essay that elucidates recurrent themes and narrative strategies as well as the achievement of the novel and its place in Welty's career.

M. E. Bradford, in "Looking Down from a High Place: The Serenity of Miss Welty's 'Losing Battles'" (*RANAM*, 1971; rptd. in Desmond), views the family in the novel, as he does in *Delta Wedding*, as representative of Southern communal life. His comments, concentrated on the threat to the community that Julia's allegiance to progressivism and rationalism represents, are chiefly thematic, although he praises the novel's authority in showing, not analyzing, the lives of the characters. Employing a similar approach to the novel is Thomas Landess in "More Trouble in Mississippi: Family vs. Antifamily in Miss Welty's *Losing Battles*" (*SR*, Autumn 1971). He sees "opposing concepts of group" as lying at the heart of the novel. The group concepts are represented of course by the family and Miss Julia, whom he sees as thoroughly exemplifying the modern "abstractionist" tendency. Landess finds the two sides portrayed with a "fine impartiality," though his sympathies seem to lie with the communal family, with all its irrational, personal ways. Interestingly, his aesthetic view differs slightly from his world view, for he faults the novel's structure for lacking unity and clarity of action, for having too much "spillage" not "gathered in and highlighted by proper action."

Most of the subsequent essays have focused in one way or another on the family-versus-Julia Mortimer dialectic as a major theme of the novel or have analyzed the style and structure of the book. Michael Kreyling treats the paired opposites in "Myth and History: The Foes of *Losing Battles*" (*MissQ*, Fall 1973) in his discussion of the mythical consciousness, expressed through family ritual and the circle motif, and the historical consciousness, shown in the individual's (Julia's) dedication to progressive change. With only slight revisions, the article forms a chapter in Kreyling's book. James Boatwright's related analysis is important and should be read. In "Speech and Silence in *Losing Battles*" (*Shenandoah*, Spring 1974), he contends that the novel is not simply made of speech, that it is "*about* speech and silence"—speech as a strategy of survival and silence as the means of asserting the soul's separateness. Boatwright's emphasis on speech as the family's ultimate weapon is more convincing than the interpretations of several other essayists. Carol A. Moore, in "The Insulation of Illusion and *Losing Battles*" (*MissQ*, Fall 1973), sees the family as making a strength of weakness by willfully maintaining their illusions about themselves, and, in "Enlightening Darkness: Theme and Structure in Eudora Welty's *Losing Battles*" (*JNT*, Spring 1978), Larry J. Reynolds, sounding like a Julia partisan, claims that the family's survival depends upon its ignorance, which it struggles to protect. In "Conflict and Resolution in Welty's *Losing Battles*" (*Crit*, No. 1, 1973), William McMillen makes some very general observations about the two opposing sides in the central conflict, and in a comparable essay in 1978, "Circling-In: The Concept of Home in Eudora Welty's *Losing Battles* and *The Optimist's Daughter*," in Desmond, he examines Welty's portrayal of home as the focus of rebellion by the younger generation against the family.

In addition to the several studies of marriage and the family, the Prenshaw collection includes five essays specifically devoted to *Losing Battles*, most of which treat the style and structure of the novel. Robert B. Heilman has written an important, penetrating analysis of the novel's technique. Accomplishing his aim, which is to convey "the sense of magnitude" the novel creates, he concentrates chiefly on the language of the book, the rhetorical patterns that give shape to the seemingly spontaneous, colloquial dialogue. He goes beyond Holland's early comments on *The Ponder Heart* and Boatwright's study of speech in *Losing Battles* to explore how meaning is expressed through style, how "community"—the struggle for survival, family feeling, feuds and battles—is communicated through the language of speech. In the course of his analysis he draws many useful comparisons with other writers and works of American, European, and classical literature.

Mary Anne Ferguson's "*Losing Battles* as a Comic Epic in Prose" is a persuasive study showing that the novel draws on the traditional epic not only for narrative material but for the structure. Ferguson claims that Fielding's phrase for *Tom Jones*, "a comic epic in prose," provides an instructive approach to the novel. Seymour Gross finds the comic vision the predominant quality of the novel in "A Long Day's Living: The Angelic Ingenuities of *Losing Battles*." Differing with other critics who discover an elegiac or even tragic tone in the novel, Gross stresses the book's life-affirming balance in depicting a family who has its sufferings and a Miss Julia who has her comic aspect. Ultimately, he contends, there are no "sides"; the novel's purpose is not to argue but to show "what it would be like *really* to believe in life." Louise Y. Gossett furthers the study of the novel's "celebratory mode" in her examination of the patterns of ceremonial behavior that confirm and sustain communal life, in "*Losing Battles:*

Festival and Celebration." Finally, Douglas Messerli, in "'A Battle with Both Sides Using the Same Tactics': The Language of Time in *Losing Battles*," proposes that the nature and different uses of language are both the method and theme of the novel. In some ways suggesting Boatwright's earlier analysis, Messerli shows that language for the family is ritualistic, used as a shield against time, whereas for Julia, language is a source of knowledge that leads ultimately to acknowledgment of time.

One Time, One Place

Several reviewers of this collection of photographs, taken in Mississippi during the depression, have more to say of Welty's foreword than of the pictures. Daniel Curley, for example, in "A Time Exposure" (*NMW*, Spring 1972), writes that "nothing wiser than this Foreword will ever be said about the connection between her experience and her art" (Welty's essay is included in *The Eye of the Story*). Madison Jones (*NYTBR*, 21 November 1971) views the technical performance of the photographs as having "uneven value," but like the fiction, they reflect the "joy and serenity and appetite for life." Two essays in Prenshaw consider *One Time, One Place*. Barbara McKenzie's "The Eye of Time: The Photographs of Eudora Welty" goes into considerable detail about the technical qualities of the pictures, but both McKenzie and Elizabeth Meese, in "Constructing Time and Place: Eudora Welty in the Thirties," explore the relation between the pictures and the fiction. They further consider what the photographs reveal of Welty's experience in rural Mississippi in the 1930s and what they illustrate of her growing awareness as an artist. Of related interest is Patti Carr Black's exhibition catalogue, *Welty* (Jackson: Mississippi Department of Archives and History, 1977), which, drawing from the same collection of 1930s photographs, links selected pictures with passages from the fiction.

The Optimist's Daughter

Granville Hicks's review, "Universal Regionalist" (*NLd*, 7 August 1972), typifies the reaction to the book: "Meanings within meanings unfold in the narrative until one is awed by the novella's richness." Michael Wood, in "Cunning Time" (*NYRB*, 29 June 1972), writes of the novel as "powerful," though he finds the symbolism transparent and he misreads the "withering sarcasm," which he attributes to Welty's use of the word "optimist." Reviewing the novel in the *Hudson Review* (Autumn 1972), Patricia Meyer Spacks locates the central action in the character Laurel Hand's effort to *see*: "Really to look at what is there, and what has been, is to come to terms with actuality without succumbing to it." Spacks offers further insights into the novel in *The Female Imagination* (Alfred A. Knopf, 1975), exploring a "faint ambiguity of value" that links the book with *Delta*

Wedding and *Losing Battles*. Spacks examines the balancing of Fay and Laurel, noting not only Laurel's commitment to memory but her withdrawal from life, and concludes that the victorious self-knowledge that Laurel attains at the end is that "memory must be independent of possession."

Much less sympathetic with Fay and her kind are Cleanth Brooks, John Edward Hardy, William J. Stuckey, and Thomas Daniel Young. In an article on theme and character, "The Past Reexamined: *The Optimist's Daughter*" (*MissQ*, Fall 1973), Brooks contrasts Fay's obliviousness to the past to Laurel's recovery of the past and the "pieties that bind one generation back to another." Hardy reaches a similar conclusion about Fay in his essay in Prenshaw, discussed above in the section on marriage and the family. Stuckey, in "The Use of Marriage in Welty's *The Optimist's Daughter*" (*Crit*, Vol. 17, No. 2, 1975), takes a strongly pro-Becky position in his study of the encounter between Fay and Laurel as the expression of "two different conceptions of marriage: Becky's and Laurel's on the one side and Fay's and her mother's on the other." In "Social Form and Social Order: An Examination of *The Optimist's Daughter*," in Prenshaw, Young declares that, in Fay, Welty portrays the "poverty of a life unsupported by a sustaining tradition," which is unmatched by any other character in her fiction.

These thematic studies all make useful observations about the novel's treatment of life, unexamined and examined, of experience enacted and perceived. Writing an early review of the *New Yorker* version of the story, Reynolds Price makes some wise comments about the role of the onlooker and the act of seeing as the central issues of the work. Based on the story's ending, which differs from that of the novel, Price concludes that the onlooker's stance is "the human stance," and that "the aims of participation are union, consolation, continuance"—all "doomed" (*Shenandoah*, Spring 1969). In a chapter that appeared originally in the *Southern Review*, "Life with People: Virginia Woolf, Eudora Welty and *The Optimist's Daughter*" (April 1977), Kreyling contends that the final version of the story significantly changes the nature of Laurel's (the onlooker's) discovery. He persuasively shows that Laurel's understandings about herself, about what is embraced in "family," and about what is required and not required by memory lead ultimately to participation, to a connection with others and the world: "The unity is created by the act of seeing." John F. Desmond's concluding essay in his collection, "Pattern and Vision in *The Optimist's Daughter*," offers a broad study of the themes, structure, and imagery of the novel. Most suggestive is his analysis of "Welty's structural technique of shifting between raw experience and memory, past and present," in ways that correspond to the thematic shifts between the public life of Judge McKelva and the private interior life of Laurel. Finally,

Welty's own essay about the novel, her preface to the 1980 Franklin Library edition, gives unique insights into the composition of the novel, the central themes, and autobiographical parallels.

The Eye of the Story

Like most reviewers, Victoria Glendinning, in "Eudora Welty in Type and Person" (*NYTBR*, 7 May 1978), found the collected essays "invigorating" and illuminating. Calling to mind Curley's judgment of the foreword to *One Time, One Place*, she writes that "the pieces in this book about the climate of the fiction writer's mind should be prescribed reading for all literary critics." Her observation that Welty "writes not so much as a critic as a sensitive reader" is further developed by Michael Kreyling and Ruth Vande Kieft, who discuss the collection in the two concluding essays in Prenshaw. In "Words into Criticism: Eudora Welty's Essays and Reviews," Kreyling identifies certain key words that signify Welty's main concerns and aims in fiction. He finds "*imagination, love* and *communication, passion*" to be the "hallmarks of Welty's criticism." In a warm, appreciative reading of the essays and reviews, Kreyling finds at the "vital heart" of the criticism, as with the fiction, a "reverence for words," "for the physical world," and "for the individual soul." Vande Kieft, in "Looking with Eudora Welty," should be consulted for her careful reading of the various critical and personal pieces in the collection, her analysis of the links between Welty's fiction and criticism, and her perceptive account of the "life patterns" or designs that give form to—and reflect—the artist Welty's eye.

The Collected Stories of Eudora Welty

Reviewing the volume in *Time* (3 November 1980), Paul Gray's "Life, with a Touch of the Comic" notes that "a collection of stories is the writer's equivalent of a retrospective exhibit, handily displayed in a portable museum without walls." He finds Welty surviving "the ordeal of retrospection beautifully," a judgment shared universally by other reviewers of the collection. Walter Clemons, in "A Short-Story Bonanza" (*Newsweek*, 3 November 1980), writes that the favorites, mainly stories set in Mississippi, are deservedly well known, but "what isn't so well known is that Welty is an experimental writer with access to the demonic. . . . She ranges wider than usually believed." Although the variety of Welty's fiction surprises no one familiar with the stories, the attention that reviewers have given "range" suggests that the stereotyping of Welty as regionalist, with the limitations implicit in the term, may still have some currency or is thought to have. If so, the retrospective readings of these forty-one stories have corrected the critical myopia. In "A Collection of Discoveries" (*NYTBR*, 2 November 1980), Maureen Howard admires the range of the stories, observing that "there is so much virtuosity in 'The Collected Stories,' such a testing of the form, we cannot help but see that the writing was always fresh to her and of great interest. That is the mark of genius." One of the most instructive reviews is Reynolds Price's "The Collected Stories of Eudora Welty" in the *New Republic* (1 November 1980). After raising the issue of whether a different arrangement of stories, ordered by composition date rather than by sequence of original publication, might have been desirable, Price goes on to discuss the nature and significance of Welty's achievement as represented by the collection. He identifies a central vision of human experience in Welty's fiction that unifies the stories "from first to last": "'Human creatures are compelled to seek one another in the hope of forming permanent bonds of mutual service, not primarily from an instinct to continue the species' (children are only minor players in her cast), 'but from a profound hunger, mysterious in cause, for individual gift and receipt of mutual care.' ('Tenderness' is Welty's most sacred word.) 'So intense is the hunger however that, more often than not, it achieves no more than its own frustration—the consumption and obliteration of one or both of the mates.' (The words 'bitter' and 'shriek' occur as frequently, and weightily, as 'tenderness.')" He concludes that "the breadth of Welty's offering is finally most visible not in the variety of types—farce, satire, horror, lyric, pastoral, mystery—but in the clarity and solidily and absolute honesty of a lifetime's vision." Price's review, along with numerous other retrospective essays, gives evidence of the growing literary stature of Eudora Welty in this country and abroad.

The literary achievement of Eudora Welty is impressive, as this present survey bears witness. Her stature as a writer has grown steadily—*Losing Battles* and *The Optimist's Daughter* are two of her strongest works. And there is promise of publication of new work in the near future. Perhaps the most pleasurable activity ahead for critics will be the reading and reviewing of the new work. For the present, there are many areas of the literary career and approaches to the existing fiction where scholarly and critical attention is needed. One would hope to see a complete descriptive bibliography of works by Welty and the continued updating of checklists of secondary material, manuscripts and letters, and interviews. A collection of the most important interviews would be an invaluable biographical aid. As for critical studies of the fiction, much of the work in the past has dealt with single stories or books. Full-length studies by Vande Kieft and Kreyling have given a more comprehensive treatment of Welty's development as a writer, but more attention to the relation between works and to the career as a whole is needed. The publication of *The Collected Stories of Eudora Welty* has already spurred study in this direction, with retrospective reviews taking account of Welty's achievement over the past forty years. Other critical approaches that will likely bear fruit, some of which Kreyling follows in his recent book, are studies of literary influences and sources, psychological patterns, sociological and historical sources and themes, and Welty's use of humor and comedy. There has been little feminist criticism of Welty's fiction, but one would expect to see such study, with attention to the treatment of marriage and the family, as well as to the psychological and sociological roles of the women characters. A final impression from reviewing the present critical work on Welty is that, despite the considerable study of structure and technique, poetic and colloquial language, plot and character, the fiction of Eudora Welty has not yet received the scale and depth of critical analysis that it warrants.

10 MARTHA E. COOK

Flannery O'Connor

Flannery O'Connor (1925-1964) has been properly labeled a "major-minor" American writer. During her lifetime O'Connor's work was recognized by fellowships from the *Kenyon Review* and the Ford Foundation; her posthumous *Complete Stories* (1971) received a National Book Award. Though many readers and critics prefer the stories, her novels *Wise Blood* and *The Violent Bear It Away* have received the most critical attention.

The body of O'Connor's work is small, but the body of critical material is unusually large. By mid-1981 two pamphlets, two collections of essays, and eighteen book-length critical or bibliographical studies had appeared. In 1958 the first major critical attention came with the Fall issue of the journal *Critique*, devoted to the fiction of O'Connor and J. F. Powers. The prestigious *Sewanee Review* published the novella "The Lame Shall Enter First" with two seminal critical essays (July-September 1962) and later a group of four articles on O'Connor's work (April-June 1968). The annual *Flannery O'Connor Bulletin* was founded in 1972. In March 1976 the French journal *Delta* published an O'Connor Issue. The Summer 1981 issue of the Catholic quarterly *Renascence* indicated that over the years it has included twenty-five articles on O'Connor's fiction, with a special issue for Autumn 1969.

All of the major anthologies of American literature—Norton, Macmillan, St. Martin's, Wiley—reprint stories by O'Connor. On the other hand, the journal *American Literature* has published only one article focusing on O'Connor's fiction (March 1974), though scholarly and critical books on her work are regularly reviewed in its pages.

O'Connor's work has also been popular with filmmakers. "The Life You Save May Be Your Own" was produced for CBS television in 1957; "The Displaced Person," for the PBS American Short Story Series in 1977. Most significant is the commercial feature film of *Wise Blood* (1980), directed by

John Huston and produced by Michael and Kathy Fitzgerald, with a screenplay by Benedict Fitzgerald.

There has been considerable disagreement among critics about the relative significance of O'Connor's religious themes and her artistry. Too much has been written with a worshipful tone, yet the finest artistic elements of her work have not received the critical attention they deserve. As often happens, O'Connor criticism has begun to repeat itself. Critics—or fans—analyze her work without considering the mass of criticism that has gone before. At the same time, there are important topics that go untouched. However, O'Connor has been well served by two major bibliographies, one primary, the other secondary (including work published through 1973).

BIBLIOGRAPHY

There is a full-length bibliography of the criticism of O'Connor's work in the G. K. Hall series of Reference Guides in Literature: Robert E. Golden's *Flannery O'Connor: A Reference Guide* (Boston: G. K. Hall, 1977). Because it is published in the same volume as Mary C. Sullivan's shorter guide to Caroline Gordon, it is in some ways less accessible than it should be; but it is a very useful work. Golden lists books and shorter writings (articles, reviews, and parts of books) for each year in the usual G. K. Hall format. Of course a chronological listing has both advantages and disadvantages. Golden's work is careful (a check reveals only a few errors in citation, and he corrects mistakes seen in many earlier bibliographies of critical work on O'Connor) and thorough (the bibliography appears to be essentially complete through 1973, but other bibliographical sources must be consulted for subsequent years). His descriptive annotations are clear and helpful. His list of sixty-five dissertations (through 1975) is the most complete yet compiled. The work contains an accurate, useful index.

There is also a book-length bibliography of writings by O'Connor: David Farmer's *Flannery O'Connor: A Descriptive Bibliography* (Garland, 1981). As Farmer states, his purpose is "to set forth and describe all her published writings." He includes all first printings of O'Connor's work, fiction, nonfiction, letters, interviews, and later reprintings by O'Connor, but not other reprints such as textbooks or anthologies. Section A, "Books," contains twenty-five entries of different editions or platings, each described in meticulous detail. Other sections include contributions to books; contributions to periodicals (including sixty-nine book reviews); miscellaneous appearances in print; early published art work; translations of O'Connor's work; film and television adaptations; and parodies. Although the last section seems somewhat out of place in a descriptive bibliography, it is both useful and interesting. The book also contains thirteen illustrations: reproductions of dust jackets, book covers, and original cartoons. Farmer's work fills a major gap in O'Connor scholarship, superseding all earlier efforts at primary bibliography. However, Lorine M. Getz, in *Flannery O'Connor: Her Life, Library, and Book Reviews* (Edwin Mellen, 1981), lists seventy-three published book reviews by O'Connor and reprints seventy-one (they are all very brief).

Most earlier bibliographies of O'Connor criticism are superseded by Golden's reference guide. Some were helpful, but others were incomplete and error-filled. Today one need consult only a few specialized listings. Joan Brittain and Leon V. Driskell's critical study, *The Eternal Crossroads: The Art of Flannery O'Connor* (Lexington: University Press of Kentucky, 1971), contains a listing of thirty-five "Biographical Articles." Allen Lackey (*BB*, October-December 1973) includes a few anthologies that contain stories by O'Connor, some master's theses, and a few reviews of critical works on O'Connor, which one might otherwise have difficulty locating.

Melvin J. Friedman's section on O'Connor in *A Bibliographical Guide to the Study of Southern Literature*, edited by Louis D. Rubin, Jr. (Baton Rouge: Louisiana State University Press, 1969) includes a brief perceptive essay summarizing the significant critical attention which O'Connor had received up to that point and suggesting what remained to be done in O'Connor criticism and scholarship. The short bibliography includes twenty-eight critical articles or parts of books, two pamphlets, and a collection of essays. Friedman's essay remains provocative, since some of what he suggests still needs to be done; and his bibliography serves to identify important early work on O'Connor.

For the student or beginning critic of O'Connor's work, Dorothy Walters's *Flannery O'Connor* (Twayne, 1973) provides the best selected bibliography of secondary sources, with brief, helpful annotations. Each entry that Walters has chosen is a significant one, and her citations are for the most part accurate.

Two other useful bibliographies are focused on specific topics or techniques. Jackson R. Bryer and Nanneska N. Magee's "The Modern Catholic Novel: A Selected Checklist of Criticism," in *The Vision Obscured: Perceptions of Some Twentieth-Century Catholic Novelists*, edited by Melvin J. Friedman (Fordham University Press, 1970), includes thirty-five entries on O'Connor that concern religious aspects of her fiction. In *The Pruning Word: The Parables of Flannery O'Connor* (Notre Dame, Ind.: University of Notre Dame Press, 1976), John R. May gives "A Selected Bibliography of Textual Analyses," containing forty-seven entries organized by subject.

EDITIONS

O'Connor's first novel, *Wise Blood*, was published in 1952 by Harcourt, Brace, as was her first collection of short stories, *A Good Man Is Hard to*

Find and Other Stories, in 1955. O'Connor later moved to the publishing house of Farrar, Straus and Cudahy, which published her second novel, *The Violent Bear It Away*, in 1960 and reissued *Wise Blood* in 1962 with a brief preface by O'Connor. In 1964 the important Signet paperback *Three by Flannery O'Connor*, containing the two novels and the stories in *A Good Man Is Hard to Find*, was published by New American Library. The second collection of stories, *Everything That Rises Must Converge*, was published by Farrar, Straus and Giroux in 1965, the year after O'Connor's death, with an introduction by Robert Fitzgerald.

Farrar, Straus and Giroux also published *Mystery and Manners: Occasional Prose*, selected and edited by Sally and Robert Fitzgerald, in 1969, and *The Complete Stories*, including in order of composition the stories from O'Connor's University of Iowa master's thesis, other uncollected stories, and the two volumes mentioned above, as well as an introduction by Robert Giroux, in 1971.

Apparently the volume *A Good Man Is Hard to Find* is no longer in print, and *The Violent Bear It Away* is available only in paperback from Farrar, Straus and Giroux. In 1980 the Franklin Library published an elaborately bound limited edition of *The Complete Stories* in its series of The Collected Stories of the World's Greatest Writers. The introduction and the text are the same as the 1971 edition, but several illustrations by Ben F. Stahl are added.

David Farmer's descriptive bibliography lists many important translations of O'Connor's stories, novels, and nonfiction.

MANUSCRIPTS AND LETTERS

The chief repository for manuscripts of O'Connor is the Flannery O'Connor Collection of the Ina Dillard Russell Library at Georgia College in Milledgeville. The bulk of the material was given to the library by Regina Cline O'Connor, the author's mother. The collection includes manuscripts of her fiction, lectures, and book reviews. Some of this material was used in the volume *Mystery and Manners*. The largest single portion of the collection is approximately 2,000 pages of *Wise Blood* in various stages of composition. The collection also contains letters to and from O'Connor, approximately 600 books that belonged to O'Connor or members of her family, editions and translations of her work, film, tapes, photographs, and so on. For a partial catalogue of the manuscripts, see Gerald Becham, "Flannery O'Connor Collection" (*FOB*, Autumn 1972). Becham, who is curator of the collection, gives some additional information in "The Flannery O'Connor Collection: GC's Vital Legacy" (*Columns*, Georgia College, Fall 1975).

Robert J. Dunn says in "The Manuscripts of Flannery O'Connor at Georgia College" (*FOB*, Autumn 1976) that he has prepared a catalogue for the collection that will be published; according to Becham, Dunn's catalogue has not been completed. In this article Dunn describes his method of organizing the manuscripts, so it should be consulted by scholars who plan to use the manuscripts.

Scholars who wish to use the Flannery O'Connor Collection must make arrangements in advance with the curator. Anyone may visit the Flannery O'Connor Memorial Room in the Ina Dillard Russell Library.

Other manuscripts and letters are scattered throughout the country. For listings, readers can consult *American Literary Manuscripts*, 2d ed., edited by J. Albert Robbins (Athens: University of Georgia Press, 1977). A major collection is 114 letters to the novelist Brainard Cheney and his wife Frances Neel Cheney, which are housed in the Special Collections, Vanderbilt University Library. This collection has four other letters by O'Connor, including two to Andrew Lytle. Another substantial group is O'Connor's seventeen letters to Roysce Smith, which can be found in George Marion O'Donnell's papers in the Special Collections, University Libraries, Washington University in St. Louis. This library also holds one letter to James Dickey.

A large number of Flannery O'Connor's letters has been published in *The Habit of Being*, edited by Sally Fitzgerald (Farrar, Straus and Giroux, 1979). Interesting and often exciting to read, the letters provide a wealth of biographical information. J. O. Tate (*FOB*, Autumn 1978), writing before the publication of the volume, calls it "an epistolary autobiography." The letters also shed light on O'Connor's methods of composition and her theories of fiction. John R. May's updated entry on O'Connor in the *Dictionary of Literary Biography Yearbook: 1980* (Detroit, Mich.: Gale, 1981) includes a detailed discussion of the significance of this volume of letters, with quotations from a number of positive reviews.

What is missing from *The Habit of Being* is the editorial apparatus that the scholar expects and needs. Fitzgerald usually puts a letter in context if necessary, but she does not always identify the correspondents fully enough. Neither does she anywhere list the correspondents. Not until page eighty-nine is the reader made aware even of the existence of "A," the one correspondent who declined to be named in the volume. Fitzgerald is not scrupulously accurate, either. She calls Father James McCown "John" throughout the volume, which includes several letters to him (see John R. May, "Blue-Bleak Embers: The Letters of Flannery O'Connor and Youree Watson," (*NOR*, September 1979). A comparison of the texts of letters to Maryat Lee published earlier (*FOB*, Autumn 1976) indicates that Fitzgerald deleted one passage from the letter of March 10, 1957, without indicating so by "dots" as is her stated editorial policy.

In her "Introduction" Sally Fitzgerald indicates that O'Connor's letters to her mother are excluded from the volume; but she speaks of "her letters" or "the letters" as if these in the volume constitute an organic whole, giving no information about other extant letters or about the depth and breadth of her search. In fact, she does not seem to have formulated a principle of selection, and she mentions no library collection other than the one at Georgia College.

Thus many questions are raised by the volume of letters, interesting and useful though it is. For example, one expects more letters to Caroline Gordon. Only in a later article, "A Master Class: From the Correspondence of Caroline Gordon and Flannery O'Connor" (*GaR*, Winter 1979), does Fitzgerald explain that Gordon had loaned several letters to a graduate student who had not returned them before. Jan Nordby Gretlund (*FOB*, Autumn 1979) explains that the two letters to Katherine Anne Porter which he is reprinting there were not found in time for inclusion in *The Habit of Being*.

Fitzgerald also does not mention any O'Connor letters that were published prior to *The Habit of Being*. Sister Mary-Alice, O.P., quotes excerpts from O'Connor's letters to her in "My Mentor, Flannery O'Connor" (*SatR*, 29 May 1965). Apparently none of these letters is included in Fitzgerald's selection. Richard Stern, who corresponded with O'Connor from 1959 to 1964, published "Flannery O'Connor: A Remembrance and Some Letters" (*Shenandoah*, Winter 1965); Fitzgerald chooses two late letters, but does not mention the earlier publication. There are a number of letters to William Sessions in *The Habit of Being*, with no indication that a substantial group of letters to Sessions was included in *The Added Dimension: The Art and Mind of Flannery O'Connor*, edited by Melvin J. Friedman and Lewis A. Lawson (Fordham University Press, 1966).

A classmate at the University of Iowa, Jean Wylder, writes of her relationship with O'Connor and gives brief excerpts of letters from 1952 to 1964 in "Flannery O'Connor: A Reminiscence and Some Letters" (*NAmRev*, Spring 1970). Wylder's letters are not mentioned in the Fitzgerald edition. Fitzgerald reprints several letters to Thomas F. Gossett and his wife Louise Gossett, without noting that Gossett has used these with letters to other correspondents in "Flannery O'Connor on Her Fiction" (*SWR*, Winter 1974) and "Flannery O'Connor's Opinions of Other Writers: Some Unpublished Comments" (*SLJ*, Spring 1974).

Other letters by O'Connor published prior to *The Habit of Being* are a group to one of her French translators, Maurice Edgar Coindreau (1958-1964), which show a side of O'Connor not seen in the volume (*Delta*, March 1976), and those to Maryat Lee already mentioned. Since the volume appeared we have seen more letters to Gordon, those to Porter, and the fascinating exchange between O'Connor and Father Watson, who is only mentioned in the volume in a 1960 letter to "A." Not even alluded to by Fitzgerald is the large body of letters to the Brainard Cheneys, who are mentioned many times in letters in *The Habit of Being*. The existence of these letters again raises questions about Fitzgerald's editorial method. The reader wonders if there was a principle of selection that Fitzgerald did not choose to reveal or perhaps one of which she was not even aware. The idea becomes more significant when one learns that Sally Fitzgerald is now at work on a biography of O'Connor. While not questioning her love and admiration for O'Connor, one wonders if she has the scholarly interest necessary for a sound literary biography.

BIOGRAPHY

There is still no full-length biography of Flannery O'Connor. The longest biographical treatment is Part I of Lorine M. Getz's *Flannery O'Connor: Her Life, Library, and Book Reviews* (Edwin Mellen, 1980). The sixty-page essay traces "her roots in the Catholic and Southern tradition, her literary apprenticeship amid Northern artistic leaders and contemporary intellectual currents, and the achievement of her artistic maturity based upon the integration of her regional materials and theological concerns." Getz does not seem to have done much original research, and her documentation is sketchy and sometimes incorrect. According to Getz, Sally Fitzgerald "read and edited Part I, adding and clarifying biographical detail." Scholars who have worked extensively on O'Connor will not find Getz's biography particularly useful.

Martha Stephens's "[Mary] Flannery O'Connor (1925-1964)," in *Southern Writers: A Biographical Dictionary*, edited by Robert Bain, Joseph M. Flora, and Louis D. Rubin, Jr. (Baton Rouge: Louisiana State University Press, 1979), gives a brief, accurate sketch, which can serve as the starting point for biographical research.

There are many short accounts of aspects of O'Connor's life by friends and associates in Milledgeville. An early one is by Margaret Inman Meaders, who was adviser to the student newspaper at the Georgia State College for Women (GSCW—now Georgia College) when O'Connor was a student. In "Flannery O'Connor: 'literary witch'" (*ColQ*, Spring 1962), she gives details about O'Connor as a student and about her life in Milledgeville in the early 1960s. Meaders's title is somewhat misleading; she gives a very interesting and positive view of O'Connor. William Kirkland, Episcopal rector, recounts details of the last years of her life in "Flannery O'Connor, the Person and the Writer" (*East-West Review*, Summer 1967). More recently, Rosa Lee Walston, former head of the English and Speech Department at GSCW, has written two articles whose titles indicate their tone: "Flannery: An Affectionate Recollection" (*FOB*, Autumn 1972) and "Flannery O'Connor as Seen by a Friend" (*Carrell*, June & December 1973). Walston includes delightful anecdotes such as the account of a luncheon at which O'Connor proclaimed that the book that meant most to her as a child was the Sears Roebuck catalogue.

Other biographical sources are by close friends whom O'Connor knew outside Milledgeville or who visited her there. Robert Fitzgerald's "Introduction" to *Everything That Rises Must Converge* (1965), written not long after O'Connor's death, is a valuable account of the year O'Connor lived with the Fitzgerald family in Connecticut. Fitzgerald gives important details concerning the progression of her illness. Louise Hardeman Abbott, a writer who sought out O'Connor's advice and soon became her friend, provides in "Remembering Flannery O'Connor" (*SLJ*, Spring 1970) a beautifully written, warm view of her visits and correspondence with O'Connor (some of her letters from O'Connor are included in *The Habit of Being*). Particularly moving is her account of the Requiem Mass for O'Connor at Sacred Heart Church in Milledgeville.

Another fine reminiscence is that by Maryat Lee, "Flannery, 1957" (*FOB*, Autumn 1976). A New York playwright whose brother became president of GSCW in 1956, Lee tells of the first year of her friendship with O'Connor, whose mother gave permission for some of her letters to be published here. On the occasion of the publication of *The Habit of Being*, James H. McCown, "Remembering Flannery O'Connor" (*America*, 1-8 September 1979), recalls his years of friendship with O'Connor while he was serving as a priest in Macon. This essay is especially valuable for the view of O'Connor's relationship with her mother. Also valuable are the reminiscent articles by Richard Stern (*Shenandoah*, Winter 1965) and Jean Wylder (*NAR*, Spring 1970) mentioned above.

Other views of O'Connor come from those who knew her only briefly. Granville Hicks in "A Writer at Home with Her Heritage" (*SatR*, 12 May 1962) recounts a visit with O'Connor. Katherine Anne Porter's essay "Gracious Greatness" (*Esprit* [University of Scranton], Winter 1964) is warm and appreciative. The essay is illustrated with a number of photographs of O'Connor's home by Paul Lowry. This memorial issue of *Esprit* also contains "Flannery O'Connor—A Tribute," with brief contributions by forty-eight persons, many of whom were personally acquainted with her. In a review of *Mystery and Manners* (*NYRB*, 21 August 1969), Richard Gilman provides an account of a visit to O'Connor in 1960, with a very interesting picture of O'Connor's mother. In "Memoir by Humpty Dumpty" (*FOB*, Autumn 1979), Russell Kirk recalls his only meeting with O'Connor in October, 1955. Kirk was inspired by reading a letter to "A" in *The Habit of Being* in which O'Connor described him as "Humpty Dumpty."

Robert Giroux, in the "Introduction" to O'Connor's *Complete Stories* (1971), gives a different view of O'Connor from that in other published accounts. He begins with a reminiscence from Paul Engle, her teacher at the University of Iowa; he also recounts his first and subsequent meetings with O'Connor as her editor and discusses her relationships with Thomas Merton, Elizabeth McKee (her agent), and others.

Interviews with O'Connor are also important biographical sources, though most are relatively difficult to obtain. Several in student publications took place when O'Connor was making frequent appearances on college campuses. "Motley Special: Interview with Flannery O'Connor" (*Motley* [Spring Hill College, Mobile, Ala.], Spring 1959) is described as "a proxy report" of a discussion with students. "An Interview with Flannery O'Connor," edited by Cyrus Hoy and Walter Sullivan (*Vagabond* [Vanderbilt University], February 1960; rptd. in *Writer to Writer: Readings on the Craft of Fiction*, edited by Floyd C. Watkins and Karl F. Knight, Boston: Houghton Mifflin, 1966), is a group interview with students and faculty members. "An Interview with Flannery O'Connor" by Katherine Fugina, Faye Rivard, and Margaret Sieh (*Censer* [College of St. Teresa, Winona, Minn.], Fall 1960) contains an important statement on the treatment of blacks in O'Connor's fiction. Two other significant interviews appear in Catholic periodicals, one by Gerard E. Sherry (*Critic*, June-July 1963), the other by C. Ross Mullins, Jr. (*Jubilee*, June 1963). Mullins's article is illustrated with excellent photographs of O'Connor on the farm.

Another article that is of some biographical significance is by the black poet and novelist Alice Walker, who grew up in a sharecropper's shack down the road from Andalusia, the O'Connors' country home. In "Beyond the Peacock: The Reconstruction of Flannery O'Connor" (*Ms.*, December 1975), Walker tells of making a visit to the area with her mother. While she expresses appreciation for O'Connor as an artist, O'Connor as a person comes to symbolize for Walker much of the tension between blacks and whites in the South of her youth.

Barbara McKenzie's *Flannery O'Connor's Georgia* (Athens: University of Georgia Press, 1980) consists of a brief text, photographs of rural middle Georgia by McKenzie, and reproductions of some photographs from the O'Connor Collection at Georgia College. Many of the photographs were published earlier in articles by McKenzie (*GaR*, Summer 1975, Summer 1977, and Winter 1977). Although some of the pictures are interesting, the book does not add a new dimension to O'Connor's life or to her fiction.

Although Josephine Hendin's *The World of Flannery O'Connor* (Bloomington: Indiana University Press, 1970) is primarily a critical study, she opens with a view of O'Connor as a woman. Hendin tries to see O'Connor as a product of Southern society, always torn between the roles of "the perfect daughter" and "the enigmatic writer." But Hendin's complete lack of sympathy for the South keeps her interpretation of O'Connor's personality from being convincing.

Robert Coles, in *Flannery O'Connor's South* (Baton Rouge: Louisiana State University Press, 1980), attempts to shed light on O'Connor's fiction by looking in detail at the South in which she lived and wrote. He is particularly interested in race and class conflicts in the 1950s and 1960s in this region, in Southern fundamentalist religion, and in the intellectual life of O'Connor herself. Coles, who knew O'Connor briefly toward the end of her life, uses quotations from *Mystery and Manners* and *The Habit of Being*, along with extensive material gleaned from interviews and experiences he and his wife had in the South. Coles offers little new information about O'Connor's life, but a reader unfamiliar with the region might find that he offers some insight into O'Connor's fiction.

CRITICISM: BOOKS AND PAMPHLETS

The first substantial study of O'Connor's work is Robert Drake's pamphlet, *Flannery O'Connor: A Critical Essay*, in the Contemporary Writers in Christian Perspectives series (Grand Rapids, Mich.: William B. Eerdmans, 1966). As Stuart L. Burns has pointed out, Drake "set the standard for the nature and thrust of most subsequent criticism of her work" when he focused on the central theme of the encounter with Christ (*MissQ*, Fall 1974). Drake also expresses the controversial opinion that O'Connor's "real *forte* is the short story. . . ." Praising *A Good Man Is Hard to Find* as probably her best volume, Drake notes that readers who don't share her "Christian concerns" may not be able fully to understand and appreciate her work; this point has provoked much discussion as well. Excerpts from this work are published as a chapter in *Religion and Modern Literature*, edited by G. B. Tennyson and E. E. Erickson, Jr. (Grand Rapids Mich.: William B. Eerdmans, 1975). In a more recent article, "Flannery O'Connor and American Literature" (*FOB*, Autumn 1974), Drake defines her place in the canon as "a kind of major-minor figure."

A second pamphlet was published the same year as Drake's, Stanley Edgar Hyman's *Flannery O'Connor*, No. 54 of the University of Minnesota Pamphlets on American Writers (Minneapolis: University of Minnesota Press, 1966). Calling her "a fiction writing theologian," Hyman enters the controversy of whether O'Connor's beliefs interfere with the acceptance of her art. Opposing Drake, Hyman calls O'Connor's novels "better and more important than even the best of her stories" and sees *The Violent Bear It Away* as her masterpiece. Probably the strongest aspect of Hyman's study is his perceptive identification of the recurring themes and symbols in O'Connor's fiction.

The first major work on O'Connor is a collection of essays edited by Lewis A. Lawson and Melvin J. Friedman, *The Added Dimension: The Art and Mind of Flannery O'Connor* (Fordham University Press, 1966). In his introduction Friedman gives an excellent overview of O'Connor's fiction, which remains very helpful for the beginning reader or critic. Then follow ten critical essays commissioned for the volume: Frederick J. Hoffman, "The Search for Redemption: Flannery O'Connor's Fiction"; Louis D. Rubin, Jr., "Flannery O'Connor and the Bible Belt"; C. Hugh Holman, "Her Rue with a Difference: Flannery O'Connor and the Southern Literary Tradition"; P. Albert Duhamel, "The Novelist as Prophet"; Irving Malin, "Flannery O'Connor and the Grotesque"; Caroline Gordon, "An American Girl"; Nathan A. Scott, Jr., "Flannery O'Connor's Testimony: The

Pressure of Glory"; M. Bernetta Quinn, O.S.F., "Flannery O'Connor, A Realist of Distances"; Harold C. Gardiner, S.J., "Flannery O'Connor's Clarity of Vision"; and Melvin J. Friedman, "Flannery O'Connor's Sacred Objects." Lawson and Friedman chose a fine variety of critics, and each of these essays represents an important perspective from which to view O'Connor's work.

The Added Dimension also includes a section entitled "Flannery O'Connor in Her Own Words," containing an important group of letters edited by William Sessions, "A Collection of Statements" from O'Connor's essays and interviews edited by Lawson, the lecture "Fiction Is a Subject with a History—It Should Be Taught that Way," and a lecture on the grotesque in fiction edited by Norman Charles. Lawson's primary and secondary bibliography, the first substantial one, closes the volume.

The second edition of *The Added Dimension* (paperback, 1977) dropped the section "Flannery O'Connor in Her Own Words" because of "copyright considerations" (perhaps caused by the publication of *Mystery and Manners* in 1969). Added were two helpful essays by Friedman, "'The Perplex Business': Flannery O'Connor and Her Critics Enter the 1970s," which is especially important since the bibliography is not updated, and "Postscript: A Personal Note," which summarizes the critical attention paid to O'Connor in France and describes the French translations of her fiction.

A second collection of essays on O'Connor's work is a volume in the Christian Critic Series, *Flannery O'Connor*, edited by Robert Reiter (St. Louis, Mo.: B. Herder, 1968). It contains ten previously published essays, all emphasizing the Catholic or Christian element in O'Connor's fiction: Brainard Cheney, "Flannery O'Connor's Campaign for Her Country"; Melvin J. Friedman, "Flannery O'Connor: Another Legend in Southern Fiction"; John Hawkes, "Flannery O'Connor's Devil"; Brainard Cheney, "Miss O'Connor Creates Unusual Humor Out of Ordinary Sin"; Lewis Lawson, "Flannery O'Connor and the Grotesque: *Wise Blood*"; Robert Fitzgerald, "The Countryside and the True Country"; Sister M. Joselyn, O.S.B., "Thematic Centers in 'The Displaced Person'"; P. Albert Duhamel, "Flannery O'Connor's Violent View of Reality"; Sister Jeremy, C.S.J., "*The Violent Bear It Away*: A Linguistic Education"; and Ted R. Spivey, "Flannery O'Connor's View of God and Man." Although these essays are not difficult to obtain in the original sources, together they represent a substantial part of the critical attention that O'Connor had received up to this time.

The first book-length critical study of O'Connor's fiction is Carter Martin's *The True Country: Themes in the Fiction of Flannery O'Connor* (Nashville, Tenn.: Vanderbilt University Press, 1969). Martin's study grew out of a 1967 dissertation. Seeing, as Robert Fitzgerald does, that the genre of O'Connor's work is "Christian tragicomedy," Martin asserts that she "writes from an orthodox Christian point of view but grinds no theological ax. . . ." In his first three chapters Martin effectively analyzes types of characters in the fiction: "Corruptions of the Spirit" (those ignorant of grace), "The Presence of Grace" (the few characters who are positive by nature), and "Manifestations of Grace" (those who experience epiphanies). However, the last three chapters lack coherence and are not as effective. He analyzes the Gothic or grotesque element of the fiction, the functions of grim humor and comic humor, and the use of satire and irony and throughout perhaps raises more questions than he answers.

The reviewers were generally kind to Martin. Louise Gossett praised the work as a whole (*AL*, November 1969), as did Miles Orvell (*SR*, January-March 1970). Maurice Bassan spoke positively of *The True Country* too, though he also noted that Martin does not consider O'Connor's "inflexibility" and "unfortunate smugness" (*MissQ*, Fall 1969). Martin has continued to publish on O'Connor, analyzing the thesis stories in "Flannery O'Connor's Early Fiction" (*SHR*, Spring 1973) and discussing the still thorny subject of "Comedy and Humor in Flannery O'Connor's Fiction" (*FOB*, Autumn 1975).

The next study is the controversial *The World of Flannery O'Connor* by Josephine Hendin (Bloomington: Indiana University Press, 1970). Reactions of reviewers range from that of Brom Weber, who writes that Hendin possesses "the kind of knowledge and tact required to deal with so unique a writer as O'Connor" (*SatR*, 18 July 1970), to that of Walter Sullivan, who flatly states that "Mrs. Hendin writes of Flannery O'Connor not because she admires her work, but because she despises her values. . . ." (*AL*, March 1971). Although Melvin J. Friedman sees Hendin as helpful in providing a balance to overly religious interpretations of O'Connor's work, he acknowledges that "Hendin emerges from her book as the very type of the Northern 'interleckchul' whom Flannery O'Connor felt so uncomfortable with" (*SLJ*, Spring 1973).

Hendin opens with a look at O'Connor herself and her "world." Emphasizing that there is more to O'Connor's fiction than Catholicism, Hendin places it somewhere between the symbolism of Faulkner and the objective realism of Robbe-Grillet, though most later critics do not find her categorization helpful. Likewise, few readers would agree that O'Connor's work resembles William Burroughs and "the literature of disgust." In a kind of psychoanalytical approach, Hendin finds that the themes in the fiction, such as the past versus the present and the parent versus the child, reflect the conflicts that O'Connor faced in her life. Hendin labels *Wise Blood* and *The Violent Bear It Away* "novels of initiation"; to her both illustrate "the impossibility of either growth or adult life" and lack "the power and force" of the short stories. Hendin sees O'Connor as failing to portray "the interpenetration of the past and the present" and thus remaining out of the mainstream of Southern literature. Although some of

Hendin's material is thought-provoking, most of what she says seems too far removed from what O'Connor wrote.

Leon V. Driskell and Joan T. Brittain's critical study, *The Eternal Crossroads: The Art of Flannery O'Connor* (Lexington: University Press of Kentucky, 1971), is less controversial than Hendin's work. Four earlier articles by Driskell and Brittain plus Brittain's earlier bibliographical work (*BB*, September-October 1967, January-April 1968) are incorporated into this volume. Their primary emphasis is on form; they also study a variety of influences on O'Connor's fiction: the somewhat superficial influence of Nathanael West, the "kinship" with Hawthorne, and the transcendence of material from Mauriac. Louise Y. Gossett, in reviewing *The Eternal Crossroads*, sees this study of influences as the weakest aspect and the study of O'Connor's revisions as the strongest (*AL*, November 1972). Stuart L. Burns rightly praises Driskell and Brittain's analysis of unifying images and symbols in the short story volumes (*MissQ*, Fall 1974). They argue effectively, for example, that O'Connor was right to substitute "Parker's Back" for "The Partridge Festival" in the volume *Everything That Rises Must Converge*. The most admirable quality of *The Eternal Crossroads* is that Driskell and Brittain see O'Connor as both a religious writer and an artist.

Gilbert H. Muller's *Nightmares and Visions: Flannery O'Connor and the Catholic Grotesque* (Athens: University of Georgia Press, 1972) was lauded by the reviewers. On the dust jacket Walter Sullivan hails it as "the best book on Flannery O'Connor that has been published thus far." Louise Y. Gossett calls it "a distinguished study" (*AL*, January 1973), while David Farmer describes it as "a clear and refreshingly concise" work (*FOB*, Autumn 1973). Although Muller's study (which began as a 1967 Stanford University dissertation) covers a fairly grim subject, it is a delight to read. He connects O'Connor solidly with the grotesque tradition in art, illustrating her affinities with painters such as Bosch: "Flannery O'Connor creates a landscape wherein life is already hellish. . . ." After giving an overview of the grotesque tradition in American literature, Muller makes the important distinction between the Gothic and the grotesque that so many critics have found difficult. He concludes that O'Connor uses "Catholic and broadly Christian doctrines to illuminate emotions and experiences that emerge from a grotesque perspective." Mueller's brief work offers insights into O'Connor's work not to be found in many longer studies. He also has a more detailed analysis of "The Artificial Nigger," which he groups with "Parker's Back" and "The Displaced Person" as O'Connor's best stories, in "The City of Woe: Flannery O'Connor's Dantean Vision" (*GaR*, Summer 1969).

Miles Orvell's study, *Invisible Parade: The Fiction of Flannery O'Connor* (Philadelphia: Temple University Press, 1972), received praise from several reviewers for placing O'Connor's work in the tradition of the American Romance (J. O. Tate, *FOB*, Autumn 1973, and Stuart L. Burns, *MissQ*,

Fall 1974). Melvin J. Friedman calls *Invisible Parade* "as good a book as we have on the Georgia writer," although he deplores Orvell's "rather too cute geographical introduction" (*AL*, May 1973). Orvell, who quotes in his preface O'Connor's own statement from *Mystery and Manners* about the impossibility of a New York critic's understanding a Southern writer, should have been sensitive enough not to open his critical discussion with a tasteless story about going to Milledgeville and meeting black people who reminded him of the characters in "Everything That Rises Must Converge."

But Orvell offers much that is rewarding to his reader, not only his placing of O'Connor in the Southern, Catholic, Romance, and native American humor traditions, but also his analyses of the fiction. Like Drake and Hendin, he sees the stories as superior to the novels; one wishes for more of the detailed explications that he gives of "Good Country People," "The Displaced Person," "The Artificial Nigger," "The Comforts of Home," and "Parker's Back." Orvell is helpful in confronting two problems that O'Connor's readers often experience: the seeming "repetitiousness" of her fiction, which is especially noticeable if one reads several works together, and the misunderstanding often experienced by the non-Catholic reader. Orvell's appendices and bibliography were valuable contributions to O'Connor scholarship; though much of his work is superseded by the recent bibliographies, his specific statements on O'Connor's revisions remain useful. Orvell's work, like Martin's and Muller's, grew out of a dissertation (Harvard University, 1970), another indication of the attention that O'Connor received in graduate study in the late 1960s and 1970s.

David Eggenschwiler's *The Christian Humanism of Flannery O'Connor* (Detroit: Wayne State University Press, 1972) is not nearly as valuable as Muller's and Orvell's studies. Although Eggenschwiler clearly wants to defend O'Connor against charges of narrowness by showing the similarity of her work to that of various theologians, sociologists, and psychoanalysts, he perhaps does a disservice to a body of fiction that he seems to admire. For example, he readily applies to O'Connor's work Freudian concepts which he admits she did not accept. Irving Malin, with whose ideas Eggenschwiler essentially disagrees, praises him as "an adept explicator of texts" (*AL*, March 1973), as does Stuart Burns, though Burns finds the thesis of Eggenschwiler's study of little value (*FOB*, Autumn 1973).

Sister Kathleen Feeley, S.S.N.D., in *Flannery O'Connor: Voice of the Peacock* (New Brunswick, N.J.: Rutgers University Press, 1972) seeks to illuminate the meaning and artistry of O'Connor's work through a study of her reading, using as evidence her underlinings and marginal comments in books from her library. In the book, which began as a 1970 Rutgers dissertation, Feeley presents a wealth of interesting and perhaps valuable material; for example, she cites passages that O'Connor marked in Mircea Eliade's *Patterns in Comparative Religion* in discussing "A Good Man Is Hard to Find" and "The Life You Save May Be Your Own" and refers to a book entitled *Memoirs of a Tattooist* in connection with "Parker's Back." Louise Y. Gossett sees much of value in Feeley's study of O'Connor's reading (*AL*, November 1972). However, as Frederick Asals notes, Feeley does not assimilate and digest the material enough to fulfill her goal of explaining "the union of reality and mystery" in O'Connor's fiction (*FOB*, Autumn 1972). Even though O'Connor's friend and admirer Caroline Gordon provided a foreword for Feeley's study, it only begins the work in this important area. Feeley's scholarly naiveté may be indicated by the fact that she calls the writer "Flannery" throughout her book.

Martha Stephens's *The Question of Flannery O'Connor* (Baton Rouge: Louisiana State University Press, 1973), a volume in the Southern Literary Studies series edited by Louis D. Rubin, Jr., has been highly praised. Both Charles Shapiro (*Novel*, Fall 1974) and Melvin J. Friedman (*SLJ*, Spring 1974) call it the best book yet on O'Connor; Friedman also labels it "usefully irreverent." On the dust jacket C. Hugh Holman is quoted as saying, "the most persuasive reading of Flannery O'Connor's work which I have seen," and Lewis Simpson as calling it "provocative criticism." While Claire Katz praises Stephens's analyses of "emotional tone and surface texture," she perceptively points out that Stephens's "critical preference for a fiction which engages the reader's empathy intrudes upon her judgment" (*AL*, May 1974).

Stephens, who first worked on O'Connor for her dissertation (Indiana University, 1968), is straightforward about what she calls "the problem of assent to O'Connor's view of life," but expresses admiration for the "high technical brilliance" that characterizes O'Connor's fiction. The analysis of what Stephens labels the "tonal dimension" of the fiction is the key element in her study. Thus she demonstrates the shift in "A Good Man Is Hard to Find" from "domestic comedy" to something quite different, a shift that troubles many readers of the story. Stephens analyzes the novels in detail, finding *The Violent Bear It Away* much stronger than *Wise Blood*, though weakened in the second part by what she calls the "too-mechanical working out of the O'Connor formula." Seeing the stories as a whole as "too predictable," Stephens provides detailed analyses of only "A Temple of the Holy Ghost," "A Circle in the Fire," and "Parker's Back." After reading *The Question of Flannery O'Connor*, one might ask why Stephens, who is obviously an intelligent critic, chose to focus on the work of O'Connor rather than to study an author whose view of life she can accept.

Dorothy Walters's *Flannery O'Connor*, No. 216 in Twayne's United States Authors Series (Twayne, 1973), follows a predictable format; and most of its ideas are fairly predictable. Seeing as she does O'Connor's work in the mode of "Christian tragicomedy," Walters offers little that is new, yet much that is sound and sensible. As a Twayne volume should, this work can serve as a good introduction to the study of O'Connor's fiction. Walters analyzes the two novels, then the stories in groups such as "Excursions into Catastrophe" and "Studies in Black and White," which in a body of fiction so unified as O'Connor's could hardly be definitive. Like Walters's analyses, her bibliography is useful for the student or beginning critic.

Another work entitled simply *Flannery O'Connor*, by Preston M. Browning, a volume in the Crosscurrents/Modern Critiques series (Carbondale: Southern Illinois University Press, 1974), returns to the view that O'Connor's "religious concerns fortified rather than weakened the artistic integrity of her creations." As one might expect, Martha Stephens castigates Browning for viewing O'Connor's fiction as "a stainless treasure" (*AL*, November 1975). Browning sees, indeed, no weaknesses in the work, which he analyzes primarily in terms of the tension of the holy and the demonic. Although throughout his study Browning corrects what he sees as misreadings by earlier critics, especially Stanley Hyman (1966), he offers little that is new in his readings of the novels and several stories.

John R. May, in *The Pruning Word: The Parables of Flannery O'Connor* (Notre Dame, Ind.: Notre Dame University Press, 1976), offers a refreshingly different, but difficult approach to the fiction of O'Connor. Although Lewis A. Lawson in "Flannery O'Connor and the Grotesque: *Wise Blood*" (*Renascence*, Spring 1965; rptd. Reiter, 1968) compares her technique to that of the parable, and J. Oates Smith in "Ritual and Violence in Flannery O'Connor" (*Thought*, Winter 1966) views her work as "a series of parables." May differs in finding the unifying principle of the fiction in the New Hermeneutic's concept of the "word" as interpreter of human existence. May's book incorporates most of his earlier articles, though one might still look at "Flannery O'Connor: Critical Consensus and the 'Objective' Interpretation" (*Renascence*, Summer 1975), in which he gives a fuller version of the material in his introduction.

May, in *The Pruning Word*, notes that many stories have not received close textual analysis, providing a bibliography of those which have. So he treats every story and novel, giving less space proportionally to the novels because they have received more critical attention. His purpose is to show the function of language in each work: "The dramatic center of Flannery O'Connor's fiction is invariably the word of revelation spoken to the protagonist that either achieves conversion or announces simple condemnation." Because he treats the entire body of fiction, May's work is particularly useful; and many of his individual explications are illuminating. However, Dean Dover finds May's approach too narrow (*JML*, No. 4, 1977); and John Ditsky feels that May "tells us in the end far more about himself than of his subject" (*AL*, November 1976). Yet Ditsky still finds the readings of the stories "persuasive"; likewise, Melvin J. Friedman praises May's close readings of the texts, especially of *Wise Blood*, "Revelation," and "Parker's Back" (*SLJ*, Spring 1980). Many readers who do not take the same approach to literature as May will still find his analyses meaningful.

Dorothy Tuck McFarland's brief *Flannery O'Connor*, in the Modern Literature Monographs Series (Frederick Ungar, 1976), treats each of O'Connor's volumes separately. McFarland especially praises O'Connor's imagery and the structure of her works. She is one of the few critics yet to treat the theme of death in the works in relation to O'Connor's illness, though she does so only sketchily. In her conclusion McFarland cites Hendin's and Stephens's volumes as evidence of the "tension between [O'Connor's] prophetic stance and the mood of the contemporary literary world." Friedman lauds McFarland for treating both "the religious dimensions of the work" and "the narrative and stylistic aspects" (*SLJ*, Spring 1980). Like Walters's Twayne volume, McFarland's study would probably be helpful for the novice reader.

In *Flannery O'Connor's South* (Baton Rouge: Louisiana State University Press, 1980), Robert Coles essentially relates his own attempt to understand O'Connor's fiction by looking beneath the surface of the South in which she lived and wrote. Thus his work is of slight biographical significance. This material was originally delivered as the Walter Lynwood Fleming Lectures in Southern History at Louisiana State University, and Coles provides no documentation except a brief bibliographical essay. Neither does he adhere to an acceptable scholarly method for using material such as interviews; in fact, he admits to having "tampered with" some of his primary material to emphasize his point. Likewise, he is too ready to speculate about what O'Connor's social and political views might have been had she lived to see the changes taking place in the South in the 1960s and 1970s. Joel Connaroe finds the overriding weakness in the volume to be that Coles "invariably sees characters as case histories, stories as tracts" (*AL*, March 1981).

As another reviewer points out, "Robert Coles is the kind of person Flannery O'Connor most distrusted: a professional academic, a psychiatrist, a Northerner, a social crusader" (*Choice*, November 1980). Yet Coles writes with admiration and respect for O'Connor and her work, and his book is very interesting. In the first lecture, "The Social Scene," he considers O'Connor's portrayal of class distinctions and racial problems, especially in "The Displaced Person" and "Everything That Rises Must Converge." The second part, "Hard, Hard Religion," includes detailed discussions of *Wise Blood* and "Parker's Back." In "A Southern Intellectual" Coles analyzes "The Lame Shall Enter First" from his own experience as a psychiatrist. Coles's book is limited in value, but he offers a view of O'Connor and her fiction that might be useful to the reader who feels alienated from the characters and settings of the stories and novels.

Carol Shloss, in *Flannery O'Connor's Dark Comedies: The Limits of Inference* (Baton Rouge: Louisiana State University Press, 1980), offers the first extended analysis of O'Connor's work from the approach of reader-response criticism. Her first two chapters are theoretical, though they are not as firmly grounded in the earlier scholarship as one might wish; she identifies her emphasis "on the qualities inherent in the work of art that are capable of eliciting certain reading responses," rather than "on the individual reader's idiosyncratic associations. . . ." Shloss makes several errors in citation, which indicate that she has not gone to original sources but has picked up incorrect information from earlier critics and bibliographers, and she has a few inexplicable misreadings. For example, she indicates that in "Revelation" Mary Grace bites Mrs. Turpin on the neck.

In analyzing seven of O'Connor's best stories and *The Violent Bear It Away*, Shloss moves toward a positive conclusion about O'Connor's fiction; but she is often forced to acknowledge either what she sees as the limitations in O'Connor's method or what she believes O'Connor would see as the limitations in her readings of the works. Shloss's reader is easily convinced that O'Connor knew that her audience had to be manipulated and that she often did so quite effectively; but the tone of some of Shloss's remarks, such as the following on "The Artificial Nigger," is disturbing: "For a statement of faith is easier for an agnostic reader to accept than O'Connor's usual tendency toward oblique insult, which ensues from the intimation that her fictional world is fraught with portentous meanings that we could see if only we were not such monstrous readers, and too limited to understand." Since Shloss praises O'Connor's style in general terms, she could have offered a more balanced study of O'Connor's fiction if she had included other aspects of the work.

Marion Montgomery's long, complex study, *Why Flannery O'Connor Stayed Home* (LaSalle, Ill.: Sherwood Sugden, 1981), is the first volume in a trilogy entitled *The Prophetic Poet and the Spirit of the Age*. Montgomery incorporates many of his earlier articles, ranging back to 1965, into this volume; but he does not always provide strong enough transitions between his many short chapters, nor does he eliminate some annoying repetition. In addition, he makes errors that should have at least been caught by a careful editor, including misspellings of characters' names and misquotations. The most disturbing is the consistent spelling of the name of Solace Layfield in *Wise Blood* as "Silas." Perhaps Montgomery sometimes goes too far in drawing analogies to contemporary events, as when he juxtaposes the thought of Eric Voegelin with an allusion to the recent fad for pet rocks.

On the other hand, a careful reading of *Why Flannery O'Connor Stayed Home* reveals an illuminating approach to O'Connor's writing. Montgomery uses O'Connor's reading and her nonfiction more effectively than has any critic to date. Seeing O'Connor as a prophetic poet offers insight into her themes of recovery of tradition and truth, as does Montgomery's extended comparison of O'Connor with T. S. Eliot. The heart of Montgomery's work, however, is the relationship between the philosophy of Eric Voegelin and the fiction of O'Connor, for to Montgomery "Miss O'Connor is a corrective to those gnostic confusions that separate heart and head, body and mind, ideas and matter—grace and nature being the final separation."

The reader who seeks thorough analyses of individual works will find only longer discussions of "A Good Man Is Hard to Find," "Everything That Rises Must Converge," and *Wise Blood*; the reader who seeks a concise, unified analysis of the whole of the fiction will be disappointed as well. But the reader who seeks a deeper understanding of O'Connor's artistry and her thought and is willing to work for it will be rewarded.

CRITICISM: ARTICLES AND PARTS OF BOOKS

Much good O'Connor criticism is to be found among the now hundreds of articles on her fiction, though some articles are not useful because they do not consider the earlier scholarship and criticism. Emphasis here is on the best or most influential; also, proportionally more attention is devoted to the articles from 1974 through 1980, both because these recent articles indicate the direction of O'Connor criticism and because the articles through 1973 have been well annotated by Robert Golden in his reference guide.

Several of the major critics of Southern literature have published significant discussions of O'Connor's work. Walter Sullivan in "Flannery O'Connor, Sin, and Grace: *Everything That Rises Must Converge*" (*HC*, September 1965; rptd. in his *Death by Melancholy: Essays on Modern Southern Fiction*, Baton Rouge: Louisiana State University Press, 1972) acknowledges that O'Connor is "not successful" with her novels, but praises "her ear for dialogue, her eye for human gestures, . . . and her vision. . . ." Though some critics feel that O'Connor lacks compassion, Sullivan sees her characters as all "loved" and "saved . . . by God's mercy." Sullivan's appreciation of the concrete reality in O'Connor's fiction is very helpful. Sullivan also contributed "Southerners in the City: Flannery O'Connor and Walker Percy" to *The Comic Imagination in American Literature*, edited by Louis D. Rubin, Jr. (New Brunswick, N.J.: Rutgers University Press, 1973).

Louis D. Rubin, Jr., in "Flannery O'Connor and the Bible Belt" (*Added Dimension*, 1966, 1977; rptd. in his *The Curious Death of the Novel: Essays in American Literature*, Baton Rouge: Louisiana State University Press, 1967), analyzes the tension in her work that derives from the "insight into religious experience." Rubin focuses on the novels, though like Drake, Sullivan, and others he sees her short stories as superior. In "Flannery O'Connor's Company of Southerners: or 'The Artificial Nigger' Read as Fiction Rather than Theology" (*FOB*, Autumn 1977), Rubin places O'Connor squarely in the tradition of "Middle Georgia humor" in the company of Augustus Baldwin Longstreet and Johnson Jones Hooper. Rubin, who calls O'Connor "a master artist," skillfully analyzes the language of the narrator in this story in great detail. From *The Habit of Being* (1979) we can now learn how conscientiously O'Connor, under the guidance of Caroline Gordon, worked to perfect her narrative voice. She was well aware, as Rubin realizes, that her narrator and her characters could not speak in the same tongue. The method that Rubin uses so effectively here could be profitably applied to other stories.

Some of the most important work on O'Connor seen in the tradition of Southern literature has been done by C. Hugh Holman. In "Her Rue with a Difference: Flannery O'Connor and the Southern Literary Tradition" (*Added Dimension*, 1966, 1977), Holman defines her South as the Piedmont, then shows how she transcends mere regionalism. In "The View from the Regency-Hyatt: Southern Social Issues and the Outer World" (in *Southern Fiction Today: Renascence and Beyond*, edited by George Core, Athens: University of Georgia Press, 1969), he compares her fiction with that of T. S. Stribling, Thomas Wolfe, and Erskine Caldwell. Both of these essays are reprinted in Holman's *The Roots of Southern Writing: Essays on the Literature of the American South* (Athens: University of Georgia Press, 1972).

Although Lewis P. Simpson has written only briefly of O'Connor, his comments identify an important difference between her and other Southern writers. In "The Southern Aesthetic of Memory" (*TSE*, 1978) and the chapter "Southern Fiction" in the *Harvard Guide to Contemporary American Writing*, edited by Daniel Hoffman (Cambridge, Mass.: Harvard University Press, 1979), Simpson emphasizes what distinguishes O'Connor from a writer like Faulkner: "Although she has a keen sense of place and writes at times with a genuine feeling for the language and humor of her region, she has no basic regard for mundane place in history or for the pieties of memory and tradition. In her stories the sense of the past is abrogated." Other critics might find it rewarding to follow up Simpson's ideas with detailed analyses of these themes—or the lack of them—in O'Connor's fiction.

Recently Thomas Daniel Young has approached O'Connor's difference from other modern Southern writers from another angle, emphasizing her concern with religious dogma. In "Redeeming Grace: Flannery O'Connor's *The Complete Stories*," in his *The Past in the Present: A Thematic Study of Modern Southern Fiction* (Baton Rouge: Louisiana State University Press, 1981), Young concludes that in O'Connor's work everything is "secondary to its Christian theme." Like writers of the Southern Renaissance, O'Connor sees value in the past, but for her that past is "the continuing tradition of orthodox Christianity."

Various other approaches have been taken to the question of the Southernness of O'Connor. P. Albert Duhamel in "The Novelist as Prophet" (*Added Dimension*, 1966, 1977) looks at her affinities with the Southern Agrarians, especially Allen Tate, in analyzing *The Violent Bear It Away*. William Koon's fascinating essay, "'Hep Me Not to Be So Mean': Flannery O'Connor's Subjectivity" (*SoR*, April 1979), explores "her transformation of traditional themes in Southern fiction into Christian themes." He emphasizes particularly her treatment of the grotesque and of the land. In "Flannery O'Connor and the Social Classes" (*SLJ*, Spring 1981), Barbara Tedford studies her use of "the traditional social structure in the South."

A number of studies have compared O'Connor with other Southern writers in addition to those already mentioned. There are several on Poe and O'Connor, including Marion Montgomery's "Of Cloaks and Hats and Doublings in Poe and Flannery O'Connor" (*SCR*, November 1978), in which he concludes that O'Connor's language is more subtle than Poe's. In an early article, "Suggs and Sut in Modern Dress: The Latest Chapter in Southern Humor" (*MissQ*, Fall 1960), Willard Thorp illustrates the parallels between O'Connor's humor and that of the humorists of the Old Southwest. Louise Westling's "The Perils of Adolescence in Flannery O'Connor and Carson McCullers" (*FOB*, Autumn 1979) indicates that while O'Connor disliked McCullers's fiction, McCullers thought that she had influenced O'Connor.

There are many other studies of influences on O'Connor or of her affinities with other writers. Many, like Orvell, see her in the tradition of romantic literature in America. For example, Thomas F. Walsh compares O'Connor with Hawthorne, finding her writing "more comic," in "The Devils of Hawthorne and Flannery O'Connor" (*XUS*, June 1966); and Frederick Asals studies O'Connor's "legacy" from Hawthorne in "Hawthorne, Mary Ann, and 'The Lame Shall Enter First'" (*FOB*, Autumn 1973). Recently Paul W. Nisly, "The Prison of the Self: Isolation in Flannery O'Connor's Fiction" (*SSF*, Winter 1980), identifies O'Connor's place in the tradition of romance in American literature as it is defined by Richard Chase. Caroline Gordon has studied the spiritual kinship of O'Connor and James in two interesting essays, "An American Girl" (*Added Dimension*, 1966, 1977) and "Rebels and Revolutionaries: The New American Scene" (*FOB*, Autumn 1974). She has also compared O'Connor with Flaubert in "Heresy in Dixie" (*SR*, April-June 1968).

Other studies focus on O'Connor in connection with religious writers or thinkers. J. O. Tate in "Flannery O'Connor's Counterplot" (*SoR*, Autumn 1980) discusses her affinities with Milton, concluding that "O'Connor imagined cosmologically all along." There are several different views of O'Connor and the thought of Teilhard de Chardin. In "Convergence of Flannery O'Connor and Chardin" (*Renascence*, Fall 1966), John J. Burke, Jr., S. J., analyzes Chardin's influence on the stories in *Everything That Rises Must Converge*, while Ralph C. Wood, "The Heterodoxy of Flannery O'Connor's Book Reviews" (*FOB*, Autumn 1976), concludes that her "fiction constitutes a critique rather than a vindication of Teilhard's naturalistic faith." (For a view similar to the latter, see Marion Montgomery, who in *Why Flannery O'Connor Stayed Home*, expresses a view similar to Wood's.) In an early article, "View from a Rock: The Fiction of Flannery

O'Connor and J. F. Powers'' (*Crit*, Fall 1958), Sister M. Bernetta Quinn, O.S.F., shows that O'Connor sees more deeply than Powers. Recently Carola Kaplan, in ''Graham Greene's Pinkie Brown and Flannery O'Connor's Misfit: The Psychopathic Killer and the Mystery of God's Grace'' (*Renascence*, Winter 1980), studies the affinities of these two modern Catholic writers, using their nonfiction as well as their fiction.

William Esty started one of the major lines in O'Connor criticism with a reference in ''In America, Intellectual Bomb Shelters'' (*Commonweal*, 7 March 1958) to O'Connor as part of ''the cult of the Gratuitous Grotesque.'' Jane Hart, in what seems to be the first critical article on O'Connor, ''Strange Earth, the Stories of Flannery O'Connor'' (*GaR*, Summer 1958), acknowledges O'Connor's connection with the Southern Gothic, but also praises ''the strong sense of rich red-clay reality'' in the fiction. Over twenty years later, little has been done with this aspect of O'Connor's work in relation to the amount that has been written about her religious themes. In ''The Grotesque in Flannery O'Connor'' (*America*, 13 May 1961), James F. Farnham replies to Esty and defends O'Connor's artistic and thematic use of the grotesque.

Another seminal article is John Hawkes's ''Flannery O'Connor's Devil'' (*SR*, July-September 1962; rptd. Reiter, 1968). Admitting that O'Connor has already disagreed with his position, Hawkes argues that in her fiction she uses ''the devil's voice as a vehicle for . . . satire.'' He also emphasizes her ''exploitation of the 'demolishing' syntax of the devil.'' Brainard Cheney immediately responded to Hawkes with ''Miss O'Connor Creates Unusual Humor out of Ordinary Sin'' (*SR*, October-December 1963; rptd. Reiter, 1968). According to Cheney, O'Connor uses the demonic in her fiction for quite a different purpose from that perceived by Hawkes: her ''art is committed to religious revolution against a secular world.'' Later Melvin J. Friedman, in ''John Hawkes and Flannery O'Connor: The French Background'' (*BUJ*, Autumn 1973), praises Hawkes's essay, refuting Cheney's position, and shows how the fiction of Hawkes and O'Connor, though dissimilar in many techniques, is similar in the use of the picaresque and the affinity with the literature of things.

Other essays continue the discussion of the grotesque, the demonic, and the violent aspects of O'Connor's fiction. Irving Malin in ''Flannery O'Connor and the Grotesque'' (*Added Dimension*, 1966, 1977) emphasizes ''her psychological awareness, not her Christian faith which, I think, often conflicts with this awareness.'' Malin also includes O'Connor in *New American Gothic* (Carbondale: Southern Illinois University Press, 1962). In *Violence in Recent Southern Fiction* (Durham, N.C.: Duke University Press, 1965), Louise Y. Gossett includes a chapter entitled ''The Test by Fire: Flannery O'Connor,'' in which she analyzes O'Connor's use of violence as ''a religious evaluation of modern life,'' a view similar to

Cheney's. Gossett only sees O'Connor's humor as "an accompaniment to the violence and grotesqueness." Harold C. Gardiner, S.J., in "Flannery O'Connor's Clarity of Vision" (*Added Dimension*, 1966, 1977), connects her introduction to *A Memoir of Mary Ann* with the element of the grotesque in her fiction.

The related problems of the use of satire and irony by O'Connor have been treated recently in articles by Mark G. Edelstein and Judith F. Wynne. Edelstein, in "Flannery O'Connor and the Problem of Modern Satire" (*SSF*, Spring 1975), notes that she is not usually viewed as a satirist—perhaps because her satire, which is from "a religious perspective," is so effective. In "The Sacramental Irony of Flannery O'Connor" (*SLJ*, Spring 1975), Wynne calls "sacramentality . . . an enriching characteristic of satiric irony," which in O'Connor's fiction "operates as a vehicle of revelation."

Several articles have focused on O'Connor's characterization and different character types in her fiction, though there is still more work to be done in this area. John F. McCarthy treats her attitude toward intellectuals in "Human Intelligence versus Divine Truth: The Intellectual in Flannery O'Connor's Works" (*EJ*, December 1966). In "Judgment in the Fiction of Flannery O'Connor" (*SR*, April-June 1968), Ruth M. Vande Kieft analyzes the character type of the "young rebel-prophet." Taking a psychoanalytical approach, Claire Katz in "Flannery O'Connor's Rage of Vision" (*AL*, March 1974) concludes that "she addresses rage and contempt to characters who at least partially represent herself." In "Flannery O'Connor and the Integration of Personality" (*FOB*, Autumn 1978), George D. Murphy and Caroline L. Cherry argue that O'Connor denies her characters this integration. From a feminist viewpoint, Louise Westling sees O'Connor's female characters as a "protest against the lot of womankind," in "Flannery O'Connor's Mothers and Daughters" (*TCL*, Winter 1978).

Two imporant articles focus on O'Connor's black characters. In "Black and White: A Study in Flannery O'Connor's Characters" (*BALF*, Spring 1978), Melvin G. Williams concludes that "Black characters are for the most part only 'issues' instead of people for O'Connor." On the other hand, Claire [Katz] Kahane in "The Artificial Niggers" (*MR*, Spring 1978) perceptively notes the differences in the characterization of blacks over the years as the struggle over civil rights became a central problem in the South. Kahane emphasizes the metaphor of the Negro as "divine humility," the masks of the Negro characters, and O'Connor's "use of the Southern stereotype."

Various thought-provoking studies analyze O'Connor's artistic techniques in order to expand the reader's understanding of the themes of her fictional works. There are very few linguistic analyses of stories or novels; but Mary Jane Kinnebrew's "Language from the Heart of Reality: A Study of Flannery O'Connor's Attitudes toward Non-Standard Dialect and Her

Use of It in *Wise Blood, A Good Man Is Hard to Find*, and *The Violent Bear It Away*'' (*LNL*, September 1976) concludes that the purpose of this dialect is "to make her characters seem to live in a real world, no matter how grotesque that world might be." In "Seduced by Language: The Case of Joy-Hulga Hopewell" (*SAF*, Autumn 1979), Cheryl Z. Oreovicz analyzes O'Connor's awareness "of how people use and are used by language. . . ."

Other studies of the artistry of O'Connor are by Melvin J. Friedman and Patricia D. Maida. In "Flannery O'Connor's Sacred Objects" (*Added Dimension*, 1966, 1977; rptd. in his *The Vision Obscured: Perceptions of Some Twentieth-Century Catholic Novelists*, Fordham University Press, 1970), Friedman sees her fiction in the context of the "literature of Things," with very helpful documentation. His many examples of the significance of things to O'Connor are convincing, though they deserve more comment than he makes. Maida has studied the imagery of blindness and vision, with related nature images, in "Light and Enlightenment in Flannery O'Connor's Fiction" (*SSF*, Winter 1976). However, she only begins what could be a profound analysis of the kind that O'Connor's fiction deserves but only infrequently gets.

Much can be learned about O'Connor's method of composition from published sources as well as manuscripts. Roy R. Male has studied "The Two Versions of 'The Displaced Person'" (*SSF*, Summer 1970); he finds the second version a great improvement, noting especially the addition of the symbolic peacock. In articles that appeared at about the same time, both Stuart Burns and Margaret Harrison analyze the composition of *Wise Blood*. Burns, in "The Evolution of *Wise Blood*" (*MFS*, Summer 1970), studies all of the early stories that were incorporated into O'Connor's first novel. Harrison, in "Hazel Motes in Transit: A Comparison of Two Versions of Flannery O'Connor's 'The Train' with Chapter I of *Wise Blood*" (*SSF*, Spring 1971), looks at the revisions from the thesis to the *Sewanee Review* version to the novel.

Burns has also studied the manuscripts in the Flannery O'Connor Collection. In "How Wide Did 'The Heathen' Range?" (*FOB*, Autumn 1975), he indicates that he found nothing publishable in the 378 pages of manuscript thought to be an unfinished novel. Actually, he says, 122 pages contain material that went into the story "The Enduring Chill"; much of the other material also appears in various published stories. Burns's article is very important for what it tells us about O'Connor's method of composition.

Another source for studying the process of composition is newspapers, of which O'Connor was an inveterate reader. Harvey Klevar has made a fascinating study of her use of material from the Milledgeville *Union Recorder* in "Image and Imagination: Flannery O'Connor's Front Page Fiction" (*JML*, September 1974). Klevar reprints articles that O'Connor seems to have used in "The Displaced Person" and "A Late Encounter with the

Enemy," which he uses to analyze "the concrete reality" of her fiction. J. O. Tate has analyzed the sources of "A Late Encounter" even more thoroughly in "O'Connor's Confederate General: A Late Encounter" (*FOB*, Autumn 1979), though to illuminate the story he also uses material which O'Connor could not have seen.

Many more articles have been written on O'Connor's novels than on the individual stories. In an early analysis Caroline Gordon, "Flannery O'Connor's *Wise Blood*" (*Crit*, Fall 1958), emphasizes that O'Connor, unlike most of her contemporaries, provides a "frame of reference larger than the individual action." Jonathan Baumbach, in "The Acid of God's Grace: The Fiction of Flannery O'Connor" (*GaR*, Fall 1963; rptd. in his *The Landscape of Nightmare: Studies in the Contemporary American Novel*, New York University Press, 1965), uses the novel as an example of the evocation of horror. In "Flannery O'Connor and the Grotesque: *Wise Blood*" (*Renascence*, Spring 1965; rptd. Reiter, 1968), Lewis A. Lawson sees Hazel Motes as a St. Anthony figure. Daniel L. Littlefield, Jr., responds to Lawson in "Flannery O'Connor's *Wise Blood*: 'Unparalleled Prosperity' and Spiritual Chaos" (*MissQ*, Spring 1970). Focusing on a minor character, Donald Gregory has analyzed the way in which doubling both emphasizes isolation and adds comedy in "Enoch Emery: Ironic Doubling in *Wise Blood*" (*FOB*, Autumn 1975). Thomas LeClair takes yet another approach in "Flannery O'Connor's *Wise Blood*: The Oedipal Theme" (*MissQ*, Spring 1976).

The early analysis by Robert M. McCown, S.J., "The Education of a Prophet: A Study of Flannery O'Connor's *The Violent Bear It Away*" (*KanMag*, 1962), is particularly significant because O'Connor herself praised it in a conversation with Joel Wells (*Critic*, August-September 1962). McCown sees the characters in the novel as allegorical, but also "passionately alive." Sister Jeremy, C.S.J., takes an interesting approach to the different "voices" in the novel in "*The Violent Bear It Away*: A Linguistic Education" (*Renascence*, Fall 1964; rptd. Reiter, 1968). William A. Fahey once more responds to Hawkes in "Out of the Eater: Flannery O'Connor's Appetite for Truth" (*Renascence*, Autumn 1967), in which he analyzes the images of eating and hunger in *The Violent Bear It Away*. Another solid analysis of the novel is that by Clinton W. Trowbridge in "The Symbolic Vision of Flannery O'Connor: Patterns of Imagery in *The Violent Bear It Away*" (*SR*, April-June 1968), in which he studies the recurrence of hunger images and the related images of loaves and fishes.

A quite different approach is taken by David R. Mayer in "*The Violent Bear It Away*: Flannery O'Connor's Shaman" (*SLJ*, Spring 1972), where Mayer uses "the phenomenon of shaman spirit possession" to interpret the character of Tarwater. One of the few examples of reader-response criticism of O'Connor's work is the excellent study of this novel by Robert H. Brinkmeyer, Jr., "Borne Away by Violence: The Reader and Flannery

O'Connor'' (*SoR*, April 1979), in which he analyzes *The Violent Bear It Away* as "the apprenticeship novel of a prophet." Readers and critics have long been aware that O'Connor as author manipulated their responses; Brinkmeyer has the appropriate approach to show how.

Peter T. Zoller effectively analyzes one of O'Connor's early stories in "The Irony of Preserving the Self: Flannery O'Connor's 'A Stroke of Good Fortune'" (*KanQ*, Spring 1977). Charles W. Mayer's "The Comic Spirit in 'A Stroke of Good Fortune'" (*SSF*, Winter 1979) shows briefly but convincingly how O'Connor's revisions add to the comedy in this story.

In an early analysis of a favorite story of many readers, "Advertisements for Grace: Flannery O'Connor's 'A Good Man Is Hard to Find'" (*SSF*, Fall 1966), W. S. Marks, III, sees O'Connor as "an incorrigible allegorist." William S. Doxey analyzes a significant problem, the shift in point of view from the grandmother to the Misfit, in "A Dissenting Opinion of Flannery O'Connor's 'A Good Man Is Hard to Find'" (*SSF*, Spring 1973). Doxey's essay may provide an answer for readers who are confused by the story but cannot understand why.

In "Flannery O'Connor's Salvation Road" (*SSF*, Spring 1966), Albert J. Griffith briefly discusses the Christ figure in "The Life You Save May Be Your Own." John F. Desmond takes a different approach in "The Shifting of Mr. Shiftlet: Flannery O'Connor's 'The Life You Save May Be Your Own'" (*MissQ*, Winter 1974-1975), where he views the main character as changing from "the potential redemptive agent" to "a satanic figure." In another religious interpretation, John D. Chapin in "Flannery O'Connor and the Rich Red River of Jesus' Blood" (*C&L*, Spring 1976) reads "The River" as "a metaphor for the process of salvation."

Robert Fitzgerald in his early article "The Countryside and the True Country" (*SR*, July-September 1962; rptd. Reiter, 1968) analyzes "The Displaced Person," looking particularly at the theme of displacement as "a religious condition." Sister M. Joselyn, O.S.B., continues this analysis in "Thematic Centers in 'The Displaced Person'" (*SSF*, Winter 1964). In "Memories of a Southern Catholic Girlhood: Flannery O'Connor's 'A Temple of the Holy Ghost'" (*Renascence*, Winter 1979), Suzanne Allen focuses on the "sexual and spiritual initiation." Seeing the story in the context of both Catholicism and Southern society is a convincing approach.

In "Dante, Tobit, and 'The Artificial Nigger'" (*SSF*, Spring 1968), Peter L. Hays concludes that Mr. Head "comes to God." An opposite reading of the story by Turner F. Byrd, "Ironic Dimension in Flannery O'Connor's 'The Artificial Nigger'" (*MissQ*, Fall 1968), declares that Mr. Head does not have "a true moment of grace," but remains "stubborn, misguided." Rubin's excellent analysis of this story takes yet another approach.

Frederick Asals explores "The Mythic Dimensions of Flannery O'Connor's 'Greenleaf'" (*SSF*, Summer 1968), both Christian and pagan. In "Blood and Land in 'A View of the Woods'" (*NOR*, Spring 1969), Don

Riso, S.J., begins his analysis in the context of myth, but sees the story primarily as a movement toward agrarianism. David Aiken, "Flannery O'Connor's Portrait of the Artist as a Young Failure" (*ArQ*, Autumn 1976), reads "The Enduring Chill" in relation to the fiction of James Joyce.

Two recent readings of "Everything That Rises Must Converge" reach opposite conclusions. In "Julian's Journey into Hell: Flannery O'Connor's Allegory of Pride" (*MissQ*, Spring 1975), John V. McDermott sees Julian in darkness at the end of the story. Robert Denham, in "The World of Guilt and Sorrow: Flannery O'Connor's 'Everything That Rises Must Converge'" (*FOB*, Autumn 1975), sees Julian positively at the conclusion. Doreen Ferlaino Fowler's "Mrs. Chestny's Saving Graces" (*FOB*, Autumn 1977) indicates that Julian's mother "exhibits both the weaknesses and strengths of the old Southern tradition," though Mary Frances Hopkins in "Julian's Mother" (*FOB*, Autumn 1978) explains that the mother is not Mrs. Chestny.

While there are far fewer close readings of O'Connor's stories than one might wish for, Frederick Asals offers a model of the New Critical method in "Flannery O'Connor's 'The Lame Shall Enter First'" (*MissQ*, Spring 1970). He analyzes in appropriate detail "the richness and coherence of language and imagery" in this novella. In another detailed study, "'Large and Startling Figures': The Place of 'Parker's Back' in Flannery O'Connor's Canon" (*AntigR*, Winter 1977), William V. Davis explains the biblical parallels and allusions in this story; he also praises O'Connor for the subtlety of "her message."

Using published versions of "The Geranium" and "Judgement Day," Ralph C. Wood has plotted the development of O'Connor's thought in "From Fashionable Tolerance to Unfashionable Redemption: A Reading of Flannery O'Connor's First and Last Stories" (*FOB*, Autumn 1978). Jan Nordby Gretlund has published "An Exile in the East," with an introduction (*SCR*, November 1978); this material is thought to be an interim version of the revision of "The Geranium" into "Judgement Day." In "Home to the True Country: The Final Trilogy of Flannery O'Connor" (*SSF*, Summer 1980), Diane Tolomeo has studied the way in which the reader is allowed to see not only visions but also their results in "Revelation," "Parker's Back," and "Judgement Day."

The greatest body of foreign criticism on O'Connor's work has come from France. As Melvin J. Friedman has explained in "Flannery O'Connor in France: An Interim Report" (*RLV*, No. 5, 1977), almost all of her work has been translated, primarily by Maurice Edgar Coindreau and Henri Morisset (see also *Added Dimension*, 1977). An early brief recognition is Michel Gresset's "Le petit monde de Flannery O'Connor" (*Mercure de France*, January 1964). In March 1976, *Delta*, published at Université Paul Valéry in Montpellier, devoted a whole issue to O'Connor, with critical articles such as Daniel Lesgoirres's "'The Displaced Person' ou 'Le Christ

Recrucifié,''' a bibliography of all translations, and one of criticism in French. Christiane Beck published "Flannery O'Connor, ou la persécution" in a special section on "Romanciers du sud" (*RANAM*, 1976). André Bleikasten contributed "The Heresy of Flannery O'Connor" (in English) to *Les Américanistes: New French Criticism on Modern American Fiction*, edited by Ira D. Johnson and Christiane [Beck] Johnson (Port Washington, N.Y.: Kennikat Press, 1978).

There is still much to be done in O'Connor scholarship and criticism; one hopes for what is needed rather than a repetition of what has already been done. The annotated secondary bibliography will need to be updated periodically. Perhaps above all there is a need for a literary biography which will illuminate both O'Connor the artist and O'Connor the woman. In criticism one looks for further application of the principles of psychoanalysis to O'Connor's characters and for more use of the techniques of reader-response criticism in studying the fiction. Finally, there can certainly be many more sound studies of her artistry, especially of her narrative techniques, her imagery, and her characterization.

11 VIRGINIA SPENCER CARR AND JOSEPH R. MILLICHAP

Carson McCullers

Carson McCullers died in 1967 at the age of fifty. Her literary canon is relatively small: five novels (one of novella length), two plays, nineteen short stories, some two dozen nonfiction pieces, a slim volume of children's verse, and a handful of poems. Although she was hailed as a *Wunderkind* when she published her first novel at twenty-three, the reviews of her subsequent books were mixed. Her works continue to be read with profound appreciation and enthusiasm throughout the world. Her fictional region is most often the American South during the 1930s and 1940s, yet there is a timelessness and universality in her that speaks to readers in a personal fashion regardless of sex, age, or background. McCullers never won a major literary prize nor wide popular acclaim, but she is frequently called to mind, by scholars and informed readers alike, and included in any listing of the major American writers of the twentieth century.

Although a resourceful researcher could locate some five hundred published essays and reviews of her work, she has been given considerably less critical attention than the major contemporary American writers with whom she is compared. However, there is a larger body of writing about her work than most scholars realize. This essay will introduce the most important parts of this extensive body of writing.

BIBLIOGRAPHY

The place to begin any study of McCullers bibliography is with *Carson McCullers: A Descriptive Listing and Annotated Bibliography of Criticism*, by Adrian M. Shapiro, Jackson R. Bryer, and Kathleen Field (Garland, 1980). Part I is an updated version of Shapiro's fine dissertation, "Carson McCullers: A Descriptive Bibliography" (Indiana University, 1977). It contains a chronological list and description of all books, plays, and separate publications, including all first printings (American and English editions), plus detailed descriptions of all subsequent printings and editions; a chronological list of McCullers's materials in books and pamphlets by other authors with subsequent appearances of these works also listed; a chronological list of the first publications of McCullers's materials in magazines and newspapers with each entry designated according to genre; adaptations of her works; recordings of McCullers; English language foreign editions of her works. (Shapiro's dissertation also lists published interviews or articles based on interviews with McCullers as well as foreign translations of her work.)

Part II of the book is an annotated bibliography of writing about McCullers compiled by Jackson R. Bryer and Kathleen Field. It is the most thorough gathering of materials to date, including many local newspaper and magazine pieces about McCullers and her work—many reviews, interviews, news stories, and editorials. It includes books and sections of books devoted to McCullers, periodical articles, reviews of McCullers's books, reviews of McCullers's plays in performance, dissertations, and foreign language material. The materials are arranged alphabetically by author's name in each section.

The first annotated list of criticism and other writings about McCullers was Robert F. Kiernan's *Katherine Anne Porter and Carson McCullers: A Reference Guide* (Boston: G. K. Hall, 1976). The spine of the book identifies it as *Carson McCullers and Katherine Anne Porter: A Reference Guide*, which somewhat confuses readers, who find the Porter material listed first. (A subsequent edition should correct the inconsistency.) Kiernan's checklist is comprehensive only through 1973. A five-page introduction summarizes the immediate critical reception of each of McCullers's books, indicates the scope and thrust of most of the academic essays, and makes valid recommendations regarding the books and articles offering the best critical assessments of McCullers's writings. It is arranged chronologically, allowing the reader to survey the development of McCullers criticism.

Kiernan's book updates and corrects earlier checklists: Stanley Stewart's "Carson McCullers, 1940-56: A Selected Checklist" (*BB*, January-April 1959); Robert S. Phillips (*BB*, September-December 1964); and William T. Stanley (*BB*, October-December 1970).

Graduate students and other scholars may want to utilize, also, J. E. Dorsey's "Carson McCullers and Flannery O'Connor: A Checklist of Graduate Research" (*BB*, October 1975), which provides a good comparative look at the graduate writings about both of these authors.

EDITIONS

All of McCullers's books are in print in American editions except *Clock Without Hands* (voted out of print on 15 November 1971, and all components ordered destroyed on 9 May 1975) and the slim volume of children's verse, *Sweet as a Pickle and Clean as a Pig* (it had one printing in 1964 and all components were ordered destroyed on 20 April 1976). For details of the editions of all of McCullers's books, both foreign and English language editions, see Shapiro's bibliography. All of McCullers's books were published first by Houghton Mifflin except the play version of *The Member of the Wedding* (New Directions, 1951). The acting version of *The Square Root of Wonderful* (Samuel French, 1959) was published after the Houghton Mifflin first edition (and only printing) in 1958, which included McCullers's "A Personal Preface."

There is no complete or definitive edition of McCullers's writings. To read all of her published works—they span four decades—one might wish to begin with the volume published last, *The Mortgaged Heart* (Boston: Houghton Mifflin, 1971), a posthumous collection consisting of her apprentice pieces (fiction) that had not been published before, as well as her poetry and a number of other pieces (fiction and nonfiction) that had been published but uncollected in the writer's lifetime. The editor, McCullers's sister Margarita G. Smith, explained in her introduction that the material selected was "to illuminate in part the creative process and development" of the author.

To find all nineteen of her published short stories, the reader should start with *The Mortgaged Heart* (for "Sucker," "Court in the West Eighties," "Poldi," "Breath from the Sky," "The Orphanage," "Instant of the Hour After," "Like That," "Wunderkind," "The Aliens," "Untitled Piece," "Correspondence," "Art and Mr. Mahoney," "The Haunted Boy," and "Who Has Seen the Wind?"). In the "Omnibus" collection, *The Ballad of the Sad Café and Other Works* (Boston: Houghton Mifflin, 1951) are "The Sojourner," "A Domestic Dilemma," "A Tree. A Rock. A Cloud," "Madame Zilensky and the King of Finland," "The Jockey," and the longer works: *The Ballad of the Sad Café, The Heart Is a Lonely Hunter, Reflections in a Golden Eye*, and *The Member of the Wedding*.

Her only uncollected published short story, "The March," appeared in *Redbook* (March 1967). This was the last short story published before her death; it was written as the first of a trilogy about blacks in the contemporary South. The other two stories, "The Man Upstairs" and "Hush Little Baby," remain unpublished (they are in the McCullers Collection at the Humanities Research Center, University of Texas at Austin).

Clock Without Hands (Boston: Houghton Mifflin, 1961) has never been published in combination with any other work. It is most easily found in its 1971 Bantam paperback edition, its last printing.

Other books published only as individual volumes are *The Square Root of Wonderful* (more easily found than the Houghton Mifflin 1958 edition is a reprint edition published by Norman S. Berg ("Sellanraa," Dunwoody, Georgia, 1971); the play version of *The Member of the Wedding*; and the volume of light verse: *Sweet as a Pickle and Clean as a Pig* (if the reader cannot find the 1964 Houghton Mifflin volume, it is more readily accessible in *Redbook* [December 1964] with a different illustrator).

To read her nonfiction prose, one might start, also, with *The Mortgaged Heart*, which includes "Author's Outline of 'The Mute'" (McCullers's working title for *The Heart Is a Lonely Hunter*), "Look Homeward, Americans," "Night Watch Over Freedom," "Brooklyn Is My Neighborhood," "We Carried Our Banners—We Were Pacifists, Too," "Our Heads Are Bowed," "Home for Christmas," "The Discovery of Christmas," "A Hospital Christmas Eve," "How I Began to Write," "The Russian Realists and Southern Literature," "Loneliness . . . an American Malady," "The Vision Shared," "Isak Dinesen: *Winter's Tales*" (book review), "Isak Dinesen: In Praise of Radiance," and "The Flowering Dream: Notes on Writing."

To read the uncollected nonfiction prose, one must consult the individual periodicals: "Author's Note" (*NYTBR*, 11 June 1961); "Books I Remember" (*HB*, April 1941); "A Child's View of Christmas" (*RB*, December 1961); "The Dark Brilliance of Edward Albee" (*HB*, January 1963); "The Devil's Idlers" (a review of Howard Coxe's *Commend the Devil, SaR*, 15 March 1941): "Look Homeward, Americans" (*Vogue*, 1 December 1940); "A Note from the Author" (*SEP*, 28 September 1963); and "Playwright Tells of Pangs" (Philadelphia *Inquirer*, 13 October 1957).

As earlier noted, all of her "serious" poetry can be found collected in *The Mortgaged Heart*.

According to the Shapiro dissertation, as of 1977 there were twenty-seven foreign editions or printings of *The Heart Is a Lonely Hunter* and four English; fourteen foreign editions or printings of *Reflections in a Golden Eye* and two English; twenty-three foreign editions or printings of *The Ballad of the Sad Café* (with and without the various collected stories) and four English; twenty-one foreign editions or printings of *The Member of the Wedding* and six English; twenty-two foreign editions or printings of *Clock Without Hands* and two English; no foreign editions of *The Square Root of Wonderful*, two English; no foreign edition of *Sweet as a Pickle and Clean as a Pig* and one English; no foreign edition of *The Mortgaged Heart* and one English. The countries in which her books have been most often translated and published are Germany (sixteen), Switzerland (fifteen), and Japan (nine). The countries in which all five of her novels have been published are Denmark, Germany, Italy, Poland, and Switzerland.

McCullers's short stories have been anthologized many times. Most frequently found are "A Tree. A Rock. A Cloud," "The Jockey," "A Domestic Dilemma," "The Sojourner," "Sucker," and more recently, "Correspondence." *The Ballad of the Sad Café* and *The Member of the Wedding* have been anthologized, as have parts of *The Heart Is a Lonely Hunter*. Probably the most often reproduced nonfiction pieces have been

"The Flowering Dream: Notes on Writing" and "Brooklyn Is My Neighborhood."

What is doubtless needed next is a *Portable McCullers* in the tradition of selected/collected works by such contemporary writers as Faulkner, Hemingway, Fitzgerald, and Steinbeck. Such a volume would be welcomed by teachers of Southern literature and general readers alike.

MANUSCRIPTS AND LETTERS

The bulk of McCullers's materials—manuscripts, galley and page proofs, letters to and from her, publishers' correspondence, photographs, and a variety of other memorabilia—is at the Humanities Research Center (HRC) of the University of Texas in Austin. Known as the Carson McCullers Collection, it includes the papers owned by her at the time of her death, the papers relating to her estate, and a cache of family papers. Most of it was acquired in 1974-1975 through the McCullers literary estate, which retained permission rights for any scholars wishing access to read or photocopy the materials.

A more detailed description of materials in the Collection at the HRC is as follows:

Works by McCullers: manuscripts of many of her early stories, lectures, children's books, and autobiographical writings ("The Flowering Dream," "Illumination," and "Night Glare"), plus many manuscripts relating to the major works; *The Heart Is a Lonely Hunter* (galley and page proofs; screenplay and filmscript by Thomas C. Ryan); *Reflections in a Golden Eye* (galley and page proofs; two versions of the screenplay by Chapman Mortimer, Gladys Hill, and John Huston); *The Member of the Wedding* (novel: two typescripts [one incomplete], galleys, and page proofs; play: at least nine drafts, including Greer Johnson's version revised by McCullers; musical: manuscripts of lyrics); *The Ballad of the Sad Café* (typescript, galleys, and page proofs of *Collected Stories* and *Ballad of the Sad Café*; play: manuscripts of Edward Albee's stage adaptation; musical: manuscripts of lyrics); *The Square Root of Wonderful* (holograph manuscript, at least twelve typescript and carbon typescript drafts, several mimeographed copies of later version); *Clock Without Hands* (holograph manuscript, three typed and typed carbon drafts, galleys, and mimeographed copies; manuscript of Arthur J. Vander's stage adaptation); *The March* (typescript and carbon typescript); *The Mortgaged Heart* (several xeroxes of each work collected for book; galleys, page proofs). In the section entitled "Letters from Carson McCullers" are forty-six letters to Reeves McCullers, her husband, and sixty from him, dating from 1943-1951; other than these, most of the letters in this section are carbons of dictated letters that date from the 1950s. "Letters to Carson McCullers" are business letters, fan letters, and letters from such friends as John and Simone

Brown, Annemarie Clarac-Schwarzenbach, Klaus Mann, Mary Mercer, and Tennessee Williams; along with letters from such famous people as Richard Burton and Marlon Brando, who wrote as admirers. The "Publishers Correspondence" contains the papers of McCullers's agents, lawyers, and publishers, including Floria Lasky at Fitelson & Mayers, Audrey Wood at ICM and Liebling-Wood, Maxim Lieber, Robert Lantz, and Houghton Mifflin. These papers include correspondence with McCullers herself and with the estate after her death. In a section labeled "Miscellaneous" are many personal financial records of McCullers, her mother, and sister; security transactions, bank records, insurance policies, materials relating to the houses in Columbus and Nyack, wills, and estates of various family members; some of McCullers's medical records, including transcripts of her meditations during analysis, form part of the collection. A large group of materials relates to the funerals of McCullers and her mother.

Also at the Humanities Research Center are materials in the Tennessee Williams Collection relative to McCullers; the Oliver Evans Collection (which includes all materials used in researching the first McCullers biography: *Carson McCullers: Her Life and Work* [London: Peter Owen, 1965]; reprinted as *The Ballad of Carson McCullers* [Coward-McCann, 1966]). Also catalogued in the Margo Jones Collection, the Harpers Collections, the Edith Sitwell Collection, and the Eugene Walter Collection are a few additional letters to or from McCullers.

The second largest collection of McCullers materials is at the Perkins Library of Duke University, Durham, North Carolina (known as the Robert Flowers Collection of Southern History and Literature). In 1977 the library acquired some 4,000 items of correspondence, notes, and clippings compiled for the research, writing, and publishing of Virginia Spencer Carr's *The Lonely Hunter: A Biography of Carson McCullers*. These resources are available to scholars without restriction.

Also housed in the Robert Flowers Collection at Duke University are the Lula Carson (Smith) McCullers Papers, 1941-1978, which include a large body of correspondence to and from Jordan Massee (McCullers's cousin and long-time friend), Tennessee Williams, Paul Bigelow, Edith Sitwell, Edward Albee, and other notables; photographs; and significant miscellaneous materials.

Notable, too, in the Flowers Collection at Duke is the Mary Tucker Collection, which includes correspondence between Mrs. Tucker (McCullers's piano teacher) and McCullers, and between Mrs. Tucker and Dr. Mary Mercer. Perkins Library also is in the process of acquiring several other private collections relative to McCullers, confirming its place as one of the two major repositories of McCullers materials.

Other libraries with useful McCullers holdings include the Beinecke Rare Book and Manuscript Library of Yale University; the Library of Congress; the Robert Woodruff Library of Emory University; the University of

Georgia; University of Iowa; the Lilly Library of Indiana University, Bloomington; the Houghton Library of Harvard University; Washington University Library, St. Louis; the Berg Collection of New York Public Library; the American Academy of Arts and Letters in New York City; the Ford Foundation Library in New York City; the Charles Patterson Van Pelt Library at the University of Pennsylvania; the Cyrus Hall McCormick Library at Washington and Lee University; the University of Maryland Library, College Park; and Dalton Junior College Library, Dalton, Georgia.

The W. C. Bradley Memorial Library of Columbus, Georgia (McCullers's hometown), has significant biographical materials relative to the author's early years, but no McCullers manuscripts. When the director of the library approached McCullers by letter in 1958 to request that she consider placing some of her manuscripts there, she declined on the grounds that the library was insufficiently integrated, thus not "public" to all races. Once the library was, indeed, fully integrated, it was too late to acquire any materials directly from her.

There has been no collection of McCullers's letters published. Such an edition would illuminate in rich detail McCullers's life and career in that her letters contain some of her best writing. Since Carr was denied permission to quote from the letters in her biography of McCullers, such a volume would be especially valuable. An additional volume of selected letters written by members of the family to each other—McCullers, her husband, mother, sister, and brother—would also make a splendid collection.

BIOGRAPHY

Since McCullers's death in 1967, only one comprehensive biography has appeared, Virginia Spencer Carr's *The Lonely Hunter: A Biography of Carson McCullers* (Garden City, N.Y.: Doubleday, 1975). The book was researched and written without the cooperation of the McCullers literary estate. The literary executors asked a number of people who knew McCullers well not to cooperate with Carr, but to save their materials for an approved biographer who would be appointed at some later date. When Carr seemed bent on pursuing her research anyway, having considered the writings of McCullers in the course of her doctoral dissertation ("Carson McCullers and the Search for Meaning," Florida State University, 1969) and having moved to McCullers's hometown of Columbus, Georgia, to teach at the college there, the McCullers literary executors denied her access to all unpublished materials in the possession of the estate (before the McCullers Collection was established at the Humanities Research Center at the University of Texas). Carr was also denied permission to quote from any of the hundreds of letters from McCullers or other members of the family she had turned up independent of the estate. Nevertheless, she found some five hundred friends, acquaintances, classmates, and relatives who were willing to talk freely about the facets of McCullers they knew best (for example, McCullers's brother cooperated with Carr, though her sister did not).

Carr discovered that her subject was seldom the *same* person to any two people; to some, she played the "wounded sparrow," to others, an "iron butterfly." With scars both psychic and actual, a life both real and fantasized, McCullers herself seldom distinguished between the two. She also took childlike delight in creating and perpetuating for others the tales and myths that abounded about her.

The Lonely Hunter was reviewed in newspapers, magazines, and scholarly journals across the country and was widely acclaimed. Most reviewers thought the portrait a sympathetic, yet honest one. They appreciated its being descriptive rather than psychoanalytic and judgmental. They liked it most, perhaps, because Carr seemed to re-create McCullers—whose life and works were one—so that the reader lived at her elbow and bedside during her troubled and pain-ridden life. Negative reviewers thought the book too long and were disappointed that Carr had not taken a strong critical stance regarding the value of each book and McCullers's over-all place or rank in twentieth-century American letters. Such was not Carr's purpose, though one cannot read this biography and not be aware that she holds McCullers's work in high esteem. As a literary biographer, Carr felt her primary role was to lead readers of the biography back to McCullers's writings themselves, "which is what good literary biography is all about," she added.

Essay-reviews of Carr's biography that also comment upon McCullers's life include: *Antioch Review* (Summer 1976), *Books and Bookmen* (May 1978), *Book World* (*Washington Post*, 17 October 1976), *Choice* (November 1975), *Journal of American Studies* (August 1978), *Listener* (5 May 1977), *London Observer* (10 April 1977), *New Statesman* (6 May 1977), *New York Times Book Review* (24 August 1975), *Prairie Schooner* (Fall 1977), *Southwest Review* (April 1976) *Southern Humanities Review* (Winter, 1978), *Times Literary Supplement* (20 May 1977), and *Virginia Quarterly Review* (Winter 1976).

The introduction to *The Lonely Hunter* ("Some Words Before") is by Tennessee Williams. The book is indexed, has seventy-five photographs, twenty-three pages of footnotes, an appendix of genealogies, a twelve-page chronology of McCullers's life, and a primary bibliography of her published works.

The only other book-length biography is Oliver Evans's *Carson McCullers: Her Life and Work* (London: Peter Owen, 1965; rptd. as *The Ballad of Carson McCullers*, Coward-McCann, 1966). It is a fair introduction to McCullers's life and works, especially in view of the fact that it was published during McCullers's own lifetime and with her cooperation. At the time she granted Evans a number of interviews, she was in critically ill health and her memory was faulty. Evans has said that he was not as candid as he would have liked, since McCullers herself would be reading the manuscript, and that there were inadvertent errors in it because he had accepted her "word" for a number of recollections presented as "fact" whereas the truth might well have been ascertained elsewhere. All of the materials used in Evans's biography are housed at the Humanities Research Center of the University of Texas.

Evans's book had one printing and sold under 3,000 copies. Though not widely reviewed, it was generally well received by the critics, who liked it for its detailed analysis of each major work, its summaries of contemporary critical reactions, and its comparison of McCullers's own life in the South to that experienced by her fictional counterparts (especially as seen in *The Heart Is a Lonely Hunter* and *The Member of the Wedding*). Evans, a university professor, scholar, and poet, had already received good response to his several critical essays published on McCullers before bringing out his biography. Until the publication of McCullers's posthumous collection, *The Mortgaged Heart*, Evans's book contained the only published version of "The Mute," the author's essay/outline of the book that eventually became known as *The Heart Is a Lonely Hunter*. It was this outline (and the first five or six chapters of the novel itself) that won for McCullers a cash advance and contract with Houghton Mifflin for publication of the book. McCullers stayed with this conservative Boston house for the rest of her life and was considered one of its most prized authors. Robert F. Kiernan's *Katherine Anne Porter and Carson McCullers: A Reference Guide* lists reviews of the Evans biography.

Three other books of interest with good introductory biographical chapters are by Lawrence Graver, Dale Edmonds, and Richard M. Cook, each entitled *Carson McCullers*. These books are described more fully below.

A two-page biographical sketch by Carr is found in *Southern Writers: A Biographical Dictionary*, edited by Robert Bain, Joseph M. Flora, and Louis D. Rubin, Jr. (Baton Rouge: Louisiana State University Press, 1979). This brief overview is useful as a first step in interesting readers in the pursuit of McCullers's books themselves. The dictionary is comprised of many hundreds of such sketches and is the most comprehensive biographical compendium of Southern writers (both living and dead) to date.

For a unique look at Reeves McCullers, the author's husband, to whom she was twice married (he committed suicide), one might try locating a little known periodical, *This Issue* (Atlanta: McKee Publishing, 1973) for an article by Delma Eugene Presley, "The Man Who Married Carson McCullers." Presley also has written several significant articles about McCullers.

There are also several articles based on interviews with McCullers. Perhaps the most memorable is Rex Reed's affectionate portrait, "'Frankie Addams' at 50" (*NYT*, 16 April 1967); it is more easily accessible in Reed's collected essays, *Do You Sleep in the Nude?* (New American Library, 1968).

For details of McCullers's death, see Carr's biography or obituary notices in the *New York Times* (30 September 1967), *Newsweek* (9 October 1967), *Publishers' Weekly* (9 October 1967), *Time* (6 October 1967), or *Contemporary Biography Yearbook* (1967-1968).

A biography that has been in progress for several years which should interest critics and lay readers alike is by Margaret Sue Sullivan (a native of McCullers's hometown), reportedly to be published by Scribner's. If it is anything like Sullivan's earlier dissertation, "Carson McCullers, 1917-47: The Conversion of Experience" (Durham, N.C.: Duke University, 1966), it should be very good indeed.

CRITICISM

Carson McCullers's critical reputation presents a complicated, curious history. She was hailed as a *Wunderkind* for her first novel, *The Heart Is a Lonely Hunter* in 1940; her subsequent books, *Reflections in a Golden Eye* in 1941 and *The Member of the Wedding* in 1946, were less well received. The stage version of *The Member of the Wedding* in 1950 solidified her popular if not her critical success. The publication of the omnibus edition of her work under the title of *The Ballad of The Sad Café* in 1951 gathered her work of the past decade, including her three novels, the title novella, and six of her best stories. For the first time academic critics joined reviewers and fellow writers in praise of McCullers's unique talents. Her ensuing silence, caused by her serious illness, once again weakened her critical reputation, which was not enhanced by her play *The Square Root of Wonderful* in 1958, or her novel *Clock Without Hands* in 1961. Since her death in 1967 and the publication of the posthumous collection *The Mortgaged Heart* in 1971, criticism again has treated McCullers more favorably, comparing her with the other women writers of the Southern Renaissance.

In general McCullers criticism has varied in appreciation and evaluation, but presented a consensus in terms of analysis and interpretation. In this view McCullers is a writer of considerable talent, insight, and artistry, whose development was limited by her health and other personal circumstances, though the writing collected in the omnibus volume of 1951 represents an interesting achievement. Most critics consider *The Heart Is a Lonely Hunter* and *The Ballad of the Sad Café* as her best works, with *The Member of the Wedding* (both novel and play) and *Reflections in a Golden Eye* following in that order of decreasing importance. *The Square Root of Wonderful* and *Clock Without Hands* are admitted failures, as are her later stories. About a half dozen of her early stories are considered fine work, as are a few of her essays, mostly concerned with her own writing; while her poetry is little regarded.

For the most part, McCullers's critics locate her fiction within the traditions of the Southern Gothic or grotesque school; in particular, she is often compared with other Southern women writers such as Katherine Anne Porter, Eudora Welty, and Flannery O'Connor. In most criticism McCullers is seen as a modern writer who uses the South as a convenient symbol of a universal wasteland. Again and again the criticism finds the same motifs. In her works loneliness, alienation, and estrangement are created by the failure of love, religion, and communication, which are symbolized in sexual ambivalence, physical abnormality, and psychological aberration. Her people are losers, freaks, and gawky adolescents who fail to make social, personal, or sexual contact with one another. Her characters are lost in violent epiphanies, only partially redeemed by fitful flashes of human insight among the ruins of their dreams. Almost all of the criticism of McCullers has accepted this general consensus of analysis and interpretation. Most of the writing about McCullers is, in fact, just this sort of interpretive criticism. Few critics consider sources or influences, textual or biographical problems, social or intellectual backgrounds. Most surprisingly, critics have neglected McCullers in terms of the major critical movements of recent years such as structural, semiotic, Marxist, or feminist approaches. Finally, the McCullers criticism seems both less interesting and less insightful than the fiction it considers.

This consensus of analysis and interpretation makes a chronological survey of the McCullers criticism most appropriate. The general view of McCullers in criticism began with the reviews of her first novel, *The Heart Is a Lonely Hunter*, in 1940. Even the title was the result of a critical consensus, as her editor forced it on the book against McCullers's wishes. This line from a second-rate poem suggested themes of love, loneliness, and questing to the critics. Most of this criticism was positive, if not insightful, in these terms. Among the more important positive reviews were Clifton Fadiman's in the *New Yorker* (8 June 1940), Rose Feld's in the *New York Times Book Review* (16 June 1940), and Robert Littell's in the *Yale Review* (Autumn 1940). These reviewers and others were impressed by the raw talent evidenced in this first novel by a twenty-three year old Southern woman. Comparisons with Faulkner and Caldwell were inevitable, but she was also contrasted, not unfavorably, with Dostoevsky, Chekhov, and even Van Gogh. Richard Wright, in the *New Republic* (16 June 1940), found her "the first white Southerner to deal with Negroes easily and with justice"; for Wright her despair was "more authentic and natural than Faulkner's." Not all the critics were ecstatic, however. Notable negative reviews include *Time* (10 June 1940) and *Times Literary Supplement* (27 March 1943).

Negative response definitely outweighed the positive when McCullers's second novel, *Reflections in a Golden Eye*, was published less than a year after the first. Such reaction was perhaps inevitable given the adulation visited on the young writer. Her second novel differed in subject, size, and mood from the phenomenal *The Heart Is a Lonely Hunter*. Most critics found *Reflections in a Golden Eye* difficult going—morbid, bizarre, and pretentious. Typical were the reactions of Clifton Fadiman, Rose Feld, and

Robert Littell, all of whom had publicly praised her first novel. Writing in the *New Yorker* (15 February 1941), Fadiman found the second novel "completely unconvincing." Feld, now reviewing for the *New York Herald Tribune Books* (16 February 1941), was more positive, though still disappointed. Littell wrote in the *Yale Review* (Spring 1941) that the novel "is something for her admirers to forget as soon as possible." However, *Time*'s anonymous reviewer was quite positive, indeed almost ecstatic (17 February 1941), as were a few other scattered reviews.

During the war years, McCullers continued to write and to publish, most notably the story, "A Tree. A Rock. A Cloud." (*HB*, November 1942; included in the O Henry *Prize Stories of 1943*), and the novella, *The Ballad of the Sad Café* (*HB*, August, 1943; included in *The Best American Short Stories of 1944*). She began work on the novel that would become *The Member of the Wedding*, supported by a number of prestigious grants and fellowships. However, her already declining health and her problematic emotional relationship with her husband, Reeves McCullers, extended the gestation period of this work through the war. McCullers was only occasionally mentioned by critics during the war, and she did not receive further critical attention until the publication of her new novel in 1946.

The Member of the Wedding is McCullers most accessible and popular book, one which was well received by general critics, less so by literary ones. It was more widely reviewed than the first two novels, and the majority of the reviews were favorable. Reviewers were taken with the more normal subject matter, the brilliant style, and the sensitivity of the portraiture. It is almost as if the critical majority found the book a relief after McCullers's other works. Notable examples of majority approval were Paul Engle (*Chicago Sunday Tribune*, 31 March 1946), Ralph McGill (*Atlanta Constitution*, 23 March 1946) and Orville Prescott (*NYT*, 19 March 1946). Representative of an important negative minority were Diana Trilling (*Nation*, 6 April 1946), D. S. Savage (*Spectator*, 7 March 1947), and Edmund Wilson (*NY*, 30 March 1946). Wilson wrote a scathing review, concluding that "The whole story seems utterly pointless." His attack is balanced by Marguerite Young's sensitive review-essay in *Kenyon Review* (Winter 1947) which explores *The Member of the Wedding* as metaphysical fiction depicting the universal "confusions of life through the symbolism of turbulent adolescence."

The reviews of McCullers's play version of *The Member of the Wedding*, which opened on Broadway early in 1950, were similar in pattern to those of her novel. The majority were positive, citing the work's "magic," "poetry," and "humor"; while a minority were negative, usually in terms of "sketchiness," "slowness," and "lack of drama." Strong reviews (all anonymous) included *Newsweek* (16 January 1950), *Life* (23 January 1950), and *Theatre Arts* (March 1950). Less favorable responses were written by Howard Barnes (*NYHT*, 6 January 1950), John Mason Brown (*SatRL*, 28 January 1950), and Wolcott Gibbs (*NY*, 14 January 1950). All of these attacks are important because they fault the work for inherent melodrama as well as its lack of formal plot progression. Their remarks seem worthy of note after seeing the 1952 movie version of the play, produced by Stanley Kramer and directed by Fred Zinnemann, with the Broadway cast nearly intact. Reviews of the film were generally positive, though the movie was not a box-office success. Again a few movie critics read back from film to play to novel, questioning the literary seriousness of the original work.

Nineteen-fifty also saw the reissue of *Reflections in a Golden Eye* by New Directions with a new preface by Tennessee Williams. In a sense, Williams's introductory essay might be viewed as the beginning of serious McCullers criticism as differentiated from occasionally insightful reviewing. In this process he presents both an encomium for the younger writer and an imprimatur for the "consensus" view of her work. He declared, "*Reflections in a Golden Eye* is one of the purest and most powerful of those works which are conceived in that Sense of the Awful which is the desperate black root of nearly all significant modern art."

Williams's points were often echoed in the outpouring of critical writing that followed the publication of the omnibus volume of McCullers's work under the title of *The Ballad of the Sad Café* in 1951. Since the volume united her three earlier novels with the previously uncollected title novella and several other stories, it provided an opportunity for a critical overview. For the most part, this assessment proved quite positive. On the front page of the *New York Herald Tribune Books*, Coleman Rosenberger exclaimed: "What an impressive and unified body of work has been produced by Mrs. McCullers at an age when many a writer has hardly started on his career . . . each [fiction] takes its place in an expanding structure in which each part augments and strengthens the rest." Other enthusiastic reviews included Ben Ray Redman in *SatR* (23 June 1951), William P. Claney in *Commonweal* (4 June 1951), and Paul Engle in the *Chicago Tribune* (10 June 1951). The omnibus volume also solidified McCullers's English reputation; see V. S. Pritchett's laudatory review in the *New Statesman* (2 August 1952), Elizabeth Bowen's pronouncements in *SatR* (13 October 1951), and the praise of Cyril Connolly in the London *Times* (20 July 1952). It is also important to note that McCullers's novella, which gave a title to the omnibus volume, won almost universal praise from the critics. Although there were a few exceptions to this critical acclaim, McCullers was at the height of her popular reputation.

The omnibus edition also elicited the first academic criticism of the McCullers canon. In an early and influential piece (*CE*, October, 1951), Dayton Kohler unifies her work around the theme of loneliness and longing. Oliver Evans also found loneliness the central concern of McCullers's fiction in another widely influential essay, "The Theme of Spiritual Isolation in Carson McCullers," which appeared in *New World Writing: First Mentor Selection* (New American Library, 1951). Evans's views may be considered the primary statement of the consensus view of McCullers's fiction. According to Evans, McCullers's people are spiritually alone because of the failure of love, a universal condition dictated by the very nature of human attraction. As evidence, Evans cites the narrator's theory of love in *The Ballad of the Sad Café*. Moreover, the evolution of her vision toward this statement in the novella provides the pattern of her career. Another early article that presents a quite similar view is Jane Hart's "Carson McCullers, Pilgrim of Loneliness" (*GaR*, Spring 1957).

McCullers's later works did little to support the critical reputation earned by the omnibus volume. Her play, *The Square Root of Wonderful* (1957), was almost universally panned. Most critics wondered along with the anonymous reviewer for *Theatre Arts* (January 1950) if this play really could have been written by the author of *The Member of the Wedding*. Important condemnations include those by Brooks Atkinson (*NYT*, 31 October 1957), John Chapman (*New York Daily News*, 31 October 1957), and Wolcott Gibbs, (*NY*, 9 November 1957). McCullers's long-awaited "new" novel received similar rough treatment in 1961. *Clock Without Hands* proved a major disappointment to most of the critics. Irving Howe's perceptive review (*NYT*, 17 September 1961) stated the case against the book succinctly. Howe pointed out the book's weak structure, particularly the lack of symmetry between the Malone and Clane strands of the plot, its unreal picture of the contemporary South, and the lack of "inner conviction and imaginative energy." Other negative reviews include those of Whitney Balliett (*NY*, 23 September 1961), and Orville Prescott (*NYT*, 18 September 1961). McCullers still had her defenders, however, and positive judgments can be found in reviews by Jean Martin (*Nation*, 18 November 1961), Penelope Mortimer (*Time and Tide*, 19 October 1961), and Edna O'Brien (*Books and Bookmen*, October 1961). These defenders of the work were decidedly in the minority, however, as McCullers's critical fortunes again suffered a reversal.

In the decade between the success of the omnibus volume and the failure of *Clock Without Hands*, academic critics continued to confirm the importance of McCullers's early achievement. During these years McCullers also elicited a generally positive response in foreign language criticism; unfortunately this writing is for the most part introductory, simplistic, and repetitive. Some of the more important American academic considerations include Frederick I. Carpenter's study of "The Adolescent in American Fiction" (*EJ*, September 1957), which discussed McCullers's use of adolescence as a symbolic theme. Frank Durham's "God and No God in *The Heart Is a Lonely Hunter*" (*SAQ*, Autumn 1955) sees an ironic religious allegory in the structure of failed character relationships in McCullers's first novel. Another allegorical reading of McCullers's fiction was provided by Frank Baldanza in his influential article, "Plato in Dixie" (*GaR*, Summer 1958). Baldanza develops parallels between McCullers's fiction and Plato's dialogues both in theme and technique. For Baldanza, McCullers is most Platonic in her distinction between spiritual and physical love.

Another important academic critic of McCullers's fiction is Ihab Hassan; his first essay on her work, "Carson McCullers: The Alchemy of Love and the Aesthetics of Pain," appeared in *Modern Fiction Studies* (Winter 1959). Hassan explained the tension between love and pain in her vision, linking her with Faulkner and the other masters of the Southern Renaissance. Portions of this essay have been reprinted eight times, indicating the importance of Hassan's extension of the consensus view of McCullers's work. In the same year a Canadian critic, Hugo McPherson, provided a more socially oriented reading in "Carson McCullers: Lonely Huntress" (*TamR*, Spring 1959). Like Tennessee Williams, McPherson sees *Reflections in a Golden Eye* as her best work, but his emphasis is on its disturbing picture of a tragically conformist society. McPherson's essay was not as widely influential as Hassan's, but many of his points were expanded by criticism of the 1970s.

Another social view of McCullers was provided by Leslie Fiedler in his influential study *Love and Death in the American Novel* (Stein and Day, 1959). Fiedler surprisingly calls *The Heart Is a Lonely Hunter* "a Depression book, the last of the proletarian novels." He also makes some perceptive remarks about the homosexual ambiance of McCullers's writing, which seem confirmed by the revelations of the Carr biography. Fiedler's view on the depression qualities of McCullers's first novel are also reflected in Horace Taylor's "*The Heart Is a Lonely Hunter*: A Southern Waste Land," in *Studies in American Literature*, edited by Waldo McNeir and Leo Levy (Baton Rouge: Louisiana State University Press, 1960). John B. Vickery's "Carson McCullers: A Map of Love" (*Wisconsin Studies in Contemporary Literature*, Winter 1960), though smoothly written, reiterates the consensus view once more.

Nineteen-sixty-two, the year following the negative reception of *Clock Without Hands*, saw several important academic studies. Donald Emerson (*WSCL*, Fall 1962) and Nick Aaron Ford (*Phylon*, Summer 1962) both try, unsuccessfully, to save the last novel from its negative reception. Oliver Evans (*EJ*, May 1962) and Ihab Hassan (*EJ*, January 1962) both extended their earlier arguments about McCullers's achievements. Irving Malin developed the Gothic aspect of the critical consensus in his book *New American Gothic* (Carbondale: Southern Illinois University Press, 1962). Gore Vidal echoed Tennessee Williams's praise of McCullers in *Rocking the Boat* (Boston: Little, 1962), while Alfred Kazin provided a more judicious overview in *Contemporaries* (Boston: Little, Brown, 1962). Perhaps the most insightful study, however, was "The Sad, Sweet Music of Carson McCullers" by Barbara Nauer Folk in *Georgia Review* (Summer 1962). Although Folk's views of McCullers's subjects and themes are similar to earlier critics' judgments, her remarks on the musical structures of McCullers's fictions provided one of the first important considerations of the writer's artistic forms.

Klaus Lubbers also considers structure carefully in the first important foreign consideration of McCullers, "The Necessary Order: A Study of Theme and Structure in Carson McCullers' Fiction" (*Jahrbuch für Amerikastudien*, No. 8, 1963). His thematic judgments were not new, but they were carefully ordered in the chronology of McCullers's career and solidly anchored in structural analysis. Wayne Dodd's "The Development of Theme Through Symbol in the Novels of Carson McCullers" (*GaR*, Summer 1963) provides a careful reading of McCullers's symbolism, most interestingly in terms of music and art symbols. In his study, *Fiction of the Forties* (Chicago: University of Chicago Press, 1963), Chester Eisinger also deals with structure and symbol in a discussion of McCullers as one of the new "antirealistic" writers of the decade who eschewed the proletarian spirit of the 1930s. Mark Schorer developed a similar position in "McCullers and Capote: Basic Patterns" in *The Creative Present: Notes on Contemporary American Fiction*, edited by Nona Balakian and Charles Simmons (Garden City, N.Y.: Doubleday 1963). A brief but accurate assessment of McCullers in her time is found in John M. Bradbury's *Renaissance In the South: A Critical History of the Literature, 1920-1960* (Chapel Hill: University of North Carolina Press, 1963). Similar insights are presented by British critic Walter Allen in *The Modern Novel in Britain and America* (Dutton, 1964).

The consensus view of McCullers's fiction was supported by several articles published in 1964. Oliver Evans published two pieces (*GaR*, Spring 1964; and *Nation*, 13 July 1964) that anticipated his critical biography of the next year. Marvin Felheim contrasted McCullers with another important woman writer of the Southern Renaissance in "Eudora Welty and Carson McCullers." His essay appeared in *Contemporary American Novelists*, edited by Harry T. Moore (Carbondale: Southern Illinois University Press, 1964). Robert Phillips published two critical articles along with his checklist of McCullers criticism in 1964. In *Studies in Short Fiction* (Spring 1964) he saw a source for *The Ballad of the Sad Café* in Isak Dinesen's Gothic tale, "The Monkey." His essay "The Gothic Architecture of *The Member of the Wedding*" (*Renascence*, Winter 1964) treats the most "normal" of McCullers's novels as a Gothic romance. Nineteen-sixty-four also saw the first doctoral dissertation concerned with McCullers, Simeon Smith's "Carson McCullers: A Critical Introduction" (University of Pennsylvania), essentially a consensus view.

The first book-length study of the writer was Oliver Evans's *Carson McCullers: Her Life and Work* (London: Peter Owen, 1965). It was published a year later in the United States as *The Ballad of Carson McCullers* (Coward-McCann, 1966). Evans tried to trace the development of McCullers's fiction from her biography. Unfortunately, the biographical background is often inaccurate, and the critical estimates do not proceed beyond the consensus views presented in Evans's earlier articles, including "The Case of the Silent Singer—A Reevaluation of *The Heart Is a Lonely Hunter*" (*GaR*, Summer 1965). The book was probably most important for simply pulling together a good deal of information about McCullers in one place.

A more interesting critical view of McCullers in 1965 was Louis Auchincloss's discussion of her in *Pioneers and Caretakers: A Study of Nine American Women Novelists* (Minneapolis: University of Minnesota Press, 1965). Two other essays focused on the topics of violence and violation in McCullers's writing: Louise Y. Gossett's "Dispossessed Love: Carson McCullers's" is a chapter in her *Violence in Recent Southern Fiction* (Durham N.C.: Duke University Press, 1965), while Marion Montgomery's "The Sense of Violation: Notes Toward a Definition of 'Southern' Fiction," was published in *Georgia Review* (Fall 1966).

Several articles considered McCullers's two most important works—*The Heart Is a Lonely Hunter* and *The Ballad of the Sad Café.* Jack B. Moore's "Carson McCullers: The Heart Is a Timeless Hunter" (*TCL*, July 1965) compares Mick's initiation in *The Heart Is a Lonely Hunter* to the archetypal patterns analyzed by Joseph Campbell in *The Hero With a Thousand Faces*. In "The Paradox of the Need for Privacy and the Need for Understanding in Carson McCullers's *The Heart Is a Lonely Hunter*" (*L&P*, No. 2/3, 1967), David Madden demonstrates the frustration created by the contradictions implied in his title. Another psychological reading of the novel is provided by Rowland A. Sherrill in "McCullers's *The Heart Is a Lonely Hunter:* The Missing Ego and the Problem of the Norm" (*KRev*, February 1968). Sherrill suggests that lack of societal norms precludes the formation of a solid ego in the personalities of McCullers's people.

Articles on *The Ballad of the Sad Café* prove less stimulating as they echo the consensus view of that most intriguing of McCullers's works. Robert S. Phillips sees the work as a grotesque parable of sexual identity in "Painful Love: Carson McCullers' Parable" (*SWR*, Winter 1966). In "Carson McCullers's Myth of the Sad Café" (*GaR*, Spring 1967), Albert Griffith traces mythic elements in the work. C. W. E. Bigsby interprets Edward Albee's dramatic version of McCullers's *The Ballad of the Sad Café* from a consensus viewpoint in "Edward Albee's Georgia Ballad," (*TCL*, January 1968).

McCullers's death in 1967 occasioned a number of reconsiderations of her work, for the most part very positive ones. Major obituaries appeared in the *New York Times* (30 September 1967), the *London Times* (30 September 1967), and *Time* (6 October 1967). McCullers's long-time friend and admirer, Ralph McGill, wrote a moving piece for the *Saturday Review* (21 October 1967). Substantial summaries of McCullers's achievement include

Frederick J. Hoffman's assessment in his *The Art of Southern Fiction: A Study of Some Modern Novelists* (Carbondale: Southern Illinois University Press, 1967). George Hendrick was also positive about McCullers's achievement in his short article, "Almost Everyone Wants to Be the Lover: The Fiction of Carson McCullers" (*BA*, Summer 1968). Robert Drake took a negative stance in "The Lonely Heart of Carson McCullers" (*CC*, 10 January 1968). He asserts that McCullers often lost thematic and formal control of her fiction, mixing up the spiritual and structural centers of her works.

A more specialized study from this period is W. R. Robinson's "The Life of Carson McCullers' Imagination" (*SHR*, Summer 1968). Robinson's argument is stimulating, basically asserting that a tension between emotion and intellect, or heart and head, dominates her fiction. The complication of this vision comes in Robinson's notion of a changing attitude toward this central tension from early to late novels. Also interesting is Robert Rechnitz's "The Failure of Love: The Grotesque in Two Novels by Carson McCullers" (*GaR*, Winter 1968). The two novels are McCullers's earliest, *The Heart Is a Lonely Hunter* and *Reflections in a Golden Eye*, which Rechnitz sees as demonstrating the grotesquerie created by the failure of love in the modern world. Rechnitz's article was drawn from his 1967 dissertation (University of Colorado), which partially considered McCullers.

Important dissertations specifically considering McCullers include Margaret Sullivan's "Carson McCullers: 1927-1947: The Conversion of Experience" (Duke University, 1967), a valuable biographical and critical source written by a native of McCullers's hometown. Virginia Spencer Carr's "Carson McCullers and the Search For Meaning" (Florida State University, 1969), which became the basis of the same author's major biography of McCullers; Joseph R. Millichap's "A Critical Reevaluation of Carson McCullers's Fiction" (Notre Dame University, 1970), which viewed McCullers's canon from the perspective of social realism, judging her fictions individually on the basis of achievement in theme, form, and mode.

Two fine pamphlet-length introductions to McCullers appeared in 1969. Dale Edmonds's *Carson McCullers* was published in the Southern Writers Series (Austin, Texas). Although not widely known, Edmonds's work remains perhaps the best short introduction to the writer and her work. The interpretations are judicious and surprisingly free of the jargon that has limited McCullers's critics. Lawrence Graver's *Carson McCullers* in the University of Minnesota Pamphlets on American Writers Series also provides a reliable introduction. Graver sees McCullers as a lyric artist, at her best when she balances mood and realism as in *The Member of the Wedding*. Graver's reading of *The Ballad of the Sad Café* also proves sensitive in the probing of that work's grotesque atmosphere.

Other interesting studies include A. S. Knowles, Jr.'s "Six Bronze Petals and Two Red: Carson McCullers in the Forties," which was printed in *The*

Forties: Fiction, Poetry, Drama, edited by Warren French (Deland, Fla.: Everett/Edwards, 1969). Knowles's essay is interesting for its analysis of the 1940s mood in McCullers's important fictions; in particular he notes the effect of the era's sentimentality on her work. Alice Hamilton's neoplatonic study of McCullers, "Loneliness and Alienation: The Life and Work of Carson McCullers" (*DR*, Summer 1970), extends earlier observations on the writer's philosophy. Ray Mathis provides one of the few readings of McCullers's neglected second novel in "*Reflections In a Golden Eye*: Myth Making in American Christianity" (*Religion in Life*, Winter 1970). The article finally is better on failure of religion in American society than on McCullers's irreligious novel. Another article considering an individual novel is Joseph R. Millichap's "The Realistic Structure of *The Heart Is a Lonely Hunter*" (*TCL*, January 1971). The article, developed from his earlier dissertation, approaches the novel from the perspectives provided by psychological and social realism to reveal "the failure of communication, the isolation, and the violence prevalent in modern society."

Nineteen-seventy-one also saw the publication of *The Mortgaged Heart*, the posthumous volume of unpublished and uncollected pieces that was edited by Margarita Smith, McCullers's younger sister and a writer herself. The intention and editing won general praise, and only a few popular critics found the pieces published here slight or embarrassing. Negative responses include Walter Clemons's review in the *New York Times* (7 November 1971); Clemons saw the beginnings of her decline even in these very early pieces. He asserts that McCullers's decline has little to do with her weakening health but stemmed from her inherent sentimentality. Similar negative views include John Alfred Avant (*Library Journal*, 1 January 1972), Thomas A. Gullason (*SatR*, 13 November 1971), and Jeanne Kinney (*Best Sellers*, 15 November 1971). Almost all the other reviews found merit, and even sparks and embers of genius in the early and late stories. McCullers's several essays on writing also won praise when viewed together for the first time. Even the sympathetic critics rejected the occasional essays and the poetry, however, suggesting that they should have been left out. Perhaps the best judgment is novelist David Madden's essay-review, "Transfixed Among the Self-Inflicted Ruins: Carson McCullers' *The Mortgaged Heart*" (*SLJ*, Fall 1972). Madden admits the volume contains mediocre work in all forms, but the better pieces remind the reader of McCullers's best work, particularly as they chart her creative course toward *The Heart Is a Lonely Hunter*. Madden saw that the publication of *The Mortgaged Heart* would substantiate the more positive reevaluation of McCullers that had begun with her death in 1967.

The posthumous volume increased critical interest in McCullers's shorter works. For example, Dale Edmonds analyzed a previously uncollected story in "'Correspondence': A 'Forgotten' Carson McCullers Short Story" (*SSF*, Winter 1972). In "Delving 'A Domestic Dilemma'" (*SSF*, Summer 1972), James N. Grinnell gave a new reading to another minor McCullers story. However, his attack on the story's protagonist was refuted by Laurence Perrine in "Restoring 'A Domestic Dilemma'" (*SSF*, Winter 1974).

The Ballad of the Sad Café is the subject of three complementary studies that emphasized the novella's complexity of mood and narrative stance. In "The Presence of the Narrator in Carson McCullers's *The Ballad of the Sad Café*" (*MissQ*, Fall 1972), Dawson Gaillard presents a convincing reading of the narrator as a character who "lifts the story beyond the commonplace facts." John McNally comes to similar conclusions in his article, "The Introspective Narrator in 'The Ballad of the Sad Café'" (*SAB*, November 1973), concluding that "In the process of telling his tale, the narrator discovers new meaning in his existence." The narrator also draws the analytical attention of Joseph R. Millichap in "Carson McCullers's Literary Ballad" (*GaR*, Fall 1972), but he sees the narrator as a typical ballad maker, spinning a timeless tale of love and violence from the Georgia backcountry.

Several new readings of McCullers's entire canon also appeared during this period of reevaluation. In his article, "The Moral Function of Distortion in Southern Grotesque" (*SAB*, May 1972), Delma Eugene Presley argues that images of incompleteness demonstrate what humanity ought to be, and thus McCullers can be seen as a more positive writer than she is generally considered. Even more impressive is Presley's "Carson McCullers and the South" (*GaR*, Spring 1974), which argues cogently that McCullers's genius was Southern in origin, and it declined when she cut herself off from her Southern roots. An East German critic, Irene Skotnicki, proposes an interesting Marxist reading of McCullers in her short article "Die Darstellung der Entfremdung in den Romanen von Carson McCullers" *Zeitschrift Für Anglistik und Amerikanistic* (January 1972). A Freudian reading, which involves the fear of incest in McCullers's work, is found in Irving Buchen's "Carson McCullers: The Case of Convergence" (*BuR*, Spring 1973). Buchen's "Divine Collusion: The Art of Carson McCullers" (*DR*, Autumn 1974) moves toward more metaphysical speculation, defining her aesthetic as "the square root of heaven on earth." None of these readings proves completely convincing, but they all provide new methods of approach to McCullers's art.

Nineteen-seventy-five saw two important publications concerned with Carson McCullers and her writing. Virginia Spencer Carr's definitive biography, *The Lonely Hunter*, is discussed under the heading above. Carr chose not to include literary criticism in her work, but the book forms the basis for all serious later criticism of McCullers. A monograph by Richard Cook, *Carson McCullers* (Frederick Unger, 1975) provides an excellent introduction to McCullers criticism, though the author was unable to profit from Carr's biographical revelations. Cook's biographical introduction is adequate, however, and his critical readings of the individual works are both sensible and insightful. *The Heart Is a Lonely Hunter* is McCullers's most realistic book according to Cook, while *Reflections in a Golden Eye* is her most grotesque. *The Member of the Wedding* demonstrates pathos and humor, while *The Ballad of the Sad Café* counterpoints humor with tragic love. *Clock Without Hands* is McCullers's most ambitious novel, but it fails to realize its ambitions in terms of character, plot structure, and theme. In general, Cook's *Carson McCullers* does not go beyond earlier criticism, but it does create a synthesis that generally avoids the jargon of the earlier work while fulfilling the purpose of its series format (Ungar Modern Literature Monographs) quite nicely.

Different approaches to several individual works in the McCullers canon were advanced in articles of the mid-1970s. Panthea Reid Broughton presented a feminist reading in her essay "Rejection of the Feminine in Carson McCullers' *The Ballad of the Sad Café*" (*TCL*, January 1974). She argues persuasively that rejection of feminine characteristic twists and perverts both the individual and the social structure. McCullers's last novel receives a positive reconsideration in Charlene Clark's "Selfhood and the Southern Past: A Reading of Carson McCullers' *Clock Without Hands*" (*SLM*, Spring 1975). Clark's assertion that the novel is McCullers's most Southern shows new approaches to the book. Mary Dell Fletcher's "Carson McCullers's Ancient Mariner" (*SCB*, Winter 1975) compares "A Tree. A Rock. A Cloud" with Coleridge's poem, emphasizing the use of the Cain figure in the story. Francis Dedmond examines the important differences between the novel and play versions of *The Member of the Wedding* in his essay, "Doing Her Own Thing: Carson McCullers's Dramatization of *The Member of the Wedding*" (*SAB*, May 1975).

The Member of the Wedding was adapted as a film, as were *The Heart Is a Lonely Hunter* and *Reflections In a Golden Eye*. The film version of the novel/play is the subject of Louis D. Giannetti's article, "*The Member of the Wedding*" (*LFQ*, Winter 1976). Giannetti finds the cinematic version a moving realization of the themes and meanings of the novel/play. Contrasting conclusions are reached in Robert Aldridge's essay, "Two Planetary Systems: *The Heart Is a Lonely Hunter*," which appears in *The Modern American Novel and the Movies*, edited by Gerald Perry and Roger Shatzkin (Frederick Ungar, 1978). Aldridge shows how the movie version of McCullers's first novel violates its intricate planetary structure and distorts its themes and meanings. The relationship of McCullers and the movies is also the subject of a paper presented by Joseph R. Millichap at the South Atlantic Modern Language Association Convention in 1980 and now awaiting publication.

The most important recent study of McCullers is Louis Rubin's "Carson McCullers: The Aesthetic of Pain" (*VQR*, Spring 1977). Rubin utilized the biographical insights provided by the Carr volume to define McCullers's aesthetic in terms of the pain of loneliness and of creativity. These were overwhelmed by the physical and psychological pain of her later life. Rubin sees her undoing as a writer in her inability to rise above pain and her perceptions of it to "the truths that, in Proust's words, 'take the place of sorrows.'"

Other interesting articles have considered individual works, particularly *The Heart Is a Lonely Hunter*, from the perspectives provided by the new biography. Among them is a consideration from a social point of view, Nancy Rich's "The 'Ironic Parable of Fascism' in *The Heart Is a Lonely Hunter*" (*SLJ*, Spring 1977). Rich utilizes McCullers's cryptic description of her novel as a key to social meanings, specifically the death struggle of fascism and democracy in the 1930s. Two other studies consider form in the first novel. Joseph R. Millichap's "Distorted Matter and Disjunctive Form: The Grotesque as Modernist Genre" (*ArQ*, Winter 1977) compares *The Heart Is a Lonely Hunter* with Sherwood Anderson's *Winesburg, Ohio* and William Faulkner's *The Sound and the Fury* as works that demonstrate the convergence of grotesque subject matter with disjunctive structural form. In "A Voice in a Fugue: Characters and Musical Structure in *The Heart Is a Lonely Hunter*" (*MFS*, Summer 1979), Michael C. Smith uses McCullers's remarks about a fugal pattern in the novel as the basis of a convincing reading that views structure in terms of counterpoint, repetition, and continuity. Smith's article is partially drawn from his fine 1976 dissertation, "Self and Society: The Dialectic of Themes and Forms in the Novels of Carson McCullers" (University of North Carolina at Greensboro). Patricia S. Box also considers the first novel in "Androgyny and the Musical Vision: A Study of Two Novels by Carson McCullers" (*SoQ*, January 1978). In *The Heart Is a Lonely Hunter* and *The Member of the Wedding*, Box finds the metaphorical use of music supportive of the theme of androgyny: "only androgyns are capable of expressing the sexless love that can ultimately unite all of mankind and change the condition of humanity from isolation to community." Robert S. Phillips uses *The Mortgaged Heart* to consider the figure of the freak in "Freaking Out: The Short Stories of Carson McCullers" (*SWR*, Winter 1978). He concludes that the novels used images of physical freakishness, while the stories show psychic abnormality, "or inner freaking out."

The long awaited Twayne United States Authors Series volume, *Carson McCullers* (Boston, Twayne), was published in 1980. Margaret B. McDowell's study takes advantage of the Carr biography and recent criticism to provide both a good general introduction to the writer and a scholarly analysis of the individual works. Although McDowell provides some new insights, especially in regard to *The Member of the Wedding, Clock Without Hands*, and the stories, most of her analysis does not go beyond the general consensus of McCullers criticism. McDowell underrates *The Heart Is a Lonely Hunter*, and she falls back on critical generalizations in her chapters on *Reflections in a Golden Eye* and *The Ballad of the Sad*

Café. The later works are somewhat overrated, but some good points are made from feminist perspectives. Finally, McDowell's Twayne volume remains more a competent general introduction than a breakthrough study.

The Twayne volume unfortunately represents the major problem of McCullers criticism stressed through this chronological survey—its unfortunate consensus. Reviewing the criticism, the reader begins to hear a litany of "gothic and grotesque," of "loneliness and love," of "adolescence and alienation." Of course, these elements are present in the McCullers canon, but the critics have echoed them to the point of distraction. It seems far past the time for new approaches, for feminist and Marxist studies, structuralist and semiotic readings, connections with other literary and intellectual traditions, or comparisons with other art forms. The renewed interest in women writers and the Southern Renaissance promises continued developments in these directions. Only then will the criticism fulfill the most significant task, that of rendering ultimate justice to the universe created by a literary artist such as Carson McCullers.

Zora Neale Hurston

> She was flamboyant and yet vulnerable, self-centered and yet kind, a Republican conservative and yet an early black nationalist.
>
> Robert Hemenway, *Zora Neale Hurston.* Urbana: University of Illinois Press, 1977

There is certainly no more controversial figure in American literature than Zora Neale Hurston. Even the most common details, easily ascertainable for most people, have been variously interpreted or have remained unresolved issues in her case: When was she born? Was her name spelled Neal, Neale, or Neil? Whom did she marry? How many times was she married? What happened to her after she wrote *Seraph on the Suwanee*? Even so immediately observable a physical quality as her complexion sparks controversy, as is illustrated by Mary Helen Washington in "Zora Neale Hurston: A Woman Half in Shadow," Introduction to *I Love Myself When I Am Laughing...And Then Again When I Am Looking Mean and Impressive*, edited by Alice Walker (Old Westbury, N.Y.: The Feminist Press, 1979), who cites Fannie Hurst's description of her as "light yellow"; Theodore Pratt's description of her as "black as coal"; and Alzeda Hacker's description of her as "reddish light brown." But more important than these issues are some essential questions about her basic personality and philosophy, which continue to be debated: Did she love black people or did she view them with condescension and contempt? Did she have self-respect or was she a shameless suppliant of white patrons? Was she a militant racial

---

I wish to acknowledge the assistance of the Robert R. Moton Foundation, from which I received a research grant during the period that this study was completed.

I am grateful to the following persons for providing information that assisted me in the preparation of this study: Robert Hemenway; S. J. Boldrick of the Miami-Dade Public Library; Lisa Browar of the Yale University Library; C. R. Williams of the University of Florida Library; J. C. Hickerson and Paul T. Heffron of the Library of Congress; E. E. Bhan of the Howard University Library; A. A. Shockley of the Fisk University Library; and Stephen Catlett of the American Philosophical Society. I also wish to thank the staffs of the Virginia Commonwealth University and Virginia Union University Libraries for their assistance.

chauvinist or a groveling Uncle Tom? Was she dedicated to her craft and ideals or would she compromise her work and her convictions for fame and fortune? Did she tacitly accept and ignore racial indignations or did she strike out against them? Some new information is occasionally being ferreted out that may help to cast additional light on some of these issues, but quite clearly Zora Neale Hurston will remain something of an enigma—too complex a figure to reach any easy conclusions about, except perhaps that she defies simple characterization. People responded to her (and still do) very emotionally: her detractors despise her bitterly; her defenders love her passionately. All agree that she was eccentric, colorful, entertaining, humorous, and unforgettable.

Perhaps the most crucial question to pose about her is why one of the most important figures in the Harlem Renaissance, the most prominent and productive black folklorist on the scene, the most prolific black female writer that this country had ever produced, one of the most widely known and honored black writers of her time, and one of the most influential authors on contemporary literature (Ernest Gaines asserts, "Probably the only black writer who has influenced my work is Zora Neale Hurston" [*Essence*, July 1975]) was ignored for so long a period by scholars, critics, anthologizers, and the American reading public. Some of the essays discussed herein consider just that question, and certainly this study attests that the problem is being attacked. The enthusiasm and the dedication of the Hurston scholars that began cropping up in the seventies promise that she will no longer be ignored.

BIBLIOGRAPHY

> I wrote "Their Eyes Were Watching God" in Haiti. It was damned up in me, and I wrote it under internal pressure in seven weeks. I wish that I could write it again. In fact, I regret all of my books. It is one of the tragedies of life that one cannot have all the wisdom one is ever to possess in the beginning. Perhaps, it is just as well to be rash and foolish for a while. If writers were too wise, perhaps no books would be written at all.
>
> Zora Neale Hurston, *Dust Tracks on a Road*

Hurston produced a remarkable number of books, and she therefore had more to "regret" than any other black woman of her day. As a matter of fact, for many years she remained the most prolific black female writer in America, having written four novels, one autobiography, two folklore studies, and numerous plays, short stories, and essays.

The most complete listing of the primary works of Zora Neale Hurston is found in Robert E. Hemenway's *Zora Neale Hurston*, (Urbana: University of Illinois Press, 1977). Within his biography Hemenway cites more secondary sources than any other study, but unfortunately he does not compile a secondary bibliography. Perhaps the most useful bibliography to date is found in Carol Fairbanks and Eugene A. Engeldinger's *Black American Fiction: A Bibliography* (Metuchen, N.J.: Scarecrow Press, 1978). Their listing of the primary works is not, however, as inclusive as Hemenway's, and they do not include Hurston's essays. Their list of biographical and critical studies is useful, and they also include reviews. Another helpful bibliography is found in *Black American Writers Past and Present: A Biographical and Bibliographical Dictionary*, edited by Theresa Gunnels Rush, Carol Fairbanks Myers, and Esther Spring Arata (Metuchen, N.J.: Scarecrow Press, 1975). One shortcoming of this work is that the editors list the anthologies and periodicals in which the short stories and essays appear, but they do not list the titles of the works. They do include a useful listing of biographical and critical sources. Another noteworthy listing of secondary sources may be found in Roseann P. Bell et al., *Sturdy Black Bridges: Visions of Black Women in Literature* (Garden City, N.Y.: Doubleday, 1979). The listing of primary sources is limited, however. Ora Williams's *American Black Women in the Arts and Social Sciences: A Bibliographic Survey* (Metuchen, N.J.: Scarecrow Press, 1978) includes several entries for Hurston, but the awkward and confusing arrangement of her book detracts from its usefulness. In her listings according to genre she includes only one short story and one play by Hurston. In the individual bibliography she lists six stories and three plays. A few essays are listed under her "Miscellaneous Subjects" section. Esther Spring Arata and Nicholas John Rotoli in *Black American Playwrights, 1800 to the Present: A Bibliography* (Metuchen, N.J.: Scarecrow Press, 1976) include a good listing of Hurston's plays and her essays that relate to drama and the theatre. However, they incorrectly attribute "The Negro in the American Theatre" (*Theatre Arts*, August 1942) to Hurston. Arata's *More Black American Playwrights: A Bibliography* (Metuchen, N.J.: Scarecrow Press, 1978) is not a very useful update. It cites only three plays by Hurston, two of which were listed in the earlier collection, and three critical articles. In his introduction to the selection from *Dust Tracks on a Road* in *Mother Wit from the Laughing Barrel: Readings in the Interpretation of Afro-American Folklore* (Englewood Cliffs, N.J.: Prentice-Hall, 1973), Alan Dundes includes a helpful listing of items dealing with Hurston's folklore studies. Very limited listings may be found in Darwin T. Turner's *Afro-American Writers* (Appleton-Century-Crofts, 1970); Dorothy B. Porter's *A Working Bibliography on the Negro in the United States* (Ann Arbor, Mich.: University Microfilms, 1969); Maxwell Whiteman's *A Century of Fiction by American Negroes, 1853-1952: A Selective Bibliography* (Philadelphia: Albert Saifer, 1974); Geraldine O. Matthews's *Black American Writers, 1773-1949: A Bibliography and Union List* (Boston: G. K. Hall, 1975); and Edward Margolies and David Bakish's *Afro-American Fiction, 1853-1976* (Detroit: Gale, 1979).

Brief Hurston bibliographies are included in a few anthologies of Black American literature, such as Arthur P. Davis's *Cavalcade: Negro American*

Writing from 1760 to the Present (Boston: Houghton Mifflin, 1971); and Richard Barksdale and Keneth Kinnamon's *Black Writers of America: A Comprehensive Anthology* (Macmillan, 1972).

EDITIONS

She is out of circulation and all her books are out of print. One cannot be rectified. The other should be.

Theodore Pratt, "Zora Neale Hurston,"
Florida Historical Quarterly (July 1961);
reprinted as "A Memoir: Zora Neale Hurston,
Florida's First Distinguished Author" (*ND*, February 1962)

FULL-LENGTH WORKS

Though Zora Neale Hurston's works were out of print for thirty years, all of her full-length works except *Tell My Horse* (Philadelphia: J. B. Lippincott, 1938; published in 1939 in England under the title *Voodoo Gods: An Inquiry into Native Myths and Magic in Jamaica and Haiti,* London: J. M. Dent and Sons) have been reprinted, and all except *Seraph on the Suwanee* are now in print. *Jonah's Gourd Vine* (Philadelphia: J. B. Lippincott, 1934) was reprinted in 1971 by Lippincott. *Mules and Men* (Philadelphia: J. B. Lippincott, 1935) was reprinted in 1969 by Negro Universities Press (Westport, Conn.), in 1970 by Harper & Row, and in 1978 by the Indiana University Press (Bloomington). *Their Eyes Were Watching God* (Philadelphia: J. B. Lippincott, 1937) was reprinted in 1965 by Fawcett Publications (Greenwich, Conn.), in 1969 by the Negro Universities Press, and in 1978 by the University of Illinois Press (Urbana). *Moses, Man of the Mountain* (Philadelphia: J. B. Lippincott, 1939) was reprinted in 1974 by Chatham Bookseller (Chatham, N.J.). *Dust Tracks on a Road* (Philadelphia: J. B. Lippincott, 1942) was reprinted in 1969 by Arno Press and in 1971 by J. B. Lippincott. *Seraph on the Suwanee* (Charles Scribner's, 1948) was reprinted in 1971 by University Microfilms (Ann Arbor, Mich.) and in 1974 by AMS Press.

Alice Walker has recently edited an anthology of Zora Neale Hurston's works (*I Love Myself When I am Laughing, and Then Again When I am Looking Mean and Impressive* [hereafter referred to as *I Love Myself*; the title is taken from a comment made by Hurston in a letter to Carl Van Vechten referring to photographs he had made of her]). The collection includes selections from *Dust Tracks on a Road, Mules and Men, Tell My Horse, Jonah's Gourd Vine, Moses, Man of the Mountain*, and *Their Eyes Were Watching God*, all of the longer works except *Seraph on the Suwanee.* Also reprinted are two short stories ("Sweat" and "The Gilded Six-Bits"), five essays and articles, and "The Eatonville Anthology." A dedication and an afterword by Alice Walker present a moving portrait of Zora Neale Hurston by a woman whose devotion could easily become mere sentiment, but whose talent as a writer and whose objectivity as a scholar result in tributes that are moving but also substantive. The introduction by Mary Helen Washington, who like Walker has been instrumental in the Hurston revival, presents a noteworthy discussion of Hurston's life, works, and critical reception, which should do much to promote a more balanced, objective, and accurate view of this much-maligned woman.

Twenty-five selections from *Mules and Men* appear in B. A. Botkin's *A Treasury of American Folklore* (Crown, 1944). A selection from *Dust Tracks on a Road* appears in Richard Long and Eugenia Collier's *Afro-American Writing: An Anthology of Prose and Poetry*, Vol. 2 (New York University Press, 1972); and Alan Dundes's *Mother Wit from the Laughing Barrel*. A Selection from *Jonah's Gourd Vine* appeared in *L'arbalète; revue de littérature* (Autumn, 1944) as "La Calebasse de Jonas" (translated by Marcel Duhamel).

SHORT STORIES

Despite the fact that Hurston wrote numerous short stories, no collection has ever been published. Except for the few popular and commonly reprinted ones, her short stories are difficult to locate, many of them having been published in obscure journals, black journals of limited circulation, and now out-of-print books.

"John Redding Goes to Sea" (*Stylus*, May 1921) was reprinted in *Opportunity* (January 1926). "O Night" appeared in *Stylus* in May 1921. "Drenched in Light" was published in *Opportunity* in December 1924 and has been reprinted in *Readings from Negro Authors for Schools and Colleges*, edited by Otelia Cromwell et al., (Harcourt, Brace, 1931); and Mary Butters McLellan and Albert V. DeBonis's *Within Our Gates: Selections on Tolerance and the Foreign Born of Today* (Harper, 1940). "Spunk" (*Opportunity*, June 1925) has been reprinted in Alain Locke's *The New Negro* (Albert and Charles Boni, 1925) and in Charles L. James's *From The Roots: Short Stories by Black Americans* (Dodd, Mead, 1971). "Magnolia Flower" appeared in *Spokesman* for July 1925. "Muttsy" was published in *Opportunity* for August 1926. "Sweat," which came out in *Fire!!* in November 1926, has been reprinted in Darwin Turner's *Black American Literature: Essays, Poetry, Fiction, Drama* (Columbus, Ohio: Merrill, 1970), Nathan Irvin Huggins's *Voices from the Harlem Renaissance* (New York: Oxford University Press, 1976), and *I Love Myself*. The popular "The Gilded Six-Bits," first published in *Story* in August 1933, has also been reprinted in Whit Burnett and Martha Foley's *Story in America* (Vanguard, 1934), Langston Hughes's *The Best Short Stories by Negro Writers: An Anthology from 1899 to the Present* (Boston: Little, Brown, 1967), Martha Foley's *200 Years of Great American Short Stories* (Boston:

Houghton Mifflin, 1975), Whit Burnett's *Black Hands on a White Face: A Timepiece of Experiences in a Black and White America: An Anthology* (Dodd, Mead, 1971), John Henrik Clarke's *American Negro Short Stories* (Hill and Wang, 1966), Susan Cahill's *Women and Fiction: Short Stories By and About Women* (New American Library, 1978), and *I Love Myself*. "The Fire and the Cloud" was published in *Challenge* in September 1934. "Cock Robin, Beale Street" appeared in the *Southern Literary Messenger* in July 1941. "Story in Harlem Slang" was published in *American Mercury* for July 1942 and is reprinted in Dundes's *Mother Wit from the Laughing Barrel*. "Conscience of the Court" was published in the *Saturday Evening Post* on 18 March 1950. "Escape from Pharoah" was published in Ruth Selden's *Ways of God and Men: Great Stories from the Bible in World Literature* (Stephen Daye Press, 1950). "The Tablets of Law" appeared in Frances Brentano's *The Word Lives On: A Treasury of Spiritual Fiction* (Garden City, N.Y.: Doubleday, 1951). "Hurricane" is published in Ann Watkins's *Taken at the Flood: The Human Drama as Seen by Modern American Novelists* (Harper, 1946).

Not many plays by Hurston have been published. "Color Struck" came out in *Fire!!* in November 1926. "The First One" appeared in Charles S. Johnson's *Ebony and Topaz: A Collectaniea* (National Urban League) in 1927. Act three of the controversial "Mule Bone," on which Hurston and Langston Hughes collaborated, was published in *Drama Critique* in the Spring 1964 issue.

Essays and Other Writings

Hurston wrote numerous essays, but they have never been collected and many of them are not readily available. They demand attention from the Hurston scholar because they present many of her views on and her studies of black folk life, history, and culture. A brief scanning here will give an impression of the variety of subjects that concerned her over a period of years.

"The Eatonville Anthology," a collection of fourteen sketches growing out of Eatonville life, was published in the *Messenger* in September, October, and November of 1926 and reprinted in *I Love Myself*. The first selections are character sketches. The two sketches in the second issue are short stories. The last sketch is an animal tale. These sketches contain episodes and materials that Hurston later used in *Seraph on the Suwanee* and *Their Eyes Were Watching God*. In *Forum* (September 1926) Hurston gives a version of the popular black folk tale, "Possum or Pig." "Dance Songs and Tales from the Bahamas" appeared in the *Journal of American Folklore* in the July-September 1930 issue. Her famous account of hoodoo in America and her own initiation rites under Samuel Thompson, a hoodoo doctor of New Orleans, the grand nephew of the famous Marie Leveau, are detailed in "Hoodoo in America" (*JAF*, October-December 1931). An account of this experience also appears in *Mules and Men*. In 1934 Nancy Cunard included several pieces by Hurston in *Negro: An Anthology* (London: Wishart; rptd. in 1969 by Negro Universities Press), including "Characteristics of Negro Expression," "Conversions and Visions," "Shouting," "The Sermon," "Mother Catherine," "Uncle Monday," and "Spirituals and Neo-Spirituals." Nathan I. Huggins (*Voices from the Harlem Renaissance*, Oxford University Press, 1976) reprints "Characteristics of Negro Expression," "Shouting," "The Sermon," "Uncle Monday," and "Spirituals and Neo-Spirituals." "Lawrence of the River," an account of a "con man," which bears a great resemblance to tall tales about folk heroes, appeared in the *Saturday Evening Post on 5 September* 1942. It was condensed in *Negro Digest* as "King of the Cow Country" (March 1943). "High John de Conquer," a poignant account of the black folk hero, appeared in the *American Mercury* in October 1943. It is reprinted in Dundes's *Mother Wit from the Laughing Barrel*. "Communications," an account of the settlement of Negroes in Fort Moosa and their fights against General Oglethorpe in the eighteenth century, was published in the *Journal of Negro History* in October 1927. "The Last Slave Ship," a moving account of the life and experiences of Cudjo Lewis, who was one of the last boatload of Africans brought to America in 1859, was published in *American Mercury* (March 1944). The account was condensed in *ND* in May 1944 under the title "Black Ivory Finale."

In numerous other essays Hurston comments on American life and politics, commentaries which are indispensable in trying to assess the Hurston personality and philosophy. "The Hue and Cry about Howard University" (*Messenger*, September 1925) is an impassioned defense of its white president, Dr. Durkee. In her review of Lance G. E. Jones's *The Jeanes Teacher in the United States* (Chapel Hill: University of North Carolina Press, 1937) in the *NYHTBW* ("Rural Schools for Negroes," 20 February 1938) Hurston joins in the condemnation of the reconstruction period and delights in the optimistic view of the future of the "New South," which will assuredly "work out all of its problems." In "The 'Pet Negro' System" (*AMer*, May 1943) she paints a picture of the black class in the South whose success she claims is often due to the support of some white friend. This article was condensed in *ND* (1 June 1943) under the title "The South's Other Side," and reprinted in *I Love Myself*. In "Negroes without Self-Pity" (*AMer*, November 1943), Hurston applauds speakers at a meeting of the Florida Negro Defense Committee who rejected the need to ask for pity for the Negroes but counseled rather assertiveness in participating in community life and correcting the irresponsible elements in the race. "My Most Humiliating Jim Crow Experience" (*ND*, June 1944) is an account of the humiliation she suffered when a white doctor, to whom her patron, Mrs. R. Osgood Mason, had referred her, examined her in the closet when he discovered her race. Hurston, who often attacked those who saw racism as unique to the South, emphasizes the fact that this incident occurred in the North. "The Rise of the Begging Joints" (*AMer*, March 1945; rptd. in *ND*, May 1945 as "Beware the Begging Joints") is an attack on small, inefficient black colleges. In "Crazy for This Democracy" (*ND*, December 1945; rptd. in *I Love Myself*), Hurston lambasts that democratic form of government of which the West and the United States in particular, brags, and notes its worldwide oppression of colored people. "I Saw Negro Votes Peddled" (*American Legion Magazine*, November 1950) is an account of Negroes selling votes, which reflects the kind of gullibility and naiveté for which her critics assail her. In "What White Publishers Won't Print" (*ND*, April 1950; rptd. in *I Love Myself*) Hurston criticizes the publishers and the reading public for their refusal to accept materials that do not reinforce their stereotyped views of minorities. Hurston attacks communism in "Why the Negro Won't Buy Communism" (*American Legion Magazine*, June 1951) and supports Robert Taft in "A Negro Voter Sizes up Taft" (*SEP*, 8 December 1951).

Also of interest are Hurston's accounts of the trial of Ruby McCollum, a well-to-do black Florida woman charged with killing her white lover, a prominent doctor and politician. Hurston's numerous accounts of the trial and portraits of Mrs. McCollum appear in the *Pittsburgh Courier* from October 1952 through May 1953; selections also appear in William Bradford Huie, *Ruby McCollum: Woman in the Suwanee Jail* (E. P. Dutton, 1956).

Hurston's interest in blacks in other parts of the African diaspora is revealed in some of her book review-essays. In a review-essay titled "Bible, Played by Ear in Africa," which is a review of Lorenz Graham's *How God Fix Jonah* (Reynal and Hitchcock, 1946) in the *NYHTBR* on 24 November 1946, she praises the author's capturing of the music of Africa in the telling of the Bible tales, but laments the fact that "The feeling of Africa is lost to a great extent through the omission of native material [such as the tales of the Mandingos, the Golahs and the Krus]." In "Thirty Days Among Maroons" (*NYHTBW*, 12 January 1947), Hurston applauds the description of life among the Maroons in Jamaica and the collection of tales and songs compiled by Katherine Dunham in *Journey to Accompong* (Henry Holt, 1946).

In "The Transplanted Negro" (*NYHTBW*, 9 March 1947), a review of Melville J. and Frances S. Herskovits's *Trinidad Village* (Alfred A. Knopf, 1974), Hurston praises the "laboratory examination" of the life of the inhabitants of Toco, but notes that the authors are sometimes mistaken in what they identify as African survivals. In "At the Sound of the Conch Shell" (*NYHTBW*, 20 March 1949) Hurston describes Vic Reid's *New Day* (Alfred A. Knopf, 1949) as "a liquid, lyrical thing of wondrous beauty." She applauds the author's historical accuracy and his effective rendering of

Jamaica: "The speech, the attitudes, the geographical descriptions are as Jamaican as a mouthful of ackee in season."

Her comments about her contemporaries also deserve mention. Of special interest is her account of her employer, "Fannie Hurst," which appeared in the *SatRL* for 9 October 1937. "Stories of Conflict" (*SatRL*, 2 April 1938) is a critical review of *Uncle Tom's Children* by Richard Wright, whom she considered talented, but whom she attacked for his subject matter, which she found too dismal and violent.

In 1947 Hurston published *Caribbean Melodies for Chorus of Mixed Voices and Soloists*, arranged by William Grant Still (Philadelphia: Oliver Ditson).

MANUSCRIPTS AND LETTERS

You have to read the chapters Zora left out of her autobiography.

Student, Special Collections Room,
Beinecke Library, Yale University,
cited in *I Love Myself*

Numerous Hurston manuscripts and letters are housed in various collections throughout the country and are indeed necessary to help paint a more complete and accurate picture of this complex personality. Many of these unpublished sources have aided scholars such as Robert Hemenway and Mary Helen Washington to begin to highlight the portrait of Zora Neale Hurston.

Upon Hurston's death a janitor in the welfare home in which she died proceeded to set fire to her effects, including the manuscript of her final work "Herod the Great," but the fire was luckily extinguished by a deputy sheriff (Hemenway, *Zora Neale Hurston*). The charred remains of this and other Hurston papers are a poignant symbol of the precarious survival of this woman within a society all too often completely insensitive to and unappreciative of her talents.

A significant number of Hurston manuscripts, letters, and other materials are housed in the Beinecke Rare Book and Manuscript Library at Yale University. In addition to the manuscripts of *Dust Tracks on a Road, Moses, Man of the Mountain, Tell My Horse*, and *Their Eyes Were Watching God*, Yale has the manuscripts of the following pieces: "Are We Citizens" (a fragment); "Book of Harlem" (short play); "The Chick with One Hen" (article); "The Emperor Effaces Himself" (short story); "Harlem Slanguage" (vocabulary); "Mule Bone" (play); "How You Cookin' with Gas" (short story—two versions); and "Polk County: A Comedy of Negro Life on a Sawmill Camp, with Authentic Negro Music" (three-act play written with Dorothy Waring), all unpublished except for the third act of "Mule Bone." Included in this collection are hundreds of letters to, from, or regarding Hurston, written by or to Carl Van Vechten, Ruby Harmon, Langston Hughes, James Weldon Johnson, Harold Jackman, Walter White, Fannie Hurst, Arna Bontemps, and Barrett H. Clark. Also of interest are a folder of clippings and some photographs.

Considerable Hurston materials may also be found in the Marjorie Kinnan Rawlings Collection at the University of Florida. There is an incomplete (some pages were burned) publisher's typescript with holograph additions and deletions of *Seraph on the Suwanee*. The University of Florida also has the partially burned manuscript of the unpublished work, "Herod the Great," including Hurston's notes for the work. Among the unpublished shorter works in this collection are the following: "The Elusive Goal—Brotherhood of Mankind" (essay); "The Enemy" (essay); "The Migrant Worker in Florida" (essay); "The Seventh Veil" (short story); "The South Was Had" (essay); "Take for Instance Spessard Holland" (essay); "Unique Personal Experience" (an early version of "The Enemy"); "The Woman in Gaul" (short story); "The Fiery Chariot" (play); "Folklore" (selection from "The Florida Negro"); "Notes on Cuban Music" (notes made by Hurston when locating folk singers); "Art and Such" (essay); and "Cross City: Turpentine Camp" (notes). The University of Florida also has a large number of letters exchanged among Hurston, Marjorie Kinnan Rawlings, Frank Alexander, Martin Anderson, Frederick Augustine, Richard Bardolph, Jesse V. Bates, T. C. Beam, R. Burdell Bixby, Willie Brown, LeRoy Collins, John K. Crippen, Ronald Cutler, Virginius Dabney, Woodrow Darden, George Beebe, Grace Davis, B. H. Dennis, Larry Eisenberg, Robert Emms, M. Mitchell Ferguson, Hoyt Fuller, Harold Gartley, Neil Gandy, P. H. Goddard, E. O. Grover, F. W. Grover, Prudence Hetherington, T. L. Hill, Mary Holland, William Huie, Everett E. Hurston, Sr., Iva Hurston, J. C. Hurston, Harper Brothers, Jean Waterbury, Joseph Keeley, Clennon King, William F. Knowland, J. Edwin Larsen, David Lawrence, Josephine Leighton, H. A. Leonard, J. P. Lippincott, B. L. Lippincott, A. C. Locke, Eva Lynd, Rosine MacLusk, William Morgan, John Scott Mahon, Clark Maxwell, Marjorie Meyer, Maurice Michael, Levi Miller, Helen and Burroughs Mitchell, Richard Moore, William Nunn, Frederick Nelson, Dorothy Owen, F. Pfeiffer, Juanita Russel, Nelson Rutledge, Edna Savoya, T. J. Seller, Waldo Sexton, Constance Sheen, Frank Smathers, W. W. Taylor, Irene Traffero, Louis Waldman, Maudie H. Warfel, Jean Parker Waterbury, D. E. Williams, Madeline Wiltz, Mary Wolfe, Fanny Hurst, and Corita Corse.

Also in the University of Florida collection are several copies of newspaper clippings regarding Hurston, programs presented by Hurston, flyers announcing her productions, and photographs. In addition there are copies of bills, unemployment compensation statements, royalty statements, and life insurance forms.

Interesting materials are also located in the Moorland-Spingarn Research Center at Howard University. In addition to several drafts of "Mule Bone" with holograph corrections, Howard University Library has a box of materials relating to the controversy surrounding the play, which served as the major source of Robert E. Hemenway's important reconstruction of that traumatic conflict between Zora Neale Hurston and Langston Hughes (see Hemenway, *Zora Neale Hurston*, Chapter 6, "Mule Bone"). There is, in addition, at the Howard University Library a holograph and typescript draft of "Barracoon" (play) and the manuscript of "The Bone of Contention" (short story). Also included in that collection are several letters regarding Hurston exchanged between Langston Hughes, Arthur Spingarn, Rowena Jelliffe, Samuel French, and Louise Thompson. There are letters exchanged between Hurston and Hughes, Alain Locke, and Arthur Spingarn. In addition there are thirty-nine letters and five telegrams from Hurston to Mrs. R. Osgood Mason. Also of interest are a contract between Hurston and Mrs. Mason, dated 1 December 1927; a contract between Hurston and Fast and Furious, Inc., New York, dated 6 July 1931; some financial statements regarding the John Golden Theatre; notes by Hurston regarding a conference with Harry Block on 26 February 1931; some newspaper clippings; and three photographs of Hurston.

The Archive of Folk Songs at the Library of Congress has 227 discs made by Hurston, Alan Lomax, and Mary Elizabeth Barnicle in Georgia, Florida, and the Bahamas during the summer of 1935. They also have twenty-three songs sung by Hurston and recorded in Florida and Haiti in 1935, 1936, and 1939. Also in this collection is a manuscript titled "Proposed Recording Expedition into the Floridas," written by Hurston when she was with the Florida Project of the Federal Writers Project, Works Progress Administration (WPA) in 1939. There are letters exchanged between Hurston, Dr. Ben Botkin, and Dr. Harold Spivack. Of further interest are field recording notes, newspaper articles, and some prints and photographs.

In the National Association for the Advancement of Colored People Records at the Library of Congress is correspondence between Hurston and Walter White.

The Manuscript Division of the Library of Congress has correspondence between Hurston and Carter G. Woodson.

The Metropolitan Dade County, Florida, Library has a Czech language edition of *Their Eyes Were Watching God*, which is autographed by Hurston (23 January 1950) and an autographed Danish language edition of the same novel. In addition there is an extensive newspaper clipping file on Hurston from the Dade County and other Florida newspapers.

The Julius Rosenwald Fund Archives, Fisk University Library, has a folder of letters regarding Hurston's application for a fellowship to pursue anthropological study in Negro folklore at Columbia University under Dr. Franz Boas, including payment vouchers, budget, letters of recommendation, and newspaper clippings by and about her. Fisk University also has the manuscript of "Black Death," a short story entered in the 1925 *Opportunity* contest.

The American Philosophical Society has a typed manuscript of Hurston's "The Florida Expedition," a report on Negro folklore, in the Franz Boas Collection. They also have correspondence between Hurston and Boas, the Julius Rosenwald Fund, and O. Klineberg. The manuscript of *Jonah's Gourd Vine* is in the Schomburg Collection in the New York Public Library. The manuscript of "The Florida Negro," a collection of stories, songs, games, slave narratives, and miscellaneous other folk items collected in the Florida WPA project, is in the Florida Historical Society Papers in the University of South Florida Library.

Robert Hemenway (*Zora Neale Hurston*) cites the Charles Scribner's Sons' Hurston files, which he notes contain 102 items, mainly their correspondence with Hurston.

Also of interest may be the series of interviews regarding Hurston that Hemenway made during his research for his biography of her. The interview with Arna Bontemps is at the University of Florida Oral History Collection. Other interviews, still in Hemenway's possession, were conducted with May Miller, George Schuyler, Bruce Nugent, Arthur Paul Davis, Saunders Redding, Herbert Sheen, Taylor Gordon, Sterling Brown, Louise Thompson Patterson, Arthur Huff Fauset, Alan Lomax, Everette Hurston, Sr., Bertram Lippincott, Tay Hohoff, W. Edward Farrison, Dean Elder, Paul Green, Mary Holland, Dorothy Waring, Grant Reynolds, Burroughs Mitchell, Louis Waldman, Jean Parker Waterbury, Everett Hurston, Jr., Sarah Peek Patterson, an unidentified cast member of *The Great Day*, and the unidentified woman for whom Hurston worked as a maid in 1950.

BIOGRAPHY

> The truth is that nobody, not even the closest blood relatives, ever really knows anybody else. The greatest human travail has been in the attempt at self revelation, but never, since the world began, has any one individual completely succeeded. There is an old saying to the effect that: "He is a man, so nobody knows him but God."
>
> Hurston, "The Life Story of Mrs. Ruby J. McCollum," *Pittsburgh Courier*, 28 February 1953

The life of Zora Neale Hurston is as puzzling, exciting, colorful, poignant, romantic, fascinating, and tragic as her fiction and has proven to be an important ingredient of most of the critical studies. An extremely private person, Hurston often concealed from her friends certain aspects of her life, such as, for example, her marriages to Herbert Sheen and to Albert Price III. While her own autobiography, *Dust Tracks on a Road*, provides some details of her life, it is perhaps more notable for what it doesn't tell us about her. The sincerity of much that she writes there is also highly debatable. Perhaps the most cogent comment on that work is the previously-quoted statement of the student in the Beinecke Library, Yale University: "You have to read the chapters Zora left out of her autobiography." (For a discussion of much of the deleted material see Hemenway, *Zora Neale Hurston.*) Further, as Hurston herself warns: "But pay no attention to what I say about love, for as I said before, it may not mean a thing. It is my own bathtub singing. Just because my mouth opens up like a prayer book, it does not have to flap like a Bible. And then again, anybody whose mouth is cut cross-ways is given to lying, unconsciously as well as knowingly" (*Dust Tracks on a Road*).

Numerous details of Hurston's life remained unclear or unknown, at least until the 1970s when Hurston scholars, notably Hemenway, uncovered certain facts about her life and began to unravel at least some parts of the puzzle. Until that time most biographies of her presented the well-known details that she chose to discuss publicly and which she included in *Dust Tracks on a Road*—mainly her life in Eatonville, her education, and her employment.

Such are the accounts that appear in sources such as B. Alsterlund's "Zora Neale Hurston, a Biographical Sketch" (*WLB*, May 1939); *Current Biography: Who's News and Why, 1942*, edited by Maxine Block (H. W. Wilson Co., 1942); Rebecca Chalmers Barton's *Witnesses for Freedom: Negro Americans in Autobiography* (Harper, 1948); *Who's Who in Colored America*, edited by C. James Fleming and Christian E. Burckel (Yonkers-on-Hudson, N.Y.: Christian E. Burckel and Associates, 1950), which contains several errors in the titles of the short works; Richard Bardolph's *The Negro Vanguard* (Rinehart, 1959); Stanley J. Kunitz and Howard Haycraft's *Twentieth Century Authors* (H. W Wilson, 1942; updated in their 1955 supplement); Russell L. Adams and others' *Great Negroes Past and Present* (Chicago: Afro-American Publishing Co., 1964); *American Women Writers: A Critical Reference Guide from Colonial Times to the Present*, edited by Lina Mainiero (Frederick Ungar, 1970); *Afro-American Encyclopedia*, edited by Martin Rywell and others (North Miami, Fla.: Educational Book Publishers, 1974); Wilhelmena S. Robinson's *Historical Afro-American Biographies* (Cornwells Heights, Pa.: The Association for the Study of Afro-American Life and History, 1976); and James A. Page's *Selected Black American Authors: An Illustrated Bio-Bibliography* (Boston: G. K. Hall, 1977).

Another source of biographical information about Hurston may be found in Langston Hughes's treatment of the Harlem Renaissance in "Harlem Literati in the Twenties" (*SatRL*, 22 June 1940; rptd. in *The Big*

Sea, Alfred A. Knopf, 1940). Most of his discussion rather sarcastically treats Hurston's personality: her playing the part of the perfect darkie for the whites, her ability to get whatever she needed from others, her wide contacts in Harlem, her entertaining humor.

Having disappeared from the public view for some years, Hurston popped up briefly working as a maid, and then died impoverished in a welfare home in Florida (her friends solicited money for her burial—including a $2.50 donation from a group of students [Hemenway, *Zora Neale Hurston*]). Her death (an uncanny fulfillment of her prophesy: "I am not materialistic. . . .If I happen to die without money somebody will bury me though I do not wish it to be that way" [quoted in Hemenway, *Zora Neale Hurston*]) was as melodramatic an episode as the rest of her life, and like the events of her life it provided good copy. Accounts of her death appeared in numerous papers and magazines. In addition to many local papers, obituary notices appeared in the *New York Times* (5 February 1960); *Time* (15 February 1960); *Newsweek* (15 February 1960); *Publishers' Weekly* (15 February 1960); *Wilson Library Bulletin* (April 1960); *Current Biography* (1960); and *Current Biography Yearbook* (1960, 1961). Three memoirs deserve note. Alan Lomax's "Zora Neale Hurston—A Life of Negro Folklore" (*Sing Out*, October-November 1960) recalls his experiences with her, mainly in quest of folklore, and pays tribute to her ability as a folk collector. He laments the lack of recognition of this woman who "was far ahead of her time," and praises *Mules and Men* as "the most engaging, genuine, and skillfully written book in the field of American folklore." He observes the irony of the fact that the week of 28 January 1960, was "a peak week in the great American folk song revival. This was also the week that the most skillful and talented field collector and writer that America has thus far produced died in a third rate hotel in Florida without a penny in her purse or a friend in the world." Theodore Pratt's "Zora Neale Hurston" (*FHQ*, July 1961) recounts her life, presents some interesting episodes from his relationship with her, and gives an account of her funeral. He laments the fact that Florida's only "first-class native-born" author has suffered literary obscurity and pleads for the recognition that she deserves. Fannie Hurst's "Zora Hurston: A Personality Sketch" (*YULG*, July 1961) is a fond memorial of her former secretary, chauffeur, and companion, one which is alternately impassionately moving and embarrassingly condescending. The lovable, irresponsible, colorful figure to whom Hurst immediately (in Zora's words) "took a shine" the first time she saw her, is remembered for "her gay unpredictability," and her being as "uninhibited as a child" and "an effervescent companion of no great profundities but dancing perceptions."

Virginia Burke's "Zora Neale Hurston and Fannie Hurst as They Saw Each Other" (*CLAJ*, June 1977) is based almost entirely on Hurst's "Zora Hurston: A Personality Sketch" and the autobiographies of the two principals. Burke notes the tendency of each to view the other in exaggerated extremes, so that, for example, Hurston pictures Hurst's family background as richer and more prominent than it was, and Hurst views Hurston's family background as being more impoverished than it actually was. Burke concludes that Hurst did not understand Hurston as well as Hurston understood Hurst, who was unable to see anything beyond the surface exotic primitive image of Hurston's personality. For Hurst, Hurston was merely a diversion; for Hurston, Hurst was a major event.

The only full-length biographical study of Hurston is Robert Hemenway's impressive *Zora Neale Hurston: A Literary Biography*. It is a tremendous undertaking and represents years of extensive research and study. It would be extremely difficult to suggest any sources (manuscripts, publications, letters, individuals) that Hemenway did not consult. His work is carefully documented and interestingly presented. The combination of the fascinating personality of his subject, the drama of her life, and his flair for telling a good story (was he influenced by Hurston?) results in a book that is as hard to put down as an intriguing novel. Hemenway traces Hurston's life from her arrival in New York "with one dollar and fifty cents in her purse, no job, no friends, but filled with 'a lot of hope'" (interspersing flashbacks to her Eatonville childhood and other intervening incidents) to its melodramatic and tragic end, reinforcing all of the paradoxes, ironies, and frustrations that he has detailed so meticulously with his forceful and simple concluding paragraph: "Zora Neale Hurston was buried in the Garden of the Heavenly Rest, the city's segregated cemetery."

Hemenway has introduced new information about some unknowns in Hurston's life and has scrupulously reconstructed certain events that had previously been shrouded in mystery. Though he does not completely resolve the issue of her birthdate, he does present an enlightening discussion of causes for the confusion and makes a convincing case for 1901. He offers interesting new information about her marriages, her relationship with Mrs. Rufus Osgood Mason (the "guardmother who sits in the twelfth heaven and shapes the destinies of the primitives" [Hurston, cited in Hemenway]); he presents a lengthy and objective clarification of the issues surrounding the "Mule Bone" controversy (the argument over the rights to the play on which they had collaborated that irrevocably destroyed the friendship of Langston Hughes and Hurston); and he gives a detailed review of the morals charges lodged against Hurston in 1948, accusing her of committing an immoral act with a ten-year-old boy. Briefly stated, Hemenway introduces additional new information and presents an intensive view of every period of the author's life, including in particular the latter years about which little had been written. He also reproduces several photographs of Hurston.

Hemenway's work is as important a critical study as it is a biography. He not only offers noteworthy discussions of all of her full-length published works, and most of the shorter ones; but he also discusses many of the unpublished texts as well. Each discussion offers critical and interpretive evaluations as well as interesting information about the inception, the composition, the publication, and the reception of each piece.

Hemenway presents his work with something of a disclaimer, motivated no doubt by the fact that he is a white man working on a black female subject during a period in which both blacks and women were jealously guarding their own against outsiders: he observes that he is not attempting a "'definitive' book—that book remains to be written, and by a black woman." Whatever limitations the writer may have placed on himself because he is a white man, he has, in spite of himself, written what must be called the definitive book on Zora Neale Hurston. And while a black woman might indeed bring to a study of Hurston some sensibilities, some perceptions, that only she could share, Hemenway has nonetheless presented her with a formidable yardstick by which to measure her achievement.

In the foreword to Hemenway's book ("Zora Neale Hurston—A Cautionary Tale and a Partisan View"), Alice Walker details her discovery of Hurston and her dedication to correcting the image of this writer who had suffered such vicious misinterpretation: "I began to fight for Zora and her work, for what I knew was good and must not be lost to us." Both Walker and Hemenway in this and other works have certainly done much to achieve that goal.

CRITICISM

I suppose that you have seen the criticism of my book in the *New York Times*. He means well, I guess, but I never saw such a lack of information about us.

Hurston, letter to James Weldon Johnson,
dated 8 May 1934, Yale University,
cited in Hemenway

Despite the fact that Zora Neale Hurston's works were rather widely reviewed and frequently lauded, the critics often praised them for the wrong reasons and showed a remarkable ignorance of or insensibility toward some of the issues with which Hurston was concerned. All too often the reviewers did not have the knowledge or sensitivity to appreciate fully the writer's efforts, and she has suffered as a result. Well-meaning whites, titillated by the exoticism of her blacks, black sophisticates embarrassed by the folk emphasis, male chauvinists alienated by her feminism, and so on, have tended to focus the discussion of her works on isolated issues rather than to initiate intensive evaluations of complete texts. Though Mary Helen Washington may be accused of some slight exaggeration, the basic truth of her assertion is irrefutable: noting the "groundswell of criticism that would become the intellectual lynching of Zora Neale Hurston" in the 1930s, she declares, "she was a black woman whose entire career output was subjected to the judgment of critics, both white and black, who were all men" (*I Love Myself*).

STUDIES OF INDIVIDUAL WORKS

Jonah's Gourd Vine

Zora Neale Hurston's first novel, *Jonah's Gourd Vine* (1934), was enthusiastically received, especially by the white press whose excessive praises sometimes suggested condescension and racism. Margaret Wallace ("Real Negro People," *NYTBR*, 6 May 1934) hailed it as "the most vital and original novel about the American Negro that has yet been written by a member of the Negro race," from which one must infer that more "vital and original" novels had been written by someone of another race. She goes on to note that though the Negro race "is as different from ours as night from day," Hurston succeeds in making her Negro characters "appeal to us . . . as human beings." Like most of the reviewers, she praised Hurston's "excellent rendition of Negro dialect." The review in *Booklist* (July 1934) likewise praised the novel as being "rich in dialect and folklore." The reviewers were almost unanimous in hailing its accurate portrayal of Negro life in the South: William Plomer (*Spectator*, 4 January 1935) called it "a genuine and in many ways admirable tale of Negro life." The *NYHTBW* reviewer praised the understanding of Negro life and the objectivity of portrayal. Herschel Brickell (*New York Post*, 5 May 1934) noted the authenticity and objectivity and called the sermon "simply magnificent." Martha Gruening (*NewR*, 11 July 1934) applauded Hurston's candor, something which she notes is "still sufficiently rare among Negro writers." The reviewer in *The Nation* (13 June 1934) did note faults in the construction of the novel, but he found much to praise. Andrew Burris (*Crisis*, June 1934) also lauded the "rich store of folklore" and the effectively reproduced dialect, but he found *Jonah's Gourd Vine* "disappointing and a failure as a novel," weak both in character and plot development.

In his introduction to the 1971 edition of the novel, Larry Neal praises it as "a remarkable first novel" and notes that "the theme, man's search for spiritual equilibrium, is large, mythic, and timeless."

Mules and Men

Zora Neale Hurston's collection of black folklore, *Mules and Men* (1935), received an enthusiastic reception similar to that accorded *Jonah's Gourd Vine*, largely from white critics, who were delighted with this colorful inside view of Negro life. Lewis Gannett (*NYHT*, 11 October 1935) declared, "I can't remember anything better since Uncle Remus." The richness of the dialect and the quality of the tales were praised by reviewers in the *New York Post* (Herschel Brickell, 26 October 1935); the *NYTBR* (H. I. Brock, 10 November 1935); the *SatRL* (Jonathan Daniels, 19 October 1935); and the *NAR* (T. C. Chubb, March 1936). The reviewer in the *NYHTBW* (13 October 1935) lauded it as a "milestone" in Negro literature. H. L. Moon (*NewR*, 11 December 1935) noted her failure to evaluate her materials or to trace origins but praised her style, which enabled the reader "to feel himself a part of [the storytellers'] circle." Sterling Brown ("Old Time Tales," 1936, unindentified clipping, James Weldon Johnson Collection, Yale University Library, cited in Hemenway, *Zora Neale Hurston*) deplored the unbalanced picture of Southern life, noting her omission of the unattractive aspects of Negro life in the South.

In his introduction to the 1978 edition of *Mules and Men*, Robert E. Hemenway discusses Hurston's development as a folklorist and the events that led to the writing of *Mules and Men*. He emphasizes the fact that the work is not merely a collection of quaint, childish tales, but rather a collection of tales that are "the complex cultural communications permitted an oppressed people." He notes some objections to the book, such as "its lack of cross-cultural analysis, comparative notes, and scholarly apparatus" as well as the absence of social consciousness among the storytellers. But, he argues, Hurston subordinated all of these matters in order to "address the negative image of the black folk publicly held by most Whites and Blacks."

Their Eyes Were Watching God

Hurston's second novel, *Their Eyes Were Watching God* (1937), was received with less enthusiasm by the American critics. They continued to applaud her reproduction of folk dialect and her portrayal of "simple Florida Negroes" (Otis Ferguson, *NewR*, 13 October 1937), but technical weakness in this work were criticized by S. A. Brown (*Nation*, 16 October 1937), Otis Ferguson, and George Stephens (*SatRL*, 18 September 1937). Lucy Tompkins (*NYTBR*, 26 September 1937) considered the novel a bit sententious at the beginning but concluded that it is nonetheless "a well-nigh perfect story." Richard Wright, in "Between Laughter and Tears" (*NewM* 5 October 1937), lambasted it as having "no theme, no message, no thought," and attacked Hurston for perpetuating a minstrel image for the entertainment of whites.

Their Eyes Were Watching God has received a great deal more attention from scholars than any other work by Hurston, particularly from black females who applaud its picture of love between a black male and a black female and its portrayal of the quest for freedom and selfhood on the part of the heroine, Janie Stark. Representative of the enthusiastic responses to it are Mary Helen Washington's assertion that it is "probably the most beautiful love story of a black man and woman in literature" (*Black-Eyed Susans: Classic Stories by and about Black Women*, Garden City, N.Y.:

Doubleday, 1971). June Jordan, in "On Richard Wright and Zora Neale Hurston" (*BlackW*, August 1974), insists that it is the "most successful, convincing and exemplary novel of blacklove that we have. Period." And Alice Walker (*I Love Myself*) exclaims, "Reading *Their Eyes Were Watching God* for perhaps the eleventh time, I am still amazed that . . . it speaks to me as no novel, past or present, has ever done. . . . There is enough self-love in that one book—love of community, culture, traditions—to restore a world. Or create a new one." And again in her introduction to *Zora Neale Hurston* she simply asserts, "*There is no book more important to me than this one.*"

Lloyd W. Brown's "Zora Neale Hurston and the Nature of Female Perception" (*Obsidian*, Winter 1978) is an interesting discussion of Hurston's presentation of the difference between the male and female modes of perceiving reality. He traces in detail Janie's ability throughout her life to transcend her adversities by living in dreams and concludes that "both as heroic affirmation and as escape, then, Janie's capacity to 'make dreams truth' emerges as an intrinsic part of her limited experiences as woman." Erlene Stetson, in "*Their Eyes Were Watching God*: A Woman's Story" (*RFI*, 1979), considers the novel a work about "survival motions, the survival of one black woman." Tracing Janie's development and maturity through her three "marriages," she notes that Janie "stands alone in relation to previous mulattos in literature." She is an "anti-romantic symbol of the mulatto 'type.'" James R. Giles, in "The Significance of Time in Zora Neale Hurston's *Their Eyes Were Watching God*" (*NALF*, Summer 1972), considers the varying views of time in the novel and concludes that those who view time in a rational, materialistic way and whose value system is modelled on the white world's lose out in this novel to those who view time "emotionally and hedonistically" and live for the momentary sexual pleasures. Peter Schwalbenberg, in "Time as Point of View in Zora Neale Hurston's *Their Eyes Were Watching God*" (*BALF*, Spring [should have been designated Fall] 1976), also considers the treatment of time in the novel. He notes that at first in the novel time is of no time—there is timelessness. Janie remains static until her marriage to Jody, where time remains exterior. Time becomes interior only with the arrival of Tea Cake. In "The Black Woman's Search for Identity" (*BlackW*, August 1972) Mary Helen Washington details the experiences and the folk traditions of black people, which help to explain Nanny's attitudes toward love and her aspirations for her granddaughter. She discusses the manner in which Janie's quest for freedom and identity lead her away, however, from those white-inspired values of Nanny, Jody Starks, and Mrs. Turner and lead her into the true values of her own culture. Her descent into the Everglades with Tea Cake is a further retreat from white models and a further movement into blackness, Washington notes. Sister Mary Ellen Doyle, in "The Heroine of Black Novels" (*Perspectives on Afro-American

Women, edited by Willa D. Johnson and Thomas L. Green, Washington, D.C.: ECCA Publications, 1975), notes that the novel is representative of the Harlem Renaissance's "rejection of imitation-white refinements and restrictions," but cautions that it is not merely a study in primitivism but rather "a sensitive study...of the ideal man/woman relationship... [asserting] that natural living and loving, working and playing, in an equal partnership worth waiting for, well considered, freely chosen and faithfully sustained make the only real satisfaction or security for a black and womanly soul." Observing the general lack of enthusiasm for the female liberation movement in the black community, S. Jay Walker, in "Zora Neale Hurston's *Their Eyes Were Watching God:* Black Novel of Sexism" (*MFS*, Winter 1974-1975), points out that *Their Eyes Were Watching God* is unusual in black literature as a work dealing more with sexism than racism. He traces the steps by which Janie fights against male domination and asserts her own dignity and independence and equality until she attains a relationship where there are no sex roles or places.

Several general surveys of black American literature discuss *Their Eyes Were Watching God*. Catherine Juanita Starke, in *Black Portraiture in American Fiction* (Basic Books, 1971), briefly discusses Janie as an example of a "youthful female seeker for identity and fulfillment." Judith R. Berzon's *Neither White nor Black: The Mulatto Character in American Fiction* (New York University Press, 1978) cites Janie as an exception to the usual female character who lacks depth and points out that she is a woman of spirit and will who "moves steadily toward self-definition." In *Black Fiction* (Cambridge, Mass.: Harvard University Press, 1974) Roger Rosenblatt observes Janie's progress toward personal freedom.

Tell My Horse

Hurston's next work, *Tell My Horse* (1938), a collection of miscellaneous commentaries and items concerning Haitian and Jamaican life and folklore, including accounts of voodoo in Haiti (which Hemenway calls her "poorest book," in *Zora Neale Hurston*) did not receive the wide nor enthusiastic response that her earlier folklore study inspired. Carl Carmer (*NYHTBW*, 23 October 1938) did praise it for its "unbelievably rich" harvest of West Indian folklore; and the *New York Times* reviewer (23 October 1938) called it an "unusual and intensely interesting book." In a mixed review Harold Courlander (*SatRL*, 15 October 1938) described it as "a curious mixture of remembrance, travelogue, sensationalism, and anthropology." The anthropology, he continued, is "a melange of misinterpretation and exceedingly good folk-lore."

Moses, Man of the Mountain

Moses, Man of the Mountain (1939, Hurston's retelling of the Biblical story, with Moses and his people being pictured as Egyptians who speak and act like black Americans, met with mixed reviews. Carl Carmer (*NYHTBW*, 26 November 1939) praised her "uncommon gifts as a novelist" and her characterization. Percy Hutchinson (*NYTBR*, 19 November 1939) characterized the work as a "narrative of great power . . . literature in every best sense of the word." His enthusiastic response was colored, however, by his condescending attitude. Speaking of American blacks he notes, "even they have traditions that will not die." Louis Untermeyer (*SatRL*, 11 November 1939) praised the characterization, the style, and the setting, but concluded that the total effect was disappointing. Philip Slomovitz (*CC*, 6 December 1939) considered the book "weak in its interpretations of the ethical contributions of the prophet and its treatment of the code of laws handed down by him," but praised Hurston's study of slave emancipation from a Negro viewpoint. Ralph Ellison, in "Recent Negro Fiction" (*NewM*, 5 August 1941), considered it, like her other work, marred by "the blight of calculated burlesque." Noting that she attempts in the work to do for Moses what *Green Pastures* did for Jehovah, he concluded, "for Negro fiction it [*Moses, Man of the Mountain*] did nothing."

Despite the fact that several scholars have acknowledged the significance of *Moses, Man of the Mountain* (Hemenway calls it Hurston's "most ambitious book" in *Zora Neale Hurston* and Darwin Turner asserts that "If she had written nothing else Miss Hurston would deserve recognition for this book" in *In a Minor Chord*), only one study has been devoted to it: Blyden Jackson's "Some Negroes in the Land of Goshen" (*TFSB*, June 1953). Jackson details Hurston's faithful rendition of the Biblical story of Moses with characters who are familiar Negro folk characters and praises it for its "beauty of simplicity." He concludes that Hurston succeeds in showing that "a Negro folk experience of life [can] be seen as what it substantially is, the reliable counterpart of every other human being's experience of the same life." While retaining the local charm of the folk she shows that "Negro life need not be parochial, but may anchor securely its substratum in the universal mind."

Dust Tracks on a Road

Dust Tracks on a Road (1949), Hurston's highly controversial autobiography, received the Anisfield Award in Racial Relations given by the *Saturday Review of Literature* for the best book of the preceding year concerned with racial problems ("Anisfield Awards to Hurston and Pierson," *PW*, 27 February 1943). The book was reasonably well-received by most white critics while it was attacked by many black critics. The reviewer in the *New Yorker* (14 November 1942) called it "warm, witty, imaginative . . . a rich and winning book." Phil Stong (*SatRL*, 28 November 1942) praised the style of the work but noted that it was more summary than autobiography. Ernestine Rose (*LJ*, 1 November 1942) noted a lack of finish, but observed that "this literary crudity may have been chosen deliberately, to heighten effect." Arna Bontemps, in "From Eatonville, Florida to Harlem"

(*NYHTBW*, 22 November 1942) sarcastically observed, "Miss Hurston deals very simply with the more serious aspects of Negro life in America—she ignores them." Harold Preece (*Tomorrow*, February 1943; cited in Hemenway, *Zora Neale Hurston*) called *Dust Tracks on a Road* "the tragedy of a gifted, sensitive mind, eaten up by an egocentrism fed on the patronizing admiration of the dominant white world."

In "*Dust Tracks on a Road*: Zora Neale Hurston and the Form of Black Autobiography" (*NALF*, Summer 1975), Ann Rayson argues that because of her colloquial and informal language and style, Hurston can get away with saying things that would ordinarily elicit hostility. She observes that Hurston "portrays herself as a reincarnation of the Melvillian isolato on a continual search for an unknown kind of holy grail" and that she also portrays herself as "a kind of black female Ben Franklin." She concludes that despite the avoidance of political and social issues and despite the contradictions, "Zora Neale Hurston succeeds in portraying her real self, which is all that any autobiographer can hope to do." Mary Burgher, in "Images of Self and Race in the Autobiographies of Black Women" (*Sturdy Black Bridges*, Garden City, N.Y.: Doubleday, 1979), uses *Dust Tracks on a Road* to illustrate her thesis that "more often than not, the route to Black womanhood is fast and direct." She observes that quite typically, Hurston enjoyed little childhood and had to grow up fast, but despite the fact that she had to accept adult responsibility when she was young, she "remains forever youthful in her optimism and her curiosity about life."

Seraph on the Suwanee

In *Seraph on the Suwanee* (1948), Hurston attempted for the first time to portray the lives of Southern whites. Initially the novel was relatively well received, though later critics, particularly her most ardent admirers, tended either to ignore it or to attack it as a futile effort to abandon the source of her inspiration and creativity—black culture. Worth Heddon (*NYHTBW*, 10 October 1948) called it "an astonishing novel" and expressed surprise that someone outside the "breed," even though a neighbor and an anthropologist, could portray the group so well. Edward Hamilton (*America*, 1 January 1949), who mistakingly assumed this was "Hurston's first novel," praised the reproduction of the speech of Florida whites and the picturing of the relationship between Arvay and Jim. Eddie Shiman (*Common Ground*, Spring 1948) viewed it as a study of white Southern culture by an anthropologist, an authority on folk culture "who happens to be a Negro." Frank Slaughter (*NYTBR*, 31 October 1948) also observed her knowledge of the people and the area that she pictures and commented on the Freudian psychology applied in the study of Arvay.

Carl Milton Hughes, in *The Negro Novelist: A Discussion of the Writings of American Negro Novelists, 1940-1950* (Citadel Press, 1953), asserts that *Seraph on the Suwanee*, "her most finished novel," places Hurston in "the avant-garde in Freudian literature among Negro authors." He considers Arvay a perfect example of the hysterical female. He notes also a talent in Hurston that many women writers lack: "she portrays a man's man." He also praised Hurston for her reproduction of the idiom of Florida whites and for her evocation of the Florida locale, especially "her precise description of shrimping on the Atlantic ocean."

General Studies

Distinguishing between the critical and biographical studies of Zora Neale Hurston is quite difficult, because most of the critiques of her work also emphasize her life and her personality. Thus some of the studies in this section may immediately appear more appropriate to the section on biography. If, however, the critic presents his work as a study of Hurston's writings, I have accepted his characterization and noted his work in this section.

The controversies about what Hurston did and didn't do, what she believed and didn't believe, what she wrote and didn't write continue in the general studies that treat her work. Hugh Gloster, in *Negro Voices in American Fiction* (Russel and Russell, 1965; reprint of University of North Carolina 1948 edition) briefly discusses *Jonah's Gourd Vine* and *Their Eyes Were Watching God*, praising her handling of folk materials in both books, but observing her weakness in character development and the analysis of social problems in the former. He notes that she is generally "more interested in folklore and dialect than in social criticism" and that she neglects racial tensions. Noel Schraufnagel's *From Apology to Protest: The Black American Novel* (Deland, Fla.: Everett/Edwards, 1973) dispenses with Hurston in two short paragraphs, which present cursory summaries of *Jonah's Gourd Vine* and *Their Eyes Were Watching God*. He does observe that Hurston does not stress social problems. Most of Nathan Irvin Huggins's consideration of Zora Neale Hurston in his study, *Harlem Renaissance* (Oxford University Press, 1971) is devoted to determining whether or not Hurston was really playing the "darky" role. He presents the views of some of her associates that she was putting on an act to fool her white patrons, but notes that her autobiography suggests a sincerity on her part in these relations. He concludes that if she were putting on an act earlier, "by the time she wrote the story of her life, she had become the act." He observes that though Hurston was better trained as a folklorist than Arthur Huff Fauset, she "was far less pure in her handling of folk materials." He describes her folk materials and concludes that Fauset "could complain as much about the sentimentality and artificiality here as in Joel Harris' work."

Arthur Paul Davis, in *From the Dark Tower: Afro-American Writers, 1900-1960* (Washington, D.C.: Howard University Press, 1974), praises the use of folk customs, superstitions, and speech in her works, but finds all of the novels lacking in some respects. Her folklore collections are her most important contributions. He notes her tendency in her works to ignore unpleasant aspects of Southern racism and comments, "This shutting of the eyes on Miss Hurston's part is a kind of artistic dishonesty." Noting her omissions from *Dust Tracks on a Road*, he says that while such ordering of experience is common in autobiographies, "the liberties Miss Hurston takes come dangerously close to plain dishonesty." In "The Negro Novelist and the South" (*SHR*, Spring 1967) Darwin Turner observes that Hurston's novels tend to exaggerate language and overemphasize certain aspects of Negro life, such as the storytelling, at the expense of the work. He notes that her settings are atypical—all-Negro community—and that she emphasizes the exotic.

Darwin Turner's *In a Minor Chord* (Carbondale: Southern Illinois University Press, 1971) is a pioneering work, the first major study that presented new information and more intensive interpretation of the life and works of Zora Neale Hurston. His contempt for the woman overshadows his respect for the writer, however, and the overall tone is one of "apparent indifference to her own dignity or that of other blacks." He observes the comments of Hughes, Bontemps, and Hurst, which suggest her assumption of the role of happy darkie. He contrasts her affable reactions to whites in *Dust Tracks on a Road* with her violent and antagonistic reactions to blacks. He accuses Hurston of denouncing some efforts of blacks to secure equal opportunities and concludes that Hurston may be characterized as "an imaginative, somewhat shallow, quick-tempered woman, desperate for recognition and reassurance to assuage her feelings of inferiority." Despite her "psychological limitations," Turner argues that her novels "deserve more recognition than they have received." He notes certain weaknesses, previously detailed in an article cited earlier in this study, but praises her "ear for dialect, . . . appreciation of the folktale, . . . lively imagination, and . . . understanding of feminine psychology." He observes a progressive improvement in the creation of her novels with *Their Eyes Were Watching God* being superior to *Jonah's Gourd Vine*, and *Moses, Man of the Mountain* being her "most accomplished achievement in fiction." Turner considers her final novel, *Seraph on the Suwanee*, "her most ambitious novel and her most artistically competent." Of her work in folklore Turner says that she is a talented reporter but a weak scholar. His general conclusion about *Tell My Horse* represents his assessment of both collections of folklore. He writes, "*Tell My Horse* reveals Miss Hurston's unusual talent for gathering material, her skill in reporting it, and her characteristic inability to interpret it." Turner concludes his study with this harsh assessment: "Always, she remained a wandering minstrel. It was eccentric but perhaps appropriate for her to return to Florida to take a job as a cook and maid for a white family and to die in poverty. She had not ended her days as she once had hoped. . . . Instead she had returned to the level of life which she proposed for her people."

Turner's study represented a kind of culmination of the harsh male attacks on Hurston, beginning with Hughes, Bontemps, and Wallace Thurman, and continued by Harold Preece, Richard Wright, Ralph Ellison, and Nathan Huggins. It was an attack which brought out Hurston's defenders in large numbers during the 1970s. And their defense of her is motivated as much by attraction to Hurston's personality as the attacks are motivated by resentment of her personality. Their defenses may often become as emotional and as subjective as some of the detractor's attacks, for to many Hurston is the representative par excellence of black strength and pride, of self-love, and of female assertiveness; and they tend to speak as often of love for her as they do of appreciation for her art.

In a general survey of the "pervasive narrow views of many male critics towards black women's novels," Rita B. Dandridge, in "Male Critics/ Black Women's Novels" (*CLAJ*, September 1979), considers three basic approaches: "apathy, chauvinism, and paternalism." Most of her essay is devoted to a scathing attack on Darwin Turner's "chauvinistic" criticism of Hurston. In a point-by-point analysis, she defends Hurston against many of Turner's charges and attacks Turner for taking a different approach to the study of Hurston than he took with Countee Cullen and Jean Toomer (the other two principals of his study), using hearsay statements and irrelevant remarks to disparage her while completely overlooking "Cullen's alleged homosexuality and Toomer's alleged partiality for white women." She attacks Turner for distorting the facts and characterizes him as "an arrogant fault-finder." She even attacks his choice of placing Hurston last in his study, "a position for a put down." Mary Helen Washington, in "Zora Neale Hurston: A Woman Half in Shadow" (*I Love Myself*), likewise attacks Turner for evaluating Hurston's work on the basis of her personality while forgiving Toomer's comparable quirks as "philosophically viable and utterly sincere" (Turner, *In a Minor Chord*).

June Jordan, in "On Richard Wright and Zora Neale Hurston" (*BW*, 23 August 1974), argues that Hurston's obscurity results from the fact that the American media generally determine what figures will be given the dominant place, and in Hurston's era Richard Wright was the solitary black figure presented. One reason that he was acclaimed and Hurston was ignored was the assumption that what we needed was protest writing; and Hurston chose to affirm blackness rather than to protest against whites. She notes that there is a definite defiance in Hurston's works and concludes that it is not necessary to choose between Bigger and Janie: "our lives are as big and as manifold and as pained and as happy as the two of them put together. We should equally value and equally emulate Black Protest and Black Affirmation, for we require both." "In Search of Zora Neale Hurston" (*Ms.*, March 1975; rptd. as "Looking for Zora" in *I Love Myself*) is Alice Walker's poignant account of her search for Hurston's unmarked grave, which is symbolically a quest for the elusive personality of Hurston. Walker's visit to Eatonville and her conversations with some of the residents who knew Hurston help to explain the pride of those from this all-black town, who like Hurston, never felt any need to integrate. Walker's quest is poignantly reinforced when, alone in a snake-infested, overgrown graveyard, she yells in frustration, "Zora! . . . are you out there?" Though she never locates the gravesite, it is quite clear that Alice Walker does find Zora Neale Hurston, and her moving portraits in this essay, in the introduction to Hemenway's book, and in the introduction to her recent collection of Hurston's works, *I Love Myself*, suggest her dedication to the proposition that finding Zora Neale Hurston will prove a source of strength to all black women and will help them to love themselves. Carole Gregory, in "A Likely Possibility: Conversation Between Zora Neale Hurston and Carole Gregory" (*Black Collegian*, April/May 1980), argues that Hurston's lack of popular acclaim is a result of her celebration of plain folks, her unsuccessful marriages, racism, color prejudice, and sexism. She applauds the "rediscovery" of Hurston today and the fact that she is now honored for revealing "the heart of Black women." Gregory imagines a dialogue between herself and Hurston, which makes use of views expressed by Hurston in her works, a dialogue which reinforces her dedication to the folk culture and her concerns with Black women, without being a "feminist."

Lillie P. Howard's "Marriage: Zora Neale Hurston's System of Values" (*CLAJ*, December 1977) notes that the marriage relationship and its problems are themes in four of Hurston's short stories and three of her novels and observes that of the eleven marriages she treats, only three succeed. From these three marriages Howard concludes that the necessary qualities for a successful marriage, according to Hurston, are "courage, honesty, love, trust, respect, understanding, and a willingness to work together." She notes that in the unsuccessful marriages, "the male is always eliminated, i.e., killed" and concludes, "A flawed man is obviously less forgiveable [*sic*] in the Hurston world than a flawed woman."

Ann Rayson's "The Novels of Zora Neale Hurston" (*SBL*, Winter 1974) presents a rather extended discussion of the four novels but also makes some questionable observations. She calls Arvay a return "to the successful female protagonist she had created in *Their Eyes Were Watching God*," a comparison that is highly debatable. She suggests that the theme of Hurston's works is the need to go beyond the "quest for bourgeois life to a comprehension of what is ultimately meaningful—love, fun, a full relationship with one of the opposite sex." This theme is discussed in *Jonah's Gourd Vine* and *Their Eyes Were Watching God*, but Rayson forgets the theme in *Moses, Man of the Mountain* during the main part of her discussion, which is a comparison with *Ol' Man Adam an' His Chillun*, by Roark Bradford. Later she tries to tie this work in with her main thesis by noting that here Moses strives to form a good relationship with God.

In "Zora Neale Hurston" (*Carrell*, June-December 1970), Evelyn Thomas Helmick gives a lengthy account of Hurston's life and a helpful overview of all of her longer works with a few commentaries on the short stories and essays.

Though many folklore studies have ignored Hurston's work, some anthropologists and folklorists have applauded and noted her contributions. Franz Boas's introduction to *Mules and Men* (1935 edition; rptd. in the 1969 edition) praises Hurston's ability to enter into the lives of blacks as one of them, gain their confidence and thereby penetrate the "affected demeanor by which the Negro excludes the White observer from participating in his true inner life." He also praises "the charm of a loveable personality and of a revealing style." In his discussion of the verbal traditions and the images and roles of black women, Roger D. Abrahams, in "Negotiating Respect: Patterns of Presentation among Black Women" (*JAF*, January-March 1975), cites passages from *Their Eyes Were Watching God*. He uses illustrations from *Their Eyes Were Watching God* and *Jonah's Gourd Vine* in his discussion of courtship patterns and "fancy talk." Lawrence Levine, in *Black Culture and Black Consciousness: Afro-American Folk Thought from Slavery to Freedom* (Oxford University Press, 1977), frequently cites Hurston's observations concerning matters such as the importance of the phonograph and its impact on blacks and her comments on blues, jazz, and work songs. In "Folklore Field Notes from Zora Neale Hurston" (*BlackSch*, April 1976), Robert Hemenway observes that the emphasis on Hurston's art by critics "has led to the neglect of her career as a folklorist." He goes on to detail her formal training and her career as a folklorist and notes that her work did much to illuminate the distinctive culture of black Americans. He then presents several notes that Hurston had intended to publish in "The Negro in Florida," including a discussion of the characteristics of black verbal lore, folk rhymes, and narratives.

It is most unusual that the subject which Ellease Southerland treats, "The Influence of Voodoo on the Fiction of Zora Neale Hurston" (*Sturdy Black Bridges*), has not been considered before. After effectively summarizing Hurston's exposure to and experiences with voodoo doctors and ceremonies, Southerland considers various aspects of voodooism in her works, including the use of the numbers three, six, and nine, the emphasis on the colors blue and yellow, the use of the tree in *Their Eyes Were Watching God*, and the portrayal of Moses as a voodoo man. This is a good introductory, ground-breaking article, which suggests the need for further investigation in this area. James W. Byrd's "Zora Neale Hurston: A Negro Folklorist" (*TFSB*, June 1955) reviews Hurston's use of folklore in *Mules and Men, Tell My Horse, Moses, Man of the Mountain, Jonah's Gourd Vine, Their Eyes Were Watching God*, and *Seraph on the Suwanee*. Citing numerous examples, Byrd praises her reproduction of black folk speech, rhymes, games, and superstitions. He acclaims her reproduction of white Southern folkways in *Seraph on the Suwanee*, but points to some instances where the author attributes black speech patterns to her white characters. Theresa Love's "Zora Neale Hurston's America" (*PLL*, Fall 1976) begins as a discussion of the use of folk materials in the works of Hurston and ends as a discussion of the theme of the need for love in *Jonah's Gourd Vine*, *Their Eyes Were Watching God*, and *Seraph on the Suwanee*, as well as in some short stories. Hugh Gloster, in "Zora Neale Hurston, Novelist and Folklorist" (*Phylon*, Second Quarter 1943), attempts to illustrate that "all of Miss Hurston's major works stem from her anthropological interests and investigations." He then goes on to discuss her "capacity for appropriating folklore to the purpose of fiction." Gloster concludes that her folk studies are not scientific: she does not consider sources, but rather treats her materials "much in the manner of the over-enthusiastic tourist." He also observes that her emphasis on folklore has resulted in a lack of attention to style, plot construction, character development, and the like: "As a result, her fiction lacks . . . literary finish, . . . structural craftsmanship, [and] psychological penetration."

Ellease Southerland's "Zora Neale Hurston: The Novelist-Anthropologist's Life/Works" (*BlackW*, August 1974) is a good overview of Hurston's life and works, with the exception of *Seraph on the Suwanee*. Southerland calls attention to some of the comments in *Dust Tracks on a Road*, which have provoked the criticism that Hurston lacks racial consciousness, but argues that her other works counter this criticism. Southerland's assertion that Hurston and Wright wrote the best novels of the Harlem Renaissance period is not clear, however, since neither author wrote any novels during the period generally referred to as the Renaissance.

In *The Way of the New World* (Garden City, N.Y.: Doubleday, 1975), Addison Gayle considers *Jonah's Gourd Vine* as a tragedy with John Pearson the tragic hero whose flaw is his sexual promiscuity. He considers the most important aspect of this novel the depiction of the character of the black woman. He considers also Hurston's portrayal of the modern liberated black woman in *Their Eyes Were Watching God*. He notes that her female characters do not castrate the black male, but are rather the "foundations of a new order, . . . from whose loins will eventually come the new man." Gayle concludes that Hurston was one of those authors who, "despite flaws in perception which often limited their vision, believed in the sanctity of the black spirit, who sought, through their art, to elevate a race of people."

Larry Neal's "Eatonville's Zora Neale Hurston: A Profile" (*BlackR*, No. 2, edited by Mel Watkins, Morrow, 1972; rptd. as "A Profile: Zora Neale Hurston," *Southern Exposure*, Winter 1974) is a good overview of her life and works. Neal gives a detailed explication of *Their Eyes Were Watching God*, which he says is "clearly her best novel." He asserts that her most significant contributions are her studies of folklore, and he praises her for her approach—that of identifying with the folk rather than the scientific approach of most folklorists. Neal attempts to explain why so little is known about such an important writer and suggests that perhaps her conservative political views and the morals charges against her in 1948 were responsible for her disappearance from the creative scene.

Robert Bone's discussion of Hurston in *The Negro Novel in America* (rev. ed., New Haven: Yale University Press, 1965) is reprinted as "Zora Neale Hurston" in *The Black Novelist*, edited by Robert Hemenway (rev. ed., Columbus: Charles E. Merrill, 1970). Bone considers *Jonah's Gourd Vine* a novel which "has style without structure, a rich verbal texture without dramatic form, 'atmosphere' without real characterization." *Their Eyes Were Watching God* is labeled her best novel and "possibly the best novel of the period, excepting *Native Son*." In his overview of Hurston's life and works James Rambeau, in "The Fiction of Zora Neale Hurston," (*MarkhamR*, Summer 1976), characterizes her folk collections as of "the personal and anecdotal nature of the amateur rather than the professional nature of the trained anthropologist." He praises her use of dialect in her works but criticizes plot construction and narration in *Jonah's Gourd Vine*. He suggests that her efforts to leave her own experiences in the black community with *Seraph on the Suwanee* led to her decline. Roger Whitlow, in *Black American Literature* (Totowa, N.J.: Littlefield, Adams, 1974), gives a cursory summary of her life and work and reproduces a lengthy folktale from *Mules and Men* and a long passage from *Their Eyes Were Watching God*. Among the few brief comments that he makes about the works is the highly questionable statement that *Seraph on the Suwanee* explores a popular new theme, "the relationship between sex and racism." Emma L. Blake, in "Zora Neale Hurston: Author and Folklorist" (*NHB*, April 1966), gives a brief overview of Hurston's life and works, incorrectly referring to Arvay as a mulatto. Robert Hemenway presents a helpful overview of Hurston's life and works in "Zora Neale Hurston and the Eatonville Anthropology" (*The Harlem Renaissance Remembered*, edited by Arna Bontemps, Dodd, Mead, 1972), which is expanded in his *Zora Neale Hurston*. Benjamin Brawley's *The Negro Genius* (Biblio and Tannan, 1972; rptd. from the 1937 edition) characterizes *Jonah's Gourd Vine* as a poorly integrated book with little merit but observes that Hurston struck her true vein with *Mules and Men*. In *The Negro in American Fiction* (Washington, D.C.: The Associates in Negro Folk Education, 1937), Sterling Brown summarizes *Jonah's Gourd Vine, Mules and Men*, and *Their Eyes Were Watching God*, praises Hurston for her poetic rendering of folk speech, but notes her lack of fully-developed characters in the two novels. He applauds her delightful tales in *Mules and Men*, but observes that she "does not uncover so much that white collectors have been unable to get." S. P. Fullinwinder's *The Mind and Mood of Black America* (Homewood, Ill.: Dorsey Press, 1969) gives a brief account of Hurston's life with an emphasis on her personality and discusses *Jonah's Gourd Vine* as a "recapitulation of her early life in Florida." Nancy M. Tischler's *Black Masks: Negro Characters in Modern Southern Fiction* (University Park: Pennsylvania State University Press, 1969) briefly summarizes *Their Eyes Were Watching God* and cites John Buddy of *Jonah's Gourd Vine* as an example of the Negro preacher-womanizer. Noel Schraufnagel's *From Apology to Protest: The Black American Novel* (Deland, Fla.: Everett/Edwards, 1973) gives a cursory examination of *Jonah's Gourd Vine, Their Eyes Were Watching God*, and *Seraph on the Suwanee.* George Kent does not treat Hurston at all in his *Blackness and the Adventures of Western Culture* (Chicago: Third World Press, 1972), but he does mention her "distinguished novels and brilliant book-length folklore studies" and comments, "She still awaits the thorough-going critical analysis that will properly place her in the patterns of American fiction." Marion Kilson's "The Transformation of Eatonville's Ethnographer" (*Phylon*, Summer 1972) traces Hurston's "transformation from ethnographic artist to critical ethnographer," a change which he suggests occurred in the early 1940s. Considering *Mules and Men*, *Tell My Horse*, and *Dust Tracks on a Road* as fiction, he notes that after *Dust Tracks on a Road* her primary form changed from fiction to the essay.

The most intensive study of Zora Neale Hurston's short fiction is found in Robert Bone's *Down Home: A History of Afro-American Short Fiction* (G. P. Putnam's Sons, 1975). He considers Hurston's "thirst for experience" a strong aspect of her personality, noting that she constantly rebelled against those who tried to limit her experience because of her race. He notes that "This thrust toward freedom, whose literary mode is the picaresque, is dramatized in three early stories, 'Drenched in Light,' 'John Redding Goes to Sea,' and 'Magnolia Flower.'" He observes that another noteworthy aspect of her early fiction is the local color strain. He also notes the fact that Hurston absorbed the storytelling tradition in Eatonville and "worked primarily within its terms. Her standard plot, for instance, pits the weak against the strong." He considers most of her short stories "apprentice work," and characterizes "Magnolia Flower" and "Muttsy" as "hopelessly incompetent." "Drenched in Light" is labeled a "remarkable first story . . . a portrait of the artist as a young girl." "John Redding Goes to Sea" is a sequel, with the protagonist changed to a boy who longs to escape the confines of the provincial folk community. "Spunk" and "Sweat" are related to the Brer Rabbit tales in their accounts of conflicts between the weak and the strong. Bone considers "The Gilded Six-Bits" "Hurston's principal achievement in the short-story form," noting that it suggests the maturity of style which is reflected in her longer works of fiction. In *Silence to the Drums: A Survey of the Literature of the Harlem Renaissance* (Westport, Conn.: Greenwood Press, 1976), Margaret Perry discusses three short stories. She praises the vitality of the autobiographical heroine Isis in "Drenched in Light." She considers the folklore strain in "Spunk" and notes that although "John Redding Goes to Sea" is one of her weakest stories, it is successful in its portrayal of a strong relationship between a black father and son. Perry concludes that while Hurston's dialogue may occasionally be stilted, she successfully handles "the important elements of the short story form—plot, diction, narration, and, especially, mood."

CONCLUSION

A study such as this one would not have been possible ten years ago. I expect that ten years hence numerous such studies will have, of necessity, appeared. This is the period (a period of increasing black and female awareness) when a figure such as Zora Neale Hurston is eagerly embraced—she was definitely a woman ahead of her time. And while, even now as in previous years, her own overwhelming personality still tends to overshadow her work, the increasing accessibility of her writings will ultimately lead to a fuller evaluation and perhaps a greater appreciation of her works. There will certainly be much debate about how she should be ranked within the scale of American writers. Whatever the ultimate assessment of Zora Neale Hurston, it seems eminently appropriate to apply to her a comment which she made about Ruby J. McCollum:

> Whatever her final destiny may be, she has not come to the bar craven and whimpering. She has been sturdy and strong. . . . She had dared defy the proud tradition[s] . . . openly and she awaits her fate with courage and dignity.

"The Life Story of Mrs. Ruby J. McCollum," *Pittsburgh Courier*, 28 February 1953

13 SAMUEL I. BELLMAN

Popular Writers in the Modern Age: Constance Rourke, Pearl Buck, Marjorie Kinnan Rawlings, and Margaret Mitchell

The four popular writers discussed here—Constance Mayfield Rourke (1885 – 1941), Pearl Sydenstricker Buck (1892-1973), Marjorie Kinnan Rawlings (1896–1953), and Margaret Munnerlyn Mitchell (1900–1949)—have, despite their literary awards and various other tokens of professional recognition, been somewhat neglected by the academic and journalistic critics. Clearly this has not been the case with many of America's most highly-regarded *male* popular writers of the modern age: Frost, Hemingway, Wolfe, Fitzgerald, Faulkner, and Steinbeck, for example. Is this disparity due to the sexist prejudice of American readers and critics? The answer must be, essentially *no*. At least half of the readers are women, as are many of the latter; moreover, such popular women writers of this period as Katherine Anne Porter, Ellen Glasgow, Willa Cather, and Carson McCullers, have generated considerable literary criticism and analysis.

While the quite modest response, by and large, of critics to the other women writers (Rourke, Buck, Rawlings, Mitchell) may be due in some small measure to those prejudiced against the subject matter, and to literary fashions and politics, these four ladies failed to maintain a sufficiently high level of quality and a consistency of fearless probing, whether they wrote many dozens of volumes (Buck) or one single long novel (Mitchell). This, in my opinion, goes far to explain their stunted critical reputations. Yet each writer has her distinctive merits: in style, in philosophy, in characterization, or in an ability to relate to a deeply-rooted common need. It may be helpful, then, in the course of this survey, to try to locate those somewhat elusive strengths.

CONSTANCE ROURKE

BIBLIOGRAPHY

As of May 1980 few detailed studies had been made of the life and work of the folk-culture critic Constance Rourke. An extensive bibliography of writings by and about her is to be found in a 1974 Yale University dissertation in modern history, by Joan Shelley Rubin, "A World Out of a Wilderness: Constance Rourke and the Search for a Usable Past." This listing (in which a few errors of detail may be found) includes Rourke's numerous book reviews in such periodicals and newspapers as the *New Republic*, *New York Herald Tribune, Yale Review, The Nation* and *The Freeman*. Far more complete is the bibliography in Rubin's published revision of her dissertation: *Constance Rourke and American Culture* (Chapel Hill: University of North Carolina Press, 1980). This bibliography, insofar as it covers primary sources, will doubtless be a standard reference source on the subject for a long time. But as regards secondary sources, there are two caveats. First, Rubin does not separate, as one might have wanted her to do, writings about Rourke from writings about American culture generally; thus entries concerned with various aspects of Rourke's background and her career are inconveniently lumped with what are really tertiary reference sources. Second, in this latter portion of her bibliography there are strange omissions. Two significant unpublished essays on Constance Rourke's personal life and her work, one by Nelle A. Curry and the other by Margaret Marshall, are not listed. Yet Rubin acknowledges having made use of them. These two essays, which are most helpful to an understanding of the writer, have also been used by Samuel I. Bellman in his Twayne United States Authors Series biography of Rourke. In addition, Rubin fails to list her own article, taken apparently from her dissertation, "Constance Rourke in Context: The Uses of Myth" (*AQ*, Winter 1976).

The bibliography in Bellman's *Constance Rourke* is selective; it omits, among other things, Rourke's early pieces in the *Vassar Miscellany* and certain of her book reviews, difficult to obtain but listed in Rubin. However, secondary sources are clearly indicated and annotated. One curious feature relating to a definitive bibliography of Rourke must be mentioned. In Stanley Edgar Hyman's seminal chapter on her work, "Constance Rourke and Folk Criticism" in his *The Armed Vision: A Study in the Methods of Modern Literary Criticism* (Alfred A. Knopf, 1948; rptd. 1952), he says this: "I am informed that Miss Rourke published magazine pieces over a pseudonym before this [1927], but so far I have been unable even to learn the pseudonym." This possibility is not clarified in Rubin's 1980 biography, which draws on a sizable body of Rourke letters, papers, and manuscripts, and any supportive evidence for the pseudonymous-author theory has yet to come to light.

EDITIONS

Harcourt Brace Jovanovich (earlier Harcourt, Brace; later, Harcourt, Brace & World) is Constance Rourke's publisher. Between 1927 and 1942 the Harcourt Brace firm brought out all seven of her books in hardcover editions; the 1942 volume, *The Roots of American Culture and Other Essays*, with an introduction by Van Wyck Brooks, was posthumously published. No standard edition of Rourke's works has been issued, nor has the great bulk of her magazine pieces (articles, book reviews, and two quasi-fictional sketches) been collected in book form. A paperback edition of her best-known work, *American Humor: A Study of the National Character* (1931), was brought out in 1955 by Doubleday Anchor Books. In 1959 *American Humor* was issued as a paperback in the Harvest Books series of Harcourt Brace Jovanovich. Rourke's *Trumpets of Jubilee* (1927) was reprinted in paperback as a Harcourt, Brace & World Harbinger Book in 1963. A third paperback reissue, the essay collection titled *The Roots of American Culture*, was published as a Harcourt, Brace & World Harvest Book [n.d.].

Rather than a new uniform edition of Rourke's published books, what is really needed is a judicious selection of her most significant writings on American culture brought together in one or more volumes. Such a collection might well include portions of *American Humor* and *Trumpets of Jubilee*, as well as her two experimental quasi-fictions from 1921, "The Porch" and "Portrait of a Young Woman."

MANUSCRIPTS AND LETTERS

A sizable store of Rourkeana—papers, correspondence, unpublished writings, part of her library—is in the possession of the Carl Shoaff family of Carbondale, Illinois. These are privately held, uncatalogued documents. Important as the personal letters here are, it appears from the work of J. S. Rubin who was given access to these holdings by Rourke's heirs, that the most valuable resource in this collection is the fragmentary manuscript of Rourke's proposed three-volume magnum opus, "A History of American Culture." Certain important records and letters pertaining to the Rourke family are held by Mrs. William Butler of Tucson, Arizona, a close friend of Constance Rourke and the executrix of her estate. A collection of manuscripts (uncatalogued) belonging to the late Margaret Marshall, another close friend of Rourke, is located in the Beinecke Rare Book and Manuscript Library at Yale University.

BIOGRAPHY

There are, first, the brief biographical entries in encyclopedias and standard reference works. Certain of these sketchy surveys contain errors of fact. Constance Rourke's father was *not* a lawyer, and he died when she was only two or three years old. The account of Rourke's career in Kunitz and Haycraft's *Twentieth Century Authors* (H. W. Wilson, 1942) is more significant than the ordinary run-of-the-mill reference book writeup because it contains a personal statement written by Rourke not long before her death. Certain journalistic articles from her hometown (Grand Rapids, Michigan) press dealing with her career-in-progress or providing posthumous appreciations and tributes are also helpful, but they are not easily available. One such piece, illustrated with photographic reproductions of Constance Rourke, her mother, interior views of their home, and so on, is the anonymously prepared "Miss Rourke" (*Grand Rapids Mirror*, Fall 1938). Included are Rourke's statements regarding her views on modern art, the American artistic tradition, and her book on the American artist Charles Sheeler.

More important are the biographical sections in the two new books, mentioned above: Rubin's *Constance Rourke and American Culture* and Bellman's *Constance Rourke*. Both draw from the unpublished memoirs of Rourke by Nelle A. Curry and Margaret Marshall, and both deal at some length with the obsessively-close mother-daughter relation that shaped Rourke's life. Each was all-in-all to the other, until the daughter's death in 1941. This odd attachment was noted by Kenneth S. Lynn in his introduction to the 1963 Harbinger Edition of *Trumpets of Jubilee*. Availing herself of the Shoaff family papers and the Margaret Marshall manuscripts, Rubin provides extensive details of the effects on Constance Rourke's career of her overdependence on her mother. Both Rubin and Bellman engage in psychological speculation here, while Bellman extends his commentary to an analysis of the female protagonist in each of Rourke's two strange sketches, "The Porch" and "Portrait of a Young Woman."

Future researchers in Rourke studies may be obliged to look further into the matter of why Constance Rourke, while pursuing an intellectual career (wherein she responded wholesomely to her mother's example and encouragement), severely restricted her emotional development by never permanently abandoning the maternal nest. Bellman's book, drawing on a somewhat different range of sources than Rubin's, discusses Rourke's Grand Rapids (once a great furniture-manufacturing center) and its effect on her as a cultural historian. Here too is an interesting line of investigation which, properly carried out, may yield important results in the future.

CRITICISM

There has not been a great deal of critical commentary on Rourke's contributions to American cultural studies. However, five items may be selected for mention, against the general background of the mild and brief controversy in 1942 between Alfred Kazin and Margaret Marshall in the pages of *The Nation* and the *New Republic*. This involved, as any serious discussion of Rourke would have to involve (sooner or later), the value for future American artists of Rourke's "diggings" in America's rich cultural past. Since there is no easy way to settle that argument, it is more desirable to focus on broader or otherwise more fruitful concerns.

First there is Stanley Edgar Hyman's now-famous chapter on Rourke. Hyman surveyed her contributions as a cultural historian, and while having no illusions as to Rourke's limitations, gave her credit for her complementary approaches—the analytic and the synthetic—in her investigations regarding our folk traditions. Together these two modes, Hyman felt, represented one of American criticism's "most promising activities," but since her death no one has continued her work—according to him. This assertion is arguable, in the light of scholarship since the later 1940s, when Hyman wrote. For example, John Kouwenhoven, author of *Made in America: The Arts in Modern Civilization* (Garden City, N.Y.: Doubleday, 1948; rptd. W. W. Norton, Norton Library, 1967), has been mentioned as one follower, of sorts. It is important to note that Hyman is credited with calling scholars' attention to Rourke's great discovery, in her inquiries into American folk tradition in the arts (for example, folk, practical, and fine arts): *form* rather than *subject matter* makes for a tradition. In line with the title of his chapter, however, Hyman breaks away from a clearly focused discussion of Rourke (who fades in and out of the latter part of the essay) and sweeps through broad areas of folkloric, mythological, and anthropological criticism. Thus, specifics in Rourke blur into considerations of primitive ritual and drama, Mencken's *Prejudices*, Malcolm Cowley's work on our writers' "cultural climate," and other assorted matters.

Kenneth S. Lynn's "Introduction to the Harbinger Edition" of *Trumpets of Jubilee* (1963 edition) pays tribute to her work as a cultural historian and credits her with influencing, for over thirty-five years, those writing about our national past. Lynn crowds into only a few pages considerable American cultural history, arguing that the "make it new" creed of Rourke's generation (those coming of age between 1900 and 1915) was reflected in *Trumpets of Jubilee*'s biographical subjects (Lyman Beecher, Harriet Beecher Stowe, Henry Ward Beecher, Horace Greeley, P. T. Barnum), who for the most part were active in the first two-thirds of the nineteenth century. In other words, by choosing these particular figures, Rourke could illustrate, to a generation strongly at odds with surviving manifestations of Puritanism, both the revitalization of Puritanism in America and Puritanism's sharp curtailment. Rourke could also focus attention on how ties of tradition linked her contemporary America with a still-meaningful past. In the course of his essay Lynn touches on such essential background matters as Rourke's subscribing to Herder's theory of artistic diffusion *upward* from the common folk, and Van Wyck Brooks's strictures on America's deleterious effects on its native artists, who require a "usable past" to be truly productive. And Lynn makes this important point about

Rourke's unmatched accomplishments in *Trumpets*: Only she, out of all her contemporaries determined to explore America's "cultural resources . . . was willing to honor the spokesmen of an older America for their own sake as well as for the sake of present and future American artists."

Joan Shelley Rubin's "Constance Rourke in Context: The Uses of Myth" (*AQ*, Winter 1976) is a later version of the "Myth" chapter in her Ph.D. dissertation on Rourke, and is thus closely related to the comparable section in her published biographical study, *Constance Rourke and American Culture*. Cogently, Rubin illuminates these points: Rourke used the term "myth" so frequently that it "loses precise meaning," and her "deliberate, persistent emphasis on myth-making suggests that she used the idea of myth as a strategy to attain some intellectual goals or emotional satisfactions."

The two new literary biographies, by Rubin and by Bellman, must now be considered. Far from being mutually comparable and diverging even in the area of Rourke's personal background, *Constance Rourke and American Culture* (Rubin) and *Constance Rourke* (Bellman) are actually complementary. The former examines Rourke's writing career against a complex background of American-culture criticism, primarily that of Van Wyck Brooks (who would finally incline to a more positive attitude toward America's capacity for nurturing its artists) and secondarily that of F. O. Matthiessen, Bernard DeVoto, Lewis Mumford, and V. L. Parrington. Rubin's essential thesis is that Rourke's major contribution is actually not in the realm of folklore or of literary criticism and scholarship, but instead has to do with the manner in which she dealt "with issues confronting the intellectual in modern America." Accordingly, Rubin specifies five basic Rourkean issues (allotting a chapter to each): "the adequacy of American traditions, the definition of culture, the character of myth, the effects of popular prose style, and the connection between politics and criticism." To deal with Rourke's underlying assumptions, Rubin's book "establishes the context for Rourke's defense of American culture—the controversies that engaged her, the books that influenced her thinking, the premises that lay beneath her vocabulary." Often drifting far away from Rourke's actual writings, though the book's subtitle provides for this (*and American Culture*), Rubin seems to fall into the same trap so astute a reader as Stanley Edgar Hyman had fallen into: taking Rourke's "Voltaire Combe" article (*The Nation*, 7 October 1939) as the biographical sketch of a real person. A close reading of the piece, in light of Rourke's other experimental fictions, shows this to be "made up"; such subtle hoaxing on Rourke's part must make us take her even more seriously as a student of American humor. It may be noted that Van Wyck Brooks's Preface to his Harcourt, Brace & World Harvest Book edition of *The Roots of American Culture* is a helpful introduction to Rubin's book.

Bellman's *Constance Rourke*, while by no means ignoring the Brooks-Rourke differences and similarities, deals largely and far more closely with

Rourke's own writings. Her major studies (*Trumpets of Jubilee* and *American Humor*) are analyzed for major themes and arguments; her biographies (far less important, with the exception of *Charles Sheeler*) are also discussed in terms of the overall patterns of her work. Likewise, some of Rourke's magazine pieces are analyzed so that they may throw light on her aims and lines of investigation as a historian of American culture. Though Rourke's accomplishments are treated appreciatively, certain of her careless and unsupportable judgments are frankly disputed, something which other commentators on Rourke have seemed unwilling to do. In the final analysis Bellman sees her as a "comic poet" (a term she employed as a chapter-title in *American Humor*) making a world out of a wilderness (another Rourkean term, used by Rubin in the title of her dissertation). The wilderness is our earlier cultural history, far richer and more nourishing than Brooks had realized. The world is a variegated population shaped by Rourke's imaginative fancies, love of the theater, and dedication to her scholarly research. It includes comic stereotypes—Yankee, Negro minstrel, gamecock of the wilderness, comic poet—as well as folk-hero giants and popular-success leaders like those in *Trumpets:* the Beechers, Greeley, Barnum. Rourke's suggestive force remains far greater than that of any of her more illustrious scholarly confreres.

In addition to the possible lines of inquiry for future scholars touched on at the end of the Biography section, much more does remain to be done, as Rourke was so fond of saying. One of the most important things would be a strenuous testing of her facile assertion (made in *Charles Sheeler*) that our folk tradition is basically abstract rather than naturalistic. Another would be a clear tracing of our early form-patterns over the decades and into the music and magazine art of the early twentieth century and, from there, into the popular arts and mass-media "art" of the 1980s.

PEARL BUCK

BIBLIOGRAPHY

A listing of Pearl S. Buck's numerous volumes of fiction and nonfiction prose, together with a small handful of biographical/critical sources, is given in *Contemporary Authors*, Vols. 1-4, edited by James M. Ethridge and Barbara Kopala, first revision (Detroit: Gale, 1967). Paul A. Doyle's *Pearl S. Buck* (Twayne, 1965) provides a selective bibliography of thirteen items dealing with the author herself. Oddly enough, for a Twayne United States Authors Series volume, Doyle's book does not—as one would expect it to—include a bibliography of writings by the author. The most complete bibliography, which appeared four years before her death (at the age of eighty) is in the first volume of Theodore F. Harris's *Pearl S. Buck: A Biography* (written in collaboration with Mrs. Buck) (John Day, 1969).

Still, Harris's listing has many omissions. For example, the matter of paperback editions—generally under the Pocket Books imprint—of her novels, rearrangements of short-story collections, and original paperback titles (such as, apparently, the Pocket Books Cardinal Edition of a 1962 novelette, *Satan Never Sleeps*), has never been taken into account. Hence it is not necessarily accurate to credit her with a mere eighty-five published books, as one reference-listing does: it seems likely that she had brought out more separate titles. In addition, a listing of her uncollected magazine and journalistic writings and speeches ought also to have been part of Harris's bibliography, despite his having limited it to books. Some of these fugitive pieces have been intercalated in the first volume of Harris's official biography. But one magazine item in particular deserves special mention: the autobiographical essay "A Debt to Dickens" (*SatRL*, 4 April 1936). This account of her childhood experiences in China and her using the stories of Dickens as a sanctuary from the somewhat hostile environment has been anthologized a number of times in Freshman Composition readers and is still being reprinted.

EDITIONS

No standard edition exists of Buck's collected works, but this is hardly surprising in view of the gargantuan amount and the uneven quality of the fiction. These include works that deal with China and the Orient generally and published under the author's own name, and the American novels, including the five published under the pseudonym of John Sedges. The John Day Company has been Pearl Buck's official publisher, and most of the volumes cited in Harris's official biography, volume one, were published by John Day. One extremely useful feature of this bibliography compiled by Harris is that it lists the large number of foreign editions of her various books. What appears more desirable than a formal collected edition of Buck's John Day publications is a "reader's choice" edition, in a small number of volumes, of the best that she has written: *The Good Earth* (1931); excerpts from various novels; individual short stories, journalistic pieces, speeches, and so on. The utility value of this would be enhanced by a brief and dispassionate single volume survey of her life in China and the United States and her efforts to improve the lot of retarded children and children of mixed racial background. A complete up-to-date bibliography of her publications, fugitive pieces too, would also be desirable—for the record, in such a "reader's choice" edition. This need is illustrated by the fact that since Harris's 1969 bibliography was printed in his biography of Buck, at least two more of her books appeared: *Mandala* (1970), and *The Kennedy Women* (1970).

MANUSCRIPTS AND LETTERS

Pearl Buck's personal letters are located in the Yale University Library (she had received an honorary M.A. from Yale). A readily available sampling of her personal communications is available to the reader in the two volumes of her official biography, by Theodore F. Harris (1969, 1971) —both done in consultation with the author herself, and both published by the John Day Company. Harris's first volume has only a few letters to and from Pearl Buck; his second volume, subtitled *Her Philosophy as Expressed in Her Letters*, is largely devoted to her correspondence—the greater part drawn from the 1940s and 1950s.

Paul A. Doyle, in his Twayne biography of Buck, mentions his use of the resources (letters, documents, and other materials on Pearl Buck) at the following libraries: The Lipscomb Library, Randolph-Macon Woman's College (where she received her B.A. degree in 1914); Yale University Library; Massachusetts Institute of Technology Library; Allegheny College Library; Allentown, Pa., Free Library; Berea College Library; Colby College Library; Dartmouth College's Baker Library; Duke University Library; Harvard University Library; Haverford College Library; Historical Society of Pennsylvania; Newark, N.J., Public Library; Newberry Library, Chicago; the New York Public Library; Asheville, N.C., Pack Memorial Public Library; State Historical Society of Wisconsin; Vassar College Library; and University of Virginia Library. Doyle does not specify in particular what resources dealing with Pearl Buck's life and career each library contains.

BIOGRAPHY

Possibly because she has written far more books than any two or three reasonably prolific writers, certain of Pearl Buck's works are difficult to obtain, and those will be mentioned very briefly here. First, however, there is her sister Cornelia's biography, which is noted in Doyle's *Pearl S. Buck* —Cornelia Spencer, *The Exile's Daughter, A Biography of Pearl S. Buck* (Coward McCann, 1944); covering certain features of her earlier years, according to Doyle, it works up to the time of World War II.

Three volumes of memoirs appeared before Theodore F. Harris's two volumes of official biography, written in consultation with the author and mentioned earlier. These three were: *My Several Worlds: A Personal Record* (John Day, 1954); *A Bridge for Passing* (John Day, 1962); *For Spacious Skies*; *Journey in Dialogue* (written with Theodore F. Harris) (John Day, 1966). The first, which emphasizes her early life in China, discusses also a rapprochement between the United States and a deeply alienated China. *My Several Worlds* won strong praise for its warm humanitarian impulses; reviewers in *Kirkus* and *Saturday Review* judged it her finest work to date. The second volume deals at length with the severe emotional effects on her of the death of her second husband, Richard J. Walsh, president of the John Day Company; critics treated this memoir sympathetically. The volume written with T. F. Harris concerns the Buck-Harris fund-raising campaign to set up a Pearl Buck Foundation for needy Asiatic children; here, as regards critical response, a special situation arises, which will be discussed momentarily. First, parenthetically, Pearl Buck wrote a biographical account of each of her parents (*The Exile* and *Fighting Angel*—both published in 1936, by the John Day Company); there are in the books a number of details of her own earlier life with these two unshakably committed Presbyterian missionaries, who were apostles to the Chinese. The biographies were very highly regarded as character studies and were singled out for special mention by the Nobel Prize Committee when it awarded Buck the Nobel Prize for Literature in 1938.

Ironically, just at the time that T. F. Harris came on the scene, Paul A. Doyle brought out the Twayne biography of Pearl S. Buck (1965). A convenient overview of her life and career up to about 1964, this study contains useful plot summaries of certain of her important books; emphasis is placed, quite properly, on *The Good Earth*, though *The Exile* and *Fighting Angel* are also dealt with at some length. But the book is quite outdated.

The Harris matter is referred to tersely in a *Time* review (22 July 1966) of *For Spacious Skies*, which was unfavorable to the book. In 1964 Buck hired Harris—an instructor of ballroom dancing, and something like forty years her junior—to teach her how to rhumba. The two got on well together, and she appointed him president and executive director of her tax-exempt Pearl S. Buck Foundation. *Of Spacious Skies*, says *Time*, is "an undisguised campaign for funds. . . ." Note: strange as Harris's entire role in Buck's life may be—and it has a bearing on literary matters concerning Buck, or it would not be mentioned in this article—something else about Buck, so lavishly praised for her selfless dedication to deprived Asian children, deserves mention. In Harris's second biographical volume, *Her Philosophy as Expressed in Her Letters*, he quotes at least one of her letters that shows Buck as distinctly ungenerous, quite unwilling to help a group that requested her aid, and not even financial aid, but merely moral aid.

Be that as it may, what strikes the reader as remarkable in Harris's collaborative biographical preparations is his unabashed and self-righteous hero-worship of Buck. So effusive is his reverential flattery of her charms, her writing skill, her very being, that it is difficult not to suspect either a hidden self-serving motive or a subtly-disguised attempt at self-parody. All of this is regrettable because Buck deserves a more level-headed and realistic Boswell if she is to be seen as a kind of Johnson. Her nonfiction writings on Chinese life and modern Chinese history are often intelligent and highly informative, based as they are on an observant writer's first-hand experiences, over many years, in a region that few Westerners have ever known much about. If her fictions have often been too sentimentally optimistic, superficial and contrived, she nonetheless has had much of importance to say about the Orient; and it is to be hoped that her solid base of expertise will not be devalued, in the light of the publicity campaign and fund-raising activities that have been associated with her name since the 1960s. In the words of a review of *For Spacious Skies*, in the 15 July 1966 issue of *Best Sellers*: "One of the most interesting threads to follow is that which binds Miss Buck to Theodore F. Harris."

CRITICISM

Malcolm Cowley, in "The Good Earthling" (*NewR*, 23 January 1935), a review of Pearl Buck's novel *A House Divided* (1935), gives this third part of her House of Earth trilogy (*The Good Earth, Sons, A House Divided*) qualified praise. It "is honest, rich, full-bodied and in general good enough to justify the adjectives that reviewers will lavish on it." While two other roughly-comparable works—Malraux's *Man's Fate* and Tretiakov's *A Chinese Testament*—are literarily superior, *A House Divided* provides a far more knowledgeable picture of Chinese life, in Cowley's opinion, which leads him to comment on how the Chinese themselves have responded to Buck's writings. They are by and large "eager to praise her work" and "many of them say that no native writer has painted a more accurate picture. . . ." She has been assailed by a small number of Chinese critics, "usually because they stood to the left or right of her" in a political sense. Phyllis Bentley's "The Art of Pearl Buck" (*EJ*, December 1935) is a warmly sympathetic discussion of Buck's achievements: her depicting China and the Chinese from an insider's perspective with no cultural bias, and her habitual use of effective and quite appropriate language to describe a culture so vastly different from that of her English-language readers. This early tribute to Buck's humanity and artistry as a writer seeks her "figure in the carpet"—her controlling idea, in the famous Henry James metaphor—and finds it to be "the continuity of life."

Henry Seidel Canby, in an effusive note, "*The Good Earth*: Pearl Buck and the Nobel Prize" (*SatRL*, 19 September 1938), admits that Buck's overall achievement to date is not quite as substantial or impressive from an international perspective, as the achievement of either of the two earlier American Nobel Laureates, Sinclair Lewis and Eugene O'Neill. But he singles out *The Good Earth* as a unique masterpiece which, in part because of its world-wide appeal, "richly deserves exalted recognition," such as that conferred by the Nobel Prize.

Four years after his generally favorable assessment of *A House Divided* (which deals with the grandchildren of Wang Lung, protagonist of *The Good Earth*), Malcolm Cowley revised his rating sharply downward. In "Wang Lung's Children" (*NewR*, 10 May 1939), which deals with Buck's current novel, *The Patriot*, as well as with the House of Earth trilogy, Cowley's hostility to *A House Divided* seems strangely intemperate. "On a second reading, I wasn't far from thinking it was the worst book ever written by a competent novelist. Its most obvious weakness is its style." But its plot "is essentially even weaker than its style." The book "is a failure that ought to be destroyed." Buck should replace it in her Wang Lung canon with *The Patriot*, making the necessary name changes.

Oscar Cargill, in *Intellectual America: Ideas on the March* (Macmillan, 1941), surveys Pearl Buck's work to date, relating her to the tradition of Naturalism and seeking parallels in her writings with those of such Naturalists as Zola. Recognizing that her work has been quite uneven—*The Good Earth* being her best book—Cargill acknowledges that her stories have "universal appeal" as well as an uncommon degree of "comprehensibility." James Gray's brief tribute to Pearl Buck in his collection of newspaper reviews, *On Second Thought* (Minneapolis: University of Minnesota Press, 1946), has the tone and thrust of a publisher's publicity release. She is pictured as a literary phenomenon, single-handedly redeeming a stout-hearted and progressive China from the degrading falsification of outrageous Western stereotyping. Her having won the Nobel Prize for Literature in 1938, to the dismay of certain critics, is energetically if unconvincingly defended, largely on the basis of her role of "internationalist." As the latter, she showed how true it is that, to quote the title of the Chinese novel she translated for the West, *All Men Are Brothers*.

Paul A. Doyle, in the concluding section ("Final Estimate") of his 1965 Twayne USAS biography of Pearl Buck, singles out *The Good Earth* and her biographies of her parents, *The Exile* and *Fighting Angel*, for special praise. One reason Doyle gives for her lack of critical success in her later work is that she followed "the old-fashioned Chinese story practice of emphasizing event and characterization." The Chinese were not given to experimentation in the novel, nor were they concerned with developing its artistic possibilities. Among Doyle's other reasons for Buck's neglect by serious critics are "her best-seller status," her being a woman, and her outlook, reflecting optimism and affirmation. There is much more in Doyle's book concerning such matters as Buck's literary theories, her having been influenced by the low esteem in which the novel was held by the Chinese and by her parents, and the mixed response she received upon winning the Nobel Prize.

C. A. Cevasco's "The Image of the Chinese Family in Pearl Buck's Novels" (*ChC*, October 1966) is a brief review-note on a book of that title, by Doan-Cao-Lý, published in Saigon in 1964. Paying tribute to Buck for her rare insider's understanding of China, Cevasco remarks on the small number of serious studies done on her writings and gives the Saigonese book credit for being among "the most substantial." Avoiding sociology and anthropology both, the author is primarily concerned "with the ways the image of the Chinese family have been [*sic*] artistically introduced into Pearl Buck's novels." The book's final chapter, according to Cevasco, "is a critical evaluation of the female characters in the most important novels." Interestingly, despite Buck's close familiarity with Chinese tradition, which values men above women, she has characterized Chinese women more effectively than Chinese men, presented the ideals of the women as being higher, and apparently even made the women superior to the men.

Paul A. Doyle's article, "Pearl S. Buck's Short Stories: A Survey" (*EJ*, January 1966), examines the writer's method of composition and faults many of her stories for their contrived plots, simplicity of style, and lack of sophistication in depicting human problems. However, Doyle feels that Buck's earliest short stories were of considerably higher quality than her later ones. Doyle throws a good deal of light on her old-fashioned approach to story-telling—with what some might describe as a tendency toward pathos and melodrama—by pointed references to her direct statements about literary influence. Early in 1932, in two lectures presented in Peiping, as well as in her Nobel Prize lecture in 1938, she "traced her own techniques to the traditional Chinese narrative," with its omniscient if unobtrusive author and character depiction through action and dialogue rather than interior monologue.

The long analysis of Buck's literary career, in the light of her having been raised by particularly forceful missionary parents deep in the Chinese interior—Dody Weston Thompson's "Pearl Buck," in *American Winners of the Nobel Literary Prize*, edited by Warren G. French and Walter E. Kidd (Norman: University of Oklahoma Press, 1968)—is absolutely indispensable for the reader wishing to understand Buck's strengths and weaknesses as a writer, the complex issues related to her winning the Nobel Prize, and the American and European literary scenes as they contrasted so sharply with her own fictive world of simplistic Chinese family dramas. Among the important matters covered in Thompson's superb explication are why Buck "never mastered either form [that of the Western novel or the Chinese narrative] in its purity, nor succeeded in her efforts at a synthesis," and why "hers has been an essentially feminine career."

While readers of other nations—Sweden, for example—have loved Buck's writings, the Chinese have long opposed them. A short memoir of Buck, with valuable comments on Chinese reactions (before and after the Communist takeover of China) to *The Good Earth* and her other Chinese fictions, was written by another old China hand, the wife of the foreign correspondent Edgar Snow. Helen F. Snow's obituary article, "'An Island in Time'" (*NewR*, 24 March 1973), discusses what the Chinese have long objected to: Buck's having violated traditional taboos regarding childbirth and sex, her treatment of Chinese women (the Chinese felt she had debased them), and (in the view of the Chinese Communists) her glorification of "the worst features of the old society."

Perhaps the most needed line of research and criticism for future Buck projects at the present time, particularly in view of the restoration of American-Chinese diplomatic relations at the turn of the 1980s, is a close comparison of Buck's uncomplicated pictures of Chinese life, with fictional narratives of Chinese life (from the 1930s up to the time of Buck's death in 1973), written by native Chinese and Taiwanese, and reflecting contemporary politics, sociology, and psychology.

MARJORIE KINNAN RAWLINGS

BIBLIOGRAPHY

There are two available bibliographies of Marjorie Kinnan Rawlings. Gordon E. Bigelow's introduction, *Frontier Eden: The Literary Career of Marjorie Kinnan Rawlings* (Gainesville: University of Florida Press, 1966), includes a "Checklist of Publications,"which itemizes her writings and also briefly mentions some of the meager criticism and commentary on her work to date. There are a number of typographical errors in this checklist. An annotated, selected bibliography is also to be found in a 1974 biography by Samuel I. Bellman, *Marjorie Kinnan Rawlings* (Twayne). (On p. 155 there is an error in dating: *When the Whippoorwill* was originally published in 1940, *not* 1943.) A few scholarly or reference-guide articles on Rawlings have been appearing in recent years; in the next decade or so there may be enough continued interest or augmented interest in her work to justify a thorough bibliography of her writings, which would begin by simply encompassing the incomplete bibliographies in the Bigelow and Bellman volumes.

EDITIONS

There is no standard edition of Rawlings. Charles Scribner's is her American publisher, and American readers will be most familiar with the Scribner's hardcover volumes of *The Yearling*, *Cross Creek*, and a few of the other titles. Her Pulitzer Prize novel *The Yearling* (1938) was an enormous best-seller in its early publishing history, and on into the 1980s it has remained a perennially-appealing "children's classic"—though it is sophisticated enough to appeal to sensitive adults also. Among the many different editions this novel has gone through is an elegant children's edition with Wyeth illustrations; the best-known Scribner's illustrator of such Rawlings titles as *The Yearling* and *Cross Creek* is Edward Shenton.

Attention should be called to one particular Scribner's edition of *The Yearling*, printed in 1941 (reprinted 1947), with the Edward Shenton illustrations and a convenient map of Florida, highlighting the scrub country near Lake George, where the Baxter family of that story lived. Designed as a special school text, this edition is distinguished primarily by the six-page introduction by Rawlings. This introduction is a reply to all of those who had been asking her how she came to write the book. Rawlings states that since it will now "be part of your English study course," I have attempted mentally to retrace "some of the steps by which an idea and a feeling became a book." And so she speaks of two of the book's most important features: the sad thrill of nature-awareness that suddenly transfixes Jody Baxter near the beginning of the story, on a day in April—which was based on a mystical experience she herself had had as a small child; and Jody's being forced by his father to kill his beloved yearling deer, which was destroying the family's crop—an episode described to her, from his own experience, by an "old-timer" in the scrub, Cal Long.

A number of Rawlings's works are still readily available in paperback, an indication that she has by no means been forgotten by a diverse reading public. These include, in a Scribner's edition, *The Yearling* (there are several different editions), *Cross Creek Cookery*, and *The Secret River* (a very slight story, written for very young children, and published posthumously). In a Mockingbird Books series there *Cross Creek*, *South Moon Under*, and *When the Whippoorwill.*

In 1956 Julia Scribner Bigham, the daughter of the publisher, brought out her own selection of what she considered to be Rawlings's "best writing": *The Marjorie Rawlings Reader* (Charles Scribner's). Bigham's Introduction includes long excerpts from Rawlings's correspondence with her Scribner's editor, Maxwell E. Perkins, in which she describes her life in the Florida backwoods, relative to her writing; her experiences as a child; and her working on a boy's book (which would become *The Yearling*) at Perkins's suggestion. An excerpt from a letter Perkins wrote her, dealing with the boy's book, is also given here. As far as the "best writing" is concerned, the entire text of *South Moon Under*, but only two chapters of *The Yearling*, made it into this *Reader*. What clearly are the three best short stories from *When the Whippoorwill* may be found here ("Gal Young Un," "Cocks Must Grow," "Jacob's Ladder"), as well as three *New Yorker* stories from the earlier 1940s. Two of these, the marvelously evocative "Jessamine Springs" and "The Pelican's Shadow," reveal very interesting autobiographical elements. Bigham (Rawlings's literary executor) includes nothing from, nor does she say anything about, Rawlings's provocative and hard-to-forget last novel, *The Sojourner*, which is set not in the Florida scrub or hammock country, but in up-state New York.

MANUSCRIPTS AND LETTERS

Aside from the small sampling of correspondence in Bigham's *The Marjorie Rawlings Reader*, there are numerous letters to Rawlings from her Scribner's editor (relative to her writing) in *Editor to Author: The Letters of Maxwell E. Perkins* (Charles Scribner's, 1950) edited by John Hall Wheelock. The University of Florida Library, Gainesville, houses the bulk of available Rawlings papers—manuscripts, correspondence, photographs, and personal documents. At least five unpublished theses dealing with Rawlings's work are also on deposit in the library.

BIOGRAPHY

Leaving aside obvious overlapping in coverage of Rawlings's life and work, the biographies by Bigelow and Bellman have essentially different orientations and thus are in a number of ways mutually complementary. Bigelow's book draws heavily on the Rawlings papers in the University of Florida Library; thus it reveals certain personal facts, details of abandoned literary projects, and so forth, that would have been unavailable to the other author. In addition, Bigelow, because of his on site location (he was in the English Department of the University of Florida at Gainesville), and his personal fondness for the Florida terrain about which Rawlings wrote, provides a geographical and topographical perspective as he treats her literary career.

Bellman's book draws, in part, on the personal reminiscences, papers, manuscripts, documents, memorabilia, of Rawlings's three paternal aunts, the Misses Grace, Wilmer, and Marjorie Kinnan, formerly of Phoenix, Arizona. They graciously made available to the author their archival collection. Primarily, the Bellman biography provides a close and analytical reading of Rawlings's major (and many of her minor) works. On the basis of her very earliest writings, her newspaper pieces in the 1920s, and her published fiction (particularly "A Mother in Mannville," *Mountain Prelude*, and *The Yearling*), Bellman carefully develops a thesis regarding what appears to be her most deeply-cherished but never-to-be-fulfilled wish: that she might have a little boy of her own. Another deeply-rooted element in her psyche, noted here as also being very influential in her fiction, was her profound, almost irrational hatred of cities and urban life; this is summed up in a memorable sonnet, published in 1935, "Having Left Cities Behind Me." In line with the psychological interpretation and literary analyses offered in his *Marjorie Kinnan Rawlings*, Bellman devotes considerable attention to Rawlings's neglected final novel, *The Sojourner*. Like so very much of her fiction, this story is filled with overt and covert autobiographical elements that continually linger on in the sensitive reader's mind. A haunting and tragic story of two brothers and their deranged mother, *The Sojourner* (completed a short time before Rawlings's death) actually sums up the joy and pain, fulfillment and soul-wrenching yearning, of Rawlings's entire life.

There are a number of brief biographical overviews. Bigelow's "Marjorie Kinnan Rawlings," in *Dictionary of American Biography, Supplement Five 1951-1955*, edited by John A. Garraty (Charles Scribner's, 1977), discusses her writings and provides a physical description of the novelist. Bellman's article, "Marjorie Kinnan Rawlings," in *Notable American*

Women, The Modern Period: A Biographical Dictionary, edited by Barbara Sicherman and others (Cambridge, Mass.: Harvard University Press, Belknap Press, 1980), and his article in *Dictionary of Literary Biography, American Novelists 1910-1945*, edited by James J. Martine (Columbia, S.C.: B C Research, 1981), attempt to go beyond the informative introduction. Both of these pieces seek to provide something of a psychological perspective, better to acquaint the reader with the work of a many-sided writer who still, despite the success of *The Yearling* and *Cross Creek*, has been inadequately appreciated by the American reading public.

CRITICISM

Setting aside the two Rawlings biographies by Bigelow and Bellman, criticism of Rawlings's work has not been very extensive, nor has it produced anything like the lively and stimulating debates found in the Margaret Mitchell criticism.

Lloyd Morris's very appreciative review of *The Yearling* and his commentary on Rawlings's other works to date, "A New Classicist" (*NAmRev*, Autumn 1938), describes the author as "a classicist in her perception of life," because of her "concern for ultimate rather than relative values" and her "intention to present experience in its most simple and enduring forms." Nevertheless, "she is a romantic in her literary endowment," her sensibility. Morris also draws interesting comparisons between *The Yearling* and Steinbeck's *Of Mice and Men*. Harry Evans's two-part article, "Marjorie Kinnan Rawlings" (*The Family Circle*, 7 May 1943, and 14 May 1943), provides an excellent description of the author in her Florida setting and of her literary productions. Amy Porter's "Growth of *The Yearling*" (*Collier's*, 29 September 1945) is a useful account, with illustrations, of the motion picture production of *The Yearling*. James Gray's commentary on Rawlings's work, originally published as book reviews in the *St. Paul Pioneer Press* and *Dispatch* and reprinted in *On Second Thought* (Minneapolis: University of Minnesota Press, 1946), deals mainly with *The Yearling* and *Cross Creek*. The brief article is superficial in its coverage, though extremely favorable to Rawlings.

Also quite superficial in its coverage is Margaret Gillis Figh's "Folklore and Folk Speech in the Works of Marjorie Kinnan Rawlings" (*SFQ*, September 1947). Figh cites only a few examples of Rawlings's use of Florida Cracker folklore in her writings, and instead of providing a substantial theoretical base for Rawlings's cultural borrowings, she quotes at length from only a few of her works: *South Moon Under, Cross Creek, The Yearling*, and a couple of short pieces. By way of conclusion, Figh acknowledges that "Rawlings has been of service to the folklorist in that she has unearthed much hitherto unrecorded material and has preserved it in its own rhythmic language pattern." Julia Scribner Bigham's introduction to

The Marjorie Rawlings Reader (Charles Scribner's, 1956) is a valuable resource, which discusses Rawlings's relations with her publisher (Scribner's) and includes some of the important correspondence between Rawlings and her illustrious editor, Maxwell Perkins.

Gordon E. Bigelow, in "Marjorie Kinnan Rawlings' Wilderness," (*SR*, Spring 1965), discusses her literary career against the background of the north Florida woods, where she lived for a number of years. A longtime enthusiastic resident of the Gainesville area, and thus well qualified to speak of the topography of Cross Creek, the hammock country, and the Big Scrub, Bigelow has a good bit to say about the symbolic and philosophical significance of this wilderness area to Rawlings. Samuel I. Bellman's extended overview of Rawlings's life and work, "Marjorie Kinnan Rawlings: A Solitary Sojourner in the Florida Backwoods" (*KanQ*, Spring 1970), attempts to give the actual feel of her characters in their north Florida locale and in upstate New York (in her last novel, *The Sojourner*). The latter article thus emphasizes the literary and the psychological, whereas the former article stresses the socio-geographical.

Bellman's "Marjorie Kinnan Rawlings' Existentialist Nightmare: *The Yearling*," in *Costerus*: *Essays in English and American Language and Literature* (No. 9, 1973), is a closer look at the dark side of *The Yearling*. His "Writing Literature for Young People: Marjorie Kinnan Rawlings' 'Secret River' of the Imagination," in the same volume of *Costerus* examines her brief fairy-tale parable and places it against the writer's story-telling career, beginning at age six. Finally, Lamar York's "Marjorie Kinnan Rawlings's Rivers" (*SLJ*, Spring 1977) is an interesting examination of one geographical-topographical aspect of her writings about the Florida backwoods folk: the waterways.

Since the salient features of her life have been reiterated sufficiently by now, what seems most needed in Rawlings scholarship is a definitive and unblinking biography. Such a study would embody the materials and arguments in the Bigelow and Bellman biographies, would make extensive use of the Rawlings papers at the University of Florida Library, and would trace in considerable detail her earliest years, before she moved to Florida in 1928. Treating of her childhood in the Washington, D.C. area, her college days in Madison, Wisconsin, and her newspaper career in Rochester and Louisville, this biography would seek some basis in her experience for her curiously intense detestation of cities. It would take up the matter of her unsatisfactory married life (1919-1933) with Charles A. Rawlings, writer and boating enthusiast. His published fiction such as the numerous *Saturday Evening Post* stories would be examined interpretively, with the idea of discovering possible influences on her work. (He seems clearly to represent the character of the unbearable husband, while she seems to figure as the put-upon wife, in the provocative *New Yorker* story, "The Pelican's Shadow" [6 January

1940].) In the final analysis the biography, while facing squarely up to her inferior writing—what she herself called "interesting trash instead of literature"—would attempt to show what went into the making of her most important and still underappreciated work. This includes *Cross Creek* and *The Yearling*, but particularly *The Sojourner*: accounts of the ordinary individual treated, perhaps quite accurately, as a lost soul yearning to return to a home that is not of this earth.

MARGARET MITCHELL

BIBLIOGRAPHY

In a sense Margaret Mitchell is an author of one book (*Gone With the Wind*, 1936—abbreviated hereafter as *GWTW*), for although she planned and wrote other stories, apparently all that remains of her literary efforts is the phenomenally-successful 1,037-page novel. Hence such bibliographies as are available tend to be listings of biographical details in reference books, references to Mitchell in more general works, book-review inventories, and citations of obituary notices in newspapers. Considering the popular as opposed to critical appeal of *GWTW* over the decades, it would be difficult to imagine a significant bibliography of serious critical articles appearing prior to the 1970s. One such list is that appearing at the end of the biographical review by Louise Y. Gossett: "Mitchell, Margaret Munnerlyn," in *Notable American Women 1607-1950*, II, edited by Edward T. James and others (Cambridge, Mass.: Harvard University Press, Belknap Press, 1971). Gossett's assortment of items in her extended list is certainly helpful as an introduction to the earlier comments and information sources on Mitchell; and Gossett acknowledges the assistance of the biographical outline, with bibliography, that was prepared by Malathi Reddy of Emory University's Division of Librarianship. A very brief list of assorted references is given at the end of the 1942 edition of Stanley J. Kunitz and Howard Haycraft's *Twentieth Century Authors* (H. W. Wilson).

EDITIONS

The standard edition of *GWTW* is for all intents and purposes the one published by Macmillan in 1936 and reprinted innumerable times thereafter. Two editions were still available in Avon paperback in 1980 (1974; 1976). Sales figures are almost unavoidable in any discussion of the book. To give a very small sample: almost twelve million copies had been sold by 1965, over five million of which were printed in foreign translations in various parts of the world; by May 1976 *GWTW* had sold twenty-one million copies. [Sources: Finis Farr, *Margaret Mitchell of Atlanta: The Author of Gone With the Wind* (William Morrow, 1965); *Newsweek*, 17 May 1976.]

MANUSCRIPTS AND LETTERS

Acutely sensitive about how her personal correspondence might be interpreted, Margaret Mitchell (who devoted a good deal of her post-*GWTW* life to answering her readers' letters) drew the curtain of privacy tightly around what she had written. Louise Gossett, in *Notable American Women*, points out that Mitchell's instructions in this regard were followed, and "most of her correspondence and papers," the *GWTW* manuscript included, "were destroyed, except for pages preserved to authenticate her authorship. The Margaret Mitchell Room of the Atlanta Public Library contains material bequeathed by her husband."

Much valuable documentation from personal archival sources is provided in Finis Farr's definitive biography. Farr, in an authorial note at the beginning, states that the book's "foundation . . . is in the papers of the Margaret Mitchell Marsh Estate and in an unpublished memoir by Stephens Mitchell [the author's brother]." However, by far the best available source of Mitchell correspondence is Richard Harwell's edition of *Margaret Mitchell's Gone With The Wind Letters 1936-1949* (Macmillan, 1976).

In his preface, Harwell tells us that Stephens Mitchell, who inherited his sister's literary rights after her husband (John R. Marsh) died in 1952 (three years after Margaret Mitchell), "has steadfastly opposed any invasion of them." However, at this time he reluctantly agreed to allow Harwell to bring together a collection of her correspondence, but added a caveat. She believed "'a false view of people was reached, when the evidence on which the view was based, was from private letters.'" And, Harwell explains, since Margaret Mitchell feared that her correspondents would allow her letters to be printed, "many of them are more restrained than she might have wished." Thus, notwithstanding Louise Gossett's statement about the destruction of most of Margaret Mitchell's papers and correspondence, Harwell obtained the letters for his book from the "magnificent collection" of her papers "in the University of Georgia Libraries." Here are "well over fifty thousand items: file copies of letters from Mrs. Marsh [Margaret Mitchell], letters to her, clippings, pictures, and a variety of miscellaneous items." With only a few exceptions, Harwell limited his choices to the store of over ten thousand letters (in the form of carbon copies) that she herself wrote; not included in the Margaret Mitchell Marsh Papers, for example, and printed here, are a holograph letter (3 July 1936) to the Librarian of the University of Georgia, Mr. Duncan Burnet, and two letters (10 February 1939 and 17 April 1939) to Susan Myrick.

Fortunately for future studies of Mitchell's career and the *GWTW* phenomenon, in 1970 Stephens Mitchell bequeathed his sister's letters to his alma mater, the University of Georgia, thus providing a convenient archival repository where scholars like Harwell might some day work. In regard to the actual scope of these letters, Harwell indicates that they begin on the eve of the publication of *GWTW* and end at the time of her death (16 August 1949). Essentially they have to do with the books, the films, and the author's friendships that can be traced to *GWTW*. But to return to an earlier point, which should be tantalizing to Margaret Mitchell scholars: Gossett was not wrong in what she said about the disposition of the Margaret Mitchell papers. According to Harwell, "her private letters were destroyed after her death."

BIOGRAPHY

Most of the important biographical sources have already been mentioned. There are short overviews in standard reference volumes. The two primary sources are Finis Farr's definitive *Margaret Mitchell of Atlanta* and Richard Harwell's *Margaret Mitchell's Gone With The Wind Letters*. As a supplement to Farr's biography, Harwell's introduction is quite helpful, particularly when Harwell points up the comparisons between Scarlett O'Hara and the city of Atlanta, and Margaret Mitchell herself and Scarlett.

One particular biographical item, details of which are to be found in the Jones article and in Farr's biography, deserves mention here. Mitchell, in her earlier, pre-*GWTW*, years, had attempted a number of fiction works. When in her teens, she completed a novel about boarding-school girls ("The Big Four") and a story about a girl who kills her sister's rapist ("Little Sister"); when in her twenties, she began a novel about adolescents in the 1920s and finished a novelette dealing with a Southern white girl's love for a mulatto. All of these manuscripts are lost.

CRITICISM

The critical commentaries on *GWTW* and the character of Scarlett O'Hara have been particularly interesting and baffling: baffling, because the novel's extraordinary success seems to defy not only the interpretations of the more discerning critics, but the human imagination as well. Harry Levin, in a 1949 lecture, "Some European Views of Contemporary American Literature" (reprinted a number of times since) refers to the vast amount of American cultural exporting—of products, and hence culture not in Matthew Arnold's terms but in Ruth Benedict's—and then adds: "All this helps to explain what European critics can justify no better than we could: why the world's best-seller, second only to the Bible, should be *Gone With the Wind*" (*Contexts of Criticism* [Cambridge, Mass.: Harvard University Press, 1957; rptd. Atheneum, 1963]).

But we might begin with a very revealing statement by the author herself in a letter to a friend. She could not, Mitchell admitted, explain *GWTW*'s incredible popularity. "Despite its length and many details it is basically just a simple yarn of fairly simple people. There's no fine writing, there's no philosophizing, there is a minimum of description, there are no grandiose thoughts, there are no hidden meanings, no symbolism, nothing sensational —nothing, nothing at all that made other best sellers best sellers." (Quoted in Finis Farr's definitive biography.)

Malcolm Cowley's early review, "Going with the Wind" (*NewR*, 16 September 1936), seems now, in the 1980s, to have been written with little serious reflection. The novel "is an encyclopedia of the plantation legend," repeated by Mitchell for the first time "as a whole, with all its episodes and all its characters and all its stage settings." Despite the fact that "the legend is false in part and silly in part and vicious in its general effect on Southern life" at the present time, it yet "retains its appeal to fundamental emotions." The author strengthens the legend "by telling it as if it had never been told before, and also by mixing a good share of realism with the romance." Mitchell "makes us weep at a deathbed (and really weep), exult at a sudden rescue and grit our teeth at the crimes of our relatives the damyankees." Though not "a great novel," and allowing for its "triteness and sentimentality," *GWTW* possesses "a simple-minded courage that suggests the great novelists of the past." There is no wonder, Cowley concludes, that copies of the book are living up to its title.

W. J. Cash, in *The Mind of the South* (Alfred A. Knopf, 1941; rptd. Vintage-Knopf-Random House, 1961), mentions the enormous morale-boosting effect on Atlantans and other Southerners, when Selznick's motion-picture version of *GWTW* was shown locally. And, "It was the measure of something that, after fifteen years of the new spirit in Southern writing," this "sentimental novel . . ., which had curiously begun by a little offending many Southerners, ended by becoming a sort of new confession of the Southern faith." Harry Levin, in his 1949 address, argues that *GWTW*'s "European success . . . has significantly coincided with a decade of invasion, occupation, displacement, dispossession, and reconstruction." He sees in this regard two "signs that life occasionally does better than literature": the South's "lost cause," appealing "so strongly to readers in occupied countries," and "the implied analogy between the Yankees and the Nazis." While Stowe's *Uncle Tom's Cabin*, which swept "the Continent, was a happier omen," foreshadowing "liberation for the slaves," *GWTW* "cultivates the unreconstructed nostalgia of the masters."

Heinrich Straumann, a professor of English Literature at the University of Zurich, in his 1951 publication, *American Literature in the Twentieth Century* (3d ed. rev., Harper & Row, 1965), tried his hand at explaining the success of Mitchell's novel. In his view—as given in this very slightly changed version from the original edition—*GWTW* is consistent in its "purely pragmatic outlook on life." After three husbands, Scarlett O'Hara, "modelled after Becky Sharp," realizes "that the one man she idolizes and never gets is a creation of her dreams"; however, "her indomitable energy" and "supreme power of adjustment" will make for material success, though at the expense of a love relationship. Drawing partly from recorded opinions, Straumann lists possible reasons for Mitchell's publishing phenomenon: Scarlett's "toughness of character"; Rhett Butler's "Byronic aspect"; "the make-believe realism of the background," blending "historic accuracy" with "a shot of magnolia myth." But, in his own view, considering the book's "incredible length and . . . tiresome repetitions," the answer lies in "an ideal fusion of the pragmatic current" and the American readers' "love of the past."

Much interesting and provocative criticism on *GWTW* and the character of Scarlett O'Hara has appeared since 1958. Robert Y. Drake, Jr., in "Tara Twenty Years After" (*GaR*, Spring 1958), reads *GWTW* as "an epic treatment of an epic theme," and is thereby not overly concerned about its lack of subtlety and conscious craftsmanship. Scarlett is at the center of the book's essential conflict—tradition versus antitradition. She does not yield to adversity, but is bent on survival at all costs. She wants "the strength of the Southern tradition," but fails to "realize it until the end," only then submitting to it. *GWTW* dramatizes the fact that a traditional society cannot be destroyed merely by having its machinery destroyed. Such a society, deriving its strength from vital "intangibles," may be defeated, but not reconstructed. This suggests a recurring question in *GWTW* criticism. If the book is not artistically written, does it have other redeeming features?

An overall negative answer is given by Louis D. Rubin, Jr., in *The Curious Death of the Novel: Essays in American Literature* (Baton Rouge: Louisiana State University Press, 1967). Mitchell gave *GWTW* "the requisite qualities of sweep and range," but she failed "in her perception of character." Beneath the novel's "often rich and glittering" surface, "behind the events," one finds nothing.

But another issue will be raised by the critics and admirers of *GWTW:* What about the roles played by Scarlett, Rhett Butler, and some of the other characters? More specifically, what becomes of the traditional role of the Southern [White] Woman, which Scarlett seems to reject? This suggests Eric Berne's transactional psychology, with its games-people-play and the roles of the three players: Parent, Child, Adult. Dawson Gaillard, in "*Gone With the Wind* as *Bildungsroman*; or Why Did Rhett Butler Really Leave Scarlett O'Hara?" (*GaR*, Spring 1974), confronts the matter directly. Scarlett finally grows up, matures, and becomes emancipated in her final scene with Rhett. Thus the figure of the "Southern Lady as myth . . . [and] as a viable social pattern of behavior" is dead. "The female parent, the old order has passed away." The author "implies . . . that when the woman-wife-child created by the Southern Lady myth awakens to her complete selfhood and matures, the parent-man walks out." Passing reference to Mitchell's *GWTW* is made in Raymond A. Cook's *Thomas Dixon* (Twayne, 1974). Cook suggests an influence, on Mitchell's proud and unyielding Sutherners, by the characters in Dixon's Reconstruction novels (*The Clansman* et al.).

Clearly one of the most valuable essays dealing with *GWTW* (though the novel is mentioned only near the end), is Earl F. Bargainnier's "The Myth of Moonlight and Magnolias" (*LaS*, Spring 1976). Surveying at great length the literature dealing with the antebellum South, Bargainnier specifies the two major literary motifs: life among the poor whites and "the myth of moonlight and magnolias." He devotes his attention to the latter, with its six essential stereotypes, "the planter-colonel, the plantation mistress, the plantation belle, the cavalier-cadet, the faithful male house slave, and the black mammy." While *GWTW* is the most successful exemplar of "moonlight and magnolias," certain of its elements betoken the weakening of that myth. Southern aristocracy can be achieved, as Robert A. Lively showed in *Fiction Fights the Civil War* (Chapel Hill: University of North Carolina Press, 1957), through "wealth and 'blustery good fellowship'" instead of through "ancestry and manners." More significantly, Mitchell splits her plantation belle and cavalier into four distinct individuals: Melanie and Scarlett for the former, Ashley and Rhett for the latter. Scarlett and Rhett, "'outlaws' to the myth," nevertheless "dominate the novel." Thus, "when Mitchell abstracts the energy present in both stereotypes, and gives it to characters so that they can express their individuality, those stereotypes collapse."

Leslie Fiedler's "Fictions of the Thirties" (*Revue des Langues Vivantes*, U.S. Bicentennial Issue, 1976) is a particularly erratic, egotistically obsessive, and hence unconvincing preachment to the effect that *GWTW* is central in importance to Fiedler's titular subject (which he had originally projected as a book). These are some of the reasons Fiedler seems to suggest for what may well be another of his attempts to spoof and shock the bourgeoisie. He sees *GWTW* as the "most popular book of the '30s, then and now"; it is sentimental enough to have caused him, on rereading it, to weep at the finale—no happy ending for its long-suffering leading characters, who endure unforgettable "scenes of deprivation and violence." Its story is, for him, intimately bound up with various forms of politics: military, racial and racist, and particularly sexual. In view of all the well-reasoned and highly respectable criticism that *GWTW* has evoked, it is embarrassing but nevertheless instructive to mention Fiedler's free-wheeling parody of a literary survey.

A fascinating account of David O. Selznick's filming of *GWTW*, with the vital assistance of scriptwriter Sidney Howard, is given by Sidney Howard White in his biography, *Sidney Howard* (Boston: Twayne, 1977). The movie, whose production involved other writers also (including Ben Hecht), won eight Academy Awards (a record number), while Howard himself won his second Oscar for a screenplay.

As if to counter the myriad laudatory appreciators of *GWTW* (William Lyon Phelps, Eleanor Roosevelt and FDR, Stephen Vincent Benét, Leslie Fiedler, and how many millions of others?), Floyd C. Watkins, in "*Gone With the Wind* as Vulgar Literature," chapter three of his *In Time and Place: Some Origins of American Fiction* (Athens: The University of Georgia Press, 1977), hits the book where it is most vulnerable. *GWTW* "propagandizes history, fails to grasp the depths and complexities of human evil and the significances of those who prevail." The single reason that it lacks depth is that "it leaves evil out of the garden of Tara. . . . Much in [*GWTW*] is bad, false to the facts of rural and southern life particularly, false to history, and, worst of all, false to human nature."

Louis D. Rubin, Jr.'s "Scarlett O'Hara and the Two Quentin Compsons," in *The South and Faulkner's Yoknapatawpha: The Actual and the Apocryphal*, edited by Evans Harrington and Ann J. Abadie (Jackson: University Press of Mississippi, 1977), analyzes the two 1936 novels about the South, *GWTW* and Faulkner's *Absalom, Absalom!* As Richard Harwell, in his 1976 edition of the *GWTW Letters*, likened Scarlett to Atlanta, Rubin discusses what she and the city had in common: a rugged, unladylike adaptability to the violent changes of the 1860s. Here Rubin's general discussion seems to follow what Mitchell herself wrote in 1936 about the "remarkably tough" real-life ladies of the Old South, braving it through the terrible upheavals of the Civil War period (Harwell, *Letters*).

Rubin both criticizes *GWTW* and praises it. He quotes Floyd Watkins on the novel's being "vulgar literature" (Watkins's essay appeared originally in *SLJ*, Spring 1970), but he finds in the sad consequences of Scarlett's self-expediency, "melodrama of a very high sort." It is "psychologically . . . authentic, and historically quite accurate": Scarlett was mirroring Atlanta's own experiences. Most importantly, Rubin relates, somewhat to the advantage of Faulkner's novel over *GWTW*, the two Quentin Compsons (the listener to all the ghost-voices playing back the Civil War- and Thomas Sutpen-past; and the judge of the terrible events narrated by the ghosts) to Mitchell's Scarlett ("the opportunist, the woman") and Melanie Wilkes ("the traditionalist, the lady"). These females, and Mitchell should have faced up to the fact, really are (like the two Quentins) "one and the same flawed human being."

There is a discussion of *GWTW* and its heroine, relative to earlier Southern fiction, in the recently published biography of Grace King by David Kirby (Boston: Twayne, 1980). As though unfamiliar with Mitchell's own clear explanation of the seeming manliness of Scarlett and the tough old ladies of the Civil War South, Kirby provides his own rationale, in the form of a five-step process, to describe the masculinization of Scarlett O'Hara.

Also in 1980 Leslie Fiedler published a booklet of essays on *GWTW* and other novels of the antebellum and postbellum South entitled *The Inadvertent Epic from Uncle Tom's Cabin to Roots* (Simon and Schuster Touchstone Books). As were the others, this small work's fourth essay, "The Anti-Tom Novel and the Great Depression: Margaret Mitchell's *Gone With the Wind*," was based on a five-part radio broadcast of the Canadian Broadcasting Corporation's 1978 Massey Lectures in the IDEAS series. A bit more restrained than his quite insubstantial essay, "Fictions of the Thirties" in *Revue des Langues Vivantes*, Fiedler's *GWTW* piece in *The Inadvertent Epic* nevertheless continues to stress fantasies and mythic elements, shock value, and popular-versus-elitist reading tastes. Thus for example, in Fiedler's rereading of *GWTW*, Scarlett O'Hara's Mammy emerges as not only an inalienable source of security to Scarlett: she "is really Uncle Tom, the Great Black Mother of us all"; and, *GWTW* "is as much a sado-masochistic work as *Uncle Tom's Cabin*, *The Clansman*, *The Birth of a Nation* and *Roots*, for like them, it is based on a fantasy of inter-ethnic rape as the supreme expression of the violence between sexes and races." But despite all of its preenings and stage tricks, its commissions and omissions, the essay and the others in *The Inadvertent Epic* are worth looking at.

Interesting as these analyses of gender-role-reversal, sexual politics, and social stratification of reading tastes in Southern fiction may be, what seems to be needed more than anything else in *GWTW* criticism is something slightly different. That is to say, a far more searching examination than we have yet had of the essential factors that have made so poorly written a novel so extraordinarily successful with the lay public as well as with certain academic critics.

CINDY HOFFMAN, CAROL DUANE,
14 KATHAREN SOULE, AND LINDA WAGNER

Three Contemporary Women Poets: Marianne Moore, Anne Sexton, and Sylvia Plath

Criticism of these three poets, whether published in 1920 or in 1980, is surprisingly consistent. No matter what the subject or style of the poems reviewed—for until the last decade, most notice of these poets was in reviews—Marianne Moore, Anne Sexton, and Sylvia Plath were pictured as being iconoclastic, and their work was considered outside the mainstream of contemporary poetry. Moore's syllabic verse of witty definition, Sexton's cries to a mysteriously unforgiving god, Plath's angry "light verse" about dirty kitchens and betraying husbands—in no way did these poems represent any acceptable literary tradition.

Criticism of Moore's poetry in particular shows the academic community at its patronizing worst. We know more about Moore's red braids and her fascination with obscure animals than we do about the important ways in which her syllabic verse helped shape the transition from accentual poetry to organic form. However, other poets, such as Robert Creeley and Donald Hall, have recognized the central importance of her line and stanza in the development of contemporary poetics. Unfortunately, too few critics have done more than tell anecdotes about her.

An even worse kind of snobbery colors criticism of the work of Anne Sexton and Sylvia Plath. Their poems were consistently attacked as being too personal in subject matter and immodest in their revelations. They were especially unsuitable when read as the works of "lady" writers. Reaction to the poems of Sexton and Plath gave rise to the term "confessional," which is seldom used positively and is often coupled with the adjective "hysterical." Only during the 1970s has adequate attention been given to the unusual speed with which both poets move from image to image, creating what Moore had referred to in the 1920s as "the white light of meaning," the place where all images intersect. That speed of movement in poems by

Plath and Sexton helps create the density of impression, the sheer impact of their work. In context too, what seem to be personal comment may well be archetypal. Not only poets feel alienation and loneliness. Between them, Plath and Sexton have written some of the finest poems to children in this century. They have also written moving poems of both love and rejection. And Sexton has also explored relationships with parents, society, and God. Somehow, these subjects extend past the "too-personal."

It is difficult to think of any of these poets—gentle women all—as outlaws or mavericks to the estate of modern and contemporary poetry. Serious consideration of the work of Marianne Moore, Anne Sexton, and Sylvia Plath may instead lead to a reassessment of the so-called main currents in this century's diverse and rich poetry. Recent criticism has begun that reassessment; we would hope that it will continue.

MARIANNE MOORE

BIBLIOGRAPHY

Although there is no thoroughly satisfying bibliography of Marianne Moore's work or the writings about her, Craig Stevens Abbott's *Marianne Moore: A Descriptive Bibliography* (Pittsburgh: University of Pittsburgh Press, 1977) is an admirable effort in primary bibliography. He describes Moore's published works from 1907 to 1970, including information on textual changes and the printing histories of individual poems. The weaknesses of the book arise primarily from Moore's renowned exactness, which inclined her to add to, subtract from, and at times truncate poems with startling frequency; and Clive Driver, Moore's literary executor at The Rosenbach Foundation in Philadelphia (2010 DeLancy Place), has sternly criticized Abbott's book for its limitations in this respect (*MMN*, Fall 1977). Nonetheless, it remains a useful body of work, certainly superseding the only previous bibliography, Eugene Sheehy and Kenneth Lohf's *The Achievement of Marianne Moore: 1907-1957* (New York Public Library, 1958).

Sheehy and Lohf's work, though incomplete even for the years covered and now outdated, offers a checklist of criticism in addition to listing first appearances of individual poems. The most complete secondary bibliography, however, is Craig Stevens Abbott's *Marianne Moore: A Reference Guide* (Boston: G. K. Hall, 1978), which lists 818 items, including books, articles, and reviews of Moore's work. Abbott also provides descriptive annotations and an index.

Producing a complete bibliography will be difficult as long as much of the Moore collection remains unexamined, held as it is by The Rosenbach Foundation. *The Marianne Moore Newsletter*, published biannually by the foundation since 1977, frequently prints formerly lost poems and reviews written anonymously or under pseudonyms.

EDITIONS

Very little of Moore's work is currently available in any form at all, let alone in a definitive edition. Compiling such an edition will be made difficult by Moore's flamboyant tastes in revision and her persistent retiring of poems. Moore's prose has never been completely assembled, but the largest selections of it can be found in *Predilections* (Viking Press, 1955) and *A Marianne Moore Reader* (Viking Press, 1961), though both are now out of print. In 1979 her essay "Henry James as a Characteristic American" was still available in *Homage to Henry James 1834-1916* (Mamaroneck, N.Y.: Paul Appel, 1971), and during her lifetime numerous single essays or poems were published in limited gift editions.

Moore was also critical about publishing her poems; the 1961 edition of *Complete Poems* (Macmillan/Viking Press) bore the warning epigraph that "Omissions are not accidents." Over the course of her career, she seems to have tried to hone down the body of her work. Many of the pieces that appeared in *Poems* (London: Egoist, 1921) were republished in *Observations* (Dial, 1924); T. S. Eliot, in his introduction to Moore's *Selected Poems* (Macmillan, 1935), says that it contains all she wished to preserve from previous volumes. Only *Collected Poems* (Macmillan, 1951) is still in print and has survived several editions, some of which involved substantial revision by Moore. It prints poems from *Selected Poems, What Are Years* (Macmillan, 1941), and *Nevertheless* (Macmillan, 1944), along with a few new poems.

The so-called *Complete Poems*, overseen by Moore, was selected from *Collected Poems, Like a Bulwark* (Viking Press, 1956), *O To Be a Dragon* (Viking Press, 1959), *Tell me, Tell me* (Viking Press, 1966), and *The Fables of La Fontaine* (Viking Press, 1954). Although *Complete Poems* apparently represents all that Moore wished to preserve of her work, it is far from "complete," and is, in any case, out of print.

In spite of the inaccessibility of these collections, Moore continues to be well represented, if not broadly, in anthologies. The Rosenbach Foundation holds many of Moore's unpublished poems, some of which are unfinished and many of which are expressly not to be thought of as part of her final work. Occasionally, however, *MMN* presents previously unknown poems or early versions of familiar ones. Clearly, any definitive or variorum edition of Moore's work will have a variety of special problems to consider. As early as 1968, Roy B. Fuller called for a "chronological delineation of her work" (*TLS*, 30 May), but so far his call is unmet and seems likely to remain so for some time.

MANUSCRIPTS AND LETTERS

The largest body of Moore's manuscripts and letters, including notebooks and diaries, is to be found at the Rosenbach Foundation. Much of this material is still unexplored, but findings are regularly reported in

MMN, and it is a useful and interesting guide. Moore was a prolific letter writer and had a circle of correspondents as varied as her interests, ranging from family and friends to anthropologists and the Ford Motor Company. Her letters, then, are understandably scattered, many of them being held among the papers of other writers. Besides those at the Rosenbach Foundation, large numbers of her letters and manuscripts are held by the Humanities Research Center of the University of Texas, the Beinecke Rare Book and Manuscript Library at Yale University, and the Newberry Library in Chicago.

A few of Moore's letters have appeared in print, but perhaps the best known are those exchanged with the Ford Motor Company. They were first published in the *New Yorker* (13 April 1957), then printed later in a limited edition by the Pierpont Morgan Library (1958) and again in *A Marianne Moore Reader* in 1961. Thomas B. Brumbaugh has published his personal correspondence with Moore concerning his habit of autograph collecting (*MissQ*, Spring 1962), and Laurence Stapleton, in his *Marianne Moore: The Poet's Advance* (Princeton: Princeton University Press, 1978), quotes extensively from unpublished letters and notebooks. Other letters are occasionally printed in *MMN*, particularly those which shed light on particular poems. Because Moore frequently talked about her writing in her letters, they are useful for critical study as well as being of biographical interest, and it is unfortunate that so little of this material is generally available.

BIOGRAPHY

As in other areas of Moore scholarship, very little has been done with biography. So far, the most accessible source for information on her life is probably the *New York Times*. Moore's informal position as poet-laureate of Brooklyn meant that interviews with her were frequent and her activities duly noted in the newspapers. In 1964 M.J. Tambimuttu edited *Festschrift for Marianne Moore's 77th Birthday By Various Hands* (Tambimuttu & Mass), which has an interesting collection of tributes to Moore and personal recollections of her. Though not particularly useful for scholarly purposes, it does provide some insight into Moore's character, at least as she was remembered by her friends.

There have been some attempts at a bio-critical approach to Moore's work, but for the most part there is still too little known about her for such an approach to produce much fruit. One article of some interest, however, is Margaret Newlin's "'Unhelpful Hymen!': Marianne Moore and Hilda Doolittle" (*EIC*, July 1977). To date, however, the most important work in Moore biography is Laurence Stapleton's bio-critical study, *Marianne Moore: The Poet's Advance*. Though far from a complete biography, it provides the most information yet available. Clive Driver is reportedly at work on a full-scale biography, but such work is bound to be slow and until his work reaches print we must rely on Stapleton, the *New York Times*, and, of course, when possible, the resources of the Rosenbach Foundation.

CRITICISM

Critical estimation of Marianne Moore has long been a contradictory assortment of views. One finds her charged with "obscurity" and praised for her "clarity"; accused of being "elitist" and censured for being "too mundane." She has been grouped rather uncomfortably with the Imagists and similarly classed with the "Objectivists"; hailed as a truly "modern" poet and lambasted as an "anachronism." While alive she received nearly every poetry prize available, but in 1979, just seven years after her death, only her *Collected Poems* was still in print. In short, the critical establishment has made little headway in assessing Marianne Moore's standing or her contribution to American poetry.

Moore's early reputation, however, did not suffer such ambivalence. By the time her second volume, *Observations*, appeared in 1924, Moore had made an astonishing entrance into the literary world. In 1925 Yvor Winters exclaimed that she had "dumbfounded most of those readers whom she has not completely subjugated" (*Poetry*, April 1925), and he clearly spoke for a much larger group of followers. Among her early admirers were fellow-poets H.D., Ezra Pound, William Carlos Williams, Wallace Stevens, T. S. Eliot: nearly the whole of the poetically-inclined community. Their comments are instructive: she was "American," "modern," "unique," and "brilliant." Her technical excellence and "precision" became standard topics in discussions of her work, as did enthusiastic responses to her "vision" and "morality." Reading those early responses to Moore corroborates Winters's comment: "she had conquered a large and discriminating audience."

If in the midst of all this praise, the reading public remained a little baffled about her meanings—W. H. Auden admitted that when he first tried reading her poems he "simply could not make head or tail of them" (*The Dyer's Hand and Other Essays*, Random House, 1962)—all was forgiven because she seemed so clearly "one of them." In 1925 Rolfe Humphries wrote that she was a just representative of the era, "as good as we deserve" (*Measure*, 23 July). Faint praise, perhaps, or praise destined to be short-lived if a poet offers nothing else. In fact, there were such rumblings of discontent. Gorham Munson argued vehemently in 1926 that Moore was "amazing" but "limited" (*LR*, Spring-Summer), and it is exactly this "she's superb, but . . ." echo which has doggedly tagged along behind the swell of tributes to Moore.

In spite of such hesitations, Moore received consistently favorable attention throughout her long poetic career, albeit mostly in the form of book reviews. Some slight testiness began to develop in response to later volumes like *O To Be a Dragon* and *The Artic Ox* (London: Faber and Faber, 1964), but those reviewers expressed an uneasy deference to the majority opinion. Strangely, those critical of Moore disliked exactly the things that others thought were her greatest accomplishments. As early as 1936, Morton Dauwen Zabel could make the ironic observation that her admirers and detractors were "fairly eye to eye" (*Poetry*, March). What was lacking was not awareness or attention to her work, but clear examination and evaluation of it. In 1968 Charles Tomlinson still lamented that she had been treated "as a national pet," and that, due to a lack of "clear-minded essays," had "suffered more from lax adoration than almost any other significant poet of our century" (*Agenda*, Autumn-Winter).

Not that the clear minds had abdicated entirely. Those early responses to Moore's work—bewildered and adoring as they were—had placed their literary fingers on points of life and these were taken up by the more "academic" examiners. T. S. Eliot (*Dial*, December 1923) and R. P. Blackmur (*The Double Agent*, Arrow Editions, 1935) attempted to trace her technical innovations and apparent insouciance to literary expectations; Kenneth Burke sought to delineate the movement of her mind in its approach to poetry (*Accent*, Spring 1942); Hugh Kenner tried to understand her view of the world (*Poetry*, May 1963). These same categories have outlined the shape of Moore scholarship since then, but none has yet been adequately examined.

Surprisingly little attention has been given to Moore's strong personal views. Apart from uncomfortably noting the "morality" in her poems, most critics—Bernard Engel excepted—have shied away from any exploration of Christianity's influence on her poetry. Its thematic import has scarcely been touched upon, let alone its outgrowth into her tone and form. But scattered throughout her essays are clues to the beliefs that first shaped her thought and subsequently her poetry, and any clear understanding of the thrust of her poetic energy must take these into account.

The 1960s produced three full-length studies of Moore's work. The first of these, Bernard Engel's *Marianne Moore* (Twayne, 1964), takes as its primary focus the "statements" that lie behind or within the poems. In considering her work chronologically, he is able to delineate rough periods in the development of Moore's values and finds that she moves from an "aloof individualism" to a more active ideal of participation. Although Engel finds Moore conventional in the values she affirms, he believes her virtues as a poet lie in her ability "to give a poetic realization" to those otherwise outworn ideals. He gives relatively little attention to matters of form except insofar as they are related to her personal ethic of "discipline" and "restraint," but as a first book on Moore, Engel is useful and offers the fullest discussion of Moore's thought to date. Sister M. Thérèse's brief *Marianne Moore: A Critical Essay* (Grand Rapids, Mich.: William B. Eerdmans, 1969) is useful in tracing specifically Christian elements in Moore's ethics, and also offers some discussion of stylistic patterns as well.

George Nitchie's *Marianne Moore: An Introduction to the Poetry* (Columbia University Press, 1969) makes an interesting companion to Engel since he traces her development out of a strict prosody into a more "prosaic naturalness," though he finds her later work "feeble." Nitchie's book, intended as a general introduction to various aspects of Moore's work, suffers somewhat from this lack of focus, but is valuable for its consideration of her prosody and for its attempt to relate Moore's "sensibility" to the larger cultural environment of World War II.

In reaction to the critical attention paid to Moore's technical innovations and "surface brilliance," Donald Hall's *Marianne Moore: The Cage and the Animal* (Pegasus, 1970) attempts to correct this imbalance by demonstrating the emotional power beneath her strict forms. While offering occasional insights, Hall essentially provides a chronological tour of his favorite poems, and his book is of limited use for critical purposes. The limitations of all three of these first books on Moore arise primarily from the scant amount of previous criticism, which forces each author to cover tremendous territory in a relatively small space, often sacrificing depth for breadth.

Certainly one of the most useful contributions to Moore scholarship in the 1960s was Charles Tomlinson's *Marianne Moore: A Collection of Critical Essays* (Englewood Cliffs, N.J.: Prentice-Hall, 1969). While perhaps too heavily weighted toward "tribute" essays written by Moore's contemporaries, Tomlinson's collection does provide a fine selection of critical essays from the 1950s and early 1960s and offers a sense of the range within Moore criticism. Kenneth Burke's "Likings of an Observationist" (*Poetry*, January 1956) reviews her volume *Predilections* and raises the issue of the relationship between Moore's ethic and her aesthetic; Robert Beloof's "Prosody and Tone: The Mathematics of Marianne Moore" (*KR*, Winter 1958) gives voice to the concern with her precise prosody and technical abilities; Henry Gifford's "Two Philologists," first published here, demonstrates the interest in Moore's use of a specifically American idiom and the attempt to place her in a larger poetic tradition.

It was during the 1960s in particular that portions of books and articles began to examine this latter issue, though there is little agreement apparent. There is in the criticism a clear sense of Moore as one of the modernists, and yet also a sense of her decisive difference from them. Of special interest in this regard are Roy Harvey Pearce's "Marianne Moore," printed in *The Continuity of American Poetry* (Princeton, N.J.: Princeton University Press, 1961), Elizabeth Jennings's "Idea and Expression in Emily Dickinson, Marianne Moore, and Ezra Pound," in *American Poetry* (Stratford upon Avon Studies, No. 7, St. Martin's Press, 1965), Bernard Engel's "Marianne Moore and 'Objectivism'" (*Papers of the Michigan Academy of Science, Arts, and Letters*, 1963), and Hugh Kenner's "The Experience of the Eye: Marianne Moore's Tradition" (*SoR*, Autumn, 1965). On a somewhat larger scale is A. K. Weatherhead's *The Edge of the Image: Marianne Moore, William Carlos Williams, and Some Other Poets* (Seattle: University of Washington Press, 1967). Weatherhead continues the emphasis of earlier criticism in his examination of similarities and differences between Williams and Moore, linking both to the "beat poets," but he unfortunately relies rather too heavily on his distinction between imagery of "fancy" and that of "imagination." Anticipating Hall, Weatherhead examines Moore's use and development of images for poetic restraint and the relationship between this restraint and deep feeling.

Although journal articles and portions of books continued to appear sporadically throughout the 1950s and 1960s, along with numerous reprintings of older criticism, if Moore's literary reputation stayed alive, it owed more to book reviews and the *New York Times* (who had, it seems, adopted her as "New York's very own poet") than to the literary critics. Moore did become a kind of "national pet," and interviews with her frequently turned up in newspapers, *McCall's*, *Harper's*, *Life*, *Time*, and various other magazines not expressly geared toward literary-guild types. She even threw out the first ball at the 1968 World Series, an honor probably never before conferred upon, or, for that matter, coveted by a poet.

Throughout all this, her actual readership was perhaps small, though she often received the appelation "Best Living Poet" from the media. There is scarcely another term so likely to send a poet into critical purgatory upon leaving the book-publishing world as that one, but fortunately Moore has fared quite well. Critical interest has begun to pay her its long-overdue attentions, even though, to the discredit of the publishing profession, nearly all of her work is out of print.

The years since Moore's death in 1972 have produced the Abbott bibliographies discussed above, Gary Lane's *A Concordance to the Poems of Marianne Moore* (Haskell House, 1972), and two full-length studies devoted to Moore, Laurence Stapleton's critical biography *Marianne Moore: The Poet's Advance*, mentioned above, and Pamela White Hadas's *Marianne Moore, Poet of Affection* (Syracuse, N.Y.: Syracuse University Press, 1977). Stapleton works quite extensively from much previously unpublished material from Moore's letters and notebooks as he chronologically explores her literary relationships, sources for her poetry, and publishing history. He gives lengthy explications of numerous poems, his emphasis throughout being Moore's technical and thematic development. Of particular interest is Stapleton's chapter on Moore's prose, of which little has been said. Hadas's competent book aims primarily at characterizing Moore's style. He sees it as motivated by her concerns with "survival, conversation, discovery, and self-hood," in his attempt to describe the links between her strict observations and her sense of mystery and morality.

Criticism in the 1970s began a reassessment of Moore's place in the poetic tradition, an emphasis that promises to admit to Moore a place of greater influence than she has previously held. Several portions of books have been devoted to this reassessment, and of particular interest are Marie Boroff's *Language and the Poet: Verbal Artistry in Frost, Stevens, and Moore* (Chicago: University of Chicago Press, 1979); Walter Sutton's *American Free Verse: The Modern Revolution in Poetry* (New Directions, 1973), which develops the philosophical implications of her unique, organic style; and Hugh Kenner's "Disliking It" in his *A Homemade World: The American Modernist Writers* (Alfred A. Knopf, 1975), which emphasizes her "pivotal discovery" of a twentieth-century American poetic.

The 1970s also considered Moore as a specifically female writer, and most of this criticism, written by women, is characterized by ambivalence. Josephine Jacobsen, in her published lecture "From Anne to Marianne: Some Women in American Poetry" (*Two Lectures*, Washington, D.C., Library of Congress, 1973), finds she must contrast Moore and Dickinson. Margaret Newlin's "'Unhelpful Hymen!': Marianne Moore and Hilda Doolittle" (*EIC*, July 1977) contrasts her to H.D., and Emily Stipes Watts sets Moore against the broader tradition of women's poetry as a whole in her *The Poetry of American Women from 1632 to 1945* (Austin: University of Texas Press, 1977). Suzanne Juhasz, the most extreme of these critics, recognizes Moore's "technical brilliance," but uses her as an example of female poets who have separated their poetry from their womanhood, saying Moore opts instead for "nonsexuality" (*Naked and Fiery Forms*, Harper Colophon Books, Harper & Row, 1976). Once again, Moore falls readily into certain categories, but does not rest comfortably in them.

It is clear that Moore scholarship has only begun its work and that vast gaps remain in nearly all areas. There is still room here, then, for critics to add, as Moore says, "a hue to the spectrum of another's mind" (*CSM*, 24 December 1958).

ANNE SEXTON

BIBLIOGRAPHY

A definitive bibliography of Sexton's writings is badly needed. To date the only bibliography which attempts comprehensiveness is Cameron Northouse and Thomas P. Walsh's *Sylvia Plath and Anne Sexton: A Reference Guide* (Boston: G. K. Hall, 1974). Including primary and secondary material only through 1971, it is, of course, badly out of date and covers neither the appearance of nor the critical response to Sexton's last five collections. Still useful, however, it records the appearance of individual poems through 1971, includes reviews of Sexton's early work, and provides helpful annotations. In addition, J. D. McClatchy's *Anne Sexton: The Artist and Her Critics* (Bloomington: Indiana University Press, 1978) provides a selected bibliography, as does Karl Malkoff's *Crowell's Handbook of Contemporary American Poetry* (Thomas Y. Crowell, 1973).

EDITIONS

Houghton Mifflin published ten volumes of Sexton's work, all of which are still in print and most of which were issued in paper and hardcover. Collections whose publication was supervised by Sexton herself include *To Bedlam and Part Way Back* (1960), *All My Pretty Ones* (1962), the Pulitzer Prize-winning *Live or Die* (1966), *Love Poems* (1967), *Transformations* (with drawings by Barbara Swan [1971]), *The Book of Folly* (1972), *The Death Notebooks* (1974), and *The Awful Rowing Toward God* (which appeared posthumously in 1975). Two more volumes were edited by Linda Gray Sexton after the poet's death: *45 Mercy Street* (1976) and *Words for Dr. Y: Uncollected Poems and Three Stories/Anne Sexton* (1978). Sexton and her close friend Maxine Kumin also coauthored four children's books: *Eggs of Things* (1963) and *More Eggs of Things* (1964) were published by Putnam; *Joey and the Birthday Present* and *The Wizard's Tears* (McGraw-Hill, 1971 and 1975, respectively) are still in print. Sexton's play, "Mercy Street," has never been published.

Most of Sexton's poetry has also been published in England. *Selected Poems* (London: Oxford University Press, 1964), samples her first two collections; subsequent volumes were issued separately.

LETTERS AND MANUSCRIPTS

All of Anne Sexton's extant manuscripts and letters have been moved from the Anne Sexton Archives at Boston University, awaiting sale arrangements; at this time, they are not available to the public. Sexton was a prolific letter writer, and her correspondence with friends and fellow poets was extensive. In 1977 Linda Gray Sexton and Lois Ames brought out a handsome and useful edition of her correspondence, *Anne Sexton: A Self-Portrait in Letters* (Boston: Houghton Mifflin). In creating "a documentary of her life," the editors say, they "sifted through over 50,000 pieces of paper" dating from Sexton's childhood to her death; until the appearance of a definitive biography by Sexton's designated biographer, Lois Ames, this volume is the only substantial record of her life we have. Carefully indexed, with narrative connections provided by the editors, its usefulness is diminished only minimally by the numerous editorial excisions for reasons of privacy.

In the early years of her career Sexton revised her poems continually, draft after draft. Worksheets for two poems have been published: "Wallflower" (*MHRev*, April 1968) and "Elizabeth Gone" (in McClatchy's 1978 festschrift cited above).

BIOGRAPHY

No biography as such is available but, in addition to its other merits, Linda Gray Sexton and Lois Ames's *Anne Sexton: A Self-Portrait in Letters* provides a detailed chronology of Sexton's personal and professional life. A. Poulin's "A Memorial for Anne Sexton" (*APR*, May-June 1975) offers a collection of remembrances in prose and verse. J. D. McClatchy's *Anne Sexton: The Artist and Her Critics* includes a generous selection of biographical and personal reminiscences by the poet's colleagues and friends; it also reprints some of Sexton's most important interviews, which frequently offer insight into her life as well as her work.

CRITICISM

The response to Sexton in the 1960s was intimately bound up with the response to confessional poetry in general, especially the subspecies that confessed mental disorder. In the quest for appropriate critical standards, there was much emphasis on the need to distinguish between poetry and autobiography, poetry and therapy. Despite repeated insistence on the need to deal with Sexton's poems as poems rather than as personal documents, however, critics all too often sought explanations in biography. The critical landscape was further complicated by the impact of A. Alvarez's doctrine of Extremism—that the poet must put him/herself at psychic risk, that the willingness to risk destruction may be a necessary condition for creation. In Sexton's case, the disorder obviously preceded the poetry, but her explicit and repeated emphasis on the therapeutic function of her work—not only in interviews and epigraphs but in the poems themselves—served to perpetuate that critical confusion.

Moreover, the secondary material about Sexton in the 1960s reveals the extent to which criticism was limited by the topical, often descriptive and often superficial, nature of its primary instrument, the review, which accounts for more than 80 percent of critical notices in that decade. This rather bleak picture is, happily, balanced by a handful of lucid and intelligent discussions of Sexton's earliest work. Some of the earliest appraisals are also, in retrospect, some of the most thoughtful: reviewing *To Bedlam and Part Way Back*, Hal Smith seeks "to praise her best by examining as carefully as possible what she has written" (*Epoch*, Fall 1960); Geoffrey Hartman, similarly, focuses on craft as well as theme (*KR*, Autumn 1960). James Dickey represents the other extreme: "one is tempted to drop [the poems] furtively in the nearest ashcan, rather than be caught . . . in the presence of so much suffering" (*Poetry*, February 1961). Variations on Dickey's theme are a persistent if minor obligato: indeed, as late as 1973, Robert Phillips found it necessary to reiterate in *The Confessional Poets* (Carbondale: Southern Illinois University Press) that Sexton's work seemed so much a part of her life that a criticism of one was a criticism of the other.

Reaction to 1962's *All My Pretty Ones* was generally favorable: Thom Gunn's perceptive and representative assessment found Sexton still heavily influenced by Lowell but saw her second volume as an advance over her first, both in tightness of structure and in control of her material (*YR*, October 1963); May Swenson, praising the "solid form" behind the "seemingly effortless diction,'' found Lowell's influence lessening (*Nation*, 23 February 1963).

British response to the 1963 publication of *Selected Poems*, which contained works from the first two volumes, was uneven; over the years, Sexton would receive less praise in England than she would at home.

In the mid-1960s Sexton's work began to receive more careful critical attention and greater critical esteem. Observing that the ''basic pattern of derangement in literature was surely set by King Lear,'' A. R. Jones established a much-needed perspective on Sexton's rendition of the landscape of Bedlam (*CritQ*, Spring 1965) and argued that her treatment of human suffering was redemptive, not exploitative. Jones was also one of the first critics to call attention to Sexton's ''ultimately religious'' but ''not theological'' frame of reference—an insight that would have special relevance for her final volumes.

Jones's contribution was complemented by Ralph Mills's important chapter in *Contemporary American Poetry* (Random House, 1965). Mills's well-focused essay praises her ''brilliant technical mastery'' and sophisticated handling of rhythm and diction. Developing his argument that Sexton is a ''bold and impressive poet,'' he credits her with a ''marvellously lucid eye'' and a compassion for others that is ''without self-pity.''

The 1966 publication of Sexton's Pulitzer Prize-winning third volume, *Live or Die*, generated an enthusiastic response, though occasional reservations centered on the appropriateness of her subject matter and the extent of her control over her material. Preoccupation with Plath's suicide was perhaps inevitable, as were comparisons between the two poets; as they charted the progress of Sexton's return trip from Bedlam, critics tended to view this volume as documentary evidence of her growing mental stability. Robert Boyers, for example, praises her ''determination to live with her eyes open'' (*Salmagundi*, Spring 1967). Acknowledging her shortcomings—occasional crudities and ineffective similes—he nevertheless claims that *Live or Die* is the ''crowning achievement'' of the confessional mode and has a ''universal relevance.''

Nineteen-sixty-seven was a banner year: acceptance of Sexton continued to grow as critics like M. L. Rosenthal offered increasingly sophisticated approaches to her work. In *The New Poets* (Oxford University Press), Rosenthal conceded that Sexton's work contains less explicit cultural criticism than that of Plath or Lowell; he nevertheless asserts that in certain poems, especially in ''Music Swims Back To Me,'' she breaks through to a ''magnificent fusion of private and universal motifs.''

Complimentary essays by Beverly Fields and Richard Fein were also helpful. Like Rosenthal, Fields invited readers to appreciate Sexton's use of the dramatic monologue and control of sound in *Poets in Progress*, edited by Edward Hungerford (Evanston, Ill.: Northwestern University Press). Fields goes beyond intelligent readings of individual poems to consider the ways in which Sexton's use of recurrent themes creates relationships among the poems in the first two volumes. Crediting Sexton with a much wider thematic range than do most critics, Fein discovers "the verve of Hogarth" in "Woman with a Girdle" and links the "brilliantly childlike diction" that concludes "The Operation" with Pope's "puffs, powders, patches, Bibles, billets-doux" (*EngR*, October 1967).

The reception of *Love Poems* in 1969 was less enthusiastic than that accorded *Live or Die*: William Dickey found it self-indulgent (*HudR*, Summer 1969); Mona Van Duyn, solipsistic (*Poetry*, March 1970). On the positive side, Joyce Carol Oates discovered, among heavy echoes of Plath, some "minor masterpieces" and a sense of humor that tempers the poet's self-absorption (*UWR*, Spring 1970).

Also in 1969, Richard Howard's *Alone with America* (Atheneum) contributed to the understanding of Sexton's handling of formal elements; he singles out for special praise her rhythmic subtlety, her use of intermittent rhyme, and her mastery of the idiosyncratic stanza, all of which reveal "a care . . . for the poem's making."

The 1971 publication of *Transformation* evoked wide praise, but that praise revealed an observable divergence in critical perspectives. On one hand, Sexton was congratulated for a new-found objectivity and distance from self; on the other, readers were told that her best poems were those which were closest to her own center of suffering. William Pitt Root's late review (*Poetry*, October 1973) represents the former approach, which sees implicit social criticism in this handsome volume. The poems, designed to "amuse and appall," attack not just the fairy tales themselves, but also "the aspects of our culture which have used them."

Over the years critics frequently referred in passing to Sexton's treatment of feminine experience, but the first feminist criticism per se came with Carol Jennings's "The Woman Poet" (*NYQ*, Autumn 1972) and Nancy J. Hoffman's "Reading Women's Poetry: The Meaning and Our Lives" (*CE*, October 1972). A year later appeared Linda Mizejewski's brief but provocative "Sappho to Sexton: Woman Uncontained" (*CE*, December 1973), in which she traces a metaphorical tradition, shared by women writers, of images of flight, of "splitting," of breaking away from the earth, which is opposed to the Greek/Hebraic ideal of "woman-as-held," as "holding," or as "container."

In addition to essays articulating a feminist perspective, 1972 and 1973 marked chapter-length attempts by Paul Lacey and Robert Phillips to provide a retrospective view of Sexton's achievements to date. In *The Inner War* (Philadelphia: Fortress Press, 1972), Lacey continues to explore the relationship between confessionalism and craft, observing that "the poets who handle the most dangerous material are also most concerned with poetic form." Sexton, he argues, is involved in the "making of rituals," and her best poems are "built around rites of communion, prayer, and gift-giving." In light of his twin perceptions that her poetry is "ritually coherent" and is "largely shaped by attempts to enlarge a traditional Christian framework which has been a chief source of the psychological suffering she has endured," one looks forward to the time when Lacey will address himself to her final volumes.

Phillips's chapter in his previously cited *The Confessional Poets* is less sharply focused than Lacey's, perhaps because it is a composite of two earlier review-articles, but he makes an intelligent plea for the acceptance of Sexton's work as at least partly fictional. Analyzing her development volume by volume, he sees *Transformations* as a "giant leap in 'progress in personalization'... the ancient is remythologized into the modern"; in his suggestion that her best and most characteristic work, however, is her most autobiographical, he seems ambivalent.

In the same year appeared Karl Malkoff's helpful discussion of confessionalism in general and Sexton in particular in his *Crowell's Handbook of Contemporary American Poetry* (Thomas Y. Crowell, 1973). Malkoff's informed and perceptive introductory essay reviews critical responses to confessionalism and places the genre in a broad historical context of symbolism, surrealism, and projectivism. More mythic than biographical, confessional poetry is less a revelation of personal exprience than an attempt to redefine human identity, he suggests, and argues that its "basic tensions" are embodied poetically in the conflicting tendencies toward formal control and formal freedom. As for Sexton herself, Malkoff offers a lucid and coherent treatment of her development through 1972, paying as much attention to formal concerns as to theme.

"Reticent" perhaps best describes the response to *The Book of Folly* (1972); the few critics who dealt with it directly did so more belatedly than usual. In addition to balanced reviews by Arthur Oberg and Hayden Carruth (*Shenandoah*, Fall 1973, and *HudR*, Summer 1974, respectively), J. D. McClatchy's assessment (*CP*, Spring 1974) is, not surprisingly, the most lucid and helpful. McClatchy, Sexton's most consistent and most committed critic, suggests that in these poems, the confessional mode tends to assume a narrative structure, which effectively dramatizes and validates an experience lived through time.

Publication of *The Death Notebooks* early in 1974 was followed by Sexton's October suicide; a few months later, *The Awful Rowing Toward God* appeared. Response to both volumes was complicated by Sexton's death, an event which raised anew the old speculation about the connections between life, health, and art. If the recurrent critical problem of the 1960s was the persistent tendency to evaluate Sexton's poems as signs of progress toward mental stability, toward an affirmative objectivity, then the corollary—to link her most recent work to her death—tended to dominate the criticism of the mid-1970s. Moreover, critics who had taken special delight in Sexton's careful crafting of her early poems were faced with a special challenge in these volumes, which were frequently seen as evidencing poetic as well as psychic disintegration. Sandra Gilbert's review of *The Death Notebooks* was singularly laudatory: despite its "Rod McKuen-ish passages," she asserts, it far surpasses Sexton's earlier work; "narrowly skirting melodrama," the poet "wins through to a kind of grandeur" (*Nation*, 14 September 1975).

Of literary post-mortems in 1975, those by Denise Levertov, J. D. McClatchy, and Joyce Carol Oates stand out. Oates observes that Sexton, like her critics, saw her solipsism as a serious limitation and not as a key to creation; her provocative but undocumented suggestion that the poems in *The Awful Rowing Toward God* attempt an "intelligent and sometimes highly critical analysis of the suicidal impulse" has promising implications for future criticism (*NYT*, 23 March 1975). Levertov argues similarly that the relationship between the creative impulse and the self-destructive impulse is "distinctly acausal" (*Ramparts*, January 1975) and links Sexton's suicide, instead, to an exploitative society that "romanticizes its victims." McClatchy's valuable and insightful retrospective essay (*CentR*, Spring 1975) asserts Sexton's permanent importance to American poetry. Sexton is "stripped bare" of the covers and disguises available to other confessional poets; while her use of form invests her poems with a sense of immediate involvement rather than retrospective observation, *The Death Notebooks* has a retrospective quality of having been written beyond death. In addition, McClatchy underscores a growing critical agreement that, despite her drive to escape from writing of the self, Sexton's strongest poems are found in a narrow thematic range.

Other helpful discussions of *The Death Notebooks* and *The Awful Rowing Toward God* include those by J. Mazzocco (*NYRB*, 3 April 1975), who points out her pervasive guilt; Steven Gould Axelrod (*MPS*, Autumn 1975), who contrasts the "psychological jottings" and "prophetic notes" of the late poems to her earlier "highly crafted" style; and Ben Howard (*Poetry*, February 1976). Howard's essay, perhaps the most incisive, traces Sexton's development as he exchanged the formalism of her early years for an episodic structure, an increasing indifference toward subtlety and polish, and a diction reduced to the level of "Run-Spot-Run": "It remains puzzling," he observes, "why an artist capable of eloquence should have chosen so limiting an idiom."

In the same year, Patricia Meyer Spacks took a similarly negative view of *45 Mercy Street*, the first posthumous collection edited by Linda Gray Sexton, the poet's daughter. Pointing to Sexton's apparent "incapacity for self-criticism, either moral or aesthetic," she concludes that "the verse implicitly argues that anguish is self-justifying" (*NYTBR*, 30 May 1976).

An important contribution to Sexton criticism was Suzanne Juhasz's *Naked and Fiery Forms: Modern American Poetry by Women, A New Tradition* (Harper and Row, 1976). In addition to an excellent introductory chapter defining the "double bind" of the woman poet, Juhasz offers a helpful reading of "The Death Baby" and a different approach to Sexton's development. Examining the relationships with her mother and daughters that dominate the early volumes, Juhasz argues that Sexton's affirmation of life, and not just her madness and accompanying desire for death, were grounded in her womanhood.

Nineteen-seventy-seven saw a handful of articles, but the major event was the appearance of Linda Gray Sexton and Lois Ames's edition of Sexton's letters. A trio of comparative articles appeared in the following year: Marilyn Stall Hubbart's "Fairy Tale Stereotypes: A Study of Iris Murdoch and Anne Sexton" (*PAPA*, Fall 1978); Myra Stark's "Walt Whitman and Anne Sexton: A Note on the Uses of Tradition" (*NConL*, Winter 1978); and Beverly Tanenhaus's "Politics of Suicide and Survival: The Poetry of Anne Sexton and Adrienne Rich" (*BuR*, Winter 1978). For the first time, Sexton's work was being linked to writers other than Lowell, Plath, and Snodgrass.

More important was the appearance of J. D. McClatchy's *Anne Sexton: The Artist and Her Critics*. This indispensable volume makes available a generous sample of much of the best commentary on her work over the years; it also includes some of the poet's most important interviews and offers personal reminiscences by colleagues and friends. In addition to an expanded and even more helpful version of McClatchy's earlier essay, "Anne Sexton: Somehow to Endure" (*CentR*, Spring 1975), it also includes an important new feminist study by Jane McCabe. Agreeing with Juhasz that Sexton is a feminine but not a feminist poet, McCabe raises important questions about the practice of feminist criticism as she traces Sexton's attempt to find "new ways to think and feel about the female body and about nonsexual relationships with women."

Three previously unpublished horror stories as well as some previously uncollected poetry were made available in *Words for Dr. Y: Uncollected Poems and Three Stories/Anne Sexton*, but the volume attracted relatively little notice. Robert Pinsky found it "mechanical" (*NYTBR*, 26 November 1978); Harvey Curtis Webster assessed the stories as expert—especially "The Bat"—but the poems as less than satisfactory (*Poetry*, January 1979).

For twenty years criticism of Sexton has seemed tied to the appearance of each new volume; as publication has waned, so has the quantity, if not the quality, of critical attention. It remains to be seen whether the 1980s will generate a renewed interest in the kind of close scrutiny and perceptive analysis that was produced, as McClatchy's festschrift makes clear, in the recent past.

SYLVIA PLATH

BIBLIOGRAPHY

Students of Plath will find two recent bibliographies useful. One is *Sylvia Plath and Anne Sexton: A Reference Guide* by Cameron Northouse and Thomas P. Walsh (Boston: G. K. Hall, 1974). It contains well over two-hundred annotated references on Plath alone, covering material from 1960 to 1973. The second is Gary Lane and Maria Stevens's *Sylvia Plath: A Bibliography* (Metuchen, N.J.: Scarecrow Press, 1978). Although it omits annotation, this source is a thorough follow-up to the 1974 work. It cites over 1,000 references and contains helpful appendices on the chronology of Plath's poems, differences between American and British editions of the primary texts, a list of critical works forthcoming, and a roster of anthologies in which Plath's poems have appeared.

EDITIONS

In 1960 William Heinemann (London) published Plath's first volume of poetry, *The Colossus*. It contains forty-four poems including "Poem for a Birthday," a collection of seven individual components ("Who," "Dark House," "Maenad," "The Beast," "Flute Notes from a Reedy Pond," "Witch Burning" and "The Stones"). The American edition, published in 1962 by Alfred A. Knopf under the title *The Colossus and Other Poems*, differs in content from the British edition. It omits "Maudlin" "Metaphor," "Ouija" and "Two Sisters of Persephone" and presents only two components of "Poem for a Birthday" as separate works. Paperback editions were issued by Random House (United States) and Faber & Faber (England) in 1968 and 1972, respectively, with no alterations in contents or form. Heinemann (London) first issued *The Bell Jar* under Plath's pseudonym, Victoria Lucas, in 1963. Faber & Faber reissued it in 1966, both in cloth and paper, under Plath's name. The 1971 edition, with a biographical introduction by Lois Ames and eight drawings by Plath, was produced by Harper & Row. Bantam followed it in 1972 with a paper edition identical to the Harper & Row issue. *Ariel* was published first by Faber & Faber in 1965, and then again, with the addition of a foreword by Robert Lowell, by Harper & Row in 1966. The American edition seems somewhat misordered; its inclusion of "Mary's Song," "Lesbos" and "The Swarm" differentiates it from its British counterpart. *Ariel* was issued twice in paper, once by Harper & Row in 1966 and once by Faber & Faber in 1968. The "transitional" poems *Crossing the Water* were released in 1971 by both Harper & Row and Faber & Faber. The American edition is less credible; it omits several of the important poems of this period, such as "Among the Narcissi" and "Pheasant." It also includes six poems published earlier in the British edition of *The Colossus* (1960). Paperback editions, which duplicated earlier releases, were issued by both presses in 1975. The Faber & Faber edition of *Winter Trees* (1971) contains "Lesbos," a poem normally assigned to the *Ariel* period, but is otherwise nicely presented. Harper & Row's edition (1972) is handsome, but also longer because it includes several poems found in the British edition of *Crossing the Water*. Paperback editions were issued by both houses in 1975. *Letters Home* is an American publication, released in cloth by Harper & Row in 1975 and by Bantam in paper in 1977. Faber & Faber (England) issued the

1977 *Johnny Panic and the Bible of Dreams*, a collection of largely unpublished short stories, prose, and diary excerpts, edited and introduced by Ted Hughes. The Harper Colophon edition of this appeared in 1979.

MANUSCRIPTS AND LETTERS

Letters Home: Correspondence 1950-1963, edited and with commentary by Aurelia Schober Plath (Harper and Row, 1975), is the only collection of letters to date. Covering the period from Plath's first year at Smith College to her death in England at age thirty, the letters provide an interesting if uncritical picture of the poet as scholar, daughter, mother, wife, and neighbor. Most of the letters were written to Mrs. Plath herself, which may cause one to question their reliability. Whether or not they provide a cohesive picture of the development of Plath as a poet may be questionable; for although they reflect the various, and at times opposed, patterns of her intellectual and emotional growth, one should remember that they were written to her mother as conscious attempts to construct a self portrait for Mrs. Plath's benefit. The letters do show "Sivvy" as a vulnerable, real person.

Much Plath material is housed at the Lilly Library, Indiana University, Bloomington, Indiana, and at Smith College.

BIOGRAPHY

Despite a tendency to view Plath's work through the fabric of her life, few full-length studies have treated the circumstances of that life. The only formal biography to date is Edward Butscher's *Sylvia Plath: Method and Madness* (Seabury Press, 1976), a book marred by an overreliance on Freudian perspective. Butscher went to considerable lengths to speak with or write to those who knew Plath; if the book has a strength, it is his careful assembling of detail.

In Butscher and in David Holbrook's *Sylvia Plath: Poetry and Existence* (London: Athlone, 1976), both unfortunately see Plath as "sadly pseudo-male," in the words of the latter. Both seem to have been unduly influenced by the early treatment of Plath as embodiment of the demonic death wish, her genius equated with that wish, given in A. Alvarez's *The Savage God: A Study of Suicide* (London: Weidenfeld and Nicolson, 1972). More recent studies have tended to read the poems as poems, with a more appropriate emphasis on craft and Plath's interest in craft. The only other studies that maintain any kind of biographical emphasis are Nancy Hunter Steiner's *A Closer Look at Ariel: A Memory of Sylvia Plath* Harper's Magazine Press, 1973) and Eileen Aird's *Sylvia Plath* (Barnes and Noble, 1973). Steiner was Plath's roommate during her last year at Smith; much of her book deals with that period of time. Aird's study makes use of the materials as yet unpublished. Her tendency to rely on Ted Hughes's memories undermines some of her own useful perceptions.

CRITICISM

Perhaps no contemporary poet has been so misread and so maligned by her own history as Sylvia Plath. Critical examination of her work—until very recently—has been filtered consistently through biography. This filtering, instead of affording a consistent and informed analysis of the work, has led to the fragmentation of her poetic persona and a general misrepresentation of the facts of her life and the choice she made to end it. In short, criticism of the past two decades, and particularly that of the past seven years, relies heavily upon the circumstances of the life and death of the poet, instead of upon the work. As a result, rarely is there in the criticism as vivid a sense of the poet-persona as Plath herself achieves in her poetry. Only very recently—in the work of Rosenblatt, Perloff, Uroff, Broe, and a few others—has the work itself found accurate and informed critics.

Little has been written on Plath's early fiction, but reviews of the 1977 *Johnny Panic and the Bible of Dreams* have brought some attention to this work. Christopher Butler's comment (*New Review*, December 1977/ January 1978) concludes that the stories show "a major creative artist subduing herself to alien modes of speech and a tired series of generic expectations"; while Katha Pollitt's *Harper's* review (February 1979) sees Plath as determined to succeed as a writer of successful commercial fiction. She denies that Plath is the victim of the 1950s view of women as subservient, blaming the direction of her early fiction on her understanding of the commercial market at that time.

Plath's novel, *The Bell Jar*, has been the subject of vehement acclaim as well as disapproval. It has been called a treatise on madness, on the subjugation of women and the beginnings of the feminist movement, on the relationship between art and artifice, on the effect of an imperialist American culture on a sensitive young woman, and on the link between suicide and creativity. It has been claimed both to complement the poetry and to do it injustice. Its narrative has been called both "pedestrian" and "artful and skillful."

The essays and reviews most conducive to a thorough study of Plath's control of fiction are those that see in the novel more than a simple biography of Plath's life. Marjorie Perloff's succinct "'A Ritual for Being Born Twice': Sylvia Plath's *The Bell Jar*" (*ConL*, Autumn 1972) both relates the novel to Plath's poetry and uses R. D. Laing as touchstone in assessing Plath's appeal to readers. Perloff contends that, rather than being inordinately subjective, Plath depicts "the general human condition." We are willing to recognize its accuracy through her detachment and humor. Robert Phillips's approach in "The Dark Funnel: A Reading of Sylvia Plath" (*MPS*, No. 2, 1972) is to trace "the trajectory of her father's memory" in both poems and novel. Stan Smith, in "Attitudes Counterfeiting Life: The Irony of Artifice in Sylvia Plath's *The Bell Jar*" (*CritQ*, Autumn 1975), claims that the novel is "a highly and originally structured novel, which has transmuted its raw material in a manner consonant with Plath's own comments on the relationship between art and personal experience." Joyce Hurlburt (*WCR*, January 1973) emphasizes that Esther is Everywoman, searching for identity in an uncaring and violent world. The novel's strength lies in its vivid poetic images and its intense sequencing of reality.

The recent books on Plath all see the novel as integral to her development as a writer, giving her the opportunity to deal with subjects and emotions not always given space in her earlier poetry.

Plath's *Letters Home* has received a similar disparate critical reaction. While nearly every review of the collection finds Aurelia Plath, Sylvia's mother and the editor of the book, less than objective in her editing, few reviewers find the letters without merit as intimate expressions of at least some facets of Plath's personality. Peter Ackroyd, in "Dear Mummy, I Hate You" (*The Spectator*, April 1976)—despite his estimation of Plath as a minor poet—is sensitive to the letters as evidence of the separation she must have felt between life and art. Harriet Rosenstein, in "To the Most Wonderful Mummy . . . A Girl Ever Had" (*Ms.*, December 1975), takes this idea of separation further, stating that behind the plurality of persona is selflessness, an impersonation act that allows Plath's full spectre of genius and power to show brilliantly in *Ariel*.

Criticism of Plath's poetry is at least as divided as that of *The Bell Jar*. It has been described as breath-taking and nerve-wrenching; a major contribution to the development of contemporary poetry; a feminist cry; the pronouncement of a confessional poet; the shriek of a schizophrenic finally out of control; the curse of the "bitchgoddess" seeking revenge on all who did her harm. The answer to "but is it any good" has varied with the times.

Critics prior to 1973 thought that the poetry in *The Colossus* was good, excellent in fact. They admired the visible control of technique, comparing Plath often to Roethke and Stevens. Since *The Colossus and Other Poems* appeared in 1960 in England, and only in 1962 in the United States, the first reviews were by British critics. Only Roy Fuller ("Book Reviews," *London Magazine*, March 1961) wondered whether the control was, in fact, too tight. John Wain ("Farewell to the World," *Spectator*, 13 January 1961), A. Alvarez ("The Poet and the Poetess," *London Observer*, 18 December 1960), Bernard Bergonzi ("The Ransom Note," *Manchester Guardian*, 25 November 1960), and others highly praised the book, as did American reviewers Reed Whittemore (*Carleton Miscellany*, Fall 1962), William Dickey ("Responsibilities," *KR*, Autumn 1962), and Nicholas King (*New York Herald-Tribune*, 26 August 1962).

With Plath's suicide in 1963, commentary emphasized the relationship between art that probes too deeply into life and Plath's recent poems, published widely in journals before *Ariel* appeared in 1965. Some was positive (A. Alvarez in the *London Observer*, 17 February 1963 and the *Review*, October 1963), but more was negative, seeing Plath's poems as a reflection of her "psychological disintegration" (P. N. Furbank in *Listener*, 11 March 1965; Alan Ross in *London Magazine*, May 1965). In 1965 began the tendency to relate Plath's work to that of Robert Lowell, using the term "confessional poetry" (see M. L. Rosenthal, "Poets of the Dangerous Way," *Spectator*, 19 March 1965; and George Steiner's essay, which terms "Daddy" the "'Guernica'" of modern poetry, in *The Reporter* 7 October 1965).

In 1966 Dan Jaffe began the current of criticism that saw Plath as a "dead-end" romantic, whose work fails finally because it does little but reinforce that attitude ("An All-American Muse," *SatR*, 15 October 1966). This approach is used positively by Charles Newman in "Candor is the Only Wile: The Art of Sylvia Plath" (*TriQ*, Fall 1966) and leads to his editing *The Art of Sylvia Plath*. Joyce Carol Oates takes the same stance much later in "The Death Throes of Romanticism: The Poems of Sylvia Plath" (*SoR*, July 1973), pointing out that Plath's "moral assumptions" condemned her to death. Oates summarizes these attitudes as a willingness to be beaten by unworthy forces, a lack of community with nature, and an inability to recognize intellect or mysticism.

Ariel itself, Plath's major work, has evoked every kind of critical response imaginable. That madness and a preoccupation with death are major themes (T. E. Kalem, *Time*, 28 January 1974); that women in the poetry are symbols of the destiny of modern civilization (Rose Kamel, *MPS*, Winter 1973); that the suicide made Plath into a cult goddess (Saul Maloff, *Commonweal*, 4 June 1976); that the poems in *Ariel* are a means to control a suicidal tendency, not the result of surrendering to it (Andrew Taylor, *Meanjin*, September 1976); that mothering and its joys is an important theme (Margaret D. Uroff, *MQ*, October 1973), and that through *Ariel*, Plath's life and literary reception is "the best example we have . . . of what it means to grow up female and talented in this country" (James E. Miller, Jr., *CR*, Summer 1974)—all these approaches have been taken and argued well. Irving Howe, in the cutting "Sylvia Plath: A Partial Disagreement" (*Harper's*, January 1972), faults Plath for using the tragedy of the holocaust as an image for personal tragedy, while Brian Murdoch (*CLS*, June 1974) calls the same use "the logical aesthetic step into the pure image."

This critical issue is probably the most important in all of Plath criticism. Frederick Buell's essay "Sylvia Plath's Traditionalism" (*Boundary 2*, Fall 1976) states that Plath uses the "tradition of post-Romantic, symbolist writing" even though she finally went beyond those traditions. In that extension lay her greatness as poet. Buell sees Plath as a true artificer, dehumanized, depersonalized in the process of her art, so that "those private experiences have been so completely absolutized that personal vision becomes also cosmic." M. D. Uroff goes a step further in "Sylvia Plath and Confessional Poetry: A Reconsideration" (*IowaR*, Winter 1977) as she points to Plath's creation of a series of personae. "From her earliest madwomen and hysterical virgins to the late suicides and father-killers, Plath portrays characters whose stagey performances are subversions of the creative act.... If she reveals herself in these poems, she does so in the grotesque mirror of parody." Uroff's view informs several of the late critical books on Plath, but the casual critic seems far from appreciating the complexity of the Plath poetic personae.

The last five years have seen many defenses of Plath's art as nonconfessional, and more than personal statement. Jon Rosenblatt's "The Limits of the 'Confessional Mode' in Recent American Poetry" (*Genre*, Summer 1977) points to the similarities between so-called confessional poetry and the traditional lyric. This theme is the subject of the excellent book by Arthur Oberg, *Modern American Lyric: Lowell, Berryman, Creeley and Plath* (New Brunswick, N.J.: Rutgers University Press, 1977) and an equally provocative study by Karl Malkoff, *Escape from the Self: A Study in Contemporary American Poetry and Poetics* (Columbia University Press, 1977). That critics see Plath as integral to the mainstream of contemporary poetics, rather than as an isolated female voice in the wilderness, may be the best corrective for her somewhat confused critical reception.

To negate Plath's femininity is, however, also an error. Suzanne Juhasz speaks to the distinctive female persona in her *Naked and Fiery Forms, Modern American Poetry by Women: A New Tradition* (Harper & Row, 1976) just as do Sandra Gilbert in "'My Name Is Darkness': The Poetry of Self-Definition" (*ConL*, Autumn 1977), and Linda W. Wagner ("Modern American Literature: The Poetics of the Individual Voice," *CR*, Fall 1977). One of the most important statements about Plath as female poet is the book by Mary Lynn Broe, *Protean Poetry: The Poetry of Sylvia Plath* (Columbia: University of Missouri Press, 1980), which studies closely Plath's themes from a feminist perspective. Broe's work with the bee-sequence of poems is especially impressive, as is her essay, "A Subtle Psychic Bond: The Mother Figure in Sylvia Plath's Poetry" in *The Lost Tradition: Mothers and Daughters in Literature*, edited by Cathy N. Davidson and E. M. Broner (Frederick Ungar, 1980).

Another book-length study is Caroline King Barnard's *Sylvia Plath* (Boston: Twayne, 1978), in which Barnard emphasizes the "speaking voice" of the poetry and the changes it undergoes as the poems move from an early visual orientation to a later aural one. Somewhat limited in focus, perhaps because of the prescribed form for the Twayne United States Authors series, Barnard's study takes less cognizance of other criticism than it might. Another less than fully realized book is Judith Kroll's *Chapters in a Mythology: The Poetry of Sylvia Plath* (Harper & Row, 1976). Kroll's use of mythic criticism to the exclusion of all else leads her to misread some of Plath's poetry.

One of the most satisfying books about any contemporary poet is Jon Rosenblatt's *Sylvia Plath: The Poetry of Initiation* (Chapel Hill: University of North Carolina Press, 1979). Rosenblatt traces through his study the "personal ritual process" that Plath charted through her poetry. In linking her private images into sequences, Plath provided a means of capturing both her personal world and that of a larger, mythic existence. The mythic, symbolic enactment was especially forceful in her late poems, the culmination of her "poetry of personal process in which the central development was an initiation, a transformation of the self from a state of symbolic death to one of rebirth." Rosenblatt treats what he calls Plath's "drama of initiation" and landscapes and bodyscapes with particular acuity.

Until the 1979 publication of Margaret Dickie Uroff's *Sylvia Plath and Ted Hughes* (Champaign-Urbana: University of Illinois Press), the only assessment made of the poetic relationship between the two poets was that of Anthony Libby, "God's Lioness and the Priest of Sycorax: Plath and Hughes" (*ConL*, Summer 1974). Working from sources previously untapped, Uroff's study is a major contribution to the understanding of this partnership and its effect on both writers' lives and work. Uroff's analyses of Plath's poems are some of the best in print.

The diversity of approaches to Plath's work is perhaps best served in the three important collections of criticism now available. Charles Newman's excellent *The Art of Sylvia Plath: A Symposium* (Bloomington: Indiana University Press, 1970) began the fine tradition. Newman included a complete bibliography and a checklist of secondary criticism, as well as an important appendix of uncollected and unpublished work of Plath (an excerpt from "Three Women," pen drawings, manuscript versions of the poem "Thalidomide," and thirteen other poems, and the essay "Ocean 1212-W"). Of the critical essays (many of which had appeared in *Tri-Quarterly* 7), those by Newman himself, A. Alvarez, and M. L. Rosenthal are classics in Plath criticism. Others of interest are the retrospective piece by Richard Howard, Edward Lucie-Smith's study of sea imagery, John Frederick Nims's technical analyses of the poems, and a structuralist analysis that emphasizes the nonpersonal nature of Plath's poems, Annette Lavers's "The World as Icon."

Other essays of interest in the Newman collection are those by Mary Ellmann on *The Bell Jar* and A. R. Jones on "Daddy." The biographical essays included are by Lois Ames, Wendy Campbell, Ted Hughes (on the chronology of Plath's poems), and Anne Sexton (the latter, titled "The Barfly Ought to Sing" includes Sexton's poem, "Sylvia's Death").

In 1977 Edward Butscher edited *Sylvia Plath: The Woman and the Work* (Dodd, Mead). Divided into those two parts, the collection mixes commissioned essays with those already published. Biographical essays commissioned include those by Gordon Lameyer, Plath's beau at Smith; Dorothea Krook, her professor at Cambridge; Clarissa Roche, a close friend from 1957 to 1958 and 1962; and Elizabeth Sigmund, a close friend from the last year.

Critical essays are nearly all reprints, and include those by Joyce Carol

Oates, Robert Phillips, Constance Sheerer, Arthur Oberg, Pamela Smith, and Marjorie Perloff on the so-called "transitional" poems. This is a good collection, though somewhat uneven.

The 1979 collection by Gary Lane (*Sylvia Plath: New Views on the Poetry*, Baltimore: The Johns Hopkins University Press) has the distinction of being almost entirely commissioned. Calvin Bedient provides a new assessment of Plath's romantic qualities; J. D. McClatchy sees her as a "period poet" and finds her chief value in her "experiments with voice and the relationships among tone and image and address."

J. D. O'Hara writes a significant essay on "Plath's Comedy" in which he describes both her comic techniques and her use of "self-comedy." He argues that her poems are comic because "they recognize a cul-de-sac, a fixed situation in which words cannot successfully conjure, supplicate, transform, or otherwise improve upon the status quo." He compares Plath with Beckett, Kafka, and Donald Barthelme. Other important essays are those by Carole Ferrier (who treats the feminism inherent in Plath's work) and Marjorie Perloff ("Sylvia Plath's 'Sivvy' Poems: a portrait of the poet as daughter").

Other essays in the collection are those by Hugh Kenner, David Shapiro, Richard Blessing, Sister Bernetta Quinn, Barnett Guttenberg, Murray M. Schwartz and Christopher Bollas, and Jerome Mazzaro. Lane himself contributes a study of Plath's poetic ancestors.

Other books that might be mentioned are the montage of Plath's writing, Barry Kyle's *Sylvia Plath*: *A Dramatic Portrait* (London: Faber and Faber, 1976) and these critical studies: Ingrid Melander, *The Poetry of Sylvia Plath: A Study of Themes* (Stockholm, Almqvist & Wiksell, 1972); Lawrence R. Ries, *Wolf Masks: Violence in Contemporary Poetry* (Port Washington, N.Y.: Kennikat Press, 1977), in which Plath appears to illustrate "the internalized response"; Ginevra Bompiani's *Lo Spazio Narrante: Jane Austen, Emily Brontë, Sylvia Plath* (Milano: La Tartaruga, 1978); and Lynne Salop, *Suisong* (Vantage, 1978).

Index

About the Contributors

RUTH M. ALVAREZ is a graduate student at the University of Maryland, College Park. She has been published in *American Quarterly* and assisted Jackson R. Bryer in editing *"The Theatre We Worked For": The Letters of Eugene O'Neill to Kenneth Macgowan.*

SAMUEL I. BELLMAN (B.A., University of Texas, 1947; M.A., Wayne University, 1951; Ph.D., The Ohio State University, 1955) is Professor of English at California State Polytechnic University, Pomona, where he has taught since 1959. In Summer 1968 he was Visiting Professor at the University of Southern California, and in 1975-1976, Visiting Exchange Professor at Portsmouth Polytechnic, Portsmouth, Hampshire, England. Editor of two college readers—*The College Experience*, 1962, and *Survey and Forecast*, 1966—he is the author of two literary biographies in the Twayne United States Authors Series: *Marjorie Kinnan Rawlings*, 1974, and *Constance Mayfield Rourke*, 1981. He is also the author of numerous published poems, and book reviews and articles on education and on English and American literature. Most recently three of his articles, in addition to the work included in the present volume, have appeared in literary sourcebooks: studies of Marjorie Kinnan Rawlings, in *Notable American Women: The Modern Period* and in *Dictionary of Literary Biography*; and a study of Constance Mayfield Rourke in *Women and Western Literature*. Many of his other articles and reviews have been reprinted (whole or in part) in other collections and in various volumes of two of the Gale Research series, *Contemporary Literary Criticism* and *Twentieth-Century Literary Criticism*.

VIRGINIA SPENCER CARR is a Professor of English at Columbus College, Columbus, Georgia, where she has taught for twelve years. Her B.A.

and Ph.D. degrees are from Florida State University, Tallahassee; her M.A. from the University of North Carolina at Chapel Hill. Her biography of Carson McCullers, *The Lonely Hunter* (Doubleday, 1975) won the Francis Butler Simkins Prize awarded by Longwood College and The Southern Historical Association "in recognition of distinguished writing in Southern history." She spent the 1980-1981 academic year at the University of Wroclaw (Poland) as a Fulbright-Hays senior lecturer of American Literature. Her biography of John Dos Passos will be published by Doubleday in 1983.

MARTHA E. COOK, presently Associate Professor of English at Longwood College and co-editor of *Resources for American Literary Study*, received her Ph.D. from Vanderbilt University with a dissertation on the Fugitive poets Allen Tate and Donald Davidson. Her publications, primarily in the field of Southern Literature, include critical articles in *Appalachian Heritage*, *Southern Literary Journal*, *Mississippi Quarterly*, and *Southern Review* and several entries in *Southern Writers: A Biographical Dictionary* and *American Women Writers: A Critical Reference Guide*.

DARYL CUMBER DANCE, Associate Professor of English at Virginia Commonwealth University, received the A.B. and M.A. degrees in English from Virginia State College, and the Ph.D. degree in English from the University of Virginia. She is the author of *Shuckin' and Jivin': Folklore from Contemporary Black Americans*.

JANE DEMOUY received her Ph.D. from the University of Maryland in 1978. Her book on women in Katherine Anne Porter's fiction will be published in the spring of 1983 by the University of Texas Press. She is a writer.

CAROL DUANE is completing her Ph.D. at Michigan State University, specializing in the English Renaissance.

PHILIP B. EPPARD was born in Cumberland, Maryland in 1945. He received his A.B. from Lafayette College, his M.A. from Andover Newton Theological School, and his Ph.D. in American Civilization from Brown University. He has contributed to *American Literature*, *Resources for American Literary Study*, *Papers of the Bibliographical Society of America*, *American Literary Realism*, and the *Dictionary of Literary Biography*. He is co-author, with George Monteiro, of a forthcoming book on the Contributors' Club of the *Atlantic Monthly* and is also working on a reference guide to John O'Hara. Currently he is an archivist at Baker Library, Graduate School of Business Administration, Harvard University. In addition he is editor of *First Printings of American Authors*.

JOAN GIVNER was born in Manchester, England. She received her B.A. and Ph.D. from the University of London and an M.A. from Washington

University in St. Louis, Missouri. She is currently an associate professor of English at the University of Regina, in Canada. Ms. Givner has published widely on Katharine Anne Porter, as well as on Eudora Welty, Jean Rhys, and Virginia Woolf. Her biography, *Katharine Anne Porter: A Life*, was published by Simon and Schuster in 1982. She has also published short stories in a number of periodicals.

BARBARA J. GRIFFIN is an Associate Professor of English at the University of Richmond in Richmond, Virginia where she also serves as a coordinator of the Women's Studies Program. She teaches two courses in that program, one of which focuses particularly on the lives, careers and problems of women writers. Her Ph.D. is from Indiana University with an emphasis in Victorian Studies. She is currently engaged in editing for publication the papers of a nineteenth-century newspaper editor and political figure.

CINDY HOFFMAN received her M.A. from Michigan State University in 1979. She is now teaching and completing her doctoral work at the University of Pittsburgh.

TONETTE BOND INGE is an Assistant Professor of English at Randolph-Macon College, Ashland, Virginia, where for six years she has directed the Writing Assistance Center and taught a variety of writing and literature courses. Her scholarly interests include the British Romantic writers and Southern women writers.

EDGAR E. MACDONALD is a Professor of English at Randolph-Macon College and a widely published scholar in the area of Southern letters. A Richmond native, he has written studies of Glasgow, Cabell, Henry Sydnor Harrison, and others. He is the editor of *The Education of the Heart: the Correspondence of Rachel Mordecai Lazarus and Maria Edgeworth* (North Carolina, 1977) and the co-editor *of James Branch Cabell: Centennial Essays* (Louisiana, 1982). He holds degrees from Virginia Commonwealth University, the University of Richmond, and the University of Paris.

JOSEPH R. MILLICHAP studied at St. Peters College and received his Ph.D. in English from Notre Dame University. After teaching at the Universities of North Carolina (Greensboro) and Montana, he came to the University of Tulsa, where he is now Associate Professor. During 1977-1978 he was Fulbright Professor of American Literature in Finland. Dr. Millichap's primary field is American studies, particularly American fiction and film. In addition to these areas he teaches and publishes in the fields of communications, humanities, and creative writing. His scholarship includes monographs on Hamilton Basso, painter, George Catlin, and film director, novelist, Lewis Milestone. In the area of Southern studies, he has published articles and delivered papers on many aspects of Southern literature, including several on Carson McCullers. His most recent research projects are a book length study of John Steinbeck and film, to be published in 1982, and a monograph on McCullers now being polished for publication.

PEGGY W. PRENSHAW is Professor of English and Assistant Dean of the Graduate School at the University of Southern Mississippi. She is also the editor of *Southern Quarterly*. A scholar of Southern literature and women's studies, her works have appeared in a number of periodicals. She is also the editor of *Eudora Welty: Critical Essays* and co-editor of *Sense of Place: Mississippi* and *Order and Image in the American Small Town*, all published by the University of Mississippi Press.

KATHAREN L. SOULE is a systems documentalist and documentation seminar instructor in the greater Detroit area. She also works as a consultant on communications and training projects in the data processing industry. Soule received her B.A. and M.A. in English from Michigan State University, where she was a teaching assistant.

ANN STANFORD, Professor of English at California State University, Northridge, is the author of *Anne Bradstreet, The Worldly Puritan: An Introduction to Her Poetry* (1974) as well as numerous essays on Bradstreet, Sarah Kemble Knight, and Mary Rowlandson. Her book, with Professor Pattie Cowell, *Critical Essays on Anne Bradstreet* is forthcoming from G.K. Hall. She has edited an anthology, *The Women Poets in English* (1973) and has written on modern poetry as well. For her own six volumes of poems she has received the Award in Literature from the National Institute-Academy of Arts and Letters.

JAMES W. TUTTLETON, Chairman of the Department of English at New York University, is the author of *The Novel of Manners in America*, *Thomas Wentworth Higginson*, and editor of *Henry James's The American*.

LINDA WAGNER is Professor of English at Michigan State University. She has published widely in American literature, with recent books being *Dos Passos, Artist as American* and her selected essays, *American Modern*.

JAYNE L. WALKER recently completed a book on Gertrude Stein, *THREE LIVES TO TENDER BUTTONS* and is currently working on a study of James Joyce. She is an Assistant Professor of English and Comparative Literature at the University of California at Berkeley.

About the Editors

MAURICE DUKE is Professor of English and Director of Creative Writing at Virginia Commonwealth University in Richmond. He has edited many works on bibliography and has written on American literature. He was the literary editor of the Richmond *Times-Dispatch* for twelve years.

JACKSON R. BRYER is Professor of English at the University of Maryland, College Park. The editor of *Sixteen Modern American Authors: A Review and Criticism*; *"The Theatre We Worked For": The Letters of Eugene O'Neill to Kenneth MacGowan*; and, most recently, *The Short Stories of F. Scott Fitzgerald: New Approaches in Criticism*, he is one of the foremost bibliographers of American literature.

M. THOMAS INGE is Head of the English Department at Clemson University in South Carolina. He has compiled the three-volume work, *Handbook of American Popular Culture* (Greenwood Press, 1979-1981), and the paperback original, *Concise Histories of American Popular Culture* (Greenwood Press, 1982).